Situated Lives

Situated Lives

Gender and Culture in Everyday Life

edited by
LOUISE LAMPHERE,
HELENA RAGONÉ,
AND PATRICIA ZAVELLA

ROUTLEDGE
New York and London

Published in 1997 by

Routledge
29 West 35th Street
New York, NY 10001

Published in Great Britain in 1997 by

Routledge
11 New Fetter Lane
London EC4P 4EE

Printed in the United States of America
Design: Jack Donner

Library of Congress Cataloging-in-Publication Data

Situated lives: gender and culture in everday life / edited by Louise Lamphere, Helena
Ragoné, and Patricia Zavella.

    p.   cm.

   Includes bibliographical references and index.

   ISBN 0-415-91806-5   ISBN 0-415-91807-3 (pbk.)

1. Sex role—Cross-cultural studies. 2. Social change—Cross-cutural studies. 3. United
States—Social conditions—1980- 4. Sex role—United States. 5. Feminist anthropology.

I. Lamphere, Louise. II. Ragoné, Helena. III. Zavella, Patricia.

GN479.65. G495 1997

305.3—dc21   96-51900

                                              CIP

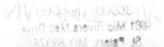

Contents

Copyright Information

Introduction

LOUISE LAMPHERE, HELENA RAGONÉ,
AND PATRICIA ZAVELLA

This collection brings together the most important recent feminist and critical research illuminating the lived experience of ordinary women and men. The essays we have selected focus on gender and culture, but they also place gender in relation to the historical and material circumstances where gender, race, class, and sexual orientation intersect and shape everyday interaction. Our choices emphasize recent changes in the global economy, capitalism, and postcolonial societies that have transformed families, workplaces, and daily lives. These structural transformations within political economies in turn lead us to reevaluate gender within colonial and postcolonial societies and to examine issues related to representation, conceptions of power, and alternative forms of portraying human agency and resistance. More-over, these structural transformations accompany new approaches to ethnographic research that lead us to rethink our position as ethnographers engaged in the practice of cultural studies.

We argue that cultural conceptions are being transformed by those who control hegemonic institutions *and* by workers, clients, patients, family members, and citizens affected by these institutions. Equally, we emphasize how material conditions and political realities shape the practices that women and men forge, and we stress the importance of human agency and resistance. Moreover, the decline in funding for research abroad has pushed anthropologists and other ethnographers to turn our attention to pressing contemporary issues in our own society. Many of the transformations that are taking place across the world are also occurring in our own country, making the U. S. an ideal site for the ethnographic study of new cultural and technological processes. For this reason some of the most exciting recent ethnography has been conducted at "home." Each section of this book includes ethnographies of the U. S. as well as essays examining field research and women's and men's lives in developing countries. We use this structure to point out important areas of contrast as well as continuities between the U. S. and the developing world.

Culture

Culture is a concept with a long history in anthropology. The term was originally used by nineteenth-century evolutionists who equated culture with "Civilization" and thought of it as a "complex whole" composed of knowledge, beliefs, and customs and as a tool for ranking humans from the primitive to the civilized (Tyler [1871] 1958). In the hands of Franz Boas and his students in the early twentieth century, culture was shorn of its evolutionary and racist origins and used to describe the complex patterns of elements, traits, and configurations that constituted the lifeways in separate but equal "cultures." Departing from this view, Clifford Geertz (1973) suggested that we view culture as the categories, meanings, and values that people use to understand their world. This emphasis shifted attention from the description of bounded cultures to the interpretation of shared meanings in varied contexts, primarily through interpretative writing.

This Geertzian sense of culture and interpretive analysis has become the heart of cultural studies, where literary scholars and specialists in popular culture focus on language and identity and examine the power of representation in contemporary literature, art, performance, or media. Cultural studies scholars theorize about diasporas, emerging discourses, new cultural tropes, and the hybridity of identities that characterize a "postmodern" world. Even though they have adopted the language of cultural anthropology, cultural studies theorists often focus more on power through cultural representation and less on the pragmatics of power or on individual and collective responses to power. Some anthropologists have incorporated interpretation of representation and cultural meaning with an analysis of economic, political, and historical underpinnings to engage a "culture and political economy" approach (di Leonardo 1991). As feminists who see ourselves as part of this perspective, we are interested in the layered meanings of cultural forms, but feel it is also important to understand how culture and historical and social processes *together* affect women's and men's lives.

Over the last thirty years, four important processes related to the globalization of capital have shaped cultural meanings on a global scale. First, transnational corporations are increasingly establishing fragmented and dispersed production processes, which in turn require workers to be more mobile. In other words, components are being manufactured in different parts of the world and assembled and marketed elsewhere, while women and men are being forced into an international wage labor force where workers must migrate away from their cultures of origin, often at great cost to their families and their personal lives. Moreover, those who remain in their own countries often produce goods for the world market as more and more products from the third world—everything from illicit drug crops, pharmaceuticals, and rain-forest products like handicraft textiles, rugs, and baskets—are marketed in industrialized countries.

Second and closely related to this globalization of production are new forms of technology, particularly those connected with high-tech electronics; for example, computerization, communication via the Internet or satellite television, and the modernized factory based on automation and robotic technology that contribute to this globalization process. The manufacture of various components of these new high-tech products often occurs in factories in the developing world, while first world managers use them to better find or communicate with far-flung sites of production.

Third, the rapid development of biotechnology has also reshaped the global market. Examples include reproductive medicine and assisted reproductive technologies (in vitro fertilization, sonograms, ultrasound, amniocentesis, and new forms of birth control), genetics (the Human Genome Project, genetic testing, and gene slicing), and medical approaches to disease (organ donation, AIDS research, and the tracking of deadly viruses). The globalization of biotechnology is evident in the use of diagnostic tests like amniocentesis (a technique to detect birth defects) for sex selection purposes, which in India, for example, has resulted in the abortion of female fetuses. Pharmaceutical firms often export and test products on women in the developing world: in Egypt, the subcutaneous birth control device Norplant has been implanted without the recipients' full knowledge or consent.

Finally, the breakthrough in electronic technology has made possible the increased globalization of media through worldwide computer networks, satellite television circuits, and fiber optic connections. The conglomeration of media industries further contributes to the U. S.'s hegemony in the circulation of film, music, and television, including the creation of media icons. Cultural studies scholars often focus on popular cultural representations emanating from this last set of developments, examining film, rock music, and television. They interpret the power of representation, the multilayered nature of texts, and the translatability of images, at the expense of discussing the material relations and economic forces making possible these cultural representations and creating new forms of power. In borrowing anthropological concepts (like culture) and critiques of anthropological writing (see Marcus and Fischer 1986), cultural studies scholars often ignore anthropologists' emphasis on the political/economic contexts in which cultural meanings and ethnographic texts are created.

Second-wave feminists and critical anthropologists have expanded our view about writing and interpretation, suggesting that we see theories as historically constructed and embedded in political, social, and cultural contexts. We now question the nature of our relationship to our subjects and examine the way in which our writing reflects the power relations embedded in the research setting. This self-critical and reflexive approach has produced innovative research, experimental writing, and attention to culture in relation to history, economic analysis, and political critique.

The new anthropological approach, the one that informs our own research and the essays in this collection, recognizes the inextricable connection of culture to politics, economics, and history. Events like the collapse of the iron curtain make ever more clear the naivete in treating culture as timeless and bounded. Despite the boundaries imposed by race, ethnicity, nation, work, or family, men and women construct cultural meanings in their everyday lives which interconnect these domains. This collection highlights these interconnections and points to new ways of thinking about culture.

Gender

The analysis of gender is crucial for understanding recent global processes and the importance of culture in everyday lived experience. The globalization of capital, transnational production, biotechnology, and the internationalization of media are all gendered: all four affect the lives of women and men in both common and different ways. While women and men may view these processes out of disparate sets of experiences, their location within the same institutional and social structures produces overlapping experience on the basis of such structural commonalties as class position, national identity, and racial status.

When feminist anthropologists first examined gender, the focus was on an "Anthropology of Women," exploring the nature of women's lives that had been hidden from view in traditional ethnographies and in anthropological theory as well. A handful of important ethnographies of the late 1950s through the 1970s focused on women's lives in an attempt to make up for the lack of research on women in earlier decades (see Fernea 1969; Murphy and Murphy 1974; Strathern 1972; Weiner 1976; Wolf 1968). While this research was much needed and long overdue, it became increasingly clear that we could not just "add women's voices" to our ethnographic texts. Any formulation about women had to include men, since gender is socially constructed and produced relationally (Rubin 1975, 1984; Ortner and Whitehead 1981; Collier and Yanagisako 1987). These relations are now understood to be constituted within a cultural, economic, and political system that is also historically situated. Such systems involve race, ethnicity, class, and other forms of inequality that must be integrally incorporated into any gender analysis. Moreover, sexuality and gender are intimately connected to the social construction of race and political economy (Lancaster and di Leonardo 1997). Whether we are talking about volatile political issues like abortion, new reproductive technologies (in vitro fertilization or surrogacy), or colonialism, notions about sex, gender, and the proper relationship between gendered/sexed and racialized individuals are all part of powerful cultural constructions that shape human interaction.

In selecting these essays, we have drawn on a culture *and* political-economy perspective, integrating the analysis of cultural meanings with a dissection of political issues and material realities. Gender is historically contingent and constructed, simultaneously embedded in material relations, social institutions, and cultural meanings. Finally, gender is intimately bound up with inequalities, not only in the often dominant relation of men to women but also to those of class and race (di Leonardo 1991, 28–32). Some essays in this book focus primarily on cultural constructions of gender while others emphasize the economic forces shaping gender relations, but taken as whole, the collection integrates both approaches to analyze changing gender configurations.

Practice, Agency, and Resistance

Beginning in the 1980s, many anthropologists embraced a "practice approach" to explicate the relation between cultural meanings and material realities. Integral to this approach is the notion of "praxis," a term borrowed from Marx: "The coincidence of the changing of circumstances and human activity or self-changing can only be grasped and rationally understood as revolutionary practice.... All social life is essentially practical. All the mysteries which lead theory towards mysticism find their rational solution in human practice and the comprehension of this practice" (Marx [1845] 1964, 68–69).

More recently other formulations inspired the current focus on practice. Bourdieu (1977, 78) suggested the concept of "habitus"—structured dispositions that are put into action through concrete practices—while Giddens (1979, 71) argued for a theory of structuration or a mutual dependence of agency and structure that emphasizes "situated practices." Ortner (1989, 12) summarized this new concept when she wrote: "Practice is action considered in relation to structure: that is, in contrast with the position taken in 'symbolic interactionism,' say, structure is not bracketed analytically, but is central to the analysis of action or practice itself. Practice emerges from structure, it reproduces structure, and it has the capacity to transform structure." Furthermore, Ortner added that "it is only in historical contexts that one can see the relationship between practice and structure fully played out" (Ortner 1989, 12).

In *Woman, Culture and Society*, feminist anthropologists offered the precursor of practice anthropology. Jane Collier (1974) argued for viewing women's agency, while others (Wolf 1974; Lamphere 1974) stressed the importance of different interests among women. As feminist anthropologists began to study gender, more attention was given to women in different positions within the same society (wives, widows, lineage sisters, rural rather than town-dwelling peasant women) and in relation to different categories of men (see Bourque and Warren 1981; Collier and Yanagisako 1987; Ortner and Whitehead 1981; Sacks 1979). Furthermore, the variation among women within the same category—their individual voices as well as the strategies they forged vis-à-vis bosses, husbands, male lineage heads, or ritual practitioners—became central to feminist anthropological analysis (Abu-Lughod 1993; di Leonardo 1984; Lamphere et al. 1992; Sacks 1988; Zavella 1987). The feminist ethnographers in this collection combine strands of both practice theory and a culture and political-economy approach.

In many ways we are borrowing from Donna Haraway's notion of "situated knowledges," a feminist epistemological stance that privileges the historicized and social location of the writer, where knowledge is always partial but also embedded in the differing visions of active subjects (Haraway 1991, 183–201; see also Rosaldo 1989; Behar and Gordon 1995). We view our own knowledge as critical feminist ethnographers as partial and situated, and, in analyzing women's and men's lives, we view our subjects as positioned actors who forge "situated knowledges" in order to act within their material circumstances.

It is not surprising, then, that the emphasis on practice and situated knowledges leads feminist anthropologists to reexamine our relationships with our subjects, with the process of fieldwork itself, and with the nature of ethnographic writing. This questioning reveals that ethnography is not only deeply gendered but is also situated within relations of power and subordination. The anthropologist's own positionality is multidimensional and changing, depending on context and historical circumstance. For these reasons, it is important to begin our discussion of culture, gender, and ethnographic practice within the debates concerning the practice of ethnography.

Originating in Marxism, practice also carries a more overt political meaning, where active human subjects respond to the conditions in which they live and construct alternatives. Feminist anthropologists are concerned with how women resist subordination through their activities in everyday life, whether in renouncing the cultural prescriptions that control their bodies or rejecting pejorative self-perceptions. This book considers how some women and men resist by developing a critical consciousness regarding the constraints of social life as they confront individuals, institutional agents, development projects, or powerful discourses, and how others, the more activist-oriented, create collectivities that change their social worlds.

The Power of Representation: Gendered Ethnography in Practice

The first section of the book deals with the initial boundary any observer of everyday practice must confront—that between the Self and the Other, between the investigator/writer and the women and men with whom she interacts, observes, and interviews. In the 1960s, anthropologists began to examine the nature of field research, writing about the politics of relationships with field assistants and informants and about the roles anthropologists assumed in the communities they studied (Golde 1970; Hymes 1969; Weaver 1973). Jean Briggs's *Never in Anger* (1970) and Paul Rabinow's *Reflections on Fieldwork in Morocco* (1977) placed the authors in narratives about the field situation itself, highlighting their interactions with a variety of others.

Feminist ethnographers question whether anthropology can or should be constructed differently when feminists study women (Abu-Lughod 1990; Stacey 1988). Stacey stresses the potentially manipulative aspects of the feminist/subject relationship and is deeply skeptical about the possibilities of a feminist ethnography. In a similar vein, Marilyn Strathern (1987) takes a negative position and asserts that the problem of feminist ethnography lies in the somewhat uneasy or ambivalent relation between feminism and anthropology, since each mocks the way the contrasting discipline conceives of the Self/Other dichotomy.

Abu-Lughod, on the other hand, argues for a feminist ethnography that works "with the assumption of difference in sameness, of a self that participates in multiple identifications, and an other that is also partly the self" (1990, 25). Abu-Lughod suggests that feminist anthropology disrupts boundaries, brings to light what it means to be a woman in other places with different conditions, and replaces the presumption of a female experience with a grounded sense of our commonalities and differences (1990, 27).

From our point of view, ethnographies written by feminists and other critical anthropologists pose several important dilemmas, including: How can we, as ethnographers, convey the nuances of our status as both outsiders and insiders—relations that exist even when we come from the same class, ethnic background, or community as our subjects? How can we alter the power relations between ethnographers and their subjects when we frame the topic for study and the questions asked and receive professional benefits from the publication of our results? And how can we write about our subjects without objectifying them? Although we cannot ever completely solve these dilemmas, as the essays in this section demonstrate, we can create new fieldwork practices and writing strategies that will help mitigate them.

Kirin Narayan's "How Native is a 'Native' Anthropologist?" addresses an important issue that many anthropologists must confront: their identity. In this essay, Narayan deconstructs her own status as a "native" anthropologist, showing us the multiple identities inherent in her American mother's and Indian father's past. She argues that she is regarded differently (as a visiting kinswoman, a "foreigner," and a foreign academic with dubious motives) at different times and in varied contexts during her field research in India.

Patricia Zavella's "Feminist Insider Dilemmas: Constructing Ethnic Identity with 'Chicana' Informants" grapples with the conundrum that researchers are simultaneously insiders and outsiders. Here Zavella shows that only when she deconstructing her own Chicana feminism could she "hear" that her informants were not Chicanas like herself, but were working-class women who used a variety of self-identifying terms, including Mexicana, Mexican-American, Spanish, or even Tex-Mex. She argues that a "self-reflexive analysis of our own experience will push us to provide 'provisional' analyses that are always incomplete, but which make clear whose viewpoint is being represented."

José Limón's "*Carne, Carnales,* and the Carnivalesque: Bakhtinian *Batos,* Disorder, and Narrative Discourses" confronts another dilemma: the power of representation. His contestation of pejorative representations of working-class Mexicanos reveals his own access to power. Here Limón narrates a story by a college dropout (a man attending a *carne asada* and farewell party for Limón) that pokes fun at the male anthropologist and thereby suggests that we can never erase class (and ethnic or gender) differences, but that we can "decenter our own narrative of self-assurance lest it be saturated with dominating power."

The essays in this section and throughout the collection demonstrate ways of writing that do not objectify our subjects. These include presenting women's voices in detail, paying attention to the variety among women's situations (rather than presenting one universal type of experience), and historically contextualizing ethnographic material. These writing strategies, along with the inclusion of the ethnographer within the narrative and an analysis of the anthropologist's position (the decentering Limón proposes), move anthropology toward creating more dialogic rather than objectifying accounts.

Reproducing the Body: Reshaping Conception and Birth

The essays in this section focus on women's bodies, and thereby contribute to one of the most exciting, expanding, and innovative areas of feminist research. Together they explicate the ways in which the analysis of cultural meanings and the attention to women's agency and practice are intertwined. Feminists have argued that reproduction, with its locus in women's bodies, is "inextricably bound up with the production of culture" (Ginsburg and Rapp 1995, 2), with world views and cosmology (Delaney 1986, 495), and with concepts of personhood and the production of knowledge (Strathern 1991, 1992c). The essays here take up different aspects of culture as well as the cultural reconfiguration of reproduction.

Emily Martin's "The Egg and the Sperm: How Science Has Constructed a Romance Based on Stereotypical Male-Female Roles" shows how the traditional narrative about the sperm fertilizing the egg recapitulates gender stereotypes.

Martin notes how the egg is either portrayed as the "damsel in distress," "the hard to get prize" (both passive metaphors), or a female aggressor who "captures and tethers the sperm," while the sperm is active, mobile, and penetrating.

Assisted reproductive technologies have led to interesting reconceptualizations of reproduction beyond this fable. As Sarah Franklin points out in "Making Sense of Missed Conceptions," for those involved in assisted reproduction (a whole array of techniques designed to help infertile couples) conception can no longer be seen as "natural" so much as an "obstacle course." In this context, each stage of conception is broken down into further stages, with "more hurdles to overcome and more things that can eventually go wrong." Martin and Franklin illustrate how medical discourses which are thought to be objective are imbued with potent cultural meanings.

Surrogate motherhood, as analyzed by Helena Ragoné in "Surrogate Mothers, Adoptive Mothers, and Fathers," also reveals the remolding and reshaping of cultural meanings surrounding reproduction. Surrogates and adoptive mothers often ignore the class divisions between those who can afford surrogacy (affluent couples) and those who bear the child (working-class women) by culturally dividing the birth process. Surrogates are seen as "biological mothers," while adoptive mothers are seen as the "social mothers," a cultural restructuring of the notion of maternal nurturance that privileges social motherhood.

In contrast, Right-to-Life activists described in Faye Ginsburg's essay, "The 'Word-Made' Flesh: The Disembodiment of Gender in the Abortion Debate," use more traditional notions of nurturance. They ally pro-choice women with destructive, decadent, and usually male sexuality, while portraying women who undergo unwanted pregnancies as "truly female," because they engage in "a heroic act in which a woman's capacity for nurturance has been tested." Both Ragoné and Ginsburg demonstrate that notions like nurturance are historically contingent and can be strategically transformed by women to deal with different reproductive dilemmas.

Rayna Rapp's study, "Constructing Amniocentesis: Maternal and Medical Discourses," finds that through Medicaid and the city's health department working-class Black and Hispanic women in New York City have access to the same prenatal diagnosis technologies as white, middle-class women. In addition to creating their own discourses concerning a positive amniocentesis diagnosis, they engage in a variety of practices in seeking support and making a decision to carry the fetus to term or have an abortion. White, middle-class women often accept medical discourse, while Black women use dreams, alternative healers, and kin as resources to interpret the meaning of their pregnancies, and Latinas often invoke religious imagery and stress maternal sacrifices.

The strategic shaping of cultural meanings leads us to the important role of agency, a central concern in a practice approach to reproduction. Who has access to various forms of birth control or reproductive technologies is one of the most important issues in this literature. As Iris Lopez's essay, "Agency and Constraint: Sterilization and Reproductive Freedom Among Puerto Rican Women in New York City," demonstrates, working-class women of color exercise agency within the context of a powerful set of constraints. Since Puerto Rican women are given limited information about other means of birth control, and they shoulder the burden of family fertility management, sterilization represents a means of maintaining control over their own reproduction and a way of improving the quality of their lives. Rather than seeing these women as victims or as simply manipulated by the medical establishment, Lopez stresses the ways that their decisions "make sense" and invites us to look at the systemic changes that would make it possible for Puerto Rican women to make other "choices."

Selections by Ginsburg and Rapp attend to cultural constructions and emphasize agency in the same analysis. Right-to-Life definitions of the fetus as a life to be saved and a clinic patient as a woman to be counseled are embedded in concrete practices. Right-to-Life activists staged prayer vigils outside abortion clinics, attempted "sidewalk counseling" with clinic patients, and established a "problem pregnancy" center that was designed to persuade women to consider alternatives to abortion. Pro-life activists shore up and sharpen their commitment to a set of cultural conceptions through these concrete rituals and actions. For women involved in surrogacy relationships, there were also important practices that solidified the radically new cultural concepts mentioned above. Adoptive mothers "bond" with their surrogates when they shop for baby clothes and attend childbirth classes and medical appointments together and, of course, when they are present at the birth (along with the father and the surrogate's husband).

All of these essays show how feminist ethnographers represent gendered cultural constructions about the body, and how women and men display historical agency through the everyday practices of reproduction.

Constructing Family: Creating Household and Community

Just as reproductive technology is shaping alternative notions of family, changes in the U. S. economy have fueled a vast transformation of family structures at home and in developing countries. In the period after World War II, the expansion of the U. S. economy propelled the building of suburbs, the growth of well-paying union jobs (particularly for men), and a rise in working-class and middle-class consumerism. After a sharp post-war rise, divorce rates decreased and birth rates rose, creating the "baby boom" and a cultural emphasis on the nuclear family—the father as provider and the mother as homemaker. This contrasted with earlier patterns where nuclear families were part of neighborhood or small-town networks of kin; the suburban, isolated nuclear family was a historically new pattern (Coontz 1992, 25–29).

This new situation contained contradictions, however, and even in the 1950s there were cracks in the idealized picture of American families. A full 25 percent of families were living below the poverty line, and people of color were excluded from white suburban affluence. Beneath the veneer of a nation of happy, homogeneous nuclear families, there were indications of sexual abuse, child battering, alcoholism, and stressful marriages (Coontz 1992, 29–37). "A successful 1950s family was often achieved at enormous costs to the wife, who was expected to subordinate her own needs and aspirations to those of both her husband and her children" (Coontz 1992, 36). Betty Friedan labeled women's malaise as the "problem that has no name" in her bestseller *The Feminine Mystique* (1963).

A series of economic transformations beginning in the early 1960s created new family patterns and again brought to light the class, racial, and ethnic differences in family organization that had been suppressed in 1950s ideology. Black migration to the North, which began in the nineteenth century, accelerated during World War II, and continued into the 1960s, was fueled by changes in southern agriculture that forced 3.5 million African Americans off the land and into northern cities (Stack 1974, 1). In 1974–75, and again in 1982–83 and 1992–93, the U. S. suffered a severe recession. These three economic downturns were part of the globalization of production and the restructuring of the American economy that continue to the present. During each recession, manufacturing plants were relocated to the American South and West and to the Third World. At first light industries like apparel, textiles, toys, and shoes were affected, but during the early 1980s, rubber, steel, and auto manufacturing also declined precipitously. Over a half million jobs were lost in the first two recessions (Bluestone and Harrison 1982, 25–26).

This began a period of irreversible structural unemployment (where the U. S. tolerated relatively high rates of joblessness and a decline in men's labor force participation). As high-paying male jobs disappeared, new jobs were created in the service sector, many of them low-paying "Macjobs"—after McDonald's, the epitome of low-wage, high-turnover positions (Garson 1988). Workers have become more productive, but inflation during the 1980s and stagnant incomes during the 1990s have meant that inflation-adjusted incomes have fallen since 1972. Women's labor force participation rose to a high of 58 percent in 1993, while men's declined to 75 percent. For women of childbearing age, labor force participation increased to 75 percent in 1993. High unemployment rates and stagnating wages also brought half a million African American men and women back to the South by 1990. Many returned to their home places of "persistent poverty" where people feel an obligation to help their kin or redeem a lost community (Stack, this volume). Declining family incomes produced more working women and the trend toward dual-worker families, while higher divorce rates and high unemployment rates increased the proportion of single-parent families to 31 percent of all families by 1994 (U. S. Census Bureau 1994). In the midst of these structural transformations, lesbian mothers challenged the very idea of the family by creating households of their own with children from their prior heterosexual marriages or artificial insemination, or they constructed "blended families" with their partners and their children.

Added to the restructuring of the American economy and increasing unemployment has been the rising cost of urban housing, the gentrification of inner cities (see Williams 1992), and the dismantling of state-funded safety nets such as institutional care for the mentally ill. These factors have contributed to the rise in domestic violence rates, divorce, and the feminization of poverty and have created a new population of homeless: women and children (Liebow 1993). Families and individuals, then, are forced to rely on neighbors, kin, friends, or community-based organizations to cope with the effects of these social problems.

The economic forces pressing on Third World families are even greater, due to the impact of structural adjustment policies on developing countries. In response to high levels of debt, the International Monetary Fund (IMF) has forced countries to devalue their currency, raise taxes, lift price controls, and cut public sector services. This has usually resulted in cuts in real wages, often pushing people out of their rural homes, and a rise in prices, squeezing working-class and poor families and creating the necessity for women's labor force participation in places like Mexico City.

"Constructing Family" contains essays that emphasize the creation of new cultural meanings of family, or illustrate how more traditional meanings are mixed with alternative conceptions of the family. Some of the cultural themes encountered in "Reproducing the Body" are echoed here. Old definitions of family are being stretched to include new individuals (lesbian partners and stepchildren), alternative roles (the providing mother and the nurturing husband), or new genetic connections (the child born of a surrogate mother and genetic father). At the same time, old constructs are being packed with new meanings, reminding us that meanings are always historically contingent. In addition to their attention to changing cultural constructions, these essays also describe the concrete practices that have resulted in new forms of family, household, and community. They illustrate the ways families are coping with the new economic realities they face. Examining the practices that women and men construct in daily life provides important insights into how structural and cultural transformations are experienced on the ground.

Brett Williams in "Reinventing the South" blends both cultural and material analysis in her account of how Black migrants to Washington, D. C., created a community. In this neighborhood sociability centered on gendered activities like gardening, fishing, and watching over neighborhood children, and on the enjoyment of regional food created by dense ties that "celebrate cycle, repetition, and texture." By focusing on texture, Williams evokes "dense, vivid, woven, detailed narratives, relationships, and experiences" that also characterize African American storytelling, blues music, children's games, and jazz (Williams 1992, 47). Ties between northern cities and southern rural communities continued as kin moved back and forth, men and women to find jobs in the North, children to spend time with families in the South. In Williams's essay, there is equal attention given to the economic realities that have brought these families from South Carolina and to their construction of meaningful notions of kin and community.

Ellen Lewin's article, "'This Permanent Roommate,'" shows that lesbian families (like heterosexual ones) construct cultural notions of motherhood rooted in traditional families. Lesbians face unique dilemmas, however, when they confront and resist the stigma attached to households with women-loving women.

Nurturance, a crucial trope for pro-life activists and women involved in surrogacy, is also central to the way in which lesbian mothers define themselves; many focus on motherhood rather than their sexual orientation. At the level of concrete practice, lesbian households vary widely. Some women shield their children from their partners and suppress their own identities, partly to protect their children from painful experiences with peers or to avoid difficult custody battles, while others create "companionate" households with their children, partners, and their partner's children.

At the level of practice in both the U. S. and developing countries, women and men are confronting changes in household configurations, divisions of labor, and forms of community, some resisting local power structures. Beatríz Pesquera's "'In the Beginning He Wouldn't Lift Even a Spoon'" shows how class shapes the struggle over "the second shift" inside Chicano families. She argues that women's contribution to the family economy is a central feature in women's ability to resist men's power in the home.

In Mexico, Matthew Gutmann, in his essay "The Meanings of Macho: Changing Mexican Male Identities," demonstrates how the struggle over the division of labor in Colonia Santo Domingo chips away at notions of "macho" among working-class men. Younger men define themselves as "neither macho nor *mandilon*" (apron-wearers), since they wash dishes, sweep, shop, change diapers, and help in raising their children. Women are still subordinate, Gutmann maintains, but women's economic participation (in formal and informal economic activities) and their history of community activism create the basis for changing the traditional gender order.

By using family ties and kin networks, women also bring about community change. Carol Stack describes the founding of "Holding Hands," an African American organization formed out of return migration to the "new South." She shows how the women used their knowledge of government funding opportunities to organize the community against white opposition to bring federally funded day care to Chestnut County.

Consciousness, Transformation, and Resistance at Work

The same economic forces that have transformed gender relations and family forms have also changed the nature of work sites. There are two important trends: reproductive work (cooking; cleaning; caring for children, the aged, and the sick) has moved out of the home and into workplaces in the private sector (restaurants, motels, dry cleaning establishments) or into bureaucratized service organizations (hospitals, nursing homes, day-care centers, and schools) (Glenn 1985, 1992). Further, industrial production has moved abroad, and those workplaces that remain in the United States incorporate participatory management techniques with more traditional managerial practices as they attempt to lower wages and increase productivity. At the same time, women in Third World countries such as Malaysia, Taiwan, Mexico, and Jamaica are experiencing new forms of capitalist work discipline as they sew clothes, sit behind microscopes, engage in word processing through telecommunications, or assemble electrical products in factories producing for global markets.

Workplaces are gendered spaces. Historically wage work has been divided into "men's jobs" and "women's jobs," categories that owe much of their persistence to culturally stereotyped notions of males and females. Men's work is more highly paid (since men are assumed to be family providers); often more physically strenuous; and, in some cases, connected to a "job ladder" so that men have more job mobility than women. As it moves from the domestic to the public sphere, paid reproductive work often continues to be "women's work." Occupations like commercial cleaner, waitress, nurse's aid, and day-care provider are regarded as "female jobs," as are professional positions like teacher, nurse, and social worker. These "feminized" occupations are defined in terms of the assumed and certainly essentialized female traits of empathy, sensitivity, an ethic of care, and an ability to communicate well (Hochschild 1989). It is not surprising, therefore, that as reproductive work has moved out of the home, women have been recruited for these positions. Racial and ethnic categories also hold an important place at work, since most low-wage workers in the U. S. and abroad are women of color, while managers, supervisors, and skilled technicians remain positions dominated by men.

Some paid reproductive work—such as housecleaning and child care—remains in the home, where race and class differences shape relations between women. As more upper-middle-class women pursue professions, they often hire domestic workers and nannies—typically women of color and immigrants—to clean their houses and care for their children. In "Invisibility, Consciousness of the Other, *Ressentiment*," Judith Rollins explores the relationship between domestic workers and their female employers, showing us how domestics often remain invisible, privy to private conversations that ignore their presence or literally locked in when the employer leaves. Domestic workers, particularly African American women, experience powerful feelings of injustice because of the maternalistic treatment of their white employers and resist through a consciousness that distances them from their employers.

Individual reactions to domestic work, and even the labor market itself, can be altered through collective action, as Leslie Salzinger demonstrates in "A Maid by Any Other Name: The Transformation of 'Dirty Work' by Central American Immigrants," a study of two Latina domestic worker cooperatives in the San Francisco Bay area, Amigos and Choices. While Amigos fostered low expectations and a willingness to accept relatively low wages among its new immigrant Latina workers, Choices dedicated itself to professionalizing housecleaning by establishing training programs, setting standards, and demanding higher wages.

Women of color are entering into clerical jobs, positions that may be low paid, but they represent considerable upward mobility for Mexican American women of working-class backgrounds. In "Chicanas in White-Collar Jobs: 'You Have to Prove Yourself More,'" Denise Segura shows that Chicanas are acutely aware of sexual harassment and racism on the job. These women mitigate the negative aspects of their jobs by affirming their relationships with Chicano students and reinforcing their ethnic and gender identities at work.

Industrial work is increasingly the domain of immigrants, as women and men find themselves in jobs that use traditional, hierarchical forms of management and emphasize productivity over safety, benefits, or worker autonomy. Donald Stull's "Knock 'Em Dead: Work on the Killfloor of a Modern Beefpacking Plant" outlines the difficulties men encounter in the recently opened meat-packing plants in rural Kansas, where many of the workers on the killfloor are either Mexican or Vietnamese immigrants who are pushed to get the product "out the door." Women, employed in skinning and trimming in the slaughter department or boning and trimming in fabrication, often find little sympathy for their child-care difficulties.

In "Women's Resistance in the Sunbelt: Anglos and Hispanas Respond to Managerial Control," Louise Lamphere and Patricia Zavella focus on the strategies and tactics women workers forge in relation to both hierarchical forms of management and new participative policies in plants located in Albuquerque, N. M. Women often use individual tactics and strategies to combat managers' attempts to build a loyal work force in hierarchical plants. Women appreciate some participative management policies, but see through them if they mask authoritarian relations. Resistance is clearly shaped by the production process and management systems of control and loyalty building.

Resistance is also the theme of Aihwa Ong's study of Malay factory workers in "Spirits of Resistance." Young unmarried women work in Japanese-owned factories assembling electronic components in a free-trade zone. They adopt stylish Western clothing and makeup and choose their own husbands, but they also face capitalist discipline on the shop floor. Resistance takes the form of spirit possession, where women are seized by spirits emanating from the "filth" of the factory and stop production for days. Ong suggests their resistance speaks out against male oppression (from supervisors and male managers), expresses a deep sense of moral decentering, and insists on equality rooted in a common humanity.

Thus, these essays show how men and women engage in resistance in individual and collective ways, with varied outcomes. While the transformation of work sites from rigid, sexually segregated to nongendered domains has been slow, workers in the United States and in the Third World (especially as we'll see below in Devon Peña's piece) struggle to make work a place of their own.

Colonizing Gender and Sexuality: Representation and Practice

The final section returns to the issues of representation raised in the beginning of this collection, but focuses on colonial and postcolonial societies. In these contexts, representations of the Other can be found in the writings of colonial administrators, merchants, and missionaries as well as in the writings and pictures of journalists, art critics, collectors, and tourist boards in the contemporary postcolonial world. We seek to place these representations in the context of colonial and postcolonial political economies, interrogating the practices of particular regimes—as seen in laws; civil ordinances; missionary practices; trading company and, more recently, international monetary policies; and local tourist marketing strategies. Colonialism, however, is not the steamroller of history; rather, women and men resist the imposition of colonial regimes, construct a pastiche of old and new cultural forms, or preserve their cultural heritage within changing contexts.

Ann Stoler's "Making Empire Respectable: The Politics of Race and Sexual Morality in Twentieth-Century Colonial Cultures" reminds us that colonialism was a deeply gendered and racialized project. Here Stoler emphasizes that Europeans in the colonies were not a homogeneous population, but were divided by class and gender. Sexual regulation over time meant that the lines between colonizer and colonized were increasingly sharpened, sometimes with the effect of masking divisions within the colony itself. Over time, European women became the bearers of morality; colonial communities became more bourgeois and the protection of white women went hand in hand with racist rhetoric, fear of rape, and the popularization of eugenics (which saw "degeneration" in race mixing). The overall result was to police and control colonized males, working-class white men, and white women of all classes.

While Stoler focuses on the sexual policing of bodies, in "The Empire's Old Clothes: Fashioning the Colonial Subject," Jean Comaroff highlights the clothing of colonized subjects. She imparts a sense of how missionaries in South Africa went about changing the clothes of the Tswana as well as saving their souls. However, she also shows how the Tswana were active agents in this transformation: Tswana elites developed costumes that were a pastiche of Western and native elements. Tswana women became the bearers of "ethnic dress" (made from conservative "mission blue" cloth) and helped put the brakes on consumption, a Western system of fashion, and increased dependency on the market.

The representation of the Tswana as naked, red, and greasy that Comaroff deconstructs markedly contrasts with the romanticized image of the Pueblo woman carrying a pot on her head as an "olla maiden" described by Barbara Babcock in "Mudwomen and Whitemen: A Meditation on Pueblo Potteries and the Politics of Representation." In postcolonial America, the olla maiden is a redemptive figure—a bourgeois dream of an alternative life and a symbol of a timeless past—whose image is marketed for tourists. But Pueblo women are not passive pawns in these interactions. Helen Cordero, a potter from Cochiti, revived figurative pottery through the storyteller doll. She used a mode of production (pottery) that women control to transform an arena of men's cultural reproduction (storytelling), and eventually altered gender politics in the pueblo.

The interplay between image, tradition, and agency is vivid in Mary Moran's "Warriors or Soldiers? Masculinity and Ritual Transvestism in the Liberian Civil War." As Cynthia Enloe (1989) reminds us, violence and warfare do not arise naturally. It takes a lot of power to turn a man into a soldier and a woman into a wife or mother of a martyr. Violence in Liberia is intimately involved with cultural production. After the 1980 Liberian coup, Samuel K. Doe's regime became more repressive. Various rebel armies were photographed in appropriated women's wigs and lingerie. Moran traces this behavior to adult male age grades of warrior societies, whose ritual war dances often combined Western and indigenous male and female elements in order to signal the warrior's control over them. This apparently bizarre behavior was an attempt by rebel soldiers to retrieve the power of the indigenous warrior as well as an implicit protest against the image of the soldier that the Doe regime promulgated.

The practices of women in postcolonial societies are often bound up not so much with issues of representation as with efforts to deal with concrete economic realities. Faye Harrison and Devon Peña illuminate the individual and collective practices of women who are facing the consequences of structural adjustment in Jamaica and Mexico, respectively. In "The Gendered Politics and Violence of Structural Adjustment: A View from Jamaica," Harrison clarifies how structural adjustment in the Third World created gendered fields of power. With few jobs, men get caught up in a masculinized order where virility, physical prowess, and toughness hold sway in urban "no man's lands." These spaces are contested by women who assert "mother-like" responsibility as center women and peacemakers and claim a "mother's yard," shared community space apart from violent areas. Harrison also shows how one unemployed woman used her transnational networks, moving through a series of informal sector activities in her community and then abroad when she reluctantly traveled to visit relatives. Her savings accounted for her family's survival once she returned to Jamaica.

In "The Mirror of Exploitation," Devon Peña analyzes COMO (Centro de Orientación de la Mujer Obrera), a center for community and workplace organizing in Ciudad Júarez, and gives a sense of collective strategies by women in the Third World. The center was originally founded in the late 1960s in an effort to help women *maquila* workers adapt to their roles, but its organizers eventually became more militant. Pushed by women who were developing a critical consciousness, COMO turned toward organizing worker cooperatives, offering training programs to ex-*maquila* workers, and involving students in research on local issues, who then acted as community organizers and labor activists. They developed outreach and provided advice and counseling to local farm workers, *maquila* independent unions, and worker cooperatives. Peña argues that these activities constitute a form of collective resistance that altered development along the U. S.-Mexican border.

Conclusion

Providing nuanced case studies of ethnographic sites around the globe, the essays included here analyze cultural transformation, gendered practice, and varied forms of resistance. While we learn about hybrid identities and cultural expressions, diasporas, power and representation, they provide fresh, grounded analyses of ethnography, reproduction, family, work, and colonialism. As critical and feminist scholars, mindful of a globalized world increasingly interconnected and multi-layered with meaning, these authors provide insight into the experiences of women and men situated in time and place. As well, they present situated knowledges of themselves as self-reflexive researchers and writers, or of their subjects who engage in quotidian struggles against the material and cultural constraints on their lives. Collectively these scholars give us a sense of hope, for even when faced with the most fouled work sites, repressive regimes, rigid notions of family, segregated neighborhoods, or blocked opportunities, ethnographic subjects express their own cultural meaning, take matters into their own hands, and work together. These are classic stories we need to hear again and again.

Works Cited

Abu-Lughod, Lila. 1990. Can There Be a Feminist Ethnography? *Women and Performance: A Journal of Feminist Theory* 5(1):9.

———. 1993. *Writing Women's Worlds: Bedouin Stories.* Berkeley: University of California Press.

Avineri, Shlomo. 1968. *The Social and Political Thought of Karl Marx.* Cambridge: Cambridge University Press.

Behar, Ruth, and Deborah Gordon, eds. 1995. *Women Writing Culture.* Berkeley: University of California Press.

Bluestone, Barry, and Bennett Harrison. 1982. *The Deindustrialization of America: Plant*

Closings, Community Abandonment, and the Dismantling of Basic Industry. New York: Basic Books.

Bourdieu, Pierre. 1977. *Outline of a Theory of Practice*. Cambridge: Cambridge University Press.

Bourque, Susan C., and Kay Barbara Warren. 1981. *Women of the Andes: Patriarchy and Social Change in Two Peruvian Towns*. Ann Arbor: University of Michigan Press.

Briggs, Jean. 1970. *Never in Anger*. Cambridge: Harvard University Press.

Collier, Jane. 1974. Women in Politics. In *Women, Culture, and Society*. Ed. Michelle Zimbalist Rosaldo and Louise Lamphere. Stanford: Stanford University Press, pp. 89–96.

Collier, Jane, and Sylvia Yanagisako, eds. 1987. *Gender and Kinship: Essays Toward a Unified Analysis*. Stanford: Stanford University Press, pp. 89–96.

Coontz, Stephanie. 1992. *The Way We Never Were: American Families and the Nostalgia Trap*. New York: Basic Books.

Delany, Carol. 1986. The Meaning of Paternity and the Virgin Birth Debate. *Man* 21:494–513.

di Leonardo, Micaela. 1984. *The Varieties of Ethnic Experience: Kinship, Class, and Gender Among California Italian-Americans*. Ithaca: Cornell University Press.

———, ed. 1991. *Gender at the Crossroads of Knowledge: Feminist Anthropology in the Postmodern Era*. Berkeley: University of California Press.

Enloe, Cynthia. 1989. *Bananas, Beaches, and Bases: Making Feminist Sense of International Politics*. Berkeley: University of California Press.

Fernea, Elizabeth. 1969. *Guests of the Sheik*. New York: Anchor Books.

Friedan, Betty. 1963. *The Feminine Mystique*. New York: Dell Publishing Co., Inc.

Garson, Barbara. 1988. *The Electronic Sweatshop: How Computers Are Transforming the Office of the Future into the Factory of the Past*. New York: Simon and Schuster.

Geertz, Clifford. 1973. *The Interpretation of Culture*. New York: Basic Books.

Giddens, Anthony. 1979. *Central Problems in Social Theory: Action, Structure and Contradiction in Social Analysis*. Berkeley: University of California Press.

Ginsburg, Faye, and Rayna Rapp, eds. 1995. *Conceiving the New World Order: The Global Politics of Reproduction*. Berkeley: University of California Press.

Glenn, Evelyn Nakano. 1985. Racial Ethnic Women's Labor: The Intersection of Race, Gender, and Class Oppression. *Review of Radical Political Economy* 17(3):86–108.

———. 1992. From Servitude to Service Work: Historical Continuities in the Racial Division of Paid Reproductive Labor. *Signs* 18 (1):1–43.

Golde, Peggy. 1970. *Women in the Field*. Chicago: Aldine Publishing Company.

Haraway, Donna. 1991. *Simians, Cyborgs, and Women: The Reinvention of Nature*. New York: Routledge.

Hochschild, Arlie. 1989. *The Managed Heart: Commercialization of Human Feeling*. Berkeley: University of California Press.

Hymes, Dell, ed. 1969. *Reinventing Anthropology*. New York: Vintage Books.

Lamphere, Louise. 1974. Strategies, Cooperation, and Conflict Among Women in Domestic Groups. In *Women, Culture and Society*. Ed. Michelle Zimbalist Rosaldo and Louise Lamphere. Stanford: Stanford University Press, pp. 97–112.

Lamphere, Louise, Patricia Zavella, and Felipe Gonzales with Peter Evans. 1992. *Sunbelt Working Mothers: Reconciling Family and Factory*. Ithaca: Cornell University Press.

Lancaster, Roger N. and Micaela di Leonardo, eds. 1997. Introduction: Embodied Meanings, Carnal Practices. In *The Gender/Sexuality Reader: Culture, History, Political Economy*. New York: Routledge.

Liebow, Elliot. 1993. *Tell Them Who I Am: The Lives of Homeless Women*. New York: Free Press.

Marcus, George, and Michael Fischer, eds. 1986. *Anthropology as Cultural Critique: An Experimental Moment in the Human Sciences*. Chicago: University of Chicago Press.

Marx, Karl. [1845] 1964. Theses on Feuerbach. In *Selected Writings in Sociology and Social Philosophy*. Trans. T. B. Bottomore. New York: McGraw-Hill, pp. 67–70.

Murphy, Robert, and Yolanda. 1974. *Women of the Forest*. New York: Columbia University Press.

Ortner, Sherry B. 1989. *High Religion: A Cultural and Political History of Sherpa Buddhism*. Princeton: Princeton University Press.

Ortner, Sherry, and Harriet Whitehead, eds. 1981. *Sexual Meanings: The Cultural Construction of Gender and Sexuality*. New York: Cambridge University Press.

Rabinow, Paul. 1977. *Reflections on Fieldwork in Morocco*. Berkeley: University of California Press.

Ragoné, Helena. 1994. *Surrogate Motherhood: Conception in the Heart*. Boulder: Westview Press.

Rosaldo, Renato. 1989. *Culture and Truth: The Remaking of Social Analysis*. Boston: Beacon Press.

Rubin, Gayle. 1975. The Traffic in Women. In *Towards an Anthropology of Women*. Ed. Rayna Reiter. New York: Monthly Review Press, pp. 157–210.

———. 1984. Thinking Sex: Notes for a Radical Theory of the Politics of Sexuality. In *Pleasure and Danger: Exploring Female Sexuality*. Ed., Carol S. Vance. London: Routledge & Kegan Paul, pp. 267–319.

Sacks, Karen. 1979. *Sisters and Wives: The Past and Future of Sexual Equality*. Westport, Conn.: Greenwood Press.

———. 1988. *Caring by the Hour: Women, Work and Organizing at the Duke Medical Center*. Urbana: University of Illinois Press.

Said, Edward. 1978. *Orientalism*. New York: Vintage Books.

Stacey, Judith. 1988. Can There Be a Feminist Ethnography? *Women's Studies International Forum* 11 (1):21–27.

Stack, Carol B. 1974. *All Our Kin*. New York: Harper and Row.

Strathern, Marilyn. 1972. *Women in Between: Female Roles in a Male World*. London: Seminar Press.

———. 1987. An Awkward Relationship: The Case of Feminism and Anthropology. *Signs* 1 (2):276–94.

———. 1991. The Pursuit of Certainty: Investigating Kinship in the Late Twentieth Century. Paper presented at the American Anthropology Association Meetings, Chicago, Illinois.

———. 1992a. The Meaning of Assisted Kinship. In *Changing Human Reproduction*. Ed., Meg Stacey. London: Sage Publications, pp. 148–169.

———. 1992b. *After Nature: English Kinship in the Late Twentieth Century*. Cambridge: Cambridge University Press.

———. 1992c. *Reproducing the Future*. New York: Routledge.

Tyler, Sir Edward Burnett. [1871] 1958. *The Origins of Culture*. New York: Harper and Row.

U. S. Census Bureau. 1994. *Household and Family Characteristics*. Washington, D. C.: U. S. Government Printing Office.

Yanagisako, Sylvia, and Carol Delany, eds. 1995. *Naturalizing Power: Essays in Feminist Cultural Analysis*. New York: Routledge.

Weaver, Thomas. 1973. *To See Ourselves: Anthropology and Modern Social Issues*. Glenview, Ill.: Scott, Foresman and Company.

Weiner, Annette. 1976. *Women of Value, Men of Renown*. Austin: University of Texas Press.

Williams, Brett. 1992. *Upscaling Downtown: Stalled Gentrification in Washington, D.C.* Ithaca: Cornell University Press.

Wolf, Margery. 1968. *House of Lim: A Study of a Chinese Farm Family*. New York: Appleton Century-Crofts.

———. 1972. *Women and the Family in Taiwan*. Stanford: Stanford University Press.

———. 1974. Chinese Women: Old Skills in a New Context. In *Women, Culture and Society*. Ed. Michelle Zimbalist Rosaldo and Louise Lamphere. Stanford: Stanford University Press, pp. 157–172.

Zavella, Patricia. 1987. *Women's Work and Chicano Families: Cannery Workers of the Santa Clara Valley*. Ithaca: Cornell University Press.

Part One

The Power of Representation

Gendered Ethnography in Practice

How Native Is a "Native" Anthropologist?

KIRIN NARAYAN

How "native" is a native anthropologist? How "foreign" is an anthropologist from abroad? The paradigm polarizing "regular" and "native" anthropologists is, after all, part of received disciplinary wisdom. Those who are anthropologists in the usual sense of the word are thought to study Others whose alien cultural worlds they must painstakingly come to know. Those who diverge as "native," "indigenous," or "insider" anthropologists are believed to write about their own cultures from a position of intimate affinity. Certainly, there have been scattered voices critiquing this dichotomy. Arguing that because a culture is not homogeneous, a society is differentiated, and a professional identity that involves problematizing lived reality inevitably creates a distance, scholars such as Aguilar (1981) and Messerschmidt (1981a:9) conclude that the extent to which anyone is an authentic insider is questionable. Yet such critiques have not yet been adequately integrated into the way "native" anthropologists are popularly viewed in the profession.

In this essay, I argue against the fixity of a distinction between "native" and "non-native" anthropologists. Instead of the paradigm emphasizing a dichotomy between outsider/insider or observer/observed, I propose that at this historical moment we might more profitably view each anthropologist in terms of shifting identifications amid a field of interpenetrating communities and power relations. The loci along which we are aligned with or set apart from those whom we study are multiple and in flux. Factors such as education, gender, sexual orientation, class, race, or sheer duration of contacts may at different times outweigh the cultural identity we associate with insider or outsider status. Instead, what we must focus our attention on is the quality of relations with the people we seek to represent in our texts: are they viewed as mere fodder for professionally self-serving statements about a generalized Other, or are they accepted as subjects with voices, views, and dilemmas—people to whom we are bonded through ties of reciprocity and who may even be critical of our professional enterprise?

I write as someone who bears the label of "native" anthropologist and yet squirms uncomfortably under this essentializing tag. To highlight the personal and intellectual dilemmas invoked by the assumption that a "native" anthropologist can represent an unproblematic and authentic insider's perspective, I incorporate personal narrative into a wider discussion of anthropological scholarship. Tacking between situated narrative and more sweeping analysis, I argue for the *enactment of hybridity* in our texts; that is, writing that depicts authors as minimally bicultural in terms of belonging simultaneously to the world of engaged scholarship and the world of everyday life.

The Problem in Historical Perspective

The paradigm that polarizes "native" anthropologists and "real" anthropologists stems from the colonial setting in which the discipline of anthropology was forged: the days in which natives were genuine natives (whether they liked it or not) and the observer's objectivity in the scientific study of Other societies posed no problem. To achieve access to *the native's* point of view (note the singular form), an anthropologist used the method of participant-observation among a variety of representative natives, often singling out one as a "chief informant" (Casagrande 1960). A chief informant might also be trained in anthropological modes of data collection so that the society could be revealed "from within." As Franz Boas argued, materials reported and inscribed by a trained native would have "the immeasurable advantage of trustworthiness, authentically revealing precisely the elusive thoughts and sentiments of the native" (Lowie 1937:133, cited in Jones 1970:252). Or better yet, a smart and adequately Westernized native might go so far as to receive the education of a bona fide anthropologist and reveal a particular society to the profession with an insider's eye. Ordinary people commenting on their society, chief informants friendly with a foreign anthropologist, or insiders trained to collect indigenous texts were all in some sense natives contributing to the enterprise of anthropology. Yet, it was only those who received the full professional initiation into a disciplinary fellowship of discourse who became the bearers of the title "native" anthropologist.

Even if such a "native" anthropologist went on to make pathbreaking professional contributions, his or her origins remained a perpetual qualifier. For example, writing the foreword to M. N. Srinivas's classic monograph on the Coorgs, Radcliffe-Brown emphasized that the writer was "a trained anthropologist, himself an Indian" and went on to add that he had "therefore an understanding of Indian ways of thought which it is difficult for a European to attain over many years" (Srinivas 1952:v). As Delmos Jones has charged, it is likely that "natives" who could get "the inside scoop" were first admitted into the charmed circle of professional discourse because they were potential tools of data collection for white anthropologists (Jones 1970:252). Admittedly, in an era prior to extensive decolonization and civil rights movements, that "natives" were allowed to participate at all in professional discourse was remarkable. In this context, calling attention to, rather than smoothing over, "native" identity perhaps helped to revise the ingrained power imbalances in who was authorized to represent whom.

Viewed from the vantage point of the 1990s, however, it is not clear that the term *native anthropologist* serves us well. Amid the contemporary global flows of trade, politics, migrations, ecology, and the mass media, the accepted nexus of authentic culture/demarcated field/exotic locale has unraveled (Appadurai 1990, 1991; Clifford 1992; Gupta and Ferguson 1992). Although many of the terms of anthropological discourse remain largely set by the West, anthropology is currently practiced by members (or partial members) of previously colonized societies that now constitute the so-called Third World (Altorki and El-Solh 1988; Fahim 1982; Kumar 1992; Nakhleh 1979; Srinivas, Shah, and Ramaswamy 1979). These scholars often have institutional bases in the Third World, but some have also migrated to Europe and the United States. Furthermore, in the First World, minority anthropologists also hold university positions and their contributions to ongoing discourse have helped to realign, if not overthrow, some of the discipline's ethnocentric assumptions (Gwaltney 1981; Jones 1970; Limón 1991). Feminist scholarship questioning the formulation of "woman as Other" has underscored the differences between women and the multiple planes along which identity is constructed, thus destabilizing the category of "Other" as well as "Self" (Abu-Lughod 1990; Alarcon 1990; Lauretis 1986; Mani 1990; Mohanty and Russo 1991; Strathern 1987). It has also become acceptable to turn the anthropological gaze inward, toward communities in Western nations (Ginsburg 1989; Ginsburg and Tsing 1990; Martin 1987; Messerschmidt 1981b; Ortner 1991). The "field" is increasingly a flexible concept: it can move with the travels of Hindu pilgrims (Gold 1988), span Greek villagers and New Age American healers (Danforth 1989), or even be found in automobile garages of South Philadelphia (Rose 1987). In this changed setting, a rethinking of "insider" and "outsider" anthropologists as stable categories seems long overdue.

Multiplex Identity

"If Margaret Mead can live in Samoa," my mother is reputed to have said when she moved to India, "I can live in a joint family." The daughter of a German father and American mother, she had just married my Indian father. Yet these terms—*German, American, Indian*—are broad labels deriving from modern nation-states. Should I instead say that my mother, the daughter of a Bavarian father and a WASP mother who lived in Taos, New Mexico, became involved with her fellow student at the University of Colorado: my Indian-from-India father? Yet, for anyone familiar with India shouldn't I add that my father's father was from the Kutch desert region, his mother from the dense Kathiawari forests, and that while he might loosely be called "Gujarati" his background was further complicated by growing up in the state of Maharashtra? Should I mention that Mayflower blood supposedly mingles with that of Irish potato famine immigrants on my maternal grandmother's side (I'm told I could qualify as a "D. A. R."), or that as temple builders, members of my paternal grandfather's caste vehemently claimed a contested status as Brahman rather than lower-ranking carpenter? Should I add that my father was the only Hindu boy in a Parsi school that would give him a strictly British education, inscribing the caste profession-based title "Mistri" (carpenter) onto the books as the surname "Contractor"? Or would it better locate my father to say that he remembers the days when signs outside colonial clubs read "No Dogs or Indians"? Also, is it useful to point out that my mother—American by passport—has now lived in India for over 40 years (more than two-thirds of her life) and is instructed by her bossy children on how to comport herself when she visits the United States?

I invoke these threads of a culturally tangled identity to demonstrate that a person may have many strands of identification available, strands that may be tugged into the open or stuffed out of sight. A mixed background such as mine perhaps marks one as inauthentic for the label "native" or "indigenous" anthropologist; perhaps those who are not clearly "native" or "non-native" should be termed "halfies" instead (cf. Abu-Lughod 1991). Yet, two halves cannot adequately account for the complexity of an identity in which multiple countries, regions, religions, and classes may come together. While my siblings and I have spent much of our lives quipping that we are "haylf" (pronounced with an American twang) and "hahlf" (with a British-educated accent), I increasingly wonder whether any person of mixed ancestry can be so neatly split down the middle, excluding all the other vectors that have shaped them. Then too, mixed ancestry is itself a cultural fact: the gender of the particular parents, the power dynamic between the groups that have mixed, and the prejudices of the time all contribute to the mark that mixed blood leaves on a person's identity (cf. Spickard 1989).

Growing up in Bombay with a strongly stressed patrilineage, a Hindu Indian identity has weighed more than half in my self-definition, pushing into the background the Pilgrim fathers and Bavarian burghers who are also available in my genealogical repertoire. This would seem to mark me as Indian and, therefore, when I study India, a "native" anthropologist. After all, researching aspects of India, I often share an unspoken emotional understanding with the people with whom I work (cf. Ohnuki-Tierney 1984). Performing fieldwork in Nasik on storytelling by a Hindu holy man whom I called "Swamiji," I had the benefit of years of association with not just Swamiji himself but also the language and wider culture. Since Nasik was the town where my father grew up, a preexisting identity defined by kinship subsumed my presence as ethnographer (cf. Nakhleh 1979). Similarly, researching women's songs and lives in the Himalayan foothills, I bore the advantage of having visited the place practically every year since I was 15, and of my mother having settled there. All too well aware of traditional expectations for proper behavior by an unmarried daughter, in both places I repressed aspects of my cosmopolitan Bombay persona and my American self to behave with appropriate decorum and deference (cf. Abu-Lughod 1988).

In both Nasik and in Kangra, different aspects of identity became highlighted at different times. In Nasik, when elderly gentlemen wearing white Congress caps arrived and Swamiji pointed me out as "Ramji Mistri's granddaughter," my local roots were highlighted, and I felt a diffuse pride for my association with the Nasik landmark of the Victorian bungalow that my grandfather had built in the 1920s. Visiting Nathu Maharaj, the barber with buckteeth and stained clothes, to discuss interpretations of Swamiji's stories, I felt uncomfortable, even ashamed, of the ways in which my class had allowed me opportunities that were out of reach for this bright and reflective man. My gender was important in the observance of menstrual taboos not to touch Swamiji or the altar—injunctions that left me so mortified that I would simply leave town for several days. Borrowing the latest Stevie Wonder tapes from one of "the foreigners"—a disciple from New Jersey—I savored a rowdy release, becoming again a woman who had lived independently in a California university town. When Swamiji advised that in written texts I keep his identity obscure ("What need do I have for publicity?"—yet his doctor took me aside to advise that I disregard such modesty and identify him by name, "so people abroad will know his greatness"), I felt my role as culture broker with the dubious power to extend First World prestige to Third World realities. Yet, when Swamiji challenged my motives for taking his words on tape "to do a business," I was set apart from all planes of locally available identification, thrown outside a circle of fellowship forged by spiritual concerns, and lumped instead with academics who made it their business to document and theorize about other people's lives (Narayan 1989:59–62).

For my second extended research project in the Himalayan foothills region of Kangra, I had no deep local roots. I was unmoored from a certain base for identification, and the extent to which *others* can manipulate an anthropologist's identity came into dizzying focus (Dumont 1978; Stoller 1989). Explaining my presence, some of the village women I worked with asserted that I was from such-and-such village (where my mother lives), hence local. At other times I was presented as being "from Bombay," that is, a city dweller from a distant part of the country although still recognizably Indian. A wrinkled old woman I once fell into step with on an outing between villages asked if I was a member of the pastoral Gaddi tribe (to her, the epitome of a close-by Other). At yet other times, and particularly at weddings where a splash of foreign prestige added to the festivities, I was incontrovertibly stated to be "from America . . . she came *all* the way from there for this function, yes, with her camera and her tape recorder!" In the same household at different times, I was forced to answer questions about whether all Americans were savages (*jangli log*) because television revealed that they didn't wear many clothes, and to listen as a member of a spellbound local audience when a dignified Rajput matron from another village came by to tell tales about how she had visited her emigrant son in New Jersey. In the local language, she held forth on how, in America, people just ate "round breads" of three sizes with vegetables and *masalas* smeared on top (pizza); how shops were enormous, with everything you could imagine in them, and plastic bags you could rip off like leaves from a tree; how you put food in a "trolley" and then a woman would press buttons, giving you a bill for hundreds and hundreds of rupees! Bonded with other entranced listeners, my own claims to authoritative experience in this faraway land of wonders seemed to have temporarily dropped out of sight.

Now it might be assumed that I had experienced these shifting identifications simply because of my peculiar background, and that someone who was "fully" Indian by birth and upbringing might have a more stable identity in the field. For a comparison, I could turn to Nita Kumar's lively and insightful *Friends, Brothers, and Informants: A Memoir of Fieldwork in Banaras* (1992), which makes many of the same points. Instead, I look further back (to pre-postmodern times) and draw out some of the implications about identity from M. N. Srinivas's compelling ethnography, *The Remembered Village* (1976). Srinivas is one of India's most respected anthropologists, although given the division of labor between anthropologists as those who focus on the Other (tribal groups) and sociologists who research the Self (village and urban dwellers), in India he is known as a sociologist. Srinivas was educated in Oxford in the 1940s. On Radcliffe-Brown's advice, he planned to do fieldwork in a multicaste village called Rampura in Mysore (Karnataka State). Srinivas's ancestors had moved several generations before from neighboring Tamil Nadu to rural Mysore; his father had left his village for the city so that his children could be educated. In returning from Oxford to live in a village, Srinivas stated his hope that "my study . . . would enable me better to understand my personal cultural and social roots" (1976:5).

But did the presence of these roots mean that he was regarded as a "native" returning home to blend smoothly with other "natives"? No, he was an educated urbanite and Brahman male, and the power of this narrative ethnography lies very much in Srinivas's sensitivity to the various ways in which he interacted with members of the community: sometimes aligned with particular groups, sometimes set apart. As he confesses, "It was only in the village that I realized how far I (and my family) had travelled away from tradition" (1976:18). From his account, one gets the impression that the villagers found him a very entertaining oddity. He struggled regularly with villagers' expectations that he behave as a Brahman should (1976:33–40). Growing up in the city, he had not internalized rules of purity and pollution to the extent that they bound local Brahmans, and he found himself reprimanded by the headman for shaving himself *after* rather than before a ritual bath. On the other hand, a political activist criticized him for his involvement with the headman, rather than with all sections and factions of the village (1976:22). When he did move throughout the village, he found himself received with affection: "word must have gone round that I did not consider myself too high to mix with poor villagers" (1976:24). Yet, as he was a respected guest and outsider, villagers as a group also colluded in keeping details of unpleasant "incidents" regarding sex, money, and vendettas from him (1976:40–47). In a lighter vein, many villagers knew him by the exotic object he sported, a camera that fulfilled not just their ends (such as the use of photographs in arranging marriages) but also his anthropological responsibilities of recording for a foreign audience. He became "the camera man—only they transformed 'camera' into 'chamara' which in Kannada means the fly-whisk made from the long hair of yak tails" (1976:20). Villagers plied him with questions about the English, and the headman even planned a tour of England in which Srinivas was to be adopted as guide (1976:29). In short, his relationships were complex and shifting: in different settings, his caste, urban background, unintended affiliations with a local faction, class privilege, attempts to bridge all sectors of the community, or alliance with a faraway land could be highlighted.

Even as insiders or partial insiders, in some contexts we are drawn closer; in others we are thrust apart. Multiple planes of identification may be most painfully highlighted among anthropologists who have identities spanning racial or cultural groups (Abu-Lughod 1988, 1991; Kondo 1986, 1990; Lavie 1990). Yet, in that we all belong to several communities simultaneously (not least of all the community we were born into and the community of professional academics), I would argue that *every* anthropologist exhibits what Rosaldo has termed a "multiplex subjectivity" with many crosscutting identifications (Rosaldo 1989:168–195). Which facet of our subjectivity we choose or are forced to accept as a defining identity can change, depending on the context and the prevailing vectors of power. What Stuart Hall has written about cultural identity holds also for personal identity:

> Cultural identities come from somewhere, have histories. But like everything which is historical, they [identities] undergo constant trans-formation. Far from being eternally fixed in some essentialised past, they are subject to the continuous "play" of history, culture, and power. Far from being grounded in a mere "recovery" of the past, which is waiting to be found, and which, when found, will secure our sense of ourselves into eternity, identities are the names we give to the different ways we are positioned by, and position ourselves within, the narratives of the past. [Hall 1989:70]

Rethinking Connections through Fieldwork

We are instructed as anthropologists to "grasp the native's point of view, his relation to life, to realize *his* vision of *his* world" (Malinowski 1961 [1922]:25). Yet who is this generic subject, "the native"? To use a clump term is to assume that all natives are the same native, mutually substitutable in presenting the same (male) point of view. Yet even received anthropological wisdom tells us that in the simplest societies, gender and age provide factors for social differentiation. To extend conceptual tools forged for the study of heuristically bounded, simple societies to a world in which many societies and subgroups interact amid shifting fields of power, these very tools must be reexamined. We would most certainly be better off looking for the natives' points of view to realize *their* visions of *their* worlds while at the same time acknowledging that "we" do not speak from a position outside "their" worlds, but are implicated in them too (cf. Mani 1990; Mohanty 1989; Said 1989): through fieldwork, political relations, and a variety of global flows.

Arjun Appadurai (1988) has persuasively teased out some of the underlying assumptions in anthropological use of the term *native* for groups who belong to parts of the world distant and distinct from the metropolitan West. As he argues, the concept is associated with an ideology of *authenticity*: "Proper natives are somehow assumed to represent their selves and their history, without distortion or residue" (1988:37). Those in the position to observe "natives," however, exempt themselves from being authentic and instead represent themselves in terms of complexity, diversity, and ambiguity. Furthermore, the term is linked to *place*. "Natives" are incarcerated in bounded geographical spaces, immobile and untouched yet paradoxically available to the mobile outsider. Appadurai goes on to show how in anthropological discourse, "natives" tied to particular places are also associated with particular *ideas*: one goes to India to study hierarchy, the circum-Mediterranean region for honor and shame, China for ancestor worship, and so on, forgetting that anthropological preoccupations represent "the temporary *localization* of ideas from *many* places" (1988:46, emphasis in original).

The critique that Appadurai levels at the term *native* can also be extended to *native anthropologist*. A "native" anthropologist is assumed to be an insider who will forward an authentic point of view to the anthropological community. The fact that the profession remains intrigued by the notion of the "native" anthropologist

as carrying a stamp of authenticity is particularly obvious in the ways in which identities are doled out to non-Western, minority, or mixed anthropologists so that
exotic difference overshadows commonalities or complexities. That my mother is
German-American seems as irrelevant to others' portrayal of me as "Indian" as the
American mothers of the "Tewa" Alfonso Ortiz, the "Chicano" Renato Rosaldo, or
the "Arab" Lila Abu-Lughod. For those of us who are mixed, the darker element in
our ancestry serves to define us with or without our own complicity. The fact that
we are often distanced—by factors as varied as education, class, or emigration—
from the societies we are supposed to represent tends to be underplayed. Furthermore, it is only appropriate (and this may be the result of our own identity quests)
that sooner or later we will study the exotic societies with which we are associated.
Finally, while it is hoped that we will contribute to the existing anthropological
pool of knowledge, we are not really expected to diverge from prevailing forms of
discourse to frame what Delmos Jones has called a genuinely "native" anthropology
as "a set of theories based on non-Western precepts and assumptions" (1970:251).

"Native" anthropologists, then, are perceived as insiders regardless of their
complex backgrounds. The differences between kinds of "native" anthropologists
are also obliviously passed over. Can a person from an impoverished American
minority background who, despite all prejudices, manages to get an education and
study her own community be equated with a member of a Third World elite group
who, backed by excellent schooling and parental funds, studies anthropology
abroad yet returns home for fieldwork among the less privileged? Is it not insensitive to suppress the issue of location, acknowledging that a scholar who chooses an
institutional base in the Third World might have a different engagement with
Western-based theories, books, political stances, and technologies of written production? Is a middle-class white professional researching aspects of her own society also a "native" anthropologist?

And what about non-"native" anthropologists who have dedicated themselves to
long-term fieldwork, returning year after year to sustain ties to a particular community? Should we not grant them some recognition for the different texture this
brings to their work? It is generally considered more savvy in terms of professional
advancement to do fieldwork in several different cultures rather than returning to
deepen understandings in one. Yet to use people one has lived with for articles and
monographs, and not maintain ties through time, generates a sort of "hit-and-run"
anthropology in which engagement with vibrant individuals is flattened by the
demands of a scholarly career. Having a safe footing to return to outside the field
situation promotes "a contemplative stance . . . [that] pervades anthropology, disguising the confrontation between Self and Other and rendering the discipline
powerless to address the vulnerability of the Self" (Dwyer 1982:269). Regular
returns to a field site, on the other hand, can nourish the growth of responsible
human ties and the subsuming of cultural difference within the fellowship of a
"We-relation" (Schutz 1973:16–17). As George Foster and the other editors of the
book *Long-Term Field Research in Social Anthropology* point out in their concluding
comments, an ongoing personal involvement with people in the communities studied often makes for an interest in "action" or "advocacy" work (Foster et al.

1979:344). Looking beyond the human rewards to the professional ones, long-term fieldwork leads to the stripping away of formal self-presentations and the granting of access to cultural domains generally reserved for insiders, thus making better scholarship. Returns to the field allow for a better understanding of how individuals creatively shape themselves and their societies through time. Finally, repeated returns to the field force an anthropologist to reconsider herself and her work not just from the perspective of the academy but also from that of the people she purports to represent. As Paul Stoller has written about his long-term fieldwork among the Songhay in Niger:

> Besides giving me the perspective to assess social change, long-term study of Songhay has plunged me into the Songhay worlds of sorcery and possession, worlds the wisdom of which are closed to outsiders—even Songhay outsiders. My insistence on long-term study forced me to confront the interpretive errors of earlier visits. Restudying Songhay also enabled me to get a bit closer to "getting it right." But I have just begun to walk my path. As Adamu Jenitongo once told me, "Today you are learning about us, but to understand us, you will have to grow old with us." [Stoller 1989:6]

While Stoller was not born Songhay, his ongoing engagement has given him a niche in the society, a place from which he is invited to "grow old" *with* his teacher. Like all long-term relationships, his encounters in the field have had exhilarating ups and cataclysmic downs, yet persevering has brought the reward of greater insight. Do not anthropologists who engage sensitively in long-term fieldwork also deserve respect from their professional colleagues as partial insiders who have through time become bicultural (cf. Tedlock 1991)? Need a "native" anthropologist be so very different?

It might be argued that the condescending colonial connotations of a generic identity that cling to the term *native* could be lessened by using alternative words: *indigenous* or *insider*, for example. Yet the same conceptual underpinnings apply to these terms too: they all imply that an authentic insider's perspective is possible, and that this can unproblematically represent the associated group. This leads us to underplay the ways in which people born within a society can be simultaneously both insiders and outsiders, just as those born elsewhere can be outsiders and, if they are lucky, insiders too. Also, as Elizabeth Colson has bluntly stated, "'Indigenous' is a misnomer, for all of us are indigenous somewhere and the majority of anthropologists at some time deal with their own communities" (Fahim et al. 1980:650). We are *all* "native" or "indigenous" anthropologists in this scheme, even if we do not appear so in every fieldwork context. Rather than try to sort out who is authentically a "native" anthropologist and who is not, surely it is more rewarding to examine the ways in which each one of us is situated in relation to the people we study.

Situated Knowledges

Visiting Nasik as a child, I knew better than to touch Maharaj, the chubby Brahman cook, as he bent over to fill our shining steel *thalis* on the floor; yet, if asked, I would never have been able to explain this in terms of "purity and pollution." I knew that servants were frequently shouted at and that they wore ill-fitting, cast-off clothes, but I did not call this "social inequality." I observed that my girl cousins were fed after the boys and that although they excelled in school they were not expected to have careers, but I did not call it "gender hierarchy." I listened raptly when the Harveys, a British couple who had stayed on after 1947, told us stories about viceroys and collectors, but I did not know the words "colonization" or "decolonization." When, amid the volley of British authors who shaped our minds in school, we finally came across poems by Rabindranath Tagore, I noticed that these were different but could not call them "nationalist." Reflecting on India with the vocabulary of a social analyst, I find that new light is shed on many of the experiences that have shaped me into the person—and professional—I am today.

In some ways, the study of one's own society involves an inverse process from the study of an alien one. Instead of learning conceptual categories and then, through fieldwork, finding the contexts in which to apply them, those of us who study societies in which we have preexisting experience absorb analytic categories that rename and reframe what is already known. The reframing essentially involves locating vivid particulars within larger cultural patterns, sociological relations, and historical shifts. At one further remove, anthropological categories also rephrase these particulars as evidence of theoretical issues that cross cultures and are the special province of trained academics.

Yet, given the diversity within cultural domains and across groups, even the most experienced of "native" anthropologists cannot know everything about his or her own society (Aguilar 1981). In fact, by opening up access to hidden stores of research materials, the study of anthropology can also lead to the discovery of many strange and unfamiliar aspects of one's own society (cf. Stewart 1989:14). I have learned, for example, a good deal more about village life, regional differences, and tribal groups than what my urban upbringing supplied. Institutions and belief systems that I took for granted as immutable reality—such as caste or Hinduism— have been dismantled as historical and discursive constructions. Even for a purported insider, it is clearly impossible to be omniscient: one knows about a society from particular locations within it (cf. Srinivas 1966:154).

As anthropologists, we do fieldwork whether or not we were raised close to the people whom we study. Whatever the methodologies used, the process of doing fieldwork involves getting to know a range of people and listening closely to what they say. Even if one should already be acquainted with some of these people before one starts fieldwork, the intense and sustained engagements of fieldwork will inevitably transmute these relationships. Fieldwork is a common plane binding professional anthropologists, but the process and outcome vary so widely that it is difficult to make a clear-cut distinction between the experiences of those with prior exposure and those who arrive as novices. As Nita Kumar writes in her memoir of fieldwork in Banaras (which she had only visited before as the sheltered, Anglicized daughter of a highly placed Indian government official): "Fieldwork consists of experiences shared by all anthropologists; the personal and the peculiar are significant as qualities that *always* but *differently* characterize each individual experience" (1992:6, emphasis in original).

To acknowledge particular and personal locations is to admit the limits of one's purview from these positions. It is also to undermine the notion of objectivity, because from particular locations all understanding becomes subjectively based and forged through interactions within fields of power relations. Positioned knowledges and partial perspectives are part of the lingo that has risen to common usage in the 1980s (Clifford 1986, 1988; Haraway 1988; Kondo 1986; Rosaldo 1989). Yet, let us not forget the prescient words of Jacques Maquet from an article in which he argued that decolonization laid bare the "perspectivist" character of anthropology in Africa, showing anthropology's claim to objectivity as entwined with power relations in which one group could claim to represent another. Arguing against objectivity in a polemic at least 20 years ahead of its time, he writes:

> A perspectivist knowledge is not as such non-objective: it is partial. It reflects an external reality but only an aspect of it, the one visible from the particular spot, social and individual, where the anthropologist was placed. Non-objectivity creeps in when the partial aspect is considered as the global one. [Maquet 1964:54]

Enacting Hybridity

"Suppose you and I are walking on the road," said Swamiji, the holyman whose storytelling I was researching in 1985. "You've gone to University. I haven't studied anything. We're walking. Some child has shit on the road. We both step in it. 'That's shit!' I say. I scrape my foot; it's gone. But educated people have doubts about everything. You say, 'What's this?!' and you rub your foot against the other." Swamiji shot up from his prone position in the deck chair, and placing his feet on the linoleum, stared at them with intensity. He rubbed the right sole against the left ankle. "Then you reach down to feel what it could be," his fingers now explored the ankle. A grin was breaking over his face. "Something sticky! You lift some up and sniff it. Then you say, 'Oh! This is *shit*.'" The hand that had vigorously rubbed his nose was flung out in a gesture of disgust.

Swamiji turned back toward me, cheeks lifted under their white stubble in a toothless and delighted grin. Everyone present in the room was laughing uncontrollably. I managed an uncomfortable smile.

"See how many places it touched in the meantime," Swamiji continued. "Educated people always doubt everything. They lie awake at night thinking, 'What was that? Why did it happen? What is the meaning and the cause of it?' Uneducated people pass judgment and walk on. They get a good night's sleep."

I looked up at Swamiji from my position on the floor and tried to avoid the eyes of the others, who watched me with broad smiles on their faces. "What was that? Why did it happen? What is the meaning and the cause of it?" rang in my ears as a parody of my own relentless questioning as an anthropologist interviewing both Swamiji and his listeners. I had to agree that among the academics I represented analysis could often become obsessive. But I also felt awkward, even a little hurt. This parable seemed to dismiss all the years that education had dominated my life. It ridiculed my very presence in this room. In his peculiar mixture of sternness and empathy, Swamiji must have read the discomfort on my face. When he settled back into his deck chair, he turned to me again. "It's not that you shouldn't study," he said, voice low and kind. "You should gain wisdom. But you should realize that in the end this means nothing."

Once again, Swamiji was needling any possible self-importance that might be ballooning inside me as self-appointed documenter and analyst of what to others was everyday life. While others enjoyed his stories and learned from them, I brought the weightiness of perpetual enquiry to the enterprise. Every action was evaluated (at least partially) in terms of my project on folk narrative as a form of religious teaching. Now Swamiji had turned his technique of instruction through stories on me. Through a parable, he dramatized how we both coexisted in shared time and space, "walking the same road," yet each with a different awareness. The power relations of "structured inequality" (Dwyer 1982; Rabinow 1977) that allow anthropologists to subsume their subjects in representation had been turned upside down with such a critique.

This uncomfortable scene dramatizes how the issue of who is an insider and who is an outsider is secondary to the need for dismantling objective distance to acknowledge our shared presence in the cultural worlds that we describe. Pioneering works on "native" anthropology emphasized the need for such anthropologists to achieve distance. Yet, distance, as Dorinne Kondo (1986) has observed, is both a stance and a cognitive-emotional orientation that makes for cold, generalized, purportedly objective and yet inevitably prejudiced forms of representation. As Kondo argues, it can be replaced with the acceptance of "more experiential and affective modes of knowing" (1986:75) in which the ethnographer's identity and location are made explicit and informants are given a greater role in texts. This is what Michael Jackson (1989) more recently called "radical empiricism": a methodology and discursive style that emphasizes the subject's experience and involvement with others in the construction of knowledge (cf. Stoller 1992).

To question the discipline's canonical modes of objective distance is not, however, to forfeit subjective distance and pretend that all fieldwork is a celebration of communitas. Given the multiplex nature of identity, there will inevitably be certain facets of self that join us up with the people we study, other facets that emphasize our difference. In even the closest of relationships, disjunctures can swell into distance; ruptures in communication can occur that must be bridged. To acknowledge such shifts in relationships rather than present them as purely distant or purely close is to enrich the textures of our texts so they more closely approximate the complexities of lived interaction. At the same time, frankness about actual interactions means that an anthropologist cannot hide superficial understandings behind sweeping statements and is forced to present the grounds of understanding. Further, as Lila Abu-Lughod has argued in regard to what she calls "ethnographies of the particular," by writing in terms of "particular individuals and their changing relationships, one would necessarily subvert the most problematic connotations of culture: homogeneity, coherence, and timelessness" (1991:154).

These insights hold radical implications for anthropological modes of representation. As I see it, there are currently two poles to anthropological writing: at one end stand accessible ethnographies laden with stories, and at the other end stand refereed journal articles, dense with theoretical analyses. We routinely assign narrative ethnographies in "Intro to Anthro" classes (even if these are written not by professional anthropologists, but by their wives [Fernea 1965; Shostak 1981]) because it is through narratives lively with people, places, and events that we know recalcitrant undergraduates are likely to be seduced by the discipline. Reading these ethnographies, we ourselves may forget we are judgmental professionals, so swept along are we in the evocative flow of other people's experiences. Narrative ethnography is one arena in which the literary critic Mary Louise Pratt's blunt diagnosis that ethnographic writing is boring (1986:33) simply does not apply. Journal articles, on the other hand, tend to be exclusively of interest to academics initiated into the fellowship of professional discourse, and subscribing members of a particular, academically formed society. Journal articles are written according to formulas that include a thesis introduced in the beginning and returned to at the end, and the convention that theoretical frameworks and generalized statements should be emphasized, suppressing vivid particulars. We read these articles with our minds more than our hearts, extorting ideas and references from their pages.

Need the two categories, compelling narrative and rigorous analysis, be impermeable? Increasingly, they seep into each other, and here I want to argue for an emerging style in anthropological writing that I call the *enactment of hybridity* (cf. Abu-Lughod 1992; Behar 1993; Jackson 1989; Kondo 1990; Lavie 1990; Rosaldo 1989; Rose 1987; Stoller 1989; Tedlock 1992). In using the word "enactment," I am drawing on Dorinne Kondo's view that "the *specificity* of . . . experience . . . is not opposed to theory; it *enacts* and *embodies* theory" (1990, emphasis in original): any writing, then, represents an enactment of some sort of theory. By "hybridity," I do not mean only a condition of people who are mixed from birth, but also a state that all anthropologists partake of but may not consciously include in our texts. As Edward Bruner (1993) has elegantly phrased it, every anthropologist carries both a personal and an ethnographic self. In this scheme, we are all incipiently bi- (or multi-) cultural in that we belong to worlds both personal and professional, whether in the field or at home. While people with Third World allegiances, minorities, or women may experience the tensions of this dual identity the most strongly, it is a condition of everyone, even of that conglomerate category termed "white men." Whether we are disempowered or empowered by prevailing power relations, we must all take responsibility for how our personal locations feed not just into our fieldwork interactions but also into our scholarly texts. When professional personas altogether efface situated and experiencing selves, this makes for misleading scholarship even as it does violence to the range of hybrid personal and professional identities that we negotiate in our daily lives.

Adopting a narrative voice involves an ethical stance that neither effaces ourselves as hybrid nor defaces the vivid humanity of the people with whom we work. Narrative transforms "informants" whose chief role is to spew cultural data for the anthropologist into subjects with complex lives and a range of opinions (that may even subsume the anthropological enterprise). At a moment in which scholarship has a "multinational reception" (cf. Mani 1990), it seems more urgent than ever that anthropologists acknowledge that it is *people* and not theoretical puppets who populate our texts, and that we allow these people to speak out from our writings. Also, narratives are not transparent representations of what actually happened, but are told for particular purposes, from particular points of view: they are thus incipiently analytical, enacting theory. Analysis itself is most effective when it builds directly from cases evoked through narrative, providing a chance to step away, reflect on, and reframe the riveting particulars of the story at hand. In including the perspective of the social analyst along with narratives from or about people studied, a stereoscopic "double vision" can be achieved (Rosaldo 1989:127–143). Some skillfully constructed analyses are as gripping as good mystery stories, starting from a conundrum, then assembling clues that finally piece together. Narrative and analysis are categories we tend to set up as opposites, yet a second look reveals that they are contiguous, with a border open even to the most full-scale of crossovers.

Calling for a greater integration of narrative into written texts does not mean that analysis is to be abandoned, but rather that it moves over, giving vivid experience an honored place beside it. By translating professional jargon into "the language of everyday life" (cf. Abu-Lughod 1991:151), analysis can also be made intriguing to audiences who would otherwise be compelled only by narrative. Admittedly, writing cannot singlehandedly change the inequalities in today's world; yet, in bearing the potential to change the attitudes of readers, ethical and accessible writing unquestionably takes a step in the right direction. As companions clothed in nontechnical language, narrative and analysis join to push open the doors of anthropological understanding and welcome in outsiders.

Conclusions

I have argued for a reorientation in the ways that we perceive anthropologists as "outside" or "inside" a society. The traditional view has been to polarize "real" anthropologists from "native" anthropologists, with the underlying assumption that a "native" anthropologist would forward an authentic insider's view to the profession. This view sprang from a colonial era in which inegalitarian power relations were relatively well defined: there was little question about the "civilized" outsider's ability to represent "primitive" peoples, and so it was worthy of note when a person excluded from dominant white culture was allowed to describe his or her own society. With changing times, however, the scope of anthropology has shifted to include industrialized societies, even as it is also practiced in "Third World" countries and by minority and "Third World" scholars. Identity, always multiplex, has become even more culturally complex at this historical moment in which global flows in trade, politics, and the media stimulate greater interpenetration between cultures.

In this changed setting, it is more profitable to focus on shifting identities in relationship with the people and issues an anthropologist seeks to represent. Even if one can blend into a particular social group without the quest of fieldwork, the very nature of researching what to others is taken-for-granted reality creates an uneasy distance. However, even if one starts out as a stranger, sympathies and ties developed through engaged coexistence may subsume difference within relationships of reciprocity. "Objectivity" must be replaced by an involvement that is unabashedly subjective as it interacts with and invites other subjectivities to take a place in anthropological productions. Knowledge, in this scheme, is not transcendental, but situated, negotiated, and part of an ongoing process. This process spans personal, professional, and cultural domains.

As we rethink "insiders" and "outsiders" in anthropology, I have argued that we should also work to melt down other, related divides. One wall stands between ourselves as interested readers of stories and as theory-driven professionals; another wall stands between narrative (associated with subjective knowledge) and analysis (associated with objective truths). By situating ourselves as subjects simultaneously touched by life-experience and swayed by professional concerns, we can acknowledge the hybrid and positioned nature of our identities. Writing texts that mix lively narrative and rigorous analysis involves enacting hybridity, regardless of our origins.

Acknowledgments

This essay emerged from fieldwork in Nasik between June and September 1983 and July and October 1985, as well as an association with the place since birth. Formal fieldwork in Kangra took place between September 1991 and August 1992, although I have visited there since 1975. I am extremely grateful for an array of grants and fellowships through the years. In building on insights garnered collectively from research enabled by these different funding sources, I lump them together here: a National Science Foundation Graduate Fellowship, a University of California at Berkeley Graduate Humanities Research Grant, a Robert H. Lowie Fellowship, a Charlotte W. Newcombe Dissertation Writing Fellowship, support from the University of Wisconsin Graduate School, an American Institute of Indian Studies Senior Fellowship, and a National Endowment for the Humanities Fellowship. My deep thanks to Ruth Behar, Eytan Bercovitch, Ed Bruner, Janet Dixon-Keller, Ann Gold, Smadar Lavie, Maria Lepowsky, Renato Rosaldo, Janis Shough, Paul Stoller, Barbara Tedlock, Anna Tsing, and Kamala Visweswaran for conversations about and comments on issues raised in this essay.

Works Cited

Abu-Lughod, Lila

    1988. Fieldwork of a Dutiful Daughter. In *Arab Women in the Field*. S. Altorki and C. Fawzi El-Solh, eds. Pp. 139–161. Syracuse: Syracuse University Press.

    1990. Can There Be a Feminist Ethnography? *Women and Performance: A Journal of Feminist Theory* 5:7–27.

    1991. Writing Against Culture. In *Recapturing Anthropology*. Richard Fox, ed. Pp. 137–162. Santa Fe, NM: School of American Research Press.

    1992. *Writing Women's Worlds: Bedouin Stories*. Berkeley: University of California Press.

Aguilar, John

1981. Insider Research: An Ethnography of a Debate. In *Anthropologists at Home in North America*. Donald Messerschmidt, ed. Pp. 15–26. Cambridge: Cambridge University Press.

Alarcon, Norma

1990. The Theoretical Subject(s) of This Bridge Called My Back in Anglo-American Feminism. In *Making Face/Making Soul: Creative and Critical Perspectives on Women of Color*. G. Anzaldua, ed. Pp. 356–369. San Francisco: Aunt Lute Foundation.

Altorki, Soraya, and Camillia Fawzi El-Solh, eds.

1988. *Arab Women in the Field: Studying Your Own Society*. Syracuse: Syracuse University Press.

Appadurai, Arjun

1988. Putting Hierarchy in Its Place. *Cultural Anthropology* 3:36–49.

1990. Disjuncture and Difference in the Global Cultural Economy. *Public Culture* 2:1–24.

1991. Global Ethnoscapes: Notes and Queries for a Transnational Anthropology. In *Recapturing Anthropology*. Richard Fox, ed. Pp. 191–210. Santa Fe, NM: School of American Research Press.

Behar, Ruth

1993. *Translated Woman: Crossing the Border with Esperanza's Story*. Boston: Beacon Press.

Bruner, Edward M.

1993. Introduction: The Ethnographic Self and the Personal Self. In *Anthropology and Literature*. Paul Benson, ed. Pp. 1–26. Urbana: University of Illinois Press.

Casagrande, Joseph, ed.

1960. *In the Company of Man: Twenty Portraits by Anthropologists*. New York: Harper and Row.

Clifford, James

1986. Introduction: Partial Truths. In *Writing Culture: The Poetics and Politics of Ethnography*. James Clifford and George Marcus, eds. Pp. 1–26. Berkeley: University of California Press.

1988. *The Predicament of Culture*. Cambridge, MA: Harvard University Press.

1992. Travelling Cultures. In *Cultural Studies*. L. Grossberg, C. Nelson, and Paula Treichler, eds. Pp. 96–116. New York: Routledge.

Danforth, Loring

1989. *Firewalking and Religious Healing: The Anasteria of Greece and the American Firewalking Movement*. Princeton: Princeton University Press.

Dumont, Jean Paul

1978. *The Headman and I*. Austin: University of Texas Press.

Dwyer, Kevin

1982. *Moroccan Dialogues: Anthropology in Question*. Prospect Heights, IL: Waveland Press.

Fahim, Hussein

1982. *Indigenous Anthropology in Non-Western Countries*. Durham, NC: Carolina Academic Press.

Fahim, Hussein, Katherine Helmer, Elizabeth Colson, T. N. Madan, Herbert C. Kelman, and Talal Asad

1980. Indigenous Anthropology in Non-Western Countries: A Further Elaboration. *Current Anthropology* 21:644–663.

Fernea, Elizabeth
1965. *Guests of the Sheik: An Ethnography of an Iraqi Village.* New York: Doubleday.

Foster, George M., T. Scudder, E. Colson, and R. V. Kemper, eds.
1979. *Long-Term Field Research in Social Anthropology.* New York: Academic Press.

Ginsburg, Faye
1989. *Contested Lives: The Abortion Debate in an American Community.* Berkeley: University of California Press.

Ginsburg, Faye, and Anna Lowenhaupt Tsing
1990. *Uncertain Terms: Negotiating Gender in American Culture.* Boston: Beacon Press.

Gold, Ann
1988. *Fruitful Journeys: The Ways of Rajasthani Pilgrims.* Berkeley: University of California Press.

Gupta, Akhil, and Ferguson, James
1992. Beyond "Culture": Space, Identity, and the Politics of Difference. *Cultural Anthropology* 7:6–23.

Gwaltney, John L.
1981. Common Sense and Science: Urban Core Black Observations. In *Anthropologists at Home in North America: Methods and Issues in the Study of One's Own Society.* D. Messerschmidt, ed. Pp. 46–61. Cambridge: Cambridge University Press.

Hall, Stuart
1989. Cultural Identity and Cinematic Representation. *Framework* 36:68–81.

Haraway, Donna
1988. Situated Knowledges: The Science Question in Feminism and the Privilege of Partial Perspective. *Feminist Studies* 14:575–599.

Jackson, Michael
1989. *Paths Towards a Clearing: Radical Empiricism and Ethnographic Enquiry.* Bloomington: Indiana University Press.

Jones, Delmos J.
1970. Toward a Native Anthropology. *Human Organization* 29:251–259.

Kondo, Dorinne
1986. Dissolution and Reconstitution of Self: Implications for Anthropological Epistemology. *Cultural Anthropology* 1:74–96.
1990. *Crafting Selves: Power, Gender and Discourses of Identity in a Japanese Workplace.* Chicago: University of Chicago Press.

Kumar, Nita
1992. *Friends, Brothers, and Informants: Fieldwork Memoirs of Banaras.* Berkeley: University of California Press.

Lauretis, Teresa de
1986. Feminist Studies/Critical Studies: Issues, Terms, and Contexts. In *Feminist Studies/Critical Studies.* T. de Lauretis, ed. Pp. 1–19. Bloomington: Indiana University Press.

Lavie, Smadar
1990. *The Poetics of Military Occupation.* Berkeley: University of California Press.

Limón, José
1991. Representation, Ethnicity, and the Precursory Ethnography: Notes of a Native

Anthropologist. In *Recapturing Anthropology*. Richard Fox, ed. Pp. 115–136. Santa Fe, NM: School of American Research Press.

Lowie, Robert

    1937. *A History of Ethnological Theory*. New York: Holt, Rinehart and Winston.

Malinowski, Bronislaw

    1961 [1922]. *Argonauts of the Western Pacific*. New York: E. P. Dutton.

Mani, Lata

    1990. Multiple Mediations: Feminist Scholarship in the Age of Multinational Reception. *Feminist Review* 35:24–41.

Maquet, Jacques

    1964. Objectivity in Anthropology. *Current Anthropology* 5:47–55.

Martin, Emily

    1987. *The Woman in the Body: A Cultural Analysis of Reproduction*. Boston: Beacon Press.

Messerschmidt, Donald

    1981a. On Anthropology "at Home." In *Anthropologists at Home in North America: Methods and Issues in the Study of One's Own Society*. D. Messerschmidt, ed. Pp. 1–14. Cambridge: Cambridge University Press.

    1981b. [ed.] *Anthropologists at Home in North America: Methods and Issues in the Study of One's Own Society*. Cambridge: Cambridge University Press.

Mohanty, Chandra, and Ann Russo, eds.

    1991. *Third World Women and the Politics of Feminism*. Bloomington: Indiana University Press.

Mohanty, Satya

    1989. Us and Them. *New Formations* 8:55–80.

Nakhleh, Khalil

    1979. On Being a Native Anthropologist. In *The Politics of Anthropology: From Colonialism and Sexism to the View from Below*. G. Huizer and B. Mannheim, eds. Pp. 343–352. The Hague: Mouton.

Narayan, Kirin

    1989. *Storytellers, Saints, and Scoundrels: Folk Narrative in Hindu Religious Teaching*. Philadelphia: University of Pennsylvania Press.

Ohnuki-Tierney, Emiko

    1984. "Native" Anthropologists. *American Ethnologist* 11:584–586.

Ortner, Sherry

    1991. Reading America: Preliminary Notes on Class and Culture. In *Recapturing Anthropology*. Richard Fox, ed. Pp. 163–189. Santa Fe, NM: School of American Research Press.

Pratt, Mary Louise

    1986. Fieldwork in Common Places. In *Writing Culture*. James Clifford and George Marcus, eds. Pp. 27–50. Berkeley: University of California Press.

Rabinow, Paul

    1977. *Reflections on Fieldwork in Morocco*. Berkeley: University of California Press.

Rosaldo, Renato

    1989. *Culture and Truth: The Remaking of Social Analysis*. Boston: Beacon Press.

Rose, Dan

    1987. *Black American Street Life: South Philadelphia, 1969–71*. Philadelphia: University of Pennsylvania Press.

Said, Edward
  1989. Representing the Colonized: Anthropology's Interlocutors. *Critical Inquiry*
    15:205–225.
Schutz, Alfred
  1973. *Collected Papers, Volume 1: The Problem of Social Reality.* The Hague: Mouton.
Shostak, Marjorie
  1981. *Nisa: The Life and Words of a !Kung Woman.* Cambridge, MA: Harvard University
    Press.
Spickard, Paul R
  1989. *Mixed Blood: Intermarriage and Ethnic Identity in Twentieth Century America.*
    Madison: University of Wisconsin Press.
Srinivas, M. N.
  1952. *Religion and Society among the Coorgs of Southern India.* New Delhi: Oxford Uni-
    versity Press.
  1966. Some Thoughts on the Study of One's Own Society. In *Social Change in Modern
    India.* M. N. Srinivas, ed. Pp. 147–163. Berkeley: University of California Press.
  1976. The Remembered Village. Berkeley: University of California Press.
Srinivas, M. N., A. M. Shah, and E. A. Ramaswamy
  1979. *The Fieldworker and the Field: Problems and Challenges in Sociological Investigation.*
    Delhi: Oxford University Press.
Stewart, John D.
  1989. *Drinkers, Drummers, and Decent Folk: Ethnographic Narratives in Village Trinidad.*
    Albany: State University of New York Press.
Stoller, Paul
  1989. *The Taste of Ethnographic Things.* Philadelphia: University of Pennsylvania Press.
  1992. *The Cinematic Griot: The Ethnography of Jean Rouch.* Chicago: University of
    Chicago Press.
Strathern, Marilyn
  1987. An Awkward Relationship: The Case of Feminism and Anthropology. *Signs*
    12:276–294.
Tedlock, Barbara
  1991. From Participant Observation to the Observation of Participation: The Emer-
    gence of Narrative Ethnography. *Journal of Anthropological Research* 47:69–94.
  1992. *The Beautiful and the Dangerous: Encounters with the Zuni Indians.* New York: Viking.

2 Feminist Insider Dilemmas

Constructing Ethnic Identity

with "Chicana" Informants

PATRICIA ZAVELLA

What happens when the ethnographic "others" are from the same society, and are members of the same race or ethnicity, gender, and class background as the ethnographer? This paper articulates the dilemmas I faced as a member of the group I was studying—Chicana working mothers—particularly regarding the terms of ethnic identification. My purpose here is twofold: I will discuss how my status as a simultaneous cultural "insider" and Chicana feminist researcher reflected a conundrum. My sense of Chicana feminist identity, constructed through participation in the Chicano movement, ironically hindered my understanding of the nuances of the ethnic identity of the women I studied and regarded as historical actors. My status as insider also posed the dilemma of how to present the ethnographic "other" to my peers, Chicano/Latino scholars who privileged the term Chicano. (As a product of the movement, I will use Chicano and Mexican American interchangeably here, except when referring to Mexican Americans from New Mexico.) These dilemmas eventually provided insight into the power relations involved when women of Mexican origin identify themselves ethnically. My discussion will contextualize the meaning of ethnic identity for working-class Mexican American women workers in two field research settings with different historical contexts.

There is debate among ethnographers about conducting field work with subjects who are of the same gender and/or race or ethnicity as the researcher. Chicano scholars assert that insiders are more likely to be cognizant and accepting of complexity and internal variation, are better able to understand the nuances of language use, will hopefully avoid being duped by informants who create cultural performances for their own purposes, and are less apt to be distrusted by those being studied. Some assert that ethnic insiders often have an easier time gaining access to a community similar to their own, and that they are more sensitive to framing questions in ways that respect community sensibilities.[1]

Others however, note that being a member of a subordinated group under study carries particular problems and creates personal and ethical dilemmas for social scientists on the basis of their race, ethnicity, gender, political sympathies, or even personal foibles. Maxine Baca Zinn found that being an insider woman conducting ethnographic research with Mexican Americans meant continually negotiating her status, since members of the community being studied often had assumptions about her intents, skills, and personal characteristics. She reminds us that insider researchers have the unique constraint of always being accountable to the community being studied. Along with the cooperation engendered by one's insider status comes responsibility to construct analyses that are sympathetic to ethnic interests, and which will somehow share whatever knowledge is generated with them: "These problems should serve to remind us of our political responsibility and compel us to carry out our research with ethical and intellectual integrity."[2] Patricia Hill Collins discusses how Black women intellectuals have creatively used their "outsider within" status, drawing on their own personal and cultural biographies to analyze the interlocking oppression of Black women, and suggests that others use this approach.[3]

Women anthropologists and feminist field workers have long been concerned about relationships with informants and have grappled with the dilemmas of being insiders, particularly when they have important similarities with the population being studied.[4] Some have argued that ethnographic methods are ideally suited to research by women because of the contextual, involved, experiential approach to knowledge that includes the sharing of experiences with one's subjects, and which contrasts with the features of positivist approaches.[5] Susan Krieger, for example, discusses how being an insider in a lesbian community enabled her to see how interviews were reflections of community norms, and her personal interpretations are sources of sociological insight.[6] Particularly since the late 1960s and early 1970s, paraphrasing Joan Acker and her colleagues, a social science *for* women has emancipatory possibilities for the researchers as well as the researched, for as women researchers we also have been absent and our views discounted within the main social science traditions. Feminist ethnographers can potentially voice many women's concerns.[7]

Increasingly, feminist and other field workers realize that we need to be sensitive to differences between our subjects and ourselves; aware of the possible power relations involved in doing research by, about, and for women; and aware that feminist studies must include a diversity of women's experiences based on race, class, and sexual preferences, among others. Lynn Weber Cannon and her colleagues critique the white, middle-class bias of much qualitative feminist research and suggest that feminists take extraordinary measures to recruit women of color so as to include a variety of perspectives.[8] Catherine Kohler Riessman points out that white women must be careful about analyzing interviews with women of color using their own narrative forms, lest they miss important nuances in meaning.[9]

Women field workers do not agree, however, on what constitutes feminist ethnography, nor do they agree on the role of the feminist insider as researcher. Judith Stacey, for example, suggests that feminist ethnography draws upon "such traditionally female strengths as empathy and human concern, allows for an egalitarian, reciprocal relationship between knower and known." She questions whether there can be a truly feminist ethnography, arguing that the personal and ethical dilemmas inevitably pose insurmountable problems. In contrast to the goals of mutuality, non-exploitation, and empathy that she hoped for with feminist field research, Stacey argues that ironically this approach places informants at greater risk in the power relations inherent to any field research. By being involved in

closer friendships, Stacey claims, informants are subject to betrayal and abandonment by the researcher and thus feminist ethnography "masks a deeper, more dangerous form of exploitation."[10]

There are two implicit assumptions in Stacey's formulation (and others who
think of feminist methodology in this way): that all women share some authentic
feminine selfhood—with characteristics like being more cooperative, empathetic,
attentive to daily life, or relational than men—so that women can thus bond with
one another across time and space; and that feminist ethnography can somehow
transcend the inequalities between women researchers and subjects. Clearly these
assumptions are problematic, particularly when Western ethnographers are doing
research in the Third World or in working-class and poor communities in the
United States. Micaela di Leonardo labels this perspective, which assumes that all
women share common experiences or interests, as "cultural feminism" and argues
that these assumptions form a "women's culture as invented tradition."[11] Moreover,
without "marking" the social location of the ethnographer and informants—their
status based on class, race, or ethnicity, sexual preference, or other relevant attributes—we cannot judge whether and how the ethnographer indeed has more power
and privilege than those being researched. This lack of context leads us to assume
researchers and subjects are more similar than they really are.

Similarly, Marilyn Strathern asserts that there is a "particularly awkward dissonance between feminist practice and the practice of social anthropology," and she
implies that feminist anthropology is virtually impossible since the two fields
"mock" one another on the basis of fundamental differences in how the ethnographic "other" is construed. Ideally, anthropologists interpret the experiences of
traditionally non-Western, pre-industrial, or peasant cultures by respecting their
own emic view of the world, and more recently by creating space for other voices;
yet the ultimate purpose serves the discipline. On the other hand, feminists,
Strathern argues, construe the ethnographic "other" as men and patriarchal institutions, and therefore there can be no shared experience between them and feminists. Within her framework, feminists and their informants "have no interests in
common to be served" by collaborating on producing an ethnographic text.[12]
Those of us who consider ourselves feminist ethnographers wonder where we and
our women informants fit into her schema.

Stacey and Strathern are correct in noting the inevitable ambivalence involved in
doing ethnographic work. Their particular feminist positions, however, beg the
question when conducting research in real field sites. Feminist ethnographers must
move beyond posing simple dichotomous methodological approaches to discussing
how we as individual "marked" researchers—contextualized in our own milieu of
research goals, ethics, sensitivities, and academic affinities—have grappled with the
contradictions of feminist research. In other words, rather than assume some type
of pan-female solidarity (with inevitable betrayal) or lack of shared experience
between researchers and subjects, we should realize that we are almost always
simultaneous insiders and outsiders and discuss what this means for our particular
research projects.

I will argue that my Chicana feminism itself was an example of "outsider within" status. Framed by larger historical forces and political struggles, identifying myself as a Chicana feminist meant contesting and simultaneously drawing from Chicano nationalist ideology and white feminism—being an insider and outsider within both movements and ideologies. It was only in retrospect, when I came to understand how Mexican American women informants from New Mexico constructed their ethnic identity in very different ways, that I realized I needed to deconstruct and problematize my own sense of Chicana feminism so that I could "see" the nuances of ethnic identity among my informants.

My experience was a form of what Micaela di Leonardo suggests is a general feminist fieldwork conundrum: we simultaneously seek out women's experiences and critically analyze male domination in societies whose customs anthropology has defended under the stance of cultural relativism.[13] Thus feminists now face the dilemma of seeing those customs as patriarchal, and rather than defend their existence, want to advocate change for women's benefit. There is growing acceptance in the field that feminist and other researchers, then, must self-consciously reflect upon their status within the field site, examine how they are situated within social and power relations, and place their own work within the changing tides of academic discourse as well. José Limón reminds us that "however 'liberating' a narrative discourse that we propose to write, it is one always intimate with power, and many of our 'informants,' 'subjects,' 'consultants,' 'teachers,' 'friends' know it. . . . We must always decenter our own narrative self-assurance lest it be saturated with dominating power."[14] Such self-reflexive analysis of our own experience will push us to provide "provisional" analyses that are always incomplete, but which make clear whose viewpoint is being represented.[15]

Constructing Chicana Identity

As part of my own process of becoming a Chicana feminist, beginning in the early 1970s, I became conscious of the critical importance of ethnic identity. I and others of my generation who were involved in Chicano movement activities deliberately rejected the hyphenated term *Mexican-American*, which to us connoted assimilation. We adopted the highly politicized term *Chicano*, which designated pride in our rich Pre-Columbian heritage and the importance of celebrating our mestizo racial and cultural mixtures, and rejected the influence of the Spanish colonizers. The term Chicano also signaled the history of racism of North American society toward people of Mexican descent; it claimed the right to self-determination and control over institutions within the Chicano community and called for the spiritual and organizational unity of the Chicano people. An integral part of reclaiming our Mexican heritage was speaking Spanish and celebrating cultural values of communalism, the family, and brotherhood (*el pueblo, la familia, y carnalismo*). Chicano movement ideology also had separatist leanings, suggested the importance of recognizing *Aztlan*—the mythical northern part of Pre-Columbian society—as a symbolic celebration of our spiritual unity, and explicitly rejected white culture. The Marxists among us argued that Chicanos and Mexican immigrants were the same people, that is, we were a primarily working-class community *sin fronteras* (without borders) who held common interests as a racialized class. These activists pushed for political strategies and organizations that would encourage the development of class consciousness between Chicanos and *Mexicanos* (that is, Mexican immigrants) regardless of the U. S.-Mexican border.[16]

At the time, Chicana activists proudly embraced movement ideology, yet our identity as feminists was submerged. It was difficult to identify as a feminist because it was seen as a white, middle-class term and itself a reason for dismissing women's views.[17] Chicanos often tried to silence feminists by baiting us as cultural betrayers, white-identified, man haters, and lesbians. Despite these travails, many of us maintained our critiques of the Chicano movement, with its male-oriented organizational concerns, the outright sexism of some leaders, the lack of recognition of women, and the unquestioning acceptance of the patriarchy inherent in the ideology of *la familia*. I further embraced the feminist principles that household decision making and the division of labor should be shared equally between partners, that women should feel good about their participation in the labor force, and that labor organizing should include women. This was my construction of Chicana feminism when I entered the field.

As I have discussed previously,[18] I started my field research in 1977–1978 with assumptions that my identity would provide me with an entrée to women cannery workers. I assumed that being a woman from a working-class background myself would provide ready access to this community of informants. Although women were generous with their time and insights, I found that indeed there were important differences between us. In retrospect, my expectations were naive, for these were predominantly middle-aged, seasonal cannery workers who were being displaced from cannery employment in the Santa Clara Valley. These women (and men) were acutely conscious of my privileges as an educated woman, and assumed I had resources that as a poverty-stricken graduate student I did not have. More important, the very research questions I posed alerted them to important political differences between us. I asked about how women made decisions, how they organized the household division of labor, how they felt about being working mothers, and about racism and sexism on the job. Implicit in my questions were Chicana feminist notions. As I came to understand, these women struggled to live independent lives—working in strenuous jobs, participating in the decisions as to how their wages were spent, taking pride in enduring the demanding labor process, and finding meaning in constructing a work culture with other women workers. Like many North American women, these informants supported feminist notions like "equal pay for equal work" and affirmative action.

Yet they also had very "traditional" notions about family, originally seeking seasonal employment because it allowed them to fulfill their familial obligations; they identified themselves as "homemakers" for most of the year. With a few notable exceptions, these were women who "happened to work" and whose seasonal employment did not challenge the traditional notions that their spouses should be breadwinners and heads of the family and that they should do most of the domestic work, although some did contest these notions somewhat. My feminist questions, then, pointed out the contradictions of their constructions of selves, and led to some awkward moments when women often preferred silence to full discussion of problems in their families or with their spouses. It was at these times that my outsider status seemed glaring.

Furthermore, those who were politically involved in the attempts to reform the Teamsters Union from within were also aware of possible political differences between us. Thus my experience of "establishing rapport" often meant discussing my political sensibilities and commitments in great detail, and I worried about "contaminating the field" with my own biases.

Although my cannery worker informants identified themselves ethnically in varied terms, ranging from *Mexicana*, Mexican American, and Chicana to Spanish, as a self-identified Chicana, I was not particularly concerned with variation in ethnic identification at the time I wrote the book, merely noting it in passing. I was more concerned with their political consciousness and activities, and wrote a critique about how race and gender were incorporated into strategies for organizing cannery workers.[19] I did not explicitly analzye the connection between ethnic identity and politics, however, and I now see that that would have been an interesting relationship to pursue.

Reflecting back, I recall that most were of the second generation (their parents were born in Mexico, but they were born in the United States). Among the second generation, those who identified themselves as Spanish or Mexican American were often the most conservative. Those cannery workers who were usually the most militant and deeply involved in the Teamster reform movement explicitly called themselves Chicanos or *Mexicanos*. Moreover, the ideological polarities that often erupted in organizational conflicts were present among the cannery worker activists with whom I did participant observation, and ethnic identification was central to ideological posturing. Some of the nationalist Chicanos advocated political strategies that focused on Chicano demands, while the more moderate or leftist Chicanos and *Mexicanos* pushed for multi-ethnic reformist strategies centered on "bread and butter" issues and downplayed ethnic differences between workers.

In sum, my cannery research experience challenged my Chicana feminist perspective, but more in terms of the gender politics within "the movement," and how class consciousness was framed in daily life. It was only in retrospect that I came to see the importance of ethnic identification with different political strategies. My shortsightedness was in tune with the field at the time.

Recognizing Heterogeneity

Writing in 1980, anthropologist José Limón pointed out that Chicano was a problematic term because it was rooted in folklore performances that were usually private (among fellow Mexican Americans), where it held both pejorative and positive connotations. To assimilated middle-class Mexican Americans, Chicano connotes the proletarian Mexican immigrant experience and later the militancy and celebration of indigenous ancestry of the movement. When used by working-class Mexican Americans through customary nicknaming practices or in situations that are culturally ambiguous, Chicano can convey affection or intimacy or legitimize one's status as an authentic Mexican American. Thus, Limón argues, through the construction of a Chicano *public* ethnic identity (in discourse where English was used or in Anglo-dominated contexts), academics and activists drew upon its highly charged symbolic power that already held intraethnic tensions and "added political meanings to the term which did not meet with the approval of the larger community."[20] Despite his cautions, the term Chicano—with its nationalist and gender-contested connotations that were added by the movement—is still the predominant term in the field of Chicano studies.

It has only been within the past few years that we are seeing theoretical analyses that explicitly look for fine-tuned differences among Chicanos and distinguish Chicanos from *Mexicanos* and other Latinos. Researchers have found variation in how Chicanos identify themselves, with regional difference being very important.[21] New Mexico, where there is a long-standing "ethnic sensitivity," has always posed a unique case in how Mexican Americans identify themselves. According to this analysis, Mexican Americans in New Mexico identified with their Spanish heritage and sought to dissociate themselves from racist sentiments directed at Mexican immigrants.[22] Thus people preferred the terms Spanish or Spanish American, and women especially rejected the term Chicano.[23]

The term Spanish (or the synonymous Spanish American) became hegemonic in New Mexican society after World War I, and clearly demarcated native-born Mexican Americans from those who migrated from Mexico,[24] yet challenged racism and discrimination against the Mexican American working class in education, politics, and the economy.[25] This hegemony can be seen in the casual usage of Spanish throughout the state today; it is a term that has become part of daily experience for Mexican Americans generally, and for our informants in particular. It wasn't until the 1980s that recent Mexican immigrants became a large presence in economically undeveloped northern New Mexican cities. Mexican migrants became integrated into a society where the major social categories of Anglo, Indian, and Spanish were already clearly established.

Constructing Hispana Ethnicity

In a second research project conducted during the 1982–1983 recession, Louise Lamphere, Felipe Gonzales, Peter B. Evans, and I studied the effects of industrialization in the sunbelt on working-class families, comparing Mexican Americans and whites.[26] We found that women's work in apparel factories and electronics production facilities sometimes brought important changes in family life as women became coproviders, mainstay providers, or, in the case of single parents, sole economic providers for their families. We argued that these working-class families are changing as women deal with the contradictions of full-time work and family commitments. Our women informants were more committed to full-time work than their mothers were, while their spouses were doing more housework and child care than we expected. Without the economic resources of highly paid professional women, these women constructed varied strategies to help mediate the contradictions of daily life—dividing up economic upkeep, finding day care for their children, negotiating a division of household chores and child care with spouses, roommates, or kin, and seeking emotional support and social exchange from relatives or friends. Mexican American and white women had similar experiences rooted in a common class status and family circumstances, yet within each group there was nuanced variation.

This project relied more on in-depth interviews with eighty-nine Mexican American and Anglo informants than on participant observation, and we explicitly questioned our informants about their own sense of ethnicity and ethnic identity. After completing our interviews with Spanish-surnamed couples and single mothers, we researchers had to grapple directly with their particular ethnic identity. We came to use the term Mexican American advisedly since the majority of our Mexican American informants identified themselves as Spanish or Spanish American, a custom at odds with my sense of ethnic identification.

Upon moving to Albuquerque before getting involved in this project, I became aware of the New Mexican prejudice toward Californians in general, and Californian Mexican Americans in particular as being arrogant and assimilated, and I began to downplay my California connections. I had lived in Albuquerque for almost a year prior to embarking on research, so I had become accustomed to hearing the term Spanish in daily conversation, and to hearing colleagues—aware of the ethnic sensitivity—referring to the local Mexican Americans with hyphenated terms like "Chicano-*Mexicano*-Spanish community." When I found Spanish rather than Chicano or Mexican American on institutional forms where I was supposed to designate my ethnic identity, I even became accustomed (with only slight hesitation) to checking the Spanish box, even though that seemed to deny my Chicana identity. As a feminist, I was aware of the possible offense of using this term and restricted it to contexts within higher education where it was more acceptable.

As I began interviewing women, then, in the course of chatting informally prior to starting the interview, I let them know how aspects of our identities coincided: I was a working mother with a young child myself who struggled to find day care and juggle work and family; my partner had been reared in Albuquerque; and we lived in the predominantly Mexican American South Valley. Further, my great-grandparents had lived and farmed in the northern New Mexican village of Tierra Amarilla, and were part of the migration northward to southern Colorado, considered by scholars and laypeople to be part of the northern New Mexico culture region. In short, my own experience seemed to parallel those of our informants. While I only got a chance to discuss our common heritage on a few occasions, having kinship ties in "the north" on the face of it made me a *manita*—figuratively a cultural compatriot. (New Mexicans use the terms *Hispano* and *manito* [literally, little brother] interchangeably, and use *Mexicano* when speaking in Spanish.) I hoped that my brief disclosures about my own ethnic heritage would allow my informants openly to express their own sense of ethnicity.

We asked questions about ethnic identity toward the end of the second interview, presumably when rapport was established and informants were comfortable with the interview format. Our strategy was to evoke their own terms by first asking them to designate a term for the Spanish-surnamed or Spanish-speaking people in Albuquerque, ask if that was the term they used for themselves, then ask for clarification about the meaning of whatever term they had selected. We also asked how whatever group they had identified (usually Spanish) differed from Mexicans, and what they thought of the term Chicano. Similar to previous research on ethnic identification in New Mexico, about two-thirds of our informants found that responding to questions about ethnic identity was a very sensitive issue. People made comments like, "I was afraid that you'd ask that." One man explained: "I'd play it by ear. Some people get offended real easy—because if other people's Chicano, they get real upset—others, uh, Spanish American." One could argue that these respondents were aware that ethnic identification expresses power relations, where being labeled or "naming" oneself can be a reflection of opposing or acquiescing to the subordination of the ethnic group.[27] Or one could argue that since ethnic identification is so influenced by context, our informants were not aware of the norms within the interview situation and thus felt that choosing a term meant taking some risk.[28]

Yet when we asked further questions, they had difficulties articulating their meaning of Spanish American, in part because their lives were so ethnically bounded. My first interview immediately cued me that these informants were different from other Mexican Americans and that they did not characterize their ethnicity in ways that were familiar. Geri Sandoval, a taciturn woman from the northern village of Mora, seemed reluctant to even discuss ethnicity. When I probed, however, she related that her family still owned a farm with a private *campo santo* (cemetery) that had been in her family for generations; that she was related to "everyone" in the general area; that her grandparents had been active members of the Catholic but renegade religious group *los penitentes*; and that they regularly celebrated Easter with traditional ethnic foods. She readily identified herself as Spanish American, but when asked how Mexicans and Spanish Americans differ, she said, "I don't know," and her tone of voice indicated she did not want to discuss it further. I let the matter drop.

In another interview, when asked about her ethnic identity, Delores Baca asked for clarification and then responded, "I don't know, I'm just me. I've never had that question asked of me." It turned out that this woman had the largest and most dense ethnic networks of any informant, and she had participated in ethnic activities. Like Geri Sandoval, Delores Baca's grandparents had owned a small farm in a northern village, but had sold it and settled the family on property in Bernalillo near Albuquerque. Thus her parents lived across the street, and her eight siblings and several other extended kin all lived within walking distance, some with their own families. Delores had rich social exchanges with her relatives—her mother provided daily day care while she worked, and her relatives often borrowed and lent money, car repairs, or clothes—and they socialized frequently. Her wedding had been "traditional," with three attempts at mock kidnapping and finally a collective "ransom" so the festivities could continue, and a *marcha*, where the godparents led the bridesmaids and attendants in a ritualized dance. When asked to describe her ethnic heritage or special traditions in her family, Delores didn't know how to respond. After some probes she described an elaborate festival in honor of San Lorenzo, where her parents had been sponsors, and told me she had participated in *matachines*—ritualized, costumed dances. When pressed about what ethnic terms she would use, Delores responded, "I'd say I'm Spanish-Mexican, Mexican-Spanish, whatever. I'd tell them where I work, what I do, I guess." Despite being totally immersed in ethnic culture, Delores did not immediately see herself as having any special ethnic heritage or identity, and distanced herself from it by coupling ethnicity with occupational identity.

One of the final interviews, with Christina Espinosa, who was the child of a "mixed marriage," drove home these informants' points about the sensitivity of ethnic identity and added meaning that was new to me. On the basis of her looks, Christina's ethnicity was ambiguous since she had fair-colored skin but dark brown hair, and she had a Spanish surname from a former marriage. It wasn't until the second interview, when we took information on extended kin, that I realized that Christina's German American father had left when she was young and that she was close to her Mexican American mother and maternal kin. When asked directly, Christina refused to provide a term for her own ethnic identity:

PZ: For the Spanish-surnamed population in Albuquerque, what word would you
      use to call them?
CE: I'd just call people by name. I don't like putting tags on people.
PZ: So if someone asked you what you are, what would you say?
CE: An Albuquerquian; I was born in Albuquerque, that's all I know. I don't know
      what my mom and dad did, that's their problem. You ask them what I am, that's not
      my problem. . . . I have a hard time 'cause I really don't see no difference. To me
      people are the same.
PZ: How are Spanish people here different from Mexicans?
CE: I don't really know. I don't really think they are. See I have a hard time when
      people say, you know, "Well look at that Mexican." I go, "How do you know they're
      not Spanish?" Because I really don't see no difference. To me they're the same. But
      now you can't tell them that 'cause they get angry. And I don't know why.

What was this, I wondered? Christina's kin network had a texture that seemed Mexican American, yet she refused to identify with any group and to characterize herself ethnically. Christina believed that Spanish and Mexicans, like all people, were "the same." Her defensive tone of voice and body language, however, indicated that this was difficult for her to discuss, for she had a "hard time" when people noticed Mexicans, who looked like the Spanish, who perhaps looked like her. Clearly she was trying to distance herself from claiming any ethnic identity.

Similarly, other informants emphasized the more neutral term *New Mexican*. One woman, who had lived in the northern city of Española through high school and who was close to her spouse's extended kin from the same area, could only explain: "I am what I am and I'm Spanish."[29] In general, our research reinforced previous findings that women had more aversion to the use of Chicano than the men did.

Part of our dilemma was in figuring out how to convey the seemingly contradictory evidence: our informants did not necessarily characterize their ethnic identity in ways with which we were familiar—they did not convey explicit pride in their ethnic heritage and their use of the term Spanish seemed on the face of it to identify with the colonizer part of their heritage. Yet our informants did not disclaim their ethnic heritage. They were mainly third generation, born in the United States with parents who had migrated to Albuquerque from predominantly Spanish villages in northern New Mexico. Though they spoke English as their first language, they did not seem assimilated. They believed that maintaining the Spanish language was important and wished their children could learn it, but since they did not consider themselves fluent (often speaking to grandparents and elders in broken Spanish) this value could not be fully realized. They did not reject their ethnic heritage, but also did not have strong views about its content.

Ethnic and gender subordination can be found in many forms in contemporary Albuquerque. Spanish Americans make up only about a third of the population. The city of Albuquerque historically was segregated by class and race/ethnicity so that predominantly Anglos lived in the Northeast Heights while the Spanish lived primarily in Old Town, and in the North and South Valleys, with some pockets of Anglos in the two valleys. (There has been some recent residential dispersal, however, so that the Southeast and North Valley and central areas have integrated neighborhoods that include Blacks and Navajos as well.) The electronics and garment work sites we studied have predominantly Spanish female work forces, although because of recruiting practices only small numbers are Mexican immigrants. These women engaged in daily struggle on the shop floor to make their piece rates, cooperate with other workers, or engage in collective struggle—including staging an election for union recognition in one factory. Our informants, then, were located in working-class occupations, where the majority of their co-workers were Spanish; their daily experiences and social worlds revolved around family and kin, and work and church activities where others were predominantly Spanish. Their lives were so immersed in ethnic social worlds that they had little information about others with which to characterize how their lives were ethnically distinct.

So when our informants used the term Spanish or Spanish American in the early 1980s, the meaning included a sense of ethnic and class segmentation. We eventually realized that despite their apparent diffidence, there was a definite awareness of their membership in a distinct social category and their constructions of meaning were complex. We discuss the varied meanings of Spanish in detail elsewhere.[30]

Suffice it to say that to some, Spanish meant an ethnic category that was distinct from Mexicans. One woman said, "Spanish American is born here in America. . . . Mexicans to me are different than what we are, 'cause our language is different." Another meaning was to differentiate Mexican Americans from other ethnic or racial groups, sometimes using racial features like skin color or notions of "Spanish blood." A third meaning centered on aspects of Mexican American cultural heritage, where a family still owned land in the north, networks of relatives still lived in rural areas, or there was participation in regional cultural activities such as the *penitentes'* religious rites or the *matachines*. In short, these informants were a particular segment of the Mexican American working class, who were ethnically distinct with important regional differences from other Chicanos but who did not explicitly claim ethnic identity unless asked, such as in our interviews. While they did not explicitly express ethnic pride, their struggles to retain their way of life were inherently political, but did not include politicized terms like Chicano.

In contrast to our informants, more recent research on ethnic identity among Mexican Americans in other areas shows that generation as well as region are important.[31] Collectively, this research highlights the regional variation of our New Mexico sample. Through their refusal of the term Chicano and the straightforward (as opposed to strident) ways they described their lives, these informants pushed me to a new understanding of Mexican American ethnicity and the importance of contextualizing our informants' own terms of identity.

The Politics of Ethnic Identity in Academia

A second dilemma arose when I attempted to present our research findings to fellow Chicano or Latino colleagues in the late 1980s. On two occasions, I made presentations on our research findings in ways that respected our informants' construction of identity and tried to contextualize their meanings. Yet I was attacked and my integrity questioned when I used the term Spanish. Puerto Rican scholars in particular strongly objected to the use of Spanish. One colleague claimed—to general agreement—that he had never even heard of anyone using the term Spanish American "in the community," so he could not understand how I could use it. They grilled me about my motivations and purposes, questioned my relationships with informants, and demanded to know how I would use the data. Embedded in their questions was the assumption that I was using the term Spanish as a euphemistic way of identifying Mexican Americans, and they implied that I was identifying with the white power structure and would use the data in ways that would harm my informants. It was only after other Hispana colleagues who were from northern New Mexico rescued me, asserting that indeed Spanish American was widely used even by scholars, that they relented. To someone who saw herself as a feminist activist scholar, this felt ironic and unfair. Clearly I had violated the Chicano/Latino academic cultural norms of ethnic identification.

I found myself in an ambivalent position: I was very sympathetic to their insistence that we scholars not buy into the racism and insensitivity involved in labeling a group by terms they would not claim, or in avoiding the mestizo racial content of the terms themselves, which Spanish seemed to imply. Chicano/Latino scholars are well aware of the pressures to be token spokespeople for "our people," and the importance of resisting any type of pejorative labeling or perpetrating misconceptions about our communities. Yet I felt very uncomfortable with their assumptions that by using Spanish I was somehow a "mainstream" scholar who would be insensitive to these issues.

In response to this critique, I cautioned my co-authors and we self-consciously decided to use the term Hispanic instead, even though we felt uncomfortable with the Euro-centered sensibility it implied. This was a term agreed upon by an advisory committee formed from representatives of various Chicano and Latino political organizations, in response to efforts to sensitize the Census Bureau's accounting of people of "Spanish origin" in the 1970 census.[32] Yet because the Census Bureau then lumped together groups with very disparate histories, socio-

demographic characteristics, political interests, and treatment upon immigration to the United States—notably Cubans, Puerto Ricans, and Mexicans[33]—many activists and scholars (including us) found Hispanic problematic.[34] The preferred term by the late 1980s was Latino, which carried connotations of community self-sufficiency and empowerment and leftist political leanings. Yet Hispanic was the term selected by our informants after Spanish, and seemed to be the next best approximation of their own sense of ethnic identity.

The last piece of evidence concerning this dilemma came more recently. In 1991 the National Association for Chicano Studies passed a student-initiated resolution that condemned the use of Hispanic.[35] (In the politics of the association, students have a political voice through a plenary session on student issues, so a student-initiated resolution carries a lot of weight.) We realized that we would be violating the Chicano/Latino academic norms once again if we continued using Hispanic.

In retrospect, it is clear there were two dilemmas operating here. The more clearly recognizable one was that there are contesting principles at work—the feminist notion that we should respect our women informants' constructions of their identity while at the same time respecting Chicano/Latino academic norms regarding presenting ourselves publicly. A Chicana feminist approach to ethnography would clearly combine the two, fully aware that academic norms must include women's interests as well.

As a way of reconciling these competing dilemmas, and after much discussion, we eventually decided to use the terms Mexican American and Hispana (for women) interchangeably. *Hispano* (the generic male) is a term indigenous to northern New Mexico and approximates the use of Spanish in that working-class people use it in daily life. But Hispano is also becoming politicized in a manner similar to Chicano. In a number of contexts in New Mexico, scholars and activists have begun using Hispano to signify Mexican American political interests.[36] We hope that by using Mexican American and Hispano interchangeably we can respect both sides in this dilemma; yet we realize that no one term will please everyone. It seemed as if the "danger" that Judith Stacey identifies in doing ethnographic research was more concerning my own integrity than in violating our informants' sense of selves. They, after all, were shielded from political critique by anonymity and by having their lives placed in context. I (and my colleagues) were subject to verbal jostling without benefit of presenting our personal concerns and agendas.

I should note that we also had a similar dilemma about how to label our white informants since most of them did not identify with the term Anglo, which is widely used in New Mexico. When asked about ethnic identity, working-class white informants used terms that specified their own mixed and varied ancestry—"I'm a little bit of everything, German, Scottish, Irish, Italian, Danish, Slavic" or used terms like "Heinz 57 flavors," which conveys a sense of culture that is processed. One woman evoked racial features and responded, "freckled and fair-skinned."[37] After similar discussion and soul searching, we decided to use white and Anglo interchangeably as well. We have yet to receive criticisms from white academics or activists for using this term. Yet the term white is clearly problematic for people of European descent as well.

More telling, and a dilemma I only came to see recently, is that my Chicano/ Latino colleagues and I were operating with a rigid construction of ethnic identity. While Chicano activist generally agreed on the necessity of using Chicano, this in turn muted the internal political and theoretical differences among Chicana (and Chicano) scholars. Thus I realized that I needed to deconstruct the "Chicana" part of Chicana feminism with which I identified and reflect upon how Chicana feminism itself was framed.

Chicana feminists have long contested the male-centered intellectual and political traditions of the Chicano movement, and the white middle-class focus of the second-wave feminist movement. Yet Chicana feminists have also simultaneously used concepts from Chicano studies for analyzing the intersection of class and race oppression, and drawn from feminist studies concepts of patriarchy and male dominance in analyzing the Chicana experience.[38] Chicana feminists also identify with our long history of labor and political activism, although again many activists did not use the term feminist. Chicana studies was the product of a "mixed union," which has been problematic, and created the need for Chicana feminist institutions, organizations, and perspectives—the construction of Denise Segura's notion of "triple oppression" based on race, class, and gender, and what Emma Perez calls a Chicana "language and space."[39]

In 1988 Beatriz Pesquera and Denise Segura did a survey of 101 Chicana faculty, students, and staff who belong to *Mujeres Activas en Letras y Cambio Social* (Activist Women in Letters and Social Change), an organization of Chicana/Latina activist academics, where 83 percent of their respondents identified themselves as feminists. Pesquera and Segura argued that there have been internal differences since the late 1960s, but that these have become more noticeable in more recent years. They identified three types of Chicana feminists in their sample. Cultural nationalists emphasize the concerns of the Chicano movement, but want recognition of women's concerns and rights as well. Liberal Chicana feminists are oriented toward reform, and hope to enhance the well-being of the Chicano community with a special emphasis on improving the status of women. Insurgent Chicana feminists, immersed in radical traditions, emphasize that Chicana inequality is the product of interrelated forms of stratification, based on race-ethnicity, class, and gender—and for some, heterosexism. These women favor personal and institutional change, and compared to the other groups are more actively involved in political activities.[40]

Pesquera and Segura's analyses helped me realize that my own thinking had undergone changes. The whole field of Chicana/o Studies had become more self-reflexive and sophisticated in its analyses of the experiences of Chicanos, male and female. Insider research, then, is more complicated than we had anticipated in the early flush of nationalist fervor, and we are beginning to realize how we are insiders and outsiders within several constituencies, each with its own norms and responsibilities.

Reconfiguring Chicana Feminist Ethnography

To be sure, I will continue to honor some of the norms of Chicano academic discourse, some of which are critical, and in some ways parallel the concerns of feminist scholars—such as the importance of activist scholarship. One of our implicit norms is that we don't present internal disagreements or conflicts publicly, that is, we don't tell "them" about "us," which makes me uncomfortable discussing this issue now in a multi-cultural rather than Chicana publication. Yet I believe that Chicano studies, like feminists and others who aim to reconstruct "the canon" and the structure of the academy, should continue its self-critical reflections on ethical and research dilemmas. In contesting the dominant discourses about women, in this case giving voice to Chicanas, Mexican Americans, or Spanish women workers, we must not be seduced into thinking that our work is without its own contradictions.

In the service of Chicana—or Hispana—informants, I had unconsciously privileged the Chicano side of my identity and not listened to women carefully. After returning to our interview data, and culling from our own experiences of living in Albuquerque and observing working-class Mexican Americans, we came to see that our Hispana informants were telling us something new about ethnic identification. That is, within the constraints of their lives, Spanish meant accommodation, resistance, and struggle to these informants. They helped me to realize that I should deconstruct my own Chicana feminist viewpoint. The critiques of our Chicano/Latino colleagues notwithstanding, we must respect our informants' own constructions of identity, however politically unpalatable they appear to us.

In conclusion, I want to return to the notion of Chicana feminist ethnography. The dilemmas I raise here really have meaning within the constraints of my own life. I hold no delusions that our research was collaborative in some type of pan-female sense that was based on special bonding or that broke down status differences between us and our subjects. While women were remarkably cooperative within the interview setting, in sometimes subtle ways they pointed out the differences between us, and how I had stakes in understanding their lives in ways they did not. In the cannery research project, my informants' political ethnic senses seemed more familiar, more like mine. In the New Mexico project, our informants' sense of ethnicity and identity was so different that we were forced into rethinking so as to recognize its implicit political nature.

In both projects, as in most academic work, the self-defined interests of the research subjects were elsewhere. The researchers defined the problem to study; we asked questions about work, family, and ethnic identity that they found sensitive and even uncomfortable; and our analysis will probably have little direct effect on their daily lives. And however self-consciously provisional an account we provide, our analysis is aimed at a primarily academic community and will provide real benefits to us. In paying careful attention to our informants' sense of their selves, I came in time to see my own Chicana feminist blinders. As we are becoming all too aware, when one claims or has attributed a categorical difference based on ethnicity, the power relations involved are readily apparent. My status as Chicana feminist researcher, then, created two audiences that I should be sensitive and accountable to. Increasingly, I share our Spanish informants' sense of struggle and unease in grappling with this "name game," realizing that I too construct ethnic identity depending on the context.

Feminist dilemmas begin at home, and we cannot take a cultural feminist stance in our approach to fieldwork. As we go through the process of talking with people like ourselves who are called "other," I hope that we can understand our own feminism and political struggles. Chacana feminist ethnography, then, would present more nuanced, fully contextualized, pluralistic self-identities of women, both as informants and as researchers.

Notes

Thanks to Felipe Gonzales and Louise Lamphere for the many extended discussions that helped to clarify my ideas here. For their very helpful critiques of this paper, I thank Gloria Cuadraz, Micaela di Leonardo, Lynet Uttal, and six anonymous reviewers of *Frontiers*.

1. See Octavio I. Romano, "The Anthropology and Sociology of the Mexican American," *El Grito* 2 (1968): 13–26; Américo Paredes, "On Ethnographic Work Among Minority Groups: A Folklorist's Perspective," *The New Scholar* 6/1–2 (1977): 1–32; and John L. Aguilar, "Insider Research: An Ethnography of a Debate," in *Anthropologists at Home in North America: Methods and Issues in the Study of One's Own Society*, ed. Donald A. Messerschmidt (New York: Cambridge University Press, 1988), 15–26.

2. Maxine Baca Zinn, "Field Research in Minority Communities: Ethical, Methodological and Political Observations by an Insider," *Social Problems* 27/2 (1979): 218. Also see Yvonne Tixier y Vigil and Nan Elsasser, "The Effects of the Ethnicity of the Interviewer on Conversation: A Study of Chicana Women," in *Sociology of the Language of American Women*, ed. Betty L. Dubois and Isabel Crouch (San Antonio: Trinity University Press, 1976), 161–169.

3. "Learning from the Outsider Within: The Sociological Significance of Black Feminist Thought," *Social Problems* 33/6 (December 1986): 514–532.

4. For a select few, see Helen Roberts, ed., *Doing Feminist Research* (London: Routledge & Kegan Paul, 1981); Peggy Golde, ed., *Women in the Field: Anthropological Experiences*, 2d ed. (Berkeley: University of California Press, 1986); Renate Duelli Klein, "How to Do What We Want to Do: Thoughts about Feminist Methodology," in *Theories of Women's Studies*, ed. Gloria Bowles and Renate Duelli Klein (London: Routledge & Kegan Paul, 1983); Rosalie H. Wax, "Gender and Age in Fieldwork and Fieldwork Education: No Good Thing Is Done by Any Man Alone," *Social Problems* 26/5 (1979): 509–522; Barrie Thorne, "Political Activist as Participant Observer: Conflicts of Commitment in a Study of the Draft Resistance Movement of the 1960s," *Symbolic Interaction* 2/1 (1979): 73–88; Kath Weston, *Families We Choose: Lesbians, Gays, Kinship* (New York: Columbia University Press, 1991); and Mary Margaret Fonow and Judith A. Cook, *Beyond Methodology: Feminist Scholarship as Lived Research* (Bloomington: Indiana University Press, 1991). For a very useful, comprehensive overview of feminist methodology, see Shulamit Reinharz, *Feminist Methods in Social Research* (New York: Oxford University Press, 1992).

5. Shulamit Reinharz reviews the work of feminists who claim that feminist research has these and other characteristics, including "share the fate of our subjects." See "Experiential Analysis: A Contribution to Feminist Research," in *Theories of Women's Studies*, ed. Gloria Bowles and Renate Duelli Klein (London: Routledge & Kegan Paul, 1983), 162–191.

6. See "Beyond Subjectivity: The Use of the Self in Social Science," *Qualitative Sociology* 8/4 (Winter 1985): 309–324.

7. Joan Acker, Kate Barry, and Johanna Esseveld, "Objectivity and Truth: Problems in Doing Feminist Research," *Women's Studies International Forum* 6/4 (1983): 423–435.

8. Lynn Weber Cannon, Elizabeth Higginbotham, and Marianne L. A. Leung, "Race

and Class Bias in Qualitative Research on Women," *Gender and Society* 2/4 (December 1988): 449–462.

9. See "When Gender Is Not Enough: Women Interviewing Women," *Gender and Society* 1/2 (June 1987): 172–207.

10. Judith Stacey, "Can There Be a Feminist Ethnography?" *Women's Studies International Forum* 11/1 (1988): 21–27. Stacey's naïveté, which she claims is overstated, is nonetheless disturbing. While she confirms that conflicting interests and emotions are inherent to field research, there is not enough context in her discussion of her own "inauthenticity, dissimilitude and potential, perhaps inevitable betrayal" to assess how she tried to deal with the dilemmas she faced. A discussion of how she negotiated with those involved, or whether she reciprocated the trust and openness that her informants shared, could have convinced us that a feminist dilemma, not her expectations and behavior, was at issue.

11. See "Habits of the Cumbered Heart: Ethnic Community and Woman's Culture as American Invented Traditions," in *Imagining the Past in Anthropology and History*, ed. William Roseberry and Jay O'Brien (Berkeley: University of California Press, 1991).

12. "An Awkward Relationship: The Case of Feminism and Anthropology," *Signs* 12/2 (1987): 290. Shulamit Reinharz points out that contrasting perspectives on the relationship of the ethnographer with her subjects has a long history. See note 4.

13. See her excellent overview and critique of feminist anthropology: "Introduction: Gender, Culture, and Political Economy: Feminist Anthropology in Historical Perspective," in *Gender at the Crossroads of Knowledge: Feminist Anthropology in the Postmodern Era*, ed. Micaela di Leonardo (Berkeley: University of California Press, 1991), 1–48.

14. José Limón, "*Carne, Carnales*, and the Carnivalesque: Bakhtinian *Batos*, Disorder, and Narrative Discourses," *American Ethnologist* 16/3 (1989): 49–73.

15. Renato Rosaldo, *Culture and Truth: The Remaking of Social Analysis* (Boston: Beacon Press, 1989).

16. See John C. Hammerback, Richard J. Jensen, and José Angel Gutiérrez, *A War of Words: Chicano Protest in the 1960s and 1970s* (Westport, Conn.: Greenwood Press, 1985); Juan Gomez Quiñones, *Chicano Politics, Reality & Promise, 1940–1990* (Albuquerque: University of New Mexico Press, 1990); Ignacio M. García, *United We Win: The Rise and Fall of La Raza Unida Party* (Tucson: University of Arizona Press, 1989).

17. Marta Cortera, *The Chicana Feminist* (Austin: Information Systems Development, 1977); Ana Nieto Gomez, "*La Femenista*," *Encuentro Femenil* 1/2 (1974): 34–49; Patrícia Hernandez, "Lives of Chicana Activists: The Chicano Student Movement (A Case Study)," in *Mexican Women in the United States: Struggles Past and Present*, ed. Magdalena Mora and Adelaida R. del Castillo (University of California-Los Angeles: Chicano Studies Research Center Publications, 1980); Sylvia Gonzalez, "The White Feminist Movement: The Chicana Perspective," *Social Science Journal* 4 (April 1977): 65–74.

18. *Women's Work and Chicano Families: Cannery Workers of the Santa Clara Valley* (Ithaca: Cornell University Press, 1987).

19. Patricia Zavella, "The Politics of Race and Gender: Organizing Chicana Cannery Workers in Northern California," in *Women and the Politics of Empowerment*, ed. Ann Bookman and Sandra Morgen (Philadelphia: Temple University Press, 1988), 202–224.

20. Limón provides a discussion of the origin of the term Chicano, which has been traced to usage in 1911, and reports on surveys on ethnic identification where the majority of respondents preferred the terms *Mexicano* or Mexican American, except

in New Mexico. See José Limón, "The Folk Performance of Chicano and the Cultural Limits of Political Ideology," in *And Other Neighborly Names: Social Process and Cultural Image in Texas Folklore*, ed. Richard Bauman and Roger D. Abrahams (Austin: University of Texas Press, 1981), 214.

21. Michael V. Miller, "Mexican Americans, Chicanos, and Others: Ethnic Identification and Selected Social Attributes of Rural Texas Youth," *Rural Sociology* 41 (1976): 234–247; John A. García, "*Yo Soy Mexicano* . . . : Self-Identity and Sociodemographic Correlates," *Social Science Quarterly* 62/1 (1981): 88–98; Aída Hurtado and Carlos H. Arce, "Mexicans, Chicanos, Mexican Americans, or Pochos . . . ? *Que Somos?* The Impact of Language and Nativity on Ethnic Labelling," *Aztlan* 17 (1987): 103–129.

22. See Nancy Gonzalez, *Spanish Americans of New Mexico: A Heritage of Pride* (Albuquerque: University of New Mexico Press, 1969).

23. Joseph V. Metzger found that the use of Spanish American had actually declined between 1962 and 1972, while those who increased their use of Chicano were primarily age twenty and younger. See "The Ethnic Sensitivity of Spanish New Mexicans," *New Mexico Historical Review* (1975): 49–73.

24. Ramón A. Gutiérrez investigated ethnic categories and identity in northern New Mexico, beginning in the eighteenth century after Spanish frontier society was firmly established. He documents that the overwhelming majority of the elites could not claim pure Spanish ancestry, yet they claimed an identity as *Españoles* to differentiate themselves from the Indians and claim honor. Mestizos, the ancestors of today's working-class Hispanos, socially constructed their self-designation as Spanish for their own ideological and material benefit. See *When Jesus Came the Corn Mothers Went Away: Marriage, Sexuality and Power in New Mexico, 1500–1846* (Stanford: Stanford University Press, 1991). Even in Spain, there were so many interracial unions that it was impossible to reckon pure Spanish ancestry (Gutiérrez, personal communication).

25. Phillip B. Gonzales, "Spanish Heritage and Ethnic Protest in New Mexico: The Anti-Fraternity Bill of 1933," *New Mexico Historical Review* 61/4 (1986): 281–299. Also see "Ethnic Diffidence and Categorical Awareness: Aspects of Identity Among a Set of Blue Collar Spanish Americans," manuscript, 1992; 'The Political Construction of Ethnic Nomenclature in Twentieth Century New Mexico," manuscript, 1992.

26. See *Sunbelt Working Mothers: Reconciling Family and Factory* (Ithaca: Cornell University Press, 1993).

27. Ramón A. Gutiérrez, "Unraveling American's Hispanic Past : Internal Stratification and Class Boundaries," *Aztlan* 17/1 (1986): 79–101.

28. Focusing on Chicago, Felix M. Padilla notes the importance of context for Mexican American identity: "Encouraged by the division of labor in U. S. industrial society which created common experiences of social inequality among Mexican-Americans and Puerto Ricans, Chicano activists forged coalitions with other Latino groups and constructed a situational ethnic identity of Latinos." See *Latino Ethnic Consciousness: The Case of Mexican Americans and Puerto Ricans in Chicago* (Notre Dame: University of Notre Dame Press, 1985). Also see Josie Méndez Negrete, "What Are You? What Can I Call You? A Study of Chicano and Chicana Ethnic Identity" (Master's thesis, University of California–Santa Cruz, 1991).

29. In a similar manner, José Limón found that some Texans of Mexican descent have used *tejano* as a public referent, in part to distinguish between a *Mexicano* from Mexico and one from Texas. See note 20.

30. Lamphere, Zavella, Gonzales, and Evans (note 26); Phillip B. Gonzales (note 25).

31. In a survey of 370 respondents, Keefe and Padilla found that 25 percent had high

Mexican cultural awareness and ethnic loyalty and were most likely to identify themselves as Mexicans; 74 percent were bicultural individuals who retained moderate or high ethnic identity. Only a small percentage were highly Anglicized and preferred Americans of Mexican descent. In a survey of people of Mexican origin, Hurtado et al. found that the first generation preferred Hispanic (88 percent), Latino (86 percent), and Mexican (76 percent); the second generation preferred Hispanic (83 percent), Californian (81 percent), and American of Mexican descent (78 percent); and the third generation preferred Mexican American (85 percent), Hispanic (83 percent), and American (82 percent) as well as American of Mexican descent (82 percent). Susan E. Keefe and Amado M. Padilla, *Chicano Ethnicity* (Albuquerque: University of New Mexico Press, 1987), esp. Chapter 4; Aída Hurtado, David E. Hayes-Bautista, R. Burciaga Valdez, and Anthony C. R. Hernández, *Redefining California: Latino Social Engagement in a Multicultural Society* (UCLA: Chicano Studies Research Center, 1992), 59. Also see David E. Hayes-Bautista, Aída Hurtado, R. Burciaga Valdez, and Anthony C. R. Hernández, *No Longer a Minority: Latinos and Social Policy in California* (UCLA: Chicano Studies Research Center, 1992).

32. Based on interviews with advisory committee participants and political leaders, Laura E. Gómez argues that Hispanic represents the more "mainstream" political viewpoints of the participants, and became popularized during the 1980s. See "The Birth of the 'Hispanic' Generation: Attitudes of Mexican-American Political Elites toward the Hispanic Label," *Latin American Perspectives* 19/4 (Fall 1992): 45–58.

33. Alejandro Portes and Robert L. Bach, *Latin Journey: Cuban and Mexican Immigrants in the United States* (Berkeley: University of California Press, 1985).

34. Beginning with the 1980 census, the term Hispanic is a specially designated ethnic term that includes four subcategories: Mexican, Mexican American, Chicano; Puerto Rican; Cuban; Other Spanish/Hispanic. For the state of New Mexico, there have been bipolar self-designations, with the Mexican, Mexican American, and Chicano and the Other Spanish/Hispanic making up the largest categories. Since it is unclear how many Iberians reside in New Mexico, and since unlike other cities (like Miami, San Francisco, Los Angeles, Washington, D. C., or New York), Albuquerque (the largest New Mexican city) is not a major site of Latin American immigrant settlement, we can only conclude that some Mexican Americans are choosing Other Spanish. Thus census data are particularly imprecise for counting the Mexican American population in New Mexico.

35. See *Noticias de NACS* 9/3: 1.

36. See Christine M. Sierra, "Hispanos and the 1988 General Election in New Mexico," in *From Rhetoric to Reality: Latinos and the 1988 Election*, ed. Rodolfo O. de la Garza and Louis de Cippio (Boulder, Colo.: Westview, 1992). Metzger claims that in the 1970s, Hispano has been used almost exclusively by scholars and professional writers to describe Spanish-speaking New Mexicans and did not have widespread use in the barrios. See note 23.

37. Ruth Frankenberg argues that the social construction of "white" carries several meanings—as distinct from "white ethnic," "spoiled by capitalism"—so that brand names like Wonder Bread connote blandness or processing, and evocations of features of the body such as skin color. See "White Women, Race Matters: The Social Construction of Whiteness" (Ph. D., diss., University of California–Santa Cruz, 1988). Micaela di Leonardo shows how late-1970s white Italian American women socially construct their own sense of white ethnicity, sometimes in racist terms. See *The Varieties of Ethnic Experience: Kinship, Class, and Gender Among California Italian-Americans* (Ithaca: Cornell University Press, 1984).

38. Marta Cortera, "Feminism: The Chicana and the Anglo Versions, a Historical Analysis," in *Twice a Minority: Mexican American Women*, ed. Margarita B. Melville

(St. Louis: C. V. Mosby, 1980); Alma M. García, "The Development of Chicana Feminist Discourse, 1970–1980," *Gender and Society* 3 (June 1989): 217–238.

39. Denise Segura, "Chicanas and Triple Oppression in the Labor Market," *Chicana Voices: Intersections of Class, Race and Gender* (Austin: Center for Mexican American Studies, 1986), 47–65; Patricia Zavella, "The Problematic Relationship of Feminism and Chicana Studies," *Women's Studies* 17/1–2 (1989); reprinted in *Across Cultures: The Spectrum of Women's Lives*, ed. Emily K. Abel and Majorie L. Pearson (New York: Gordon and Breach, 1989), 23–34. Actually I said mixed marriage. Thanks to Emma Perez, who reminded me that my use of a marriage analogy is a heterosexist formulation. See "Speaking from the Margin: Uninvited Discourse on Sexuality and Power," in *With These Hands: Building Chicana Scholarship*, ed. Beatriz Pesquera and Adela de la Torre (Berkeley: University of California Press, 1993).

    In 1988 Beatriz Pesquera and Denise Segura did a survey of 101 Chicana faculty, students, and staff who belong to *Mujeres Activas en Letras y Cambio Social* (Activist Women in Letters and Social Change), an organization of Chicana/Latina activist academics, where 83 percent of their respondents identified themselves as feminists. Pesquera and Segura argued that there have been internal differences since the late 1960s, but that these have become more noticeable in more recent years. They identified three types of Chicana feminists in their sample. Cultural nationalists emphasize the concerns of the Chicano movement, but want recognition of women's concerns and rights as well. Liberal Chicana feminists are oriented toward reform, and hope to enhance the well-being of the Chicano community with a special emphasis on improving the status of women. Insurgent Chicana feminists, immersed in radical traditions, emphasize that Chicana inequality is the product of interrelated forms of stratification, based on race-ethnicity, class, and gender—and for some, heterosexism. These women favor personal and institutional change, and compared to the other groups are more actively involved in political activities.

40. Denise A. Segura and Beatríz M. Pesquera, "Beyond Indifference and Antipathy: The Chicana Movement and Chicana Feminist Discourse," *Aztlan, International Journal of Chicano Studies Research* (in press). Also see Beatriz M. Pesquera and Denise A. Segura, "With Quill and Torch: A Chicana Perspective on the American Women's Movement and Feminist Theories," in *Third Wave: Feminist Perspectives on Racism*, ed. N. J. Alarcon, S. Alexander, S. Day, L. Albrecht, and M. Segrets (New York: Kitchen Table, in press).

3   *Carne, Carnales,* **and the Carnivalesque**

Bakhtinian *Batos,* Disorder,

and Narrative Discourses

JOSÉ E. LIMÓN

> And when he came to the place where the wild things are
> they roared their terrible roars and gnashed their terrible teeth
> and rolled their terrible eyes and showed their terrible claws
> till Max said, "Be still!"
> and tamed them with the magic trick
> of staring into all their yellow eyes without blinking once
> and they were frightened and called him the most wild thing of all
> and made him king of all wild things
> "And now," cried Max, "let the wild rumpus start!"
>
> > —From the children's book by Maurice Sendak, *Where the Wild Things Are,*
> > in which a mischievous little boy, Max, visits the wild things.

At two in the afternoon a periodically unemployed working-class man in Mexican-American south Texas puts hot chunks of juicy barbecued meat with his fingers on an equally hot tortilla. The meat or *carne* has marinated overnight in beer and lemon juice before being grilled. Antoñio, or Toñio, passes the meat-laden tortilla to one of the other eight mostly working-class men surrounding a rusty barbecue grill, but as he does so, the hand holding the food brushes against his own genital area, and he loudly tells the other, "*¡Apaña este taco carnal, 'ta a toda madre mi carne!*" (Grab this taco, brother, my meat is a mother!)[1] With raucous laughter all around, I accept the full, dripping taco, add some hot sauce, and reach for an ice-downed beer from an also rusty washtub.

Some 50 years ago the Mexican thinker Samuel Ramos published his well-known and still culturally authoritative *Profile of Man and Culture in Mexico* (1934), an interpretive general narrative history of its subject since its indigenous beginnings. Ramos was trying to explain what he saw as the reduced sense of Mexican cultural life and its contradictions in his time. As part of his contemporary account, a kind of climax to his narrative, Ramos turns into an anthropological, if distanced, observer of everyday Mexican life, particularly male life. For example, the Mexican *pelado* or lower-class man

> belongs to a most vile category of social fauna; . . . a form of human rubbish. . . . Life from every quarter has been hostile to him and his reaction has been black resentment.

He is an explosive being with whom relationship is dangerous, for the slightest friction causes him to blow up [1962:59].

According to Ramos, the Mexican lower-class man's

explosions are verbal and reiterate his theme of self affirmation in crude and suggestive language. He has created a dialect of his own, a diction which abounds in ordinary words, but he gives these words a new meaning. He is an animal whose ferocious pantomimes are designed to terrify others, making them believe that he is stronger than they and more determined. Such reactions are illusory retaliations against his real position in life which is a nullity [1962:60].

For Ramos, these verbal pantomimes, these explosive linguistic reactions, are of a particular kind. This lower-class man's "terminology abounds in sexual allusions which reveal his phallic obsession; the sexual organ becomes symbolic of masculine force." The reproductive organs are a symbolic source of "not only one kind of potency, the sexual, but every kind of human power" as this man "tries to fill his void with the only suggestive force accessible to him: that of the male animal," and, continues Ramos, "so it is that his perception becomes abnormal; he imagines that the next man he encounters will be his enemy; he mistrusts all who approach him" (1962:59–61).

In this paper I discuss what Foucault calls discourses of power as these concern Mexican-American south Texas, where I was raised, my current fieldwork site, and still a place characterized by sharp class and ethnic divisions as it has been since Zachary Taylor's army first conquered the area in the 1840s during the United States–Mexico War (Foley 1978; de Leon 1982, 1983; Montejano 1987). You have already heard two examples of such discourse: one, the expressive, all-male human of a group of *batos* (guys, dudes) articulated in and through the ritualistic consumption of barbecued meat in southern Texas, an event called a *carne asada*; and two, Samuel Ramos' narratively embedded commentary on the language and culture of the Mexican male lower class, a discourse tradition continued by Octavio Paz in the 1950s and applied directly to the Mexican-Americans of south Texas in the 1960s by anthropologist Joseph Spielberg (1974).

Mindful of Marcus' recent call upon Marxist ethnographers to also provide analyses of the culture of the dominant as well as the dominated (1986), I have in another paper tried to show how this second set of discourses, this interpretive tradition begun by Samuel Ramos, functions as a discourse of power in a larger international scope (Limón 1987). At critical moments in Mexican and Mexican-American history, this interpretive tradition unintentionally helps to ratify dominance through its negative psychologistic interpretation of the Mexican male lower class and its language. As Ramos' commentary clearly illustrates, this discourse casts these classes in the idiom of human rubbish, animality, aggressiveness, and abnormality, a view, I might add, considerably shared by those—both Anglo and Mexican-American—who hold class power in southern Texas.

My chief purpose here, however, is to begin to develop an alternative understanding of this lower-class male culture; to develop a third narrative discourse, if you will, one which I would like to think Foucault might have called an archaeology of subjugated knowledges and practices, this in an effort to demonstrate the power of such knowledges and practices as a discourse of the dominated, discourses often in narrative form. My analysis will draw from recent Marxist perspectives on language, on the anthropology of natural symbols, but centrally on Bakhtin's sense of the carnivalesque.

However, even as I go about this central purpose, I want to call attention to the purpose itself. That is, I want to keep before the reader my own effort to narrativize these subjugated narratives. To be sure, this effort is in a different political direction from Ramos and Paz but is nonetheless itself an authoritative narrative, which, as Foucault would remind us, is never wholly free from the influence of dominating power. This latter issue will become more evident in my conclusion.

In the construction of our own ethnographic narratives, we are inevitably faced with the problem of rhetorically managing what we are pleased to call "the data." How much is enough so as to persuade and not bore or overwhelm? And where do we place it in the structural development of our own text? What is the proper relationship between the data and our interpretive analysis, recognizing full well that the selection and organization of the data have already taken us a long way toward our understanding of it? With these issues in mind, I continue with my strategy of juxtaposing narrative discourses from the dominant and dominated, reminding you once again of my own emerging ethnographic narrative.

Later that afternoon on a hot August Saturday in 1981, another man, an auto parts salesman, in a ten-year-old pickup drives up to our barbecue session in the outskirts of McBurg.[2] He brings with him a couple of pounds of tripe that will eventually be added to the other internal organs and to the *fajita*, or skirt steak, now turning golden brown and sizzling in its fat on the barbecue grill. His *tripitas*—for all the meat parts are expressed in the diminutive—are turned over to Poncho, house painter and the latest cook at the grill. Jaime, this new arrival (otherwise known as "el Midnight" because he is quite dark), begins to shake everyone's hand in greeting saying, "*¿Como estas?*" (How are you doing?) and so on. Expecting my turn, I put down my beer and dry my hand on my jeans, but Jaime never makes it past the second man he greets, Simón.

Simón, otherwise known as "el Mickey Mouse" because of his large ears, has been a construction laborer most of his adult life, except for the three years he spent at the state prison when he got caught on the highway to Austin transporting marijuana for the consumption of the students at the university. "*¡Que pendejada! ¡Tiré un beer can y me paró el jurado!*" (What stupidity! I threw out a beer can and the cop stopped me!)

Simón takes Jaime's hand as if to shake it but instead yanks it down and holds it firmly over his own genital area even as he responds to Jaime's "*¿Como estas?*" with a loud "*¡Pos, chínga ahora me siento a toda madre, gracias!*" (Well, fuck, now I feel just great, thank you!) There is more laughter which only intensifies when "Midnight" in turn actually grabs and begins to squeeze "el Mickey's" genitals. With his one free hand, for the other is holding a taco, el Mickey tries to pull on Jaime's arm unsuccessfully. Finally, in an effort to slip out of Jaime's grip, he collapses to the ground cursing and trying to laugh at the same time and loses his taco in the process. Jaime, however, has gone down on his knees and manages to maintain his grip even as he keeps saying over and over, "*¡Dime que me quieres, cabrón, dime que me quieres!*" (Tell me you love me, godammit, tell me you love me!) El Mickey finally says "*Te quiero, te quiero*" but as soon as he is released, he continues, "*Te quiero dar en la madre!*" (I want to beat the hell out of you) playing on the double meaning of *quiero* as "want" and "love." He takes a few semi-mock punches at Jaime's torso and receives a few in return, both carefully avoiding the face. Everyone is still laughing as el Mickey and Midnight, still on their knees, hug each other to a stop. As they help each other up, Jaime tells Mickey, "*Dejando de chingaderas, anda a traer otro taco y traile uno a tu papa*" (All screwing around aside, go get another taco and bring one for your father), referring, of course, to himself. Doing or saying *chingaderas* (fuck ups) is how these men label and gloss this activity, also sometimes *pendejadas* and *vaciladas* (stupidities, play routines). See Spielberg (1974).

In the 1950s another distinguished Mexican intellectual had this story to tell about the Mexican lower-class male personality and his language. "It is significant," says Octavio Paz, "that masculine homosexuality is regarded with a certain indulgence insofar as the active agent is concerned." The passive agent is an abject, degraded being. "This ambiguous conception," he continues, "is made very clear in the word games or battles—full of obscene allusions and double meanings—that are so popular in Mexico City" (1961:39).

> Each of the speakers tries to humiliate his adversary with verbal traps and ingenious linguistic combinations, and the loser is the person who cannot think of a comeback, who has to swallow his opponent's jibes. These jibes are full of aggressive sexual allusions; the loser is possessed, is violated, by the winner, and the spectators laugh and sneer at him [1961:39–40].

Octavio Paz continues this commentary, translated into English in 1961. "The Mexican macho," he says,

> is a humorist who commits *chingaderas*, that is, unforeseen acts that produce confusion, horror, and destruction. He opens the world; in doing so, he rips and tears it, and this violence provokes a great sinister laugh . . . the humor of the *macho* is an act of revenge [1961:81].

"Whatever may be the origins of these attitudes," Paz tells us, "the fact is that the essential attribute of the *macho*-power almost always reveals itself as a capacity for wounding, humiliating, annihilating" (1961:82).

It is almost six o'clock in this evening outside of McBurg at what our host Chema likes to call his *rancho*, which amounts to less than one-quarter acre of dry, wholly undeveloped land with only a few mesquites to provide some shade from the hot south Texas sun. Chema bought the land, called "ranchettes" by local real estate agents, when he came into a little money from a worker's compensation settlement. He fell from a truck while doing farm labor for extra money. Massaging his lower back for the still lingering pain, he says, *"El pínche abogado se quedó con la mitad"* (The fucking lawyer [Mexican-American] kept half). Chema's only real notion for improving the property is to build an inevitable brick barbecue pit, but until he can afford it, he will have to haul the portable rusty one on the black of his pickup out to the *rancho*.

A few more men have come with more meat and beer and a few have left, play-fully taunted by the others, *"Tiene que ir a reportar a la vieja"* (He has to go report to his old lady), knowing that eventually they'll have to go report to their "old ladies." The eating, drinking, and the talk are still thick, and *conjunto* polka music is playing from a portable radio, although later this will be replaced by guitar play-ing and singing of, on the one hand, *corridos* or Mexican ballads with accompanying *gritos* (cries) and, on the other, American tunes from the fifties such as "In the Still of the Night" by the Five Satins, to which everyone will sing a cacophony of appro-priate *sho do be do be doos*.

One of the men keeps insisting that he has to go; with equal insistence he is told to have another beer and to make a taco out of the very last of the cherished deli-cacy, *mollejitas* (glandular organs), but he is particularly insistent because his kids need to be picked up at the movies, where, we discover, they have been watching Steven Spielberg's *E.T.—The Extra Terrestrial*. Octavio is almost ready to leave when Chema, our host and ranch owner, asks him: *"Aye, 'Tavo. Sabes como se dice 'E.T.' en espanol?"* (Hey 'Tavo, do you know how to say E. T. in Spanish?) Before Octavio can even try to reply, a grinning Chema answers his own question correctly by saying, *"Eh Te,"* but he is also holding his hand over his genitals and gesturing twice with it as he pronounces the two syllables. *Eh Te* does of course mean E. T. in Spanish, but it is also the way a toddler might pronounce *este* (this one), dropping a consonant "s" but meaning *this* or *this one* as in *este papel* (this paper). In saying *Eh Te* and with his double gesture, Chema is calling attention, particularly Octavio's attention, to his penis—this one. But things get better . . . or worse, as the case may be. Chema continues his interrogation of Octavio: *"Y, como se llaman los dos her-manitos de E.T.?"* (And, what are the names of E. T.'s two little brothers?) Chema demonstrates the answer with another genital double gesture, this time answering his own question with the Spanish *Eh Tos*, again exploiting the baby play language pronunciation of *estos*, meaning *these*, referring of course to *these two*, meaning his own testicles. Everyone, including Octavio, is laughing and all of us cannot help but look as Chema does his gestures and baby talk, and he isn't through yet. "And what," he asks, "is the name of E. T.'s mother?" This time, however, Octavio, who has obviously been conducting his own ethnography of this speech act, beats Chema to the answer with his hand at his crotch, loudly and triumphantly pro-claiming the answer, *"¡Mama Eh Te!"*; this time, Octavio has exploited the original *este* (this one), and he has also exploited the charged ambiguity of *mama* in Span-ish, which, depending on accent and syntax can mean "mother" or "suck." Laugh-ing with the others, Octavio finally makes his way to the movie *E.T.* or *Eh Te* to pick up the kids; Chema is shaking his head and laughing and complaining about all of the meat juice he has managed to rub all over his crotch.

By seven or eight, more people start dispersing, a few latecomers arrive, a fire has been started, and one of the guitarists sings the "Corrido of Jacinto Trevino" about a brave south Texas Mexican who shot it out with the Texas Rangers in 1906 in the town of Brownsville just down the river from McBurg (Paredes 1976). Finally, thinks your ethnographer, I get some real folklore of resistance and not all of these *chingaderas.*

For at that moment, some years ago, I am troubled, at least intellectually, by what I have reexperienced, having gone through such events several times in my life in south Texas but also in a few cantinas in Monterey, in Los Angeles, in Mexico City. Are Ramos and Paz right when they speak of sexual anxiety, of wounding and humiliation? Are the *chingaderas* "unforeseen acts that produce confusion, horror and destruction" amid a "great sinister laugh"? And, at that time it did not help to have reread a recent anthropological study of such south Texas male humor specifically in this area near McBurg in which Joseph Spielberg, also a native south Texans, concludes that this humor "can be characterized as verbal aggression aimed at another when he is most vulnerable" by his "own lack of discretion in bodily functions, social circumstances or by revealing his sentiments." In the tradition of Ramos and Paz, Spielberg also believes that "the principal theme of this humor" is "humiliation" (1974:46).

These discourses troubled me then, for they did not speak well of these, my people, and perhaps they do not speak well of me, for, frankly, although with some ambivalent distance, I had a good time that Saturday afternoon and have had a good time since.

I had indeed gone to racially and structurally dominated southern Texas in 1981 looking for a folklore of resistance, carrying in my head the examples furnished by Genovese, by Gutman, by E. P. Thompson and George Rudé, and ultimately by Gramsci. I found instead a powerful sexual and scatological discourse—part of a greater Mexican working-class folk tradition, but a tradition I saw as delegitimatized by the powerful authoritative intellectual discourses of Ramos and Paz and, in a more circumscribed but still effective way, by Spielberg. And I found difficult, and perhaps still do, its relegitimization because this is at least the implicit burden of those who approach such materials from a Marxist cultural perspective. Certainly one alternative is simply to deny the burden and accept Ramos and Paz or perhaps some species of functionalist argument where these behaviors are seen as adaptive steam valves. From this perspective, as everyone leaves Chema's ranch, they feel well adjusted to the labors they will face on Monday.

How can one rethink these materials as a narrative of resistance provided by Marxist social historians, especially when the materials do not nicely lend themselves to such a reading, as do black spirituals and the crafts of English artisans? And how can one do this if one has to contend with an extant authoritative interpretive discourse, especially one developed by members of the same general cultural group, such as Spielberg?

In the intervening years I have read new sources, reread old ones, and have been developing an analysis of such discourses so as to address this question. The task is made more interestingly difficult by George Marcus, who, in the essay cited earlier,

takes Paul Willis to task, and by implication other Marxist ethnographers, for priv-
ileging working-class culture as a seamless discourse of anti-capitalist resistance
(1986). As I think of Chema, Midnight, Mickey Mouse, Octavio, and others, I ask,
how does one develop a different story about these men without lapsing into an
uncritical romanticism of resistance everywhere; how does one do this without
abandoning the concept of the social whole and one's native and political sympathy
with the dominated? And, finally, how does one produce a narrative construction,
one's ethnography, that does not wholly objectify and violate the "feel" of such
events?

Writing with a Difference

We may begin this alternative reformulation by examining the central sexual sym-
bolization that lies at the heart of the speech play and gesture that I have noted.
Toñio's, Jaime's, Simón's, Octavio's, and Chema's obvious and expressive manipulations of body and speech would certainly seem consistent with Samuel Ramos'
observation that the Mexican lower-class man's

> terminology abounds in sexual allusions which reveal his phallic obsession; the sexual
> organ becomes symbolic of masculine force. In verbal combat he attributes to his
> adversary an imaginary femininity, reserving for himself the masculine role. By this
> stratagem he pretends to assert his superiority over his opponents [Ramos 1962:
> 59–60].

For these commentators, aggression and its generative conditions—inadequacy and
inferiority—are directly expressed in this humor through anal references and the
theme of male sexual violation. I would not deny the existence of these values and
meanings, given my earlier argument for the historical production of aggression,
nor that these performances may in part be expressing them. I would, however,
argue that these might be multivocal symbols possessing *several* meanings and not
reducible to a single one that fits a preconceived psychoanalytical scheme. It is too
easy to rely on a wild psychoanalysis when dealing with such physical references.

Mary Douglas has warned us of the dangers and shortcomings of such simple
psychologistic readings when they concern rituals dealing with the human body
(1978). Some psychologists are fond of treating such rituals not as social acts, but
as the expression of private and personal infantile concerns. "There is," she
believes, "no possible justification for this shift of interpretation just because the
rituals work upon human flesh . . ." (1978:115). Those who make this interpretive
reduction

> proceed from unchallenged assumptions, which arise from the strong similarity
> between certain ritual forms and the behavior of psychopathic individuals. The
> assumption is that in some sense primitive cultures correspond to infantile stages in
> the development of the human psyche. Consequently such rites are interpreted as if
> they express the same preoccupations which fill the mind of psychopaths or infants
> [1978:115].

Douglas argues for an alternative analytical model for the understanding of the human body in relation to society—one that is "prepared to see in the body a symbol of society, and to see the powers and dangers credited to social structure reproduced in small on the human body" (1978:115). A society's definition and treatment of the body and bodily pollution is, in her estimation, a critical symbolic key for grasping its perceptions of its own structure and of its external relationships. Such pollution—all forms of matter issuing from the body's orifices as well as entering through them—may acquire symbolic proportions, as do necessarily the orifices themselves. The Coorgs of India, for example, are an isolated mountain community sharing with other castes a fear of what is "outside and below" their group. In their ritual behavior they "treat the body as if it were a beleaguered town, every ingress and exit guarded for spies and traitors" (1978:123).

I would submit that the *mexicano* on both sides of the border also has something to fear. This fear may not be simply an infantile concern with one's *palomilla* (gang) and simple sexual dominance. Rather, the themes of anality, pollution, and bodily penetration may also be symbolic expressions of an essentially political and economic concern with social domination, not from below, as with the Coorg, but from above—from the upper levels of the structure of power in both countries. The marginalized working and unemployed classes where these expressions abound constitute a body politic symbolically conscious of its socially penetrable status. What Douglas claims for the Coorgs may be at least partially applicable for Octavio, Samuel, Chema, and my other friends:

> For them the model of the exits and entrances of the human body is a doubly apt symbolic focus of fears for their minority standing in the larger society. Here I am suggesting that when rituals express anxiety about the body's orifices the sociological counterpart of this anxiety is a care to protect the political and cultural unity of a minority group [1978:124].

There is certainly some evidence for this view in the often noted tendency of the Mexican male, particularly the lower-class male, to turn to the expression *chingar*—meaning sexual violation—to also express social violation, as my friends often do when speaking particularly of their political/economic relationships: *"Me chingaron en el jale"* (I got screwed at work) or, during one of the regular political discussions at the *carne asada*, *"Pos gano Reagan, y ahora si nos van a chingar"* (Well, Reagan won, now we're really going to get screwed), and finally, *"La vida es una chinga"* (Life is being constantly screwed), which represents a quite reasonable perception of social conditions for these men in this part of the world.

Others, the dominant Mexican-American and Anglo upper classes—*los chingones* (the big screwers)—as these men commonly refer to them, always have the ability to *chingar*, and it is entirely to the point that these are also men, and it is here, I suspect, that we can find a possible reason for the conversion of this potential male social violation into the symbolic idiom of homosexuality. The routines, I will remind you, are called *chingaderas*. When Antoñio seemingly threatens me with the meat that has passed by his genitals; when Octavio triumphantly says *"¡Mama*

Eh Te!" they may indeed, as all Western men do, be expressing their latent anxiety about homosexuality. However, I am suggesting, partially following Mary Douglas' lead, that we need not just stop here.[3] These men may also be reenacting, in the idiom of homosexuality, their sense that the world beyond Chema's *rancho* is also full of constant violation by other men—*los chingones*—and one must learn to play that too-serious game as well![4]

But as I write of play and games, I want to introduce another critical alternative perspective that speaks to a central flaw in Ramos, Paz, and Spielberg's understanding—or lack of it—of this speech play. It is important to recognize that even as my friends introduce the seemingly aggressive idiom of sexual and social violation, they do so in a way that reframes that aggressive speech and gesture into play. Ramos, Paz, and Spielberg extract the sexual symbols in this play and give them their shallow reductive interpretations. They are not appreciative of these scenes as dynamic forums that interactionally produce meaning. Their focus always is on those discrete "aggressive" verbal symbols. As such they are like those anthropologists who, according to Peacock,

> tend to pay too little heed to the dynamics of (cultural) performances, to report from the performances only those tidbits of content which lend support to his portrait of the values and organization of the society in which the performances are found. . . . This kind of analysis which fails to grasp the essence of symbolic performances can yield no full appreciation of social dynamics [1968:256].

This difference in interpretive emphasis is crucial, for their "tidbits of content" analysis leads these analysts to ignore the way in which the aggressive meaning of the literal language, such as it is, is transformed into its exact opposite through the intercession of interactional speech play and art.

To begin with, *mexicanos* frame such scenes as ludic moments through native markers such as *relajando* and *llevandosale* (carrying on, bantering, playing), as in *"nomas estabamos relajando"* (we were just playing). We have a clear recognition of a play world in which open aggression can appear *only by mistake*. Such a mistake can occur when a novice or an unacculturated person fails to "recognize" the scene, or when he is less than competent in the requisite artistic skills. This latter consideration is crucial, for whatever latent aggression exists is not only rendered socially harmless but is turned into a basis for solidarity. The participants do this by interactionally creating an artistically textured discourse through skillful manipulations of allusion, metaphor, narration, and prosody.

Through interactionally produced play, the aggression of the world is transformed into mock aggression, mock fighting through artistic creativity which does not deny the existence of aggression but inverts its negativity. Ultimately this transformation is of greater social significance. What Bateson notes for nonhuman animals is also fundamentally true for these human artistic performers. These men mean something other than what is denoted by their aggressive language. Such language becomes like the "playful nips" which "denote the bite but it does not denote what would be denoted by the bite" (Bateson 1972:180). Art and play ultimately create paradox and fiction.

Paradox is doubly present in the signals which are exchanged within the context of the play, fantasy, threat, etc. Not only does the playful nip not denote what would be denoted by the bite for which it stands but the bite itself is fictional. Not only do the playing animals not quite mean what they are saying but, also, they are communicating about something which does not exist [1972:182].

Aggression is what would be denoted by an actual bite—it is that something that is the hidden textual model for the playful nip, but is itself not denoted and therefore is negated at the moment of interaction. The playful nips of skillful artistic language produce a paradoxical effect, namely, the interactional production of solidarity, or as Latin Americans everywhere would say, *confianza*. Anthony Lauria notes that in Puerto Rico, "to indulge in *relajos* of any sort in the presence of anyone is to engage in a relation of *confianza*—of trust and familiarity with that person" (1964:62). As Lauria also notes, the ultimate paradoxical social result of the expressive scene is not aggression, humiliation, and alienation, but rather *respeto*. This is the significance of ending a verbal exchange in mock punches, a hug, and a laugh. In one of Bateson's metalogues his persona and that of his daughter engage in conversation.

Daughter: Why do animals fight?
Father: Oh, for many reasons, territory, sex, food . . .
Daughter: Daddy, you're talking like instinct theory. I thought we agreed not to do that.
Father: All right. But what sort of an answer do you want to the question, why animals fight?
Daughter: Well, do they deal in opposites?
Father: Oh. Yes. A lot of fighting ends up in some sort of peace-making. And certainly playful fighting is partly a way of affirming friendship. Or discovering or rediscovering friendship.
Daughter: I thought so . . . [1972:18].

The artistic disclosure of friendship and respect in the *palomilla's* interaction is not, in and of itself, ideological. That is, in a social vacuum, one could only construe it as play, friendship, and solidarity pure and simple. But, of course, these expressive scenes do not emerge in such a vacuum; they appear and are embedded in a political economy and a hegemonic culture that produces marginalization and alienation such as prevails among this class of *batos* in south Texas.[5]

In these particular socioeconomic circumstances play and its concomitant friendship become eminently ideological. As an emergent cultural performance, they represent an oppositional break in the alienating hegemony of the dominant culture and society.

In a provocative article, Hearn correctly notes that both mainstream and orthodox Marxist social science construe play as an ontologically secondary activity to the instrumental "real" world of politics and economics (1976-77). There is in such a construal a reproduction of capitalist categories of experience, a particularly unfortunate situation for Marxists. Hearn offers a corrective formulation of play that draws upon the work of two non-orthodox Marxist theoreticians, Habermas and Marcuse. He notes the former's idea of language as symbolic interaction that "has a transcendental self-reflexive capacity which permits it to give expression to contradictions between appearance and reality, potentiality and actuality." Because it is not totally and automatically bound to reproduce the social order, "language has the potential for emancipating people from a dependence on reified cultural controls." As such, people have in their language "the capacity for reflexivity and transcendence which enables the creation of evaluative standards, allows the expression of contradictions, and supplies a conception of potentiality, of 'what can be'" (Hearn 1976–77:147). These critical possibilities are greater for that least commodified and instrumentalized language—the emergent verbal art of marginalized peoples.

Hearn finds similar properties in Marcuse's concept of play. For Marcuse human play is the autonomous production of a dramatized, albeit temporal, vision of an alternative social order. In authentic, that is, non-commodified, play, there is an emergent promise of "freedom from compulsion, hierarchy, inequality, and injustice" (1976–77:150). In its very ontology, play is neither secondary to instrumentalism nor is it its total denial. Rather it emerges as a critique, a constraint, and a transcendence of all instrumental activity. Ultimately, play—the free-flowing artistic exchanges of the men at Chema's *rancho*—has a subversive quality.

> In play while the limitations of the existing reality are exposed, a more satisfying—more equitable and just—order is celebrated.... To the extent that play affirms the possibility of a "better world" it retains the potential for highlighting the negativity of and contributing to the subversion of the prevailing arrangements [Hearn 1976–77:150–151].

Mexicans and their verbal art draw upon the domains of language and play explored by Habermas and Marcuse to produce a single phenomenon—human speech play. Through such speech play the participants continually produce a world of human value—of *confianza* and *respeto*. Created in collective equality, such momentary productions negate the alienating constraints of the historically given social order that exists for *mexicanos* and affirm the possibilities of a different social order. They momentarily overturn the alienating effects even while they remind these men of the real aggression in the world, that of *los chingones*.

Because the dominant discourse of power—that of Ramos, Paz, and Spielberg—has focused exclusively on the language of such scenes, I too have felt obligated to pay special attention to language even while recognizing that language is only part of a cultural contextual scene. Indeed, as I have suggested, it is the failure to recognize this total context of play that flaws this dominant discourse. But in the world of Chema's *rancho*, it is necessary to recognize other symbolic elements that also constitute this play world as a temporary forum of non-alienation.

For example, this play scene is itself framed in another form of play—a kind of visible joke—namely, the very existence of Chema's *rancho*, that undeveloped little piece of land surrounded on all sides by huge ranches with oil drills; just a few miles away, for example, lie the beginnings of the King Ranch, parts of which, according to Mexican legend, were bought and paid for in Mexican blood. Chema's *rancho* is itself a source of constant humor, especially when, after a few beers, Chema begins to tell the other guys of his big plans for this little place. Inevitably someone will ask him, where are you going to put the cow? And, how is the bull going to screw her when you can't get them both on the place at the same time? The ultimate joke, of course, is the existence of this "ranch" dedicated not to capitalist mass agriculture but to friendship and play. While not a necessary condition, the very existence of this visible joke—this humorous incongruity—is productive of more jokes and play. As Mary Douglas says, "if there is no joke in the social structure, no other joke can appear" (1968:366).

Finally, there is my title—*carne, carnales,* and the carnivalesque. As the name of this event—*carne asada*—clearly indicates, and as I have suggested throughout, *carne* (meat) and its preparation and consumption are of central concern here. If, as Mary Douglas says, food is a code, then where in society lies the precoded message and how does this message speak of hierarchy, inclusions, and exclusions (1971:61)? What kind of meat is this socially and what, if anything, is its message?

These men are preparing and consuming those parts of a steer—the internal organs and the *faja*, or skirt steak—that are clearly undervalued, low-prestige meats in the larger social economy, and, given their economic resources, that is not unexpected. As an old Anglo rancher in the area told me, "We used to call that stuff 'Mexican leavings.'" What interests me is the way in which such meat parts, symbolically linked to capitalist cattle ranching, are culturally mediated to convert them from low-prestige, rather tough and stringy protein into tasty, valued, social food. The use of the affectionate diminutive to name and linguistically "soften" this food—*fajita, mollejita, tripita*—is a case in point here and parallels the physical softening of the protein in much-valued, secret marinades. (Indeed, it is rumored with awe and disgust that the marinade for Chema's meat—which is considered the best—has a touch of urine in it, some say from his wife. When I hesitantly asked Chema about this, he said it was absolutely not true; he would never ask his wife to do such a thing. After a few seconds, he added, with a grin, "Only a man's piss will do!") In this cultural mediation we get food that is an ever-present reminder of their class status but which in its preparation symbolically negates that status; food material that begins with low status and exclusion results in food prepared in pride, good taste, and social inclusion.

The preparation and consumption of this meat also speaks to class difference in another way. The food is simply prepared, with the only utensils present being a sharp knife to cut the meat and the chilis, tomatoes, and onions for the sauce, and a fork to turn the meat. The sauce is prepared in the bottom parts of beer cans cut in half, and spoons are fashioned from the metal of the upper half. This preparation becomes a way for these guys to distinguish themselves from the dominant Others—*los chingones*—who use plates, knives, forks, cups, and napkins. They also eat awful things like potato salad and lettuce with their meat, which is bought and barbecued for them by their Mexican servants from across the border, who cross the bridge to work in their large, fashionable homes.

Finally, I am most interested in the way the consumption of food is a kind of international parallel to the charged language that paradoxically generates friendship. Everyone brings their low-prestige meat—a symbol of societal aggression—and contributes it to a central collective pile; everyone, at some point or another, takes a turn at shooing flies away, broiling and cutting the meat, and making the sauce.

The tacos are made by everyone in random fashion and, since there are no plates, they are passed along by hand, sometimes going through two or three sets of hands. These men at Chema's *rancho* and many others throughout south Texas and, I might add, in the Texan outposts of central California, prepare and consume their once low-prestige food collectively and non-hierarchically even as they playfully assault each other with the charged language of friendship. The felt result is another discourse of power, a power that does not dominate but liberates them, if only for brief moments, from the contexts of alienation beyond Chema's *rancho* where race and structure still prevail. In this world, Chema's *carne* is closely linked to *carnales*, a kinship term used among brothers or close male friends.

In the 1960s Chicano college students spoke in too self-conscious and slightly forced ways of *carnalismo*. These men never use this term, although, when they hear it, they can sense what it means. Rather, they freely use the term *carnal*—a folk term for brother or buddy, which seems to me to be an appropriate native gloss for their cultural practice. In one too conscious and too keenly ideological moment, Chinito ("little Chinese man"), a young man with "Asian" features and the most educated among them (one year of college), holds up a piece of raw *fajita* and says *"esta carne es pa' mis carnales, esto es el carnalismo"* (This meat is for my brothers, this is brotherhood). Another man, pained slightly by this apparent intrusion of linear ideology, immediately replies, *"Mira cabron,"* and going for his own genitals, says, *"Esta es la carne que te voy a dar"* (Look, goddammit, this is the meat I'm going to give you). And it is only at this moment, when the others laugh hesitantly, that we see the possibility and the tones of real aggression. The world of too-conscious ideology has intruded and must be rejected. One does not speak ideologically of friendship and community, one practices it in the symbolic action of meat, body, and language.

To unify these various revisionary perspectives, I want to think of these scenes as a present-day example of what Bakhtin calls the unofficial culture of the Middle Ages, the folk culture of Grotesque Realism, of the carnivalesque. The playful, sexual, and scatological language, the concern with minimalist consumption of meat taken from the internal, stomach-centered parts of the animal, the concern with the body—all of these involve what Bakhtin called degradation, a principal aspect of the carnivalesque. But this is not degradation as the imprisoning bourgeois discourse of Ramos and Paz would have it.

> Degradation here means coming down to earth, the contact with earth as an element that swallows up and gives birth at the same time. To degrade is to bury, to sow, and to kill simultaneously, in order to bring forth something more and better. To degrade also means to concern oneself with the lower stratum of the body, the life of the belly and the reproductive organs; it therefore relates to acts of defecation and copulation,

conception, pregnancy, and birth. Degradation digs a bodily grave for a new birth; it has not only a destructive, negative aspect, but also a regenerating one. To degrade an object does not imply merely hurling it into the void of nonexistence, into absolute destruction, but to hurl it down to the reproductive lower stratum, the zone in which conception and a new birth take place. Grotesque realism knows no other lower level; it is the fruitful earth and the womb. It is always conceiving [Bakhtin 1984:21].

However, in adopting this Bakhtinian perspective on unofficial culture, heteroglossia, and the carnivalesque, one also has to note its political limitations and its uneasy relationship to Marxism. In a recent critical review of this issue, Young seriously and persuasively questions the Marxist status of Bakhtin's thought on the carnivalesque in culture (Young 1985–86). Taken without critical revision, Young argues, Bakhtinian "carnival offers a liberal rather than a Marxist politics" (1985–86:92). That is, Bakhtin has offered a semi-idealist sense of an essentialist-humanistic oppositional Other expressed in the carnivalesque as a transcendence of an unspecified general Foucauldian-like domination. Only by specifying the historical moment and social location of the carnivalesque, as Fredric Jameson would have us do, only by specifically accounting for its class- (and race-) antagonistic character in a specific context, can the carnivalesque be read as an expression of class contestative discourse in the manner that I have tried to do (Jameson 1981:83–87). For it is specifically against the ruling bourgeois official culture of contemporary south Texas, including that of both Anglos *and* Mexican-Americans, that one must understand my friends. Their discourses of sexuality, the body, and low-prestige food exactly counterpoint the repression and affectation of these ruling sectors throughout the region, a dominating culture whose most visible expression, for example, is the upper-class celebration of George Washington's birthday in Laredo, Texas, not far from Chema's *rancho.*

However, a Marxist perspective on the carnivalesque also obliges us to note that its ideological and material character is not one of undiluted seamless "opposition." Two points may be made here. First, the critical carnivalesque of these men is to some considerable degree predicated on a model of their own dominating patriarchy and exclusion of women from these scenes. Second, in the long term, their feasting on beef and beer on an almost daily basis is likely contributing to serious health problems among the working-class male population of this area (Lyndon B. Johnson School of Public Affairs 1979).

> "Now stop!" Max said and sent the wild things off to bed
> without their supper.
> And Max the king of all wild things was lonely and wanted to
> be where someone loved him best of all.
> Then all around from far away across the world he smelled
> good things to eat so he gave up being king of where the wild things are.
> But the wild things cried, "Oh please don't go—
> we'll eat you up—we love you so!"
> And Max said, "No!"

The wild things roared their terrible roars and gnashed
their terrible teeth and rolled their terrible eyes and
showed their terrible claws
but Max stepped into his private boat and waved goodbye [Sendak 1963].

Epilogue: The Centipede Who Played Free Safety

So there you have my narrative, which, though now fleshed out with new theoretical references, had already begun to take this form even as I concluded the period of fieldwork that generated it. Successful, I thought, was I in producing an ethnographic account that could stand as a critical counternarrative to that of the great Mexican bourgeois thinkers and its localized application by Spielberg. Successful was I, I thought, in giving narrative critical voice to the dominated against those who in their discourses of power would reproduce and enhance the domination in their everyday lives. And, as such, this essay could have ended a paragraph ago were it not for the centipede—the centipede who played free safety.

As I prepared to leave McBurg, *los batos* decided to have a *despedida* (a farewell party) in my honor, naturally a *carne asada*. This time, however, rather than Chema's *rancho*, we decided to gather at a local bar—Tenorio's—where in addition to partying, it was also decided that I would make a "speech" (their term) about what I had "learned," the whole thing in an idiom and ethos of play consistent with the event. We all gathered outside in a kind of patio behind the bar and with *fajita* tacos and beer for fuel, I meandered my way through a kind of "folk" version of my present story. A variety of commentary followed ranging from *"bien de aquellas"* (real good) to *"puro pedo"* (pure shit) to loud "Hmmm's" to quiet long pulls on beers. Most of them at least agreed that my rendering was better than those of Ramos and Paz, which they unambivalently thought of as *"puro pedo."*

And then the centipede, unexpectedly, made his appearance. Chinito, the local college dropout who knew something about the esoterica and secret rituals of our sacred discipline, had, from the beginning, been unhappy with my fieldwork enterprise. But he had not actually said so or specified his objections until a little too much beer plus my leave-taking provided the necessary disinhibition to his repressed critique. Like one of the young antagonistic villagers that James Fernandez encountered in the Fang village of Gabon, this fellow, with even greater antagonism, wanted to know, "what reason did I have for wanting to know such things?" (Fernandez 1986:173). As with most antagonistic and therefore rhetorical questions, my questioner came equipped with his own answer, to wit: "You want to *tell* them about us!" with a heavy emphasis on "tell" and "them"—which, of course, was quite true, although I wouldn't have put it quite that way. Rather, I would have said, or tonally implied, that, yes, I did want to tell *them* about Mexican-American critical ideological responses to *their* domination. We debated the question, there next to the barbecue pit, and generated just about as much heat with raised voices, which eventually led to a bit of body posturing—he, forward, me, backward—my most vivid recollection of that instant being, "Oh, shit, did the summer grant cover health insurance?"

This emerging disorder of a different kind—this intrusion into the somewhat spontaneous *communitas* of the *carne asada* that afternoon—could not be permitted by the rest of the guys, who had a stake not only in the maintenance of the *communitas* but in making sure that I, friend/guest/ "professor," wasn't mistreated. Yet, to varying degrees, they too had probably wondered "what reason did I have for wanting to know such things?" which, after my best explanations and in the final analysis, I may not have fully answered to their total satisfaction, a probably impossible thing. It was at that point, after several of my friends persuaded my interrogator to calm down, that one of them, *"la tuerca"* (the screw nut), a car mechanic, offered the following. He opened with a local introductory marker for joking narratives:

¡Watcha, Limón. Pesca este pedo y pintalo verde! [Lookit, Limón. Catch this "fart" and paint it green.] These two *antropolocos* [anthropologists] got a grant, you know. To go to Africa to study the natives. But when they got there, all the *batos* [dudes] had split for the mountains. Left a sign in the village. "Gone to the mountains, *bros*, see you next winter!" "So now what are we going to do, Bruce?" said one of them.

"Well, gee, I don't know, Horace." So they sat around getting bored. Once in a while one of them would find some native shit, and they'd get all excited thinking they were still around. But no, it was old shit. One day, one of them said, "You know, we're not doing anything. Why don't we organize all of the jungle animals into football teams and have a game?" So they did. They chose up. A tiger for me. A tiger for you. A hippo for me. A hippo for you. We each get a gazelle for running backs.

And then they started the game. The giraffe kicked off for one team, and the other team had its cheetah back to receive. And the game went on. But since both teams had pretty much the same animals, they were tied by the end of the first quarter. But then the elephant who was playing linebacker on one team got hurt when somebody stepped on its trunk. So the other team with its hippo fullback and nobody to stop him up the middle started getting ahead. *¡En chinga carnal!* [Fucking them over, *bro*!]

They went into the third quarter, and the hippo started right up again, but all of a sudden, he went down with a crash at the line of scrimmage and he had both knees injured. So both coaches and the teams gathered around, one coach worried about his player and the other one wanted to know who brought the hippo down. "Was it you, turtle?" "No, coach, I couldn't react fast enough!" "How about you, chimp?" "No, coach, I was up on the goal posts!"

Then they heard a little voice coming from under the hippo, "I got the bastard, I got the bastard!" They turned the hippo over and there was a little centipede holding tightly to the hippo's leg. So after they got him off, the coach asked him, "How did you do it, centipede?" And the centipede said, "Well, coach, I was playing free safety and when I saw that the hippo had the ball, I just ran up and met him at the line of scrimmage!"

"But why didn't you do that in the first half?" asked the coach.

"I wasn't playing the first half, coach."

"Well, where the hell were you?"

"Say, man," said the centipede, "don't fuck with me, I was in the locker room putting on my goddamn tennis shoes!"

(Much laughter; Chinito and I look sheepish, I think.)

What is *this* about, I asked and continue to ask myself? Two anthropologists, marked as elite *and* effeminate by the use and intonation of the personal names *Bruce* and *Horace*, fail to find their "natives" when they arrive in Africa armed with their inevitable grant. Given an active presence by the narrator, the natives have "split" and by virtue of the sign they leave behind, they are also given voice. The often deactivated subject of anthropology is restored in the same way that it (they) were restored when I was questioned. So far, perhaps, so good. But why—and this was the largest piece of the puzzle for me—do our anthropologists/protagonists then turn immediately to the organization of jungle animals into football teams and a game? Are the latter so many surrogate "natives"; and is this a satirical comment on the obsessive anthropological quest for order, any order, at all costs? After all, we can't very well just sit around. Is it this that makes us "antropo-locos" (crazy anthropologists)?

But why football? Why not? Isn't it the Balinese cockfight of American culture where our capacity for highly organized systemic violence is displayed most evidently in the frame of "game" and at a profit? But juxtaposed to anthropology as its close semantic cousin? Was this what I had been doing, organizing their play this way? Is this what we all do? Order up what Fernandez calls "the play of tropes in culture" into ethnographies that organize the polyphony into narrative forms that are metaphorically related to violence and profit?

Having organized my "natives" for the sake of my own orderly narrative game, I was ready to take leave of them when the game started breaking down. For I suspect that, perhaps, in the role of one coach, I had gotten ahead of them, run up the score by having gained much with relatively little in return, save for a book that would tell "their" story for the benefit of others. Did I, in fact, as I prepared to leave, require some marked opposition to stop my tough running game?

Which brings us to the centipede. Here the animal symbolism becomes even shiftier and more multivocalic. Is this the antagonist who brought me down, reframed in narrative play and thereby given symbolic license? Why a centipede? Well, it makes for the punch line, but why a centipede who acts this way, sitting out the first half, laboriously putting on fifty pairs of tennis shoes so that he can get in the game? And why does he play free safety?

Let me momentarily avoid my own problem and digress to suggest that the centipede is a pretty good symbolic rendition not only of my personal antagonist who disordered my ethnographic narrative game, but of these guys as a group and probably of Mexican-Americans as they see themselves relative to the sociopolitical game of which anthropology is part.

To fully exploit this particular reading, you have to know your football, including the knowledge that the free safety, as his name implies, is a defensive back not bound to the standard zone defense where a defender protects a particular portion of the backfield. Rather, he is set deep in the backfield and free to roam it, protecting against deep and short passes but also free to come up and stop a running play, as our centipede did. You may, perhaps, also need to know that in the folklore of the National Football League, free safeties, along with split ends, are thought to be marginal, temperamental, moody guys who love to hit. To this knowledge, shared by my barbecue friends who are avid watchers of the sport, we can add the following concerning the centipede, which is found plentifully in south Texas. It is small and nasty, frequents dark places, and will painfully sting by clinging ferociously and venomously. Nonetheless, they are lesser creatures certainly in comparison to tigers, lions, and so on.

And that may be how Mexican-Americans see themselves and are, in fact, seen in American popular, political, *and* anthropological discourse. There at the margins, not fully dangerous or exotic; socially and politically lesser but not enough to make them a real problem or a real attraction for the imagination. To be sure, every so often they come up fast and make a hit—Cesar Chavez, Henry Cisneros—but most of the time there they are at the margins. (Like the coach, Anglo liberals sometimes ask me the political equivalent of "Where were you in the first half?" which is, "Why didn't Mexican-Americans turn out to vote in the last election?" usually for an Anglo liberal candidate. To which, like the centipede, I sometimes feel like saying, "Say, man, come on. Maybe they're in the locker room slowly and laboriously putting on the necessary social, educational, and cultural equipment to come out and play for themselves.")

But you see, here I am digressing in my own interest, once again, returning to my safe and politically hip narrative role of explaining how Mexican-Americans express their cultural opposition to *them*, including the dominant discourses of intellectual power. I am neatly avoiding the fragmenting problem for my own work, namely, what does the centipede have to do with *me*, with my ethnographic narration?

The centipede, I propose, is the critical carnivalesque turned in my direction. Even as I was rewriting their mostly oppositional voices into my own narrative, thereby rendering it oppositional to those of Ramos and Paz, my friends offered me pointed instruction on the limits of my rewriting. In their disordering deconstruction of the ethnographic project, they remind me (us) that however "liberating" a narrative discourse we propose to write, it is one always intimate with power, and many of our "informants," "subjects," "consultants," "teachers," "friends" know it. That these particular friends permit me to rewrite them is itself testimony to their understanding that there are better and worse discourses—that some are, indeed, *"puro pedo"*—that there are sites of struggle far from Chema's *rancho* where such discourses contest for hegemony in other cultural spheres and where my pale rewriting may be to some purpose.

But it is important to note that their critical reminder itself comes in the form of the carnivalesque, as if to say that anthropology itself is not and should not be immune to its disorderly character. Indeed, I want to go a step further and take this lesson at full formal value for the production of my ethnographic narrative. Used with imagination, this empowering gift of the carnivalesque can lend not only ideological content but also an ideology of critical form, as Jameson (1981) might say, to our ethnographic practice. Along with other critical resources we can incorporate the carnivalesque into our ethnographic practice, creatively disordering it so that it also stands as a formal counterhegemonic practice countering the "normal" and often dominating practice of ethnography.[6] I believe this is what Fischer is recommending when he argues for an ethnography based formally on the post-modern practices of ethnic autobiography, practices such as inter-reference, critical juxtaposition, ironic humor, parody, the return of the repressed, alternative selves, and bifocality, which, in my estimation, are synonymous with the carnivalesque (1986). To some degree at least, I have been experimenting with this formal appropriation of the critical carnivalesque here even as I also write manifestly against the *ideas* of domination. Finally, at the heart of this gift of the carnivalesque is a reflexive critical self-awareness of our status as ethno-graphers: writers of people. For, as my friends and the centipede reminded me, this postmodernity of the carnivalesque must also include the keen sense of critical reflexivity that goes with such discourse, the sense that we must always decenter our own narrative self-assurance lest it be saturated with dominating power. Ultimately, as Stephen Tyler reminds us, when ethnography is truly critical, such a function

> derives from the fact that it makes its own contextual grounding part of the question and not from hawking pictures of alternative ways of life as instruments of utopian reform [1986:139].

Notes

Portions of this paper were presented as lectures at Stanford University (1986) and at the annual meetings of the American Ethnological Society in St. Louis (1988). My special thanks to Renato Rosaldo for the former invitation and to Charles Briggs for the latter. The research was conducted under the partial auspices of a grant from the National Research Council and the Ford Foundation sponsored by the Language Behavior Research Laboratory at the University of California, Berkeley.

1. All formal names and nicknames are fictitious.
2. McBurg is also my general fictional name for the towns—very close to each other—in South Texas where these men live. It is a composite of two large Anglo-dominated towns—McAllen and Edinburg. These were established as "American" towns at the turn of the century as part of the Anglo-American agricultural capitalization and social dominance of the area. It is in this general area that Madsen (1964) and Rubel (1966) conducted their fieldwork. For a fine critical account of these two projects and their insensitivity to language and humor, see Paredes (1978).
3. I say "partially," for I appropriate only Douglas' fine descriptive insights, not her Durkheimian interpretive framework. Clearly I am moving in a different left direction.
4. In a footnote, anthropologist Patricia Zavella notes a closely related male-centered verbal performance among California Mexican-Americans *who are nonetheless from South Texas*. I have never heard the expression *chingar mentis* in South Texas, so it is possibly a California label for this same kind of verbal performance, I quote Zavella:

   > In an analysis of *chingar mentis* behavior (which means to fuck over minds), I concluded that it is a male form of verbal art similar to "playing the dozens" by young black males. I observed young Chicano males from South Texas spreading false stories or spontaneously duping someone through group verbal performance. According to the performers the point of these hilarious deceptions was just to *chingar mentis*, but I argue they develop male solidarity and prestige among the participants [Zavella 1987:25].

5. In a recent article announcing the vice-presidential nomination of Senator Lloyd

Bentsen, who is from this area, David Rosenbaum of the *New York Times* has succinctly captured this world better than any set of social statistics:

> the 67-year-old Senator has deep roots in Texas. He comes from one of the richest and most prominent families in the Rio Grande Valley of south Texas, where the great wealth of a few families contrasts with the poverty of the overwhelmingly Mexican-American citizenry [Rosenbaum 1988].

6. In a perceptive insight Young, after Benjamin, notes the way Bakhtin's *Rabelais and His World* could be read as itself a carnivalesque text in formal counterhegemonic response to Stalinist domination (Young 1985–86:78).

Works Cited

Bakhtin, Mikhail
  1984. *Rabelais and His World.* Bloomington: Indiana University Press.

Bateson, Gregory
  1972. A Theory of Play and Fantasy. In *Steps to an Ecology of Mind*, pp. 177–193. New York: Random House.

de Leon, Arnoldo
  1982. *The Tejano Community, 1836–1900.* Albuquerque: University of New Mexico Press.
  1983. *They Called Them Greasers: Anglo Attitudes Toward Mexicans in Texas, 1821–1900.* Austin: University of Texas Press.

Douglas, Mary
  1968. The Social Control of Cognition: Some Factors in Joke Perception. *Man: The Journal of the Royal Anthropological Institute* 3:361–376.
  1971. Deciphering a Meal. In *Myth, Symbol, and Culture.* Clifford Geertz, ed., pp. 61–81. New York: W. W. Norton.
  1978 [1966]. *Purity and Danger: An Analysis of the Concepts of Pollution and Taboo.* London: Routledge & Kegan Paul.

Fernandez, James
  1986. *Persuasions and Performances: The Play of Tropes in Culture.* Bloomington: Indiana University Press.

Fischer, Michael M. J.
  1986. Ethnicity and the Post-Modern Arts of Memory. In *Writing Culture: The Poetics and Politics of Ethnography.* James Clifford and George E. Marcus, eds., pp. 194–233. Berkeley: University of California Press.

Foley, Douglas
  1978. *From Peones to Politicos: Ethnic Relations in a South Texas Town.* Austin: University of Texas, Center for Mexican American Studies.

Hearn, Francis
  1976–77. Toward a Critical Theory of Play. *Telos* 30:145–160.

Jameson, Fredric
  1981. *The Political Unconscious: Narrative as a Socially Symbolic Act.* Ithaca: Cornell University Press.

Lauria, Anthony, Jr.
  1964. Respeto, Relajo, and Interpersonal Relations in Puerto Rico. *Anthropological Quarterly* 3:53–67.

Limón, José E.
  1987. Mexican Speech Play: History and the Psychological Discourses of Power. *Texas Papers on Latin America.* No. 87–06. Austin: University of Texas, Institute of Latin American Studies.

Lyndon B. Johnson School of Public Affairs
  1979. The Health of Mexican Americans in South Texas. *Policy Research Project* No. 32.
    University of Texas at Austin.
Madsen, William
  1964. *The Mexican-Americans of South Texas*. New York: Holt, Rinehart, and Winston.
Marcus, George E.
  1986. Contemporary Problems of Ethnography in the Modern World System. In
    Writing Culture: The Poetics and Politics of Ethnography. James Clifford and George E.
    Marcus, eds., pp. 165–193. Berkeley: University of California Press.
Montejano, David
  1987. *Anglos and Mexicans in the Making of Texas*. Austin: University of Texas Press.
Paredes, Américo
  1976. *A Texas-Mexican Cancionero*. Urbana: University of Illinois Press.
  1978. On Ethnographic Fieldwork among Minority Groups: A Folklorist's Perspective.
    In *New Directions in Chicano Scholarship*. Recardo Romo and Raymund Paredes, eds.,
    pp. 1–32. La Jolla: Chicano Studies Center, University of California at San Diego.
Paz, Octavio
  1961 [1951]. *The Labyrinth of Solitude: Life and Thought in Mexico*. New York: Grove
    Press.
Peacock, James
  1968. *Rites of Modernization: Symbolic and Social Aspects of Indonesian Proletarian Drama*.
    Chicago: University of Chicago Press.
Ramos, Samuel
  1962 [1934]. *Profile of Man and Culture in Mexico*. Austin: University of Texas Press.
Rosenbaum, David E.
  1988. A Candidate Who Is More Like Bush: Lloyd Millard Bentsen, Jr. *New York
    Times*, July 13, p. 1.
Rubel, Arthur
  1966. *Across the Tracks: Mexican Americans in a South Texas Town*. Austin: University of
    Texas Press.
Sendak, Maurice.
  1963. *Where the Wild Things Are*. New York: Harper and Row.
Spielberg, Joseph
  1974. Humor in a Mexican-American Palomilla: Some Historical, Social, and Psycho-
    logical Implications. *Revista Chicano-Requeña* 2:41–50.
Tyler, Stephen A.
  1986. Post-Modern Ethnography: From Document of the Occult to Occult Docu-
    ment. In *Writing Culture: The Poetics and Politics of Ethnography*. James Clifford and
    George E. Marcus, eds., pp. 122–140. Berkeley: University of California Press.
Young, Robert
  1985–86. Back to Bakhtin. *Cultural Critique* 1:71–92.
Zavella, Patricia
  1987. *Women's Work and Chicano Families: Cannery Workers of the Santa Clara Valley*.
    Ithaca: Cornell University Press.

Part Two

Reproducing the Body

Reshaping Conception and Birth

The Egg and the Sperm   4

How Science Has Constructed a Romance Based on Stereotypical Male-Female Roles

EMILY MARTIN

> The theory of the human body is always a part of a world-picture. . . .
> The theory of the human body is always a part of a *fantasy*.
>
> —James Hillman, *The Myth of Analysis*[1]

As an anthropologist, I am intrigued by the possibility that culture shapes how biological scientists describe what they discover about the natural world. If this were so, we would be learning about more than the natural world in high school biology class; we would be learning about cultural beliefs and practices as if they were part of nature. In the course of my research I realized that the picture of egg and sperm drawn in popular as well as scientific accounts of reproductive biology relies on stereotypes central to our cultural definitions of male and female. The stereotypes imply not only that female biological processes are less worthy than their male counterparts but also that women are less worthy than men. Part of my goal in writing this article is to shine a bright light on the gender stereotypes hidden within the scientific language of biology. Exposed in such a light, I hope they will lose much of their power to harm us.

Egg and Sperm: A Scientific Fairy Tale

At a fundamental level, all major scientific textbooks depict male and female reproductive organs as systems for the production of valuable substances, such as eggs and sperm.[2] In the case of women, the monthly cycle is described as being designed to produce eggs and prepare a suitable place for them to be fertilized and grown— all to the end of making babies. But the enthusiasm ends there. By extolling the female cycle as a productive enterprise, menstruation must necessarily be viewed as a failure. Medical texts describe menstruation as the "debris" of the uterine lining, the result of necrosis, or death of tissue. The descriptions imply that a system has gone awry, making products of no use, not to specification, unsalable, wasted, scrap. An illustration in a widely used medical text shows menstruation as a chaotic disintegration of form, complementing the many texts that describe it as "ceasing," "dying," "losing," "denuding," "expelling."[3]

Male reproductive physiology is evaluated quite differently. One of the texts that sees menstruation as failed production employs a sort of breathless prose when it describes the maturation of sperm: "The mechanisms which guide the remarkable cellular transformation from spermatid to mature sperm remain uncertain. . . . Perhaps the most amazing characteristic of spermatogenesis is its sheer magnitude: the normal human male may manufacture several hundred million sperm per day."[4] In the classic text *Medical Physiology*, edited by Vernon Mountcastle, the male/female, productive/destructive comparison is more explicit: "Whereas the female *sheds* only a single gamete each month, the seminiferous tubules *produce* hundreds of millions of sperm each day" (emphasis mine).[5] The female author of another text marvels at the length of the microscopic seminiferous tubules, which, if uncoiled and placed end to end, "would span almost one-third of a mile!" She writes, "In an adult male these structures produce millions of sperm cells each day." Later she asks, "How is this feat accomplished?"[6] None of these texts expresses such intense enthusiasm for any female processes. It is surely no accident that the "remarkable" process of making sperm involves precisely what, in the medical view, menstruation does not: production of something deemed valuable.[7]

One could argue that menstruation and spermatogenesis are not analogous processes and, therefore, should not be expected to elicit the same kind of response. The proper female analogy to spermatogenesis, biologically, is ovulation. Yet ovulation does not merit enthusiasm in these texts either. Textbook descriptions stress that all of the ovarian follicles containing ova are already present at birth. Far from being *produced*, as sperm are, they merely sit on the shelf, slowly degenerating and aging like overstocked inventory: "At birth, normal human ovaries contain an estimated one million follicles [each], and no new ones appear after birth. Thus, in marked contrast to the male, the newborn female already has all the germ cells she will ever have. Only a few, perhaps 400, are destined to reach full maturity during her active productive life. All the others degenerate at some point in their development so that few, if any, remain by the time she reaches menopause at approximately 50 years of age."[8] Note the "marked contrast" that this description sets up between male and female: the male, who continuously produces fresh germ cells, and the female, who has stockpiled germ cells by birth and is faced with their degeneration.

Nor are the female organs spared such vivid descriptions. One scientist writes in a newspaper article that a woman's ovaries become old and worn out from ripening eggs every month, even though the woman herself is still relatively young: "When you look through a laparoscope . . . at an ovary that has been through hundreds of cycles, even in a superbly healthy American female, you see a scarred, battered organ."[9]

To avoid the negative connotations that some people associate with the female reproductive system, scientists could begin to describe male and female processes as homologous. They might credit females with "producing" mature ova one at a time, as they're needed each month, and describe males as having to face problems of degenerating germ cells. This degeneration would occur throughout life among spermatogonia, the undifferentiated germ cells in the testes that are the long-lived, dormant precursors of sperm.

But the texts have an almost dogged insistence on casting female processes in a negative light. The texts celebrate sperm production because it is continuous from puberty to senescence, while they portray egg production as inferior because it is finished at birth. This makes the female seem unproductive, but some texts will also insist that it is she who is wasteful.[10] In a section heading for *Molecular Biology of the Cell*, a best-selling text, we are told that "oogenesis is wasteful." The text goes on to emphasize that of the seven million oogonia, or egg germ cells, in the female embryo, most degenerate in the ovary. Of those that do go on to become oocytes, or eggs, many also degenerate, so that at birth only two million eggs remain in the ovaries. Degeneration continues throughout a woman's life: by puberty 300,000 eggs remain, and only a few are present by menopause. "During the 40 or so years of a woman's reproductive life, only 400 to 500 eggs will have been released," the authors write. "All the rest will have degenerated. It is still a mystery why so many eggs are formed only to die in the ovaries."[11]

The real mystery is why the male's vast production of sperm is not seen as wasteful.[12] Assuming that a man "produces" 100 million ($10(8)$) sperm per day (a conservative estimate) during an average reproductive life of sixty years, he would produce well over two trillion sperm in his lifetime. Assuming that a woman "ripens" one egg per lunar month, or thirteen per year, over the course of her forty-year reproductive life, she would total five hundred eggs in her lifetime. But the word "waste" implies an excess, too much produced. Assuming two or three offspring, for every baby a woman produces, she wastes only around two hundred eggs. For every baby a man produces, he wastes more than one trillion ($10(12)$) sperm.

How is it that positive images are denied to the bodies of women? A look at language—in this case, scientific language—provides the first clue. Take the egg and the sperm.[13] It is remarkable how "femininely" the egg behaves and how "masculinely" the sperm.[14] The egg is seen as large and passive.[15] It does not *move* or journey, but passively "is transported," "is swept,"[16] or even "drifts"[17] along the fallopian tube. In utter contrast, sperm are small, "streamlined,"[18] and invariably active. They "deliver" their genes to the egg, "activate the developmental program of the egg,"[19] and have a "velocity" that is often remarked upon.[20] Their tails are "strong" and efficiently powered.[21] Together with the forces of ejaculation, they can "propel the semen into the deepest recesses of the vagina."[22] For this they need "energy," fuel,"[23] so that with a "whiplashlike motion and strong lurches"[24] they can "burrow through the egg coat"[25] and "penetrate" it.[26]

At its extreme, the age-old relationship of the egg and the sperm takes on a royal or religious patina. The egg coat, its protective barrier, is sometimes called its "vestments," a term usually reserved for sacred, religious dress. The egg is said to have a "corona,"[27] a crown, and to be accompanied by "attendant cells."[28] It is holy, set apart and above, the queen to the sperm's king. The egg is also passive, which means it must depend on sperm for rescue. Gerald Schatten and Helen Schatten liken the egg's role to that of Sleeping Beauty: "a dormant bride awaiting her mate's magic kiss, which instills the spirit that brings her to life."[29] Sperm, by contrast, have a "mission,"[30] which is to "move through the female genital tract in quest of the ovum."[31] One popular account has it that the sperm carry out a "perilous journey" into the "warm darkness," where some fall away "exhausted." "Survivors" "assault" the egg, the successful candidates "surrounding the prize."[32] Part of the urgency of this journey, in more scientific terms, is that "once released from the supportive environment of the ovary, an egg will die within hours unless rescued by a sperm."[33] The wording stresses the fragility and dependency of the egg, even though the same text acknowledges elsewhere that sperm also live for only a few hours.[34]

In 1948, in a book remarkable for its early insights into these matters, Ruth Herschberger argued that female reproductive organs are seen as biologically interdependent, while male organs are viewed as autonomous, operating independently and in isolation:

> At present the functional is stressed only in connection with women: it is in them that ovaries, tubes, uterus, and vagina have endless interdependence. In the male, reproduction would seem to involve "organs" only.
>
> Yet the sperm, just as much as the egg, is dependent on a great many related processes. There are secretions which mitigate the urine in the urethra before ejaculation, to protect the sperm. There is the reflex shutting off of the bladder connection, the provision of prostatic secretions, and various types of muscular propulsion. The sperm is no more independent of its milieu than the egg, and yet from a wish that it were, biologists have lent their support to the notion that the human female, beginning with the egg, is congenitally more dependent than the male.[35]

Bringing out another aspect of the sperm's autonomy, an article in the journal *Cell* has the sperm making an "existential decision" to penetrate the egg: "Sperm are cells with a limited behavioral repertoire, one that is directed toward fertilizing eggs. To execute the decision to abandon the haploid state, sperm swim to an egg and there acquire the ability to effect membrane fusion."[36] Is this a corporate manager's version of the sperm's activities—"executing decisions" while fraught with dismay over difficult options that bring with them very high risk?

There is another way that sperm, despite their small size, can be made to loom in importance over the egg. In a collection of scientific papers, an electron micrograph of an enormous egg and tiny sperm is titled "A Portrait of the Sperm."[37] This is a little like showing a photo of a dog and calling it a picture of the fleas. Granted, microscopic sperm are harder to photograph than eggs, which are just large enough to see with the naked eye. But surely the use of the term "portrait," a word associated with the powerful and wealthy, is significant. Eggs have only micrographs or pictures, not portraits.

One depiction of sperm as weak and timid, instead of strong and powerful—the only such representation in western civilization, so far as I know—occurs in Woody Allen's movie *Everything You Always Wanted To Know About Sex* *But Were Afraid to*

Ask. Allen, playing the part of an apprehensive sperm inside a man's testicles, is scared of the man's approaching orgasm. He is reluctant to launch himself into the darkness, afraid of contraceptive devices, afraid of winding up on the ceiling if the man masturbates.

The more common picture—egg as damsel in distress, shielded only by her sacred garments; sperm as heroic warrior to the rescue—cannot be proved to be dictated by the biology of these events. While the "facts" of biology may not *always* be constructed in cultural terms, I would argue that in this case they are. The degree of metaphorical content in these descriptions, the extent to which differences between egg and sperm are emphasized, and the parallels between cultural stereotypes of male and female behavior and the character of egg and sperm all point to this conclusion.

New Research, Old Imagery

As new understandings of egg and sperm emerge, textbook gender imagery is being revised. But the new research, far from escaping the stereotypical representations of egg and sperm, simply replicates elements of textbook gender imagery in a different form. The persistence of this imagery calls to mind what Ludwik Fleck termed "the self-contained" nature of scientific thought. As he described it, "the interaction between what is already known, what remains to be learned, and those who are to apprehend it, go to ensure harmony within the system. But at the same time they also preserve the harmony of illusions, which is quite secure within the confines of a given thought style."[38] We need to understand the way in which the cultural content in scientific descriptions changes as biological discoveries unfold, and whether that cultural content is solidly entrenched or easily changed.

In all of the texts quoted above, sperm are described as penetrating the egg, and specific substances on a sperm's head are described as binding to the egg. Recently, this description of events was rewritten in a biophysics lab at Johns Hopkins University—transforming the egg from the passive to the active party.[39]

Prior to this research, it was thought that the zona, the inner vestments of the egg, formed an impenetrable barrier. Sperm overcame the barrier by mechanically burrowing through, thrashing their tails and slowly working their way along. Later research showed that the sperm released digestive enzymes that chemically broke down the zona; thus, scientists presumed that the sperm used mechanical *and* chemical means to get through to the egg.

In this recent investigation, the researchers began to ask questions about the mechanical force of the sperm's tail. (The lab's goal was to develop a contraceptive that worked topically on sperm.) They discovered, to their great surprise, that the forward thrust of sperm is extremely weak, which contradicts the assumption that sperm are forceful penetrators.[40] Rather than thrusting forward, the sperm's head was now seen to move mostly back and forth. The sideways motion of the sperm's tail makes the head move sideways with a force that is ten times stronger than its forward movement. So even if the overall force of the sperm were strong enough to mechanically break the zona, most of its force would be directed sideways rather than forward. In fact, its strongest tendency, by tenfold, is to escape by attempting to pry itself off the egg. Sperm, then, must be exceptionally efficient at *escaping* from any cell surface they contact. And the surface of the egg must be designed to trap the sperm and prevent their escape. Otherwise, few if any sperm would reach the egg.

The researchers at Johns Hopkins concluded that the sperm and egg stick together because of adhesive molecules on the surfaces of each. The egg traps the sperm and adheres to it so tightly that the sperm's head is forced to lie flat against the surface of the zona, a little bit, they told me, "like Br'er Rabbit getting more and more stuck to tar baby the more he wriggles." The trapped sperm continues to wiggle ineffectually side to side. The mechanical force of its tail is so weak that a sperm cannot break even one chemical bond. This is where the digestive enzymes released by the sperm come in. If they start to soften the zona just at the tip of the sperm and the sides remain stuck, then the weak, flailing sperm can get oriented in the right direction and make it through the zona—provided that its bonds to the zona dissolve as it moves in.

Although this new version of the saga of the egg and the sperm broke through cultural expectations, the researchers who made the discovery continued to write papers and abstracts as if the sperm were the active party who attacks, binds, penetrates, and enters the egg. The only difference was that sperm were now seen as performing these actions weakly.[41] Not until August 1987, more than three years after the findings described above, did these researchers reconceptualize the process to give the egg a more active role. They began to describe the zona as an aggressive sperm catcher, covered with adhesive molecules that can capture a sperm with a single bond and clasp it to the zona's surface.[42] In the words of their published account: "The innermost vestment, the *zona pellucida*, is a glycoprotein shell, which captures and tethers the sperm before they penetrate it. . . . The sperm is captured at the initial contact between the sperm tip and the *zona*. . . . Since the thrust [of the sperm] is much smaller than the force needed to break a single affinity bond, the first bond made upon the tip-first meeting of the sperm and *zona* can result in the capture of the sperm."[43]

Experiments in another lab reveal similar patterns of data interpretation. Gerald Schatten and Helen Schatten set out to show that, contrary to conventional wisdom, the "egg is not merely a large, yolk-filled sphere into which the sperm burrows to endow new life. Rather, recent research suggests the almost heretical view that sperm and egg are mutually active partners."[44] This sounds like a departure from the stereotypical textbook view, but further reading reveals Schatten and Schatten's conformity to the aggressive-sperm metaphor. They describe how "the sperm and egg first touch when, from the tip of the sperm's triangular head, a long, thin filament shoots out and harpoons the egg." Then we learn that "remarkably, the harpoon is not so much fired as assembled at great speed, molecule by molecule, from a pool of protein stored in a specialized region called the aerosome. The filament may grow as much as twenty times longer than the sperm head itself before its tip reaches the egg and sticks."[45] Why not call this "making a bridge" or "throwing out a line" rather than firing a harpoon? Harpoons pierce prey and injure or kill them, while this filament only sticks. And why not focus, as the Hopkins lab did, on the stickiness of the egg, rather than the stickiness of the sperm?[46] Later in the article, the Schattens replicate the common view of the sperm's perilous journey into the warm darkness of the vagina, this time for the purpose of explaining its journey into the egg itself: "[The sperm] still has an arduous journey ahead. It must penetrate farther into the egg's huge sphere of cytoplasm and somehow locate the nucleus, so that the two cells' chromosomes can fuse. The sperm dives down into the cytoplasm, its tail beating. But it is soon interrupted by the sudden and swift migration of the egg nucleus, which rushes toward the sperm with a velocity triple that of the movement of chromosomes during cell division, crossing the entire egg in about a minute."[47]

Like Schatten and Schatten and the biophysicists at Johns Hopkins, another researcher has recently made discoveries that seem to point to a more interactive view of the relationship of egg and sperm. This work, which Paul Wassarman conducted on the sperm and eggs of mice, focuses on identifying the specific molecules in the egg coat (the zona pellucida) that are involved in egg-sperm interaction. At first glance, his descriptions seem to fit the model of an egalitarian relationship. Male and female gametes "recognize one another," and "interactions . . . take place between sperm and egg."[48] But the article in *Scientific American* in which those descriptions appear begins with a vignette that presages the dominant motif of their presentation: "It has been more than a century since Hermann Fol, a Swiss zoologist, peered into his microscope and became the first person to see a sperm penetrate an egg, fertilize it and form the first cell of a new embryo."[49] This portrayal of the sperm as the active party—the one that *penetrates* and *fertilizes* the egg and *produces* the embryo—is not cited as an example of an earlier, now outmoded view. In fact, the author reiterates the point later in the article: "Many sperm can bind to and penetrate the zona pellucida, or outer coat, of an unfertilized mouse egg, but only one sperm will eventually fuse with the thin plasma membrane surrounding the egg proper (*inner sphere*), fertilizing the egg and giving rise to a new embryo."[50]

The imagery of sperm as aggressor is particularly startling in this case: the main discovery being reported is isolation of a particular molecule *on the egg coat* that plays an important role in fertilization! Wassarman's choice of language sustains the picture. He calls the molecule that has been isolated, ZP3, a "sperm receptor." By allocating the passive, waiting role to the egg, Wassarman can continue to describe the sperm as the actor, the one that makes it all happen: "The basic process begins when many sperm first attach loosely and then bind tenaciously to receptors on the surface of the egg's thick outer coat, the zona pellucida. Each sperm, which has a large number of egg-binding proteins on its surface, binds to many sperm receptors on the egg. More specifically, a site on each of the egg-binding proteins fits a complementary site on a sperm receptor, much as a key fits a lock."[51] With the sperm designated as the "key" and the egg the "lock," it is obvious which one acts and which one is acted upon. Could this imagery not be reversed, letting the sperm (the lock) wait until the egg produces the key? Or could we speak of two halves of a locket matching, and regard the matching itself as the action that initiates the fertilization?

It is as if Wassarman were determined to make the egg the receiving partner. Usually in biological research, the *protein* member of the pair of binding molecules is called the receptor, and physically it has a pocket in it rather like a lock. As the diagrams that illustrate Wassarman's article show, the molecules on the sperm are proteins and have "pockets." The small, mobile molecules that fit into these pockets are called ligands. As shown in the diagrams, ZP3 on the egg is a polymer of "keys"; many small knobs stick out. Typically, molecules on the sperm would be called receptors and molecules on the egg would be called ligands. But Wassarman chose to name ZP3 on the egg the receptor and to create a new term, "the egg-binding protein," for the molecule on the sperm that otherwise would have been called the receptor.[52]

Wassarman does credit the egg coat with having more functions than those of a sperm receptor. While he notes that "the zona pellucida has at times been viewed by investigators as a nuisance, a barrier to sperm and hence an impediment to fertilization," his new research reveals that the egg coat "serves as a sophisticated biological security system that screens incoming sperm, selects only those compatible with fertilization and development, prepares sperm for fusion with the egg and later protects the resulting embryo from polyspermy [a lethal condition caused by fusion of more than one sperm with a single egg]."[53] Although this description gives the egg an active role, that role is drawn in stereotypically feminine terms. The egg *selects* an appropriate mate, *prepares* him for fusion, and then *protects* the resulting offspring from harm. This is courtship and mating behavior as seen through the eyes of a sociobiologist: woman as the hard-to-get prize, who, following union with the chosen one, becomes woman as servant and mother.

And Wassarman does not quit there. In a review article for *Science*, he outlines the "chronology of fertilization."[54] Near the end of the article are two subject headings. One is "Sperm Penetration," in which Wassarman describes how the chemical dissolving of the zona pellucida combines with the "substantial propulsive force generated by sperm." The next heading is "Sperm-Egg Fusion." This section details what happens inside the zona after a sperm "penetrates" it. Sperm "can make contact with, adhere to, and fuse with (that is, fertilize) an egg."[55] Wassarman's word choice, again, is astonishingly skewed in favor of the sperm's activity, for in the next breath he says that sperm *lose* all motility upon fusion with the egg's surface. In mouse and sea urchin eggs, the sperm enters at the *egg's* volition, according to Wassarman's description: "Once fused with egg plasma membrane [the surface of the egg], how does a sperm enter the egg? The surface of both mouse and sea urchin eggs is covered with thousands of plasma membrane-bound projections, called microvilli [tiny "hairs"]. Evidence in sea urchins suggests that, after membrane fusion, a group of elongated microvilli cluster tightly around and interdigitate over the sperm head. As these microvilli are resorbed, the sperm is drawn into the egg. Therefore, sperm motility, which ceases at the time of fusion in both sea urchins and mice, is not required for sperm entry."[56] The section called "Sperm Penetration" more logically would be followed by a section called "The Egg Envelops," rather than "Sperm-Egg Fusion." This would give a parallel—and more accurate—sense that both the egg and the sperm initiate action.

Another way that Wassarman makes less of the egg's activity is by describing components of the egg but referring to the sperm as a whole entity. Deborah Gordon has described such an approach as "atomism" ("the part is independent of and primordial to the whole") and identified it as one of the "tenacious assumptions" of Western science and medicine.[57] Wassarman employs atomism to his advantage. When he refers to processes going on within sperm, he consistently returns to descriptions that remind us from whence these activities came: they are part of sperm that penetrate an egg or generate propulsive force. When he refers to processes going on within eggs, he stops there. As a result, any active role he grants them appears to be assigned to the parts of the egg, and not to the egg itself. In the quote above, it is the microvilli that actively cluster around the sperm. In another example, "the driving force for engulfment of a fused sperm comes from a region of cytoplasm just beneath an egg's plasma membrane."[58]

Social Implications: Thinking Beyond

All three of these revisionist accounts of egg and sperm cannot seem to escape the hierarchical imagery of older accounts. Even though each new account gives the egg a larger and more active role, taken together they bring into play another cultural stereotype: woman as a dangerous and aggressive threat. In the Johns Hopkins lab's revised model, the egg ends up as the female aggressor who "captures and tethers" the sperm with her sticky zona, rather like a spider lying in wait in her web.[59] The Schatten lab has the egg's nucleus "interrupt" the sperm's dive with a "sudden and swift" rush by which she "clasps the sperm and guides its nucleus to the center."[60] Wassarman's description of the surface of the egg "covered with thousands of plasma membrane-bound projections, called microvilli" that reach out and clasp the sperm adds to the spiderlike imagery.[61]

These images grant the egg an active role but at the cost of appearing disturbingly aggressive. Images of woman as dangerous and aggressive, the femme fatale who victimizes men, are wide-spread in Western literature and culture.[62] New data did not lead scientists to eliminate gender stereotypes in their descriptions of egg and sperm. Instead, scientists simply began to describe egg and sperm in different, but no less damaging, terms.

Can we envision a less stereotypical view? Biology itself provides another model that could be applied to the egg and the sperm. The cybernetic model—with its feedback loops, flexible adaptation to change, coordination of the parts within a whole, evolution over time, and changing response to the environment—is common in genetics, endocrinology, and ecology and has a growing influence in medicine in general.[64] This model has the potential to shift our imagery from the negative, in which the female reproductive system is castigated both for not producing eggs after birth and for producing (and thus wasting) too many eggs overall, to something more positive. The female reproductive system could be seen as responding to the environment (pregnancy or menopause), adjusting to monthly changes (menstruation), and flexibly changing from reproductivity after puberty to nonreproductivity later in life. The sperm and egg's interaction could also be described in cybernetic terms. J. F. Hartman's research in reproductive biology demonstrated fifteen years ago that if an egg is killed by being pricked with a needle, live sperm cannot get through the zona.[65] Clearly, this evidence shows that the egg and sperm *do* interact on more mutual terms, making biology's refusal to portray them that way all the more disturbing.

We would do well to be aware, however, that cybernetic imagery is hardly neutral. In the past, cybernetic models have played an important part in the imposition of social control. These models inherently provide a way of thinking about a "field" of interacting components. Once the field can be seen, it can become the object of new forms of knowledge, which in turn can allow new forms of social control to be exerted over the components of the field. During the 1950s, for example, medicine began to recognize the psychosocial *environment* of the patient: the patient's family and its psychodynamics. Professions such as social work began to focus on this new environment, and the resulting knowledge became one way to further control the patient. Patients began to be seen not as isolated, individual bodies, but as psychosocial entities located in an "ecological" system: management of "the patient's psychology was a new entrée to patient control."[66]

The models that biologists use to describe their data can have important social effects. During the nineteenth century, the social and natural sciences strongly influenced each other: the social ideas of Malthus about how to avoid the natural increase of the poor inspired Darwin's *Origin of Species*.[67] Once the *Origin* stood as a description of the natural world, complete with competition and market struggles, it could be reimported into social science as social Darwinism, in order to justify the social order of the time. What we are seeing now is similar: the importation of cultural ideas about passive females and heroic males into the "personalities" of gametes. This amounts to the "implanting of social imagery on representations of nature so as to lay a firm basis for reimporting exactly that same imagery as natural explanations of social phenomena."[68]

Further research would show us exactly what social effects are being wrought from the biological imagery of egg and sperm. At the very least, the imagery keeps alive some of the hoariest old stereotypes about weak damsels in distress and their strong male rescuers. That these stereotypes are now being written in at the level of the *cell* constitutes a powerful move to make them seem so natural as to be beyond alteration.

The stereotypical imagery might also encourage people to imagine that what results from the interaction of egg and sperm—a fertilized egg—is the result of deliberate "human" action at the cellular level. Whatever the intentions of the human couple, in this microscopic "culture" a cellular "bride" (or femme fatale) and a cellular "groom" (her victim) make a cellular baby. Rosalind Petchesky points out that through visual representations such as sonograms, we are given "*images* of younger and younger, and tinier and tinier, fetuses being 'saved.'" This leads to "the point of visibility being 'pushed back' *indefinitely*."[69] Endowing egg and sperm with intentional action, a key aspect of personhood in our culture, lays the foundation for the point of viability being pushed back to the moment of fertilization. This will likely lead to greater acceptance of technological developments and new forms of scrutiny and manipulation, for the benefit of these inner "persons": court-ordered restrictions on a pregnant woman's activities in order to protect her fetus, fetal surgery, amniocentesis, and rescinding of abortion rights, to name but a few examples.[70]

Even if we succeed in substituting more egalitarian, interactive metaphors to describe the activities of egg and sperm, and manage to avoid the pitfalls of cybernetic models, we would still be guilty of endowing cellular entities with personhood. More crucial, then, than what *kinds* of personalities we bestow on cells is the very fact that we are doing it at all. This process could ultimately have the most disturbing social consequences.

One clear feminist challenge is to wake up sleeping metaphors in science, particularly those involved in descriptions of the egg and the sperm. Although the literary convention is to call such metaphors "dead," they are not so much dead as sleeping, hidden within the scientific content of texts—and all the more powerful for it.[71] Waking up such metaphors, by becoming aware of when we are projecting cultural imagery onto what we study, will improve our ability to investigate and understand nature. Waking up such metaphors, by becoming aware of their implications, will rob them of their power to naturalize our social conventions about gender.

Notes

Portions of this article were presented as the 1987 Becker Lecture, Cornell University. I am grateful for the many suggestions and ideas I received on this occasion. For especially pertinent help with my arguments and data I thank Richard Cone, Kevin Whaley, Sharon Stephens, Barbara Duden, Susanne Kuechler, Lorna Rhodes, and Scott Gilbert. The article was strengthened and clarified by the comments of the anonymous *Signs* reviewers as well as the superb editorial skills of Amy Gage.

1. James Hillman, *The Myth of Analysis* (Evanston, Ill.: Northwestern University Press, 1972), 220.

2. The textbooks I consulted are the main ones used in classes for undergraduate premedical students or medical students (or those held on reserve in the library for these classes) during the past few years at Johns Hopkins University. These texts are widely used at other universities in the country as well.

3. Arthur C. Guyton, *Physiology of the Human Body*, 6th ed. (Philadelphia: Saunders College Publishing, 1984), 624.

4. Arthur J. Vander, James H. Sherman, and Dorothy S. Luciano, *Human Physiology: The Mechanisms of Body Function*, 3d ed. (New York: McGraw Hill, 1980), 483–84.

5. Vernon B. Mountcastle, ed., *Medical Physiology*, 14th ed. (London: Mosby, 1980), 2:1624.

6. Eldra Pearl Solomon, *Human Anatomy and Physiology* (New York: CBS College Publishing, 1983), 678.

7. For elaboration, see Emily Martin, *The Woman in the Body: A Cultural Analysis of Reproduction* (Boston: Beacon, 1987), 27–53.

8. Vander, Sherman, and Luciano, 568.

9. Melvin Konner, "Childbearing and Age," *New York Times Magazine* (December 27, 1987), 22–23, esp. 22.

10. I have found but one exception to the opinion that the female is wasteful: "Smallpox being the nasty disease it is, one might expect nature to have designed antibody mol-

ecules with combining sites that specifically recognize the epitopes on smallpox virus. Nature differs from technology, however: it thinks nothing of wastefulness. (For example, rather than improving the chance that a spermatozoon will meet an egg cell, nature finds it easier to produce millions of spermatozoa.)" (Niels Kaj Jerne, "The Immune System," *Scientific American* 229, no. 1 [July 1973]: 53). Thanks to a *Signs* reviewer for bringing this reference to my attention.

11. Bruce Alberts et al., *Molecular Biology of the Cell* (New York: Garland, 1983), 795.

12. In her essay "Have Only Men Evolved?" (in *Discovering Reality: Feminist Perspectives on Epistemology, Metaphysics, Methodology, and Philosophy of Science*, ed. Sandra Harding and Merrill B. Hintikka [Dordrecht: Reidel, 1983], 45–69, esp. 60–61). Ruth Hubbard points out that sociobiologists have said the female invests more energy than the male in the production of her large gametes, claiming that this explains why the female provides parental care. Hubbard questions whether it "really takes more 'energy' to generate the one or relatively few eggs than the large excess of sperms required to achieve fertilization." For further critique of how the greater size of eggs is interpreted in sociobiology, see Donna Haraway, "Investment Strategies for the Evolving Portfolio of Primate Females," in *Body/Politics*, ed. Mary Jacobus, Evelyn Fox Keller, and Sally Shuttleworth (New York: Routledge, 1990), 155–56.

13. The sources I used for this article provide compelling information on interactions among sperm. Lack of space prevents me from taking up this theme here, but the elements include competition, hierarchy, and sacrifice. For a newspaper report, see Malcolm W. Browne, "Some Thoughts on Self Sacrifice," *New York Times* (July 5, 1988), C6. For a literary rendition, see John Barth, "Night-Sea Journey," in his *Lost in the Funhouse* (Garden City, N. Y.: Doubleday, 1968), 3–13.

14. See Carol Delancy, "The Meaning of Paternity and the Virgin Birth Debate," *Man* 21, no. 3 (September 1986): 494–513. She discusses the difference between this scientific view that women contribute genetic material to the fetus and the claim of long-standing Western folk theories that the origin and identity of the fetus comes from the male, as in the metaphor of planting a seed in soil.

15. For a suggested direct link between human behavior and purportedly passive eggs and active sperm, see Erik H. Erikson, "Inner and Outer Space: Reflections on Womanhood," *Daedalus* 93, no. 2 (Spring 1964): 582–606, esp. 591.

16. Guyton (n. 3 above), 619; and Mountcastle (n. 5 above), 1609.

17. Jonathan Miller and David Pelham, *The Facts of Life* (New York: Viking Penguin, 1984), 5.

18. Alberts et al., 796.

19. Ibid., 796.

20. See, e.g., William F. Ganong, *Review of Medical Physiology*, 7th ed. (Los Altos, Calif.: Lange Medical Publications, 1975), 322.

21. Alberts et al. (n. 11 above), 796.

22. Guyton, 615.

23. Solomon (n. 6 above), 683.

24. Vander, Sherman, and Luciano (n. 4 above), 4th ed. (1985), 580.

25. Alberts et al., 796.

26. All biology texts quoted above use the word "penetrate."

27. Solomon, 700.

28. A. Beldecos et al., "The Importance of Feminist Critique for Contemporary Cell Biology," *Hypatia* 3, no. 1 (Spring 1988): 61–76.

29. Gerald Schatten and Helen Schatten, "The Energetic Egg," *Medical World News* 23 (January 23, 1984): 51–53, esp. 51.

30. Alberts et al., 796.

31. Guyton (n. 3 above), 613.

32. Miller and Pelham (n. 17 above), 7.

33. Alberts et al. (n. 11 above), 804.

34. Ibid., 801.

35. Ruth Herschberger, *Adam's Rib* (New York: Pelligrini & Cudaby, 1948), esp. 84. I am indebted to Ruth Hubbard for telling me about Herschberger's work, although at a point when this paper was already in draft form.

36. Bennett M. Shapiro, "The Existential Decision of a Sperm," *Cell* 49, no. 3 (May 1987): 293–94, esp. 293.

37. Lennart Nilsson, "A Portrait of the Sperm," in *The Functional Anatomy of the Spermatozoan*, ed. Bjorn A. Afzelius (New York: Pergamon, 1975), 79–82.

38. Ludwik Fleck, *Genesis and Development of a Scientific Fact*, ed. Thaddeus J. Trenn and Robert K. Merton (Chicago: University of Chicago Press, 1979), 38.

39. Jay M. Baltz carried out the research I describe when he was a graduate student in the Thomas C. Jenkins Department of Biophysics at Johns Hopkins University.

40. Far less is known about the physiology of sperm than comparable female substances, which some feminists claim is no accident. Greater scientific scrutiny of female reproduction has long enabled the burden of birth control to be placed on women. In this case, the researchers' discovery did not depend on development of any new technology. The experiments made use of glass pipettes, a manometer, and a simple microscope, all of which have been available for more than one hundred years.

41. Jay M. Baltz and Richard A. Cone, "What Force Is Needed to Tether a Sperm?" (abstract for Society for the Study of Reproduction, 1985), and "Flagellar Torque on the Head Determines the Force Needed to Tether a Sperm" (abstract for Biophysical Society, 1986).

42. Jay M. Baltz, David F. Katz, and Richard A. Cone, "The Mechanics of the Sperm-Egg Interaction at the Zona Pellucida," *Biophysical Journal* 54, no. 4 (October 1988): 643–54. Lab members were somewhat familiar with work on metaphors in the biology of female reproduction. Richard Cone, who runs the lab, is my husband, and he talked with them about my earlier research on the subject from time to time. Even though my current research focuses on biological imagery and I heard about the lab's work from my husband every day, I myself did not recognize the role of imagery in the sperm research until many weeks after the period of research and writing I describe. Therefore, I assume that any awareness the lab members may have had about how underlying metaphor might be guiding this particular research was fairly inchoate.

43. Ibid., 643, 650.

44. Schatten and Schatten (n. 29 above), 51.

45. Ibid., 52.

46. Surprisingly, in an article intended for a general audience, the authors do not point out that these are sea urchin sperm and note that human sperm do not shoot out filaments at all.

47. Schatten and Schatten, 53.

48. Paul M. Wassarman, "Fertilization in Mammals," *Scientific American* 259, no. 6 (December 1988): 78–84, esp. 78, 84.

49. Ibid., 78.

50. Ibid., 79.

51. Ibid., 78.

52. Since receptor molecules are relatively *immotile* and the ligands that bind to them

relatively *motile*, one might imagine the egg being called the receptor and the sperm the ligand. But the molecules in question on egg and sperm are immotile molecules. It is the sperm as a *cell* that has motility, and the egg as a cell that has relative immotility.

53. Wassarman, 78–79.

54. Paul M. Wassarman, "The Biology and Chemistry of Fertilization," *Science* 235, no. 4788 (January 30, 1987): 553–60, esp. 554.

55. Ibid., 557.

56. Ibid., 557–58. This finding throws into question Schatten and Schatten's description (n. 29 above) of the sperm, its tail beating, diving down into the egg.

57. Deborah R. Gordon, "Tenacious Assumptions in Western Medicine," in *Biomedicine Examined*, ed. Margaret Lock and Deborah Gordon (Dordrecht: Kluwer, 1988), 19–56, esp. 26.

58. Wassarman, "The Biology and Chemistry of Fertilization," 558.

59. Baltz, Katz, and Cone (n. 42 above), 643, 650.

60. Schatten and Schatten, 53.

61. Wassarman, "The Biology and Chemistry of Fertilization," 557.

62. Mary Ellman, *Thinking about Women* (New York: Harcourt Brace Jovanovich, 1968), 140; Nina Auerbach, *Woman and the Demon* (Cambridge, Mass.: Harvard University Press, 1982), esp. 186. More specific is the connection of spider imagery with the idea of an engulfing, devouring mother.

63. Kenneth Alan Adams, "Arachnophobia: Love American Style," *Journal of Psychoanalytic Anthropology* 4, no. 2 (1981): 157–97.

64. William Ray Arney and Bernard Bergen, *Medicine and the Management of Living* (Chicago: University of Chicago Press, 1984).

65. J. F. Hartman, R. B. Gwatkin, and C. F. Hutchison, "Early Contact Interactions between Mammalian Gametes *In Vitro*," *Proceedings of the National Academy of Sciences (U.S.)* 69, no. 10 (1972): 2767–69.

66. Arney and Bergen, 68.

67. Hubbard (n. 12 above), 51–52.

68. David Harvey, personal communication, November 1989.

69. Rosalind Petchesky, "Fetal Images: The Power of Visual Culture in the Politics of Reproduction," *Feminist Studies* 13, no. 2 (Summer 1987): 263–92, esp. 272.

70. Rita Arditti, Renate Klein, and Shelley Minden, *Test-Tube Women* (London: Pandora, 1984); Ellen Goodman, "Whose Right to Life?" *Baltimore Sun* (November 17, 1987); Tamar Lewin, "Courts Acting to Force Care of the Unborn," *New York Times* (November 23, 1987), A1 and B10; Susan Irwin and Brigitte Jordan, "Knowledge, Practice, and Power: Court Ordered Cesarean Sections," *Medical Anthropology Quarterly* 1, no. 3 (September 1987): 319–34.

71. Thanks to Elizabeth Fee and David Spain, who in February 1989 and April 1989, respectively, made points related to this.

Making Sense of Missed Conceptions   5

Anthropological Perspectives
on Unexplained Infertility

SARAH FRANKLIN

Explanations of conception and procreation have long been of intrinsic interest to anthropology (see Montagu, 1937). The discipline itself was founded amidst debates concerning the negotiation of parenthood and procreation, kinship reckonings and conception stories. Central to these debates has been the issue of the relationship between the so-called "natural facts" of human reproduction and the various cultural elaborations brought to bear on what is considered to be its objective, biogenetic basis.

The classic anthropological controversy known as the "virgin birth" debates proceeded from the discovery of cultures which do not believe in the biological model of conception (see Delaney, 1986). When Malinowski visited the Trobriand Islands of Melanesia, he tried hard to convince his informants of their oversight in thinking that a male contribution was unnecessary to the production of a pregnancy. Was it not true, he insisted, that intercourse is necessary for conception to occur? His informants remained firm. Why, they replied, if there is a causal relationship between intercourse and pregnancy, do so many young girls who have intercourse not become pregnant (Malinowski, 1925)? Children, they argued, result from the return of an ancestor through the body of a woman. Hence, the matrilineage is preserved, as a woman's ancestors return through her to produce offspring. Hence, the central mechanism of Trobriand social organization, the matrilineal clan, through which new Trobrianders come into being and acquire a specific identity and meaningful kinship ties and obligations (see Malinowski, 1916, 1929; Weiner, 1976, 1988).

Anthropologists have offered many explanations of peoples, such as the Trobrianders, who reject biological accounts of conception (Leach, 1966; Spiro, 1968). These range across the entire gamut of anthropological thought, invoking a set of questions about theory, method and cross-cultural comparison which are too numerous to describe here. At the root of this controversy is the assumption that beliefs about parenthood and procreation represent key cultural constructs, the interpretation of which is therefore of critical importance, to anthropologists as well as the peoples they study.

In contemporary British culture, we are unaccustomed to thinking of our accounts of conception as cultural constructions. On the contrary, we assume that the causal relationship between intercourse and pregnancy is a matter of scientific fact. Anglicans may still debate the virgin birth, but such uncertainty is considered to be of a distinctly theological character. In secular life, we are certain about the events which cause pregnancy. Pregnancy is caused by the meeting of the sperm and egg, which fertilize to produce an embryo which develops inside the womb into a child.

However, neither natural science nor natural facts are independent of the cultural context in which they are produced. Like those of other cultures, our conception stories have changed historically, and emerge in the context of specific social formations (see Laqueur, 1986). Moreover, we are currently in the midst of a major elaboration of the biogenetic events involved in reproduction. This is partly due to the emergence of new reproductive technologies which have removed conception from inside the body and made it visible for scientific scrutiny. It is also because of the importance attributed to the events of conception in understanding the mechanisms of genetic inheritance, which are currently receiving an unprecedented degree of scientific attention, as evidenced by major global scientific efforts such as that of mapping the human genome.

While it is seen to be a set of natural facts, we are also familiar with the representation of conception as a narrative (Martin, 1991). In the standard conception narrative, authenticated by biological science, the facts of life unfold along a well-known trajectory. After the sperm are released into the vaginal cavity, they swim into the cervix and up into the uterus and fallopian tubes, where they meet the egg, which has come down to meet them from the ovary. When they meet, the sperm and egg merge, at which point fertilization takes place. As the fertilized egg begins to subdivide and develop, it implants itself into the wall of the uterus, thus establishing a pregnancy.

This standard conception narrative is more or less how all of us were told about the "natural facts" connecting intercourse and pregnancy, and accounting for the biological mechanisms of human procreation. Like all narratives, this linear construction of events involves the establishment of a causal sequence from starting point to ending point through which the various components of the narrative are linked. Under most circumstances, this narrative functions adequately as both a representation and an explanation of the causal sequence of events involved in conception. It is, after all, not a very complicated story.

New Conception Stories

One of the most immediate means of appreciating the changing cultural construction of conception is to consider how this staple narrative is changing. The most important change is that this narrative is becoming much more complex. It is also getting longer, as both the starting points and the ending points of the narrative are extended. It is also becoming less certain, as gaps are opened up in the causal sequence which holds the narrative together. It is becoming less "natural," as technology increasingly enters into this narrative as an agent in its own right. From the perspective of both social and natural facts, conception stories are becoming more elaborate.

One of the main reasons for these changes in accounts of conception is the growing awareness of the large number of people for whom the standard conception narrative does not function. We are increasingly aware, that is, of the number of people for whom intercourse does not cause pregnancy, whose egg and sperm do not fertilize, whose embryos do not implant, and so forth. These are the couples who are undergoing infertility treatment.

For such couples, and the clinicians who treat them, and the researchers who study them, the standard conception narrative is inadequate. The causal chain established by biological science and assumed as commonsense has broken down. This reveals a very interesting feature of our conception stories. The chain of causality, it is revealed, only functions as a successful explanation system *retrospectively*. It provides a wholly adequate explanation for why conception has occurred *if it has occurred*. In the situation in which the causal factor is present but the hoped-for outcome fails to occur, there is an unexplained event.

The World of Achieved Conception

Once they are excluded from the standard conception narrative, infertile couples who seek medical assistance come to inhabit a very different world of conception. This might usefully be described as the world of achieved conception. Moving into the world of achieved conception entails a number of significant shifts. From a private and personal matter, conception becomes a public event involving teams of professional experts. From a non-commercial activity, conception takes on a commercial dimension, and the couples become consumers in the marketplace of infertility services on offer. Once taken for granted as a simple natural sequence, conception becomes a technologically assisted achievement. In sum, conception is transformed from a simple narrative into a story that is much more complex, uncertain and mysterious.

Infertility guidebooks, of which there is a rapidly expanding genre, offer a useful introduction to the world of achieved conception, to the new conception narratives emerging out of the context of infertility treatment. The following is a short list of chapter headings from a guidebook of this sort:

> How the Ovaries Work
> How Men Make Sperm
> The Modern Semen Analysis
> Mechanical Obstructions
> Blocked Ducts and Other Transport Problems
> Microsurgery, Lasers and the 21st Century
> Miracle Babies
> Brave New World

This list, from a book entitled *The Fertility Handbook* (Bellina and Wilson, 1986), provides a useful introduction to the content and parameters of emergent conception stories in the context of *assisted* reproduction. To begin with, the starting point of the conception narrative has been moved back in time to encompass the production of gametes, egg and sperm, not simply their journeys from their points of origin to their eventual rendezvous. Secondly, the topology of achieved conception, heavily indebted to the analogy of plumbing, is defined in terms of the various conduits and passageways which may be obstructed or blocked. Most notably, this world is defined by a particular relationship between modern science and reproductive physiology. It is thanks to modern science that we can see, name, understand and control this new domain, and this achievement is seen as a definitively modern one, associated with the advance of scientific progress. Achieved conception foregrounds the enabling potential of technology to overcome "natural" error. Miracle babies and laser surgery are part of the brave new world of achieved conception in the twenty-first century.

Finally, the world of achieved conception is defined by specific parameters, most notably those of biological science and medical technology. These can be seen to operate discursively, in the Foucauldian sense of "the delimination of a field of objects, the definition of a legitimate perspective for the agent of knowledge, and the fixing of norms for the elaboration of concepts and theories" (Foucault, 1977: 199). Meaningful information in the context of achieved conception is information which can reveal the biological obstacles to conception, and this information is acquired through technological investigation and monitoring: ultrasound scans, laparoscopy, measurement of hormone levels and so forth. These discursive parameters frame the context within which both infertile couples and clinicians attempt to make sense of missed conceptions.

The world of achieved conception presents not only a changed landscape in the sense of changing natural facts, but a changed landscape of social facts and cultural meanings. It should be remembered that anthropological interest in conception accounts is not merely motivated by a desire to understand the social construction of natural facts. It is also motivated by the assumption that this process of social construction is quite fundamental to a culture's definition of itself. Conception stories not only tell us where we came from—they tell us who we are, how we are related to others, what our kinship obligations are, and how we are situated in patterns of inheritance and descent. They are central to the acquisition of a specific cultural identity, to definitions of sexual difference, personhood, parenthood and procreation. What a culture believes about conception, Malinowski argued, tells you what it believes about everything else. Conception stories are cultural cosmologies in microcosm.

What then are the cultural implications of the changing definition of conception? What are the consequences of this brave new world of achieved conception, miracle babies and state-of-the-art reproductive technologies which are dramatically altering our perception of "the facts of life"? To answer this question, we are indebted to the experience of those who have inhabited this new frontier and begun to chart its contours. These are the couples who have undergone extensive treatment for infertility and have thus acquired considerable experience and expertise within the world of achieved conception.

To understand these questions, and to locate the changing discursive construction of "the facts of life" within the context of lived understandings of these changes, ethnographic interviews were conducted with 20 women undergoing IVF. This fieldwork took place in the West Midlands during 1988 and 1989, and provides a means of relating changes at the level of public, or mainstream, culture to the lives of individuals with direct experience of the world of achieved conception. In the next section data from these interviews are drawn upon in the attempt to illustrate some of the consequences of inhabiting this world, this subculture, and to suggest some of their implications (see further Franklin, 1992).

Making Sense of IVF

To begin with, inhabiting the world of achieved conception, defined as it is by certain restricted parameters, opens up a number of gaps which need somehow to be resolved. The most obvious gap is that between the desire for a biological child and the inability to produce one. Related to this is the gap between the biological facts of infertility, which are a definitive component, indeed the foundation of the world of achieved conception, and the social facts of infertility, which are more or less excluded from, or at least marginal to, this world. More specifically, there are gaps in knowledge which often remain unresolved, and a gap between accumulated information and meaningful knowledge, which do not always coincide.

Let us consider the last of these examples first. For both the infertile woman and the clinician, particularly in the case of unexplained infertility, *information* which is defined as meaningful, within the parameters of the dominant discourse, does not always add up to meaningful *knowledge*. In interviews with women undergoing IVF, this problem was frequently encountered. A case which illustrates the kind of paradox this can create is that of women who are repeatedly told that "there is nothing wrong":

> Each test we had they said, "well, everything was fine in there Mrs H., everything was fine," and I kept saying I know you're smiling about this, but I wish you would turn around and say you have found something wrong, because I think in my mind I'd feel easier.

The problem for women such as Mrs H. is that the accumulation of information does not add up to knowledge. The medical information that "there is nothing wrong" directly contradicts both her knowledge and experience that there is definitely something wrong. Women in the position of Mrs H. invariably know far more technical data about the state of their reproductive physiology than many medical experts, but it serves them little in the way of coming to terms with their condition or doing anything about it.

Another gap which opens up is that between the biological facts of infertility and the social experience of it. Needless to say, infertility is not experienced as a purely biological event. An effect of this is the need somehow to bridge the gap between the technical information given about a woman's physical condition and her experience of infertility as a social condition. It is thus hardly surprising to discover that this need to bridge the gap has the effect of increasing the desire for "something to be wrong." The work of coping with the social dimensions of infertility, such as providing explanations to friends, relatives or colleagues for an inability to produce children, or even simply an unwanted absence of them, is eased with the acquisition of some explanation for why conception fails.

The desire for something to be wrong in order for it to be put right is emphasized by the trajectory established by infertility treatment. It is clear in the plumbing analogy and the mechanical sequence which defines the causal chain of biological events leading to conception. Events are *supposed* to proceed along an established path. However, the "plumbing" turns out to be composed of many mechanisms which are not very clearly understood. This is especially evident in the context of IVF.

Like the standard conception narrative, the procedures involved in assisted conception are initially quite straightforward. Descriptions of IVF need not be overly complex: the egg is removed from the woman's body, fertilized *in vitro* and returned to the womb. In this sense, IVF is represented as a means of replicating, through technological procedures, what "nature" does "herself." However, as the very high failure rates of IVF indicate, the process is far from straightforward. Indeed, many women do not even reach the stage for which IVF is named, fertilization *in vitro*, as there are so many things which can go wrong even before this point in treatment.

As conception is increasingly subject to the clinical and scientific gaze, each stage in the sequence leading to fertilization is broken down into smaller and smaller stages. For "sperm fertilizes egg" must now be substituted a long list of molecular events which are themselves being subdivided still further as the complex biogenetic process is scrutinized.

The effect of this on conception narratives is to make them appear more like an obstacle course than a process so simple it could happen if you "passed him on the stairs." Far from being as "easy as falling off a ladder," or as neat "as shelling peas," conception turns out to be a minor miracle of reproductive physiology. Human reproduction, experts now suggest, "is remarkably inefficient" (see, for example, Hull, 1986).

IVF is also described as an obstacle course by many of the women who undergo it. For every stage of conception that is broken down into further stages, there are more hurdles to overcome and more things that can eventually go wrong. Conception comes to look more and more like a badly designed process. Not only does nature need a helping hand, it sometimes appears nature would not even get off the starting blocks without the aid of modern technology.

A major component of the experience of IVF is therefore the accumulation of an increasing amount of information about the technical complexity of conception. At one level, this can be very discouraging: as one woman described it to me, IVF is like "trying to run the Grand National blindfolded and with your legs tied together." At another level, this has the effect of changing definitions of success and failure in the context of IVF. Initially, success is defined as a successful pregnancy, or a "take home baby," as it is dubbed. The further a woman goes on with unsuccessful IVF treatment, however, the lower the threshold of relative success drops. Hence, after failing at the first hurdle on the first try, some women may consider their treatment "successful" if it then moves on to fail at the third hurdle on the second try, or the fourth hurdle on the third try, and so forth. Failure can even be defined as "successful" treatment if the source of the failure reveals more about the precise problem to be overcome. Hence, for example, a failed treatment which yields diagnostic clarity may be an incentive for a woman to pursue further treatment, as the "light at the end of the tunnel" becomes more visible, and hope for a successful resolution grows.

IVF is the conception story of the world of achieved conception *par excellence*. Women who undergo this form of treatment are, as Rayna Rapp has noted, reproductive pioneers (Rapp, 1987). It is their bodies in which this domain is being explored by science. It is their lives in which the unprecedented dilemmas posed by treatment, the difficult personal and ethical decisions and choices, are being forged. It is for this reason that the world they inhabit, a world in which the social construction of natural facts takes on a daily, intimate and taxing reality, deserves considered attention. It is also for this reason that the specific dilemmas they face take on a significance that extends well beyond their own immediate circumstances.

This is so not only because public awareness of the number of couples experiencing fertility problems is increasing, but because the world of achieved conception is becoming less and less a subculture and more and more a part of mainstream cultural understandings of parenting, personhood and procreation. Television documentaries, such as "The World of the Unborn" (*Panorama*, 1988), illustrate the process whereby the meanings produced in the world of achieved conception are becoming more mainstream. In this hour-long documentary, produced by an infertility clinic but aimed at a general audience, conception is no longer the simple biological sequence it used to be. Instead, consistent with the perception of it by infertile couples, conception is represented as an epic saga. The obstacle course analogy prevails. Given the number of things that can go wrong, this documentary would seem to be suggesting, every baby is a miracle baby and it is quite remarkable that we can reproduce at all!

A similar example can be drawn from current popular cinema, where an increasing number of films address themselves to the mysteries of procreation. The genres of science fiction and horror in particular have moved from a fascination with outer space to a fascination with inner space. Commenting on such films as *Alien* and *The Fly*, film critic Barbara Creed notes:

> The sci-fi horror film's current interest in the maternal body and processes of birth points to changes taking place on several fronts. Among the most important of these are the developments taking place in reproductive technology which have put into crisis questions of the subject, the body and the unconscious. . . . In more recent years, as experiments with reproductive technology have begun to make enormous headway, [these films] have become increasingly preoccupied with alternative forms of the conception-gestation-birth process. [Creed, 1987: 56–7]

The preoccupation of such films with something going wrong in the conception-gestation-birth process is a clear indication of the widespread anxiety surrounding the current renegotiation of "the facts of life." To borrow from the parlance of postmodernism, conception might be thought of as a foundational narrative in crisis. Lost is the certainty and predictability surrounding our maternal origins. Such a loss has understandably disturbing implications.

The Changing Landscape of Reproduction

To appreciate the impact of achieved conception as an emergent cultural construction, it must be situated in the context of broader shifts occurring in the definition of human reproduction. These include the centrality of reproductive processes in general, and of conception in particular, to the rise of biogenetic sciences in recent decades. Also of significance is the increasing medicalization and technologization of the birth process. From this perspective, the "naturalness" of both human and animal reproduction must be seen as an increasingly residual concept (see Strathern 1992). As human reproduction becomes increasingly subject to technological monitoring and intervention, now extending from the preconception to postnatal stages of the birth process, and plant and animal reproduction become increasingly subject to industrial demands, their "naturalness" is diminished in relation to their pervasive, patent (and increasingly patented) artificiality.

A second consequence is related to this. The significance of the concept of human achievement in a context previously understood to occur "naturally" should not be underestimated. As it comes to be seen as less "natural," so too will conception come to be a less taken-for-granted event. This is already evident in a number of examples. The marketing of ovulation prediction tests, and the rising awareness of the higher-than-expected rates of infertility, coupled with concern about the effects of environmental toxins on fertility, will undoubtedly lead to a more widespread view of conception as an event involving calculated risk and careful reproductive planning. Already this is known as "preconceptive" or "preparental" planning. As more information from the rapidly expanding sciences of biogenetics, concerning the mechanisms of genetic determinism, enters into mainstream cultural circulation, so the events involved in conception will come to be regarded as increasingly significant. Most importantly, they will also be seen as open to increasing degrees of risk, and therefore intervention, such as that already available in the form of pre-implantation diagnosis, a technique designed to select and potentially "treat" human embryos *in vitro*.

The changing landscape of conception, then, is part of a wider set of changes in the cultural construction of human reproduction. The project to map the human genome now in progress is only one of several components in this refigured field. It is difficult to underestimate the cultural consequences of such changes.

In addition to becoming more complex, more difficult and more subject to technological intervention, conception is also becoming more public. This is true at a number of levels. Conception is now more public in a commercial sense, in so far as reproductive services (as well as reproductive tissue) have become consumer items. It is also more public in that it is now more visible than ever before, and is available in the form of icons, such as that of the unborn fetus or the "moment" of fertilization, which imagery has now become widely circulated. It is more public also as a form of property, especially in the context of animal husbandry, where the patenting of reproductive techniques and of particular genetic strains or breeds (such as the famous patented mouse) has necessitated the development of gene libraries to accompany already existing gene banks. Finally, conception is moving into the public domain via the mechanisms of state bureaucracy, as is evident in regulatory bodies such as the recently created Human Fertilization and Embryology Authority, established in 1990, which oversees licensing arrangements to register clinicians and scientists involved in various forms of assisted conception.

The Meaning of Assistance

What then of the women who enter the world of assisted conception and are at the cutting edge of a set of techniques which have already precipitated a cultural redefinition of conception to such a great extent? For most women, their venture into this territory will not lead to the desired outcome of a child. The gaps between the social and biological facts of infertility, between information and knowledge, between the desire for a child and the inability to produce one, between the conception narrative they started with and the one they came to inhabit may or may not be resolved. One way or another, they will have to find their way out, as they found their way in, with little support, guidance or precedent to see them through.

It is not therefore surprising to discover that many women have second thoughts about having attempted IVF. Having failed after several attempts, they wonder if they might not have been better able to come to terms with their infertility without it. As one woman said to me, "Years and years ago, if couples couldn't have children, they just couldn't have children. . . . I often wonder if we hadn't started going to fertility clinics right from the beginning, would we not have been better off?" Yet there is an equally strong desire to feel that every possible option has been pursued in the attempt to have a child. Almost always this is phrased in terms of not wanting to look back at a later stage in life and feel there was something that could have been tried and might have succeeded. On the one hand, new forms of technological assistance offer the possibility, however remote, of successful pregnancy. On the other hand, the costs of these largely unsuccessful forms of reproductive assistance are virtually impossible to gauge at the outset. Such are the dilemmas an increasing number of would-be parents will face, be it in the context of infertility treatment, prenatal diagnosis or the proposed treatment of genetic disorders, all of which involve a reproductive experience which is mediated by technology.

If conception stories are cultural cosmologies in microcosm, then the conception story of IVF, of the world of achieved conception, deserves comment not only because it is limited in terms of therapeutic success. The limits it imposes are also limits of cultural imagination. As the dominant analogies from the world of achieved conception become more definitive of human reproduction in general—the analogies of scientific achievement, of technological assistance, of mechanical sequences, or of an obstacle course—so too do our definitions of kinship and personhood alter accordingly. For example, as Marilyn Strathern has noted, it is unclear how the meaning of assistance in the domain of kinship will alter understandings of fundamental social ties. Such shifts are already evident in statutory definitions of "mothers," "fathers" and "pregnancies," which, by the very process of attempting to define these terms, paradoxically bring to the fore their increasing ambiguity. Similar shifts are also evident in redefinitions of the natural facts of pregnancy and childbirth, such as the redefinition of the "embryo" as the "pre-embryo." Most of all, they are evident in the dilemmas faced by infertile couples undergoing IVF, but already these are dilemmas which are facing a much wider population.

Conclusion

Looking back to the curiosity expressed by Victorian anthropologists at the puzzling conception stories of the Trobrianders, there can be seen, perhaps, a different object lesson. Instead of a culture so divergent from our own, there is a familiar pattern. In the negotiation of conception stories our most powerful cultural idioms can be seen at work: industrialism, technology, scientific progress, the advance of knowledge and the ability to control and improve natural processes for the betterment of humankind. Moreover, we see conception located in a matrix of social institutions which give it the specific meanings through which it makes sense to us, including those of medicine, law, commerce and the state. Were a visitor from Kiriwina to visit us today, in a reverse pilgrimage to that of Malinowski, he or she would likely arrive at the same conclusion: that conception stories do indeed reveal a culture's definition of itself. And such a visitor would have to be forgiven too for commenting on Malinowski's view of the Trobrianders as quite exotic in their accounts of human conception. Had Malinowski been a member of the Warnock Committee, his fieldnotes would have been copious indeed.

Works Cited

Bellina, J. and Wilson, J. (1986) *The Fertility Handbook: A Positive and Practical Guide*. Harmondsworth: Penguin.

Creed, B. (1987) "From here to modernity: Feminism and postmodernism," *Screen*, 28(2): 47–67.

Delaney, C. (1986) "The meaning of paternity and the virgin birth debate," *Man*, 21: 494–513.

Foucault, M. (1977) *The History of Sexuality*. Harmondsworth: Penguin.

Franklin, S. (1992) *Contested Conceptions: A Cultural Account of Assisted Reproduction*. PhD thesis. Department of Cultural Studies, University of Birmingham.

Hull, M. G. R. (1986) "Infertility: Nature and extent of problem," in CIBA Foundation, *Human Embryo Research: Yes or No*. London: Tavistock, pp. 24–35.

Laqueur, T. (1986) "Orgasm, generation and the politics of reproductive biology," *Representations*, 14: 1–41.

Leach, E. (1966) "Virgin birth," *Proceedings of the Royal Anthropological Institute for 1966*, pp. 39–49.

Malinowski, B. (1916) "Baloma: The spirits of the dead in the Trobriand Islands," *Journal of the Royal Anthropological Institute*, 46: 353–430.

Malinowski, B. (1925) *The Father in Primitive Society*. New York: Harcourt, Brace and World.

Malinowski, B. (1929) *The Sexual Life of Savages in North-Western Melanesia*. London: Routledge and Kegan Paul.

Martin, E. (1991) "The Egg and the Sperm," *Signs*, 16(3): 485–501.

Montagu, A. (1937) *Coming into Being Among the Australian Aborigines*. London: Routledge and Kegan Paul.

Panorama (1988) "The World of the Unborn," Genesis Productions. Transmitted BBC1.

Rapp, R. (1987) "Moral pioneers: Women, men and fetuses on a frontier of reproductive technology," *Women and Health*, 13(1/2): 101–16.

Spiro, M. (1968) "Virgin birth, pathenogenesis and physiological paternity: An essay in cultural interpretation," *Man*, 3: 242–61.

Strathern, M. (1992) *After Nature: English Kinship in the Late Twentieth Century*. Cambridge: Cambridge University Press.

Weiner, A. (1976) *Women of Value, Men of Renown: New Perspectives in Trobriand Exchange*. Austin, TX: University of Texas Press.

Weiner, A. (1988) *The Trobrianders of Papua New Guinea*. Orlando, FL: Holt, Rinehart and Winston.

6 Chasing the Blood Tie

Surrogate Mothers, Adoptive Mothers, and Fathers

HELENA RAGONÉ

> An election that's about ideas and values is also about philosophy, and I have one. At the bright center is the individual, and radiating out from him or her is the family, the essential unit of closeness and love. For it's the family that communicates to our children, to the 21st century, our culture, our religious faith, our traditions, and our history.
>
> —George Bush, Presidential Nomination Acceptance Speech, 1989

In the wake of publicity created by the Baby M Case,[1] it seems unlikely that any in the United States can have remained unfamiliar with surrogate motherhood or have yet to form an opinion. The Baby M Case raised, and ultimately left unanswered, many questions about what constitutes motherhood, fatherhood, family, reproduction, and kinship. Much of what has been written about surrogate motherhood has, however, been largely speculative or polemical in nature; it ranges from the view that surrogate motherhood is symptomatic of the dissolution of the American family[2] and the sanctity of motherhood to charges that it reduces or assigns women to a breeder class structurally akin to prostitution (Dworkin 1978) or that it constitutes a form of commercial baby selling (Annas 1988; Neuhaus 1988).

In recent years a plethora of studies on reproduction has emerged in the field of anthropology (Browner 1986; Delaney 1986, 1991; Dolgin 1993; Ginsburg 1987, 1989; Martin 1987; Modell 1989; Newman 1985; Ragoné 1991, 1994; Rapp 1987, 1988, 1990; Scrimshaw 1978; Strathern 1991, 1992a, 1992b).[3] Not since the "virgin birth" controversy have so many theorists turned their attention to the subject (Leach 1967; Spiro 1968). Many of these studies represent a response to the interest generated by the emergence of what are collectively called assisted reproductive technologies, such as in vitro fertilization, surrogate motherhood, amniocentesis, and ultrasound. Much of the relevant research examines how these technologies are affecting the relationship between "procreative beliefs and the wider context (worldview, cosmology, and culture)" (Delaney 1986:495), as exemplified by concepts and definitions of personhood and knowledge (Strathern 1991, 1992a). There nevertheless remains a paucity of ethnographic material about these technologies—in particular about surrogate motherhood, the subject of this article, which is based on fieldwork conducted at three different surrogate mother programs from 1988 to the present.

Historically there have been three profound shifts in the Western conceptualization of the categories of conception, reproduction, and parenthood. The first occurred in response to the separation of intercourse from reproduction through birth control methods (Snowden and Snowden 1983), a precedent that may have paved the way for surrogate motherhood in the 1980s (Andrews 1984:xiii). A second shift occurred in response to the emergence of assisted reproductive technologies and to the subsequent fragmentation of the unity of reproduction, when it became possible for pregnancy to occur without necessarily having been "preceded by sexual intercourse" (Snowden and Snowden 1983:5). The third shift occurred in response to further advances in reproductive medicine that called into question the "organic unity of fetus and mother" (Martin 1987:20). It was not, however, until the emergence of reproductive medicine that the fragmentation of motherhood became a reality; with that historical change, what was once the "single figure of the mother is dispersed among several potential figures, as the functions of maternal procreation—aspects of her physical parenthood—become dispersed" (Strathern 1991:32). As will be shown in the following section, the a priori acceptance of surrogates' stated motivations has often produced an incomplete profile of surrogate mothers.

Surrogate Motivations

When I began my field research in 1988, surrogate mother programs and directors had already become the subject of considerable media attention, a great deal of it sensationalized and negative in character. At that time there were ten established surrogate mother programs in the United States; in addition, there were also a number of small, part-time businesses (none of which were included in the study) in which lawyers, doctors, adoption agents, and others arranged occasional surrogate mother contracts.[4] In order to obtain as stable a sample as possible, I chose to include only firmly established programs in my study. The oldest of the programs was established in approximately 1980, and none of the programs included in my study had been in business for fewer than ten years as of 1994.

There are two types of surrogate mother programs: what I call "open" programs, in which surrogate and couple select one another and interact throughout the insemination and the pregnancy, and "closed" programs, in which couples select their surrogates from information—biographical and medical information and a photograph of the surrogate—provided to them by the programs. After the child is born in a "closed" program, the couple and surrogate meet only to finalize the stepparent adoption.[5] I formally interviewed a total of 28 surrogates, from six different programs. Aside from these formal interviews I also engaged in countless conversations with surrogates, observing them as they interacted with their families, testified before legislative committees, worked in surrogate programs, and socialized at program gatherings with directors and others. Quite often I was an invited guest at the homes of program directors, a situation that provided me with a unique opportunity to observe directors interacting with their own spouses and children, with couples and surrogates, and with members of their staffs. The opportunity to observe the daily workings of the surrogate mother programs provided me with invaluable data on the day-to-day operations of the programs. At one program I attended staff meetings on a regular basis and observed consultations in which prospective couples and surrogates were interviewed singly by members of the staff such as the director, a psychologist, a medical coordinator, or the administrative coordinator.

A review of the literature on surrogate motherhood reveals that, until now, the primary research focus has been on the surrogate mother herself, and that there have been no ethnographic studies on surrogate mother programs and commissioning couples. Studies of the surrogate population tend to focus, at times exclusively, on surrogates' stated motivations for becoming surrogate mothers (Parker 1983). Their stated reasons include the desire to help an infertile couple start a family, financial remuneration, and a love of pregnancy (Parker 1983:140). As I began my own research I soon observed a remarkable degree of consistency or uniformity in surrogates' responses to questions about their initial motivations for becoming surrogates; it was as if they had all been given a script in which they espoused many of the motivations earlier catalogued by Parker, motivations that also, as I will show, reflect culturally accepted ideas about reproduction, motherhood, and family and are fully reinforced by the programs.[6] I also began to uncover several areas of conflict between professed motivations and actual experiences, discovering, for example, that although surrogates claim to experience "easy pregnancies" and "problem-free labor," it was not unusual for surrogates to have experienced miscarriages, ectopic pregnancies, and related difficulties, as the following examples reveal. Jeannie, age 36, divorced with one child and employed in the entertainment industry, described the ectopic pregnancy she experienced while she was a surrogate in this manner: "I almost bled to death: I literally almost died for my couple." Nevertheless, she was again inseminating a second time for the same couple. As this and other examples demonstrate, even when their experiences are at odds with their stated motivations, surrogates tend not to acknowledge inconsistencies between their initially stated motivations and their subsequent experiences. This reformulation of motivation is seen in the following instance as well. Fran, age 27, divorced with one child and working as a dog trainer, described the difficulty of her delivery in this way: "I had a rough delivery, a C-section, and my lung collapsed because I had the flu, but it was worth every minute of it. If I were to die from childbirth, that's the best way to die. You died for a cause, a good one." As both these examples illustrate, some surrogates readily embrace the idea of meaningful suffering, heroism, or sacrifice, and although their stated motivations are of some interest they do not adequately account for the range of shifting motivations uncovered in my research.

One of the motivations most frequently assumed to be primary by the casual observer is remuneration, and I took considerable pains to try to evaluate its influence on surrogates. In the programs, surrogates receive between $10,000 and $15,000 (for three to four months of insemination and nine months of pregnancy, on average), a fee that has changed only nominally since the early 1980s.[7] As one program psychologist explained, the amount paid to surrogates is intentionally held at an artificially low rate by the programs so as to screen out women who might be motivated solely by monetary gain. One of the questions I sought to explore was whether surrogates were denying the importance of remuneration in order to cast their actions in a more culturally acceptable light, or whether they were motivated in part by remuneration and in part by other factors (with the importance of remuneration decreasing as the pregnancy progresses, the version of events put forth by both program staff and surrogates).

The opinion popular among both scholars and the general population, that surrogates are motivated primarily by financial gain, has tended to result in oversimplified analyses of surrogate motivations. The following are typical of surrogate explanations for the connection between the initial decision to become a surrogate and the remuneration they receive. Dismissals of the idea that remuneration serves as a primary source of motivation for surrogates of the kind expressed by Fran were frequent: "It [surrogacy] sounded so interesting and fun. The money wasn't enough to be pregnant for nine months."

Andrea, age 29, was married with three children. A high school graduate who worked as a motel night auditor, she expressly denied the idea that remuneration motivates most surrogates. As she said here, "I'm not doing it for the money. Take the money: that wouldn't stop me. It wouldn't stop the majority."

Sara, age 27, who attended two years of college, was married with two children and worked part-time as a tax examiner. Here she explains her feelings about remuneration:

> What's 10,000 bucks? You can't even buy a car. If it was just for the money you will want the baby. Money wasn't important. I possibly would have done it just for expenses, especially for the people I did it for. My father would have given me the money not to do it.

The issue of remuneration proved to be of particular interest in that, although surrogates do accept monetary compensation for their reproductive work, its role is a multifaceted one. The surrogate pregnancy, unlike a traditional pregnancy, is viewed by the surrogate and her family as work; as such, it is informed by the belief that work is something that occurs only within the context of paid occupations (Ferree 1984:72). It is interesting to note that surrogates rarely spend the money they earn on themselves. Not one of the surrogates I interviewed spent the money she earned on herself alone; the majority spend it on their children—as a contribution to their college education funds, for example—while others spend it on home improvement, gifts for their husbands, a family vacation, or simply to pay off "family debts."

One of the primary reasons that most surrogates do not spend the money they earn on themselves alone appears to stem from the fact that the money serves as a buffer against and/or reward to their families—in particular to their husbands, who make a number of compromises as a result of the surrogate arrangement. One of these compromises is obligatory abstention from sexual intercourse with their wives from the time insemination begins until a pregnancy has been confirmed (a period of time that lasts on average from three to four months in length, but that may be extended for as long as one year).

Surrogacy is viewed by surrogates as a part-time job in the sense that it allows a woman, especially a mother, to stay at home—to have, as one surrogate noted, "the luxury of staying home with my children," an idea that is also attractive to their husbands. The fact that a surrogate need not leave home on a routine basis or in any formalized way to earn money is perceived by the surrogate and her husband as a benefit; the surrogate, however, consequently spends less time with her family as a result of a new schedule that includes medical appointments, therapy sessions, social engagements with the commissioning couple. Thus surrogates are able to use the monetary compensation they receive as a means of procuring their husbands' support when and if they become less available to the family because of their employment.

The devaluation of the amount of the surrogate payment by surrogates as insufficient to compensate for "nine months of pregnancy" serves several important purposes. First, this view is representative of the cultural belief that children are "priceless" (Zelizer 1985); in this sense surrogates are merely reiterating a widely held cultural belief when they devalue the amount of remuneration they receive. When, for example, the largest and one of the most well-established surrogate mother programs changed the wording of its advertising copy from "Help an Infertile Couple" to "Give the Gift of Life," the vastly increased volume of response revealed that the program had discovered a successful formula with which to reach the surrogate population. With surrogacy, the gift is conceptualized as a child, a formulation that is widely used in Euro-American culture—for example, in blood (Titmuss 1971) and organ donation (Fox and Swazey 1992).

The gift formulation holds particular appeal for surrogates because it reinforces the idea that having a child for someone is an act that cannot be compensated for monetarily. As I have already mentioned, the "gift of life" theme is further enhanced by some surrogates to embrace the near-sacrifice of their own lives in childbirth.

Fran, whose dismissal of the importance of payment I have already quoted, also offered another, more revealing account of her decision to become a surrogate mother: "I wanted to do the ultimate thing for somebody, to give them the ultimate gift. Nobody can beat that, nobody can do anything nicer for them." Stella, age 38, married with two children, noted that the commissioning couples "consider it [the baby] a gift and I consider it a gift." Carolyn, age 33, married with two children and the owner of a house-cleaning company, discussed her feelings about remuneration and having a surrogate child in these terms: "It's a gift of love. I have always been a really giving person, and it's the ultimate way to give. I've always had babies so easily. It's the ultimate gift of love."

As we can see, when surrogates characterize the child they reproduce for couples as a "gift," they are also suggesting tacitly that mere monetary compensation would never be sufficient to repay the debt incurred. Although this formulation may at first appear to be a reiteration of the belief that children are culturally priceless, it also suggests that surrogates recognize that they are creating a state of enduring solidarity between themselves and their couples—precisely as in the practice of exogamy, where the end result is "more profound than the result of other gift transactions, because the relationship established is not just one of reciprocity, but one of kinship" (Rubin 1975:172). As Rubin summarizes Mauss's poineering work on this subject, "the significance of gift giving is that [it] expresses, affirms, or creates a social link between the partners of exchange . . . confers upon its participants a special relationship of trust, solidarity and mutual aid" (1975:172).

Thus when surrogates frame the equation as one in which a gift is being proffered, the theme serves as a counterpoint to the business aspect of the arrangement, a reminder to them and to the commissioning couple that one of the symbolically central functions of money—the "removal of the personal element from human relationships through it(s) indifferent and objective nature" (Simmel 1978:297)—may be insufficient to erase certain kinds of relationships, and that the relational element may continue to surface despite the monetary exchange.

This formulation of surrogacy as a matter of altruism versus remuneration has also proved to be a pivotal issue in legislative debates and discussions. Jan Sutton, the founder and spokeswoman of the National Association of Surrogate Mothers (a group of more than 100 surrogates who support legislation in favor of surrogacy), stated in her testimony before an information-gathering session of the California state legislature in 1989: "My organization and its members would all still be surrogates if no payment was involved" (Ragoné 1989). Her sentiment is not unrepresentative of those expressed by the surrogates interviewed for this study. Interestingly enough, once Sutton had informed the committee of that fact, several of the members of the panel who had previously voiced their opposition to surrogacy in its commercial form began to express praise for Sutton, indicating that her testimony had altered their opinion of surrogacy.

In direct response to her testimony, the committee began instead to discuss a proposal to ban commercial surrogacy but to allow for the practice of noncommercial surrogacy. In the latter practice the surrogate is barred from receiving financial compensation for her work, although the physicians and lawyers involved are allowed their usual compensation for services rendered. In Britain, where commercial surrogacy has been declared illegal, the issue was framed often in moral terms: "The symbol of the pure surrogate who creates a child for love was pitted against the symbol of the wicked surrogate who prostitutes her maternity" (Cannell 1990:683). This dichotomous rendering in which "pure" surrogates are set in opposition to "wicked" surrogates is predicated on the idea that altruism precludes remuneration. In the Baby M Case, for example, the most decisive issue was the one concerning payment to the surrogate (Hull 1990:155).

Although surrogates overwhelmingly cast their actions in a traditional light, couching the desire to become a surrogate in conservative and traditionally feminine terms, it is clear that in many respects surrogate motherhood represents a departure from traditional motherhood. It transforms private motherhood into public motherhood, and it provides women with remuneration for their reproductive work—work that has in American culture been done, as Schneider has noted, for "love" rather than for "money" (Schneider 1968). It is this aspect that has unintendedly become one of the primary foci of consideration in state legislatures throughout the United States. Of the 15 states that now have surrogacy laws in place, the "most common regulations, applicable in 11 states . . . are statutes void-ing paid surrogacy contracts" (Andrews 1992:50). The overwhelming acceptance of the idea of unpaid or noncommercial surrogacy (both in the United States and in Britain) can be attributed to the belief that it "duplicates maternity in culturally the most self-less manner" (Strathern 1991:31).

But what is perhaps even more important, the corresponding rejection of paid or commercial surrogacy may also be said to result from a cultural resistance to con-flating the symbolic value of the family with the world of work to which it has long been held in opposition. From a legal perspective, commercial surrogacy has been viewed largely by the courts as a matter of "merg[ing] the family with the world of business and commerce" (Dolgin 1993:692), a prospect that presents a challenge to American cultural definitions in which the family has traditionally represented "the antithesis of the market relations of capitalism; it is also sacralized in our minds as the last stronghold against the state, as the symbolic refuge from the intrusion of a public domain that consistently threatens our sense of privacy and self determina-tion" (Collier et al. 1982:37).

Resistance in U. S. society to merging these two realms, the domestic and the public, may be traced to the entrenched belief that the

> private realm [is] where women are most in evidence, where natural functions like sex and bodily functions related to procreation take place, where the affective content of relations is primary and [that] a public realm [is] where men are most in evidence, where culture is produced, where one's efficiency at producing goods or services takes precedence. [Martin 1987:15–16]

With the introduction of the phenomenon of public motherhood in the form of surrogacy, however, the separation of family and work has been irrevocably chal-lenged. Over time it became clear to me that many of the women who chose to become surrogate mothers did so as a way to transcend the limitations of their domestic roles as wives, mothers, and homemakers while concomitantly attesting to the importance of those roles and to the satisfaction they derived from them. That idea indeed accounted for some of their contradictory statements. Surrogates, who are for the most part from predominantly working-class backgrounds, have, for example, often been denied access to prestigious roles and other avenues for attain-ing status and power. Surrogacy thus provides them with confirmation that moth-erhood is important and socially valued.[8] Surrogacy also introduces them to a world filled with social interaction with people who are deeply appreciative of the work that they do, and in this way surrogates receive validation and are rewarded for their reproductive work through their participation in this new form of public motherhood.

Of all the surrogates' stated motivations, remuneration proved to be the most problematic.[9] On a symbolic level, remuneration detracts from the idealized cul-tural image of women/mothers as selfless, nurturant, and altruistic, an image that surrogates have no wish to alter. Then, too, if surrogates were to acknowledge money as adequate compensation for their reproductive work, they would lose the sense that theirs is a gift that transcends all monetary compensation.[10] The fact that some surrogates had experienced difficult pregnancies and deliveries and were not thereby dissuaded from becoming surrogate mothers, coupled with their devaluation of remuneration and their tendency to characterize the child as a gift, suggested that current theories about surrogate motivations provided only a partial explanation for what was clearly a more complex phenomenon.

From the moment she places a telephone call to a surrogate mother program to the moment she delivers the child, the balance of power in a surrogate's personal life is altered radically. Her time can no longer be devoted exclusively to the care and nurture of her own family because she has entered into a legal and social contract to perform an important and economically rewarded task: helping an infertile couple to begin a family of their own. Unlike other types of employment, this activity cannot be regarded as unfeminine, selfish, or nonnurturant. As I have previously mentioned, the surrogate's husband must sign a consent form in which he agrees to abstain from sexual intercourse with his wife until a pregnancy has been confirmed. In so doing he agrees to relinquish both his sexual and procreative ties to his wife and thus is understood to be supporting his wife's decision to conceive and gestate another man's child (or another couple's child, in the case of gestational surrogacy). Once a surrogate enters a program, she also begins to recognize just how important having a child is to the commissioning couple. She sees with renewed clarity that no matter how much material success the couple has, their lives are emotionally impoverished because of their inability to have a child. In this way the surrogate's fertility serves as a leveling device for perceived, if unacknowledged, economic differences—and many surrogates begin to see themselves as altruistic or heroic figures who can rectify the imbalance in a couple's life.

Fathers, Adoptive Mothers, and Surrogate Mothers

Studies on surrogate motherhood have tended to characterize the couple's motivations as lacking in complexity; in other words, it is assumed that the primary motivation is to have a child that is biologically related to at least one member of the couple (in this case the father and, in the case of donor insemination, the mother) (Glover 1990). A tendency on the part of earlier researchers to accept this theory at face value may be said to stem from the influence of Euro-American kinship ideology, particularly from its emphasis on the centrality of biogenetic relatedness, and perhaps secondarily from the fact that researchers have not had ready access to this population. Biological relatedness thus continues to be accepted as a given, "one way of grounding the distinctiveness of kin relations ... the natural facts of life that seem to lie prior to everything else" (Strathern 1992a:19).[11]

While genetic relatedness is clearly one of the primary motivations for couples' choice of surrogate motherhood, this view is something of a simplification unless one also acknowledges that surrogacy contradicts several cultural norms, not the least of which is that it involves procreation outside marriage. The case of surrogate motherhood requires that we go beyond the parameters that until now have delineated domains such as reproduction and kinship, to "pursue meaning[s] where they lead" (Delaney 1986:496). Although couples may be motivated initially by a desire to have a child that is biologically related to at least one of the partners, the fact that this can only be achieved by employing the services of a woman other than the wife introduces a host of dilemmas.

Fathers and adoptive mothers resolve the problems posed by surrogate motherhood through various and separate strategies. Their disparate concerns stem not only from the biogenetic relationship the father bears to the child and from the adoptive mother's lack of such a relationship, but also from the pressures of having to negotiate the landscape of this novel terrain. For the father the primary obstacle or issue posed by surrogate motherhood is that a woman other than his wife will be the "mother" of his child. The following quotations from fathers illustrate the considerable degree of ambiguity created by surrogate motherhood. They also reveal the couples' shared assumptions about American kinship ideology and how it is that "biological elements have primarily symbolic significance ... [whose] meaning is not biology at all" (Schneider 1972:45).

Tom and his wife, for example, had experienced 17 years of infertility. Initially opposed to surrogate motherhood out of concern that his wife would feel "left out," Tom described his early reactions: "Yes, the whole thing was at first strange. I thought to myself; here she [the surrogate] is carrying my baby. Isn't she supposed to be my wife?"

Ed, a 45-year-old college professor, described a similar sense of confusion: "I felt weird about another woman carrying my child, but as we all got to know one another it didn't seem weird. It seemed strangely comfortable after a while."

Richard, age 43, a computer engineer, described similar feelings of awkwardness about the child's biological tie to the surrogate:

> Seeing Jane [the surrogate] in him [his son], it's literally a part of herself she gave. That's fairly profound. I developed an appreciation of the magnitude of what she did and the inappropriateness of approaching this as a business relationship. It didn't seem like such a big thing initially for another woman to carry my baby, a little awkward in not knowing how to relate to her and not wanting to interfere with her relationship with her husband. But after Tommy was born I can see Jane in his appearance, and I had a feeling it was a strange thing we did not to have a relationship with Jane. But it's wearing off, and I'm not struck so much with: I've got a piece of Jane here.

Questions such as Tom's "Isn't she supposed to be my wife?" reflect the concern and confusion experienced by husbands, their ambivalence underscoring the continued symbolic centrality of sexual intercourse and procreation in American kinship, both of which continue to symbolize unity and love (Schneider 1968). The father's relationship to the surrogate, although strictly noncoital, is altered by the fact that it produces what was always, until the recent past, the product of a sexual union—namely, a child. Feelings of discomfort or "awkwardness," and concerns as to how to behave toward the surrogate and the surrogate's husband, stem from the idea that the father-surrogate relationship may be considered adultery by those unfamiliar with the particulars of the surrogate arrangement. For example, one program reported that a client from the Middle East arrived at the program office with the expectation that he would engage in sexual intercourse with the surrogate. One surrogate remarked on this ambivalence: "The general public thinks I went to bed with the father. They think I committed adultery!"

In addition to concerns about his relationship to the surrogate vis-à-vis the child, a father is aware that the child bears no genetic tie to his wife. The husband thus gains his inclusivity in the surrogate relationship through his biological contribution vis-à-vis the surrogate: he is both the genitor and pater; but it is the surrogate, not his wife, who is the genetrix. One of the primary strategies employed by both couples and surrogates is to deemphasize the husband's role precisely because it is the surrogate-father relationship that raises the specter of adultery or, more accurately, temporary polygandry and temporary polygyny. They also downplay the significance of his biological link to the child, focusing instead on the bond that develops between the adoptive and the surrogate mother.

The Surrogate and Adoptive Mother Bond

The adoptive mother attempts to resolve her lack of genetic relatedness to the child through what I have labeled her "mythic conception" of the child—that is, the notion that her desire to have a child is what first makes the surrogate arrangement a possibility. Cybil, an adoptive mother, explained the mythic conception in this way: "Ann is my baby; she was conceived in my heart before Lisa's [the surrogate's] body." Lucy, an adoptive mother, described the symbiotic relationship that developed between herself and her surrogate in a slightly different way: "She [the surrogate] represented that part of me that couldn't have a child."

The adoptive mother also experiences what can be described as a "pseudopregnancy" through which she experiences the state of pregnancy by proxy—as close to the experience as an infertile woman can be. As one surrogate said of this relationship, "I had a closeness with Sue [the adoptive mother] that you would have with your husband. She took Lamaze class and went to the delivery room with me." In fact, when geographical proximity permits, it is expected in the open programs that adoptive mothers will accompany surrogates to all medical appointments and birthing classes, in addition to attending the delivery of the child in the hospital (where the biological father and the surrogate's husband are also present whenever possible).

Together, the surrogate and the adoptive mother thus define reproduction as "women's business," often reiterating the idea that their relationship is a natural and exclusive one. As Celeste, a surrogate mother, pointed out: "The whole miracle of birth would be lost if she [the adoptive mother] wasn't there. If women don't experience the birth of their children being born they would be alienated and they would be breeders." Mary, a surrogate whose adoptive mother gave her a heart-shaped necklace to commemorate the birth of the child, said, "I feel a sisterhood to all women of the world. I am doing this for her, looking to see her holding the baby."[12] Both of the adoptive mother's strategies, her mythic conception of the child and her pseudopregnancy, are—as these quotations demonstrate—greatly facilitated by the surrogate, who not only deemphasizes the importance of her physical pregnancy but also disavows the importance of her own biological link to the child. Celeste summed up the sentiment expressed by many surrogates when she stated, "She [the adoptive mother] was emotionally pregnant, and I was just *physically pregnant*" (emphasis added).

Without exception, when surrogates are asked whether they think of the child as their own, they say that they do not.[13] Kay, a surrogate, age 35 and divorced with two children, explained her feelings in this way: "I never think of the child as mine. After I had the baby, the mother came into the room and held the baby. I couldn't relate that it had any part of me."

Mary, age 37, married with three children, similarly stated, "I don't think of the baby as my child. I donated an egg I wasn't going to be using." Jeannie, yet another surrogate, described herself as having no connection to the child: "I feel like a vehicle, just like a cow; it's their baby, it's his sperm."

The surrogate's ability to deemphasize her own biological link to the child is made possible in part by her focus upon the folk theory of procreation in which paternity is viewed as the "primary, essential and creative role" (Delaney 1986:495). Even though in the realm of scientific knowledge women have long been identified as cocreators, "in Europe and America, the knowledge has not been encompassed symbolically. Symbols change slowly and the two levels of discourse are hardly ever brought into conjunction" (Delaney 1986:509).

With the "dominant folk theory of procreation in the West," paternity has been conceptualized as the "power to create and engender life" (Delaney 1986:510), whereas maternity has come to mean "giving nurturance and giving birth" (Delaney 1986:495). Surrogates therefore emphasize the importance of nurturance and consistently define that aspect of motherhood as a choice that one can elect to make or not make. This emphasis on nurturance is embraced readily by the surrogate and adoptive mother alike since "one of the central notions in the modern American construct of the family is that of nurturance "(Collier et al. 1982:34). In the United States nurturance until now has been considered "natural to women and [the] basis of their cultural authority" (Ginsburg 1987:629). Like other kinds of assisted reproduction, surrogate motherhood is understood to "fall into older cultural terrains, where women interpret their options in light of prior and contradictory meanings of pregnancy and childbearing" (Rapp 1990:41).

For this reason surrogates underplay their own biological contribution in order to bring to the fore the importance of the social, nurturant role played by the adoptive mother. The efforts of surrogates and adoptive mothers to separate social motherhood from biological motherhood can be seen to represent a reworking of the nature/culture dichotomy. A primary strategy an adoptive mother may employ in order to resolve her lack of genetic relatedness to the child is her use of the idea of intentionality, specifically of "conception in the heart"—that is, the idea that in the final analysis it is the adoptive mother's desire to have a child that brings the surrogate arrangement into being and ultimately results in the birth of a child. The surrogate thus devalues her own genetic/physical contribution while highlighting the pseudopregnancy of the adoptive mother and the importance of the latter's role as nurturer. In this way motherhood is reinterpreted as primarily an important social role in order to sidestep problematic aspects of the surrogate's biogenetic relationship to the child and the adoptive mother's lack of a biogenetic link. This focus upon intentionality and nurturance by both surrogates and adoptive mothers is reflected in the following statement by Andy, a 39-year-old surrogate, who is the divorced mother of two children and a full-time nurse:

> Parents are the ones who raise the child. I got that from my parents, who adopted children. My siblings were curious and my parents gave them the information they had and they never wanted to track down their biological parents. I don't think of the baby as mine; it is the *parents, the ones who raise the child,* that are important (emphasis added).

The adoptive mother and father of the child attempt to resolve the tensions inherent in the surrogate arrangement, in particular its rearrangement of boundaries through the blurring of the distinctions between pregnancy and motherhood, genetic relatedness and affective bonds, wife and mother, wife and husband, and wife and surrogate mother. The surrogate's role in achieving these goals is nevertheless essential. Through the process in which pregnancy and birth are defined as being exclusively women's business, the father's role is relegated to secondary status in the relational triangle. The surrogate plays a primary role in facilitating the adoptive mother's role as mother of the child, something that is made possible by her refusal to nurture the child to which she gives birth. In the interest of assisting this process the surrogate consistently devalues her biological contribution or genetic relationship to the child.

In this process of emphasizing the value of nurturance, surrogates describe motherhood as a role that one can adopt or refuse, and this concept of nurturance as choice is for them the single most important defining aspect of motherhood. Surrogates believe that, in the case of surrogacy, motherhood is comprised of two separable aspects: first, the biological process (insemination, pregnancy, and delivery); and second, the social process (nurturance). They reason that a woman can either choose to nurture—that is, to accept the role of social mother—or choose not to nurture, thereby rejecting the role of social mother.[14]

As we have seen, surrogates, couples, and surrogate mother programs work in concert to create a new idea of order and appropriate relations and boundaries by directing their attention to the sanctity of motherhood as it is illustrated in the surrogate and adoptive mother bond. The surrogate and adoptive mother work in unison, reinforcing one another's view that it is social rather than biological motherhood that ultimately creates a mother. Nurture, they reason together, is a far more important and central construct of motherhood than nature. The decision on the part of the surrogate not to nurture the child nullifies the value of biological motherhood, while the adoptive mother's choice to nurture activates or fully brings forth motherhood.

Because of the emphasis couples place on having a child that is biologically related to at least one partner, I was initially perplexed to learn that less than five percent of couples chose to have a paternity test performed once the child had been born (although this option is offered to every couple); surrogate contracts specifically state that the couple is under no obligation to accept the child until such a test has been performed. In view of the fact that couples spend between $40,000 and $45,000 in fees to have a child who is biologically related to them, such a lack of interest in the paternity test is initially perplexing. When asked about paternity testing, wives and husbands typically give responses such as these: "We knew she was ours from the minute we saw her," or "We decided that it really didn't matter; he was ours no matter what."

While these statements may initially appear to contradict the stated purpose of pursuing a partially biogenetic solution to childlessness, they can also be understood to fulfill two important purposes. From the wife's perspective, an element of doubt as to the child's paternity introduces a new variable that serves to equalize the issue of relatedness. The husband is of course aware that he has a decisive advantage over his wife in terms of his genetic relatedness to the child. Although paternal doubt is always present for males, in the case of surrogate motherhood paternal doubt is thereby culturally enhanced. Allowing paternal certainty to remain a mystery represents an attempt to redress symbolically the imbalance created between wife and husband through the surrogate arrangement. Before the advent of these reproductive technologies, the "figure of the mother provided a natural model for the social construction of the 'natural' facts" (Strathern 1991:5); motherhood was seen as a single, unified experience, combining both the social and biological aspects—unlike fatherhood, in which the father acquired a "double identity." With the separation of the social and biological elements, however, motherhood has, in the context of surrogacy, also acquired this double identity (Strathern 1991:4–5). In this way, surrogate motherhood thus produces the "maternal counterpart to the double identity of the father, certain in one mode and uncertain in another" (Strathern 1991:4).

All the participants in the surrogate motherhood triad work to downplay the importance of biological relatedness as it pertains to women. They tend to reinforce the idea of motherhood as nurturance so that the adoptive mother's inability to give birth or become a genetrix (both wife and mother) is of diminished importance. At the same time, the husband's relationship to the surrogate vis-à-vis the child, and his biological relationship to the child, is also deemphasized. The idea that the adoptive mother is a mother by virtue of her role as nurturer is frequently echoed by all parties concerned. In this sense motherhood, as it pertains to surrogacy, is redefined as a social role. This occludes the somewhat problematic issues of the surrogate's biogenetic relationship to the child and the adoptive mother's lack of such a relationship.

Thus the decision not to have a paternity test performed provides additional reinforcement for the idea of parenthood as a social construct rather than a biological phenomenon. The importance of the bond that develops between the surrogate and the adoptive mother is twofold: it merges the adoptive mother (or mater) and the surrogate (or genetrix) into one by reinforcing and maintaining the unity of experience, erasing the boundaries that surrogacy creates; and, at the same time, it establishes and maintains new boundaries as they are needed between surrogate and father.

I have attempted here to show that surrogates' stated motivations for choosing surrogate motherhood represent only one aspect of a whole complex of motivations. While surrogates do, as they say, enjoy being pregnant, desire to help an infertile couple to start a family of their own, and value the compensation they receive, there are other equally good—if not more—compelling reasons that motivate this unique group of women to become surrogate mothers. Biological relatedness is both the initial motivation for and the ultimate goal of surrogacy, and it is also that facet of surrogacy that makes it most consistent with the biogenetic basis of American kinship ideology. Nevertheless, it must be deemphasized—even devalued—by all the participants in order to make surrogacy consistent with American cultural values about appropriate relations between wives and husbands. In addition to broadening the scope of our understanding about the motivations of the couples who choose to pursue a surrogate solution, I hope that this article has illuminated the complexity of the couples' decision-making process as well as their motivation.

As we have seen, surrogates as a group tend to highlight only those aspects of surrogacy that are congruent with traditional values such as the importance of family. Like the couples, they also tend to deemphasize those aspects of the surrogate relationship that represent a departure from conventional beliefs about motherhood, reproduction, and the family. Interspersed with surrogates' assertions that surrogate motherhood is merely an extension of their conventional female roles as mothers, however, are frequent interjections about the unique nature of what they are doing. The following quotation, for example, reflects surrogates' awareness of the radical, unusual, and adventurous nature of their actions: "Not everyone can do it. It's like the steelworkers who walk on beams ten floors up. Not everyone can do it; not everyone can be a surrogate."

It is thus not surprising, in view of their socialization, their life experiences, and their somewhat limited choices, that surrogates claim that it is their love of children, pregnancy and family, and their desire to help others that motivates them to become surrogates. To do otherwise would be to acknowledge that there may be inconsistencies within, and areas of conflict between, their traditional female roles as wives, mothers, and homemakers and their newfound public personae as surrogate mothers.

In conclusion, it can be said that all the participants involved in the surrogacy process wish to attain traditional ends, and are therefore willing to set aside their reservations about the means by which parenthood is attained. Placing surrogacy inside tradition, they attempt to circumvent some of the more difficult issues raised by the surrogacy process. In this way, programs and participants pick and choose among American cultural values about family, parenthood, and reproduction, now choosing biological relatedness, now nurture, according to their needs.

Notes

This article has benefited greatly from the comments, suggestions, and encouragement of many individuals. I would like to express my gratitude to the late David Schneider for his support of my work, and for his pioneering work on American kinship without which my own research would have been considerably less complete. I would also like to thank Marilyn Strathern for her encouragement. Many thanks to my anonymous reviewers for their incisive comments. Special thanks are due also to the following individuals: Robbie Apfel, William Beeman, Carole Browner, Sarah Franklin, Lina Fruzzetti, Louise Lamphere, Lucile Newman, Rayna Rapp, Suasan Scrimshaw, Bennet Simon, and June Starr.

1. A couple, William and Elizabeth Stern, contracted with a surrogate, Mary Beth Whitehead, to bear a child for them because Elizabeth Stern suffered from multiple sclerosis, a condition that can be exacerbated by pregnancy. Once the child was born, however, Whitehead refused to relinquish the child to the Sterns, and in 1987, William Stern, the biological father, filed suit against Whitehead in an effort to enforce the terms of the surrogate contract. The decision of the lower court to award custody to the biological father and to permit his wife to adopt the child was overturned by the New Jersey Supreme Court, which then awarded custody to William Stern, prohibiting Elizabeth Stern from adopting the child while granting visitation rights to Mary Beth Whitehead. These decisions mirrored public opinion about surrogacy (Hull 1990:154).

2. See Rapp (1978:279) and Gordon (1988:3) for a historical analysis of the idea of the demise of the American family.

3. For a more extensive review of the literature, see, for example, Ginsburg and Rapp 1991.

4. As of 1994, only seven of the original ten are now in existence. I have changed the names of programs, surrogates, couples, and directors in order to protect their identities.

5. Over the years I have interviewed surrogates who had been employed by closed programs, interviewed the administrative assistant at the largest closed program, and spoken with program directors who arrange either a closed or open arrangement (depending upon the couple's choice). Many of the data presented in this article were collected in the open programs.

6. See, for example, Ragoné 1994 for a detailed account of the role of the surrogate mother program.

7. One of the programs has, however, recently increased its rate to $15,000. Surrogates also receive an allowance for maternity clothing, remuneration for time lost from work (if they have employment outside of the home), and reimbursement for all babysitting fees incurred as a result of surrogate-related activities.

8. The quantifiable data reveal that surrogates are predominantly white, an average of 27 years of age, high school graduates, of Protestant or Catholic background, and married with an average of three children. Approximately 30 percent are full-time homemakers, and those surrogates who are employed outside the home tend to be employed in the service sector. A comparison of surrogate and couple statistics reveals pronounced differences in educational background, occupation, and income level. The average combined family income of commissioning couples is in excess of $100,000, as compared to $38,000 for married surrogates.

9. For example, Gullestad (1992) observed that girls who worked as babysitters in Norway tended to emphasize the extent to which their work was motivated by nurturance, deemphasizing the importance of the remuneration they received.

10. Surrogate motivations are diverse and overlapping, and surrogates express empathy for infertile couples as well as joy experienced during pregnancy.

11. Commissioning couples consistently articulate the belief that surrogacy is a superior alternative to adoption. Many couples have attempted to adopt, only to discover the shortage of healthy white infants and age limit criteria of adoption agencies: see Ragoné 1994. Surrogacy not only provides them with the highly desirable partial-genetic link (through the father), but it also permits them to meet and interact with the biological mother—something that is usually not possible with adoption.

12. When Robert Winston, a pioneer in assisted reproductive technologies in Britain, revealed that he had facilitated a surrogate arrangement that involved two sisters, the case tended to elicit from the public "strong and sentimental approval" (Cannell 1990:675).

13. Prospective surrogates who find themselves unwilling to dismiss their biological link to a child frequently opt for gestational surrogacy rather than abandon the idea of surrogate motherhood altogether, even though the risk of medical complication is thereby greatly increased. Over a three-year period I observed that the rate of gestational surrogacy had increased from less than five percent to close to fifty percent at the largest of the surrogate mother programs and at another well-established program. I am currently in the process of researching gestational surrogacy.

14. Giddens's theory of structuration is understood as a corrective to both the exclusively rigid structuralist worldview (which tends to eliminate agency) and phenomenologists, symbolic interactionists, and enthnomethodologists who overemphasize the plasticity of society (Baber 1991:220). Giddens has articulated the view that "all structural properties of social systems are enabling as well as constraining" (1984:177), a phenomenon that can be seen in surrogate arrangements when surrogates and couples focus upon certain elements or aspects of parenthood while deemphasizing others. The way in which these different idioms of nature and nuture are emphasized and deemphasized also parallels and substantiates Strathern's observations (1992c) about the selective weight of nature/nurture in the kinship context.

Works Cited

Annas, George
    1988. Fairy Tales Surrogate Mothers Tell. *In* Surrogate Motherhood: Politics and Privacy. Larry Gostin, ed. Pp. 43–55. Bloomington: Indiana University Press.
Andrews, Lori
    1984. New Conceptions: A Consumer's Guide to the Newest Infertility Treatments. New York: Ballantine.
    1992. Surrogacy Wars. California Lawyer 12(10):42–49.
Baber, Zaheer
    1991. Beyond the Structure/Agency Dualism: An Evaluation of Giddens' Theory of Structuration. Sociological Inquiry 61(2):219–230
Browner, Carole
    1986. The Politics of Reproduction in a Mexican Village. Signs 11:710–724.
Cannell, Fenella
    1990. Concepts of Parenthood: The Warnock Report, the Gillick and Modern Myths. American Ethnologist 17:667–686.
Collier, Jane, Michelle Rosaldo, and Sylvia Yanagisako
1982. Is There a Family? New Anthropological Views. *In* Rethinking the Family: Some Feminist Questions. Barrie Thorne and Marilyn Yalom, eds. Pp. 25–39. New York: Longman.
Delaney, Carol
    1986. The Meaning of Paternity and the Virgin Birth Debate. Man 24 (3):497–513.
    1991. The Seed and the Soil: Gender and Cosmology in a Turkish Village Society. Berkeley: University of California Press.

Dolgin, Janet
  1993. Just a Gene: Judicial Assumptions about Parenthood. UCLA Law Review 40(3).
Dworkin, Andrea
  1978. Right-Wing Women. New York: Perigee Books.
Ferree, Myra
  1984. Sacrifice, Satisfaction and Social Change: Employment and the Family. *In* My
    Troubles Are Going to Have Trouble with Me. Karen Sacks and Dorothy Remy, eds.
    Pp. 61–79. New Brunswick, NJ: Rutgers University Press.
Fox, Renée, and Judith Swazey
  1992. Spare Parts: Organ Replacement in American Society. Oxford: Oxford University
    Press.
Giddens, Anthony
  1984. The Constitution of Society. Berkeley: University of California Press.
Ginsburg, Faye
  1987. Procreation Stories: Reproduction, Nurturance and Procreation in Life Narra-
    tives of Abortion Activists. American Ethnologist 14(4):623–636.
  1989. Contested Lives: The Abortion Debate in an American Community. Berkeley:
    University of California Press.
Ginsburg, Faye, and Rayna Rapp
  1991. The Politics of Reproduction. Annual Review of Anthropology 20:311–343.
Glover, Jonathan
  1990. Ethics of New Reproductive Technologies: The Glover Report to the European
    Commission. DeKalb: Northern Illinois Press.
Gordon, Linda
  1988. Heroes of Their Own Lives. New York: Viking.
Gullestad, Marianne
  1992. The Art of Social Relations. Oslo, Norway: Scandinavian Press.
Hull, Richard
  1990. Gestational Surrogacy and Surrogate Motherhood. *In* Ethical Issues in the New
    Reproductive Technologies. Richard Hull, ed. Pp. 150–155. Belmont, CA:
    Wadsworth Publishers.
Leach, Edmund R.
  1967. Virgin Birth. *In* Proceedings of the Royal Anthropological Institute for 1966.
    Pp. 39–49. London: RAI.
Martin, Emily
  1987. The Woman in the Body: A Cultural Analysis of Reproduction. Boston: Beacon
    Press.
Modell, Judith
  1989. Last Chance Babies: Interpretations of Parenthood in an In Vitro Fertilization
    Program. Medical Anthropology Quarterly 3(2):124–138.
Neuhaus, Robert
  1988. Renting Women, Buying Babies and Class Struggles. Society 25(3):8–10.
Newman, Lucile, ed.
  1985. Women's Medicine: A Cross-Cultural Study of Indigenous Fertility Regulations.
    New Brunswick, NJ: Rutgers University Press.
Parker, Philip
  1983. Motivation of Surrogate Mothers: Initial Findings. American Journal of Psychia-
    try 140:117–119.
Ragoné, Helena
  1989. Proceedings from an information-gathering committee to the California State
    Legislature. Unpublished notes.

1991. Surrogate Motherhood in America. Ph.D. dissertation, Brown University.

1994. Surrogate Motherhood: Conception in the Heart. Boulder, CO, and Oxford: Westview Press/Basic Books.

Rapp, Rayna

1978. Family and Class in Contemporary America: Notes toward an Understanding of Ideology. Science and Society 42(3):278–300.

1987. Moral Pioneers: Women, Men and Fetuses on a Frontier of Reproductive Technology. Women and Health 13(1/2):101–116.

1988. Chromosomes and Communication: The Disclosure of Genetic Counseling. Medical Anthropology Quarterly 2:143–157.

1990. Constructing Amniocentesis: Maternal and Medical Discourses. In Uncertain Terms: Negotiating Gender in American Culture. Faye Ginsburg and Anna Lowenhaupt Tsing, eds. Pp. 28–42. Boston: Beacon Press.

Rubin, Gayle

1975. The Traffic in Woman: Notes on the Political Economy of Sex. In Toward an Anthropology of Women. Rayna Reiter, ed. Pp. 157–210. New York: Monthly Review Press.

Schneider, David

1968. American Kinship: A Cultural Account. Englewood Cliffs, NJ: Prentice Hall.

1972. What Is Kinship All About? In Kinship Studies in the Morgan Centennial Year. Priscilla Reining, ed. Pp. 32–63. Washington, DC: Anthropological Society of Washington.

Scrimshaw, Susan

1978. Infant Mortality and Behavior in the Regulation of Family Size. Population Development Review 4:383–403.

Simmel, Georg

1978. The Philosophy of Money. London: Routledge and Kegan Paul.

Snowden, R. G. Mitchell, and E. Snowden

1983. Artificial Reproduction: A Social Investigation. London: Allen and Unwin.

Spiro, Melford

1968. Virgin Birth, Parthenogenesis, and Physiological Paternity: An Essay in Cultural Interpretation. Man (n.s.) 3:242–261.

Strathern, Marilyn

1991. The Pursuit of Certainty: Investigating Kinship in the Late Twentieth Century. Paper presented at the 90th American Anthropological Association Annual Meeting, Chicago.

1992a. Reproducing the Future. New York: Routledge.

1992b. The Meaning of Assisted Kinship. In Changing Human Reproduction. Meg Stacey, ed. Pp. 148–169. London: Sage Publications.

1992c. After Nature: English Kinship in the Late Twentieth Century. Cambridge: Cambridge University Press.

Titmuss, Richard

1971. The Gift Relationship: From Human Blood to Social Policy. New York: Pantheon Books.

Zelizer, Vivian

1985. Pricing the Priceless Child. New York: Basic Books.

7 Constructing Amniocentesis

Maternal and Medical Discourses

RAYNA RAPP

> When we walked into the doctor's office, both my husband and I were crying. He looked up and said, "What's wrong? Why are you in tears?" "It's the baby, the baby is going to die," I said. "That isn't a baby," he said firmly. "It's a collection of cells that made a mistake."
>
> —Leah Rubinstein, white housewife, 39

The language of biomedical science is powerful. Its neutralizing vocabulary, explanatory syntax, and distancing pragmatics provide universal descriptions of human bodies and their life processes that appear to be pre-cultural or non-cultural. But as the field of medical anthropology constantly reminds us, bodies are also and always culturally constituted, and their aches, activities, and accomplishments are continuously assigned meanings. While the discourse of biomedicine speaks of the inevitable march of scientific and clinical progress, its practices are constantly open to interpretation. Its hegemonic definitions routinely require acceptance, transformation, or contestation from the embodied "objects" whose subjectivity it so powerfully affects.

The necessary contest over the meaning assigned embodied experiences is particularly clear in the field of reproductive health care, where consumer movements, women's health activism, and feminist scholars have sharply criticized biomedical practices. Public accusations against the demeaning and controlling nature of gynecological and obstetrical health care have led to dramatic results. Over the last 20 years, such criticisms have influenced the reform of medical services, occasionally encouraged the development of alternative health practices, and often inspired women to advocate for themselves and others. Contests over the means and meanings of women's reproductive health services are, thus, an ongoing part of American social and institutional life. These conflicts reflect the complex hierarchies of power, along which both providers and consumers of health care are organized. They cannot easily be resolved because the practices of biomedicine are at once emancipatory and socially controlling, essential for healthy survival yet essentializing of women's lives.

Reproductive medicine and its feminist critique thus share a central concern with the problem of female identity. In both discourses, as throughout much of American culture, motherhood stands as a condensed symbol of female identity. Changes in sexual practices, pregnancy, and birth are widely believed to be transforming the meaning of "womanhood" itself. This connection between women's reproductive patterns and a notion of female gender is longstanding: cries of alarm have been raised for over a century concerning the future of "the sex" as birth control practices spread, as abortion was criminalized and medicalized, as childbirth moved from the hands of female lay practitioners to male professionals, and as a discourse of explicitly female sexual pleasure became articulated. There is, of course, great diversity in women's experiences with medical care in general, and the medicalization of sexual activity and reproduction in particular. Yet, the image of "womanhood" as a central symbol in American culture has often been constructed as if motherhood were its stable and uniform core, threatened by external changes in technology, education, labor force participation, medicine, and the like.

This shared and shifting object of embodied gender is revealed when we examine what have come to be called "the new reproductive technologies," dramatic and well-publicized interventions into fertility, conception, and pregnancy management and screening. Biomedical claims about the NRTs are usually framed in the available language of neutral management of female bodies to ensure progress; feminist critiques are often enunciated as protection of women's core experiences against intrusion by "technodocs." Both discourses are fraught with old assumptions about the meaning of pregnancy, itself an archetypically liminal state. And both discourses are shot through with contradictions and possibilities for the health care providers, pregnant women, and feminist commentators who currently must make sense of the rapid routinization of new reproductive technologies.

This article presents an analysis of amniocentesis, one of the new reproductive technologies.[1] My examples are drawn from an ongoing field study of the social impact and cultural meaning of prenatal diagnosis in New York City, where I have observed more than 250 intake interviews, in which genetic counselors interact with pregnant patients; interviewed over 70 current users and refusers of amniocentesis; collected stories of 30 women who received what is so antiseptically referred to as a "positive diagnosis" (i.e., that something was wrong with their fetus); and participated and interviewed in a support group for parents of children with Down syndrome, the most commonly diagnosed chromosome abnormality, and the condition for which pregnant women are most likely to seek amniocentesis.[2]

In New York City, unlike many other parts of the United States, prenatal diagnosis is funded by both Medicaid and the City's Health Department, so it is available to a population of women whose ethnic, class, racial, and religious backgrounds are as diverse as the City itself. The City's cytogenetic laboratory through which I work reaches a population of pregnant women who are approximately one-third Hispanic, one-third African-American, and one-third white, according to the racial/ethnic categories provided by both the City and State Health Departments. But these categories undoubtedly conceal as much as they reveal. At the present time, "Hispanic" includes Puerto Ricans and Dominicans long familiar with City services and the "new migrants" of Central America, many of whom are drawn from rural backgrounds, are desperately poor, and are often undocumented, as well as middle-class, highly educated Colombians and Ecuadorians who may be experiencing downward mobility through migration. African-Americans include fourth-generation New Yorkers, women whose children circle back and forth between the City and rural Alabama, and Haitians who have lived in Brooklyn only a few months. "White" encompasses Ashkenazi and Sephardic Jews, Irish, Italian, and Slavic Catholics, Episcopalian and Evangelical Protestants, as if being neither Black nor Brown placed them in a homogenized racial category. The categories themselves thus freeze a "racial map," which ignores the historic complexity of identity endemic to New York, and many other urban areas in contemporary America. Despite any understanding of the historical processes by which such a map has been created and promulgated, it is nearly impossible to escape its sociological boundaries when conducting and describing fieldwork in New York City.

My interviews and observations are tuned to the tension between the universal abstract language of reproductive medicine, and the personal experiences pregnant women articulate in telling their amniocentesis stories. Differences among women are revealed in their reasons for accepting or refusing the test; their images of fetuses and of disabled children; and the meaning of abortion in their lives. My working assumption is that a conflict of discourses necessarily characterizes the arena of reproductive technology, where nothing is stable: scientific "information," popular struggles both feminist and anti-feminist, and the shifting meaning of maternity and womanhood for individuals and communities with diverse ethnic, racial, religious, sexual, and migration histories are all currently under negotiation.

As one of the new reproductive technologies, prenatal diagnosis makes powerful claims to reveal and characterize biological bodies. Bypassing women's direct experiences of pregnancy, prenatal diagnosis uses sonography, an amniotic tap, and laboratory karyotyping to describe fetal health and illness to the woman (and her support network) within whose body the fetus grows.[3] Prenatal diagnosis focuses on pregnancy, first decontextualizing it and then inscribing it in a universal chronology, location, and ontology. Maternal serum alphafetoprotein blood screens (MSAFP), for example, may suggest a neural tube defect if readings are too high for a given pregnancy's dates, or a fetus with Down syndrome if values are too low. But the calibration of values is tricky, and potentially abnormal results must be recalibrated against a sonogram, whose measurement of cranial circumference and femur length is commonly considered the most accurate indicator of pregnancy dates. There is thus ample room for negotiating interpretations within the biomedical model. Many women already hold firm opinions about the dating of their pregnancies before they become acquainted with this highly technical process. Any woman may insist that she knows exactly when she became pregnant, or date her own growing pregnancy by signs phenomenologically available only to herself, contesting the narrative strategy of MSAFP, LMP (last menstrual period), and sonodates. But when pregnancies are medically managed, most women learn to redescribe their bodily changes through the language of technology, rather than dating their pregnancies experientially. There is thus a continuous negotiation circling the description of any pregnancy in which a woman reveals and embeds herself and her perceptions of her fetus in a language shot through with medical, personal, and communal resources.

The Language of Testing

Women use very different language and reasons in describing their acceptance or refusal of the test. When I first began interviewing middle-class pregnant women about their amniocentesis decisions, it was hard for me to hear their cultural constructions, for, like my, own, they mirrored the progressive message of science. Most (but not all) middle-class women, a disproportionately white group, accepted the test with some variant of this statement:

> I always knew I'd have amnio. Science is there to make life better, so why not use its power? Bill and I really want a child, but we don't want a baby with Down's, if we can avoid it. (Susan Klein, white accountant, 37)

But even white, middle-class women often express ambivalence, and they do so in a language intricately intertwined with the language of medicine itself. Their fears and fantasies reflect thoughts that both question and sustain the dominant discourse itself, for example:

> I cried for two days after I had the test. I guess I was identifying with universal motherhood; I felt like my image of my womb had been shattered. It still feels like it's in pieces, not like such a safe place as before. I guess technology gives us a certain kind of control, but we have to sacrifice something in return. I've lost my brash confidence that my body just produces healthy babies all by itself, naturally, and that if it doesn't, I can handle whatever comes along as a mother. (Carola Mirsky, white school teacher, 39)

The low-income African-American women with whom I talked were far less likely to either accept, or be transformed by, the medical discourse of prenatal diagnosis. American black women who had grown up in the South, especially the rural South, often described alternate, non-medical agendas in their use of amniocentesis, invoking other systems for interpreting bodily states, including pregnancy. Dreams, visions, healing sessions, root work, and herbal teas could be used to reveal the state of a specific pregnancy. One such woman, who at 27 became the mother of a Down syndrome baby, told me she had been refused amniocentesis in five city hospitals, always because of her young age. When I asked why she had wanted the test, she described a dream which recurred throughout the pregnancy:

> So I am having this boy baby. It is definitely a boy baby. And something is wrong, I mean, it just is not right. Sometimes, he is missing an arm, and sometimes, it's a leg. Maybe it's a retarded baby. You can't really tell, it's all covered in hair. Once or twice, they give him to my husband and say, "look at your son, take him the way he is." As if the way he is isn't all right. I tried to get that test to make peace with that dream (Q: Would you have had an abortion if you'd had the test?) Oh, no. The whole thing was going back to the dreams . . . just so's I could say, "this is the baby in the dreams" and come to peace with it. (May Norris, African-American hospital orderly, 27)

Another African-American woman, pregnant with a fourth, unexpected child at the age of 42, had this to say:

> So I was three months pregnant before I knew I was pregnant, just figured it was change of life. The clinic kept saying no, and it's really the same signs, menopause and pregnancy, you just feel that lousy. So when they told me I was pregnant I thought about abortion, I mean, maybe I figured I was too old for this. But in my neighborhood a lot of Caribbean women have babies, a lot of them are late babies. So I got used to it. But the clinic doctor was freaked out. He sent me for genetic counseling. Counseling? I thought counseling meant giving reassurance, helping someone accept and find their way. Wisdom, help, guidance, you know what I mean. This lady was a smart lady, but right away she started pullin' out pictures of mongoloids. So I got huffy: "I didn't come here to look at pictures of mongoloids," I says to her. So she got huffy and told me it was about mongoloids, this counseling. So we got more and more huffy between us, and finally, I left. Wasn't gonna sit and listen to that stuff. By the time I got myself to the appointment (for the test) I'd been to see my healing woman, a healer, who calmed me down, gave me the reassurance I needed. I knew everything was gonna be ok. Oh, I wouldn't have had an abortion that late in the game. I just got helped out by the healer woman, so I could wait out the results of that test without too much fussin'. (Naiumah Foster, school teacher, 43)

And among women whose background includes no prior encounter with the scientific description of amniocentesis, the test may be accepted out of the desire to avoid the suffering of children; a respect for the authority of doctors (or the conflated image of genetic counselors in white coats); or simple curiosity. One recently arrived Salvadoran, now working as a domestic, told me, for example, that she wanted the test because science had such miraculous powers to show you what God had in store. This mixing of religious and secular discourses is no less awed (and awesome!) than that of the native-born professional woman who told me she wanted her test to be an advancement to science. She knew it was the only way geneticists could legally obtain amniotic fluid for their research, to which she ardently wished to make a contribution. Both women characterized amniocentesis as a path of enlightenment, but their motivations for its use differed sharply. The one characterized it in terms of God's grace; the other in light of scientific progress.

Even those rejecting the test often express amazement and interest in the powers of reproductive medicine. A Haitian Evangelist who said she would never accept amniocentesis wavered briefly when she learned it could tell her the sex of her baby: did such information cost more, she queried? (as the mother of four daughters, she had high hopes and great curiosity). Among those rejecting the test, reasons included anti-abortion attitudes often (but not always) articulated in religious terms[4]; fear of losing the baby after medical invasion[5]; anger and mistrust of the medical system; and fear of needles.

When I first began observing counseling sessions, it was easy for me to share the psychological lingo many counselors use privately, in evaluating patients' motives for accepting or rejecting the test. A discourse of fluent Freudian phrases is used by counselors trained in psychological-psychoanalytic thinking, as well as in human genetics. Women may easily be labeled "denying," "regressed," "passive," or "fatalistic" when their choices are seen as irrational to professionals trained to balance empathy against epidemiological statistics. Such labels, however, reduce social phenomena and cultural contexts to individual idiosyncrasies. I have often observed communication gaps, negotiated decisions, and situations of multiple meaning, which cannot be understood when reduced to a model of individual decisionmaking. When a Puerto Rican garment worker, aged 39, who is a Charismatic Catholic, replied to the offer of "the needle test," "No, I take this baby as God's love, just the way it is, Hallelujah," one genetics counselor felt hard pressed to understand what was going on. It was easier to fall back upon individualizing psycho-speak than to acknowledge the complexity of the patient's cultural life, which profoundly influenced her choices. When a Hungarian-born artist, 38, refused amniocentesis because "it wouldn't be done in my country until 40, and besides, we are all very healthy," I observed a genetics counselor probe extensively into genealogy, and finally discover one possibly Ashkenazi Jewish grandparent. Because of this, the counselor was able to recommend Tay-Sacks screening. Visibly shaken, the pregnant woman agreed. In instances such as these, the hegemonic discourse of science encounters cultural differences of nationality, ethnicity, or religion and often chooses to reduce them to the level of individual defensiveness. Yet what is being negotiated (or not negotiated, in the first example) is the power of scientific technology to intersect and rewrite the languages previously used for the description of pregnancies, fetuses, and family problems.

What Is Seen

Whether they accepted or refused amniocentesis, virtually all the women with whom I spoke had undergone a sonogram by the mid-trimester of pregnancy. My data on images of fetuses have been collected in light of the powerful restructuring of experience and understanding this piece of obstetrical technology has already accomplished. Several native Spanish-speaking women (both poor and middle-class) described their fetuses in nontechnological imagery: "it's a liquid baby, it won't become a solid baby until the seventh month"; "it's like a little lizard in there, I think it has a tail"; "it's a cauliflower, a bunch of lumps growing inside me." Their relative autonomy from technological imagery may be due as much to having recently emigrated from countries and regions where hospital-based prenatal care is both less common and less authoritative, as to anything inherently "Hispanic."

Most women were fascinated with the glimpses they received of the fetal beating heart; its imagery fits nicely into a range of Christian symbols. And several were also impressed by the fetal brain, which is measured during sonography. Heart and brain, feeling and intellect, are already subjects of prenatal speculation among women for whom fetal imaging has been objectified.

Most women born in the United States, whatever their ethnic and class background, invoked the visual language of sonography and its popular interpretation to answer my query, "Tell me what the pregnancy feels and looks like to you now?"

For one it was "a little space creature, alone in space";[6] for another it was "a crea-ture, a tiny formed baby creature, but because its eyes are closed, it is only a half baby." Another woman told me that as her pregnancy progressed, she felt the fetus's image becoming more finely tuned in, like a television picture coming into better focus. White middle-class women (especially those having a first baby) frequently spoke of following fetal development in books which included week-by-week sono-grams. Thus, technological imagery is reproduced in text as well as image, avail-able to be studied privately, at home, as well as in public, medical facilities. Learning about what the technology can do, and about what the baby appears to be, proceed simultaneously.

Poorer women were unlikely to have such primers, but they, too, had been bom-barded by the visualization of fetuses (and amniocentesis, with its attendant moral dilemmas) in the popular media. When asked where they first learned about amnio-centesis, many Hispanic and white working-class women mentioned three episodes of "Dallas" in which prenatal diagnosis plays a large part, and one African-Ameri-can woman said she knew about Down syndrome "because the Kennedys had one" in a story she'd read in the *National Enquirer.* In the weeks following a Phil Don-ahue show devoted to Down syndrome children and their families, clinic patients spoke with great interest about that condition. Increasingly, health care providers must confront the popularization of their technologies, with all its attendant ben-efits and distortions, in their interviews with patients.

The widespread deployment of sonographic imagery is hardly innocent. What-ever its medical benefits, the cultural contests it enables are by now well known: anti-abortion propaganda is shot through with sonographic images, to which those who would defend abortion rights have had to respond.[7] Some people use this tech-nology for political advantage in medical settings, as well as in popular culture. Sev-eral genetic counselors offered stories about Right-to-Life sonographers who aggressively insisted on delivering detailed verbal descriptions of fetuses and hand-ing fetal images to women who were planning to have abortions after positive diag-noses. While this punitive behavior may seem excessive, even the seemingly neutral language of reproductive medicine affects pregnant women, who sometimes describe themselves as "maternal environments" in interviews. Until well after World War II, there were no medical technologies for the description of fetuses independent of the woman in whose body a given pregnancy was growing. Now, sciences like "perinatology" focus on the fetus itself, bypassing the consciousness of the mother, and permitting her, as well as biomedical personnel, to image the fetus as a separate entity. I will return to the importance of this internal disconnection and reconnection to fetal imagery in the next section.

Because amniocentesis was explicitly developed to probe for chromosome-based disabilities and confront a woman with the choice to end or continue her pregnancy based on its diagnostic powers, my interview schedule includes questions about the images of disabled fetuses women carry and disabled children they might raise. Here, too, television and magazine representations of disability loom large. One Peruvian factory worker who had lived in New York for 14 years spoke of them as

Jerry kids (a reference to Jerry Lewis' telethons—an image hotly contested by the disability rights movement). A white working-class woman who had adopted two disabled children told this story about arriving at her maternal choices watching the telethons:

> Ever since I was a little girl, I always watched those telethons, I always knew it was a shame, a crying shame that no one loved those kids enough. So when I was a teenager, I got to be a candy-striper, and I worked with kids in wheelchairs, and I always knew I'd adopt them before I'd have them for myself. I'm not afraid of problems. I've got a daughter with spina bifida, and they said she'd be a vegetable. Fat chance! My other one's gonna be mentally retarded. I can handle it. I learned these kids need love on the telethon. (Lisa Feldman, white home maker, 26)

Most women in my sample could recall someone in their own childhood or community who had a child with Down syndrome. Their memories invoke mothers intensely involved and devoted. Many described positive relationships that women had with their mentally retarded children. And some even talked about the hidden benefits of having a "permanent child" as the mother herself grew older, and became widowed. Most middle-class women, however, drew a contrast between themselves and those Down syndrome mothers they had encountered:

> It's too much work. There's a certain kind of relationship I want to have with my child, and it isn't like that one, that's so dependent, forever. I wouldn't be any good at it; I'd resent my child. (Ilene Cooper, white college professor, 40)

> Oh, I know I'd work really hard at it, I'd throw myself into it, but I'm afraid I'd lose myself in the process. I wouldn't be like her, she was a really great mother, so self-sacrificing. (Laura Forman, white theater producer, 35)

> My aunt was terrific. But she stayed home. I know I'm going back to work after this baby is born, and I can't imagine what it would take to do it her way. (Susan Klein, white accountant, 37)

What accompanied these she/me distinctions in the discourse of white, middle-class women was a running battle over the question of selfishness and self-actualization, a problem linked to the central importance of "choice" as a cultural value and strategy. This is a subject to which I will return below.

Working-class and low-income African-American women were no less concerned about the possible diagnosis of Down syndrome, but they often saw their decision-making as taking place within networks of support. One low-income African-American single mother expressed strong anti-abortion sentiments, but requested the test. Had the results been positive, she intended to move home to Georgia, where her mother would help her to raise a baby with health problems. A Black secretary married to a Black plumber chose to end her third pregnancy after a prenatal diagnosis of Down syndrome. When I asked her how she'd made the decision, and who had given her advice, support, or criticism, she described the active involvement of clergy and community members in the church to which she belonged.

Among many Hispanic women, mostly working-class and low-income (both those choosing and refusing amniocentesis), the image of mothering a disabled child conjured less ambivalence than among white, middle-class women. Friends and relations with sickly children were recalled, and testimonies about the sacrificial qualities of maternity were offered. There was often a conflation of maternal and child suffering, including this madonna-like image:

> When they told me what the baby would suffer, I decided to abort. But it was Easter, so I couldn't do it, I just couldn't do it until His suffering was ended. Then my child could cease to suffer as well. (Lourdes Ramirez, Dominican house cleaner, 41)

The Meaning of Abortion

The meaning of abortion loomed large in the consciousness of pregnant women discussing amniocentesis. All women could articulate reasons for and against late abortion after a prenatal diagnosis of a serious condition. These included the evaluation of the child's suffering; the imagined effects of a disabled baby on other siblings and on the parents themselves; the sense of responsibility for having brought a baby into the world who might never grow to "independence"; and, sometimes, the "selfishness" of wanting one's own life to be free of the burdens a disabled child is thought to impose. For Hispanic women, fear of the child's suffering was most salient, followed closely by the effects its birth would have on other children. They were, in principle, more accepting of the sacrifices they imagined disabled children to call forth from their mothers. It is hard to disentangle ethnicity, language, class, and religion in these responses. As one Honduran domestic worker awaiting amniocentesis results told me:

> Could I abort if the baby was going to have that problem? God would forgive me, surely, yes, I could abort. Latin Catholics, we are raised to fear God, and to believe in His love and forgiveness. Now, if I were Evangelical, that's another story. It's too much work, being Evangelical. My sisters are both Evangelicals, they go to Church all the time. There's no time for abortion for them. (Maria Acosta, 41)

Many Hispanic women reported having had early, multiple abortions and did not discuss the procedure as morally problematic. Yet many also identified *late* abortion as a sin, because quickening has occurred. In this case, a set of subtle and differentiated female experiences is being developed as popular theology.

Low-income African-American women weighed non-medical agendas in deciding to accept amniocentesis and possibly consider abortion: confirmation of dreams, prior omens, and use of healers all figured in the stories they told about why the test might be of use to them. Many low-income Hispanic women appear wrapped up in intertwined images of maternal and child suffering. White middle-class women seem most vulnerable to the abortion controversy currently raging in our national, political culture. Virtually all of the women I interviewed from this group, whether Catholic, Jewish, or Protestant, provided critical exegeses on the tension between "selfishness" and "self-actualization." Again and again, in assessing the possibility or the reality of aborting a disabled fetus, women quesioned whether that decision would be selfish. Their concerns revealed something of the limits of self-sacrifice that mothers are alleged to embody.

> I share a lot of the feelings of the Right-to-Life Movement, I've always been shocked by the number of abortion clinics, the number of abortions, in this city. But when it was *my* turn, I was grateful to find the right doctor. He helped me to protect my own life, and that's a life, too. (Mary Fruticci, white home maker, 44)

This reflection over selfishness and self-actualization is mirrored in two counter-discourses, one particularly "male," one more classically "female." Several middle-class white husbands went to some length to point out that a decision to bring a disabled child into the world knowingly was, in their view, "selfish":

> If you have a child that has severe defects, the natural thing I think that would happen would be that it would die at a very early age and what you're doing is you're prolonging, artificially, the child. And I think that most of the people that do that, do it for themselves, they don't really do it for the child, and it tends to be a very selfish thing for people to do. (Jim Norton, white lawyer, 42)

Their inversion of selfishness neatly reverses the vector of blame, which Right-to-Life imagery would pin on their wives.

Several white middle-class women articulated a different discourse, one which confronted selfishness with an implicit critique of medical technology, and nostalgia for a lost and imagined maternity:

> The whole time they were doing more sonograms, checking the chromosomes, confirming their diagnosis, that whole time I kept thinking, "I'll keep the baby, I'll go to the hospital, I'll nurse right there. Who knows, in a year, two years, this baby might get better." I just kept romancing that, wanting to believe that I could be that kind of mother. (Jamie Steiner, white health educator, 33)

> If only I could have become supermom, given that baby everything she needed. But I can't even bake an apple pie, so how could I do it all? Meanwhile, I kept going for more tests, more consultations. (Q: Why did you take a month to make the decision to abort?) The technology was so interesting. And you know what, I became an interesting case. I know this sounds sick, but I've got to be honest and tell you that this technology replaced the baby in what was making me special. (Sybil Wootenberg, white artist, 41)

For some, the critique of technological reasoning is more explicit:

You know, I kept thinking after the genetic counseling, the amniocentesis, they just keep upping the ante on you, they really do. Now, I'm not even allowed to pet my cat, or have a glass of wine after a hard day's work. I'm supposed to think that three cigarettes a day is what caused my first miscarriage. They can see a lot of patterns, but they sure can't explain them. But they talk as if they could explain them. I mean, they want you to have a baby by the statistics, not from your own lifestyle. (Laura Forman, white theater producer, 35)

I was hoping I'd never have to make this choice, to become responsible for choosing the kind of baby I'd get, the kind of baby we'd accept. But everyone, my doctor, my parents, my friends, everyone urged me to come for genetic counseling and have amniocentesis. Now, I guess I'm having a modern baby. And they all told me I'd feel more in control. But I guess I feel less in control. It's still my baby, but only if it's good enough to be our baby, if you see what I mean. (Nancy Smithers, white lawyer, 36)

Why are white middle-class women so self-critical and ambivalently technological? Three themes contextualize their concerns.

The first is that the material conditions of motherhood really are changing, dramatically so, within these women's lifetimes. White women who "have careers" and postpone babies are directing their lives differently than the women in the communities from whom they learned to mother. Unlike African-American women, for whom working mothers are longstanding community figures, and motherhood is a culturally public role, and unlike many Hispanic respondents, who painted images of sacrificial motherhood, for white middle-class women, individual self-development looms large as a cultural goal.

While *all* Americans prize "choice" as a political and cultural value, large-scale changes in education, labor-force participation, and postponed marriage and childbirth have enabled many white middle-class women to maintain at least an illusion of control over their lives to a degree unprecedented for other groups. Their relative freedom from unwanted pregnancies and child illness and death is easily ascribed to advances in medical science. Medical technology transforms their "choices" on an individual level, allowing them, like their male partners, to imagine voluntary limits to their commitments to children.

But it does not transform the world of work, social services, media, and the like on which a different sense of maternity and the "private" sphere would depend. Moreover, that "private" sphere and its commitment to child bearing is now being enlarged to include men. Fathers, too, can now be socially created during the pregnancy, through birth-coaching and early bonding. These new fathers may also claim the right to comment on women's motives for pregnancy and abortion in powerful ways.

Individually, white middle-class women may be "becoming more like men," freer than ever before to enter hegemonic realms of the culture from which they were formerly barred, but at the price of questioning and altering their traditional gender identity.[8] Modern, high-technological maternity is part of the gender relations now under negotiation, and may belong to new, emergent traditions. But it presently lies in an ambivalent terrain, a kind of "no man's land" between the technological claims to liberation through science, and the feminist recovery and romance with nurturance as a valuable activity.

A second reason for white middle-class women's ambivalence about prenatal diagnosis and abortion may well be, paradoxically, their close connection with the benefits and burdens of the increasing medicalization of pregnancy. While "everybody" now undergoes pregnancy sonograms, not everybody is as committed as this group to the medical discourse, and its images in pregnancy primers. For them, a paradoxical separation and reconnection to fetuses appears to be under way. On the one hand, they can "see" their fetuses in pictures and on medical screens. This allows for the "early bonding" which runs rampant through the parenting and obstetrical literature. But a seen fetus is also a separate fetus, one to whom one connects as a "maternal environment," in obstetrical language, and as a "sanctuary" in the words of "The Silent Scream."[9] Paradoxically, white middle-class women are both better served by reproductive medicine, and also more controlled by it, than women of less privileged groups. They are likely to be educated in the same institutions in which doctors are produced, and their own language closely mirrors medical speech and its critique in both the Right-to-Life's discourse of "selfishness" and mainstream feminism's "self-actualization."

A third reason for complex and contradictory feelings about abortion is not confined to white middle-class women, although the cultural and medical importance of individualism may make them particularly vulnerable to its effects. This reason concerns the shifting historical ground on which abortion practices rest. That point was dramatically made to me in one amniocentesis story:

> For three weeks, we tried to develop further information on oomphaloceles and satellites on the chromosomes, and the whole time, my mother kept saying, "Why are you torturing yourselves, why don't you just end it now, why do you need to know more?" She'd had an abortion between her two pregnancies. And my mother-in-law had even had a late abortion when she first got to this country, and she kept saying the same thing: "I put away one, just do it, and get it over with." And I was so conflicted, and also so angry. So finally I turned on my mother and asked her, "How can you be so insensitive, it's such a hard decision for us, you can't just dismiss this." And as we talked, I realized how different their abortions were from mine. They were illegal. You've got to remember that, they were illegal. They were done when you worried about the stigma of getting caught, and maybe, getting sick. But you didn't think about the fetus, you thought about saving your own life. (Jamie Steiner, white health educator, 33)

Illegal abortions were dangerous and expensive. They were performed under the shadow of death—maternal, not fetal. Morbidity and mortality from the complications of abortion dropped sharply after 1973, in the wake of Roe v. Wade. Indeed, "abortion related deaths have decreased by 73 percent" within a decade of abortion decriminalization.[10] Criminal prosecution, morbidity, and mortality were the fears attached to illegal abortions but not "selfishness." A variety of social forces, including medical reform and feminist political organization, led to abortion law reform. On the heels of its success, the Right-to-Life movement was quickly organized. We cannot really understand the talk of "selfishness" articulated by middle-class women, and used against all women, until we locate the meaning of abortion at the intersection of culture, politics, technology, and social change.[11]

Science speaks a universal language of progress. But women express their diverse consciousness and practices in polyglot, multicultural languages. When women speak about the medicalization of reproduction, what they tell us must be placed in its historical, social context. Amniocentesis and other new reproductive technologies open a Pandora's box of powerful knowledge, constructed through scientific and medical practices. But messages sent are not necessarily messages received. New technologies fall onto older cultural terrains, where women interpret their options in light of prior and contradictory meanings of pregnancy and childbearing. Any serious understanding of how "motherhood" is changing under the influence of the new reproductive technologies depends on realizing women's stratified diversity. Otherwise, it will reproduce the vexing problem of the false universalization of gender which feminism itself initially promised to transcend.

Notes

Earlier drafts of this article were read by Faye Ginsburg, Evelyn Fox Keller, Shirley Lindenbaum, and Anna Tsing. I thank them for their criticisms and suggestions. Faye Ginsburg deserves my greatest gratitude: without her support and direction, this paper would never have been completed.

1. Support for the field research on which this article is based was provided by the National Science Foundation, the National Endowment for the Humanities, the Rockefeller Foundation's "Program in Changing Gender Roles," and the Institute for Advanced Study. I thank them all. I am especially grateful to the many health care providers who shared their experiences with me, and allowed me to observe them at work, and to the hundreds of pregnant women and their supporters who shared their amniocentesis stories with me. Where individual illustrations are provided in the text, all names have been changed to protect confidentiality.

2. Additional reports on the fieldwork from which this article is drawn can be found in "Moral Pioneers: Women, Men and Fetuses on a Frontier of Reproductive Technology," *Women & Health* 13 (1987): 101–116; "The Powers of Positive Diagnosis: Medical and Maternal Discourses on Amniocentesis," in Karen Michaelson, ed. *Childbirth in America: Anthropological Perspectives* (South Hadley, Mass.: Bergin & Garvey, 1988); "Chromosomes and Communication: The Discourse of Genetic Counseling," *Medical Anthropology Quarterly* 2 (1988): 121–142; and "Accounting for Amniocentesis," in Shirley Lindenbaum and Margaret Lock, eds., *Analysis in Medical Anthropology* (New York: Cambridge University Press, forthcoming).

3. See Ann Oakley, *The Captured Womb* (Oxford, England: Blackwell, 1984), ch. 7, for an interesting discussion of how medical technology bypasses and reconstructs knowledge of fetuses, which excludes the perceptions of pregnant women.

4. Religiously framed anti-abortion sentiments were expressed more often among Evangelicals than Catholics, at least among Hispanics and Caribbean Blacks. At the same time, many Hispanic Pentecostals and Charismatic Catholics, and Black Seventh Day Adventists accept amniocentesis in City clinics. It is important to distinguish official Church theology from local practices, including the discursive resources, social networks, and strategies particular church membership may provide.

5. Amniocentesis adds an increase of one-third of one percent to miscarriage rate. This is considered statistically insignificant, but as genetic counselors are quick to point out, no risk is insignificant when assessing a given pregnancy, rather than simply constructing statistics. And prior reproductive history powerfully shapes how this statistic is interpreted.

6. Barbara Katz Rothman, *The Tentative Pregnancy* (New York: Viking Penguin, 1986), 114, provides an excellent discussion of the implications of sonography for maternal/fetal separation. Rosalind Petchesky has written a powerful critique of the history and hegemony of fetal images, "Fetal Images: the Power of Visual Culture in the Politics of Reproduction," *Feminist Studies* 13 (1987): 263–292. See Oakley, *The Captured Womb*, for a history of sonography.

7. My understanding of the importance of fetal imagery in political struggles is deeply indebted to Rosalind Petchesky, "Fetal Images . . ." Most activists have viewed "The Silent Scream," and Planned Parenthood's video "Response to the Silent Scream," and clips from both were widely available on television in 1984 and 1985, the years of their release.

8. Faye Ginsburg, "Dissonance and Harmony: The Symbolic Function of Abortion in Activists' Life Stories," in The Personal Narrative Group, ed., *Interpreting Women's Lives* (Bloomington, Ind.: Indiana University Press, 1989).

9. Again, see Rosalind Petchesky, "Fetal Images . . ."

10. Rosalind Petchesky, *Abortion and Woman's Choice* (Boston: Northeastern University Press, 1984), 157.

11. See Faye Ginsburg, *Contested Lives: The Abortion Debate in an American Community* (Berkeley & Los Angeles, Calif: University of California Press, 1989) for an excellent analysis of these historical intersections.

8   The "Word-Made" Flesh

The Disembodiment of Gender

in the Abortion Debate

FAYE GINSBURG

> During the course of my prayer vigil, I asked God to tell me how he wanted
> me to pray. After this, the Lord showed me the house—the Abortion
> Clinic—wrapped in barbed wire. I meditated on the meaning of this, how
> impossible it would be to enter it if it were bound in this way. Then the
> wire turned into a crown of thorns, some red with the blood of Jesus. The
> words came to mind: "My love can close those doors." The prayers of the
> faithful can bring love to bear.
>
> —"Thoughts About Prayer," *LIFE Coalition Newsletter*, December 1981

These words were the thoughts of a right-to-life activist as she prayed in front of
the first and only abortion clinic in the state of North Dakota, the Fargo Women's
Health Organization.[1] Through such rhetoric, she and others like her have been
attempting to resignify not only the physical site of abortion—the clinic—but also
the pregnant bodies that enter its doors. For many other women in the region, the
clinic's opening in 1981 signalled a long-awaited blessing: it greatly increased their
access to safe, sympathetic, and reasonably priced abortions.

In the 1980s, right-to-life protests centered more and more on abortion clinics,[2]
which still are unevenly available in their delivery of services nearly two decades
after abortion's legalization.[3] The battles taking place over clinics are both more
intense and more local than those that were waged during the first wave of right-
to-life activism in the 1970s.[4] Abortion activists—pro-life or pro-choice, as they
define themselves—are primarily white, middle-class, and female. Clearly,
women—even with similar class and cultural backgrounds—do not experience
themselves and act as a homogeneous social group with a universal set of interests.[5]
It is more the case, in the abortion controversy, that competing definitions of gender are being negotiated in terms of cultural understandings and practices of procreation, sexuality, and nurturance in America.

This essay is based on the research I carried out with grassroots activists on each
side of the ongoing battle over Fargo's abortion clinic.[6] The focus here is on right-
to-life activism in particular, concentrating on the period in the 1980s when both
local and national right-to-life strategies shifted to direct efforts to win over the
members of the population most likely to have abortions: young women with

unwanted pregnancies. A close examination of this activity reveals how notions of gender are being reformulated in relation to the conditions and discourse created by legal abortion. As reproduction has become more a matter of choice, one sees a steady transformation away from essentialism, in which gender is assumed to be determined *by* the body. In the abortion debates, as each side takes a different position on "women's interests," neither can claim that there is an essential femininity. Instead, it is a woman's *stance toward* her body, and pregnancy in particular, that becomes a kind of crucible of female identity, and the focus of gender discourse.

The developments in the Fargo case presented here illuminate how the struggle over the interpretation and cultural status of reproduction is taking place. This struggle does not play out as a static demonstration of two fixed positions. Rather, one sees a dialectical process in which each side's position evolves over time in response to the other and to internal dynamics of the movements.

Stigmatizing the Clinic

Broadly sketched, the public controversy over abortion in Fargo has mirrored the course of events and sentiments fueling the conflict at the national level. The first wave of activism occurred between 1967 and 1972, over efforts to liberalize abortion laws. When the clinic opened in 1981, many Fargo residents opposed it.[7] Confronted with this symbol of undesirable social change, pro-life forces dramatized their resistance to what they saw as alternative cultural values and formed a group called LIFE Coalition. During the first year of the Fargo clinic's existence, the Coalition organized popular support to close the clinic through legal and political processes. While the initial battle made the clinic and its opponents into a local *cause célèbre* and polarized many of Fargo's citizens, the pro-life efforts to shut the clinic down through such means were unsuccessful.[8] Having tried and failed in the political arena, the Coalition members shifted their goals. LIFE Coalition activists, recognizing they were unlikely to get rid of the unwanted clinic, decided to express their concerns through public protests.

Their protests were held right outside the clinic. These pro-life activists hoped to use a variety of tactics to reframe the clinic, literally and figuratively, and attempted to stigmatize it by maintaining an oppositional presence on the edge of the building's property. This, in turn, focused attention on the clinic's actual or potential clientele, who must encounter protestors in order to have access to abortion.

Like any political controversy, the abortion debate transforms quickly as both the local and national situations change. The activities I am describing occurred while I was in the field, between 1981 and 1984. They were carried out by what I am calling "moderate" pro-life activists who were the key players at that time. Mostly, these were women born in the 1950s, many of them college-educated young mothers who were in or had recently left the work force, with modest or declining middle-class household incomes. To generalize, they are active in both civic organizations and Catholic, Lutheran, or other mainline Protestant congregations. While they and people like them are still important and active players in the movement, other pro-life groups, such as Operation Rescue, which endorse more violent activity, have become more prominent both nationally and locally since 1983. By contrast, members of the latter groups are predominantly male, often marginal to other parts of the community, and are associated mainly with Fundamentalist, Evangelical, and Charismatic churches.[9]

The staple of LIFE Coalition's activities against the clinic in its first year was what they called the Prayer Vigil. Pro-life volunteers dedicated at least two hours a week to this action, which entailed walking back and forth along the sidewalk in front of the clinic, engaged in silent prayer, often with a Bible in hand. Those who participated call themselves "Prayer Vigilantes." Their stated intention is to draw attention to the clinic and offer an alternative interpretation of its activities to passersby. They describe their actions as "a sacrifice on our part to show the outcry of concern we have over the death chamber in Fargo." Despite its obvious public aspects, the Prayer Vigil drew little general attention; the clinic is on a side street that gets little traffic and the protestors were quickly accepted as a regular and unremarkable feature by most Fargo citizens. However, LIFE Coalition members, rather than becoming *more* disruptive in order to attract attention, emphasized their larger goal of developing a reputation for moderation. This was evident, for example, in the following list of instructions given for the "Peaceful Prayer Walk."

1.   This is a two-person Vigil of prayer only, not a demonstration.
2.   Pray silently and unobtrusively.
3.   Stay on sidewalk; keep moving; do not get in anyone's way.
4.   DO NOT: Argue, explain, discuss, answer questions with [*sic*] anyone, including press. (If the press comes say only that you'll talk to them at another location when you are finished.)
5.   Do nothing demonstrative except walk and pray—no signs or gestures.
6.   Do not congregate—two cars for two people.
7.   Do not cross the boulevard, grass, etc. Stay on sidewalk.

Almost every issue of LIFE Coalition's monthly newsletter has a short piece on the subjective experience of the Vigil, in which the prominent themes are critical life choices for women, and women's responsibilities for each other's actions. Such writing reveals how actions like the Vigil generate internal conviction and support among activists. The symbolic construction of the stories and the fact of their reiteration in newsletters and meetings are essential to the process by which collective meaning is constituted from action. In the following selection, the speaker links the experiences of "the girls" seeking abortions and the counselors who advise them at the clinic in terms of her own sister's difficult life and death.

About 4 weeks to the day before Christmas, I was walking my usual time (from 10 a.m. to 11 a.m.) on the Prayer Vigil. I was alone as I usually am on the walk. I had been reading my prayer book and had been reflecting on life as a whole and the importance of each person's life—the hard things we go through, the joys—and all the help we need from each other. My oldest sister had just died on November 7. She had just dropped dead. I was missing her and thinking of her life, which included tragedy and much suffering on her part. In spite of her hardships, I thought of her faith in God, her strengths and also her failings and guilt that resulted from these weaknesses.

I then thought about the girls and families where mistakes had been made and these girls were being counseled and having abortions as I was walking there in front of the place where this was going on. I though about the counselors. I prayed for all concerned and prayed especially that counselors were doing just that—a thorough job— and my, what a disservice to the girls if life is treated lightly. Each girl's life is so important that decisions made are of utter importance. She has to live her life the day, or month, or year after the counselor has sat across from a desk and said "whatever." Anyhow, these were my thoughts that morning. ("A Walk in November," *LIFE Coalition Newsletter*, January 1982)

Like Christian conversion testimonies, such stories provide a vehicle for each participant to infuse prayer with personal meaning by constructing a narrative that links her life and immediate situation to the goals of the movement. Clearly, the Prayer Vigil is not just an activity that sustains interest and activist support. The prayers are effective in and of themselves. For those who utter and hear them, the very *act* transforms the area around the clinic from a sidewalk, lawn, and entryway into a highly charged battle zone for "prayer warriors." A Fargo pro-life leader explained her view of the power of prayer in political action:

Prayer is one method of attack and the others—whether legislation, rallies, counseling, personal opinion offered at a crucial time, are all made more effective if prefaced by prayer.

Reinterpreting the Unwed Mother

On the first-year anniversary of the clinic's opening, LIFE Coalition members decided to escalate their activities. They were responding to internal criticism that they were not doing enough to fight the clinic, and to external accusations that they showed no compassion for the women seeking abortions. The latter pro-choice critique pushed LIFE leaders to address more directly and personally the pregnant women who came to the clinic. The Coalition hired a "problem pregnancy counselor" and organized what they call a "sidewalk counseling program." Sidewalk counselors behave very much like the prayer vigilantes; they walk quietly, usually in twos, back and forth in front of the clinic. In addition, they approach people entering the clinic and give them literature and suggest they think about alternatives to abortion. By handing out business cards with LIFE Coalition's phone number, counselors convey that the organization offers sources of emotional and material support for carrying an unwanted pregnancy to term. The counselors attempt to engage clinic clientele in conversation and take them to a nearby coffee shop— named, coincidentally, "Mom's"—to talk over the decision. Generally, encounters in which the woman changes her mind about abortion are unusual. Indeed, in 1983, when a pro-life counselor succeeded in winning over a woman who, unbeknownst to LIFE members, the clinic had turned away *because* of her ambivalence, it was a local media item for a week.

Despite the difficulties in reaching women who were using the clinic, LIFE nonetheless put considerable time and effort into the counseling endeavor. LIFE's coordinator described the work involved:

> The prayer vigil only requires one or two workshops a year. The counselors have a much more involved process of training. They need workshops, meetings, phone calls, baby-sitting services. . . .

At the training workshops that I attended, at least half of those present were new volunteers. The meetings usually had about ten people, two of whom were LIFE staff or board people. Almost all the trainees were women, usually in their mid to late twenties, and generally friends of those already engaged in pro-life work who had urged them to come. The very form of LIFE's recruitment and activism tends to generate a more moderate membership, made up (usually) of women who are pro-life but not inclined toward confrontation—a conscious choice on the part of the coordinator:

> The kind of person who works best is someone who is pro-life but really feels for the women. Someone who is super anti-abortion can't do it.

Most of the talk at meetings centered on depicting and assigning meaning to the "other," the woman having the abortion. For example, at one gathering, the following typology was offered by LIFE's problem pregnancy counselor.

> There are three types you encounter going to get abortions:
>   1.   Women's Libber: She needs a lot of education. She's hostile and cold.
>   2.   Ambivalent Type: She is conflicted and lets others make up her mind for her.
>   3.   Ignorant: The kind that is really pro-life but doesn't know there is another way.

She then offered a broader interpretation of the meaning of abortion:

> With Christianity came the acceptance of the child without it having to bear its father's sins. Abortion is a sign of a decline in the culture. I view it [abortion] as the rape of motherhood, of the gender, of the uterus, of the womb. If you think sex is natural, birth is even more natural. The first love you feel is for your mother. What is the furthest reach of the devil? Not murder, not sex, not rape. It's abortion.

In such discourse—a staple of these frequent, small, face-to-face meetings, which maintain and generate pro-life membership—abortion is fused with the imagery of destructive, decadent, and usually male sexuality. In this case, "the rape of motherhood" is fused with "the decline of the culture." Abortion is contrasted to pregnancy, birth, and maternity. The latter are cast as the domain of female experience, creation, childhood innocence, pure motive, and nuturance: "the first love you feel is for your mother." Unable to make the termination of pregnancy illegal, abortion activists are attempting at least to redefine it: women who advocate or have abortions are not only misguided or immoral; they are not properly female. Sidewalk counseling thus promoted not only an interpretation of abortion but also a particular construction of (appropriate) female gender as nurturant, peaceful, and loving. Ironically, the activists were constrained in their own actions by that very construction.

In their political performances in front of the clinic, demonstrators felt obliged to display themselves according to this view of feminine identity in which nurturant love was prominent. One of the pro-life leaders explained the dilemma to me:

> In the East, they have sit-ins. I doubt that we'd get women here to do that. The community would turn against us. The women have to deal with their family and friends. Their husbands have to be supportive.
>
> I don't want to picket out there 'cause we'll scare them. It's the most we can do. If we picket we can't reach them. We've worked so hard to prove we're loving and caring.

For LIFE Coalition members, conforming to their formulated image of compassion and nurturance was at least equal to, if not more important than, the more immediate objective of stopping women from using the clinic.

The Problem Pregnancy Industry

As part of their agenda to persuade people of their compassion, in the spring of 1983, LIFE Coalition activists decided to open a "Problem Pregnancy Center" to back up its sidewalk counseling campaign. That decision was also part of a new emphasis in national pro-life strategy to promote "alternatives to abortion."[10] It indicated, as well, the shifting understandings of the young unwed mother since the legalization of abortion in 1973. She was no longer the guilty social outcast to be shunned, but the catalyst for community efforts to develop sex education and, most notably, the target for what I am calling the "Problem Pregnancy Industry," a new focus of attention in the Fargo area. The struggle to redefine and claim women with an unwanted pregnancy was not just taking place between pro-life and pro-choice activists. It extended to social service, voluntary and governmental agencies, and divided constituents within the pro-life ranks, as well. Each group has a different understanding of the "problem" and the "solution." This is all part of a political economy of gender in which power and resources are being renegotiated constantly in relation to changing attitudes toward pregnant women, especially teenagers.

In the United States, the combination of the rise in teen pregnancy and the legalization of abortion (teenagers comprise approximately one-third of all abortion clients) has contributed to the creation of this new category of "problematic women." Because such definitions are a crucial determinant of governmental, legal, and political actions and public and private allocation of benefits and services, control over their meaning is the focus of conflict. Unwed mothers are defined and redefined as possible abortion clients, potential mothers needing prenatal care, children needing protection from parents, or students unable to complete their education, to name a few possible understandings.

A short overview of a decade of changes in Fargo regarding problematic pregnancies should make clear the impact of such redefinitions in the institutions that structure daily life there. In 1973, the main home for unwed mothers in town was closed down due to disuse. That same year, a handful of pro-life veterans established a chapter of Birthright, a pro-life group that seeks to help women with unwanted pregnancies to carry, deliver, and place their babies for adoption. At that time the only professionally trained counselor for problem pregnancies in Fargo was a woman named Mary Mintz. Ten years later, in addition to Mary, three other professionally trained "problem pregnancy counselors" were hired at Lutheran and Catholic agencies. By 1982, two state-sponsored programs offering nutritional, medical and social support to pregnant single women had been organized by the N. D. State Council on Problem Pregnancy. A daycare center for single and poor mothers was, for the first time, receiving support from the United Way (although it had to redefine its purpose as "preventing juvenile delinquency" to receive funding). In 1983, several support groups for single mothers sponsored by social service agencies were in place and the local Junior League began a community advocacy group for "school-age parents." A North Dakota chapter of WEBA (Women Exploited by Abortion) started in 1984, a group "for women who have had an abortion, now realize it was the wrong decision, and want to educate other women on the trauma of abortion." At the end of that year, in addition to the Catholic social work agency, three other pro-life groups *each* had "problem pregnancy centers." They were Birthright, LIFE Coalition, and a new group called Save-A-Baby. By September 1985, a pro-life home for unwed mothers opened in a former boarding house. In short, over one decade during which the number of pregnant adolescents in North Dakota tripled,[11] new groups, including the abortion clinic, were formed in Fargo to deal with and compete for these teenagers, bringing the total number of groups to fourteen.

The competition is readily apparent to those involved in problem pregnancy groups in Fargo. When the plan for starting a problem pregnancy center was first discussed at a LIFE board meeting, members spoke of an "expanding market." In the words of one activist:

> It's like a business. If they [the abortion clinic personnel] don't get enough clients, they'll have to close the doors.

The struggle to win both the actual clientele and the power to determine the outcome of unwanted pregnancies is not merely between pro-life and pro-choice activists. As one social worker expressed it to me:

> There really is competition between agencies. They don't admit it. Nobody says we're competing but we are. The bread and butter of this agency is adoption. Sixty-five percent of unwed girls opt to have abortions. And nearly 95 percent of the rest keep their

babies who can. Very few release their babies for adoption. I want our agency to be the
best and first so of course I'm competitive.

The increasing competition divided constituents within the pro-life ranks as
well. In its initial stages, LIFE had worked together with Birthright, which had been
helping pregnant teens find "alternatives to abortion." Birthright, begun in 1973,
had been the project of the first wave of local pro-life activists, mostly older
women, many newly widowed. By 1983, most of them were in their mid to late sixties or older. New pro-life activists, primarily younger women more politically
involved in the national right-to-life movement than their predecessors, became
increasingly impatient with Birthright. In their view, it was too low key, unprofes-
sional, and insufficiently public. As LIFE focused its efforts more and more on
"reaching the woman," which is also Birthright's agenda, the conflict intensified.
Under pressure from LIFE, Birthright hired a new director who was instructed to
be more aggressive. She began active fundraising and advertised in the local paper
and on radio stations.

Despite Birthright's efforts, LIFE decided to go ahead with its own plans for a
Problem Pregnancy Center, which opened in August 1984. This competition for
sources of local support for pro-life work instensified a few months later when an
Evangelical Christian man rumored to have links with Jerry Falwell opened yet
another pro-life pregnancy support center with his wife. Backed by a group called
Save-A-Baby, the Board of Directors was made up primarily of congregants from
the Assemblies of God. Insult was added to injury when they named their center
Life Clinic. This was a rather obvious attempt to benefit from the carefully cultivated reputation of LIFE Coalition. The LIFE Board tried but was unable to stop
this new effort, although they did persuade the "clinic" to change its name. The
new name, The Women's Help Clinic of Fargo, got them into a lawsuit with the
Fargo Women's Health Organization: the abortion clinic claimed that the pro-life
group selected a name similar to their own to deceive women into thinking that the
Women's Help Clinic offered abortions.

With the other competing pro-life group embroiled in legal problems, LIFE was
determined to "control the market" and gain legitimacy as the pro-life alternative
to abortion. LIFE Coalition's Problem Pregnancy Center had only a few clients in
its first year.[12] Most were women who had mistaken it for the abortion clinic. Yet
the Coalition's investment of time, energy, and money in their center indicated
that they thought ignorance led many women to abortion. Phrased in terms of
individual motivation, the woman who seeks an abortion is, to use one counselor's
words, "confused, kind of weak, and uneducated" about the fetus. Therefore, pro-
lifers are convinced that, if she received adequate emotional and material support,
and if she had knowledge of fetal life as they see it, she would not choose to abort.

Fetal Imagery and Female Identity
The idea that knowledge of fetal life, especially confrontation with the visual image
of the fetus, will "convert" a woman to the pro-life position has been a central and
increasingly dominant theme in both local and national right-to-life activism. The

relationship between knowledge (seeing), belief, and action, draws on more general constructs regarding witnessing and conversion in American culture. It is this cultural logic that resulted in the introduction of the fetal image into pro-life political activities in the 1970s, and its persistent presence in current pro-life propaganda. A popular quip summarizes this position: "If there were a window on a pregnant woman's stomach, there would be no more abortions."

This view, that a pro-choice position is due to ignorance of fetal life, is constructed and reinforced in two of the main pro-life media pieces—the 52-minute film "Assignment Life" and the videotapes "The Silent Scream" and "The Eclipse of Reason," released in 1984 and 1987 respectively. During the time I was in Fargo, "Assignment Life" was shown not less than once a month at some pro-life gathering. To judge by audience response, it had a lot of shock value for new recruits and solidified conviction among the converted.[13] "The Silent Scream" shows an abortion "from the point of view of the unborn child" using sonogram imagery. Sonograms, part of the high-tech experience of pregnancy since the 1980s, are generally associated with confirmation of a desired pregnancy and, according to some, provide a new site for the formation of the initial maternal-fetal bond.[14] By provocatively juxtaposing this imagery with abortion, "The Silent Scream" relies on the notion of the power of the fetus to convert.

The idea that once the fetus is "seen" one has no choice but to become pro-life underscored the 1985 North Dakota Right-to-Life Convention, entitled "Rescue and Restore." The theme was explicit in the Biblical verse from Proverbs that welcomed conventioneers:

> Rescue those who are being taken to their death; and from those staggering toward slaughter will you withhold yourself? If you say, "See we did not know this," does not the One who weighs hearts perceive it? And He who watches over the soul, does He not know and shall He not repay each man for his deeds? Proverbs 24: 11–12

As is the case in conversion, the assumption conveyed in the chosen quote is that once a potential convert witnesses a certain "truth" and comes "under conviction," there is only one path to follow.[15]

The right-to-life belief that conversion will take place after seeing the "truth" about abortion relies on the root metaphor of the fetus as "the unborn child."[16] Right-to-life visual material offers two representations that are frequently shown together. The principal one is the magnified image of the fetus—for example, floating intact inside the womb, or with its tiny, perfectly formed feet held between the thumb and forefinger of an adult. These pictures are usually in warm amber tones, suffused with soft light, rendered more mysterious by their separation from the mother's body. Juxtaposed to these photographs are gruesome, harshly lit, clinical shots of mutilated and bloody fetal remains "killed by abortions." These are what pro-lifers refer to as "the war pictures." Thus, the qualities evoked by the representations of the fetus—the mystery of conception, warmth, unconditional nurturance, radical innocence, and maternity—are continually contrasted with visions of its possible violent destruction.

In the 1983 version of a popular slide show produced by National Right-to-Life Committee President Jack Willke, the associations to these images were expanded to take on more explicit political meaning. The "war pictures" of fetuses were intercut with old news photos of Southeast Asian civilians burnt by napalm. These slides are accompanied by the following narration:

> Do you remember Cambodia?
> We ignored the genocide then until our nation saw the horror through our media. These horrible pictures woke people up. There is another war going on today. This nation should also see the horror of that reality. Every citizen of this country should see what we call "the war pictures."
> [The slide on at this point shows dead fetuses from late abortions piled in garbage cans; it then switches to a shot of a 21-week fetus aborted by a saline injection, which turns the skin a shiny red color.]
> We call this the candy-apple baby. The saline must feel like napalm. Neither the abortionist nor the bombardier saw their victim.

Through such symbolic constructions, those who would participate in abortion are associated with genocidal practice.

Moreover, in drawing analogies to war, the aborted fetus becomes a sacrifice offered for the redemption of America. This is demonstrated not only in verbal and visual media, but in other forms of symbolic action. At the 1985 North Dakota Right-to-Life Convention, a permanent memorial for "All of our nation's children who have died by abortion" was erected next to the War Veteran's Memorial. As a local pro-life leader observed:

> The symbolism was clear. More babies have died through abortion than in all the wars our country has fought. Abortion on demand is clearly the war on our unborn children. The veterans died to protect freedom everywhere, yet for the unborn there are no rights. A few yards from the gravesite also stands the flagpole with the American flag overhead.

Similarly, the redemptive power of the aborted fetus informed the following comments made to me by a sidewalk counselor on the fourth of July:

> Ask yourself this question: On the fourth of July we celebrate all the people who died that we might have freedom. And I'm wondering if some of these children aren't dying so that we will appreciate life, marriage, and relationships more fully. To keep a sixteen-year-old from getting pregnant, she needs a good self-concept. If she has that, she won't get pregnant. If it makes us go back and think of that, it may not be in vain.

While the associations of the fetus with life and death are charged with historically specific meanings, these polarities are also often taken out of time and place by the analogy to Christian religious imagery. Explicitly or implicitly, the fetus is linked frequently to Jesus and the woman with the unwanted pregnancy is likened to Mary, as in a December 1986 article in the AAA Problem Pregnancy Center Newsletter entitled "Jesus Became a Fetus."

> Luke's Gospel tells us that an angel named Gabriel visited a virgin named Mary and said, "Rejoice, O highly favored daughter. The Lord is with you . . ." (Luke 1:28) . . .
>
> How does Jesus feel about an abortion? Might Jesus have said, "For I was unborn and you killed me. I became a fetus, a little one, and you turned me into property." . . . (Michael Gaworski, Pro-Life Action Ministries)

Thus, the battle over abortion is cast as one in which the sacrifices entailed in bearing an unwanted child will redeem the woman caught in the unfortunate circumstance of unwanted pregnancy. More generally, these associations give larger meaning to the struggles and everyday difficulties of life.

Given the increasing focus on "abortion-prone" teenagers and women as objects of political struggle and social redefinition, the relatively small number of images of pregnant women in pro-life visual material is striking. This absence, I believe, indicates the shifting status of pregnancy in the abortion debate, which must be understood within the broader context of an ever fluctuating cultural construction of gender.

In American culture, as in most other cultures, pregnancy (especially first conception) places women in a liminal status, a temporary condition in which the subject is in transition between two structural states. In Arnold Van Gennep's classic formulation of rites of passage,[17] the liminal subject or initiate is usually secluded from public view and only regains visibility when he or she reenters the social system with a new status—one that is ascribed, more or less culturally predetermined. Reincorporation of the liminal person into the appropriate role serves to legitimate, for the subject and observers, a particular interpretation of social reality as not only necessary but "natural." Deviation from the prescribed outcome is not only a serious violation of social rules; it also exposes the possibility that there could be alternative interpretations of a particular situation. Thus, sanctions are often severe because such "deviance," by presenting the possibility that categories and social arrangements could be different, threatens the whole cultural order.

When abortion was illegal, the assumption for a pregnant woman was that her liminality would end when she gave birth and was given the ascribed status of motherhood. Because deviations from that script were either hidden or punished, they confirmed the dominant discourse. With abortion legal and available, the liminality of pregnancy carries a new and contested semantic load. The state into which the pregnant woman can pivot is no longer predetermined; rather than become a mother, she *may* choose to end the pregnancy and return to her former state. Thus, legal abortion subverts the prior associational chain that pregnancy "must" result in childbirth and motherhood.

In other words, with the acceptance of abortion, the dominant and oppositional discourses regarding the place of pregnancy and abortion in women's lives were suddenly reversed. Although abortion is now legal, right-to-lifers clearly do not consider termination of pregnancy an option. Yet, their view now exists within the new social and discursive context created by abortion's legalization. To succeed, right-to-lifers cannot simply defend past arrangements, as stereotypes would have it, but must construct their own position in positive terms that address the current situation. In pro-life action and discourse—particularly in the focus on women with problem pregnancies—one can see how this accommodation has been made in a particular and telling way: the decision to keep the pregnancy *despite* adverse circumstances becomes an achievement, rather than the inexorable if begrudging fulfillment of an ascribed role. The woman who decides to carry an unwanted pregnancy signifies an assertion of a particular construction of female identity—now experienced as oppositional by pro-lifers—in which nurturance, achieved through accepting pregnancy and birth, despite hardships, is of paramount value.

Now, the once dominant narrative of pregnancy in American culture is only one of several acceptable scenarios associated with the image of the pregnant woman. Thus, that absence in pro-life visual imagery is less of a paradox. Otherwise, the fetal image would have to compete with the other possible associations that a representation of a pregnant woman might evoke, and which are compelling conditions justifying most abortions—poverty, age, other children, lack of a partner, etc. Instead, the right-to-life visual focus on the fetus denies the varied circumstances of women's lives that shape reproductive decisions.

Some have argued from this data that pro-life materials simply repress all consideration of the circumstances of the mother.[18] I think such a reading inappropriately decontextualizes the image from right-to-life rhetoric, in which a choice of motherhood over abortion as the outcome of problem pregnancy is reframed as a heroic achievement of nurturance over adversity. The construction of this image is clear, for example, in the following statement of a Fargo pro-life activist:

> I think we've accepted abortion because we're a very materialist society and there is less time for caring. To me it's all related. Housewives don't mean much because we do the caring and the mothering kinds of things which are not as important as a nice house or a new car. I think it's a basic attitude we've had for some time now.

Thus, abortion is generalized to signify a withdrawal of unconditional, self-sacrificing nurturance, the devaluation of human life, and a denial of the reproduction of the culture.

Abortion and Metaphors of Social Reproduction

In their vigils, sidewalk counseling, prayers, and meetings, female right-to-life activists reframe abortion as undermining the gendered bases of nurturance and compassion in our culture. In the words of a pro-life activist:

> Abortion is of crucial importance because it negates the one irrefutable difference between men and women. It symbolically destroys the precious essence of womanliness—nurturance. . . .

In the pro-life view, women who choose in the face of problematic circumstances to keep an unwanted pregnancy when abortion is a choice are "truly" female. A woman's decision to carry a pregnancy to term under these conditions is understood simultaneously as a decision not to abort, and as a heroic act in which a woman's capacity for nurturance has been tested.

This chain of associations from sex to reproduction to nurturance is central to the organization of meaning in pro-life discourse. Within that discourse, abortion undermines not only the reproductive potential of sex but also the differentiation of male and female character. As one leader phrased it:

> Pro-abortion feminists open themselves to charges of crass hypocrisy by indulging in the very same behavior for which they condemn men: the unethical use of power to usurp the rights of the less powerful.

In this view, then, abortion represents the possibility of women moving into structurally male positions and links it with the corruption of the cultural order. A woman who endorses abortion denies the links between female reproduction and nurturant character and thus becomes culturally male. Thus, the interpretation of gender that has developed in pro-life arguments in the 1980s is based not on a woman's possession of her reproductive capacities but on her responses to them. Thus, contrary to those who claim that for right-to-lifers, the category "woman" is determined by the female body, I would argue that women are distinguished ultimately not by their bodily differences from men, but by *acceptance* of their reproductive capacities and the attributes seen to follow from them.

The development of pro-life ideology and action in the abortion debate in the 1980s was clearly more than a static political debate over reproductive and fetal rights. In it one saw a renegotiation of the meaning of female gender in relation to women's reproductive capacities. As pro-choice activists set new terms in which pregnancy is seen increasingly as a *choice*, right-to-life rhetoric regarding gender has also been transformed. As motherhood is being reframed as an achievement (rather than an ascribed status change) in the construction of female identity in American culture, so a general understanding of gender is shifting as well as the players themselves recognize (and make use of) its mutability.

More generally, the changing views of women over time in this controversy shows how our own society's views of gender are altered through social action. Through the debate, then, we are increasingly made aware of a larger cultural process: the disembodiment of gender from the bodies that ultimately bear the consequences and contradictions entailed in its shifting cultural and social formulations.

Notes

Portions of the material presented in this paper also appear in my book *Contested Lives: The Abortion Debate in an American Community* (Berkeley: University of California Press, 1989). For the fieldwork on which this work is based, I gratefully acknowledge research support from the following sources: American Association of University Women Dissertation Fellowship, a Newcombe Fellowship for Studies in Ethics and Values; the David Spitz Distinguished Dissertation Award, CUNY; and a Sigma Xi research grant. I would also like to thank the women in Fargo with whom I worked, who were so generous in their time and insights. Their identities are disguised and they shall remain anonymous, as was agreed. For invaluable emotional and intellectual support, I am grateful to Fred Myers.

1. Run by a local abortion rights activist, the clinic is one of 10 such facilities set up in small metropolitan areas by the National Women's Health Organization. This business seeks to bring abortion to those parts of the country where services have not been readily available, usually due to the conservatism of the local medical community. Since the 1973 Roe v. Wade decision legalizing abortion, over 1,000 such freestanding clinics providing first-trimester abortions have been established throughout America.

2. Struggles over local delivery of abortion services have dominated the conflict in the 1980s, while legislative right-to-life efforts have been relatively unsuccessful. The judiciary is another arena for action, since the possibility remains that the Roe v. Wade decision might be reversed by the Supreme Court, particularly with the appointment of more conservative Justices, Antonin Scalia and Anthony Kennedy, by former President Ronald Reagan. The concern of people on either side is, of course, whether they will join like-minded colleagues on the Court—Rehnquist, O'Connor, and White—and thus constitute a new working majority in the Court that might overturn or erode Roe v. Wade, particularly in the wake of the 1989 Webster v. Reproductive Health Services ruling which essentially allows states to place limitations on abortion services. One effect of this decision has been a renewed mobilization of pro-choice activists, most significantly young women not involved in earlier reproductive rights battles, and Republican women who are dissenting from their party's official position.

3. Frederic Jaffe, Barbara Lindheim, and Philip R. Lee, *Abortion Politics: Private Morality and Public Policy* (NY: McGraw-Hill, 1981).

4. Raymond Tatalovich and Byron W. Daynes, *The Politics of Abortion* (NY: Praeger, 1981).

5. For arguments regarding the rather homogeneous sociological profiles of activists on each side, see Faye Ginsburg, *Contested Lives* (Berkeley: University of California Press, 1989); Daniel Granberg, "The Abortion Activists," *Family Planning Perspectives* 13, no. 4: 158–61; and Kristin Luker, *The Politics of Motherhood* (Berkeley: University of California Press, 1984).

6. I went to Fargo in order to see this critical "backstage" setting for the national abortion drama, to get a sense of the specific shape and impact it has at the local level. The conflict, which I have been following since 1981, including two six-month periods of fieldwork, illuminates larger cultural processes. During the first stint of fieldwork in 1982, I was also working as a producer for a documentary on the clinic controversy. During the second six months I spent in Fargo in 1983, I identified myself as an anthropologist. In addition to following the development of the organizations that formed for and against the clinic and participating in community life in general, I also collected life histories from 35 people involved in the conflict, in order to see how their activism and personal and historical experiences were intertwined.

7. Like Muncie, Indiana, described in the classic *Middletown* studies (Lynd and Lynd), Fargo is small enough to provide a coherent social universe, yet sufficiently large and diverse to encompass farmers and professionals, a working class, and a university community; Catholics, Lutherans, Evangelicals, a small Jewish population, and some Native Americans. While many people in Fargo view themselves as politically conservative, they also value a tradition of populism and defense of individual rights.

8. For a full discussion of that conflict, see "The Body Politic: The Defense of Sexual Restriction by Anti-Abortion Activists," in *Pleasure and Danger: Exploring Female Sexuality*, ed. Carole Vance (Boston: Routledge and Kegan Paul, 1984), 173–188.

9. See Faye Ginsburg, "And the Lord Is on Our Side: Violence in the Anti-Abortion

Movement," in *Remaking the World: Fundamentalist Impact*, ed. Martin Marty (forthcoming).

10. *National Right to Life News* 12, no. 1 (1984). Since the early 1980s, the number of pro-life "problem pregnancy centers" has mushroomed from almost none to over 2,000. Over a dozen have been the subject of litigation, including the one in Fargo. Women seeking abortion services contend the centers misled them through false advertising.

11. See North Dakota Department of Human Services, *Children Born out of Wedlock* (Bismarck, 1982), Table.

12. According to the Problem Pregnancy Center's Report in its February 1997 Newsletter, in 1986 an average of 15 clients per month came into the office and "1200 contacts were made by phone." The Center's report in the December 1986 Newsletter is instructive as to how to understand these figures: "Each girl who comes into the Center, both positive and negative tests [*sic*], view [*sic*] our educational presentation and receives individual counseling. Six of the fifteen girls had positive tests. Four girls decided to carry their babies; one girl, though still not certain, is leaning toward carrying her baby; and one was lost to abortion . . . five of the six girls came into the Center considering abortion, and changed their minds." The Center advertises in the newspaper and Yellow Pages under "Pregnancy Counseling," through public service announcements on local television and radio, posters at area colleges, and an installation of a large street sign outside the Center bearing its name.

13. "Assignment Life" is essentially a conversion tale. The main character, a young female journalist, reluctantly takes an assignment from the older male editor to cover the abortion issue. She proceeds with her investigation, conducting interviews with almost all the key leaders in the right-to-life movement, as well as "average women," such as a reformed prostitute, and a child who announces, "If abortion had been legal, I wouldn't be here." The reporter also visits a California gynecologist who allows her to film a suction abortion. At the end, she comes to the conclusion that abortion is murder. The structure of the film is a narrative model for the pro-life conviction that if a woman had knowledge of fetal life she would not choose to abort.

14. See John Fletcher and Mark Evans, "Maternal Bonding in Early Fetal Ultrasound Examinations," *The New England Journal of Medicine* 308 (1983): 392–3.

15. See Susan Harding, "Convicted by the Holy Spirit: The Rhetoric of Fundamental Baptist Conversion," *American Ethnologist* 14, no. 1 (February 1987): 167–81.

16. In his book *Dramas, Fields, and Metaphors* (Ithaca: Cornell University Press, 1974), p. 51, Victor Turner argued that such paradigms produce "a certain kind of polarization of meaning in which the subsidiary subject is really a depth world of prophetic, half-glimpsed images, and the principal subject, the visible, fully-known . . . at the opposite pole to it, acquires new and surprising contours and valences from its dark companion . . . because the poles are 'active together' the unknown is brought just a little more into the light by the known."

17. Arnold Van Gennep, *Rites of Passage* (Chicago: University of Chicago Press, 1960 [1908]).

18. See for example Rosalind Petchesky's excellent essay, "Fetal Images: The Power of Visual Culture in the Politics of Reproduction," *Feminist Studies* 13, no. 2 (Summer 1987): 263–92.

Agency and Constraint   9

Sterilization and Reproductive Freedom Among
Puerto Rican Women in New York City

IRIS LOPEZ

This article focuses on the social, historical and personal conditions that shape, influence and constrain Puerto Rican women's fertility decisions with respect to sterilization.[1] It examines the reasons why Puerto Rican women have one of the highest documented rates of sterilization in the world by concentrating on the interplay between resistance and constraints and by teasing out some of the contradictions in their reproductive decisions about sterilization.[2] It also highlights the diversity of experiences that sterilized Puerto Rican women have with *la operación*, the colloquial term used to refer to sterilization among Puerto Rican women.

With the exception of cases of sterilization abuse, this ethnographic study demonstrates that Puerto Rican women make decisions about sterilization that are limited by their sociopolitical conditions. Their reproductive decisions are based on a lack of options circumscribed by a myriad of personal, social and historical forces that operate simultaneously to shape and constrain Puerto Rican women's fertility options. Presenting women as active agents of their reproductive decisions does not suggest that they are exercising free will or that they are not oppressed but that they make decisions within the limits of their constraints. As their oral histories reveal, women do actively seek to transform and improve their lives, and controlling their reproduction is one of the primary means of which they avail themselves to do so. Yet, as their oral histories also show, the constraints of their lives play an equally significant role in shaping their reproductive decisions and experiences. Consequently, this study takes into account the role that class, race and gender play in determining the range of options that individuals have available and how much control they have over them. While it is undeniable that all women have had their fertility options limited by the types of contraceptives developed and because they have had to bear much of the burden of population control, it is imperative to recognize that poor women are even more constrained.

It is also important to note that while the social and economic forces that limit Puerto Rican women's fertility options are not more or less constraining for them than they are for other lower-income people, particularly poor women of color, the historical antecedents that have led to the high rate of sterilization among Puerto Rican women are unique. In exploring the reasons for the high rate of sterilization among Puerto Rican women, I reformulate the binary model between submission and agency as well as withstand the temptation to use the term "resistance" in a monolithic way in the context of this study. I found that there are "elements of resistance" in their attempts to forge a social space for themselves on a personal level. Some women use sterilization as an "element of resistance" against the constraints of patriarchy/female subordination which subject them to double standards and make them primarily responsible for their fertility, child rearing and domestic work. Other personal difficulties related to female subordination such as abusive relationships that involved substance abuse also play an important role in some women's decisions to become sterilized. However, these "elements of resistance" do not make their decisions entirely defiant and conscious acts of resistance nor a complete break with the social conditions that have perpetuated high rates of sterilization.

In contrast to most of the studies on Puerto Rican women's reproductive experiences, I diverge from an exclusively cultural perspective that focuses on the women themselves as the principal unit of analysis and consider women within the wider structural and historical contexts that gave rise to and continue to perpetuate the high rate of sterilization. This aspect of Puerto Rican women's reproductive experience is as much a political as a cultural phenomenon, and ultimately speaks to wider issues of reproductive control and women doing the best that they can with their lives within the parameters of their socio-political oppression.[3]

Migration and Sterilization: Two Sides of the Population Coin

In order to understand the reasons why Puerto Rican women in Puerto Rico as well as in the United States have such a high rate of sterilization, it is essential to examine the sociopolitical and ideological framework in which sterilization developed in the island. Puerto Rico became a colony of the United States in 1898. As early as 1901 government officials attributed Puerto Rico's poverty and underdevelopment to an "overpopulation problem." Though the "problem of overpopulation" in Puerto Rico was more the result of U. S. capitalist, policy and legislative interests than of uncontrollable growth in population, an ideology of population was developed and implemented as a rationale for encouraging the migration of Puerto Ricans along with the sterilization of over one-third of all Puerto Rican women (Bonilla and Campos 1983).[4] As a result of this ideology, migration was used as a temporary escape valve to the "overpopulation problem," while they experimented with more lasting and efficacious solutions, such as sterilization and diverse methods of fertility control.[5]

In New York City, sterilization became available for "birth control" purposes in the decade of the sixties. Puerto Rican women migrating to New York City in the fifties were already familiar with *la operación* because of its extensive use in Puerto Rico. By the decade of the seventies sterilization abuse in New York City had become a pervasive theme among, though not exclusively, poor women of color (CARASA 1979; Rodriguez-Trias, 1978; Velez 1978; Davis 1981). Sterilization abuse takes place when an individual submits to a tubal ligation or vasectomy without their knowledge and/or consent or because they are blatantly pressured to accept sterilization. In the seventies, many judicial cases were documented of poor women who had been threatened with having their welfare rights taken away if they did not accept sterilization, were not given consent forms at all, or were provided with consent forms to sign while they were in labor (Rodriguez-Trias 1978). In this study, I found a few cases of women who were interned in a hospital for a different kind of surgery and were sterilized without their knowledge or consent, and many cases of women who were sterilized but were not aware of the permanent nature of a tubal ligation. In 1975, after a long and harrowing struggle undertaken by women's groups, health and community activists, sterilization guidelines were implemented in New York City to protect women and men against sterilization abuse.[6]

One of the questions my work raises is how do we then talk about agency and/or freedom of reproductive choice among Puerto Rican women in the context of the historical legacy of coercion and sterilization abuse? Although sterilization abuse is an important part of Puerto Rican women's experiences, on the island as well as in the U. S., it is important to keep in mind that not all Puerto Rican women who have undergone the operation perceive themselves as having been coerced. Therefore, in examining Puerto Rican women's reproductive decisions, I take into account the diversity of their reproductive circumstances by considering the variation of their experiences, which range from sterilization abuse to those women who suggest that they have voluntarily made the decision to be sterilized. Rather than pose these experiences, in opposition to each other, I contend that all decisions are socially constrained and mediated when individuals confront them as active social agents.

The Setting and Methodology

The high rate of sterilization among Puerto Rican women on the island has been reproduced in the U. S., where Puerto Ricans in New York City have one of the highest documented rates of sterilization. In the context of New York City as a changing metropolis, in one of the inner city's oldest and poorest neighborhoods, I set out in 1981 to learn more about the individual and social conditions that shape the reproductive decisions of Puerto Rican women with respect to sterilization on a daily basis.[7] The neighborhood where these women live is located between Williamsburg and Bushwick in Brooklyn, New York. This is one of Brooklyn's oldest garment districts. It is also the home of one of the largest Puerto Rican communities in New York City. Of the households with one or more Puerto Rican women over age twenty, 47 percent included one or more sterilized women. Ninety-three percent of the sterilized women were born in the island, but they were sterilized between the ages of seventeen and twenty-one, after they migrated to New York.

The ethnographic methods used to collect the data for this study are participant observation, oral histories, and an in-depth survey of a selected sample of Puerto Rican women. Intensive interviews were conducted with 128 Puerto Rican women, 85 of whom were sterilized. After spending two months in the field doing participant observation, I developed an extensive questionnaire which contained open-ended and closed questions. This questionnaire was administered by three women from the neighborhood and myself. After completing the survey, I continued doing participant observation and collecting oral histories from a select number of women who represented different situations that led women to either accept or opt for sterilization. I collected oral histories from seven families which consisted of a total of twenty mothers, daughters and grandmothers. This intergenerational perspective is important because it enables me to compare the perceptions and experiences of women from different generations within the same families. Through the collection of oral histories, I explored the different ways that Puerto Rican women use sterilization, the constraints that they face in making reproductive decisions, and how they resist these constraints. Many use sterilization to help them solve the immediate problem of unwanted pregnancies.[8]

Revisiting the Ideology of Choice

The ideology of choice is paramount in a discussion of sterilization among Puerto Rican women. At the heart of this research lies the question of what constitutes a "choice" and what the concept of "voluntary" means in the context of the lives of Puerto Rican women. The "ideology of choice" is based on the assumption that people have options, that we live in a "free" society and have infinite alternatives from which to choose. As individual agents, we are purportedly capable of making decisions through envisioning appropriate goals, in order to increase our options. Implicitly, the higher the social and class status the greater the options. Striving toward the middle or upper class is, in part, a striving toward a "freedom" of expanded choice, which is part of the reward of upward mobility. By focusing on individual choice, we overlook the fact that choices are primed by larger institutional structures and ideological messages.

The discrepancy and contradictions between agency and constraints led me to reconceptualize the ideology of choice in order to develop and refine a new language that enables us to think in a more dialectical way about Puerto Rican women's fertility behavior. In this formulation of individual choice, a distinction needs to be made between a decision that is based on a lack of alternatives versus one that is based on reproductive freedom. A decision is said to be more voluntary when it is based on a greater space of viable alternatives and the conditions that make this possible. Moreover, it is not simply a matter of the alternatives women have available to them but also the perceptions or knowledge women have about the various alternatives that are available to them. For example, a large number of women in this study did not know about the diaphragm.

Even though today's contraceptive technology is limited for all women, the options presented to these women were constrained by their lack of knowledge about the different forms of birth control technology as a result of limited resources and staff in the clinics/hospitals available to them. Therefore, reproductive freedom not only requires the ability to choose from a series of safe, effective, convenient and affordable methods of birth control developed for men and women, but also a context of equitable social, political and economic conditions that allows women to decide whether or not to have children, how many and when (Colon et al. 1992; Hartman 1987; Petchesky 1984). Consequently, I have deliberately avoided framing the fertility decisions of Puerto Rican women within a paradigm of choice because it obfuscates the reality of their fertility histories and experiences as colonial/neo-colonial women.

Birth Control Versus Population Control

Although sterilization is technically considered birth control, a distinction needs to be made between sterilization and birth control on an analytical level as a result of the way it is used and its consequences for women's lives. For my purposes, birth control is defined as the ability to space children while sterilization entirely eliminates the management of birth control. In fact it renders the need to control fertility irrelevant. In most cases, sterilization marks the end of a woman's ability to reproduce. It is a method of population control which I have termed "fertility control" rather than "conception control." The important distinction is between population control as a state imposition and birth control as a personal right. It is not between sterilization and other forms of controlling births. Population control may be achieved through other methods: Norplant and abortion, for example, are presently considered. Population control is when a population policy imposes the control of fertility, as opposed to the individual right to control their own fertility, and even be sterilized if that is their desire. Fertility control can be defined as a population policy that imposes the curtailment of population growth on women, eliminating the individual's right to control her own fertility.

In addition to the technical differences between sterilization and birth control, sterilization also functions as fertility control when population policy is defined and implemented by health care providers to curtail the rate of population growth among a particular class or ethnic group because they are considered, in eugenic terms, a social burden, and therefore, should not procreate (Hartman 1987). Consequently, the important issue here is not sterilization technology per se, but the way population policy is defined, translated and implemented.

On the national and international levels, health care policy plays an important role in narrowing women's fertility choices. Whereas federal funding initially covered the cost of abortion, the Hyde Amendment of 1977 changed this policy by denying women on Medicaid funding for abortions except in restricted cases or special circumstances. The refusal of the state to provide public funds for abortion services, except in narrowly defined therapeutic cases, while making sterilization readily available suggests a definite predilection for sterilization over temporary methods of birth control and abortion (CARASA 1979). This reflects the goals of the director of USAID who stated in 1987 that by 1995 he wanted to sterilize one-quarter of the world's female population (Hartman 1987).

I depart from a political economic analysis of sterilization as population control in order to consider the diversity of women's experiences and the different levels of resistance they engage in. I seek to establish a much needed new paradigm of reproductive choice that explores, interrogates and expands on what consent, choice and coercion really mean within the context of these women's lives. In doing this I hope to broaden the concept of what constitutes coercive sterilization—by showing the variety of factors that lead women to sterilization, including the active participation of women in sterilization and the elements of resistance they engage in. It is then possible to distinguish between birth control and population control.[9]

Diversity of Experiences

In addition to becoming sterilized for a series of reasons, Puerto Rican women experience sterilization in a host of different ways. For example, while sterilization may give one woman a great deal of freedom, it may be oppressive to another. Moreover, at one point, a woman may perceive sterilization as independence, yet at a different point in her life she may perceive it as oppressive. For example, a woman who is glad she is sterilized may regret it later if her child dies or if she remarries and is not able to have any more children. Sometimes resistance and oppression occupy different spaces and other times they occupy the same space because different realities can, and often do, coexist within a particular content. For example, a Puerto Rican woman may decide to get sterilized because she does not want any more children. This is a vital decision for her because it gives her more control over her body, therefore giving her more self-determination over her life. In contrast, the state's motivation for encouraging her sterilization is due to her dependency on welfare, where she is considered a burden on the state. By attempting to control her fertility, motivated by considerations of economy and politics, the state imposes its double standard of "choice" and "freedom" which is potent oppression. Consequently, women and the state's interests intersect on the level that there is consensus between the woman and the state—to control her fertility. Sterilization becomes simultaneously oppressive while it offers elements of empowerment, because both the state and women's motivation for wanting to limit their own fertility are at once synchronized as well as diametrically opposed. Therefore, on this level, there is both consensus as well as conflict and oppression (Lopez 1994).

Another way that women experience sterilization differently is based on their life situations. Often, there are conflicting conditions in women's lives where resisting one set of circumstances subjects them to another, potentially oppressive set. Thus, a woman may get sterilized as a way of resisting forced maternity, submitting as well to a health practitioner's recommendation or state policy on sterilization (Colon et al. 1992).

Finally, it is also important to consider that voluntary sterilization must be available as a means of "birth control" for women to exert their reproductive freedom. Some women seek sterilization because they have achieved their desired family ties and they either decide independently or with their companion/husband that they do not desire, and/or cannot afford, to have any more children. Those women tend to use sterilization as fertility control because of their social and historical predisposition towards this technology and due to the lack of viable options. Given a women's conditions, in some cases, sterilization may be the most reasonable decision they can make. There is also the possibility that even if these women had viable alternatives and their conditions were different, they still might elect sterilization. However, for the majority of women in this study, this is not the case.

Women's Perceptions of Their Bodies and Agency

In unraveling the complicated subject of the interplay between women's resistance, constraints and agency, I begin with an examination of the ways that women exert agency. This is best illustrated through women's perceptions of their bodies and the question of who should control them, as well as through the circumstances that have led some of the women to use sterilization as an element of resistance to patriarchy and female subordination. The elements of resistance occur as each woman's individual struggle to fight sexism, versus breaking with the constraints that have led them to get sterilized.

With the exceptions of those who were openly victims of sterilization abuse, most women in this neighborhood adamantly shared the view that sterilization was their decision because it was their body and they would do with it as they pleased. Consequently, most women did not feel that they had to ask the men in their lives for permission to get sterilized. Concurrent with this attitude, men rarely objected to a woman's decision to become sterilized unless the couple disagreed about the number and gender of the children desired. This was the case because most couples in this study agreed that it was difficult to raise and provide for more than three children.

It is important to remember that the perception that sterilization was their decision and the fact that they felt they had no other viable options appear to them as two separate issues. When I asked the question: "Who influenced your decision to get sterilized?" only one out of 96 women responded that her husband directly influenced her. This does not mean that women do not consult their husbands/ companions about their sterilization decision. In most cases they did. What it means is that regardless of the man's view, most women felt that they had the right to ultimately make the final decision about sterilization, because they were the ones who were going to have the baby and would be the primary care takers. This data demonstrates the ways that women assert agency and the ways that agency and constraints sometimes intersect. It also illustrates that what may appear at first glance to be an "individual" or "cultural" factor may actually be socially or economically intermeshed. In addition to attitudes about who should control their bodies and their perceptions that they have been sterilized "voluntarily," population policy, class and poverty play a critical role in limiting the fertility options of Puerto Rican women.

Socioeconomic Considerations

While most lower-income women experience difficult socioeconomic situations, households headed by female single parents fare even worse. Sixty-six percent of the women in this study are heads of households. Almost all of the women in this study stated that they had been married at least once, though 53.1 percent said that they were separated, divorced or widowed. Almost three-quarters (70 percent) received either supplementary or full assistance from Aid to Dependent Children. The mean annual income in 1981 was $7,000 or less. This income supports a mean of 3.4 children and two adults. With this money, women support themselves and their children, buy food and clothing and also pay the rent.[10]

The employed Puerto Rican women in this neighborhood are low-wage workers with little job stability, generally working in tedious jobs and often under difficult conditions. Eighty percent of the women in this study claimed that their economic circumstances directly or indirectly strongly influenced their decisions to become sterilized. Forty-four percent felt that if their economic conditions had been better, they would not have undergone surgery. As one woman stated:

> If I had the necessary money to raise more children, I would not have been sterilized. When you can't afford it, you just can't afford it. Girl, I wish that I could have lived in a house where each of them had their own room, nice clothing, enough food, and everything else that they needed. But what's the sense of having a whole bunch of kids if when dinner time rolls around all you can serve them is soup made of milk or cod fish because there is nothing else. Or when you are going to take them out, one wears a new pair of shoes while the other one has to wear hand-me-downs because you could only afford one pair of shoes. That's depressing. If I had another child, we would not have been able to survive.

Although their socioeconomic position permeates every aspect of these women's lives, many of them did not reduce their reasons for becoming sterilized to strictly economic considerations because this was not how most of them expressed their views about sterilization and their lives. Instead they talked about the burglaries, the lack of hot water in the winter and the dilapidated environment in which they live. Additionally, mothers are constantly worried about the adverse effect that the environment might have on their children. Their neighborhoods are poor with high rates of visible crime and substance abuse. Often women claimed that they were sterilized because they could not tolerate having children in such an adverse environment and/or because they simply could not handle more children than they already had under the conditions in which they lived. However, rarely did anyone say that they were sterilized because their annual income was only $7,000. They mostly talked indirectly about the conditions that led them to get sterilized.

Lack of Access to Quality Health Care Services

On a local level, a person's resources profoundly affect the type of health care services an individual has access to, as well as their knowledge of their options. On a micro level, the quality of care and information that middle-class women receive in private hospitals broadens their choices by enabling them to make informed decisions within the limits of the contraceptive technology that is available. Conversely, the inadequate quality of care that poor women receive diminishes their ability to make informed reproductive decisions and in this way further restricts their already limited options. For instance, because public hospitals have fewer health providers, facilities, and time to spend with their patients, poor women are not always informed about all of the contraceptives that are available. This is particularly true about the diaphragm.

There is a prevalent belief among health care providers that Puerto Rican women reject the diaphragm because of a cultural aversion to the manual manipulation involved in its use. While this may be true for some Puerto Rican women, there are other equally compelling reasons why a large number of low-income Puerto Rican women do not use the diaphragm. Some of the women in this study did not use the diaphragm because they had never heard of it. This is true primarily because it is not frequently recommended to poor women, since in order to prescribe it the health provider must show the woman how to use it properly. This requires a minimum of ten to fifteen minutes of the health provider's individual time, as well as a private space. Time and space are premium commodities in municipal hospitals. Moreover, if the health providers believe that the diaphragm is a culturally unacceptable method of birth control for the poor, chances are that they are not going to recommend it. Finally, there is also the attitude among health care providers that it is better to recommend mechanical and surgical forms of fertility control to the poor because they do not have sufficient initiative or responsibility for controlling their fertility.

Problems with Birth Control

The quality of health care services a woman has access to significantly influences her knowledge of contraceptives and attitudes about them. The lack of safe and effective temporary methods of birth control prompted many women in this sample to get sterilized. Although 76 percent of the women used temporary methods of birth control before getting sterilized, they expressed dissatisfaction with the contraceptives available, especially the pill and the IUD. As one woman stated:

> The pill made me swell up. After three years, I had an IUD inserted. It made me bleed a lot so I had it removed. I was sterilized at the age of twenty-five because I couldn't use the pill or the IUD. I tried using Norforms and the withdrawal method before I was sterilized but neither method worked very well.

Thus, because women are cognizant of the constraints that their economic resources, domestic responsibilities and problems with contraceptives place on their fertility options, many of them feel that sterilization is the only feasible "choice." In addition to the combination of social and historical factors previously mentioned that limit and constrain Puerto Rican women's fertility decisions, such as socioeconomic considerations, these women's fear to allow their children to play outdoors because of the high rate of crime in their neighborhood, their lack of access to quality health care services and many of the domestic difficulties that stem from poverty, personal and familial issues also influence their fertility decisions.

Women Marry Young and Are Primarily Responsible
for Their Fertility and Child Rearing

The tendency to either marry or have their children while they are still relatively young precipitates their decision to get sterilized at a younger age: 66 percent of these women were sterilized between the ages of twenty-five and twenty-nine as compared to Euro-American and Afro-American women at the age ranges of thirty to thirty-four (New York City Health and Hospital Corporation 1982). Moreover, most of the women in this study married and had their children before the age of twenty-five.

Therefore, by their mid-twenties, they had already achieved their desired family size but still had approximately twenty years of fecundity left. Since the most effective method available to curtail fertility is sterilization, their "choice" was to accept it or continue using temporary methods of birth control for the next twenty years.

The average woman in this study had between two and three children, their perception of the ideal family size. More than half (56.7 percent) claimed that they were completely responsible for their fertility and child rearing. While this may appear as an issue of individual choice, it is part and parcel of the construction of the nuclear family in a patriarchal society in which the brunt of the responsibility of child rearing and birth control is relegated to women. This is accomplished by providing birth control mainly to women and few if any contraceptives for men.

Women's Religious Views and Familiarity with *La Operación*

Although Puerto Rico is a Catholic country, Catholicism does not appear to have a direct effect on most women's decisions to be sterilized. Eighty-seven percent of the women in this sample were raised as Catholics. Of these women only 32 percent felt that sterilization goes against their religious beliefs. In contrast, however, women's familiarity with *la operación* has had a profound affect on predisposing them towards sterilization.

The prolonged use of tubal ligation has transformed it into part of the cultural repertoire for a large segment of the Puerto Rican population. Women's perceptions about *la operación* are also strongly influenced by the large number of females within their own families who have been sterilized. The effect that almost six decades of exposure to this operation has had on predisposing Puerto Rican women to sterilization cannot be underestimated.

To acknowledge that sterilization has a cultural dimension to it does not, however, make the decision to become sterilized one based on free will since free will does not exist in a vacuum. Nor does such a decision suggest that it originates from women's "folk" culture, as some scholars have implied through the language that they have used to describe this phenomenon (Presser 1973).[11]

Although the cultural beliefs of Puerto Rican women play an important role in their fertility decisions, particularly because of their misinformation about this procedure, this approach, like the culture of poverty thesis, blames the individual (Lewis 1976). For Puerto Rican women sterilization became part of their cultural repertoire because of the political, social and economic conditions that favored it, creating the conditions for their predisposition towards sterilization through the use of population control policies and initiatives.

Misinformation and Regret

Puerto Rican women have a very high rate of misinformation about the permanency of sterilization. Eighty-two percent of the women in this study make a distinction between the "tying" and the "cutting" of the fallopian tubes, a differentiation that does not exist. In one woman's words:

I feel that if a woman is not sure if she wants any more kids, then she should have her tubes tied. If a woman has decided she absolutely does not want to have more children, then she should have her tubes "cut."

The importance of the high rate of misinformation about sterilization is that it is one of the main factors that maintains and perpetuates the high rate of sterilization.

The simplistic language used to discuss sterilization in hospitals such as "band-aid sterilization" and the "bikini cut" is another factor that contributes to Puerto Rican women's confusion about the permanency of this operation. This issue is complicated because in some cases, women have these beliefs and do not communicate them to health providers. In other cases, health providers do not tell women about the permanent nature of *la operación*, or they talk to them in a language that deemphasizes the permanency of this surgery, thus making the situation worse. This leads to a high rate of regret among the women in this study.[12]

Of the 96 sterilized women, a third (33 percent) regretted that they were sterilized. Twenty percent do not regret their decision. The others (46 percent) fall somewhere in the middle. That is, they did not regret their decision but they were not happy with it either, although they felt they made the best decision they could under their given conditions. Women tend to regret their decisions because they remarry and would like to have a child with their new spouse, their socioeconomic situation improves, or because one of their children dies.

Conclusion

In order to accentuate the interplay between elements of resistance and constraints/oppression, this study has highlighted the complex, contradictory and multidimensional nature of Puerto Rican women's experiences with sterilization. The issue of sterilization among Puerto Rican women is a complicated one indeed. On the one hand, with the exception of victims of sterilization abuse, the majority of Puerto Rican women suggest that they made a decision between getting sterilized or continuing to have children under adverse conditions. Because of the limited nature of this "choice," however, many women feel they had no other viable alternative but to opt for, or to accept, sterilization.

In the conceptualization of my work, I have deliberately rejected the language of choice. Such language invokes ideas of free will based on individual freedom, part of the liberal ideology of choice which promotes a binary framework of choice/no choice, voluntary/non-voluntary decision-making, and obscures the interplay between social constraints and human activity. Moreover, all human decisions are socially mediated but some people have more social space to make decisions than others.

In attempting to exercise control over their lives, Puerto Rican women may use sterilization as an element of resistance to forge some social space for themselves by refusing to have more children than they desire, and/or by attempting to exert some control over their socioeconomic situation, female subordination and/or problematic relationships. This forces us to reevaluate the culture of poverty thesis of Puerto Rican complacency, passivity and lack of planning.

At the same time, it is necessary to frame their reproductive decisions within the context of the constraints that they face. Despite women's desire to plan their lives, in addition to having children there are other forces operating simultaneously to shape, frame and limit their fertility choices. Puerto Rican women's "individual choice" has been substantively circumscribed by the United States/Puerto Rican colonial population policy as well as by women's poverty, race and gender oppression. The problem with sterilization is, of course, not the technology itself but the way it has been used to solve Puerto Rico's economic problem of underdevelopment and poverty by sterilizing Puerto Rican women. Then, moreover, given the social and economic constraints discussed, sterilization appears to them as the only viable alternative.

After four decades of residence in the United States, Puerto Rican women are still living in poverty, and they are still faced with the same dilemma of how to control their fertility. Although there are certainly more contraceptives today than there were in the past, after using and experiencing health problems with the pill and IUD, a large number of Puerto Rican women turn to sterilization, a method of fertility control they have now been practicing for approximately six decades. Aside from their predisposition to *la operación*, sterilization is also frequently recommended to them in municipal hospitals. Although public attention in New York City is not directed at an overpopulation problem, as it is in Puerto Rico, the "welfare problem" is an item of considerable debate since it is the poor who are considered to have too many children.

In addition to the historical antecedents, there are a host of individual and societal forces that maintain, condition and perpetuate the fertility decisions of Puerto Rican women in New York City. Women's familiarity with *la operación*, combined with the high rate of misinformation among Puerto Rican women about sterilization procedures, poverty and lack of access to quality health care, further circumscribes women's fertility decisions by limiting their knowledge about their options. Moreover, the lack of access to safe, effective, convenient and affordable birth control, in conjunction with the goals of sterilization policy to control the rate of population growth among the poor, play an equally important role in constraining women's reproductive options.

By not offering women alternatives such as quality health care services, safe and effective temporary methods of birth control for both men and women, abortion services, quality and affordable day care centers and opportunities for a better standard of living (Hartman 1987), women's fertility options have been effectively narrowed, at times making sterilization the only viable alternative. Until Puerto Rican women achieve a more equitable status in society and are able to improve their socioeconomic situation, they will continue to have one of the highest documented rates of sterilization in the world. Reproductive freedom means having all the alternatives and the conditions in order to decide whether or not to have children. As long as women continue to have children under these inequitable conditions we cannot talk about reproductive freedom.

Notes

I would like to thank my good friends, Alice Colon and Caridad Souza, for reading and discussing my paper and for their insightful and editorial recommendations.

1. Sterilization consists of cutting and suturing the fallopian tubes in the female to permanently block the flow of the sperm to the egg cell and to prevent the egg cell from entering the uterus. In its broadest meaning, sterilization includes hysterectomies and vasectomies. The latter is the method used to sterilize men. Female sterilization is also referred to as tubal ligation.

2. In 1982, a study by a Puerto Rican demographer, Vasquez-Calzada, showed that 39 percent of Puerto Rico's female population between the ages of fifteen and forty-five were surgically sterilized (Vasquez-Calzada 1982). A similar situation can be found for Puerto Rican women and other minorities in the United States. In New York City, where this research took place, Latinas have a rate of sterilization seven times greater than that of Euro-American women and almost twice that of Afro-American women (New York City Health and Hospital Corporation 1982). Although information is scarce for most cities, my study of Puerto Rican women in one neighborhood in New York found that in 47 percent of the households one or more Puerto Rican women over age twenty were surgically sterilized. Moreover, another study reveals that in Hartford, Connecticut, 51 percent of Puerto Rican females of reproductive age were sterilized (Gangalez et al. 1980).

3. Contending views of Puerto Rican women's reproductive decisions are paradoxical because they have been posed in binary terms. Puerto Rican women are either presented as victims of population policy (Mass 1976) or free agents making voluntary decisions about their reproductive lives (Stycos et al. 959; Presser 1973). There are numerous problems with this logic. The argument that the high rate of sterilization is based on reproductive freedom glosses over the importance of power dynamics in relation to Puerto Rican women as colonial and neo-colonial subjects of population programs in Puerto Rico. In contrast, the view that state-initiated Puerto Rican women are victims of sterilization abuse makes them appear passive and does not take into account the range of their diversity or the complexity of their experiences.

4. After World War II, Puerto Rico became a model for the strategy of development known as Operation Bootstrap and a testing laboratory for the pill, IUD, EMKO contraceptive cream and the development of sterilization technology. By 1937 sterilization was implemented in Puerto Rico as a method of "birth control." The legislation grew out of the Eugenics Movement that developed in the United States to sterilize people considered socially or intellectually inferior. Finally, it is also important to keep in mind that for 31 years in Puerto Rico sterilization was systematically available while temporary methods of birth control were only haphazardly available. For a complete history of Puerto Rico's birth control movement see Ramirez de Arellano and Scheipp's (1983) work.

5. Interestingly, sterilization was never official government policy in Puerto Rico (Presser 1973; Henderson 1976; Ramirez de Arellano and Sheipp 1993). It took place unofficially and became a common practice condoned by the Puerto Rican government and many of its health officials, frequently filling the gap for the systematic lack of temporary methods of birth control. Albeit many birth control clinics opened and closed throughout Puerto Rico's history, it was not until 1968 that federally funded contraceptives were made available throughout the island. It is within this context of a policy prompting population control, particularly for poor women, that decisions regarding sterilization must be analyzed.

6. This legislation mandated that a thirty-day period of time be observed between the time an individual signs a consent form to the day she is operated on. It also stipu-

lated that women under the age of twenty-one could not be sterilized with federal funds, and that a consent form must be provided in a person's native language, and administered in written and oral form.

7. Although this research originally took place in 1981, in 1993 I collected more oral histories from some of these women in order to update my ethnographic material.

8. An article on the conceptualization and methods used to collect the data for this research is forthcoming in an anthology on Puerto Rican women entitled "Negotiating Two Worlds: The Experiences of Puerto Rican Anthropologists in Brooklyn, New York," U. S. Puerto Rican Women: Creative Resistance, 1994, editors, Doris Correa Capello and Caridad Souza, Third Woman Press, California [forthcoming].

9. Time and space do not allow me to elaborate further on the distinction between sterilization and population control and on the different levels that the women in this study resist. This will be the focus of my upcoming book on this topic.

10. In 1981, more than three-quarters of the women in this study were not working outside the home, although 12.5 percent were actively looking for jobs. Of the women who have spouses, 31.3 percent had husbands who were employed and 15.6 percent had husbands who were not working at the time this study took place.

11. The language that Presser used to describe this phenomenon is problematic. In reference to sterilization she states: "Its widespread practice represents a 'grass roots' response among Puerto Rican women who sought an effective means of limiting their family size" (Presser 1973:1). The difficulty is not with the acknowledgment that there is a cultural dimension to sterilization but that she disociates culture from the social, political and historical context.

12. Although minority and poor women are likely to be misinformed about the permanent nature of sterilization, a study found that, regardless of ethnic group or class, most women are likely to be misinformed (Carlson and Vickers 1982).

Works Cited

Bonilla, Frank, and Ricardo Campos (1983). Evolving Patterns of Puerto Rican Migration. IN The Americas in the New International Division of Labor, Steve Sanderson (ed.). New York: Holms and Meir, pp. 172–205.

Carlson, Jody, and George Vickers (1982). Voluntary Sterilization and Informed Consent: Are Guidelines Necessary? New York: Women's Division of the United Methodist Church.

Colon, Alice, Ana Luisa Davila, Maria Dolores Fernos, Ruth Silva Bonilla, and Ester Vicente (1992). Salud y Derechos Reproductivos. Tercer Encuentro de Investigadoras Auspiciado por el Proyecto de Intercambio CUNY-UPR.

Committee for Abortion Rights and Against Sterilization Abuse, (1979). Women under Attack: Abortion, Sterilization Abuse, and Reproductive Freedom. New York: Committee against Sterilization Abuse.

Davis, Angela (1981). Women, Race, and Class. New York: Random House.

Gangalez, Maria V. Barrera, P. Guanaccia, and S. Schensul (1980). The Impact of Sterilization on Puerto Rican Women, the Family, and the Community, Unpublished Report. Connecticut: Hispanic Health Council.

Hartman, Betsy (1987). Reproductive Rights and Wrongs: The Global Politics of Population Control and Contraceptive Choice. New York: HarperCollins.

Henderson, Peta (1976). Population Policy, Social Structure, and the Health System in Puerto Rico: The Case of Female Sterilization. Ph.D. dissertation, University of Connecticut.

Lewis, Oscar (1976, 1966c). La Vida: A Puerto Rican Family in the Culture of Poverty. San Juan and New York: Vintage Books.

Lopez, Iris (1994). A Question of Choice: An Ethnographic Study of the Reproduction of Sterilization among Puerto Rican Women (forthcoming).

Mass, Bonnie (1976). Emigration and Sterilization in Puerto Rico. IN Political Target: The Political Economy of Population in Latin America, Bonnie Mass (ed.). Ontario: Charters, pp. 87–108.

New York City Health and Hospital Corporation (1982). Sterilizations Reported in New York City, Unpublished Data, Department of Biostatistics.

Petchesky, Rosalind. (1984). Abortion and Woman's Choice: The State, Sexuality, and Reproductive Freedom. New York: Longman Series in Feminist Theory.

Presser, Harriet (1973). Sterilization and Fertility Decline in Puerto Rico. Population Monograph No. 13. Berkeley: University of California Press.

Ramirez de Arellano, Annette and Conrad Scheipp (1983). Colonialism, Catholicism, and Contraception: A History of Birth Control in Puerto Rico. Chapel Hill: University of North Carolina Press.

Rodriguez-Trias, Helen (1978). Women and the Health Care System: Committee against Sterilization Abuse. New York: Barnard College.

Stycos, Mayone, Reuben Hill, and Kurt Back (1959). The Family and Population Control: A Puerto Rican Experiment in Social Change. Chapel Hill: University of North Carolina Press.

Vasquez-Calzada, Jose. 1982. La Población de Puerto Rico Y Su Trajectoria Historica. Edcuela de Salud Publica, Reciento de Ciencias Médicas. Puerto Rico: Universidad de Puerto Rico.

Velez, Carlos (1978). Se Me Acabo la Canción. Paper presented at the International Congress of Anthropological and Ethnological Sciences, New Delhi, India, December.

Part Three

Constructing Family

Creating Household and Community

BRETT WILLIAMS

> Knowing that there was such a thing as outdoors bred in us a hunger
> for property, for ownership. The firm possession of a yard, a porch, a
> grape arbor. Propertied black people spent all their energies, all their
> love, on their nests. Like frenzied, desperate birds, they over-decorated
> everything: fussed and fidgeted over their hard-won homes; canned,
> jellied, and preserved all summer to fill the cupboards and shelves; they
> painted, picked, and poked at every corner of their houses. And these
> houses loomed like hothouse sunflowers among the rows of weeds that
> were the rented houses. Renting blacks cast furtive glances at these
> owned yards and porches, and made firmer commitments to buy them-
> selves "some nice little old place."
>
> —Toni Morrison, *The Bluest Eye*

The varied fortunes of the Harper family illustrate the political, historical, and economic connections between the Carolinas and Washington, whose service sector
has grown from the poverty displacing blacks from the rural Carolinas. The emergence of big government, the (sometimes related) shifts in southern agriculture,
and the landmark civil rights decisions of the 1950s opened up jobs and houses in
Washington to a generation of migrants who, like Walter Harper, came north to
build better lives in the city. Their place in history, and its intersection with residential flux in Elm Valley, means that we find in this neighborhood a generation of
relatively successful migrants. Their success, as well as the ceiling most of them
eventually met, offers dramatic testimony to the opportunities and constraints that
black people from Carolina meet in Washington.

Being black, from Carolina, and in Washington is of course not the same for
everybody. However, certain experiences were characteristic of the post–World
War II generation of migrants, who have drawn up other relatives and with neighbors and kin have rebuilt Carolina traditions in the city. Members of this generation
worked very hard to make a living, support a house, care for other kin, and build a
community. They took advantage of a window in Washington time that allowed
them to rebuild rural traditions on a base of property ownership and shared safe
space. Their descendants face the problems of reworking these traditions in rented
apartments, in dispersed suburbs, or on Elm Valley's main street. Thus the story of
Walter Harper's alley is a sad one as this generation dies, and as many of their
descendants meet even harsher constraints today. This article explores the meaning
of the transplanted cultural traditions Carolina migrants rebuilt in an international,
sophisticated, and potentially alienating place. What does this rich, self-defining

constellation of traditions mean as an adaptation to city life or as a potential culture of resistance? Why should people who, by many measures at the polls, are among America's most progressive citizens keep alive the southern past?[1]

I begin by locating Carolina culture in Elm Valley's core group of women and men in their middle years, working in service jobs or recently retired, hanging on to lives they have valued in a neighborhood where today they can barely afford to stay. I trace it through the net they have woven in the interstices of the city structure, including the places where they shop and work, the homes of their kin, and the connections to Carolina. I concentrate on the processes through which Carolina culture is expressed among neighbors, friends, and kin, primarily through gardening, fishing, feasting, and the construction of an alternative economy. Elm Valley residents cast their nets both wide and deep. I conclude with a discussion of how Carolina folk culture endows both the South and the city with meaning and how it might be linked to oppositional politics.

The Alleys of Elm Valley

The developers of Elm Valley built and sold row housing, designed to offer the semblance of private houses along with the economy of shared walls and lots to the working-class and middle-class workers who first settled there. The tiny yards, inexpensive heating, solid brick construction, lovely architectural rhythms, and deep communal rear alley spaces were attractive to black families who found them suddenly, dramatically vacant in the 1950s and 1960s, in many cases being resold by speculators.

The deep alleys hold the most important clues to black Elm Valley life. Although many people sit out on their front porches as well, most interaction among neighbors without real yards occurs behind their houses. Now almost entirely paved over in an effort to solve Elm Valley's parking problems, the alleys still reserve tiny patches of soil for gardening, which complements other back-door activities such as hanging up laundry, taking out garbage, cleaning rugs, feeding animals, and minding children. Here neighbors cement neighborly interaction and reroot Carolina tradition.

Nestled between two rows of especially small houses built in the 1930s. Walter Harper's alley captures in microcosm both stability and change in Elm Valley. Framing the alley community at its two ends are a Baptist church (white, Episcopal, and local until its members moved to the suburbs and a more cosmopolitan black congregation purchased the building) and a large detached house owned by a city politician. In between, the tiny row houses open onto the alley and are oriented toward the back.

Walter lives on the Saratoga Street side, surrounded by neighbors who, like him, arrived in the early 1960s. Next door lives an eighty-year-old white woman who has been in her house since it was built in 1937. Now a widow whose children and grandchildren live in Tennessee, retired from a university position as a secretary, she remains active in a nearby church and cares for her senile neighbor across the street. The only white resident of the alley to remain after the racial shift in the 1950s, she is still surprised by the mass exodus. "You know why they left," smiles

Edna Hanrohan, "but you couldn't find better neighbors. I remember after my husband died, everyone looked out for me. They would at least send the children over each day to knock on the door and make sure I was all right."

Three doors down from Mrs. Hanrohan lives Mrs. Jones, who came to Washington in 1957 from Raleigh-Durham, North Carolina. Also a widow, she has one daughter who has moved to Pennsylvania but brings her children to live with Mrs. Jones off and on between jobs. Mrs. Jones has worked since she arrived as a housekeeper for a judge and his family. Herbert and Shirley Garrett live across the alley on the Cumberland Street side. Once residents of the Carolina coastal plain, they have lived here since 1960, when they bought their house for $12,000, "the first black on the block." Mrs. Garrett has always worked "taking care of apartments." When her first employer died she easily found another place, for her housekeeping skills are renowned in the condominium complex where she works. Mr. Garrett is a retired city worker, president of a senior citizens' organization, and head usher at his church, where his wife is active in the women's club. Next door to the Garretts lives Mrs. Walker. She has been a housekeeper at Howard University since coming to Washington from Asheville, North Carolina, in 1951, and she bought her house from an Italian-American barber in 1963. Mrs. Walker retired in the summer of 1986 because "you know after thirty-two years on the same job you get kind of cranky." Her husband, a taxi driver, died in 1980; her daughter, a single parent, lives in Maryland with two young children. Her brother Pool, somewhat retarded and severely alcoholic, lives with her; he spends much of his time caring for his dog and frequenting Elm Valley's main street. Although she suffers from arthritis, Mrs. Walker has enjoyed retirement, joining her "retiree buddy" to go to sales and meetings and visit the sick.

Her next-door neighbor is Mary Malone, a former day-care worker whose husband suffered a heart attack while having his hair cut in 1980, "when he had just begun to live, after working hard all his life." Childless, she is affectionately involved with her twenty-one nieces and nephews, whom she sees as remarkably successful: "They're doctors, lawyers, professors, and everything." (One sister died in 1986 after raising twelve children, participating actively in club, sorority, PTA, and church life, and working in hotel service for thirty-five years.) A close friend of Mrs. Hanrohan's (of whom she says, "Now *that's* a neighbor"), Ms. Malone is widely loved for her generosity and thoughtfulness.[2] Each day she brings Pool's little dog the leftovers from her own dinner; in the summertime she often greets the garbage collectors with a pitcher of lemonade; and alley children know that each holiday they can expect an Easter basket, a bag of candy, or whatever is appropriate. One summer, admiring Walter's grandnephew's skill at basketball, she sent Walter to Zayre's discount store to buy the boy a small basketball set she had seen on sale. "That boy's going to be a ballplayer," she insisted.

Ms. Malone is also renowned because, as Walter puts it, "she can talk shit." Neighbors find her always ready with a wry or barbed comment. Of a little boy she finds mischievous, she said, "Here comes hell on wheels," and of a neighbor who left a tricky will, "Can you imagine—on your way to heaven and you do something like *that*?" Seventy-six years old, retired, and active in club life, Ms. Malone rarely goes out, but she hosts frequent barbecues for relatives, club and sorority members, and friends, along with her new companion, Mr. Friendly, who has become a pillar of alley life himself. They enjoy celebrating their cross-church relationship (she is a lifelong Catholic and he is a Baptist deacon), because "there are twelve gates to heaven and you can get in any one," but both are somewhat leery of the increasingly dramatic presence of foreign newcomers in the neighborhood. Ms. Malone is especially upset about the confusing behavior of "all their children" during church services.

In the next house lives Ms. Margie Harris, formerly from South Carolina, retired from domestic work and widowed in 1984 when her husband died of heart trouble. He was a retired trucker who worked at the local grocery store offering people rides home for whatever they wanted to pay. Ms. Margie has spent the past ten years in very active church work. She particularly loves the women's choir and her work as chair of the Sick and Condolence Committee, and she has many close friends from these groups. She is an avid gardener and fisherwoman, and she has three children of whom she is enormously proud. Two have stayed in the area, including a daughter whom she picks up at 5:00 A. M. and drives to her work at a hospital and a son who lives with her. Her other daughter lives in Atlanta, but she sends Ms. Margie's grandchildren to spend each summer, and Ms. Margie returns the visit every Christmas. Walter considers Ms. Margie the heart of alley life; he looks forward to walking home through the back each day so he can joke with her, and he appreciates her watching his house whenever he is gone.

When Ms. Margie drives to Atlanta to pick up her grandchildren, she is accompanied by her young neighbor Johnnie Mae Reed, who says of Ms. Margie, "We go everywhere together." Johnnie Mae lives next to Mrs. Jones at the opposite end of the alley. She and her husband are in their early thirties, she a day-care worker and he a bulldozer driver. They moved onto Saratoga Street in 1971 after speculators had rented out their house for about ten years to people Mrs. Hanrohan believes were prostitutes, as well as to a "nice Jamaican family." Both their children were born there. In the house next to Ms. Margie live Ms. Marie, her three dogs, and her two grown sons Henry and John. Frequent visitors are her three young grandchildren, who live with their parents in a nearby apartment building.

These residents compose the core of the alley community. Longtime pillars of the neighborhood, Inez and Calvin Green, have been absent since 1985, when Mr. Green died of kidney failure and Mrs. Green moved to a senior citizens' home. As members of this original generation die, the changes in the neighborhood are accelerated. For example, the Greens' house is now occupied by a young black couple who work for the government. These dashing, handsome, socially active young people break many of the alley's rules; they drive fast through children at play, squabble over parking spaces, and leave their dog outside barking at night while they are away. Ms. Margie insists that "we *never* had any trouble in this alley until they moved in." Mr. Garrett believes their disruptiveness testifies to the fact that they are renting.

The two houses between Mrs. Hanrohan and Mrs. Jones are occupied by whites. In one house a young but high-ranking government employee lives alone. He is renovating the house himself but has angered his neighbors by first building a very high fence around the back. "I don't know what he's trying to hide," muttered Mr. Green. Mrs. Hanrohan sums it up: "Nobody likes that fence." Walter believes that black families in the alley are more likely to build decks for observing alley life and staging events, while whites are more likely to build high fences and enclosed patios to seclude themselves. This man also annoys neighbors by roaring into the alley in his car and making such announcements as "I want these children *supervised*." A long-standing, powerfully shared alley tradition holds that all the adults "look out for each other's children." His life-style and the inappropriate behaviors linked to his life course are echoed on many other streets in Elm Valley where younger owners meet older ones. Next door live the Goodnews, he a doctor, she a teacher who has chosen to stay home for a few years with their baby daughter. The Goodnews keep up close ties with kin in other states and friends throughout the region. Through their painstaking, skilled efforts at gardening and through their shared affection for alley children and especially their pets, these newer residents have tried unusually hard to fit into the alley community. Michael frequently brings his dog out to join residents' grandchildren at play and jokes about the troublesome barking dog at the other end: "We finally got the kids grown out of their Big Wheels, and now we have this."

Several features of alley life are immediately distinctive. The first is that the alley has a core of elderly, mainly retired people. All, like Walter, are part of a circle of dispersed kin; all belie popular notions that the elderly are the dependent members of kin networks or neighborhoods. In the alley as well, the elderly are in charge, and their younger neighbors rely on them to watch their houses and their children and to give them advice. Sometimes the only family members to own property, often the only ones with flexible domestic space, these residents are likely to keep and transport children and grandchildren and to house grown adults. When they die, they leave their children houses valued at nearly $100,000.

The aging population influences alley life in other ways as well. The high death rate, especially for men, makes elderly men in the alley rare and valued today. The five funerals for men during the past ten years have brought residents together to prepare food. On funeral mornings the alley mobilizes, with each household sending covered dishes and money to the home of the mourners. Death comes very hard to the alley for several reasons. Mr. Garrett said of Mr. Green's death, "It hit me more than with a relative, because I have to miss him every day. I guess I'll get over it." Alley life is so dense that each death leaves a deep, shared hole. As residents age and get sick, they are less able to tolerate long, emotional funerals and wakes, so fewer attend. Death is a stark reminder of everyone's approaching death and of the death of the alley community. Johnnie Mae, a true leader in the work of death, mobilizes neighbors to bring food, go to funerals, and come to the house later, yet she finds the death rate hard too, because she feels that her children will grow up, and she and her husband will age, in a more remote, less textured kind of place. She notes, as do others, that none of the white newcomers have ever brought food or attended a funeral.

Surviving residents appreciate having others who will bring food and care for them when they are ill and who will listen to the intricacies of their increasingly annoying ailments, such as glaucoma, arthritis, and "pressure." How, why, and when the pains come and go are topics to detail and embroider. Mrs. Garrett, who has recently began to have heart trouble, is very grateful that she can always find someone around to discuss it or to distract her when it comes. When Ms. Malone was bedridden with a bad knee, her neighbors brought her meals during the day until her daughter could come at night.

Still another striking feature of alley life is its density. Especially in the spring, as children tumble out with bikes and balls and people begin to plant, sights, sounds, and smells fill the alley and people become enmeshed in one another's lives. When a neighbor, well regarded for his care in maneuvering his white van slowly through the ever-present group of playing children, began to drive carelessly, it took almost no time for everyone to learn that his wife had been seen drinking with notorious street-corner men in a local bar, that his children were often locked out after school, and that he was no doubt distressed and distracted by the turn of events. When Walter bought a new car, he first consulted a Dodge dealer he had seen bringing home demonstration models across the street; but then opted to buy a Ford from Johnnie Mae's brother-in-law.

This density is best observed in the socialization of new residents. Although several of the people who have moved in or through in the past ten years were potentially disruptive, they have learned that the residents of the alley are lifemates, with many shared memories, stories, and terms of order. Long-term residents talk of the differences between those who are renting and those who are owning, but the density of alley life and the ways they come to know their neighbors allow them to make many exceptions, especially for those who try hard to discover alley rules. Some rules are flexible and some are not. Fast driving and improper garbage disposal are quickly censured, but the barking of two alley dogs, maddening to newer residents, is tolerated. Walter, for example, holds that "dogs have always barked in Elm Valley, and white people have nothing to say about it."

In another example, a new woman trying to call her children in to bed at 8:00 P.M. found her decision challenged by a number of grandparents arguing, "It's too early to put those children to bed. They want to play." It was daylight savings time, still light outside, and the alley was full of children. Though sometimes intrusive and annoying, this density gives more meaning to personal events and everyday life: when Walter helped his nephew learn to ride his bicycle without training wheels, most of the alley either turned out to cheer and offer advice or peeped in silent encouragement from behind curtains and doors. When another grandnephew was learning to roller skate, Mrs. Garrett was quick to offer numerous tips, including tying a string around his waist and pulling him down the alley, "so that he can do it himself." Such communal participation seemed to make these triumphs more meaningful.

Residents are nearly unanimous in their self-conscious pride in their neighborliness. Many agree that "there's no neighborhood like this one," and Mrs. Hanrohan is emphatic in claiming, "It's much, much nicer than it used to be [in the 1940s and 1950s]. We didn't use to care about each other like this." Such comments sustain the larger vision that "we never had no trouble until *they* moved in." This is a romantic, not quite accurate myth, but it shows, I believe, that in a difficult, sometimes alienating city the alley offers a safe and known place and that people who live there find life denser and richer, though harder, than in many other neighborhoods.

Transplanting the Foods of Home

The alley community highlights Carolina foodways and brings residents together to share advice, techniques, and vegetables. Since it is a seasonal place, interaction diminishes during the winter, but back doors open and people emerge as spring arrives and neighbors begin to plant. As Mr. Green once said, "Everyone puts in a little something." Mrs. Jones, Ms. Malone and Mr. Friendly, Mrs. Hanrohan, and Mrs. Garrett fill their yards with flowers, and Mrs. Goodnew found this an important way of entering the alley community, since she also plants flowers.[3] Neighbors also grow many kinds of vegetables, including okra, green beans, sweet potatoes, peppers, corn, and tomatoes. But these are widely considered supplemental crops. As Walter puts it, "Number one I gotta have my garden, and number one in my garden is my collard greens." Collard greens almost monopolize space, time, admiration, and concern (see Cornely, Bigman, and Watts 1963). In many gardens they are the most visually prominent crop; they grow very large and enjoy a seven-month season, often lasting through November.

Mrs. Walker speaks of collards as the bellwether of a garden, sometimes marking off black Carolina tastes from those of white gardeners, who place more emphasis on tomatoes. When the plants thrive they reflect one's skill as a gardener and may ratify the desire to participate in the alley community. The thick roots and great, wide leaves of these healthy blooming plants are appropriate metaphors for being settled and committed to the alley world. These neighbors' kin, if they can move to the suburbs, also plant large plots in their yards, again dominated by collards. Those who stay in apartments may let this tradition lapse.[4]

Throughout the season neighbors exchange praise, warnings, and advice about the collards. They share many tips about when to plant and harvest. Some argue that it is lucky to plant on Good Friday; others say a gardener should wait for the full moon. Ms. Margie says her grandfather insisted collards be planted on March 15. Much concern surrounds the frost at the end of the season. Most gardners believe the frost should "set on" (or "hit") their collard greens once to make them tender. The most daring and experimental will let the frost hit twice, which produces extraordinarily tender greens; but to let it hit three times is to risk their rotting or dying.

A continuing conversation follows the collard greens through to harvest, as neighbors predict and act on the vicissitudes of each season and devise ever-changing tactics to trick urban animals like rats, dogs, raccoons, and opossums. As new neighbors move in and decide to plant, they often depend on what longer-term residents have figured out about how to build soil, fertilize, and defend against pests. Mr. Green advised his neighbors to fill jars with flour, punch holes in the lids, and sprinkle the flour on their greens; this seems to keep bugs away. Many argue that fertilizing greens with fish heads produces an excellent, powerful taste; Walter claims that this is because "in Carolina there were no sewers so we had to bury our fish heads." Mrs. Garrett links this to the Cherokee practice of burying half a fish head with each kernel of corn, a tip she says Indians taught slaves. Neighbors also share tools. Before his death in the early spring of 1985, Mr. Green hung his tools on a tree in his backyard and insisted that people could borrow without asking. Gardening well in the city can entail complex, demanding research into metropolitan offerings in seeds and seedlings, trips to suburban markets to buy young plants and fertilizer, building and rebuilding soil, and constructing massive terraces. On his retirement Mr. Green took apart his own and his wife's bureaus and used the drawers outside as planters, thus avoiding large roots in his backyard. For the most part these gardens flourish, a tribute to the care that has gone into creating perfect, composite soil in the heart of the urban landscape and into nurturing the greens themselves.

Gardening is a crucial way to socialize and incorporate new residents, as Mrs. Goodnew learned when she marched out to remove the previous owner's iris so that she could plant her own flowers and vegetables. Gardening also complements an extraordinary concern in the alley for foodways and growth. Just as Ms. Malone feeds Pool's dog, Mr. Garrett takes scraps to Ms. Marie's three dogs each day and leaves a pile of crumbs for the pigeons. Mrs. Hanrohan feeds sparrows throughout the winter. People share food at birthdays and funerals. The alley is truly a dramatic stage for celebrating the annual cycle, the repetition of seasons, the return of perennials like roses and iris, the promise each year of new growth. This concern with repetition, cycles, life, and growth in old age is expressed both in child keeping and in gardening, and through it residents both root themselves in the alley community and re-create the world of Carolina in the city.[5]

Fishing and Feasting among Metropolitan Kin

Rebuilding Carolina traditions cements alley life and helps neighbors nurture community. Working at these traditions also draws residents out of the alleys for wider interactions with dispersed relatives, who are knit together through a continuing recommitment to the past. As we saw in tracing Walter's family history and the settlement patterns of the alley, Elm Valley residents are likely to house younger kin for short periods throughout their lives. For example, Walter's grown daughter Carolyn loves to joke that she is going to move back in with him, since she "can't find a husband." He responds with a collection of stories about how much she and Lonnie worried him when they lived at home. Family lore celebrates the hardships fathers suffer when living with teenage and adult daughters. Families also participate in widely dispersed metropolitan kindreds, who come together to exchange services and to gather and share foods. Many events and tasks bring Walter's family together—from a child's problems with homework or a visitor from another state through advice on a diet or a broken-down car to the exchange of foods. Most important, relatives come together to go fishing and to produce feasts.

Like gardening and cooking, fishing is shared by women and men. Several women in the alley love to fish. But in the Washington branch of the Harper family fishing, like other foodways involving meat, is monopolized by men. Beginning early in the spring and throughout the summer, men fish for herring in the Potomac and Anacostia rivers. Walter usually fishes with his nephews and with his neighbor who comes from Raleigh-Durham. Others' fishing groups include brothers, cousins, fathers and sons, and a group of Carolina in-laws and friends. Men usually bring home several buckets of the small, pungent fish, caught both with nets and with poles. Although some men occasionally go farther away to catch other fish, this early morning trip for herring is a widely shared routine, demanding specialized skills and knowledge concerning the time of year, time of day, locations, routes, and pace of the herring runs. Many choice spots, from the chain bridge to Virginia, to Thompson's Boathouse near the Kennedy Center, to Haines Point in Southeast Washington vary in value through the year. Men may leave at 3:00 or 4:00 A. M. and return by 7:00 A. M. They then clean the catch, preserve it with coarse salt in plastic buckets, and eat it for breakfast throughout the year (usually fried in cornmeal). Some eat herring only on Sundays, others all week long. This well-loved delicacy is traced without hesitation by these fishermen to rural Carolina. As the summer continues Walter and his nephews fish for perch, bluefish, and shad, and they may travel to Chesapeake Bay to go crabbing.[6]

The most important events punctuating the annual cycle are the various family feasts, outdoors and indoors, often held on holidays and birthdays. At these feasts relatives enjoy comparing the taste and cooking style of each other's greens (Childs 1933; Cornely, Bigman, and Watts 1963). Collard greens are big, tough plants that cook down into a much smaller mass. People refer to them, both raw and cooked, as "a mess of collards." They seem an unlikely object for discerning tastes. Yet they are at once highly individualized and surrounded by intricate, hotly debated, shared lore.

Within their families, gardener/cooks pride themselves on their own carefully cultivated styles, and in most families relatives characterize one another's greens vividly and precisely. The characterizations often stress cooking strategies, which vary enormously. Many cooks add pork, but they take pride in the type (and the amount) they choose. This can be fatback, neckbones, ham hocks, or bacon, varying from just a morsel to a portion equal to the greens. Some cooks stress adding lemon, vinegar, or cooking oil; those who harvest before the frost often add sugar. Some cooks prefer an extraordinary salty taste. Some chop the greens very fine; others keep the leaves long and tangled. Those who link their strategies closely to Carolina claim the most traditional way is to add potatoes and cook the dish until everything is so well done that the greens and potatoes blend. Louise, however, feels that greens cannot taste the same away from "Carolina soil."

Yet individual distinctiveness goes far beyond cooking—beginning with fertilizing, nurturing, and harvesting strategies and continuing through cooking time, seasonings, and serving style. Many people freeze collards so that they can enjoy their own throughout the winter. Each person's greens do in fact look and taste unique; they vary in sweetness, saltiness, and pungency. Collard greens stand for a process that offers opportunities for many variations on a theme. They are also deceptive in their hulking, characterless appearance. Like a painter's canvas, collards allow for striking personal creativity. In growing and cooking collards for feasts, kin express themselves by the ways they transform widely shared expectations that greens be served and by where they locate themselves in a broad field of acceptable techniques.

When relatives come together to eat, at Thanksgiving, Easter, Father's Day and Mother's Day, the Fourth of July, Labor Day, Christmas, New Year's Day, and occasionally birthdays and Memorial Day, collard greens are almost mandatory. The other compulsory item, again deeply rooted in rural Carolina culture, is pork. One man, describing his New Year's feast to me, laughed, "I cooked three kinds of pork—chitlins, pigs' feet, and ham." This same man has become famous in his family for a personal recipe for barbecuing a side of beef in his backyard. But he makes it clear that this is something he learned in Washington: "I can't remember ever eating beef in Carolina."

People share many parts of the pig, eating them both with vegetables and on their own. Although chitlins have through the years received the most publicity, in Washington pigs' feet and ears, chopped barbecue, and barbecued ribs seem to be special favorites, with barbecue—like collard greens—providing an arena for different cooks to experiment with individual styles. One man describes his barbecue sauce: "I go through my cabinet and put everything in—but always garlic and vinegar or lemon. Then I run through my bar and throw in every kind of liquor I don't want." Most barbecue chefs are more precise and more secretive, but all seem to have definite ideas about what makes their barbecue the best and about how it differs from (most typically) the barbecue of Texas. Robert and Cornelius, for example, love to tease each other about the secrets and intricacies of their own sauces. What is true of sauce is true, I believe, of the pig in general. Like collard greens, pork is also a chef's canvas, offering enormous variety in shape, size, boniness, and fleshiness of raw material. It thus gives cooks many areas for creative variety.[7]

Several distinctive styles also accompany the sharing of food. For example, some families clearly separate eating and drinking liquor. People cook a stovetop full of food for the day and then let it sit, either when having company or when spending a Sunday at home. Walter claims that his family drinks to wake up but eats to sleep. Thus an afternoon's drinking may come to an end with a large meal. Walter's nephew Robert jokes that eating pigs' feet is risky because it makes you talk in your sleep. Walter enjoys swapping stories with his relatives during these meals; one of his favorites is about the Carolina relative who had always cooked biscuits for her brother every morning. She swears that the day after his death his ghost showed up for breakfast. Both women and men cook, especially for holidays. When planning a Father's Day celebration for Walter, Lonnie had to be firm and explicit when telling her kinswomen that the women had to cook. This may reflect in part a migration strategy as mothers prepared their sons for urban life. Charles says, "My mother taught us all [listing a number of sons and nephews]. She always said, 'If you find a woman and can't live with her, at least you can cook.'" It also might well reflect some of the exigencies of a difficult rural life where men had to learn domestic skills and pull their own weight. Many men find work cooking in Washington, because the city offers mostly service jobs. In any event, in these metropolitan families the men cook often and well.

The Connection to Carolina

Washington's black families may have relatives living in other cities north along the migration corridor that extends through Baltimore and Philadelphia into New York. Most still have some kin in several generations who have remained in Carolina, in depressed Piedmont cities like Rocky Mount and in the very small towns and farms of the east, which Marjorie Harper describes as "all laid out." "It's *so* quiet there," echoes her daughter. People revive and reenact their connection to Carolina often. They travel back and forth to visit frequently, send children to spend summers hunting and fishing and farming at home, bring older relatives up for medical treatment or a rest, and reorganize households by, for example, sending an unemployed young man north to look for work. Marjorie enjoys reminiscing about Walter's first trips back after he had moved to Washington: "He came in a card and bought us fruit and everything. We thought he was rich!" Carolyn and Lonnie Harper recall that as children they spent a month and a half with one grandmother, then rode with their Uncle Cornelius to spend the next month and a half with the other. Charles's and Cornelius's children continue this practice today, spending half of each summer with Mary and the other half with Louise. To visit Carolina is to watch kin flow in and out of their home places, especially in the summer or during the holidays.

Some of these kin create more problems than others. Charles's son Joseph, for example, regularly travels back and forth, working at odd carpentry jobs in Washington arranged by his relatives at their homes or their neighbors', or sometimes at their workplaces—for example, in Robert's restaurant. Walter's sister comes to Washington for dental care. Three of Walter's grandnephews and grandnieces spend their summers with his brother on the farm so "they'll stay out of trouble." On the other hand his other nephews, who come to Washington several times a year expecting hospitality and sometimes help, are considered burdensome, for they enjoy drinking and carousing and find it difficult to get dependable jobs and stay employed.[8]

Residents of Washington also share in the fruits of the January hog killings and of the Carolina harvest, which because of the mild climate and long growing season, continues for much of the year. Men from farms often return to them in January, either because "my parents won't kill any hogs unless I'm there" or simply to appropriate one to bring back to Washington. I have never seen a hog killing, but men's descriptions make them sound very close to longtime Carolina traditions: they shoot the hogs in their very small brains or "knock them in the head with an ax." They then scald them in boiling water and butcher them, often preparing the chitlins at once. In Carolina families will sometimes barbecue hogs right away, laying them out over a pit and cooking them about eight hours, which is "not that long if you keep yourself together." One man sometimes brings a pig home to barbecue over an improvised pit made of cinder blocks rather than a hole in the ground. Many stories and legends surround the killings and barbecues. Charles Harper's favorite is about the time he dozed off while watching the pig roast and his brother and cousins "sneaked up and ate the whole pig up—they put barbecue sauce on it and everything!"

Sometimes young relatives will bring the harvest north to share. This may trigger mixed emotions, for some migrants have painful, bitter memories of sharecropping or helping out on the family farm. Robert describes digging potatoes "until my fingers were bleeding, and my uncle wouldn't even let me go to school." Also, some of the disdain for the rural South in metropolitan Washington seeps into the way people come to see their home. Thus they sometimes look with scorn on gifts of clothing from relatives in the South, for example, and may talk disdainfully about those "Carolina shoes." But mostly good humor and appreciation seem to surround the continued sharing of North Carolina crops, which may include cantaloupe, watermelon, squash, cucumber or watermelon pickles, peppermint and spearmint to be replanted in alley gardens, raw peanuts for roasting, wild pears, homemade cherry or blackberry wine, and sassafras and cherry bark for colds. The greatest emblematic gift is the delicate wild green poke sallet, available only in very small batches for a short time each spring.

Rural emissaries also give their urban kin tips, such as how to plant celery and pineapple as houseplants or when to harvest mint to dry for wintertime tea. One woman claims that only "Carolina hands" can cultivate pineapple as a houseplant. They help with making home delicacies such as cantaloupe cocktail or plum and cherry jelly. They search the urban landscape for native wild onions, which are used in healing puncture wounds, cuts, and burns.

Joseph Harper is especially skilled at making wine, tea, and liniment. He reminds his relatives how to use boiled pine needles to cure colds, peach tree leaves to cure an upset stomach, spearmint to "refresh the body," peppermint "to warm the body in winter" or cure a stomachache, and cherry, sassafras, and sage for multiple ailments. He scours the alleys and highways for herbs and has even found a number of cherry and sassafras trees along the Beltway. Most of what he knows he learned from his grandmother, a skilled healer particularly known for treating wounds with junction weed and spiderwebs. He often brings Carolina seeds during the winter so that his relatives can start them indoors; in the spring he joins his brother, uncle, and cousins to go fishing; sometimes he travels on with news and gifts to visit kin in another urban place. He returns home faithfully at the first of the month to collect money from people who buy wood from him, since they receive checks then. Men like him seem to be crucial in bringing a continuing infusion of Carolina culture into Washington. In fact their roles make it clear that culture and the Carolina connection are not items but processes and that growth and the harvest are appropriate idioms for capturing them.[9]

The Many-Layered Meanings of Carolina in the City

Thus the Carolinas are lived out in the city as neighbors gather over gardening, as dispersed families come together to produce, prepare, and enjoy the foods of home, and as friends exchange remedies and special treats. Through Carolina traditions Walter Harper and his neighbors build alley life and reach out to kin in Washington and at home. Their world is a rich if invisible one, in some ways and for some families truer to the preservation and celebration of folk traditions than to the actual communities they left behind in Carolina. I have called the activities and process of this world "culture" because I think the life of Carolina in the city expresses three important qualities: a shared appreciation of style, a reworked system of meanings, and a continuing interplay of constraint and creativity.

First, Carolinia culture celebrates cycles, repetition, and texture. By texture I refer to dense, vivid, woven, detailed narratives, relationships, and experiences. A passion for texture seems to shape such long-standing black American cultural traditions as storytelling, blues music, children's games, jazz, and the dense lyrics and heavy percussion of go-go, the newest, Washington-based style of urban black music. All these expressive forms rely powerfully on repetition, improvisation, and the exploration of sometimes narrow situations through many emotional, sensory, interpersonal, and reflective voices (Borchert 1980; Kochman 1972; Levine 1977; Snead 1984). A passion for texture is bolstered by the circumstances of renting, which encourage and reward a deep ethnographic concern for local life. We will see that this passion for repetition and texture appears in other arenas of Elm Valley life as well; in the density of apartment life, in the attention to thick, rich, interwoven local detail that shapes the street life of this and other Washington neighborhoods. A passion for texture is not always rewarded in American society, and more middle-class strategies for urban living aim at breadth instead. Yet it is an approach that ethnographers, as well as novelists, often favor. In several ways it is a style that suits the emergence of Carolina culture in the city. The particular foods central to Carolina cuisine offer opportunities for displaying individual preferences and tactics in every sensory detail. Collards, ribs, and herring—which seem bland as raw foods—end up on the table as rich, complex blends of decision making beginning with the start of organic life and widely discussed all the way along. Furthermore, North Carolina itself is an extraordinarily textured state, stretching from true islands into Appalachia through small-scale communities offering seemingly endless variations in ecology, terrain, and style of life. To be from North Carolina can mean almost anything. And in weaving Carolina folkways through Washington, those who hold onto them create an interstitial regional life linking the political and business centers of the city.

Second, Carolina culture embraces a shared system of meanings about history, race, and place. The roots of Carolina folkways are certainly in black culture, but the emphasis today seems different from the celebration of soul in the 1960s. It is also important to declare that despite the southern exodus blacks are not homogeneous and should not be so seen. It may be that these shared foodways offer continuing opportunities to make distinctions and discriminations, first between blacks and whites, but now among blacks as well. In expressing a Carolina identity, black Washingtonians celebrate regional and cultural specialties. At the same time, former Carolinians reclaim the South, invest the South with particular meanings of time, roots, and trust, and through reaffirming those meanings in Washington, reclaim it as home as well. By texturing a symbolic, international, sophisticated urban place with rural, androgynous, traditional foods, they renegotiate its identity and make it their own.

It might be most appropriate to label this folk culture, since through Carolina style and meaning people reaffirm that they are part of a group. As they do through culture nearly always, people build responses to forces and situations that then reshape their lives and that they in turn act on and sometimes transform. In Washington these forces have included labor migration, urban colonialism, a racial job ceiling in the service sector, the constraints of poverty and dense living, a taste of independence and the ever-elusive chance to shape a black-run state. The response has included a great deal of national and local activism around issues of race, class, and civil liberties. Central to the response as well have been the politics of culture, expressed in the literary, musical, and artistic renaissance of the 1920s, the celebration of soul music and soul food in the 1960s, today's go-go, and I believe, the foodways of the Carolinas.

The working people of Elm Valley increasingly feel the commercial impact of selectively nostalgic values. The gentrification of our cities, our television shows, and—through the "lite" marketing revolution—our foods means that we must take into account mainstream marketing forces as a cultural-political force. American studies scholar Warren Belasco has documented a pervasive mainstreaming process that begins when the left adopts a nostalgic folk product to make a political point (such as blue jeans, soul food, or burritos during the 1960s). In the past twenty years we have seen much of this revolt retailed through Levi Strauss and Gloria Vanderbilt, Pizza Hut and Popeye's, granola-yogurt bars and Quaker natural cereals.

Yet the neoethnic, neoregional marketing of the 1960s politically based countercuisine has left black foods in general, and Carolina foods in particular, unspoiled. Why have they escaped untainted the otherwise relentless marketing of nostalgic folk foods from Taco Bell through Po' Folks to "dirty rice" at Popeye's? If pseudo-Cajun and home-cooked Italian, why not country Carolina or neosoul? Many answers are worth exploring, from the long, hard color line in black/white foods, through the split between the black and white left at the time of the political emergence of the countercuisine, through the possibility that some whites perceive blacks as cultureless (Belasco 1989, and pers. comm.)[10]

The second puzzling question is why the residents of Elm Valley hang on so tenaciously and gladly to foodways that are received with indifference, if not disdain. It is hard to imagine foods more oppositional to self-consciously healthful, gourmet diets. Most residents chuckle at southern dress; few play Carolina blues. Is it an accident that these traditions seem very working-class based, that some more cosmopolitan black residents consider them insulting and demeaning but that, for example, the radical chair of the D. C. Statehood party is an expert on gardening traditions? Is it an accident that the grandchildren of the Carolina gardeners have built go-go—the most oppositional, longest unappropriated, nonretailed musical tradition in years? Is the combination of discrimination and defiance important in the emergence and evolution of Carolina culture?

Willis (1984) writes of novelist Toni Morrison that her "eruptions of funk" aim to repair the alienation that plagues urban blacks displaced from the South. Through sensual intrusions from the past, Morrison suggests, her characters can step out of empty, commodity-tainted relationships into a social world that is more of their own making. They reverse clichés and suggest alternatives to someone like

Toomer's "orphan woman" Avey. Perhaps one can say much the same of Carolina culture in Elm Valley.

Carolina traditions are a complicated weave of adaptation, opposition, co-optation, and response (Abrahams 1981; Day 1982; Limón 1983; Williams 1977). Carolina culture extends the hope that people can create alternative identities by anchoring themselves at the intersection of family and friendship, history and place. The life of the Carolinas in Washington has made the secret city richer and more livable as older residents build ties, save history, and offer their children the continuing possibility of constructing cultural and political choices. Displacement and poverty in Elm Valley threaten this world, however, as new grandparents in their thirties, living in apartments, gradually lose the gardening, fishing, and cooking skills of their older relatives. The transformations in Walter Harper's alley capture in a small way the larger battering that Carolina families now take in the city.

Notes

1. This city council has a long and impressive history of progressive legislation, ranging from gender-free divorce and custody laws through early divestiture of interest in companies doing business in South Africa, penalties for insurance companies that discriminate against those carrying the AIDS virus, and strict gun control. Under its home-rule authority over the District of Columbia, Congress has contested several of these measures, overruling the insurance legislation and attaching to a 1986 tax package an amendment forbidding the District to finance abortions for poor women. These actions make the autonomy of statehood very appealing. The proposed state constitution, ratified by city voters though not yet accepted by Congress, guarantees everyone a job or an income and mandates equal pay for equal work.

2. I use Ms., Mrs., and Miss as those in the alley do.

3. Although foodways appear in few ethnographies of urban life, Boggs (1929), Childs (1933), Cornely, Bigman, and Watts (1963), Halpern (1965), Jerome (1980), and Shimkin, Shimkin, and Frate (1978) do discuss their importance in knitting together migrants to the cities of the Midwest.

4. Many other researchers have noted the central place of greens in slave, soul, and Carolina diets. See, for example, Abrahams (1981),Cornely, Bigman, and Watts (1963), Cussler and De Give (1952), Hand (1965), Hendricks (1939), Joyner (1971), and Otto (1979, 1984).

5. Snead (1984) argues that repetition and improvisation, so that "the thing is there when you come back to pick it up," are fundamental qualities in black culture, emerging with particular clarity in such forms as storytelling and jazz. This may be another example of valued repetition, highlighted in the alleys by the experience of shared aging.

6. On herring in Carolina diets, see Baraka (1966), Daniels (1941), Joyner (1971), and Otto (1979, 1984).

7. Again, many writers have stressed the place of pork in southern and soul foodways, especially for the Carolinas. See Baraka (1966), Boggs (1929), Botkin (1949), Daniels (1941), Forrest (1983), Hand (1965), Hendricks (1939), Joyner (1971), Otto (1979, 1984), and Wilson and Mullally (1983). On Carolina barbecue see Botkin (1949), Daniels (1941), Hendricks (1939), Joyner (1971), and Zobel (1977).

8. The patterns Shimkin, Shimkin, and Frate (1978) sum up for Holmes County migrants to Chicago are also expressed among North Carolina migrants to Washington, who visit, foster, and reorganize households in order to get medical care,

reassemble at holidays, remove teenagers from city streets, or return the retired and disabled to the country. See also Jones (1985, pp. 159–69) and Jones (1980).

9. Ginns (1982) discusses similar North Carolina remedies including onion poultices, ginseng, sassafras, garlic, and cherry bark.

10. Rob Rubenstein pointed out to me that many whites see blacks as having no culture. For an interesting discussion of what might be the potential gentrification of some Carolina foods, see O'Brien (1983), who describes North Carolina's historic restaurants featuring sweet-potato muffins, roast pork loin, and Cornwallis yams.

Works Cited

Abrahams, Roger. 1981. Shouting match at the border. In . . . *And other neighborly names*, ed. Richard Bauman and Roger Abrahams, pp. 303–322. Austin: University of Texas Press.

Baraka, Imamu Amiri. 1966. *Home*. New York: Morrow.

Belasco, Warren. 1989. *Appetite for change*. New York: Pantheon.

Boggs, Eva. 1929. Nutrition of fifty colored families in Chicago. M. A. thesis, University of Chicago.

Borchert, James. 1980. *Alley life in Washington*. Urbana: University of Illinois Press.

Botkin, Benjamin. 1949. *A treasury of southern folklore*. New York: Crown.

Childs, Albert. 1933. Some dietary studies of Poles, Mexicans, Italians, and Negroes. *Child Health Bulletin* 9:84–91.

Cornely, P. B., S. K. Bigman, and D. D. Watts. 1963. Nutritional beliefs among a low-income population. *Journal of the American Dietetic Association* 42:131–35.

Cussler, Margaret, and Mary De Give. 1952. *Twixt the cup and the lip*. New York: Twayne.

Daniels, Jonathan. 1941. *Tar heels*. New York: Dodd, Mead.

Day, Kay Young. 1982. Kinship in a changing economy. In *Holding on to the land and the Lord*, ed. Robert Hall and Carol Stack, pp. 11–24. Athens: University of Georgia Press.

Forrest, John. 1983. Foodlore and folklife in Tidewater, North Carolina. *North Carolina Folklore* 31(2):76–84.

Ginns, Patsy. 1982. *Snowbird gravy and dishpan pie*. Chapel Hill: University of North Carolina Press.

Halpern, Joel M. 1965. The rural revolution. *Transactions of the New York Academy of Sciences*, ser. 2, 28:78–80.

Hand, Wayland. 1965. *Popular beliefs and superstitions from North Carolina*. Frank C. Brown Collection of North Carolina Folklore, vols. 6 and 7. Durham: Duke University Press.

Hendricks, W. C. 1939. *North Carolina: A guide to the Old North State*. Federal Writer's Project. Durham: Duke University Press.

Jerome, Norge. 1980. Diet and acculturation: The case of black immigrants. In *Nutritional anthropology*, ed. Jerome Norge, Randi Kandel, and Gretel Pelto, pp. 275–326. Pleasantville, N. Y.: Redgrave.

Jones, Jacqueline. 1985. *Labor of love, labor of sorrow*. New York: Random House.

Jones, Yvonne. 1980. Kinship affiliations through time: Black homecomings and family reunions in a North Carolina county. *Ethnohistory* 27(1):49–64.

Joyner, Charles. 1971. Soul food and the Sambo stereotype. *Keystone Folklore Quarterly* 16:171–78.

———. 1984. *Down by the riverside*. Urbana: University of Illinois Press.

Kochman, Thomas. 1972. *Rappin' and stylin' out*. Urbana: University of Illinois Press.

Levine, Lawrence. 1977. *Black culture and black consciousness*. New York: Oxford University Press.

Limón, José. 1983. Western Marxism and folklore. *Journal of American Folklore* 96(379): 34–52.

O'Brien, Dawn. 1983. *North Carolina's historic restaurants and their recipes*. Winston-Salem: J. F. Blair.

Otto, John S. 1979. A new look at slave life. *Natural History* 88(1):8–31.

———. 1984. *Cannon's Point Plantation*. New York: Academic Press.

Shimkin, Edith, Demitri Shimkin, and Dennis Frate. 1978. *The black extended family*. The Hague: Mouton.

Snead, James. 1984. Repetition as a figure in black culture. In *Black literature and literary theory*, ed. H. L. Gates, pp. 59–80. New York: Methuen.

Williams, Raymond. 1977. *Marxism and literature*. Oxford: Oxford University Press.

Willis, Susan. 1984. Eruptions of funk: Historicizing Toni Morrison. In *Black literature and literary theory*, ed. H. L. Gates, pp. 263–84. New York: Methuen.

Wilson, Emily, and Susan Mullally. 1983. *Hope and dignity*. Philadelphia: Temple University Press.

Zobel, Kathleen. 1977. Hog heaven: Barbecue in the South. In *Long journey home: Folklife in the South*. Special issue of *Southern Exposure*. Chapel Hill, N. C.: Institute for Southern Studies.

11   "This Permanent Roommate"

ELLEN LEWIN

"Do you have a family?" has become a commonplace euphemism for having children and, usually, a husband. Like others in our society, lesbians associate having a child with "starting a family." For women who had their children during marriages, continuing ties with children can come to represent the stability of the most meaningful of family links. For women who had their children outside of marriages, having a baby can represent their ability to overcome both concrete barriers and social disapproval, to demand a piece of family life that they value.

Daily Routines

Lesbian mothers' accounts of their relationships with their children tend to focus on the pace of daily life, the ongoing round of cooking, cleaning, shopping, laundry, and child-care arrangements that define the rhythm of existence. Particularly those who do not have partners may devote considerable energy to devising strategies for getting everything done; these strategies, however, are commonly fragile and may be easily undermined by small setbacks or unexpected obstacles.

The complex of strategies needed to manage child-care arrangements emerge as major themes in the narratives of mothers whose children are very young. Mothers not only must find adequate child care that they can afford but often are preoccupied with locating alternatives when the arrangements they have made break down. Transportation is likely to be a key issue. Mothers who do not own automobiles talk at length about the time required to travel by public transportation to child-care providers and to their jobs, and the difficulties of handling such tasks as grocery shopping and laundry. Going out in the evening may present problems so overwhelming that many mothers decide it's easier just to stay home.

Margo Adler describes how the daily routine of her twelve-year-old daughter dictates her own schedule. Because Amy is developmentally disabled, she cannot assume as much independence as most girls her age, and Margo is acutely aware that this burden will not decrease appreciably as Amy grows up.

Margo readily admits that the system of strategies she has devised for arranging supervision of Amy is subject to breakdown at virtually every point. So that she can get from her suburban home to her job in San Francisco on time, she has persuaded the school bus operators to pick up Amy at the beginning of their route; so, Amy's morning "child care" is essentially provided by the bus driver. After-school care—difficult to locate for a child as old as Amy—requires Margo to pay to have her picked up at school. All of these arrangements are workable, of course, only when school is in session.

> Every time the season changes I have to figure out a whole new thing to do with her. Child care is definitely one of the biggest hassles and issues in my life. And it's partic-ularly difficult because she's old and still needs child care.

The most recent disruption of Margo's routine came when Amy joined a soccer team. This is Amy's first experience with team sports and Margo is delighted that she wants to do it, but getting her to soccer practice has forced Margo to leave work early once a week and to rearrange her schedule to make up the time she misses. Amy's health is poor, and Margo's routine is further disrupted by the need to sched-ule medical appointments and manage her care when she is sick.

Finding baby-sitters among local teenagers has been so difficult—apparently because the kids who live in Margo's upper-middle-class neighborhood have no need to earn money—that she almost never goes out at night, though as a last resort she sometimes takes Amy to a friend's home in a nearby East Bay city. Her friend, a married woman who does not work outside the home, is someone she has known since childhood and has a child the same age as Amy. Margo hates to ask her friend to watch Amy, though, because she has no way to reciprocate.

Margo's child-care problems are even more acute during the summer. Commu-nity activities when school is not in session are not necessarily scheduled to dove-tail nearly; often there are gaps between the end of one program and the start of another. Sometimes her parents have come out from the East in the summer and have handled child care for her. At other times Margo has been forced to take Amy to work with her. This is far from an ideal arrangement, not only because her employer, a major financial institution, objects to children in the office, but because Amy's unpredictable behavior makes it difficult for Margo to concentrate on her work. The problems are even worse during school breaks at Christmas and Easter, when the school district runs no programs at all.

Margo knows that her child-care problems have affected her progress at work both because of the amount of time she misses and because she is often distracted and worried. She talks longingly of the possibility that her parents will move to the Bay Area; though she would lose some of her privacy, they would assume respon-sibility for much of Amy's care in a way she feels no one else ever will. Because Amy is a difficult and demanding child, Margo believes that few people but her parents can ever be expected to take a major role in her life.

> I think the thing that seems the most important to me now is that I feel like . . . I will be the only person that has a certain kind of responsibility and feeling for this kid. That's sometimes very heavy to me. That even if I wind up with another person, that won't be their kid. That will be my kid. No matter how they feel, it's still going to be my kid. . . . I feel like she's only my kid, and not [my ex-husband's] at all. The only time I ever think of it as being any kind of shared thing is like I think if I died, he would have to take responsibility for her. But other than that, I really feel like that's my kid.

It's sort of like I had this kid alone. I think that aspect of feeling like that will never change. It's probably the heaviest piece to me.

Some lesbian mothers find unusual solutions to their complex domestic problems. Ruth Zimmerman, a computer technician, lives in San Francisco with her five-year-old son and a male roommate. She recruited the roommate to live in her apartment in exchange for a wide range of household and child-care duties. He handles all of her baby-sitting needs, goes to the store, and takes responsibility for laundry and most of the house cleaning. Her friends think it's strange for her to be living with a man in this sort of situation, and she herself finds the arrangement a bit odd, but it meets a variety of needs and is difficult to give up. Her concern about continuing to have the roommate take this role is that she fears his becoming too attached to her and her son as his "nuclear family," something that doesn't seem appropriate in a situation she defines as temporary and justified only by its convenience.

> If I could find somebody else to be maid, butler, child-care worker, and chauffeur, all the things he does for me, for the price, of course, the price is kind of high. Financially, it's not high. But emotionally, I guess it's starting to get a little higher.

Some lesbian mothers, then, shape their accounts of being mothers in terms of the practical challenges they must successfully overcome. Perhaps because becoming a mother so dramatically alters the daily pace of life, getting through routine tasks and devising solutions to persistent difficulties stand as evidence of a woman's ability to act as a mother in the world. These narratives tell us not only how the speakers cope with their responsibilities but that they define motherhood, at least in part, as a set of concrete constraints and challenges that demand innovative, practical solutions.

"Companionate" Households

Particularly when they live alone with a single child, lesbian mothers tend to view their relationships in a way I think of as "companionate": mother and child accomplish essential tasks in much the same way roommates might, with few trappings of the sort of hierarchical authority that one typically finds in two-parent families.

This is not a pattern unique to lesbian mothers. Heterosexual mothers I interviewed expressed similar sentiments.[1] Alma White, who lives alone with her sixteen-year-old son, sees her relationship with her son as exceptionally harmonious.

> Basically, what we've tried to do since [my son is] older is to say we are two adults living in the same house. We share. We take care of each other. We take care of the house. We take care of meals, food, and chores and all of those kinds of things together collectively. We just kind of do it together and it's worked out pretty well.

Besides managing basic household chores cooperatively, Alma says, she and her son seek out each other's company for "fun" things: bowling, eating out, going to the movies, going camping. They do not share all of their meals, largely because of

Alma's busy schedule of community activities. She views the relationship as one in which each respects the autonomy of the other, so that arguments never arise. According to Alma, she and her son discuss "everything": her job, his schoolwork, household finances, and her homosexuality. They have had extended conversations about her most recent breakup, and he has expressed his hope that she will be somewhat discreet about being a lesbian. Alma says that out of respect for his wishes she has tried to make the public areas of the house "neutral" in decor so that he will feel comfortable when he brings his friends home. She keeps books on lesbian and gay subjects, posters for lesbian community events, and everything else of that sort in her bedroom.

Along similar lines, Leslie Addison views her relationship with her twelve-year-old daughter, Jennifer, as much like a marriage. A major theme in their relationship is compromise, a process whereby they work out differences and agree to accommodate each other's preferences. Leslie's admitted restlessness used to lead her to relocate herself and Jennifer to a different part of the country nearly every year. As Jennifer has grown older, however, she has become more assertive about expressing her wish to stay in the same place longer, largely because of the ties she forms in school and with neighborhood children. So they have compromised: Leslie has agreed not to move during the school year and Jennifer has agreed that they can travel in the summer and possibly not return to the same place next year.

> We've worked out little compromises like that between us. . . . It took us a long time to work out our relationship. But now that's kind of hard, too—it makes it difficult for other people to break into it, because we have our set patterns. Like when we get a roommate, or I get a lover, or she gets a new friend, it's real hard. It's just like being a couple.

The analogy between mother-child ties and those of a couple arises frequently among single mothers, lesbian and heterosexual alike. The companionate model certainly recalls the equality of an ideal couple. Many lesbian mothers, as we have seen, describe women who have no children as "single."

Tanya Petroff speaks strongly of her feeling that she does not share the same fundamental concerns as people who have no children. Though she does not have a lover, she does not see herself as single precisely because she is a mother.

> I don't seem to have the need to get together with someone of either sex as much as my single friends do. I have a real solid relationship [with my daughter] that provides me with a feeling that I am necessary and worthwhile . . . and all that other stuff.

Along similar lines, but with an added edge of anger, Leslie Addison also characterizes childless women as "single:"

> I think that the lesbian community is organized around the single lifestyle only. I've heard more than a hundred times from a woman, a lesbian—"I chose not to have kids, so don't push yours off on me."

And Tanya Petroff says:

> I've had [lesbians] tell me that I had chosen a privileged position in having a child and
> if it was going to be difficult for me then it was too goddamn bad.

Another lesbian mother, Gloria Frank, has lived on her own with her three children for most of their lives. Her experience has often been that important people
in her life, including her lovers, have not wanted to make the kinds of sacrifices she
sees as unavoidable for a mother, and she tends to feel that she cannot rely on anyone outside of the family—herself and her three kids. But there can be comfort in
ties to children, as she makes clear.

> I think what happens when you're alone with children is that you very frequently treat
> your oldest one almost as another adult; you talk to them about things that you would
> normally share with an adult, and they . . . see themselves as having much more
> responsibility . . . and they really see themselves as the other adult in your life.

Gloria points out that this closeness can backfire, particularly when she wants to
get involved with a lover. The child who has been acting as confidant does not want
to relinquish this position to a stranger, and may try to sabotage the new relationship.

The theme of equality emerges as a core value in accounts given by other lesbian
mothers about their lives with their children. Inez Escobar, who lives alone with
her twelve-year-old daughter in an isolated suburban housing tract, describes a routine that is notable for its apparent lack of routine. Although her daughter is supposed to keep her room clean and wash the dishes after dinner, and often takes
responsibility for doing the laundry or cleaning the house, Inez see their arrangement as informal and easygoing.

> We don't have anything definite set up for chores now, really. Whenever anything
> needs to be done, we just kind of decide to do it. Housekeeping is really not a prior-
> ity, I don't think. We'd just as soon do something, or go to the movies, or play a game
> as clean. . . . We're so free. Kind of answerable to no one, really. All I know for sure is
> that I have to go to work. [My daughter] knows that her job is to go to school. The rest
> of our time is just real free-flowing. Like I say, if we want to do the housework, we can
> . . . or we can just slough it off.

Part of sharing responsibility for the daily operation of family life is being aware
of the financial constraints the mother faces. If anything is a consistent theme in
the lives of both lesbian mothers and heterosexual single mothers, it is the persistence of economic pressures, the nearly constant fear that they may not be able to
manage. The mere fact of their survival becomes a mark of honor for some mothers; for others, the reality of an unpredictable financial situation is a source of
ongoing anxiety.

As part of the kind of openness lesbian mothers seek with their children, discussions about budgets and finances are described as frank and explicit. In many instances, of course, financial strains can be traced directly to nonpayment of child support, so mothers must weigh the benefits of leveling with their children against the possible harm of attacking a fragile link to their fathers. Nonetheless, most mothers told me they take pains to explain their incomes and budgeting decisions, largely in hopes that children will appreciate the efforts they make to manage on skimpy resources. These frank discussions, however, may not assuage children's desires for the luxury items their friends have.

Most of the conflicts Doris Johnson has with her eleven- and fourteen-year-old daughters focus on clothes and on the narrow limits on the kinds of purchases they can make. Doris is a graduate student, trying to complete work on a doctorate in history. She lives with her lover, June Kepler, a medical student, and her two daughters in cramped campus housing, getting by on student loans, her earnings as a research assistant, small contributions from June, and sporadic child-support payments from her former husband, who lives in another state.

All of these sources together add up to a minimal income, and Doris must plan her budget carefully. The girls become upset when they compare their wardrobes with those of their friends. Though Doris wishes she could spare her daughters this experience, she also thinks that it builds character and that they will later come to appreciate the benefits of learning to economize.

> They will never, probably, as long as they live, take for granted that you can just have whatever you want.

Similarly, Winnie Moses, who lives with her lover and her two teenage sons, has had to have frank discussions with her children about financial realities. Though her ex-husband is reliable about paying child support, he has resisted all her efforts to get the amount raised; there have been only very minor increases since they divorced twelve years ago. At one point the boys complained that she wasn't spending enough on them in view of the amount of the support payment. She took this occasion to explain the entire household budget and how she calculated the costs of raising them. This discussion apparently resolved the matter.

Anita Korman is also open about financial realities with her fourteen-year-old daughter. She discusses her plans to pursue a doctorate with her daughter, weighing the possible economic advantages of the degree against the costs they would both have to bear during the lengthy process of obtaining it. She doesn't feel that she can ask her daughter to sacrifice endlessly, but she knows that in the long run they would both benefit from an improvement in her credentials.

> I don't burden her with every bill that I owe but we talk about it a lot in a realistic way. What we can afford and what we can't and particularly lately we've been talking about if our living situation should change, how we would deal with that, how we would deal with it financially as well as the other ways. . . . I mean she wants to know and she understands the situation.

Managing Stigma

Though lesbian mothers share with single heterosexual mothers a concern with child care and family finances and a preference for an egalitarian style of interaction, they alone have to manage the stigma attached to homosexuality. Coming out as lesbians intersects in important ways with the relationships mothers maintain with their relatives, and, as we shall see, with ongoing ties with their children's fathers. But mothers' lesbianism may have other layers of meaning for children. Mothers' interpretations of the impact of their sexual orientation on their children tends, therefore, to focus both on its significance for ties to relatives and fathers and on its presumed effects on their children's friendships.

Bernice Nelson, who lives alone in a North Bay suburb with her seven-year-old daughter, describes a rather positive self-image as a lesbian and has strong views about the importance of the independence she has achieved since coming out. She lived in several communal situations when she was still with her husband, and her current lifestyle retains a counterculture flavor. Yet at the same time that she values nontraditional approaches to daily life and to child rearing and believes, at least in the abstract, that being "open" is good, Bernice is fearful about what would happen if her lesbianism became widely known.

> It's hard for me to know exactly how to get across to her that it's important for her own sake that she be discreet about who she shares her life with and yet encourage her at the same time to be willing to share her feelings with someone. . . . For her my fear is that she'll be identified in school by her teachers . . . as something real strange and unusual, because of the way I live, and that that'll change the way they relate to her. That the kids will find out the way I live and start tormenting her. You know how mean kids are to each other—your mommy's a queer, and that kind of stuff.

To ensure that other children do not accidentally have access to compromising information, Bernice has developed a set of rules that restrict her daughter's friends to her room, denying them access to other parts of the house, especially when she is entertaining her own adult guests. Bernice is afraid that being known as the daughter of a lesbian not only would subject her daughter to discrimination at school but would restrict her "options" in the future. On another level, she takes seriously her ex-husband's occasional threats to seek custody, and sees any breach of family confidentiality as providing him with potential ammunition. These fears seem closely related to similar concerns about the impact of her sexual orientation on her future career. Bernice hopes to begin studies toward certification as a psychotherapist, but worries that being known as a lesbian might prevent her from practicing or obtaining licensure.

What is noteworthy about Bernice's fears is that they do not reflect any personal history of actual discrimination. Her daughter has never, to her knowledge, been teased by friends; her husband has not made any serious attempts to gain custody; and she has not even begun to train for a career in psychotherapy or counseling. Bernice's narrative tells us more about the meanings she attaches to being a lesbian than about her concrete experiences.

In a somewhat similar vein, Lisa Stark, who has an eleven-year-old daughter and a nine-year-old son, is concerned about the impact being "out" would have on her relationships with her neighbors. She would prefer to live in a neighborhood with more gay people, but explains that at present the only place she can afford to live is a rather bleak working-class neighborhood on the Peninsula. She doubts that her neighbors are open-minded about homosexuality, though she has never raised the subject with any of them. But her relationships with them are vital: they are her principal source of the babysitters on whom she depends. An available pool of local teenagers allows her to stay at her office in a city agency for the long hours she is often required to work, or which she chooses to work in the hopes of being promoted to a supervisory position.

Some children find that knowing other children whose mothers are lesbians helps them to normalize what might otherwise seem like a deviant situation. But even these children learn that information about their mothers' sexual orientation may have to be carefully managed. Judy Tolman's nine-year-old son knows many other children in lesbian families, but Judy has

> a feeling that he senses that school is part of the world out there that doesn't like gay people. . . . Same when he goes to be with his father—I don't think he really talks about it that much.

More commonly, mothers talk about the need to maintain secrecy as rooted in the possibility of a custody challenge. To protect their children from having to manage potentially damaging information, these mothers feel the best policy is to keep their lesbianism a secret from them.

Rita García has worked out a difficult truce with her family over her homosexuality. Her former husband has failed to make contact with her for several years, has never paid child support, and has a record of alcohol abuse and battery. All the same, she fears he might suddenly return and try to take their son away from her.

> I feel that I would be laying a guilt trip on Jim if I told him that I was gay but to keep it a secret. Because if we ever had to go to court again and somebody found out, they would take him away from me.

Although virtually all of her friends are gay and she has lived with Jill for most of her son's life, Rita is convinced that he knows nothing of her sexual orientation. She elaborated on this belief several times during our conversation, despite the fact that he was in the room during the entire interview.

Theresa Baldocchi has carefully shielded her nine-year-old son, Tom, from knowledge of her lesbianism. Her former husband, John, sued her for custody at the time of their divorce, alleging (inaccurately at the time) that she was a lesbian. Despite the bitter memories of the divorce, which nearly bankrupted her, Theresa is pleased that John is willing to stay with Tom in her home every night while she is at work. But, this arrangement requires Theresa to be very careful about leaving any evidence of her lifestyle around the house; she feels certain that John examines everything while he is there. Her caution has extended to keeping her lesbianism a secret from her son.

> If John weren't around, I would probably be real open with Tom. [But] I don't want him torn between having to lie to his father and having to accept me, too. That would really be hard for him. He loves his dad a whole lot.

Laura Bergeron, who had her three children outside of marriage, is also cautious about letting her children know that is a lesbian. The primary consideration she cites is her lover, Margaret Towers, who is married, determined to do nothing that would disrupt the customary rhythm of her life, and thus adamant that the nature of their relationship be kept secret. Laura also mentions a vague worry that the father of her two sons might try to get custody of them if he knew about her sexual orientation, even though he agreed to cooperate in her two pregnancies only with the understanding that he would never have any formal obligations to their children. The man who fathered her third child, a daughter, through insemination knows that Laura is gay, so she feels more comfortable having him visit and spend time with her and the children. But she has never discussed her lesbianism with her children and is sure she will never be able to do so.

> My children don't know that I'm a lesbian. You see the relationship with my lover . . . We're very conventional. Our whole life is very conventional. My profession would be endangered, and her life is the neighborhood. . . . I mean there's just no way that we could ever be anything but heavily closeted. We have a lot of women's activities that go on here, but we don't mix the worlds. . . . That's why my children can't know.[2]

Though Laura was so eager to have children that she become pregnant three times on her own, she has more recently begun to see her children as a limitation on her ability to live spontaneously. She feels pulled between her obligations to them and her relationship with Margaret, and sees no way to harmonize these two parts of her life. Further, she believes that having children has wrecked her finances and that the expenses of child care for three children are the direct cause of her recent bankruptcy.

Laura has made arrangements for before- and after-school care, and her children also check in with Margaret, who lives next door, when they return home. To maximize the time she can spend with Margaret, Laura has installed an intercom system between the two houses, so she can listen to what is happening at her house while she is at her lover's. She fits shopping and other errands in on her lunch hour, or does them on her way home from work. These complicated arrangements have left Laura with virtually no time to herself.

> When I'm alone, I'm usually doing something with my kids, because if anything I feel guilty that I don't spend enough quality time with them. I'm more of a caretaker a lot of the time. It seems like I'm always just hurrying them up and making them do this

and that, so . . . I make myself take one evening a week, the same evening every week. This is it, this is theirs. And we either go out for pizza or go to a movie or sit around and read stories to each other. In other words, we are together as a family for sure at least one night a week.

These arrangements do little to allow Laura to enjoy the more creative aspects of motherhood that many other mothers speak of with such deep feeling. She has convinced herself that her life with Margaret can continue only if she separates herself from her children; she is left with little beyond obligation to them, and intense self-consciousness about maintaining the secrecy of her lesbianism.

> I just feel like I'm a robot sometimes. There's just not enough of me. And someday they're going to realize that, you know. And I want them to. I don't want them to grow up and look back and think my mother was a robot. But I don't know that there's much I can do about it because I've got too many things in motion now, you know.

Laura and Margaret do have a limited social life with other lesbians, hosting rather formal social gatherings such as bridge parties. These parties, however, provide additional occasions when the children must be segregated from interaction with adults and excluded from Laura's life. She comments that the boys, in particular, are "understandably" not welcome at a lesbian social event, and that, in any case, she can't risk having her children make observations on these occasions.

> So I've set my life up so that it doesn't include my children. That's what it amounts to. . . . [Being with a man] was so much easier. It seems like such a hassle to be gay. . . . But still, I might always be a little closeted. . . . I don't want to go around alienating everybody and destroying their reality and upsetting their reality. I'm not trying to convert anybody and make any stand for lesbianism. I told you I'm not in the least militant or radical or political or anything.

At the same time, Laura understands that the gulf being created between herself and her children will probably have long-term effects on their relationship, effects that she can no longer control.

> I think at some point it's probably going to be important to me that my children know I'm lesbian and I'm never going to be able to tell them as long as I'm in this relationship, you know. I guess I have fantasies about maybe we could tell [my daughter] when she's about fifteen or so or something. . . . But I guess I'm never going to be able to tell the boys and I feel a distance between me and them for that reason.

Laura's situation contrasts sharply with that of most mothers I interviewed. She has chosen, in effect, to submerge her decisions as a mother to sustain a complex system of secrecy that she and her lover have established. The system is based on the assumption that terrible consequences would flow from any revelation of their lesbianism, and that secrecy can be maintained only if Laura's identities as mother and lesbian are strictly separated. It also rests on a related, but questionable, assumption that no one knows about her lesbianism if she chooses not to talk about it.

Laura is hardly the only lesbian mother to shield her children from knowledge of her sexual orientation, but she is in the minority. Far more of the mothers I spoke to feel strongly that being open is best for everyone involved. Elaine Weinstein's daughters are twelve and fourteen. Since her divorce she has been very circumspect about her lesbianism, both because her husband sued her for custody at the time of their divorce and because her job as a teacher might be compromised. She decided to be more open with her daughters when her lover moved into the household, and since then she has been able to look forward to spending time with them.

> I used to live for the weekend that the kids would go away. . . . It was just so nice to have that break. Now I don't feel that way anymore, mostly because they know that I'm a lesbian. . . . It's like a big weight has been lifted. So I don't feel a need to have them gone.

Ruth Zimmerman, who had her son five years ago while she was living with a man, has been very open with him about her lesbianism. She does not think that her son's father will ever try to get custody, though he has retained some interest in the child and visits occasionally. Ruth believes that her son's understanding of her lifestyle can only be positive.

> He doesn't think it's strange to see two women in bed together. I mean, I can only see it as a broadening experience. It's one less thing in the world for him to find strange or different.

In a similar vein, Gloria Frank, who had three children with three men, thinks her kids have an advantage because their mother is a lesbian.

> I think it probably will just leave openings for more possibilities in their lives, I would hope. . . . I think it's incredibly valuable that my children be exposed to as many different lifestyles as possible.

Motherhood as a Central Identity

Mothers who are strongly committed to maintaining total secrecy about their sexual orientation find that segregation of their daily lives into time when they are "mothers" and time when they are "lesbians" creates constant concerns about information management. Their self-consciousness is heightened as they evaluate and analyze every episode that might breach their confidentiality. While some such mothers are motivated by fears about custody, others seem to be thinking more in terms of what they construe as broad community standards. They understand that homosexuality is generally disapproved of, and want to protect their children from being stigmatized in the way they feel themselves to be. Some of them also understand that motherhood tends to be perceived as contradictory to lesbianism, so that the mere fact of being mothers can protect them from being identified as gay. As Valerie Thompson, the mother of a twelve-year-old daughter, said, "Of course, I have the mask. I have a child. I'm accepted [as heterosexual] because I have a child and that kind of protection."

But fears about stigma are not the only reason for segregating roles. Virtually all the women I interviewed commented on the pressure they felt to do everything adequately alone. As we saw earlier, some women focus on the successes they have achieved and derive considerable self-esteem from the effort. Others tend to focus on how difficult it is to manage under the conditions that motherhood imposes in their situations, how discouraged and overwhelmed they feel, how little hope they see that their situations will become easier until their children are grown.

Both approaches revolve around a common understanding: that being a mother eclipses and overshadows all other roles. A few women, such as Laura Bergeron, in a sense keep motherhood at a distance in order to manage a particularly difficult lesbian relationship. But Laura does not find this separation easy, and as we have seen, she is haunted by the impact her segregated lifestyle has on her children.

Tanya Petroff is very much aware that being a mother overshadows being a lesbian. "The mothering thing," she says, "the thing about being a mother seems to be more important to me than my sexual orientation." She views herself and her seven-year-old daughter as an indivisible social unit, which takes first place over any other sort of relationship.

> I'm definitely part of a package deal. I come with my daughter and people who can't relate to both of us are not people I want to relate to for very long.

That being the case, Tanya sees other mothers, regardless of their sexual orientation, as the people with whom she has the most in common. Since moving to the Bay Area a few years ago from the Midwest, she has tended to avoid the lesbian community in favor of socializing with other mothers. Her past experience was that the "lesbian community" put pressure on her to make her daughter a "little amazon." As a mother, she feels strongly that her daughter should be free to develop in whatever direction she chooses, not constrained by "political correctness." When Tanya speaks of "political correctness," she is referring to the standards that lesbian feminists first imposed on themselves in the 1970s. At that time, efforts to create a "lesbian nation" gave rise to often rigid expectations in such areas as dress, political activity, sexual behavior, and language. Behavior that could be construed as "straight" or oriented toward conventional standards of success and attractiveness was generally censured, as were such traditional markers of femininity as high heels and makeup.[3]

Being a mother seems to release some lesbian mothers from pressures to be a lesbian in that "correct" way. Most women who raise this issue frame it in terms of dress or other aspects of personal appearance, but the implication that other behavior is also involved is clear. Many of the women who discussed this problem were veterans of 1970s radical feminism, and their stories resonate with resentment over the limitations this ideology placed on their ability to express themselves as individuals. It seems that once a child is on the scene, one's presentation as a lesbian is inevitably altered, and this experience may be freeing in some ways. Louise Green, who came out as a lesbian while still in her teens and has had no heterosexual experience, has relaxed her earlier efforts to be as "butch" as possible in her personal style, though it seems that dress and style are only the outward manifestations of other levels of personal change.[4]

> Since I had [my daughter] I felt it was OK to do these things I've been wanting to do real bad. One of them is to paint my toenails red. I haven't done it yet, but I'm going to do it. I felt really OK about wearing perfume and I just got a permanent in my hair. . . . I feel like I'm robbing myself of some of the things I want to do by trying to fit this lesbian code. I feel like by my having this child, it has already thrown me out in the sidelines.

Other mothers locate the centrality of motherhood in the sheer quantity of obligation that having a child imposes on one's life. Peggy Lawrence lives with her lover, Sue Alexander, her ten-year-old daughter, and Sue's two sons. Her comments on motherhood focus on the limitations it imposes on her personal freedom. Having a child makes her be more concerned with living in a stable environment than she thinks she would be otherwise, and it makes her cooperate with a social system, particularly in its educational dimension, that she personally disagrees with. Travel seems impossible when one is a mother. Making a living becomes the center of her existence because of her obligations to her daughter. She and Sue have chosen to live in a neighborhood convenient to the children's school, and though they would prefer to relocate to the Midwest, where both of them have lived before, they are reluctant to do so because they believe that the kids encounter less bigotry as the children of lesbian mothers in San Francisco. Peggy explains:

> Being a mother, to me—being a mother is more consuming than any other way that I could possibly imagine identifying myself. . . . Any other way that I identify myself is an identification of some part of my being a mother. I am a lesbian mother, I am a working mother—"mother" hardly ever modifies any other thing. "Mother" is always the primary—it's always some kind of mother, but it's never a mother-anything. "Mother" is—"mother," for mothers, is always the thing that is more consuming. Because being a mother is so big, I have much more in common with all mothers than I have in common with all lesbians. It's so big. It starts out as a twenty-four-hour-a-day job, and it just goes on and on and on.

But still other mothers locate the meaning of motherhood in the sheer intensity of feeling that exists uniquely between mother and child. Lisa Stark, who is often visibly depressed by the unrelenting obligations of single parenthood, has come to see her children as the reason she can face the obstacles that seem to make up her daily life. Since her life presumably would be easier without children, her celebration of their importance is somewhat paradoxical.

I've . . . never had to live for myself. The only reason I get up in the morning is to get them off to school. For me to trot off to work in order to earn the money to support them. I don't know what I'd do if I didn't have them. They're everything I've got. . . . I love them so much that it really is painful.

Her comments echo her description of her own relationship with her parents. She describes her parents as the only people other than her children who care about her, the only reliable source of support in her rather bleak social world. This relationship contrasts dramatically with the minimal connection she maintains with the children's father, who has cut himself off from her and the children nearly completely.

He doesn't know [the kids] and doesn't want to. He signs their cards, or his wife does, with [first names], not "Daddy" or "Your father" or anything.

Similarly, relationships with women lovers have not proved to be stable or supportive for Lisa. She is left with the intensity of her kin relations, her closest ties being those with her children.

In a somewhat different vein, Ruth Zimmerman describes the process that led her to decide to have a child on her own.

One of the reasons I probably decided to have a kid was to have a certain kind of continuity. What you call a long-term relationship. I wanted that. I wanted to feel that important to somebody else, that committed to somebody else. I guess I really am a family person, in spite of the fact that I don't feel real comfortable with my own family. But being . . . committed to people is kind of important to me. . . . I wanted more continuity in my life than going through a series of roommates and having the household change with the roommates. That just seemed . . . so transient. It just didn't feel like a life. So now I've got me this permanent roommate. . . . And the closeness that's possible with a child—I mean, I don't know where else that's possible. . . . A lover relationship can approach the intensity of a parent-child relationship, but never have that same quality of how close that is.

Thus having a child anchors one socially, puts one in the world in a way that creates meaningful connections and that reinforces, and is reinforced by, continuity with other kin. At the same time, kin relations may also be seen as *representing* valued ties with children, as validating those links. The paradox here, as we see poignantly in the case of Lisa Stark, is that children are the source of considerable difficulty and hardship at the same time that their ability to generate feelings of intimacy and links to the ineffable constitute the apparent solution to the very problems they generate. By becoming mothers, lesbians are able to negotiate a more satisfactory stance with respect to traditional gender expectations. Paradoxically, however, this very process of accommodation presents them with further problems to be resolved, frequently demanding that they reorganize their identities with motherhood at the core.

As we saw earlier, having children has the added benefit of connecting lesbians and other women to forces of "good" in the world, of allowing them to participate in the creativity of childhood, and to be altruistic. The intensity of their feelings makes the experience of motherhood meaningful, rather than just burdensome. For some women, this is almost an astonishing transformation.

Christine Richmond, who had a baby on her own about three years ago, speaks with amazement about the changes he has brought into her life. She is a successful musician, and until she became a mother she spent most of her time perfecting her skills, planning performances and tours, and being caught up in the excitement of her professional world. But her son, she says,

> brings out feelings in me that I have never experienced before, both love and anger. . . . He's the first thing in my life that means more to me than I do. I would do anything for him, I mean I would give my life for him. . . . If anything were to happen to him I don't know if I would want to go on living.

Inez Escobar sees her daughter not only as her closest friend and companion but as the person whose existence helped her to improve her life, particularly to overcome her early problems with alcohol and drugs.

> I think being responsible for somebody, and kind of like having a stake in the future. Like wanting the world to be a better place. . . . But just kind of when I started to see her mirror me, it kind of made me want to change, and be a better person.

Lesbian mothers' narratives reveal the resilience of relatively traditional notions of family, even as their structural expression may vary tremendously. More profoundly, perhaps, lesbian mothers appear to accept motherhood eagerly as a core identity, and to be willing to allow its demands to attenuate other kinds of relationships and other sources of identity. Their narratives show that links to children, and particularly the need to engage in altruistic behavior and the opportunity to be in touch with the higher order one encounters with children, may be what family means in the shifting situation of lesbians. Here ideas about one's blood kin provide a model, albeit highly idealized, of what one can expect from one's connection to one's children.

Ties with children are anchored by the twin weights of responsibility and connectedness. Having a child on one's own, whether one started on that basis or not, locates one in the world, gives a woman a partner, a collaborator in the business of living, and takes some of the uncertainty and formlessness out of daily existence. At the same time, motherhood imposes heavy burdens and feelings of obligation and inadequacy that undermine other concerns and areas of competence, relegating them to triviality. Nothing else seems as important as one's children, and women paradoxically resent the tyranny of motherhood at the same time that they derive value from their experience of it.

Notes

1. See Weiss 1979 for similar findings in a study of postdivorce families.
2. Lillian Faderman (1991:218–219) notes that lesbian feminists frequently use "wo-man" as a euphemism for "lesbian," particularly when they refer to the cultural developments—women's books, women-centers, women's music, and the like—that emerged in the 1970s.
3. Faderman 1991 and Echols 1989 discuss the pressure to be "p.c." and its effects on feminists in the 1970s.
4. Some commentators claim that "butch/femme" roles are both historically and eco-nomically situated and no longer are key dimensions of lesbian communities, but evidence points to the continuing salience of these roles and in some cases to renewed enthusiasm for their symbols. See Kennedy & Davis 1989, 1993; Nestle 1987, 1992; Newton 1984; Newton & Walton 1984; Weston 1990.

Works Cited

Arendell, Terry. 1986. *Mothers and Divorce: Legal, Economic, and Social Dilemmas.* Berkeley: University of California Press.

Echols, Alice. 1989. *Daring to Be Bad: Radical Feminism in America, 1967–1975.* Minneapo-lis: University of Minnesota Press.

Faderman, Lillian. 1991. *Odd Girls and Twilight Lovers: A History of Lesbian Life in Twenti-eth-Century America.* New York: Columbia University Press.

Faludi, Susan. 1991. *Backlash: The Undeclared War against American Women.* New York: Crown.

Hartmann, Heidi I. 1981. The Family as the Locus of Gender, Class, and Political Strug-gle: The Example of Housework. *Signs* 6(3):366–394.

Hochschild, Arlie, with Anne Machung. 1989. *The Second Shift.* New York: Viking.

Kennedy, Elizabeth Lapovsky, and Madeline Davis. 1989. The Reproduction of Butch-Fem Roles: A Social Constructionist Approach. In *Passion and Power: Sexuality in History,* ed. Kathy Peiss and Christina Simmons with Robert Padgug, pp. 241–256. Philadelphia: Temple University Press.

———. 1993. *Boots of Leather, Slippers of Gold: The History of a Lesbian Community.* New York: Routledge.

Lewin, Esther. 1984. The Mythic Mannish Lesbian: Radclyffe Hall and the New Woman. *Signs* 9(4):557–575.

Nestle, Joan. 1987. *A Restricted Country.* Ithaca, N. Y.: Firebrand Books.

——— ed. 1992. *The Persistent Desire: A Femme-Butch Reader.* Boston: Alyson.

Newsweek. 1990. The Future of Gay America. March 12, p. 21 (cited in Faderman 1991:309, n.3).

Newton, Esther, and Shirley Walton. 1984. The Misunderstanding: Toward a More Pre-cise Sexual Vocabulary. In *Pleasure and Danger: Exploring Female Sexuality,* ed. Carole S. Vance, pp. 242–250. Boston: Routledge & Kegan Paul.

Weiss, Robert S. 1975. *Marital Separation.* New York: Basic Books.

———. 1979. *Going It Alone.* New York: Basic Books.

Weston, Kath. 1990. Do Clothes Make the Woman? Butch/Fem and Gendered Transfor-mation. Paper presented at annual meetings of American Anthropological Association, New Orleans.

12 "In the Beginning He Wouldn't Lift Even a Spoon"

The Division of Household Labor

BEATRÍZ M. PESQUERA

Research on the division of household labor demonstrates a persistent pattern: married women continue to perform all or most household tasks even when they are employed (Berk, 1985; Hartmann, 1981; Vanek, 1980). Similar patterns have been reported among Chicano families, however, these patterns are analyzed and reported in diverse ways. Some researchers stress the participatory role of husbands in the division of household labor to emphasize a trend toward egalitarianism (Ybarra, 1982), but even those who adhere to this line of thought acknowledge male reluctance. Ybarra and Arce (1981) found that husbands might participate in some household chores but that tasks such as cooking and laundry are resistant to "defeminization." Flores (1982) reported a traditional sex-role division, with women doing the majority of the housework; and other researchers support the tenacity of the traditional division of household labor (Mirandé and Enríquez, 1979; Segura, 1984).

Among Chicano couples, the most significant factor affecting the redistribution of household labor is women's employment. Ybarra (1982) and Baca-Zinn (1980) argue that there is a correlation between women's employment and increased male involvement in household labor. Zavella (1987), however, points out a key fact: although women's employment somewhat altered the distribution of labor, tasks remained sex-gender segregated. Data from my study of professional, clerical, and blue-collar Chicana workers corroborate these findings. Women's employment generally does bring about greater male involvement in household labor, but it does not lead to an egalitarian redistribution of tasks.

This essay analyzes the relationship between the ideology and practice of the division of household labor among a select group of Chicana workers. It also describes the process whereby that division of labor is altered or reproduced. I suggest that the distribution of household labor is shaped by the women's level of economic contribution to the household and their employment demands.

This study is based on information obtained through in-depth interviews with professional, clerical, and blue-collar married Chicana workers between the ages of twenty-five and forty. Each category included a selected sample of eight women; each informant met three criteria: (1) spouses must be of Mexican origin, (2) children must be present in the home, and (3) the women must have been employed full-time for at least five years. The employment criterion was essential, since the study analyzes the impact of work on family life. Because most of the women interviewed were in their childbearing years, I took maternity leaves into account.

To obtain a sample with these characteristics, I contacted professional associations, community groups and agencies, human service agencies, labor unions, and key persons who have contact with Chicana women. Informants were selected from names generated through the above referral system. Generalizability of the study is limited both by the relatively small sample size and by the method of sample selection.

The informants and their spouses came from lower- and working-class backgrounds. Although some of the women had early-childhood experiences in migrant workers' families, all have lived in urban settings the majority of their lives. At the time of the study, they resided in northern California.

Chicana professionals have at least a bachelor's degree, and five earned postgraduate degrees. Three husbands have the same level of education as their wives, two are more highly educated, and the remaining three have less education (with one a college student at the time the interview took place). Chicana professionals are all concentrated in the public sector; the majority are administrators, and two are teachers. Five of the husbands are either administrators or lawyers, one is self-employed, one is a student, and the other was at the time of the interview an unemployed teacher. Clerical workers are also employed primarily in the public sector. All but one of the clerical workers have from one to two years of community college or business school training. The majority of their husbands are blue-collar workers. Except in one case, where the husband has a bachelor's degree, the clerical workers have higher levels of education than their spouses. Among blue-collar workers, 75 percent also have some community college education. Their spouses tend to have lower levels of education; half did not complete high school, two have high school degrees, one has a bachelor's degree, and one has technical training. Except for one blue-collar worker who drives a delivery truck, all the women in this category work in factories. Their spouses are mainly employed as factory workers or in the skilled trades; one is a human services professional.

Data on the division of labor were generated through the use of various techniques. On a scaled written questionnaire, the women indicated the level at which each family member participated in household tasks and their own level of satisfaction with these arrangements. In addition, in a series of personal interviews, I asked the informants to describe in detail an average workday and an average weekend; open-ended questions were used to explore women's beliefs, expectations, and strategies. Disagreements or conflicts arising from the division of household labor were explored. Significant discrepancy existed between women's answers to the scaled questionnaire and their detailed descriptions of household routines. Overall, informants tended to report a higher level of male participation in household chores and a higher level of satisfaction with existing arrangements on the questionnaire than they expressed in their interviews. These differences between written and verbal descriptions of daily life require closer examination. They should give us insight into the dynamics of household labor.

The analysis presented here emerged from the contradictions in the data and provides a glimpse into the mundane interactions of Chicana workers in this sample. These interactions represent an important area for the study of gender politics. The division of household labor is a critical factor, since it is an arena where gender relations are negotiated, altered, and reproduced.

Ideology and Practice

The following sections discuss the relationships between the ideology and the practice of professional, clerical, and blue-collar Chicana workers. The discussion will focus primarily on "gender strategies"—that is, peculiarities in types of strategies used by wives and husbands in the struggle over "who will do what." These strategies—such as "stalling" (used by men) and "coaching" (used by women)—articulate the ideological underpinnings in the "political struggle" over household labor. By *ideology*, we mean the belief system that incorporates what women "think" husbands ought to do and what they concretely "expect" them to do. The *practice* of household labor refers to "behavior," including strategies used in the struggle over household chores. The term *political struggle* is borrowed from Hartmann (1981), who proposes using housework to illustrate the conceptualization of family as a "locus of political struggle" over the fruits of labor.

The overwhelming majority of women in this study "think" that their husbands should participate equally in household labor. Expectations of actual performance, however, differ considerably. Thus, at the level of "thought," the responses are uniform. At the level of "expectations," however, this ideological convergence is altered. In particular, clerical workers did not "expect" their husbands actually to perform household labor on an equal basis.

Differences in the level of "expectation" reflect what takes place in practice within these families. Professional and blue-collar Chicana workers have greater expectations and observe greater male participation in household tasks. The different levels of male involvement reflect not only different expectations but also the women's willingness to engage in conflict and struggle with their husbands in order to increase their share of household work. That is, professional and blue-collar Chicana workers not only expect more but are willing to demand more from their husbands. Therefore, their husbands do considerably more than the husbands of clerical workers. The high level of "expectation" did not, however, translate into an equal division within these households. Although these women were firm in expressing their expectations, half of them admitted that these expectations were not actually fulfilled. As one woman stated, "It doesn't mean it's going to happen."

To understand the complex dynamic between ideology and behavior, we must examine the gender strategies of these households by occupation. As pointed out, at the level of ideology, there was a divergence by occupation; differences also exist at the behavioral level. These findings are discussed in the following sections, which are organized by occupational categories.

Professional Workers

Households of Chicana professionals are the least sex-role segregated of this sample (Table 1). Nonetheless, these women perform more of the household labor than their husbands do. Although professional women's expectations are not being translated into equitable household division of labor, half of these women reported a high degree of satisfaction with existing arrangements. The reported level of satisfaction was called into question, however, as Chicana professionals articulated their frustrations, conflicts, and struggles during the interview. Furthermore, the reported level of male involvement in the division of household labor on the scaled questionnaire often did not coincide with the women's descriptions of daily activities in the home.

Table 1   Division of Household Labor: Professional
(% of sample, in round numbers; N = 8)

	Respondent[a]	Both[b]	Spouse[a]
Plans/prepares meal	37	50	12
Cleans up after meals	50	37	12
Cleans house	62	37	—
Buys groceries/household needs	50	37	12
Does laundry	50	50	—
	High	Low	Neutral
Level of satisfaction	50	37	12

a Performs these chores all or most of the time.
b Perform these chores about equally.

The struggle over the division of household labor among professional couples tends to generate various levels of conflict. For some, it was minimal; for others, it was open warfare. Perhaps Linda was most adamant in expressing this conflict:

Well, he says that I need to do more around the house. I'm sure that whatever he says, it is because he is feeling that I'm not putting in my part. But frankly, I don't give a shit. I mean, I do, but I'm thinking I'm doing a lot, too. I tell him I'm not superwoman. And if I start taking what he says really seriously, then I would probably have a nervous breakdown. I wouldn't be able to function.

Yolanda felt that she was doing more of the household work than she should. Her husband's lack of participation and his cultural expectations were constant sources of conflict. She complained that her husband consistently compared her to other women in order to discredit her expectations. She also has come to the conclusion that other women are willing to accept a minimal amount of male participation.

What happens, what blows my mind, is I consider the fact that my husband does what to me is a minimal amount of work around the house, and my friends will come over and it will blow their minds at how much he does. Oh, Tony cooks, and washes dishes. Yeah, and it blows their mind, because their husbands do even less.

"Stalling" or not completing the task properly are strategies employed by men to avoid doing housework. Women sighed with resignation and said that often it was just easier to do the work themselves. Teresa Godinez explained:

The balance between how much is done or expected to be done creates tension. I think at any point when something isn't done there is a "who will do it." In his mind the easiest answer is that no one does it and that's okay with him. In my mind if it doesn't get done, then I'm unhappy about it, so I end up doing it. It's not so much an argument of "who will do it," but just it has to be done. It probably goes back to the superwoman image. I want a good house. I don't want somebody to walk in and see this mess. It is not going to be Mike that they think didn't clean up the mess. It's going to be me.

Selia, who has difficulties with her husband's stalling strategies, rationalized his behavior as "casual, laid-back." She stated that her husband was extremely committed to his career and spent several hours every evening on his work. His zeal and commitment to his work call into question his "laid-back" attitude toward household labor. Rather, his casual attitude toward housework appears to be a strategy to avoid the work.

Overall, men married to professional Chicanas do more household work than other men in this sample. In a few families, their involvement is not a product of constant tension. For the most part, however, the only way women have altered the distribution of labor has been through conflict and confrontation.

Clerical Workers

In marked contrast, men married to clerical Chicanas do much less housework than all other husbands in the sample (Table 2). Although women were solely or primarily responsible for the household tasks, only three expressed dissatisfaction. The division of household labor in these households did not generate the same level of conflict as was found in households of Chicana professionals. Instead of open conflict, clerical workers thankfully accepted whatever their husbands were willing to give, or they attempted to "school" their husbands through gentle non-confrontational tactics. Their behavior reflects a clear ideological division between what they "think" and "expect" regarding household labor. Some women said that they did not expect equal sharing because of their cultural upbringing. Gloria, for example, said:

I think if I was raised differently and he had been raised differently I would, but I don't expect it. I'm not going to be the type that nags and says you do your share. I don't because it makes the house a little more comfortable, rather than have the constant nagging.

Table 2 Division of Household Labor: Clerical
(% of sample, in round numbers; N = 8)

	Respondent[a]	Both[b]	Spouse[a]
Plans/prepares meals	87	12	—
Cleans up after meals	87	12	—
Cleans house	75	25	—
Buys groceries/household needs	50	37	12
Does laundry	75	25	—
	High	*Low*	*Neutral*
Level of satisfaction	37	37	25

a Performs these chores all or most of the time.
b Perform these chores about equally.

Laura, a swing-shift worker at the telephone company, whose husband is a full-time student, does not expect him to take equal responsibility and attempts to avoid conflict. Before she leaves for work in the afternoon, she usually prepares dinner for her husband and nine-year-old son. Although she arrives home after midnight, she gets up in the morning to take care of her son's needs and drives him to school.

> There are times when I wish I could come home and the sink was clean and there were no dishes from dinner. But I overlook it. They are going to get done, I'm going to do them, and I see no sense in making an upheaval about it. I never hold him accountable. So if it gets done, fine; if it doesn't, well it will get done somehow. It's not something I harp on.

Norma, a secretary, talked about how men had to be "retrained." She also attempts to avoid conflict, nagging, or demanding tactics. Instead, she has taken the advice of older Mexican women, who have told her that "tienes que hacerlo por la buena" (you have to do it on good terms).

> I usually try to do it "a la buena." I kind of play little tricks, get him into a good mood or whatever. I just make sure that everything feels kind of neutral, like at night when no one is feeling grouchy or angry. And I will say, "Oh, help me with this, or bring me that, and can you do this for me. Oh, thank you, honey" or whatever and I kind of pat him on the back.

Norma's efforts have met with some success, in that her husband is beginning to become more involved in household labor. Juan is now working a four-day, ten-hour shift and is home Fridays. "On Fridays, when he is home, he fixes his own breakfast, and he will clean up a little bit, like he washes the dishes, vacuums, and fixes things up."

Norma also recently began to "school" him on how to do the laundry. While she feels responsible for laundering his work and personal clothing, she decided that he could take care of his athletic clothing. Juan belongs to a soccer team that plays every weekend and practices several times a week, so extra work is required for the upkeep of his gym clothes. Recently, after gentle prodding from her, he began to take responsibility for doing his own gym clothes.

The division of labor has also changed somewhat over the course of the marriage in Flor's household, but she is still responsible for the majority of the work, with help from her teenage daughter.

> It's changed. In the beginning he wouldn't lift even a spoon. As they say in Spanish: "No levanta ni una cuchara." That's true. He wouldn't babysit his own children; he wouldn't pick up his things; he wouldn't take his dish to the sink. Everything had to be done for him. It remained like that while I was at home. After I started working, things weren't getting done by me. After a long time he finally decided he could carry his dish to the sink by himself, and he could watch his own kids. Little by little he has just kind of gotten into doing things for himself. If there wasn't a pair of pants ironed, well, he just had to iron them himself. He has also learned to prepare his own breakfast and lunch for himself. So now he does for himself, and he doesn't really get into any household things for anybody else. If he does, then we hear about it.

Flor's husband, like Norma's, is involved in sports tournaments and practices several times a week. Like Norma, Flor also recently decided that she should not have to be responsible for his gym clothes.

Clerical workers also complained that their husbands utilize stalling techniques. Even though women recognize these tactics, they nevertheless fall prey to their husbands' strategies. As Yvette explained:

> There were times when the garbage is there and I'll ask him, "Victor, will you please take out the garbage?" and he will say, "OK babe, I'll do it later." It's two hours later and I look and the garbage is still there and I will think, "I'll fix that." I'll get another bag and I'll start making another little garbage bag. And it's already in the evening and I'll ask him, "Aren't you going to take out the garbage?" "Oh yeah, babe, I'll do it later." Then I'll think, "I'll fix this guy, I'll do it myself." I feel like I'm torturing him because I didn't give him the opportunity to take out the garbage, but all along I'm torturing myself, right?

While clerical workers do expect their husbands to "fill in their shoes" when necessary, they cling to traditional gender-role ideology. Although Yvette's situation has changed over the course of the marriage, with her husband taking on more responsibilities, a clear division of "his" and "her" realms persists, and both view his participation as a "help" to her.

> Things have changed. Now if he takes off his clothes and leaves them around, I just put them into a little pile. So a few days later, he will say, "Where are my slacks?" You

see that pile over there? Well, what are they doing there? Look, I don't wear them, those are your clothes. If you known they are clean, you hang them up, and if they are dirty, then I will get to them.

Clerical workers in particular bring up gender-role socialization to explain contemporary gender behavior and realms of responsibility. As Yvette explained:

In my house my father did nothing, my mother did everything. The house was the responsibility of my mother and the children. So in my mind, the father was to go to work and bring home the bread and butter, and it was the mother's responsibility to have the bread and butter on the table. That is why I say, my dishes, my laundry, because those are my responsibilities up front.

Chicana clerical workers differ from women in both professional and blue-collar jobs in their acceptance of traditional gender-role divisions. They uniformly stated that they did not expect their husbands to share equally in the division of household labor, they relied on gender-role ideology to explain their situation, and they utilized nonconfrontational strategies to attempt to change this division of labor.

Blue-Collar Workers

Chicana blue-collar and professional workers articulated similar expectations and willingness to engage in household struggle. Although husbands of blue-collar workers do less housework than husbands of Chicana professionals, the level of satisfaction with the division of household labor was similar for both groups. Half of the blue-collar women expressed a high level of satisfaction (Table 3).

Table 3   Division of Household Labor: Blue-Collar Workers
(% of sample, in round numbers; N = 8)

	Respondent[a]	Both[b]	Spouse[a]
Plans/prepares meals	75	25	—
Cleans up after meals	50	37	—
Cleans house	50	50	12
Buys groceries/household needs	50	37	12
Does laundry	65	25	12
	High	Low	Neutral
Level of satisfaction	50	25	25

a Performs these chores all or most of the time.

b Perform these chores about equally.

One blue-collar worker stated that she expected her husband to do his equal share "right from the beginning," but most of the blue-collar workers adopted a militant stance on household labor later in their marriages. The overwhelming majority of blue-collar marriages started out highly sex-role segregated. During the course of the marriage, however, women began demanding—and receiving— more help from their husbands to accommodate their working schedules.

Christina, a delivery truck driver, who has the most egalitarian relationship in this sample, was very clear about what she expected from her husband from the beginning of her marriage.

> Well, in the beginning we would have arguments, but I told him, I can't do everything. Right from the beginning we said what was expected. I wanted to work but I didn't want to come home to clean up the house. Like some of my girlfriends, their husbands work and they come home and that is it. They don't do anything. And on Friday nights they go out and have fun with their friends and the women have to stay home with the kids. I can't accept that. That is not right.

Christina reported joint division of labor on almost all items on the scaled questionnaire. However, when she talked about what occurred on a daily basis, it was clear that although her husband does a considerable amount of work, she does more. At the end of the interview, she became aware of this contradiction, looked up at me, and said: "I think I do more. But he doesn't just sit around the house. He puts his share in, but I do more."

Perhaps the most dramatic change has occurred in Maria's family as a result of her demands. Maria has a full-time job in a furniture factory, working the swing shift. She also works on-call at a motel during the week and works two eight-hour shifts on the weekends. Of the women interviewed in this sample, she had the most oppressive relationship. Prior to her newfound militancy, she did all the household labor, but then things changed. As she says,

> This just started recently, about two years ago. Before, I used to do everything. Now I put my cards on the table and he is doing his chores. In other words, we have made an agreement that he does so much and I do so much. I have worked hard for this, that is why it has changed.

When I asked her what brought on the change, she replied:

> I just got tired of it. *I'm nobody's slave.* Like I told him, I never used to take care of myself. Now I'm taking care of me. Before, I was too busy taking care of everything. I didn't have time, now I have time. Before, he demanded that I get up at 4:00 A. M. to prepare his breakfast and lunch, and now he does it himself. So now I get a full rest. I don't have to worry about washing clothes because he washes every week. If I prepare dinner, he will wash dishes. And when I don't feel like preparing dinner, he makes dinner and washes dishes too.

Like Chicana professionals, blue-collar women have had to fight an uphill battle that has gained them some tangible results. But even though men are doing more, most of the women are still responsible for the majority of household labor. Although men married to blue-collar women are sharing in the household labor, there is a great deal of resistance on their part. Women, however, continue to strive for greater male involvement. Victoria discusses resistance and change in gender relations in her marriage:

> It hasn't been easy. Richard was brought up *muy macho*. When I started working, I told him, "I'm tired. Why don't you help me do this?" At first he would say, "You can do it." It was getting to be too much. To this day Richard does not bathe the girls, Richard does not cook, he doesn't wash the toilet. I do that. But he washes clothes, mops the floor, and vacuums.

Richard's subversive techniques are similar to those employed by other husbands in this sample. Victoria, like other women, falls prey to these strategies, ultimately doing the job herself.

> For Richard to give the girls dinner, he will go to Wendy's and feed them. For him to be able to pay the PG&E bill, he will wait for two months to pay it. For Richard to make sure that the floor is clean, he will let it go. He will eventually do it but not when it needs to be done. I know he can do it, *pero se hace tonto* [but he plays dumb]. So I'll say, "Get out of here and let me do it."

Victoria has attempted a variety of techniques in her struggle. Outright confrontation and nagging have netted some results. Recently she has become increasingly impatient with her husband and has gone on strike.

> So I found another way of doing it, which is I don't wash for him, I don't cook for him. I'm getting to the point at which I only make certain foods for the girls and I. Then he will come to, he gets the message.

Not only are blue-collar Chicanas willing to make demands on their husbands, but also at the ideological level they label their husbands' attitude as sexist. Victoria very adamantly told me: "One day I called Richard a male chauvinist pig. Boy, was he shocked."

Like other husbands, blue-collar men compare their wives to other women as a mechanism of social control in their attempts to maintain their privileges. Lisa related an incident that happened at her mother-in-law's house.

> He tries to pull these little numbers. Like "That is not the way my mother does it." Well, once we were at his mother's house and she had some beans on the stove, and he told his mother the way he wanted the beans cooked. And I thought to myself, if he had told me that, he would have been wearing the beans. I just thought, no way. I'm not going to put up with that, no way.

The data reveal that both men and women employ a variety of "gender strategies" to manipulate the situation to their advantage. Men use stalling tactics and perform tasks in a slipshod manner to avoid domestic work. They attempt to com-

pare their wives to other women, as a means of social control and in order to discredit their wives' requests. Women also utilize a variety of strategies in their daily
struggle: they retrain, coach, and praise husbands for a job well done. At times, they
resort to slowdowns or work stoppages, so that eventually men are forced to contribute more to household labor.

Clerical workers are unique in their underground approach, which, for the most
part, avoids verbal confrontations and open power struggles. Professional and blue-
collar workers also utilize underground resistance in combination with confrontation techniques. This tactic has been successful for blue-collar and professional
women; they have been able to alter the distribution of household labor on their
behalf to a much greater degree than clerical workers. A strong relationship
emerged between women's willingness to engage in "political struggle" and the
level of male involvement in household labor.

The analysis of the household division of labor in this sample illustrates the
complexity of the relationship between ideology (the belief system that incorporates what women "think" and what they "expect") and practice (as expressed in
their behavior). At the ideological level, all the respondents believe that their husbands should have equal responsibility for household chores. However, clerical
workers unanimously stated that they did not expect equal sharing, whereas blue-
collar and professional workers expected equal sharing but did not believe it would
actually happen. The category "expectations" operates at two levels: what women
want, and what they think will happen realistically. At the level of practice, clerical
workers behaved according to their nonexpectations. They did not demand or
struggle for male involvement. They also articulated more sex-linked attitudes
regarding male and female roles in the family. At the abstract level, they embrace an
egalitarian stance on household labor. At the same time, they also expressed strong
ideological and emotional ties to sex-typed roles. Perhaps this commitment to traditional roles accounts for their lack of expectations and their nondemanding attitudes. They could not expect their husbands to participate equally, since they
themselves were not convinced that there *should* be equal participation. Professionals and, to a lesser degree, blue-collar workers were more successful in translating
their beliefs and expectations into practice. Their willingness to struggle with their
husbands also attested to the strength of their convictions and expectations.

Analysis

I believe that women's earnings and work demands are contributing factors, at the
ideological and behavioral levels, in the "political struggle" over the distribution of
household labor. They are not the only factors, but they represent two plausible
links between employment and the division of household labor that emerged from
this sample.

Income

In *Becoming a Two Job Family*, Hood (1983) found that, in her sample of midwest-
ern American couples, income ratio strongly influenced power relations in the family. Similarly, data from this study suggest a link between women's earnings and

their ability to negotiate for greater male involvement in household labor. Most women viewed their economic contribution as a bargaining chip in the marriage power struggle. However, most of the women in this sample were unable to translate "income power" into marriage power, probably because they earned less than their spouses. This wage differential was most acute in the clerical category.

Clerical workers earned considerably less than their spouses, seven of whom are blue-collar workers and one a supervisor. Three clerical workers earned half or less than half as much as their spouses earned, and two earned $5,000 less. The other three women were primary supporters: one husband was a student on the GI bill, another collected disability insurance after an industrial accident, and a third husband received unemployment benefits.

While blue-collar Chicana women earned less than their blue-collar husbands, the gap was much less than for clerical women. In the blue-collar category, six Chicanas earned $5,000 to $10,000 less than their spouses, one earned the same salary, and one earned $2,000 more.

Among professional workers, two women were primary supporters, two earned $10,000 to $15,000 more than their spouses, two earned the same salary, and two earned $10,000 to $15,000 less than their husbands. Husbands of professional women were also professional workers, except in one case, where the husband was a student. For professional Chicanas, the economic gap was also much less than for the clerical workers.

Among the eight professional Chicanas in the sample, four of the husbands assumed considerable responsibility for household chores. In three of these four households, the women were providing most of the income to the household and had jobs with higher status than those of their husbands; one husband was a student, one held a transitional job that he was going to quit in order to study for the bar, and one was attempting to establish a law practice. In one other household, the husband was unemployed and the wife provided the sole economic support, but she was still responsible for most of the household tasks. This household exhibited a high level of conflict. In households where wives provided either similar or less income, or held similar or less prestigious employment status, women were responsible for more of the household labor.

Among blue-collar households, the relationship between women's earnings and the division of household labor was not readily apparent—probably because the earning gap between men and women was minimal. Although blue-collar men were assuming a share of the household labor, their involvement fell short of that of men married to professional women. Blue-collar households were similar to professional households in that there was a high level of struggle.

Clerical women were at an economic disadvantage vis-à-vis their husbands. This disadvantage was reflected in the lack of male participation in household work. Overall, clerical workers did most or all of the household work. In the two households where men were assuming more responsibility, the husbands were providing less household income. In one case, the husband was a student receiving GI benefits; in the other, the husband received disability benefits. Since clerical Chicanas earn considerably less than their spouses, their economic power for bargaining strategies was practically nil. Furthermore, some of the men openly utilized their earning advantage in their efforts to circumvent their wives' attempts to involve them in household labor. These husbands used their higher salaries as leverage to maintain a measure of economic and social control and justify their resistance to doing "women's work."

Work Demands

The work demands for professional and blue-collar Chicanas are greater than for clerical workers; therefore, greater male involvement in household chores is required if these women are to handle both work and family concerns. Clerical workers have set limits to their labor, whereas the demands of professional and blue-collar jobs are not so easily contained. Clerical workers, for example, have fixed schedules, and though they may bring home their work-related problems and frustrations, they are generally better able to separate work from family life. Though they generally complain about fatigue and stress from the job, they are not required to bring work home, and generally they are not required to work overtime or work a shift that conflicts with their familial duties.

For blue-collar workers, however, work schedules may vary. These workers complained that, although theoretically overtime is voluntary, they must work overtime if they are to stay in the good graces of the supervisor because a worker's willingness to put in overtime hours is taken into account when evaluations are made and promotions given. Work shifts can also vary; consequently, husbands often are forced to assume a greater share of household and child-care tasks, whether they want to or not.

Professional workers have to contend with the fatigue and stress of juggling work and family committments and are often unable to keep work from spilling into family life. Professional Chicanas have to take work home and often must attend evening meetings. Furthermore, the pressures associated with being a woman of color increase their level of tension, expectations, and stress. As Luisa stated,

> It's the double-triple role you have to uphold. Like I was telling my boss, I said, "You know, I have to succeed in this job. Because if I don't, I fail as a Chicana, as a female, and as me," where if I was a white man, it would be different. It's that responsibility that we carry.

The work demands and the political nature of their jobs give Chicana professionals a degree of leverage for negotiating greater male involvement in household labor.

Conclusion

The degree of husbands' participation in household labor varied considerably in this sample. Professional men married to professional women did a greater share than most other men. The lack of a substantial earning gap, the energy and time demands of the women's careers, and their ability to pressure their husbands into doing their share had a positive effect on male involvement.

Blue-collar men married to clerical women did the least amount of household labor. In these families, a substantial earning gap, working schedules that allowed clericals to continue to fulfill their familial responsibilities, and the women's ideological stance had a cumulative negative effect on male involvement in household labor.

The lack of earning gap between blue-collar men and women was virtually nil—in conjunction with women's demanding and often unpredictable working schedules and their willingness to press for greater male participation in household labor—produced a positive result. Blue-collar men married to blue-collar women were more involved in household labor than blue-collar men married to clerical workers; but, with few exceptions, blue-collar men did less of the household labor than professional men.

Most of the women in this study have made some gains in moving their relationships with their partners toward less sex-role-segregated arrangements. In general, however, these marriages are not egalitarian in household chore allocation. The portrait that emerges from this study is a tendency toward a reproduction of the traditional household division of labor juxtaposed with a minimal degree of task reallocation. The data collected in this study points to the important role that qualitative research plays in uncovering critical dynamics in the household division of labor.

The relationship between income, demands of work, and the ideological and behavioral dimensions of the struggle over the division of household labor needs to be tested with larger samples.

Works Cited

Baca-Zinn, Maxine.
   1980. "Employment and Education of Mexican American Women: The Interplay of Modernity and Ethnicity in Eight Families." *Harvard Educational Review* 50:47–62.

Berk, Sarah Fenstermaker.
   1985. *The Gender Factory*. New York: Plenum.

Flores, Yvette Gisele.
   1982. "The Impact of Acculturation on the Chicano Family: An Analysis of Selected Variables." Ph. D. diss., University of California, Berkeley.

Hartmann, Heidi.
   1981. "The Family as the Locus of Gender, Class and Political Struggle: The Example of Housework." *Signs* 6:336–394.

Hood, Jane C.
   1983. *Becoming a Two Job Family*. New York: Praeger.

Mirandé, Alfredo, and Evangelina Enríquez.
   1979. *La Chicana: The Mexican American Woman*. Chicago: University of Chicago Press.

Segura, Denise A.
   1984. "Labor Market Stratification: The Chicana Experience." *Berkeley Journal of Sociology* 29:57–91.

Vanek, Joann.
   1980. "Household Work, Wage Work, and Sexual Inequality." In *Women and Household Labor*, ed. Sarah F. Berk. Beverly Hills, Calif.: Sage.

Ybarra, Lea.
  1982. "When Wives Work: The Impact on the Family." *Journal of Marriage and the Family* 2:169–177.

Ybarra, Lea, and Carlos H. Arce.
  1981. "Entra Dicho y Hecho Hay Gran Trecho: The Division of Household Chores in the Chicano Family." Paper presented at the National Association for Chicano Studies conference, Riverside, Calif., April.

Zavella, Patricia.
  1987. *Women, Work and the Chicano Family: Cannery Workers of the Santa Clara Valley.* Ithaca, N. Y.: Cornell University Press.

The Meanings of Macho 13

Changing Mexican Male Identities

MATTHEW C. GUTMANN

By 1992, most of the five-year-old boys in the San Bernabé Nursery School in Col. Santo Domingo cheerfully participated in the game called *"el banño de la muñeca,"* "the doll bath." Aurora Muñoz, the director of the Nursery, noted that the boys also now swept up, watered the plants, and collected the trash. When she began working at San Bernabé in 1982, however, many of the boys would protest: "Only *viejas* do that!" (similar to "That's girls' work!"). Aurora Muñoz attributed the changes to the fact that, as the boys themselves reported, their older brothers and fathers often did these things now, so why shouldn't they?[1] In the *colonia popular* neighborhood of Santo Domingo on the southside of Mexico City, where I began conducting ethnographic fieldwork on male identities in 1992, grandfathers sometimes remark on the changes in men and women in their lifetimes. When they were young, for instance, only girls were sent shopping for food, while today being allowed for the first time to go buy fresh tortillas marks a rite of passage for boys as well as girls.

In social science as well as popular literature the Mexican male, especially if he is from the lower classes, is often portrayed as the archetype of "machismo," which however defined invariably conjures up the image of virulent sexism (see Gilmore, 1990; Mernissi, 1975/1987; Paz, 1950/1992; Ramos, 1934/1992; Stevens, 1973). On the face of it, the classifications "Mexican men" or "Spanish-speaking men" are anachronisms. Such general categories negate important differences which exist within regions, classes, age cohorts, and ethnic groups in Mexico and throughout Latin America and Spain. Yet Brandes is still one of the few scholars to point to this variety: "Over the years, I acquired an image of Tzintzuntzan, and the Lake Patzcuaro region as a whole, as deviating from the usual social-science portrait of Mexican machismo" (1988:30).

As this paper will show, the diversity of male identities in the neighborhood of Col. Santo Domingo alone is enormous. Nonetheless, despite this diversity of male identities, at the same time certain important similarities exist among men who share particular sociocultural and historical experiences. Here, in order to examine Mexican male identities and to determine whether and how they may be transforming, I will explore intergenerational differences in what *ser hombre*, to be a man, means today in a lower class area of Mexico's capital city.

The history of Col. Santo Domingo makes it a good place to examine what, if any, are some of the changes in gender relations occurring today in Mexican society, and specifically, how male gender attitudes and behavior may be experienced and perceived differently today by both women and men. Before 1971, Santo Domingo was a wasteland of volcanic rocks, caves, shrubs, snakes, and scorpions. With migration from the impoverished countryside and other parts of the capital exacerbating the housing shortage in the cities, in one 24-hour period in early September 1971, nearly 5,000 families "parachuted" into the inhospitable yet uninhabited lava fields of Santo Domingo. It still stands as the largest single land invasion in Latin American history.

In the period since the invasion, as in many other urban and rural areas of Latin America, popular movements for social services (water, electricity, schools, sewage, and so on) have been a major political force in the area. In these popular struggles, the women of Col. Santo Domingo have generally been among the most active participants, and sometimes the leaders, including in opposition to continued government attempts to stop or coopt the independent organization of the residents of Col. Santo Domingo.

Change "by Necessity"

To a great extent this activity on the part of women has reflected the fact that most men can find jobs only outside the *colonia*, and that in many families it has been at least implicitly understood that women more than men had the job of trying to resolve day-to-day deprivations in the neighborhood. In addition, while Col. Santo Domingo was struggling into existence during the 1970s and 1980s, another change was occurring in the broader Mexican society that greatly affected men's relations with women, and therefore men's own identities: women in unprecedented numbers began to work outside the home.

Table 1   Women's and Men's Participation in the Economically Active Population (as Percentage of Total Population over 12 years old) for Mexico City and Mexico in 1990

	Mexico City (%)	Mexico (%)
Women	30.66	19.58
Men	66.81	68.01
Total	47.63	43.04

Source: *Estados Unidos Mexicanos, Resumen General, XI Censo General de Población y Viviendo*, 1990. Cuadro 27, p. 316. Mexico City: Instituto Nacional de Estadística, Geografía e Informática.

The most common explanation offered by men and women of varying ages in Col. Santo Domingo as to why so many men are now taking greater responsibility for various household duties that previously were the rather exclusive duties of women is "*por necesidad*," by necessity, because they have to. What they usually mean is that in many families, especially since the economic crisis of 1982, it has become economically necessary for both husband and wife to have paid work, and that this has often required the husband to do some of the household tasks that previously may have been done by the wife alone. What few men state, but what many women discuss with a certain relish, is that *por necesidad* can refer also to men being forced by the women with whom they live to take on some of these responsibilities. That is, in terms of changes in cultural attitudes regarding housework, quite regularly it is women who change first and then make—or at least try to make—their men change.

Women's participation in remunerated employment is significantly higher in Mexico City than in any other part of the country; thus one important result of migration from the rural *campo* to this sprawling metropolis of 20,000,000 inhabitants is a change in many women's occupational patterns (see Table 1).[2]

While in Mexico City in 1990, around 30 percent of women worked for money, this figure was slightly less than 20 percent for the country overall. Statistics by age groups reveal an even starker contrast between Mexico City and the country as a whole: over 40 percent of women between the ages of 40 and 44 in the Federal District were still "economically active" in 1990. Only 22 percent of women in Mexico in the same age category were registered as having remunerated employment (see Table 2).

Table 2   Women's and Men's Participation in the Economically Active Population, by Selected Age Groups (as Percentage of Total Population over 12 years old) for Mexico City and Mexico in 1990

	Women	Men	Total
Mexico City			
20–24 years	40.14	69.61	54.28
25–29 years	44.85	88.97	65.96
30–34 years	43.94	94.48	67.75
35–39 years	43.22	95.42	67.71
40–44 years	41.06	94.93	66.37
Mexico			
20–24 years	29.10	77.10	52.02
25–29 years	28.42	89.32	57.43
30–34 years	26.87	92.11	58.10
35–39 years	24.85	92.18	57.35
40–44 years	22.56	91.17	56.00

Source: *Estados Unidos Mexicanos, Resumen General, XI Censo General de Población y Vivienda*, 1990. Cuadro 27, p. 316. Mexico City: Instituto Nacional de Estadística, Geografía e Informática.

While I sat one day on a stool in his kitchen admiring the masonry work in his brick walls, Marcos washed the morning dishes. I asked Marcos if he had always done this chore. He paused for a moment, thinking, and then turning around to face me, shrugged and said: "I began doing it regularly four years, two months ago." Skeptical by nature and more than mildly surprised by the precision of his response, I inquired how he could so clearly remember his initiation into this task. "Quite simple, really," he replied with a grin—he knew exactly what I was driving at with my questions about men doing housework—"that's when my *vieja* began working full time. Before that she was around the house a lot more."

Gilberto Echeverría, a sixty-eight-year-old grandfather, offered his own experience. "Things used to be much more simple. For 40 years, I earned the family money as an *albañil* [laborer in construction], and my wife, before she died, she was responsible for everything in the home. "Now," he mused in a meditative tone, "now it's a wonder you can tell who's who. My daughter is also making money and my son-in-law helps [*ayuda*] her all the time in the house." Doña Berta says that her husband, who is still working on the line in the same factory after 20 years, used to get ridiculed by his brother when their five children were young, because Don Antonio would hold the children, change their diapers, and in general help a lot in raising them. Her brother-in-law's attitude was fairly typical of his generation. Now, she reports with a certain satisfied look, the tables have turned a lot and "the father who doesn't do these things is more likely to be the one being ridiculed."

It is not uncommon for husbands and fathers in their 20s and 30s in Col. Santo Domingo to wash dishes, sweep, change diapers, and go shopping on a regular basis. They will tell you about it if you ask, as will some of their wives, mothers, and sisters, and you will see them in their homes, in front of their houses, and in the neighborhood markets. One friend boasted to me one day: "Why sometimes I'm the one buying my daughters their sanitary pads. And, I'll tell you, I've got no problem with this as some guys still do. Well, so long as they tell me what brand to buy. After all, I'm not going to stand there like an asshole just gaping at all the feminine hygiene products!" It is certainly more common now than at any time in the past for men in Col. Santo Domingo to participate in most chores involved in running the household.

One exception to this is cooking, which among older and younger men—and not a few women—in various classes in Mexico City is still commonly seen as the consummately female task. Therefore rare is the man who prepares his or others' meals on a regular basis. Many men do cook when their wives or other women are not around, though this generally takes the form of reheating food which the women have left for them. And a lot of men like to cook for fiestas and on festive occasions, often having a special, signature meat dish (like calf brain tacos or a spicy goat stew). When asked about their not cooking more, some men explain that their wives will not let them enter the kitchen area, much less cook. Some of these same wives clarified for me that the real issue was that their husbands are far better at giving excuses than working.

The partial and relatively recent changes within the division of labor in some households in the *colonia* are not simply a reflection of economic transformations, for example, women working outside the home, but also relate to cultural changes in what it means to be a man today in at least some working class neighborhoods of Mexico City. It is a further indication of the actual duties performed and of the cultural values still placed on these household tasks, by women as well as by men, that the expression used by nearly all to describe men's activities in the home is *ayudar a la esposa*, helping the wife. Men generally do not equally share in these responsibilities, in word or deed, and the cultural division of labor between women is still regarded as important and therefore enforced by many. The female *doble jornada*, second shift (literally double day), is an ongoing and significant feature of life for many households in Santo Domingo. In addition, and related to their often privileged position in Mexican society, men in particular sometimes admit to trying to take advantage of the situation, by attributing greater natural energy to women and greater natural *flojera* (laziness) to men.

Fathers and Sons

Even more than housework, cooking, and shopping, parenting is considered by some scholars as a habitually and often exclusively feminine domain, and the extent of shared parenting between women and men is deemed a key test of the degree of gender equality in societies (see, for example, Chodorow, 1978; Ruddick, 1989). At the same time, Margaret Mead once defined the distinctively human aspect as lying "in the nurturing behavior of the male, who among human beings everywhere helps provide food for women and children" (1949/1975, p. 188). If not nearly measuring up to Mead's idyllic classification, in various *colonias populares* in Mexico City, as in other parts of Mexico today and historically, there exists a tremendous variety in patterns of parenting, specifically with reference to the roles played by men in raising children, which may challenge findings based more exclusively on certain U. S. middle class settings.

True enough, in Col. Santo Domingo it is certainly the case that women usually spend more time with the children than men do, and in the minds of a lot of women and men there, children, especially young children, belong with their mother or other women. And it is still the case that a majority of women in *clases populares* list as their work *hogar* and *ama de casa*, housework and housewife; clearly they are still in most households the adults most responsible for parenting day in and day out. Yet historically, in certain rural regions of Mexico, for instance, men have often played a special role in raising boys, particularly after they have reached an age when they are finally deemed mature enough to help with, or at least not get in the way of, their fathers' work in the fields (see Lewis, 1951/1963; Romney & Romney, 1963).

In the cities today, some men speak with great pleasure about having jobs that allow them to spend time with their children while they are working, like those furniture repairmen or cobblers who have little workshops in their houses, or others like car mechanics who work in the street in front of their homes. In addition, while family sizes are growing smaller, in households with older children it is common to find older girls, and increasingly older brothers and male cousins, caring for younger siblings, for example after school when parents and other adults may still be working.

Some men in their 70s today who took part in the invasion of Santo Domingo 20 years ago, after their children were already grown, talk about having had a lot of responsibility for raising their boys in particular. In formal interviews conducted with men and women in Col. Santo Domingo, a common theme among older men is that their parenting role with their boys included two particular dimensions. One, frequently these men relate that they usually took the boys with them when they went out on errands or to visit friends during their "free time," especially on weekends. Two, they were responsible more than the boys' mothers for teaching the boys technical skills (a trade) that would be necessary in fulfilling their later, adult masculine responsibilities as economic providers. Significantly, older women and men both report having shared in providing moral instruction and discipline for the boys. At least with the older generation, girls were more exclusively raised by women.

Alejandra Sánchez, a mother of two teenage girls, is convinced that the main reason her husband has never taken much responsibility for the children is because they have no sons. She laments that had there been two boys instead, he would have had "to buck up," and life for her would have been very different. Her situation is felt by neighbors to be rather typical of old-fashioned relations between mothers and fathers, and in this sense more exceptional in a community that has undergone innumerable changes in cultural relations, including those between men and women. Whether she is right is impossible to say, but her perception that with boys her irresponsible husband would have been at least culturally pressured if not obligated to take on certain accepted male parenting duties is certain.

A division of labor, fathers-sons and mothers-daughters, still pertains in some younger families in Col. Santo Domingo, but many men with small children today like to claim as a point of pride that they treat their boys and girls the same. If they spend more time with the boys outside the home, they sometimes explain, it is because it simply works out that way, because it is more convenient for both the father and mother, or because the boys want to spend time with them more than the girls do. To this must be added the fact that mothers—more than fathers—are often reluctant to have their girls go out with the men. Despite the fact that men carry and walk their daughters, it remains the case that from very early on boys are shepherded off with their fathers by their mothers in a way that girls seldom are.

Changing economic conditions in Mexico, especially since 1982, have impelled further changes among broad sectors of the male population. Some older men in Col. Santo Domingo are being laid off from jobs they have held for decades, and thus find themselves unemployed (and semiemployable at best) at the age of 60. They frequently report having more daily contact with their grandchildren than they ever had with their own children, a situation only some find agreeable. Among intellectuals in the middle classes, tougher economic times have sometimes necessitated doing without the live-in maid/nanny who was ubiquitous only a short time ago. Therefore men in these strata find themselves caring for their children far more than ever in the past, and the expression "*Estoy de Kramer*," "I'm Kramering," has come into vogue, meaning "I've got the kids," recalling the U. S. movie *Kramer vs. Kramer,* and pointing to certain U. S. cultural influences regarding modern family values and practices.

All in all, it is difficult in the case of Col. Santo Domingo to argue that in terms of attitudes and behavior parenting is identified exclusively with women. To some extent historically and without question today, for a variety of reasons, active, consistent, and long-term parenting is a central ingredient there for numerous, though obviously not all, men and women in what it means to be a man.

Machos Are Not What They Used to Be

It is common to hear women and men in Col. Santo Domingo say that while there used to be a lot of macho men, they are not as prevalent today. Some people who make this comment are too young to know anything firsthand about the old days, but regardless, they are sure there was more machismo before. If some oldtimers like to divide the world of men into machos and *mandilones* (meaning female-dominated men), it is far more common for younger men in Col. Santo Domingo to define themselves as belonging to a third category, the "nonmacho" group, "*ni macho, ni mandilón,*" "neither macho nor *mandilón*."[3] Though others may define a friend or relative as "your typical Mexican macho," the same man will not frequently reject the label for himself, describing all the things he does to help his wife around the home, pointing out that he does not beat his wife (one of the few generally agreed on attributes of machos), and so on. What is most significant is not simply how the terms macho and machismo are variously defined—there is little consensus on their meanings—but more, that today the terms are so routinely regarded by men in the working class in Col. Santo Domingo, Mexico City, as pejorative and not worthy of emulation.[4] Further, while many men in Col. Santo Domingo have (re)considered the relative merits of being macho, fewer have changed the way they refer to a group of men that, for them, is beyond the pale, that is, the *maricones*, queers, homosexuals, who thus constitute an especially marginalized fourth category of Mexican masculinities.

Sociocultural changes directly involving women have propelled new ways of thinking and acting among men with regard to machismo. Such changes among women have required reevaluations and changes among men, for if womanhood no longer is so closely tied to motherhood, manhood too must be at least partially recast. As a single (and still childless!) young man of 27 explained, "For me, having a lot of kids to prove you're really macho is a bunch of bullshit. That stuff went out four decades ago." Not all would agree with his periodization, but the sentiment is more widespread than the conventional wisdom—that Mexican males need confirmation of their virility through procreation—would allow.

In 1970, the average number of children per woman (out of the female population over 12 years old) in Mexico as a whole was 4.5 and for Mexico City 2.6. In 1990, the figure for Mexico City was 2.0, while for the country two years earlier it had dropped to 2.5 (see Table 3).[5] The drop in birthrates in the last 20 years in Mexico as a whole, and its urban centers in particular, has been dramatic. This decline has not necessarily led to direct changes in parenting attitudes and behavior on the part of men, but it certainly reflects changes in cultural practices by women regarding an area long closely identified with their gender identities.

Another sign of changes in gender identities in Col. Santo Domingo, especially in the last decade, has to do with women's alcohol consumption and adultery. While no precise figures are available, male and female residents of the neighborhood uniformly agree that women are drinking alcohol and "*saliendo,*" "going out" (in the sense of cheating on their spouses), in far higher numbers than ever before. There is disagreement as to whether men are drinking and cheating more. People are also divided, and of significance not neatly along gender lines, as to whether these

Table 3   Birthrates in Mexico from 1900 to 1988:
Average Number of Children per Woman over 12 years old

Year	(at any given time)
1900	5.0
1940	4.6
1960	4.5
1970	4.5
1977	3.8
1981	3.4
1983	3.1
1985	2.8
1988	2.5

Source: Adapted from Zavala de Cosío, 1992, pp. 26, 222, 282.

developments among women are good or bad in the long run. Regardless of different individuals' opinions about how women today are "altering the rules," the changes have contributed, among other things, to the initiation of numerous discussions within families and among friends about the meaning of terms like equality when applied to gender relations.

Women Are "Natural Leaders" in Col. Santo Domingo

Aurora Muñoz of the San Bernabé Nursery School says that women "tend to be natural leaders in Santo Domingo because of the needs of the *colonia*." From the beginning of the neighborhood in 1971, women led in the fights to acquire water for all residents. Then for electricity and schools. Only recently, in 1992, were streets being torn up to lay sewage pipes for the over 150,000 residents of Col. Santo Domingo.

Older women and men seem to have an easier time responding to questions about what difference it might make to grow up in an area in which women are community organizers and leaders, as opposed to one in which even if women work outside the home they certainly do not play an integral role in the political campaigns and protests of the neighborhood. For those who have grown up in Col. Santo Domingo, or in other areas of Mexico City where "popular urban movements" have taken place in the past 15 years, it is far more difficult to even imagine a situation in which women are not community activists.

Few questions are received by younger adults in the *colonia* as being so absurd (to the point of provoking chuckles) as those which inquire about the *mujer sumisa* or *mujer abnegada*, the submissive or self-sacrificing woman. It is not that people do not recognize her to exist; everyone can point to a neighbor or aunt whom they will characterize in this way. And it is true that the disdainful laugh of some men at the question about submissive women barely conceals a defensiveness regarding their own behavior toward women. Yet even when people identify *la mujer sumisa* as a relic from the provinces, that is, a migrant from another part of the country, people commonly point out to the inquiring ethnographer that this really is not an accurate description of women in many of the villages of Mexico either.

"Sure," Manuel Ramos points out to me, "these women exist and have always existed, but with all the moving around people have done in the last 30 years do you think this has left everything the way it was once between women and men? Impossible."[6]

Further, as Fidel Aguirre, a technician working in a laboratory outside the *colonia*, took pains to explain, "with women working outside the home it's not just a question of them having their own money now, as important as this has been. What's also involved is that women have met all sorts of different people, which has changed them forever. And this has meant that the men have changed, for if they don't, more and more they're getting left behind by women. Let me tell you, this is what's happening."

In addition to these changes in the sociocultural landscape several others have of course greatly contributed to the questioning and challenging of gender relations among people in Col. Santo Domingo. Chief among these must be listed the fact that through at least the early years of college, the numbers of females and males are today roughly equivalent, and thus expectations of women themselves (and frequently, of parents for their daughters, husbands for their wives, and so on) are quite different from what they were with earlier generations. Television, and within this the cultural reach of the U. S., has had a profound impact. Some government family centers and some churches have developed forums in which such information has been disseminated as well. A grandfather of eight grinned when he said that while he had never changed the diapers on his own children he had since learned how to do it for the next generation. Where did he learn this? From a program in his church.

Finally, the women's movement and the struggles for homosexual rights have had important, if more indirect, influences in Col. Santo Domingo on the self-conceptions that women of all ages, and to a lesser extent men of especially the younger generations, have concerning being women and men. This influence is realized in a number of ways, from women's health care workers who have been active in the community for over 10 years, to feminist magazines which at times have reached a mass circulation in some of the *colonias populares*.

Changing Men

In Mexico in the last 20 years, precisely the period in which Col. Santo Domingo has come into being, the entire society has witnessed rapid and widespread upheavals involving the economy, gender roles, struggles over ethnic identity, regional development and stagnation, ecological catastrophes, international migration, and political insurgency and repression. For most of this century there was a sense among even the poor that times would get better. Now, for many, the mood is more akin to the postmodernist malaise that has struck indeterminate others around the globe.[7]

Each of these sociocultural factors has its own particular timetable and trajectory, and it is far from clear, in the case of gender relations for example, where things are truly heading. But while we must therefore be particularly cautious in our attempt to analyze changes in these phenomena, we must also guard against a perhaps even more debilitating contemporary notion that nothing ever does change, especially when it comes to life between women and men.

The changes in attitudes and behavior on the part of men and women in Col. Santo Domingo are deeply felt, and evidently part of a developing process of transforming gender relations throughout Mexico. They are not, however, uniformly experienced or acknowledged. The ethnographic research reported in this paper has been conducted primarily in a lower class urban milieu, and secondarily among middle class merchants and professionals in Mexico City.

Lomnitz and Pérez-Lizaur (1987) conducted an ethnographic study of an elite Mexican family for 7 years. As the focus of their investigation concerned kinship networks, their findings are quite pertinent here. They write that among the elites studied, the father's "participation in raising children is indirect; he may occasionally play with his small children or, when they grow up, gradually introduce his sons to certain aspects of a man's world. Child rearing is the direct and formal responsibility of the mother" (p. 210).

For at least many fathers in Col. Santo Domingo, this is hardly the situation. Simply to note the greater responsibilities that women in both elite and popular classes have in parenting misses the enormous differences in the content of fathering in each context. Fathers in Col. Santo Domingo to a far greater extent appear to be integral in all stages of their children's lives, though to be sure in practice they are present more in the evenings and on weekends, commonly more with their boys than with their girls, and more with children over 3 or 4 years old. But beyond a merely quantitative, time-allocation difference in fathers' attention to their children, men in at least certain *colonias populares* define their own and others' masculinity in part in terms of their active role in parenting.[8]

Of course, as important as fathering may be to numerous men in Col. Santo Domingo, it is not all there is to being a man. In a conversation with an older couple on what had changed between women and men in their lifetimes, the woman (whom neighbors like to describe as a classic *mujer abnegada*) offered, "Why, the liberation of the woman!" She did not care to expand on this opinion except to add that it has been women who had changed the most since her youth, implying that the men were lagging behind. Her husband, a straight-talking character, dismissed his wife's comment with a wave of his hand and countered that what was different was that: "Today there're a lot of queers who've stopped being men." Clearly the directions in which changes have occurred are not uniform, either between women and men or between generations.

As a sign of continuing subordination of women to men, and despite the greater financial liberty brought to women by earning their own salaries, far more women are still economically dependent on men than men on women in Col. Santo Domingo. Talking with women who have endured years of battering from their husbands with no end yet in sight, this point is made repeatedly.

Birthrates have dropped, and contraceptives are used more than ever before, yet it is still most common to find women being held mainly responsible for birth control: a woman from Col. Santo Domingo went to get condoms at a state health service and was told by a male government doctor that prophylactics were only for promiscuous women, and that since they are not comfortable for men anyway, she should give her husband a break and use an I. U. D.

And while the boys in the San Bernabé Nursery School today play "girls' games" and, with the girls, help to clean up more than they used to, most of the girls, when they remember, are still careful to not get their clothes dirty, and most of the boys are still embarrassed when they cry, because their mothers and fathers are still teaching them that girls don't play like that and boys don't cry.

The developments and transformations in Col. Santo Domingo do not indicate full equality, cooperation, and mutual respect suddenly blossoming in gender relations there. Nonetheless, as part of the broader society and because of certain specific conditions pertaining in this largely self-built community, the "Mexican macho" stereotypes so common in the social sciences are today inappropriate and misleading in understanding large sections of men in this area, how they see themselves and how the women with whom they share their lives see them, their history, and their future.

Notes

Fieldwork was conducted in 1992–1993, with grants from Fulbright-Hays DDRA, Wenner-Gren, National Science Foundation, Institute for Intercultural Studies, UC MEXUS, and Center for Latin American Studies and Department of Anthropology at UC Berkeley. This research is continuing under a grant from the National Institute of Mental Health. My thanks to the Centro de Estudios Sociológicos and the Programa Interdisciplinario de Estudios de la Mujer, both at El Colegio de Mexico, and to the Departamento de Antropología, Universidad Autónoma Metropolitana-Istapalapa, for providing institutional support during fieldwork in Mexico City. My thanks also to Stanley Brandes, Nelson Minello, and Francesca Lima for comments on this paper.

Address correspondence to the author at Department of Anthropology, University of California, Berkeley, California 94720.

1. I am not proposing that getting boys to play with dolls in any manner resolves the issue of male dominance, as may be inferred from some socialization theories in psychology. Rather, boys playing with dolls is used here as an indication of changing sociocultural attitudes and practices.

2. See also earlier figures and discussion in García, Muñoz, and de Oliveira, 1982, pp. 34ff.

   Both Tables 1 and 2 are based on 1990 census data which unquestionably underestimate many forms for paid employment, semi-employment, illegal employment, "informal" employment, etc. Nonetheless, for purposes of comparison (e.g., were more women employed in Mexico City or in the *campo*?), we may reasonably draw limited conclusions from these figures.

3. *Mandilón* comes from *mandil* (apron) and translates literally as "apron-er."

4. See de Barbieri's (1990) provocative paper on "possible erosions in Mexican machismo."

5. The 1970 figure for Mexico City comes from the *IX Censo General de Poblacíon*, Cuadro 30, p. 513 (Secretaría de Industria y Comercio, Dirección General de Estadística). For 1990, the figure is from the *XI Censo General*, Cuadro 24, p. 273 (Instituto Nacional de Estadística, Geografía e Informática). Since women who will

go on to have other children are averaged into these totals, these figures do not represent the fertility rates for these areas.

6. Though a friend still describes the division of labor between men and women in his Zapotec village in the sierra of Oaxaca as *"mucho, mucho más tajante"* ("much, much sharper").

7. See Bartra (1987).

8. See also Arizpe (1989) on the relation between class, gender, and household roles.

Works Cited

Arizpe, L. (1989). *Cultura y desarrollo: Una etnografía de las creencias de una comunidad mexicana*. Mexico City: Porrua/Universidad Nacional Autónoma de México.

Bartra, R. (1987). *La jaula de la melancolia: Identidad y metamorfosis del Mexicano*. Mexico City: Grijalbo. (In English: *The Cage of Melancholy: Identity and Metamorphosis of the Mexican*. Christopher J. Hall, trans. New Brunswick: Rutgers University Press, 1992.)

Brandes, S. (1988). *Power and persuasion: Fiestas and social control in rural Mexico*. Philadelphia: University of Pennsylvania Press.

Chodorow, N. (1978). *The reproduction of mothering: Psychoanalysis and the sociology of gender*. Berkeley: University of California Press.

de Barbieri, T. (1990). Sobre géneros, prácticas y valores: notas acerca de posibles erosiones del machismo en México. In J. M. Ramírez Sáiz (Ed.), *Normas y prácticas: morales y cívicas en la vida cotidiana* (pp. 83–106). Mexico City: Universidad Nacional Autónoma de México.

García, B., Muñoz, H., and de Oliveira, O. (1982). *Hogares y trabajadores en la Ciudad de México*. Mexico City: El Colegio de México/Universidad Nacional Autónoma de México.

Gilmore, D. (1990). *Manhood in the making: Cultural concepts of masculinity*. New Haven: Yale University Press.

Lewis, O. (1951/1963). *Life in a Mexican village: Tepoztlán restudied*. Urbana: University of Illinois Press.

Lomnitz, L., and Pérez-Lizaur, M. (1987). *A Mexican elite family: 1820–1980*. Princeton: Princeton University Press.

Mead, M. (1949/1975). *Male and female: A study of the sexes in a changing world*. New York: Wm. Morrow.

Mernissi, F. (1975/1987). *Beyond the veil: Male-female dynamics in modern Muslim society*. Bloomington: Indiana University Press.

Paz, O. (1950/1992). *El laberinto de la soledad*. Mexico City: Fondo de Cultura Económica. (In English: *The Labyrinth of Solitude: Life and Thought in Mexico*. Lysander Kemp, trans. New York: Grove, 1961.)

Ramos, S. (1934/1992). *El perfil del hombre y la cultura en México*. Mexico City: Espasa-Calpe Mexicana. (In English: *Profile of man and culture in Mexico*. Peter G. Earle, trans. Austin: University of Texas Press, 1962.)

Romney, K., and Romney, R. (1963). The Mixtecans of Juxtlahuaca, Mexico. In B. Whiting (Ed.), *Six cultures: Studies in child rearing* (pp. 541–691). New York: John Wiley.

Ruddick, S. (1989). *Maternal thinking: Toward a politics of peace*. Boston: Beacon.

Stevens, E. (1973). *Marianismo*: The Other Face of *Machismo* in Latin America. In A. Pescatello (Ed.), *Male and Female in Latin America* (pp. 90–101). Pittsburgh: University of Pittsburgh Press.

Zavala de Cosío, M. E. (1992). *Cambios de fecundidad en México y políticas de poblacíon*. Mexico City: El Colegio de México.

CAROL STACK

The road from home leads out to the world and back. The people in this chapter who returned to the poor southern communities I call Burdy's Bend and New Jericho in Powell County, and Chowan Springs and Rosedale in Chestnut County, had not made one-way pilgrimages to northern cities. For generation upon generation, black men and women had been leaving such places, flooding away especially in the 1940s and 1950s. But in the 1970s and 1980s the sea changed, the tide of migration turned homeward, and the story of all the decades in between can no longer be represented as a simple narrative of a people packing up and heading north. What has never been told, we know now, is the tale of the bonds that were never broken; of the ways in which the people never entirely departed and in fact foreshadowed their homecomings.

For eight years, mostly in the 1980s, I talked to people who had left the South and then moved back home again. Their homeplaces were in the rural, eastern reaches of North and South Carolina, in communities that by all statistical measures can only be assessed as some of the least promising places in all of America. The U. S. Department of Agriculture has established a dismal category for them, the "Persistent Poverty Countries," and certainly for the past fifty years or so their major contribution to the American economy has been the production of out-migrants. That such places have now become destinations for a large-scale return of African Americans is a difficult fact for standard migration theories to digest.

The homeplace communities described in this chapter share a certain statistical profile: they are far from big cities, far from Sunbelt industry, way below national and even state averages for income, linked historically to the traditional southern cash crops, and skewed demographically by generations of out-migration. Black people have traditionally made up a majority of the population in such places, though all the decades of black exodus have sometimes changed the local racial balance. My research took me to nine counties in the two Carolinas, but many other places like them exist in all the southern states.

Holding Hands wasn't the first women's service organization in Chestnut County. By the time of its official charter in December 1981, there were already two other such groups: the Chestnut Education Circle, which a woman named Menola Rountree had started back in the 1950s to sponsor an annual beauty walk and raise money for college and trade-school scholarships, and Worldly Women, which held teen dances every month or so to bring together young people from the various churches in the county, most of which were too small for youth ministries or young people's fellowships of their own. Chestnut County was still just a little country place—in 1980 census takers had counted fewer than 1,000 people in the county seat, Chowan Springs, and just 467 in Rosedale, the next-largest town—but nonetheless, the three women behind Holding Hands believed that the time had come for another women's group, an organization that would try to tackle the problems of Chestnut County head-on, taking an approach that was literally hands-on.

The idea for Holding Hands could be traced to a backyard barbecue in late October of 1981. But the history actually went much further back than that, as any of the women involved could explain. It went back to the painful lessons the women had begun learning in 1979, when the first of them moved home again from the Bronx. And then back behind those lessons were ways of dealing with the world that the Holding Hands women had developed in the 1960s and 1970s while working their way through school, selling Amway products and life insurance, moving to the city, raising families, running PTAs and scout troops, and working in corporate offices and government agencies. Even more fundamentally, the roots of Holding Hands had been planted back in the 1950s when the women were growing up in Chestnut County as the daughters of sharecroppers and as best, best, best friends who just knew that everything was going to work out all right.

The three little girls, Shantee, Isabella, and Collie Mae, eventually acquired the matronly names of Shantee Owens, Isabella Beasley, and Collie Mae Gamble. All of them kept in touch over the years and got together often, but two of them in particular, Isabella and Collie Mae, carried their girlhood friendship to a new level in adulthood. For many years they were living hundreds of miles apart and were thus unable to rely on one another for day-to-day companionship and conversation; instead, they each took over responsibility for managing the other's career. For example, on the day before Isabella married Rudy Beasley, she took Collie Mae, who had driven up to Newark so she could be maid of honor in the wedding, over to the Civil Service office and arranged for her to take the employment exam. After Isabella moved back home and told Collie Mae about the shameful state of day-care services in Chestnut County, Collie Mae asked around her church until she located a *gentleman* who owned an abandoned gas station and persuaded him to make it available rent-free for a model day-care center. Neither woman could imagine changing jobs or making any major decisions about her professional life without consulting the other.

Shantee kept a little more distance, preferred a little more privacy. She wasn't a loner exactly, and she certainly wasn't shy, but perhaps people were left with some such impression because of the contrast with her mother, the inimitable and irrepressible Orlonia Parks, de facto toastmistress of Chestnut County. In 1946 a Rosedale boy named Halliburton Parks had been detailed over to Powell County by the lumbering outfit he worked for, and ever since he robbed the cradle over there to bring back fifteen-year-old Orlonia as his bride, life in Chestnut County had not been the same. No church meeting, school function, civic event, or gathering of any kind was complete without a few words from Miss Orlonia. She was the one who could get everybody to sit down and hush up, and she was also the one who could get everybody on their feet and roaring for action. People remembered her words: for example, instead of repeating a conventional expression such as "between a rock and a hard place," Miss Orlonia would say something like "between a dog and a tree."

As soon as Shantee was old enough to toddle onto the stage behind her mother, Orlonia had dragged her along and pushed her forward at every occasion. Shantee couldn't help but grow up poised and comfortable in public, though she backed off from her mother's down-to-earth imagery and developed a reputation for delivering even the most off-the-cuff remarks in a formal and polished cadence. But she, too, could turn a phrase that set people to giggling. *I am here today*, she once told an audience, *because my mother suggested that it would be in my best interest, or her best interest—or perhaps what she meant was that it would be* interesting*—if I got out of the house a bit and, shall we say,* established *myself*. Sometimes, however, Shantee left her listeners with a sense that she knew more than she would tell. People who liked her said she was discreet, and people who didn't like her said she was secretive.

Collie Mae and Isabella liked her very much and suspected secret sadnesses in her life. She'd been the first of the three to leave home, back in 1967, one day after they all graduated from East Chestnut High. She had stayed up north the longest, till the summer of 1983; Collie Mae had returned two years earlier, and Isabella two years before that. Everybody knew all about the fancy life she'd led up in New York. Orlonia left no one in the dark about how Shantee had gone to college and taught school for a while and then gone to work for a company that ran workshops in school districts all over the country, training teachers in the use of new curricular materials. *Shantee rides an airplane to work every day*, Miss Orlonia told Chestnut County. *She teaches teachers how to teach.*

Shantee's high school boyfriend, Anthony Owens, had sulked and pined after she left. He hadn't promised to wait for her—in fact, he'd threatened *not* to wait for her—but when she didn't come home and didn't come home, he finally moved up north himself to live with his uncle in the Bronx. Shantee was going to school at the time and claimed to be much too busy for a social life, so the only way Anthony could think of to get to see her was to enroll in school himself, signing up for the same classes she was taking. He eventually became a parole officer in Harlem, and they were married in 1972. The apartment they moved into was up on the thirty-fifth floor and had shag carpeting on the floor and track lighting in the ceiling. They had two black cocker spaniels. They never had children.

Isabella, meanwhile, stayed home while she attended a community college down near the coast, about an hour's drive from Chowan Springs. She got an associate's degree and then moved in with her sister in Newark, where she met a boy from home, Rudy Beasley, who was just back from Vietnam. Their wedding was Chestnut County's social event of the year, though it took place in Newark; half the county attended. Rudy went into the home remodeling business with his brothers, and Isabella worked for a state agency that administered federal funds for Head

Start and Title XX day-care programs. They eventually had two daughters, who worried Isabella sick all day every day, especially when they became teenagers. Newark was no place to raise children.

Collie Mae had the hardest time leaving home. She had been sent up north for three years back when she was in junior high school and her mother was dying of cancer; once the family was reassembled at home on their farm near Chowan Springs, she felt personally responsible for ensuring that things went smoothly. She lived with her father and her four little sisters and her father's mother, and though she was trying to take a full-time course load at a traditionally black teachers' college sixty-five miles from the farm, she also helped her grandmother with the cooking and the ironing and the washing, and she helped her father with farm chores and kept the books for him, and she helped her sisters with their schoolwork, and she worked part-time as a maid at a motel on the highway. When her grandmother fell ill, she took over all the cooking and ironing and washing, and she killed hogs, plucked chickens, put up vegetables for winter, nursed her grandmother, took over the main responsibility for raising her little sisters—and never stopped going to school. Some semesters she had to reduce her course load, but she never once dropped out.

Her grandmother died when Collie Mae was twenty-one and about halfway finished with her degree in business administration. After the funeral, every time she thought about her grandmother, she couldn't stop herself from also thinking about her mother; she was walking in the shadow of the valley of death, fearful and uncomforted. To keep herself from dwelling on her losses, she increased her course load at school to twenty-one semester hours, well above the full-time level, and she increased her work week at the motel to forty hours, sometimes more. Her housework and farmwork didn't really let up, but it only took her one more year and two summer sessions to become a college graduate.

She still felt needed at home, so she framed her diploma and hung it on the wall over the living room sofa, and she kept her job as a motel maid and tried to figure out what she could do with her life. The idea of applying for a fancy professional job seemed unpromising; hardly ever did jobs of that sort come open in Chestnut County, but even if an opening did come up, everybody knew Collie Mae as a farm girl who cleaned motel rooms. Who would believe she'd turned herself into someone at a whole different level?

Finally, Isabella came back home and talked some sense into her. *You are one stubborn girl*, she said. *Look at how you went to school. You never gave up, you kept on fighting against the odds, you worked twenty-five hours a day, you wouldn't take no for an answer. Those are advantages—they're your strengths in life. You're persistent. What you need is a job selling something.*

So Collie Mae signed up with an insurance company that offered accident and burial policies for poor people. The policies cost twenty-five dollars and stayed in effect for six months, so twice a year she revisited her old customers to try to collect premiums. In between she and the other sales-people canvassed county by county, walking every dirt road, visiting every shack. They started off each morning with pep rallies to psych themselves up, and they practiced setting daily performance goals: how many contacts, how many successful closings. From the very first day Collie Mae was the top trainee. No matter how high she set her daily goals, she routinely exceeded them, and none of the other salespeople came close to her performance. She completed the most sales visits, earned the most in commissions, and won trophies from the company.

Her base salary was five hundred dollars a month. When her sales performance exceeded a certain quota, she earned commissions on top of the base, but when people signed up for a policy and then didn't pay, the missing premiums would be deducted from her salary. Collie Mae was surprised at first by how many customers didn't pay; it was an everyday thing for people to act as though they had the money when they really didn't. She started looking more closely at the conditions in which people were living, and what she saw turned her stomach.

I saw people living worse off than I ever imagined, and I had always thought my family was poor. I knocked on the door of one house and found people living in a part of a house that didn't have a roof! They were living in the one good room in an abandoned house that was all caved in. They used a car battery to charge their refrigerator. There was no running water. They had to tote water from way down the road. I'd say it was well over a mile to this one gas station that would let them take water. And, of course, they had no car. And they paid forty dollars a month for rent!

These folks didn't have any job, no job skills, and they had no car. Even if they got a job, how would they get to work? Who would take care of their kids? Their room was freezing cold in the winter. Some people have welfare and food stamps, but one family I met, they didn't even know to go get it. Some people don't go. There's some that can't get into town to get to the welfare office. And then there's some families that just don't want it. They'd rather be cold and hungry and do what they are doing than have somebody breathing down their backs or calling their neighbors and asking about them.

Collie Mae began to feel an urgent need to get away. Surely there was some place on earth where things were better, where she wouldn't have to live all day every day breathing in the stench of poverty and desperation. Although there was no shortage of work for her at home around the farm, her sisters were getting old enough to help out. She began taking more and more vacations—always heading to New Jersey to visit Isabella—and the family seemed to get by all right without her. The vacations began to seem absolutely necessary to save her sanity. She'd already taken and passed the state civil service exam, so the next step, the final break, was easier than she had ever dreamed: her sisters cried and her father seemed dazed, in a state of shock, but nobody told her flat out not to go. On a certain level, they understood. She took a job processing bids on government contracts in Camden, New Jersey, a town just across the Delaware River from Philadelphia.

The workload was unbelievable. For the first month she went in to work early every day and stayed late and brought huge stacks of papers home and stayed up half the night, and still she couldn't catch up. No sooner did she pick up one piece of paper than ten more appeared on her desk. No matter how hard she tried, she couldn't come close to working fast enough.

At the end of the month she figured it all out: the man who shared the cubicle with her was dumping most of his own work on her. She was trying to keep up with two people's work while he sat around sucking on peppermints and reading *True Detective* magazine. The minute she realized what was going on, she excused herself, went into the ladies' room, locked the door, and cried. Then she washed her face, figured out exactly what she should say to the man, and went back up to him and said it. That was the end of the problem.

Through her cousins in Camden, Collie Mae met a young man who also had Chestnut County roots, though he'd spent more of his life in New Jersey than he had back home. He was a journeyman electrician. They were married in 1975, and in 1976 they arranged for one of Collie Mae's sisters to come up and move in with them to help take care of their new baby, Aleisha. Camden was beginning to feel like home.

But Isabella was already plotting to leave Newark. Her daughters were entering their teenage years, and she worried about them every minute. They were supposed to walk straight home after school and call her at work the minute they got in. They had to stay in the apartment, with the door locked; they couldn't go anywhere or have anyone over while she was at work. On weekends, if they went out, they had to call when they got there, and then call again before they went anywhere else, and she always had to know exactly who they were with and what they were doing and how they were going to get there and when they would be home—and it was no way to live. The girls resented all the rules and rebelled from time to time, or snuck around behind their mother's back, covering up for each other. Isabella understood how they felt but was just plain terrified to let up on them. Even when they were at school she worried: from everything she'd heard, education was just about the last priority in some of those classrooms.

She began investigating private schools. She and Rudy both made decent money, though in the construction industry he couldn't always count on having a good year. But even with two incomes, the bills got away from them sometimes. They were still making payments on Isabella's college loans, as well as trying to send money home every month and saving up for a piece of land and a house of their own. Isabella decided that the only way they could afford private school tuition would be by adding a third source of income, and when she discussed the problem with Collie Mae, she got an instant answer: she should set herself up in some kind of business.

The business she eventually chose—over Rudy's strenuous objections, which she interpreted as lack of imagination on his part—was a distributorship for a high-priced line of cleaning supplies called Diamond. They had to put in three thousand dollars up front, an investment that they could recover slowly by selling cleaning supplies or much more rapidly by bringing in new investors. But their three-thousand-dollar check had scarcely cleared the bank before the Diamond empire collapsed, and like all the other would-be "distributors" in the pyramid, Isabella and Rudy Beasley lost every dime of their money. They learned later that their three-thousand-dollar loss ranked them among the luckiest of Diamond's victims; some people lost as much as forty or fifty thousand.

But right after it happened, when they were still feeling decidedly unlucky and were floundering emotionally, desperate for someone or something to blame, Collie Mae drove up to Newark for the weekend, with little Aleisha, to try to cheer up her old friend Isabella. Sparks of marital hostility were flaring into flame in the Beasley apartment; Isabella and Rudy seemed to be going after each other with blowtorches. *I'm warning y'all, cut that out*, insisted Collie Mae. *It's gonna be all right. I know just what it is you need to do now.*

What they needed to do now was sell Amway products. The initial investment required was less than a hundred dollars.

We'd been burned once, really burned, so it was hard for me to develop a positive attitude when I first got into Amway. My husband wasn't supportive at all—he just didn't see the opportunities. It's not that he couldn't see it, he just wouldn't see it. After that first experience we'd had, his heart wasn't in it at all. But I tell people that I am an Amway lifer.

I truly believe in their philosophy. It works. The whole basis of the Amway philosophy is positive thinking, and I have learned—they have taught me, in the seminars and so forth—that everything stems from positive thinking. I could apply that attitude in my everyday life—there are always people who are going to try to psych me out, but if I can take the approach of positive thinking, it doesn't get to me. In life there are little things every day that get to people, and they wipe a lot of people out, but I just keep saying to myself, girl, keep on going. Keep on going.

I'm still in Amway. I haven't made a fortune at it. I could have, I think. I could have done very well, especially if my husband had gotten as much out of it as I have. But aside from the money, in terms of what I have learned about life, yes, absolutely, I'm an Amway lifer.

While Isabella was plunging into Amway, Rudy tried another tack. He took the girls back home for a summer vacation and used what little was left of their savings to buy a small lot at the edge of Chowan Springs. For three weeks they all camped out in a tent on their lot while he and one of his brothers, who'd already moved home to stay, poured the foundation and a concrete slab. They went back to Newark for the school year, and then the next summer they camped on the slab while Rudy framed the house. The summer after that, in 1978, they moved back home for good, camping in the house shell while Rudy did the finishing work. The girls enrolled in East Chestnut High School.

Isabella stayed on in Newark. She didn't know what to do; at one point she was on the verge of joining the family in Carolina when she was offered a promotion at work that she just couldn't turn down. Her job was a joy: she oversaw the grant application process for Head Start and day-care funding, helped set up training programs for care providers, and visited project sites to evaluate their strengths and weaknesses. Every day she felt she was learning something new about the intricacies of government bureaucracies and community organizing efforts. She watched community organizations develop programs that grew and flourished, and she watched other organizations struggle for years and finally fail. She watched and learned and made good money and missed her family every moment.

To economize, she gave up the apartment in Newark and moved in with her sister, sleeping on the couch. Virtually every cent she earned went straight to Rudy, for plumbing fixtures, lumber, roofing shingles, electrical conduit, insulation, siding, and whatever tools he needed that he couldn't beg or borrow. Rudy and his brother were experienced builders who knew how to cut corners when they had to, but Isabella felt that watching the building process from hundreds of miles away was nerve-wracking enough without having to worry about corner-cutting. When they discussed things on the phone, she would always advise him to wait and save up until they could afford to do this or that job properly, but he would always respond that he did not need sidewalk superintendence from the sidewalks of Newark.

At one point he bought an old barn for a few dollars and spent almost a month tearing it carefully apart for the lumber. Only after he had hauled all the wood over to his lot did he look at it carefully enough to determine that termites had ruined almost all of it.

Isabella's response was to sell more Amway so she could send home more money and he could build the house faster. She rode the Greyhound bus back and forth to Chowan Springs and started selling some Amway products to friends and relatives there. Even after all her years up north, she still knew a lot of people in Chestnut County, and sales were better than she had expected. In fact, she sold so much Amway back home that she began to form a plan in her mind: maybe she could quit her job in New Jersey even before she'd found a new job in Carolina, and move back home where she belonged, with her family, relying on Amway to finish paying for the house and tide them over till she could get another real job.

In the summer of 1979, almost exactly a year behind Rudy and the girls, Isabella moved back to Chowan Springs. For the next five years she scoured Chestnut and surrounding counties for any job of any kind that she might be even remotely qualified for. But she never worked at a regular job again. Rudy's occasional construction jobs and Isabella's Amway did in fact finish the house and see the family through until she was able to bring in funds from the outside world to create steady work for herself and many dozens of other people.

Collie Mae watched enviously from New Jersey as Isabella settled herself back in at home. Ever since Aleisha's birth, she'd been paying close and nervous attention to Isabella's adventures and misadventures raising daughters up north, and even over the phone she could hear the relief in her friend's voice once the girls were safely back in Chowan Springs. Aleisha was a thriving toddler, enrolled in a Montessori preschool and happily spending weekends and evenings with her little cousins in Philadelphia. But Collie Mae was already worried about the sorts of problems that a child—a girl in particular—would have to learn to deal with growing up in a big city.

Also, the phone calls from her father begging her to return were growing more and more frequent, and more and more depressing. He always tried to sound upbeat, but she could hear undertones of stress, even desperation, in his voice. The farm was a disaster; high interest on FHA loans and a run of bad seasons were threatening to destroy a lifetime of devoted stewardship of the land. Her father was a resourceful, community-minded man; out in back of his equipment sheds, for example, he'd put up rental houses, and he'd turned an old soybean field into a baseball diamond. He didn't charge for use of the baseball field but did require all the teams to pick up paper and other litter after the games. His latest idea to save the place was to put up a trailer park out in a field where he'd once grown peanuts. *Sounds like a pretty good crop to me, growing trailers,* he told Collie Mae. *Soon as you're ready to come on back home, I believe we could raise us a right nice little crop of trailers.*

She almost felt ready to come on home. Her father seemed so lonesome, and so up against the wall. He'd had such a hard life, losing his wife and then his mother, raising five children all by himself. As the oldest of the children, Collie Mae felt by far the closest to him. And anyway, her little sisters weren't really ready yet to think about settling down. Two of them stayed in Camden with Collie Mae for a while, and then one went home to go to nursing school and the other moved in with a third sister and their aunt in Philadelphia. The youngest one had joined the army and was about to be sent to Germany. One of the ones in Philadelphia said she and her boyfriend were going to move to California as soon as he got his disability settlement from his motorcycle accident. They were kids, still eager to see the world, but as Collie Mae approached her thirtieth birthday, she was already beginning to feel old and worn down.

Her husband wasn't opposed to moving back home—as an electrician, he was sure he could find work around there somewhere—but he was loudly opposed to moving in with Collie Mae's father. *When your daddy is around me, all he sees is a new farmhand to put to work*, he complained. *I just can't be bossed around like that. I ain't cut out to be a farmboy.*

Eventually, despite his qualms, going home began to seem like the only option. They wrote a letter to one of her father's tenants, asking them to move out at their earliest convenience, which turned out to be five months later, in the spring of 1981; inexpensive housing was hard to find. They moved into the little house in back of her father's shed and got Aleisha a puppy and even a sad old spotted pony. Collie Mae's husband, anxious to make certain that her father didn't mistake him for a farmhand, dressed in a suit and tie every morning and carried an attaché case containing his résumé, which he presented to potential employers all over Chestnut and surrounding counties. Nobody hired him.

Collie Mae thought he was going about his job search all wrong.

He just looked like such a city slicker. "You don't wear fancy clothes and hand out a résumé," I kept telling him. "At least go in your blue jeans, look like you're ready to work." People here don't want a résumé. Really, in his heart, he had become a city slicker. When he finally got a job at the meatpacking company, they put him on the floor pulling off hogs—and you know, a city guy down here, this frustrated him.

It was real hard for him. And there was an old girlfriend, too, which is something I hadn't known about before we moved back, but it became obvious. She kept showing up for this excuse and that excuse, her car would just show up in the driveway. I thought about, you know, having words with her, but it wasn't the kind of life I wanted. Finally he just stopped coming home, and we separated within about six months of moving back.

A few weeks after Collie Mae's husband left, she and her father hosted a barbecue in honor of Shantee Owens and her husband, who were back home for a long weekend. Isabella and Rudy and their daughters were the other guests. It was late October and the night got chilly, but the party lasted and lasted. The kids all fell asleep in Aleisha's room. The men moved inside to watch a ball game on TV and then a movie on the VCR. Collie Mae brought blankets out onto the porch, and the three women wrapped themselves up and sat and sat, listening to October leaves scuff across the field in the wind and looking up every now and then at the skyful of stars.

Shantee was suddenly overcome by nostalgia and homesickness. *I can't believe y'all are back here and I'm still out on the highway. Remember when we were little, and we'd spend the night, and it would be so freezing cold in the morning when we woke up, and we'd all run over by the stove and just hug and hug each other?*

Remember when the fire was all gone out? asked Isabella. *And you'd get up in the morning, and your mother was trying to make a fire, and you'd be trying to get to the washpan 'round the heater and have your sponge bath and get dressed and go to school?*

Collie Mae was quiet for a long time. *When you say it like that, it sounds so nice and cozy,* she finally said. *But we don't have to live like that anymore, and there's lots of people that still do. It has been sickening to me, since I got home, how many people there are around here that have even less nowadays than we had back then—a whole lot less. There's old people, little children, people in shacks, no water, no electricity, no wood for the heater. I keep thinking it's time to do something.*

The three of them decided right then and there that they were can-do women who didn't need to just sit around and talk about things like that. They would form a club. If there was somebody without heat, this club could bring them a load of wood or lend them a down payment for a tank of oil. If somebody's porch steps were broken, or if they had children who needed coats, or if they needed a ride to town to see if they could get food stamps, or maybe it was just a matter of a sack of groceries to get through the end of the month—they could help with that. Or if there was somebody that just wanted to learn to write their name and had never been able to, well, they could help with that, too. They could help when there was an old person who couldn't get around anymore without a walker and they couldn't afford a walker. And in the wintertime, in some of those little old houses that had no ventilation, the air would get so hot from the stove you could see the heat waves ripple around the room, and there would be old people just sitting there like crabs boiled alive, no fresh air—the club could buy them a fan, something as simple as that. There were little things that would make a difference.

Isabella recalled an organization in Newark called Helping Hands, which got them started on a name: *Holding* Hands. That was exactly the idea—holding their neighbors' hands, helping out at a basic level. They would just do what they could do. But, of course, they would do everything the right way: they would need bylaws and dues and fundraising strategies and goals and objectives. They would need another meeting.

They met again two days later, as Shantee and her husband were packing up to head back to the city. The meeting was a hoot: all three women had prepared agendas and proposals written out on yellow legal pads, and all three of them had brought file folders containing model bylaws and sample brochures. From the start, Holding Hands got off on a decidedly businesslike foot.

Dues were set at ten dollars a month, and the initial membership goal was one hundred women per county in three counties. Because Shantee wouldn't be around to help with the work, she contributed five hundred dollars for start-up capital. She also told Isabella and Collie Mae to get in touch with Eula Grant over in Powell County, the daughter of Shantee's mother's old friend Pearl. Eula had been trying to fix up the old community center building in New Jericho, which might work out as a meeting place for Holding Hands or as a location for special events.

By the end of 1981 Holding Hands was incorporated as a tax-exempt nonprofit organization. On Martin Luther King's birthday in January 1982, the club held a memorial ceremony at the newly refurbished community center in New Jericho, which was rededicated that afternoon. A plaque was mounted near the front door, inscribed with the name of Eula Grant, "who gave this community center a new life." The keynote speaker was the president of the state college that Collie Mae had attended. Freshly printed brochures and membership application forms were spread out on a table, and people in the audience signed up on the spot.

In addition to Shantee's start-up money, Holding Hands raised $1,950 in its first year, much of it from a series of raffles; club members who sold twenty-five dollars' worth of raffle tickets in a given month were excused from paying dues for that month. By the end of 1982 they'd reached their goal of one hundred members in Chestnut County and had signed up fifty-eight members in Powell County and thirty-one in Harden County. Because cutting wood had become a major club activity, the bylaws were amended to admit men as members.

The maximum grant for a family was set at two loads of wood plus one hundred dollars, which usually worked out to fifty dollars in cash and fifty dollars in food. Holding Hands also supplied sheets and pillow cases, a high chair, toys, a kitchen table and chairs, whatever people needed. Families whose houses burned up got one hundred dollars plus household items and food.

Once, when Isabella approached a woman who lived on her road about buying a one-dollar raffle ticket, she was told there wasn't a dollar in the house. The woman was taking care of her grandson, and her husband had just died, and she had no money; it also turned out that she had no wood. So Isabella gave her the money she'd collected so far that day from raffle sales, which turned out to be only one dollar, and she arranged to have a load of wood delivered. The next week the woman stopped by Isabella's house and gave her the dollar back.

At the end of the second year Collie Mae wrote up a grant application for Holding Hands and applied for funding from the Z. Smith Reynolds Foundation.

A couple of weeks before we got our first grant, I got three phone calls in one day from people who would not identify themselves. They threatened that we better watch out, we're asking for trouble. Instead of hanging up on them, I asked, "Now, who is this 'we' you're talking about?" And they said, "You just keep your hands to yourself—keep your hands to yourself." In other words, the "we" was Holding Hands. Isabella got calls, too, and she also got letters, and there were at least three letters we know about that were sent to Social Services to try and discredit us. People found notes on their cars. White folks don't want us organizing, but then they never stop talking how we can't do for ourselves. But I say, let's just keep going, 'cause we're helping.

Isabella, meanwhile, was taking her Amway products to every town, every hamlet, every crossroads for miles around. Anywhere she knew anybody—which was virtually everywhere in Chestnut County's six hundred square miles—she sold her wares and visited with the folks and learned about what was going on. One thing she learned was why she was having such a hard time finding a job—why she had been rejected for one job in particular that had sounded like it would be exactly up her alley. The county social services department had advertised for someone with expertise in administering federal funds. Isabella had gotten an interview, but the director had brushed her off immediately, saying that her background was not at all what they needed. She'd been baffled by his rejection until she'd traveled the backroads of the county for a while and realized that Chestnut had no projects whatsoever funded by the federal programs she had been working with in New Jersey. No Head Start, and no day care—zero federal dollars. The only federal money that the county social services office administered went for food stamps and AFDC, even though many other programs existed that were designed specifically for areas with high levels of poverty—a description that fit Chestnut if it fit anywhere. Isabella hadn't yet heard all the explanations of local officials, but she had seen enough to realize that they preferred not to provide the poor people of the county with such services as day care, even if the services could be provided without spending a penny of local money.

About twenty thousand people lived in Chestnut County, 60 percent of them black. Almost 40 percent of the population—nearly eight thousand people—lived below the poverty line. Unemployment was high, but there were many more people working than not working, which to Isabella's way of thinking meant that demand for day-care services must be strong. And most of the jobs in Chestnut and surrounding countries paid minimum wage or thereabouts and offered nothing or next to nothing in the way of employee benefits—which to Isabella's way of thinking meant that unsubsidized day-care services must be way beyond what most working people in Chestnut could afford.

While working her Amway territory, she made a point of visiting all the day-care centers she could find; there were a few around, scattered here and there in private homes, rundown storefronts, and church basements. Conditions in most of the centers shocked her: at one overcrowded proprietary operation called The Three Bears, she noticed missing stair-boards, a broken window with jagged glass at the children's eye level, a jug of bleach sitting out on the bathroom floor, filthy rags used and reused for diaper changing, and Kool-Aid instead of milk at mealtime. Such a place could never pass even a fire inspection, much less meet minimal safety and sanitary standards for a facility jam-packed with young children—and it had a waiting list. There was no way on earth to improve a center like The Three Bears without spending a great deal of money, and the parents who had no choice but to leave their children there had no way on earth to pay any more.

Isabella knew, however, that the federal government had money available precisely for quality day care in communities too poor to afford it. She knew the money was there, she knew the procedure for applying for it, she knew the criteria for obtaining funding. And even before Collie Mae pointed it out to her, she knew that she as an individual was in a position to make a big difference in the lives of her friends and neighbors.

She began by documenting the situation. Two food-processing plants in Chestnut County employed more than 1,100 workers, and three other such plants in nearby counties employed 2,000 more. A factory sewing men's underwear employed 210 people, and a furniture maker employed more than 400. Wages in all these industries averaged just over five dollars an hour.

Isabella talked to parents, and she spoke with public officials, who admitted to her face what she had begun to suspect: *They said that they turned back these funds year after year. One lady told me she didn't believe in government subsidies at all, but her office manages AFDC and food stamps because they have to. In another office the director said it was a point of pride for him that in his county they served very few of the eligible families, much fewer than a lot of places. He said that poor people have more dignity and self-regard for it.*

Isabella believed she could organize an effort to bring Title XX day-care funds to Chestnut County. She knew the people to call upon, and she began to see herself working for herself and with others—autonomously, drawing on what she interpreted as the Amway approach.

I bring this attitude to all my work, trying to create an Amway world, where people believe they can do anything they want to. I could talk about this all day and all night. When I decided this is what I wanted, I knew it would happen. I never got uptight about it.

She was not a loner. She called on Collie Mae, of course; on Eula Grant, who had become a vice president of Holding Hands; on Menola Rountree with her teen beauty walk organization; and on somebody else recommended by Shantee, a woman named Maude Allen, who worked as director of CATS, Chestnut Action for Teenage Students. Shantee said that Maude was prickly and stand-offish but professional through and through. They didn't have to like her, but she was somebody who could make things happen.

At the first meeting Isabella warned everybody that government bureaucracy moved slowly. They gave their organization a name—MAC, Mothers and Children, Inc.—and they set up a timetable to prepare for the mandated preliminary inspection, with Collie Mae in charge of site selection. When Maude Allen asked how they planned to obtain the necessary application forms, Isabella smiled; such a question demonstrated considerable sophistication about the hard realities of local politics. She'd been thinking about that particular matter a great deal and had concluded that the only way was to circumvent the local social service agencies altogether. MAC, Inc., would have to drive all the way up to the state capital and request the packet of forms in person. *It reminds you of the old days, doesn't it? Remember how our parents used to go over to the food store, the phone company, pay all the bills in person?*

Collie Mae arranged for MAC to use the old Shell gas station in Chowan Springs for their initial demonstration project. They wouldn't have to pay rent, but every inch of the building needed repair and renovation.

The fundraising that followed was like pulling money out of the bottom of the piggy bank. All of the MAC women had overcommitted calendars and overextended bankbooks; they were swamped with work and family and civic obligations. The communities in which they had to raise the money they needed had no money to spare. But none of these problems was new to them. Around Christmastime Collie Mae organized a gift-wrapping booth inside Billie's House of Beauty on Main Street, and Maude Allen and CATS, the youth council, threw a teen dance in Rosedale with a talent show competition. Isabella in Chestnut County and Eula in Powell each set up doughnut sales, bake sales, turkey raffles, fish fries, garage sales. And then there were all the events-after-the-events, the parties and teas and receptions to show appreciation for all the volunteers. The women from Working Women's Curb Market, a produce stand on the highway outside of Chowan Springs, provided MAC with "office" space—a card table and rusty filing cabinet in the storage shed behind the stand—and the men from Dream Land, Collie Mae's cousin's Drive Inn Bar-B-Que, brought ribs to every party.

Working across county lines, MAC focused all its efforts on getting one single model day-care center established. They wrote a grant application and then, eager to lay groundwork for a close working relationship with state officials, they took a preliminary draft in person to the chief deputy director in the Day Care Section of the Department of Human Services in the state capital. After he reviewed their work, they made the suggested changes, and they made a point of calling him about every detail, consulting him on the dotting of every *i* and the crossing of every *t*. Eighteen months later they received official notification of their first grant award.

And that was when the trouble began. Notice of the grant was also sent to the county director of social services in Chowan Springs, a Mrs. Beard, who immediately announced that every penny of that money would be returned to the state. Isabella went over Mrs. Beard's head to her new friend in the state capital.

I worried the chief deputy director to death trying to find out what happened to our funds. We had renovated the building and completely furnished it. There were all the little tables and chairs, and the mats, the toys, the playground. We had interviewed day-care teachers and assistants, and we had begun training. We had checked eligibility and assembled a group of children—not all black children either, it was strictly on income. We had everything but the funds.

The chief deputy director again sent the funds to Chestnut County. This time the social services department passed the buck to the county commissioners, who were supposed to approve all funds coming into the county. At the Board of Commissioners meeting, Mrs. Beard made no secret of her department's opposition to public support of day care. Most of the commissioners were like-minded, but Maude Allen had anticipated the precise tone of the meeting and had made a suggestion that seemed to break the logjam: MAC, Inc., packed the meeting room with all the little children who were set to attend the new center. The children sat together in the first three rows of grown-up-sized chairs, squirming, occasionally whimpering, and the parents and ministers and MAC board members who had come prepared to speak never had to say a word: officially, day-care funding was approved by a murmured voice vote, and from then on local opposition to MAC was limited to behind-the-scenes tactics. Bureaucrats stalled, politicians filed to reduce the allocation, clerks said they couldn't locate the funds, officials forgot about appointments and forgot to file papers and forgot how to write a check. Eventually the commissioners informed MAC that the funding was secure but that it would be administered by none other than the county director of social services, their good friend Mrs. Beard. The MAC women learned to work through her by sneaking around her and by becoming accustomed to delays, broken promises, unmet deadlines, and the unmet needs of parents who trusted them.

After three years MAC, Inc., was able to pull the political levers that changed the procedure for funding so that money could be allocated directly to their projects. But local attempts at sabotage continued, and the endless attention they consumed ate at the hearts of the MAC women and nibbled at the nerves of civic engagement.

When I was coming up, I gave things my best shot. But better than any teacher, even better than my Amway lessons, time is the best teacher, time makes the difference!

Our saving grace was that we created alliances across at least three counties. When this all got started, we could have been in, you know, competition. But then we started helping one another out. If one group was having trouble getting the money—political problems— well, one of us from another county would call the state capital for them, help them out with our direct contacts. We began to train board members in how they could help. We approached our state representative. Only the strong survive.

By 1986 MAC was operating three day-care centers in Chestnut County, one in Powell County, and two in nearby Harden County. Rose Towers, Sunshine Center, Toddlers Club House, Lady Bug, Children's Wonderland, Rainbow Early Learning, and Teddy Bear Town were all safe and sanitary child-care facilities, with trained staffs, developmentally oriented curricula, parent participation on the boards, and sliding fee schedules. More than three hundred children were enrolled. Fifty new full-time jobs and a couple of dozen part-time jobs were created directly to staff the centers, and the availability of the centers enabled many parents to hold jobs for the first time, bringing thousands of additional dollars into the community.

Isabella became MAC's paid director; Shantee Owens was hired to manage Lady Bug Day Care Center. MAC, Inc., and Holding Hands bleed the poor to help the poor. But they also represent a new type of organizing activity in poor rural communities. Serious and sustainable services in desperately poor rural counties cannot succeed on turkey raffles and fish fries alone. They cannot be funded solely or even largely by charitable contributions from the tiny handful of black business and professional people in these communities. They might be aided to a degree by local tax support, but political resistance is unyielding. They might be aided significantly by large industries employing local people, but the history is bleak: corporate operations in places like Powell and Chestnut counties have never supported local organizations in the black community.

People who return and get involved feel they have to go it alone. One morning a four-year-old boy at Teddy Bear Town waved at a car that was driving by, and one of his classmates ran inside the center and hid. *You can't wave to a white person,* the terrified child told his teacher. *They'll shoot off your hands. They'll kill you.* Some adults remain almost that fearful; it may take more than a wave, they argue, but there is a degree of speaking out that will put a black person's life at risk. Other people believe that fear is more a white man's tool than a danger to black lives. The women of Holding Hands felt the threats against them reflected white efforts to intimidate them, which is not quite the same as actual efforts to maim or kill them.

Obviously, the new old South isn't the old old South, but distrust, fear, and hostility persist. In the midst of so much bitterness and ill will, outside money is a critical resource. Dogged self-help, with no reliance on government funding, can support some small initiatives, such as Holding Hands—although even Holding Hands eventually needed outside money, for which they turned to charitable foundations. Even a hundred such organizations, however, can't do it all.

Where large numbers of people lack the minimal necessities of life, public funds make a difference. Organizing by black women (and men) to help provide obviously needed services—firewood, say, or safe child care—is perceived by "the white community" as threatening rather than helpful. An outsider might suggest that within the white community are surely as many nuances and varieties of opinion as exist within the black community, but it often doesn't sound that way to a black person listening to the discussion at county commission meetings.

Collie Mae and Isabella and the other activists feel that the white establishment routinely, almost reflexively, tries to tear down whatever they build up, and that the strategies of white resistance are as old as Jim Crow. They say their biggest headache, year in and year out, has been the resistance of white bureaucrats who could have been allies. When bureaucratic habits of inaction and insensitivity are compounded by old racist habits of resistance and recoil, headaches can last a long time.

Collie Mae and Isabella are organizers. People who never left Chestnut County have also formed organizations around social issues but never to the same extent, or the same effect. The people returning home brought experience with structures and strategies that established them locally as people to be contended with. They created networks and coalitions that grew.

In the scholarly literature, this sort of work has been termed social-capital formation, a notion that has recently attracted public attention as a key to community uplift. The new public interest is ironic on four or five levels: for one thing, it comes along at a moment when observers have widely acknowledged a drastic decline, throughout the United States, in participation in neighborly or other voluntary associations. As at the turn of this century, perhaps, when scholars suddenly began to discuss the significance of the frontier in American life, interest seems to dawn as an era comes to a close. Uprootedness, which is related to migration, of course, among other modern habits, may contribute to—or result from—the loss of social ties. Nonetheless, a second level of irony involves the political response to the decline of voluntarism: a reduction in the public assistance that might supplement or substitute for weakened private service organizations.

A third irony is that the generation returning to rural homeplaces today—the repeatedly uprooted, the people who might be termed least suited for developing social relationships grounded in neighborliness—are the very people forging serious civic and associational involvements in these communities.

Yet a fourth irony is that, at least in places like Chestnut County, the people who proclaim most loudly the urgency and legitimacy of self-help, the bureaucrats and politicians, are the same people who, when faced with actual self-help organizations in their home communities, work to thwart them.

A fifth irony—or perhaps *irony* as a label is too elegant and neat—a last question, perhaps, or dilemma, spins on migration itself. People come into the modern world from all sorts of places; if they then choose to leave modern metropolitan life to go back home again, should they be considered uprooted, displaced, refugees—the victims, in a sense, of modernism? Or is it those among us who no longer have homeplaces and kin to return to who represent the shocking emblems of the end of modernity?

Part Four

Consciousness, Transformation, and Resistance at Work

Invisibility, Consciousness of the Other, *Ressentiment*   15

JUDITH ROLLINS

Invisibility

My field notes from my first day cleaning a large house in West Newton describe this scene:

> Mrs. Thomas and I were both cleaning in her large kitchen when her sixteen-year-old came in to make a sandwich for lunch. They talked openly as if I weren't there—about where he had gone the night before, who he had seen and how angry his father was about his staying out too late. I was surprised at how much rather personal information they exposed. During their conversation, he asked her if cats took vitamins. (The family recently got a kitten.) She answered she didn't know but she didn't think so. Despite the fact that I knew there were vitamins for cats, I said nothing because I felt that that was what was expected of me. This situation was the most peculiar feeling of the day: being there and not being there. Unlike a third person who chose not to take part in a conversation, I knew I was not expected to take part. I wouldn't speak and was related to as if I wouldn't hear. Very peculiar.

At a spacious house in Belmont where I worked a full eight-hour day during December and January (when the temperature was regularly below freezing), the psychiatrist husband and his non-working wife usually left the house in mid-morning and returned in the late afternoon. My notes from the first day describe a pattern that would be repeated every time they left the house:

> About a half an hour after they left, I noticed the house getting cooler. The temperature continued to drop to, I would guess, 50°–55°—not comfortable even with my activity. I realized that they had turned the heat down as if there were no one there! I looked for a thermostat but couldn't find it. Worked in that temperature until 5:00 when I left.

And at a more humble ranch home in Needham, where I cleaned half a day each week for a retired accountant and his wife, this event took place:

> They left around 9:30 to make a doctor's appointment for her at 10:00. About forty-five minutes after they had left, the doorbell rang. When I went to open it, I was unable to. I could see through a small circular window in the middle of the door that it was a man delivering a plant. I gestured for him to leave it outside. I remembered that Mrs. Brown

had always unlocked the door from the inside when I arrived, so I started a futile search for the key. I realized that when leaving the house, they must have locked it as they would when leaving it empty and that the only way I could get out would be to climb through a window. When they returned, I explained why the plant was sitting outside. He laughed and said, "Oh, I hadn't thought about that. You couldn't get out, could you?"

Similar kinds of incidents in which I felt I was treated as though I were not really there happened repeatedly during my seven months of domestic work. On one occasion, while sitting in a kitchen having my lunch while a couple walked and talked around me, my sense of being invisible was so great that I took out paper and started writing field notes. I wrote for about ten minutes, finished my lunch, and went back to work. They showed no evidence of having seen their domestic doing anything unusual; actually, they showed no evidence of having seen their domestic at all. (As Ralph Ellison has observed, "it is sometimes advantageous to be unseen."[1])

But such incidents were always disconcerting. It was this aspect of servitude I found to be one of the strongest affronts to my dignity as a human being. To Mrs. Thomas and her son, I became invisible; their conversation was as private with me, the black servant, in the room as it would have been with no one in the room. For the couples in Belmont and Needham, leaving me in the house was exactly the same as leaving the house empty. These gestures of ignoring my presence were not, I think, intended as insults; they were expressions of the employers' ability to annihilate the humanness and even, at times, the very existence of me, a servant and a black woman. Fanon articulates my reaction concisely: "A feeling of inferiority? No, a feeling of nonexistence."[2]

The servant position is not the only "non-person" role, but, as Erving Goffman has suggested, it may well be "the classic type of non-person in our society. . . . In certain ways [s]he is defined by both performers and audience as someone who isn't there."[3] Other categories of people sometimes treated as though they were not present include the very young, the very old and the sick. What is important about all of these groups of people is that their non-person role relates to their subordination and carries with it some disrespect. Thus the servant as non-person is a perfect fit: the position is subordinate by definition, the person in it disrespected by centuries of tradition.

It has been suggested that it was during the nineteenth century that Europeans began to consider their servants as non-persons.[4] Clearly invisibility was a desirable quality in an American domestic by the late nineteenth century. Writing about this period, David Katzman states:

One peculiar and most degrading aspect of domestic service was the requisite of invisibility. The ideal servant as servant (as opposed to servant as a status symbol for the employer) would be invisible and silent, responsive to demands but deaf to gossip, household chatter, and conflicts, attentive to the needs of mistress and master but blind to their faults, sensitive to the moods and whims of those around them but undemanding of family warmth, love and security. Only blacks could be invisible people in white homes.[5]

Thus Katzman leads us to the other, race-related, dimension of invisibility: blacks (and, I would submit, all people of color) are more easily perceived by whites as invisible or non-human than are other whites. This is an aspect of racism that has been discussed by many writers. Ralph Ellison wrote of white America's inability to see blacks because of "a matter of the construction of the inner eye, those eyes with which they look through their physical eyes upon reality." For James Baldwin, the "inner eye" of white America is constructed in such a way that despite an Afro-American presence of over four hundred years, the nation "is still unable to recognize [the black person] as a human being." From his examination of the treatment of Third World people in films, Asian scholar Tom Engelhardt concluded that such films promote "the overwhelmingly present theme of the nonhumanness of the nonwhite," thus perpetuating that idea in the minds of the viewing audience.[6]

Even observers of interracial relations in the overseas colonies have pointed to dehumanization as fundamental to such relations. Albert Memmi explained how this mechanism facilitated the control of the colonized Arabs by the French: "What is left of the colonized at the end of this stubborn effort to dehumanize him? . . . He is hardly a human being . . . [and] one does not have a serious obligation toward an animal or an object."[7] But Frantz Fanon, writing of the same colonial dynamic, added the important point that the conceptualizations of those of the more powerful group create reality only for themselves and not for the people they choose to define as other than human.

> At times this Manicheism goes to its logical conclusion and dehumanizes the native, or to speak plainly, it turns him into an animal. . . . The native knows all this, and laughs to himself every time he spots an allusion to the animal world in the other's words. For he knows that he is not an animal. . . . [During decolonization] the "thing" which has been colonized becomes man during the same process by which it frees itself.[8]

Have I gone too far? Are the conceptual leaps from the mistress ignoring the presence of her servant to Asians being portrayed as non-humans in films to the colonizer treating the colonized as an animal or an object too great? I think not. I submit that all of these behaviors are manifestations of similar mental processes. What all of these writers are describing is the reality that, having been socialized into cultures that define people of color as worth less than whites and having observed material evidence that seems to corroborate this view of them as inferior, whites (particularly those in societies with large Third World populations) do, to varying degrees, devalue the personhood of such people. This devaluation can range from the perception of the persons as fully human but inferior to conceptualizing them as subhuman (Fanon's colonized "animal") to the extreme of not seeing a being at all. And though this mechanism is functioning at all times when whites and people of color interact in this society, it takes on an exaggerated form

when the person of color also holds a low-status occupational and gender position—an unfortunate convergence of statuses for the black female domestic servant.

Consciousness of the Other

Yet the domestics I interviewed appeared to have retained a remarkable sense of
self-worth. Like the colonized described by Fanon, domestics skillfully deflect these
psychological attacks on their personhood, their adulthood, their dignity, these
attempts to lure them into accepting employers' definitions of them as inferior.
How do they do it? How do they cope with demands for deference, with maternalism, with being treated like non-persons? It seemed to me that their most powerful protections against such treatment were their intimate knowledge of the
realities of employers' lives, their understanding of the meaning of class and race
in this country, and their value system, which measures an individual's worth less by
material success than by "the kind of person you are," by the quality of one's interpersonal relationships and by one's standing in the community.

Domestics were able to describe in precise detail the personalities, habits,
moods, and tastes of the women they had worked for. (The descriptions employers
gave were, by comparison, less complex and insightful—not, it seemed to me,
because employers were any less capable of analyzing personalities but rather
because they had less need to study the nuances of their domestics.) Domestics'
highly developed observational skills may grow out of the need for maneuvering
and for indirect manipulation in this occupation, but the resulting knowledge and
understanding is critically beneficial to their maintenance of their sense of self
worth vis-à-vis their employers. Domestics' answers to my questions about their
feeling jealousy about their employers' better material conditions gave insight into
not only their assessments of their employers but also their value system. Elizabeth
Roy's, Ellen Samuel's, and Joan Fox's answers were particularly revealing:

> I used to feel envy of all the things they have. When I was younger, I did have a little
> envy. I wondered why they could have it all and we didn't have any. But I don't any-
> more because as I got older and took a good look at them, I realize material gains don't
> necessarily mean you're happy. And most of those women aren't happy, you know. I
> feel like I've done a good job. All three of my children came here to me to Boston.
> They're doing well. I'm proud of what I've done. I don't have any regrets. (Ms. Roy)

> Even today—and he's [her employer's son] a big doctor now—you know, when she
> wants to tell him something important, she calls me and asks me to call him. 'Cause
> he'll hang up on her! He hates her! When I was there [when the son was a teenager]
> he used to yell at her. He never yelled at me. Said then and he says now that I'm more
> of a mother to him than she is. I still get a birthday card and a Mother's Day card from
> him every year. Never sends her one. Now isn't that an awful way to live? (Ms. Samuel)

> I wouldn't want to be in her place. She's got nothing to do with herself. The older ones
> are the worst off. Just go to the hairdresser, go to this meeting, sit around. If you look

close, you see they're very lonely. I would never want to stop working, for one thing, even if I could. I would never want to live like that, sitting around, talking foolishness, and doing nothing. (Ms. Fox)

Working in the most private sphere of their employers' lives, domestics see their human frailties and problems. Sometimes employers volunteer the information. I was surprised by the revealing frankness of one of my employers (a Wellesley mother of two small children) the first day I worked for her. My field notes read:

> While I had my tea and she puttered in the dining area, she talked about her switch to health foods and her husband's still eating junk food. For example his breakfast, she said, is usually a Coke and a Baby Ruth bar. I commented lightly that that must be hard for a person into health foods to live with and she said, quietly and seriously, "You learn to live with it. If you want your children to have a father, you have to." She looked blankly at the wall as she spoke and when she realized that I was looking at her (with my surprise at her frankness probably showing), she nervously and quickly moved out of the room. I think she had revealed more about marital discontent to the stranger who'd come in to clean than she'd intended to.

And sometimes domestics just observe the contradiction between what employers want to present to the public and what the reality is. (Recall Odette Harris' comment: "I saw one thing [about her marriage] and she told me another thing. I was shocked.")

Thus, domestics' stronger consciousness of the Other functions not only to help them survive in the occupation but also to maintain their self-respect. The worker in the home has a level of knowledge about familial and personal problems that few outsiders do. It is not surprising that domestic workers do not take the insulting attitudes and judgments of employers seriously; they are in a position to make scathing judgments of their own. Regrettably, some of the best evidence of their evaluation of their employers cannot be captured in print: it was the cynicism and humor displayed in their derisive imitations of their employers. Raising their voices to little girl pitch, adding hand and facial gestures suggesting confusion and immaturity, my interviewees would act out scenes from their past experiences— typically scenes in which the employer was unable to cope with some problem and had to rely on the guidance and pragmatic efficiency of the domestic. It was interesting that these domestics, described historically and by some of the employers interviewed as childlike, perceived their employers as "flighty" and childlike. How *could* they buy into the evaluations of women they so perceived? When I asked a group of six domestics if they felt like "one of the family" when they heard themselves referred to as such, they laughed in agreement with Elizabeth Roy's cynical answer: "No! Of course not! [Employers] just say that in order to get more work out of you. It's just like that old Southern terminology: 'She's a good old nigger. That's my nigger. I just don't know what I'm going to do without that nigger.'"

The domestics I interviewed knew the importance of knowledge of the powerful to those without power. This significant element in relationships of domination has been discussed by writers as diverse as Nietzsche, Hegel, and Fanon.[9] Nietzsche was extreme in his view that the "slave" is a dependent lacking originality and genuine creativity:

> Slave ethics . . . begins by saying *no* to an "outside", an "other", a non-self, and that *no* is its creative act. This reversal of direction of the evaluating look, this invariable looking outward instead of inward, is a fundamental feature of rancor. Slave ethics requires for its inception a sphere different from and hostile to its own. Physiologically speaking, it requires an outside stimulus in order to act at all; all its action is reaction.[10]

Likewise Fanon, in his early writings, considered the consciousness of the colonized to be totally dependent. Colonized people, he said, "have no inherent values of their own, they are always contingent on the presence of the Other. . . . Everything that [he] does is done for the Other because it is the Other who corroborates him in his search for self-validation."[11] And at the beginning of his famous discussion of "Lordship and Bondage," Hegel appears to agree: "The one is independent, and its essential nature is to be for itself; the other is dependent, and its essence is life or existence for another. The former is the Master, or Lord, the latter the Bondsman."[12]

Domestics have been perceived as a dependent labor group in the past and, in some parts of the world, even today. (In fact, Memmi states that this is the reason servants are the only poor who have always been despised by other poor.[13]) Unquestionably, material dependence has characterized this occupation throughout time; in only a few parts of the world have the labor options of low-income women weakened this material dependence. But I suspect that the psychological independence displayed by the women I interviewed has also existed, to varying degrees, throughout time. Hegel and Fanon both recognized this as a countervailing energy within the apparent dependence—an energy, for Hegel, that developed out of the slave's labor and its effects on his or her consciousness:

> Through work and labour, however, this consciousness of the bondsman comes to itself. . . . Labour is desire restrained and checked, evanescence delayed and postponed. . . . The consciousness that toils and serves accordingly attains by this means the direct apprehension of that independent being as itself. . . . Thus precisely in labour where there seems to be merely some outsider's mind and ideas involved, the bondsman becomes aware, through this re-discovery of himself by himself, of having and being a "mind of his own."[14]

The master, on the other hand, because of his desire-and-consumption pattern of activity, becomes weaker in skills, self-discipline, and overall human development. "It is not an independent, but rather a dependent consciousness that he has achieved."[15] Fanon, too, later recognized the existence of inner-directedness and the importance of tradition in shaping the colonized's thoughts and behaviors. However, Fanon maintained his view that the extensive control exercised by the European colonizer forced the colonized to be in a state of constant awareness when among the colonizers: "The native is always on the alert. . . . The native and the underdeveloped man are today political animals in the most universal sense of the word. . . . The emotional sensitivity of the native is kept on the surface of his skin like an open sore."[16] This view of the powerless as exhibiting the elements of dependence and independence and always acutely aware of the powerful is consistent with the information my interviews yielded. While domestics were indeed "invariably looking outward," carefully scrutinizing the personality, habits, and moods of their employers, they were also inner-directed, creative, and, like Hegel's slave, "having and being a 'mind of [their] own.'"

Domestics, indeed, know the Other. And domestics know the meaning of their own lives. They know they have held down jobs typically since they were teenagers; they know they had the strength to move *alone* from the country or the South or the Islands in order to better themselves; they know they can successfully maneuver in black and white, working- and middle-class worlds; they know they are respected by their neighbors for being able to maintain a regular job in a community plagued by unemployment, for their position in the church or the Eastern Star or the Elks, and, most important, for raising good children. Domestics also know the limitations placed on them in this country because of their class and race in a way employers do not, because they need not, know. And they know they have survived and transcended obstacles their employers could not imagine. Free of illusions about equal social opportunity, domestics neither blame themselves for their subordinate economic position nor credit their female employers' superordinate position to any innate superiority of theirs. This ability to assess their employers' and their own lives based on an understanding of social realities and on a distinct moral system is what gives domestics the strength to be able to accept what is beneficial to them in their employers' treatment while not being profoundly damaged by the negative conceptualizations on which such treatment is based. And the fact that all the domestics I interviewed who had worked in both the North and the South said they preferred Southern white women as employers further attests to this extraordinary "filtering" ability.

It may be assumed that most Southern white women are more conservative politically than most Northern white women. Certainly, on the group level, the Northerner's "aversive" racism would be less obviously oppressive than the Southerner's "dominant" style.[17] Yet, the Southern white women's style of relating to the domestic worker was preferred.

Eleanor Preston-Whyte encountered a similar phenomenon in two sections of Durban, South Africa.[18] Relationships between servants and their employers were far more intimate, familiar, and maternalistic in the lower-income, more politically conservative area than in the higher-income, politically liberal neighborhood. Preston-Whyte attributed the familiarity in the low-income homes to the physical closeness of the women (because of small houses), the more informal family interaction style, which carried over into relationships with servants, and more cultural and experiential similiarities between the low-income employers (frequently of rural backgrounds) and their servants. In the higher-income areas it was not only culture which divided them but social class, experience and ambition. In the lower-income area, on the other hand, the white and African women may be said to have shared something of common social environment. They could appreciate the other's problems and offered each other genuine sympathy in times of crisis and insecurity.[19]

The apparent paradox of the conservative, apartheid-favoring white who permits intimacy in her home with her servant is explained by

the very clear acceptance of both parties of the inferior position of the employee. . . . If the groups to which individuals belong are clearly differentiated and unequal to each other, the closest contact may not only be allowed, but it may even be thought fitting. . . . In South Africa . . . close contact between employer and servant may occur at certain levels since it is thought impossible for a relationship of equality to exist between Black and white. There is thus no need for the employer "to keep his or her distance."[20]

Similarly in the American South where, until recently, racial segregation and domination were firmly embedded, the social distance between mistresses and servants, between blacks and whites, was unquestioned. Katzman states that, "since individual white action could not affect the subordinate role of blacks—Southern racial etiquette ensured this—whites could develop a far greater intimacy with their black servants than could mistresses in the North with their servants."[21] Additionally, as in Preston-Whyte's low-income area, Southern white and black women share a great deal in common culturally, certainly more than do Northern white employers and Southern black domestics. Katzman considered this to be one of the differences between the North and the South around the turn of the century:

For all the differences between black and white in the South, they had in common Southern cultural traditions. The cultural differences between whites and blacks in the South were far fewer than the dissimilarities between native-born white mistresses in the North and their immigrant or black servants.[22]

Many of my interviewees had worked in the South for blue-collar families (factory workers, small farmers). Because of the availability of a large cheap servant pool, Southerners of fairly low incomes—that is, with incomes close to that of their servants—can afford household help. One Southern-born domestic referred to the two groups as "co-related":

There's quite a difference [between Northern and Southern white women employers]. From the Southern point of view, we're kind of co-related, you know. I say "co-related" meaning the Southern black and the Southern white understand each other—whether they like one another or not. You understand their goings and comings. And you feel a little easier with them. And they understand us more than Northern whites do. And treat us better.

Closer in class and culture, operating within a clearly defined system of social and racial inequality, sharing an acceptance of maternalistic behaviors as a necessary and appropriate element of domestic service, Southern black and white women developed a kind of mistress-servant relationship that was psychologically satisfying, to some degree, to both groups of women. Northern employers, on the other hand, operating in communities with unclear rules of race relations, typically having had less experience with blacks than their Southern counterparts, administering to an employee different not only in color but in culture and class, had to struggle to create rules to define domestics' proper place in their homes and psyches. If the Northern employer was also new to the role, the struggle was one of creating both class and racial distance. In any case, this need to create the behavioral norms of racism, since they were not given to Northern employers readymade as in the South, is part of the explanation for Northerners' treating domestics more coldly. I interpret my interviewees' preference for Southern employers as an expression of both their comfort with the familiar and their desire for a more personal kind of relationship in their work situation—typically a high value, as stated, for all women. These women were able to accept and benefit from the supportive elements in Southern maternalism while at the same time rejecting the destructive belief system on which such behavior was based.

Lack of Identification

One might expect domestics' keen consciousness of employers to lead to their identifying with them. Certainly, the characterization of domestics as inevitably identifying with their mistresses is a prevalent theme in the literature on servitude throughout the world. From the upper-level servants of eighteenth-century England to the house slaves of the American South, identification has been seen as a characteristic of this occupation which brings the worker into such constant and intimate contact with the employer.

But identification is, of course, not unique to servitude. The phenomenon is a mode of coping with a situation of powerlessness that precludes overt attack against those with power. By identifying with the persons in power, one is permitted "a vicarious sharing of some of his or her strength."[23] However, this coping mechanism has the unhealthy elements of self-delusion and an admiration for one's oppressor. Bruno Bettelheim discerned it among some Nazi concentration camp prisoners:

> When a prisoner had reached the final stage of adjustment to the camp situation, he had changed his personality so as to accept various values of the SS as his own ... from copying the verbal aggressions of the SS to copying its form of bodily aggressions. ... They would try to acquire old pieces of SS uniforms ... [because] ... the old prisoners admitted that they loved to look like the guards. ... [They] accepted Nazi goals and values, too, even when these seemed opposed to their own interests.[24]

But Bettelheim added this significant observation: "These same old prisoners who identified with the SS defied it at other moments, demonstrating extraordinary courage in doing so."[25]

Likewise, writers have discussed such identification on the part of the colonized toward the colonizer. Unlike in the concentration camp, the identification in this situation is a result of direct efforts on the part of the dominant group: the culture of the colonizer is forced upon the colonized through institutions such as the educational and religious. Fanon observed:

> There is always identification with the victor.... The black schoolboy in the Antilles, who in his lessons is forever talking about "our ancestors, the Gauls", identifies himself with the explorer, the bringer of civilization, the white man who carries truth to savages—an all-white truth. There is identification—that is, the young Negro subjectively adopts a white man's attitude.[26]

And writers on the antebellum South, like Jessie Parkhurst and Eugene Genovese, have also commented on the identification of house slaves with their owners. But, like Bettelheim, Genovese sees that this identification had its limits: "On occasion ... a servant decided he or she had had enough and murdered the white family."[27] What the concentration camp, the colonial situation, and house slavery have in common is the extreme dominance of one group over another and sufficient contact between members of the two groups for those in the less powerful position to have enough knowledge of the ideas and behaviors of the powerful to be able to adopt them to some degree. The existence of contact is critical; it explains why field slaves or the less assimilated colonized are less likely to identify. And it suggests why domestic servants, more than other blue-collar workers, might identify with their employers.

Undoubtedly, servants' identifying with their employers has existed in recent history. Identification may still exist to some degree in the American South and Far West, where servants are less sophisticated and dependency more encouraged. It may even exist in the Northeast among some live-in workers. But the women I interviewed expressed no hint of it. A discussion of the phenomenon was considered appropriate because so many writers have associated it with domestic service and because, frankly, I expected to encounter it. Rather, the domestics I interviewed see themselves, their lifestyles, their values, as distinct from and, in some ways, superior to those of their employers.[28] The closest phenomenon to identification I could discern, and it is quite distinct to be sure, was the extreme consciousness of the Other. As stated, domestics as a group were far more aware of and concerned with the subtleties of personality and habits of their employers than vice versa. But this awareness was that of a distant and somewhat judgmental observer, fully cognizant of her disadvantaged position in the relationship and the society, and conscious that the greater her understanding of those wielding power over her life the greater her potential for maneuvering skillfully and profitably within the employer's world. It was the keen awareness of one who knows that knowledge is power, not the envious and hungry stare of the sycophant. Powerlessness necessitates a state of acute awareness and a stance ready to react; these qualities are not, however, synonymous with identification.

Today's domestic (or at least, the American-born woman in the Northeast), fully aware of an egalitarian philosophy of human worth and opportunity, more psychologically and materially independent than her predecessors (and less fortunate segments of the contemporary pool), defines herself by her family, her church, her organizations, her place in her community. She neither buys into the employer's definition of her nor does she base her own definition of herself on her work situation. Like other blue-collar workers who consider their "real" lives that part that is away from their jobs, domestics' "real" identities come from other than work-related activities. But while the domestics of today are, in fact, more psychologically and materially independent than domestics of the past, they are nevertheless still asked for some semblance of the traditional subservient performance, a performance, it is clear, far removed from their view of their real selves. It is this contradiction of contemporary American servitude that explains why the women I interviewed exhibited such a high degree of *ressentiment*.

Ressentiment

Ressentiment, a French term adopted by Nietzsche into the German language and later thoroughly explored by Max Scheler, denotes

> an attitude which arises from a cumulative repression of feelings of hatred, revenge, envy and the like.... When a person is unable to release these feelings against the persons or group evoking them, thus developing a sense of impotence, and when these feelings are continuously re-experienced over time, then *ressentiment* arises.[29]

> *Ressentiment* can only arise if these emotions are particularly powerful and yet must be suppressed because they are coupled with the feeling that one is unable to act them out—either because of weakness, physical or mental, or fear. Through its very origin, *ressentiment* is therefore chiefly confined to those who serve and are dominated at the moment.[30]

A critical element of *ressentiment* is the sense of injustice based on the belief that one does not deserve to be in the subordinate position. It is not surprising, then, that *ressentiment* would be "strongest in a society like ours, where approximately equal rights (political and otherwise) or formal social equality, publicly recognized, go hand in hand with wide factual differences in power, property, and education."[31]

Scheler felt that certain positions within a social structure were especially prone to produce *ressentiment*-filled people: the feminine role (especially the spinster), the mother-in-law, and the priest, for example. Individuals in these positions have a sense of deprivation relative to others' power or benefits, with no opportunity to express the anger and envy caused by the deprivation. Clearly, domestic servants are in a similar type of position; they may be, in fact, the epitome of "those who serve and are dominated." And to the degree that they do not believe in their inferiority and therefore see their situation as unjust, they too should feel *ressentiment*. And, indeed, they do.

Despite domestics' knowledge that material comforts do not bring happiness and their assessments of themselves by other than job-related criteria, their awareness of employers' unearned privileges in the society (because of their class and race) and their having to endure employers' demeaning treatment cause feelings of *ressentiment* in even the most positive domestics. Many writers on servitude, from Lewis Coser to Jean Genet, have commented on the hostility that must exist in those who serve.[32] But *ressentiment* is more than hostility; it is a long-term, seething, deep-rooted negative feeling toward those whom one feels unjustly have power or an advantage over one's life. A domestic illustrates her *ressentiment* while describing her "kind" employer:

> She was the kind of person who made up for their dullness by a great show of pride, and she got every bit of her "Yes, Ma'am, Miss Annes" from each and everybody. Since she was that kind of person, I used to see if I could feed her enough of that to choke her. . . . She was, by white standards, a kind person, but by our standards she was not a person at all.[33]

Domestics know that employers have the power to make the relationship mainly what they want it to be. Domestics may reject the degrading ideas behind the demanded "games," but, like Elizabeth Roy, they also know they have little choice but to play: "Domination. That's the name of the game. The more you know, the more you make the employer uneasy. . . . They want to dominate, exploit." If domestics do not pretend to be unintelligent, subservient, and content with their positions, they know the position could be lost. Esther Jones expresses an understanding all domestics share: "She always said I was one of the family, but I knew better. I knew just what was going on and how they could change. If you don't do the way they want, they'll change overnight!"

Thus, part of their *ressentiment* is caused by the psychological exploitation that my research indicates is intrinsic to this work relationship, and part of it is caused by domestics' knowledge of how employers have used their power to also exploit them materially. For domestics are aware of this simple fact: if employers paid better, the quality of their (domestics') lives would be better. Even egalitarian interpersonal relationships (which are non-existent, in any case) could not fully compensate for the hardships caused by not making enough money to provide adequately for oneself and one's family. I heard a Newton employer speak warmly about Mary Dixon, her domestic of fifteen years, who was "one of the family now," who worries about the employer's husband dressing warmly enough, and whom "we love and trust." I later visited Ms. Dixon's clean but rundown apartment near Franklin Park in Roxbury and heard her talk about her minister's unsuccessful efforts to get her Medicaid coverage (she was fifty-two at the time), about having to make partial payments on her bills again in order to make a vacation trip home to South Carolina, about not declaring two of her six employers in order to be eligible for food stamps, which never seem to get her through to the end of the month. And I realized what this "caring" employer's wages of $3.50 an hour meant to the quality of the domestic's life. Ms. Dixon knew, of course, far better than I:

> Ya, they're all right [her six employers]. As long as I do what I'm supposed to, they're fine. And even then, they don't always do right. Like they go on vacation for two weeks

without telling me ahead of time. Or they go for two months in the summer and not even try to help me find some other work. They're not people I consider friends. They're takers. Take as much as you let them. And then grab a little more.

I visited a sixty-four-year-old domestic's apartment heated only by a kitchen stove, and a sick domestic's efficiency heated by only a small space heater. I saw thirty-seven-year-old Edith Lincoln's face when she told me how she'd like to put her daughter in pre-school but because of her financial situation had to leave her with relatives. And I heard domestics' dreams, like Nell Kane's . . .

I would have liked to get training for better jobs than just domestic work, maybe secretarial work or bookkeeper or something that would be upgrading.

. . . Dorothy Aron's . . .

If I'd been able to get the education, I would have preferred to teach. I always thought I would be good at that. And I love children. But I just didn't have that opportunity.

. . . and Elizabeth Roy's . . .

I always wanted a brick home. I always wanted my family together. But didn't any of that materialize.

In addition to having to cope with low pay, most domestics have experienced or heard about outright cheating by employers. Mary Dixon was one of the domestics who told me about a new practice in the Boston area:

What's happening now, you have to be careful about checks. I won't take a check on the first day any more. This woman in West Newton was very nice, but she gave me a check for thirty-five dollars and it bounced. So I called her and she said I should redeposit the check, she just forgot to put money into her account. So I redeposited it and it bounced again. That's what they're doing today. It's happened to a lot of the girls.

Did you go to her house to get your money?

No, I didn't have the time for that. They know you're not going all the way back out there. That's why they know they can get away with it. They found a new way to get a free day's work for nothing.

Stories of such trickery are part of the ugly folklore of domestic service. The worst and most pervasive of such practices were apparently during the Depression in the notorious "Bronx slave markets," but stories of cheating by employers persist and are passed around in this labor group, feeding the anger shared among workers toward "these white people." Domestics do not forget employers' abuse of their power even when it is, from the employer's point of view, a minor infraction.

Sixty-five-year-old Nell Kane vividly remembered an experience she had in the 1940s:

> She was a wealthy lady. They owned a gladiola farm. I had already learned to cook and serve when I went to work for her. My regular people, were away, so I went to work for her for the holidays.
>
> From my working in different wealthy homes, I used to write up my own recipes. If I got an idea of something nice to serve, I would build a recipe up and try it. And if it was a success, I'd put it in this little book. I had created a lot of little decorations for their teas and dinners that I had written in there too. Whenever the ideas came, I'd write them down. And whenever you do, it's like a precious little thing that you do because you want to show your work.
>
> And I worked for her and she took my book. I remember her asking the evening I was packing to leave if she could borrow the book and copy some of the recipes. I said, "Well, these are the recipes I built from the time I began working and it's kind of precious to me," I said, "but you can take a look at it." My brother drove me out there a few days later to pick it up and she says, "Nell, I've looked everywhere for that book and can't find it." So I looked around but didn't see it. Do you know, they moved away and I never got that book back. That was one of the most upsetting experiences I've had. That book was so valuable to me. I wanted my children to read it.
>
> I think she took it deliberately. It hurt me. I cried. At that age, I didn't think anyone would do that to you. But some of these women! She had so much more than I did and that little book was my joy. It was a history I would like to have kept.

Telling me this story almost forty years after it happened, Nell Kane once again cried. As Nietzsche said, the *ressentiment*-filled person inevitably becomes "expert in silence, in long memory, in waiting."

Employers' exploiting their advantaged position has been both institutionalized (as in the pay system) and underhanded, both material and psychological. But domestics recognize the exploitation for what it is and know their comparative powerlessness to change it. This knowledge of their powerlessness as a group combines with their inability to express their outrage to those who have caused it to form the basis of the deep and pervasive *ressentiment* in the women I interviewed. The presence of such *ressentiment* attests to domestics' lack of belief in their own inferiority, their sense of injustice about their treatment and position, and their rejection of the legitimacy of their subordination.

Domestics' ways of coping with employers' degrading treatment have been effective, then, in protecting them from the psychological damage risked by accepting employers' belief system but have not been effective in changing the behaviors themselves. All of the behaviors that are generated from the mistress—the demands for various forms of deference, treating domestics as non-persons or children, the encouragement of unattractiveness and of performances of low intelligence and general incompetence (except for physical labor)—all of these conventions of the mistress-servant relationship have in common the quality of affirming the employer's belief in or of her asking for evidence of the domestic's inferiority. The behaviors and feelings that emanate genuinely from domestics (those not demanded by the mistress) indicate their rejection of the ideas of their own inferiority, of the greater worth of the mistresses, and of the legitimacy of the hierarchical social system.

Domestics do not identify with their employers; they evaluate themselves by criteria other than the society's and their employers' views of those who do domestic work; they show no evidence of considering themselves inferior because of the work they do. But domestics do exhibit the extreme consciousness of the Other that is characteristic of those in a subordinate position; and they do express the *ressentiment* of oppressed who do not accept the justness of their oppression. The elements in the relationship generated by domestics, however, form a weak counterpoint to the deference rituals and maternalism that are the essence of the dynamic between employers and domestics. The employer, in her more powerful position, sets the essential tone of the relationship; and that tone is one that functions to reinforce the inequality of the relationship, to strengthen the employer's belief in the rightness of her advantaged class and racial position, and to provide her with justification for the inegalitarian social system.

Notes

1. Ralph Ellison, *Invisible Man* (New York: Vintage, 1972), p. 3.

2. Frantz Fanon, *Black Skin, White Masks* (New York: Grove, 1967), p. 139.

3. Erving Goffman, *The Presentation of Self in Everyday Life* (Garden City, N. Y.: Doubleday Anchor, 1959), p. 151. Although the terms "invisible," "non-person," or "object" to describe servants are not synonymous, I will discuss them without distinguishing between the subtle differences in their meaning. This is because writers use the terms differently but are, in my opinion, referring to closely related mental and social processes (for example, Goffman's use of "non-person" is quite similar to Ellison's use of "invisible person").

4. Theresa McBride, *The Domestic Revolution* (New York: Holmes & Meier, 1976), p. 29.

5. David Katzman, *Seven Days a Week: Women and Domestic Service in Industrializing America* (New York: Oxford University Press, 1978), p. 188.

6. Ellison, *Invisible Man*, p. 3; James Baldwin, *The Fire Next Time* (New York: Dial, 1963), p. 114; Tom Engelhardt, "Ambush at Kamikazee Pass," in *Majority and Minority*, ed. Norman R. Yetman and C. Hoy Steele (2nd ed.; Boston: Allyn & Bacon, 1975), pp. 522–31.

7. Albert Memmi, *The Colonizer and the Colonized* (Boston: Beacon, 1965), p. 86.

8. Frantz Fanon, *Wretched of the Earth* (New York: Grove, 1963), pp. 43 and 37.

9. Elsewhere, I have discussed in greater detail the ideas of these three writers on the consciousness of the Other and *ressentiment* of those in a subordinate position. See Judith Rollins, "And the Last Shall Be First: The Master-Slave Dialectic in Hegel, Nietzsche and Fanon," in "The Legacy of Frantz Fanon," ed. Hussein A. Bulhan, unpub. manuscript.

10. Friedrich Nietzsche, *The Birth of Tragedy and the Genealogy of Morals*, trans. Francis Golffing (New York: Doubleday Anchor, 1956), p. 171.

11. Fanon, *Black Skin, White masks*, pp. 212–13.

12. G. W. F. Hegel, *The Phenomenology of Mind*, trans. J. B. Baillie (New York: Harper Colophon, 1967), p. 234.

13. Albert Memmi, *Dominated Man* (New York: Orion Press, 1968), pp. 178–79.

14. Hegel, *Phenomenology of Mind*, pp. 238–39.

15. Ibid., p. 237. I did not, however, detect dependence in most of the employers I interviewed. This may have been because most had held jobs outside their homes and none currently had full-time domestic help. The few whose personalities suggested dependence were older women of less than good health (including the two widows). Their dependency seemed to stem from these factors rather than overreliance on their domestics.

16. Fanon, *Wretched of the Earth*, p. 45.

17. For a full discussion of aversive and dominant racism, see Joel Kovel, *White Racism: A Psychohistory* (New York: Vintage, 1971), especially ch. 2.

18. Eleanor Preston-Whyte, "Race Attitudes and Behaviour: The Case of Domestic Employment in White South African Homes," *African Studies* 35, no. 2 (1976): 71–89.

19. Ibid., p. 82.

20. Ibid., pp. 86–87.

21. Katzman, *Seven Days a Week*, p. 200.

22. Ibid.

23. Alfred Lindesmith, Anselm Strauss, and Norman Denzin, *Social Psychology* (5th ed.; New York: Holt, Rinehart & Winston, 1977), p. 420.

24. Bruno Bettelheim, *Surviving and Other Essays* (New York: Alfred A. Knopf, 1979), pp. 77–79.

25. Ibid., p. 82.

26. Fanon, *Black Skin, White Masks*, pp. 146–47.

27. Eugene Genovese, *Roll, Jordan, Roll: The World the Slaves Made* (New York: Vintage, 1976), p. 337.

28. The area of employers' lives most frequently criticized by domestics was their child-rearing practices. Domestics described seeing children grow up who no longer speak to their parents; a number said their female employers had expressed envy of the respect and caring the domestic's children demonstrated. For a fuller discussion on comparative childrearing practices and the women's views on it, see Bonnie Thornton Dill, "Across the Boundaries of Race and Class: An Exploration of the Relationship Between Work and Family Among Black Female Domestic Servants," Ph. D. diss., New York University, 1979.

29. Lewis Coser, "Introduction," in Max Scheler, *Ressentiment*, trans. William Holdheim (Glencoe, Ill.: Free Press, 1961), pp. 23–24.

30. Scheler, *Ressentiment*, p. 48.

31. Ibid., p. 50.

32. See Lewis Coser, "Servants: The Obsolescence of an Occupational Role," *Social Forces* 52, no. 1 (Sept. 1973): 31–40, and Jean Genet, *The Maids*, trans. Bernard Frechtman (New York: Grove, 1954).

33. John L. Gwaltney, *Drylongso* (New York: Vintage, 1981), p. 6.

A Maid by Any Other Name   16

The Transformation of "Dirty Work" by
Central American Immigrants

LESLIE SALZINGER

I am teaching an English class at Choices, a cooperative of immigrant Latina domestic workers.[1] We are practicing tenses of the verb "to be." "In El Salvador I was a teacher, here I am a housekeeper." "In Nicaragua I was a businesswoman, here I am a housekeeper." Embarrassed laughter ripples through the group at the end of each sentence. "Oh, how the mighty have fallen," I say, reflecting the discomfort in the room. Another co-op member comes in and a woman in the class explains what's going on, quoting my comments in summary. But then she turns back to the group. "It makes us embarrassed, but it shouldn't. We're trained, we do good work, and they pay us well. We haven't fallen." Everyone nods in agreement.

A few weeks later I am teaching a similar class at Amigos, another local domestic worker cooperative. As we go around the room the sentences falter and trail off into uncertainty. "In El Salvador I was a cashier, here I am. . . ." "In Guatemala I was a laundress, here I am. . . ." I suggest "domestic worker." They agree matter-of-factly, but there is no conviction to their responses. Whether positive or negative, they have not claimed this identity as their own.

I spent the fall of 1988 observing and sometimes participating in the meetings, gossip, English classes, and job-reception work of two immigrant Latina domestic worker cooperatives in the Bay Area. As the months passed, a few questions began to surface with increasing frequency. Many of these women had been in the United States for close to a decade. Why were they doing domestic work after so many years here? Domestic work is a paradigmatic case of immigrant "dirty" work—of work that is irredeemably demeaning.[2] Why did some of these women speak with such pride of their work? And even more puzzling, what accounted for the dramatically different attitudes members of the two groups held toward their work? As my attention was drawn to these anomalies, I realized that many of the explanations were to be found not within the cooperatives that had generated them, but in the market for domestic work. In this chapter I look at the occupational strategies of these women and locate them in the structural context within which they were formed. I argue that the human capital resources they brought—or failed to bring—with them account for little of their work experience in this country. Rather, it is within the context of the constraints and opportunities they encountered here that we can understand their occupational decisions, their attitudes toward their work, and ultimately their divergent abilities to transform the work itself.

Why Domestic Work?

Although many immigration theorists emphasize the role of culture or human capital in explaining occupation,[3] such arguments provide us with little help in accounting for the occupational strategies of many of the women in Choices and Amigos. Teachers, cashiers, peasants, laundresses, housewives, recent immigrants, longtime residents, persecuted organizers, jobless mothers, documented recipients of political asylum, undocumented refugees, Nicaraguans, Guatemalans, Colombians, Salvadorans, single women, wives, widows, mothers . . . the most striking thing about the women I encountered was their diversity. No group seemed to lack its representatives. There are some whom we might expect to find: those who did domestic work in their countries of origin, or who come from rural areas, or who never obtained legal documents. However, we find others whose presence is harder to account for: urban, previously professional women who have been here long enough to obtain work permits. Why are they doing domestic work after so many years in this country?

The work of Saskia Sassen-Koob[4] moves away from the characteristics of individual women, or even of individual ethnic groups, to focus directly on the structural context entered by contemporary immigrants to American cities. During the last twenty years, immigrants have entered the United States' "declining" cities in ever-increasing numbers, and contrary to all predictions they continue to find enough work to encourage others to follow them. Sassen-Koob asks how these immigrants can be absorbed by an economy that is rapidly losing its industrial base. Her explanation for this apparent anomaly is that while these cities are losing their place as manufacturing centers, they are simultaneously undergoing a rebirth as "global cities," dedicated to the coordination of scattered factories and to the production of "producer services" such as banking and insurance for an international corporate market. Retaining her focus on the niche filled by immigrant workers in contemporary cities, she emphasizes the direct support services and one-of-a-kind luxury goods financed by this new, export-directed service economy. Thus her analysis points not only to the financial analysts but to the clerical workers who punch in their data, not only to the advertising executives but to the workers who stuff their futons and sew their quilts, not only to the commodity brokers but to the workers who clean their offices, buildings, and apartments. Like early analyses of household labor, her schema makes visible the denied: the work that enables the smooth operation of both the offices and the lives of those who run them.

Sassen-Koob's research points to the way in which a new international division of labor affects the opportunities and constraints directly facing job seekers. She distinguishes between the suburban middle class of 1950–1970, based in a manufacturing economy, and the urban middle class of the 1970s and 1980s, based in the new service economy, and she traces the impact of their divergent life-styles on the market for low-level service work. Her claim is that whereas suburbs were made possible by the construction of roads and cars and household "labor-saving" devices, new professional life-styles depend on the creation of labor itself. She identifies two historically specific systems: the manufacturing-based middle class with life-styles undergirded by a physical infrastructure constructed by past immigrants, and the service-based middle class with life-styles supported by a labor infrastructure made up of recent immigrants.

Such an analysis highlights not only the existence of low-level jobs, but the two-tiered nature of contemporary economies. The bulk of available jobs generated by the growing service sector either require formal training—generally certified by North American credentialing institutions—or presuppose and provide no training at all. Mobility, when it occurs, is achieved through off-the-job training. There is no way to "advance" from clerical worker to executive or from janitor to nurse without formal education. Unless one enters the country with transferable professional credentials, there is no way to cash in on previous status unless one has the resources, either in capital or in family support, to get formal training and credentials here.

Many of the women I met are aware that a lack of locally legitimated training is what is holding them back. An Amigos board member ran a trucking business in which she bought and sold goods throughout Guatemala, Honduras, and El Salvador. In Guatemala, her husband and children did almost all the housework, and she hired someone to come in and do the extensive preparation required for festivals. However, since her arrival in this country ten years ago she has consistently done one form or another of domestic work. "I hope I don't keep doing cleaning," she says. "First of all, because I'm forty-eight years old, and I'm worked out. And to tell you the truth, I don't like cleaning. In two years my daughter will start working and then maybe she can support me and I can study something. Then I could do something else. We'll see."

It is not that the only jobs in this bottom tier are domestic work. Sassen-Koob remarks on the emergence of sweatshops to manufacture the "craft goods" so attractive to the new professional class. And in fact, among these women there are frequent references to the choice to do domestic work over low-paid factory jobs. A man who called Amigos in search of women to work full-time sewing sequins and beads found few takers. At $5 (taxable) an hour, it would have meant a cut in pay. A woman who had worked as a seamstress in Nicaragua commented, "I worked sewing for a while when I first got here, but the boss yelled all the time. The only thing he missed was plugging us in." Another commented, "I've done everything, packing, inventory, stuffing pillows. . . . But I like this work. You don't have to punch in. You can negotiate your own terms." Domestic work, for at least some of these women, is a choice. But it is a choice made within limits.

We can better understand why such a heterogeneous group of Latina immigrants are doing domestic work when we shift our gaze from them to the society they face. The diversity of the human capital they bring to the labor market is matched—and made irrelevant—by the lack of diversity in the opportunities they find there. If we look at these women outside the context of the local economy, their occupational strategies are opaque. It is only when we pay attention to what they are choosing *between* that their strategies become comprehensible. The contours of the job market, rather than the limits of skill, vision, and ambition of those entering it, construct the boundaries of possibility.[5]

Two Domestic Cooperatives

Latina domestic workers in the Bay Area find jobs in a multitude of ways: through friends, churches, agencies, chance street contacts, radio and newspaper advertisements, recommendations, and job-distribution cooperatives. Cooperatives are a recent addition to the list. They emerged in the 1980s in response to the incoming flood of undocumented Central American refugees unable to turn to the American state.[6] Their presence is a reflection not only of the growing numbers of job seekers, but of the changing nature of domestic work. Today, employers often hire someone to clean once a week or once a month rather than to work full-time. This means that workers need a large number of employers to support themselves. In addition, the rise in professional cleaning agencies has accustomed many employers to finding domestic workers through advertisements, rather than through personal networks. Cooperatives provide workers with an alternative to agencies; the co-ops give them access to a pool of jobs gathered through advertising without having to surrender a large percentage of their salaries to an intermediary.

Amigos was the first Bay Area Latina domestic worker cooperative. It was established in 1983 by a neighborhood social service organization to alleviate the most pressing needs of its clientele. The only requirement for admittance is being a Latin American refugee.[7] There is a great deal of turnover in membership. Currently, the group has about sixty members who pay $15 monthly for the right to take jobs. Twenty to thirty people show up at any given meeting. The group is roughly half Salvadoran, half other Central Americans, with a scattering of Mexicans and South Americans. Most, but not all, come from urban areas. Their class backgrounds are extremely varied, ranging from medical technician to country washerwoman. There is a wide range of ages, but the bulk of members are between twenty and forty. The overwhelming majority have been in the country for less than five years, more than half for under a year. Only about a fifth of the group have long-term work permits, although roughly the same number are involved in a drawn-out asylum process through which they are issued work permits as well. No one in the group speaks English fluently, and most speak too little to communicate at even the most basic level.

The current staff person, Margarita, originally came to the cooperative as a member and did domestic work for several years. She stopped housecleaning as soon as her husband found work, however, and she considers it work of last resort. In response to the application of an Argentine woman who has been in the United States for twenty-six years, she comments: "Look, Leslie, if I'd been here twenty-six years, I'd have learned something else by now. I wouldn't be turning up here looking for cleaning work. . . . I put her on the waiting list." This is the land of opportunity, she asserts frequently; people should not content themselves with cleaning; they should study, better themselves, do something else.

Like Margarita, the co-op's founders saw the group as a stopgap solution, designed to provide as many refugees as possible with a way to survive until they found other work. They assumed there was a trade-off between quality and quantity, and quantity was always their priority. Thus, from the outset their marketing strategy was for members to undercut other workers by entering the market at the bottom. This framework was, and is, reflected in their advertising. Their listing in the local paper, two lines under "Domestic Jobs Wanted" rather than under "Domestic Agencies," reads simply, "HOUSECLEANING Garden. Latin American Refugees," with the phone number. The crookedly photocopied flyers they leave under doors convey the same mix of amateurism and desperation. Their ads proclaim not their expertise, but their need and their vulnerability. The subtext of such publicity is exploitability.

The emphasis on quantity over quality of jobs is also evident in the group's wage scale, which is relatively low for domestic work. Members are paid $6 an hour plus transportation for cleaning jobs, $4.50 an hour for child care, and $4 an hour for child care that takes over twenty hours a week. The group charges a formal minimum of $450 monthly for live-in work, but in fact sometimes accepts jobs that pay less. During one meeting Margarita raises the issue of pay, evidently in response to rumors that some members have been asking employers for higher wages: "You all deserve $10 (an hour), but $6 is the going rate. If we ask for more, we're going to lose jobs."

Pay is the only aspect of the work for which the co-op sets any standards at all. In fact, the few times an employer complained that a worker had attempted to negotiate other aspects of the relationship, Margarita and board members sided decisively with the employer. One woman who had been having problems with a live-in employer attempted to get her to sign a contract in November promising to keep her through January. When the employer called complaining that one of the board members had suggested this course of action, the office was in an uproar. Ana stoutly denied doing any such thing: "God forbid," she said. "If I don't like a job, I just leave. I don't stick around complaining and negotiating!" Incredulous irritation swirled through the office at the incident. "Imagine!" "Can you believe it?" "If she doesn't like it, she should just leave!"

Staff and board member expectations for workers are almost as low as are their expectations for employers. The group does no training of new cooperative members, and since most of the group cannot read the (English) instructions on cleaning products and machinery, there are constant mishaps. Virtually every week there is a new complaint from an employer: someone left the gas on and almost blew up the house; someone used the wrong cleaning product and destroyed an antique wooden table. According to Margarita, they used to have a cleaning workshop "to avoid problems," but it eventually took too much time, money, and energy. In any case its purpose was always to forestall disaster, never to transform members into "skilled" workers. Today new members set off for their first jobs without even this minimal introduction, armed only with a bilingual list of common household tasks.

Weekly job-allocation meetings are simultaneously authoritarian and fractious. Board members, three previous members who volunteer their time, read job descriptions and then go down a list of names until the job is claimed. At any given meeting, about a quarter of those present receive jobs—usually for one four-hour stint every two weeks, although most weeks at least one live-in job is taken as well. Since many employers request some knowledge of English, and since board members often warn people not to assume that "just knowing how to say hello" is enough, jobs are often taken by the same women week after week. There is never any collective discussion during meetings; instead, there is the constant hum of private ("unauthorized") conversation between members who are or have become friends. Favoritism based on ethnicity and the unfairness of job allocation are constant topics of discussion among these cliques. There is a sense that members have gathered to compete with each other for a scarce resource, not that they have gathered either to create a collectivity or to support each other as workers.

Conversations at meetings not concerned with problems within the group generally revolve around survival issues: rent, documents, the scarcity of jobs. Strategies for handling bad employers or filthy houses—even complaints about these occupational problems—are conspicuously absent. It is as if the work they spend their days on is not worthy of comment, purely a means to survive and thus significant only in those terms. This attitude is best summed up by Nora, a young Guatemalan woman who has been in the country for a little over a year. When I ask her if she thinks cleaning is good work, she is taken aback: "Any work's fine with me. The thing is to make money." She is not looking for a career, she is looking for a job.

Choices was set up in 1984, inspired by the success of Amigos during the preceding year. The group accepts any Latina woman who is over forty years old. Today, it has about fifty members who pay $3 weekly to participate. Jobs are allocated during twice-weekly meetings. About twenty-five women attend each meeting. Although new members join almost every meeting, at least half of the group at any given time have been members intermittently over several years. They come from all over Latin America, and although there are still many more Central Americans than South Americans, Salvadorans constitute less than half of the group. The membership is overwhelmingly urban. More than half come from middle-class backgrounds, and several come from quite elite families. In their countries of origin, they worked as teachers, secretaries, cashiers, or housewives; some ran small businesses of their own. Almost none were manual laborers or domestic workers before their arrival in this country. Many of the women have been in this country as long as ten years, and almost every member who did not already have a work permit has recently qualified for the federal amnesty that requires proof of continuous presence in the country since 1982.[8] About half of the group's members speak enough English to get around, although very few speak with any fluency.

The group was set up by a feminist organization dedicated to helping older women establish meaningful and self-directed careers. Founders initially attempted to serve Latina women in the same program in which they served their other, primarily Anglo and middle-class constituencies. However, to their frustration, they found that gaps in language and formal credentialing were keeping them from placing anyone. Hearing of the relative success of the Amigos Cooperative, they turned reluctantly to domestic-work placement. Unlike the founders of Amigos, however, they framed this work in the context of a commitment to career development, not survival. Thus, within the constrained context of domestic work, they continued to focus on the development of secure, dignified, and relatively decently paid work for their members and on the right of members to determine the course of their own work lives.

When Choices was founded it charged $5 hourly, taking its cue from its model. However, members soon began to push for higher wages. Unlike Amigos, where such a move was seen as subversive, Choices staff were supportive of the shift. In fact, the push by members for higher wages made it easier for Lisa, the group's first staff person, to come to terms with "just channeling women of all different abilities into domestic work," because it not only increased wages, but also meant that group members were beginning to take control of, and define, the work on their own. Today members charge $10 hourly for the first cleaning and, if it is an ongoing job, $8 hourly thereafter. They charge a minimum of $6 hourly for child care, but they do very little, engaging mostly in cleaning work. They have no formal set of standards for live-in jobs, but the current staff person, Lilian, says that she would tell anyone considering paying under $800 a month that she wouldn't be able to find anyone in the group willing to take the job.

The experience of raising prices and continuing to get work orders gave Choices staff a different view of the demand for domestic work than that held by staff at Amigos. Lisa comments that there are "different markets" and mentions advertising in particular newspapers as a way of targeting "better" employers. The group also runs a display ad in the *Yellow Pages* offering "Quality HOUSECLEANING at affordable rates. [Choices] domestic referral service." At the bottom in fine print it says "A non-profit community service by [Choices' sponsor]." Their advertisements look essentially like those for profit-making cleaning agencies and contain no reference to the Latin background of workers. Leaflets do not figure in the marketing strategy at all.

When employers call in, the intake call continues in this professional tone. Lilian mentions that all the workers are Latina women, but makes it clear that anything the employer needs to communicate can be communicated through her. She also lets them know that all workers are "trained." There is a sense that employers will be taken care of. From the employer's point of view, apart from the fact that the worker is paid directly, the group could easily be any one of a number of for-profit cleaning agencies, run by Anglos, that hire Latina women to do the actual work. This sense of worker connection to a white agency is enhanced by the fact that every worker takes an envelope from the office to each new job. The envelope contains Lilian's card, a bilingual household task sheet, a list of appropriate cleaning products, and an evaluation form to be filled out by the employer and mailed to the office. These evaluations not only function to provide employers with a sense of worker accountability, but are also used by co-op members when employers request a worker with references. This process allows workers, as well as the group as a whole, to develop marketable personas.

The professional context within which the co-op sells itself has led it to develop its own standards for members. Soon after raising its prices, the group instituted a short training for members "in order to earn those two dollars," according to Lisa. The training is currently conducted by a member who is paid by the sponsoring organization. It involves going through cleaning tasks and products and discussing how one solves specific cleaning problems, particularly when the employer does not have the standard cleaning products. Trainings also discuss the use of nontoxic cleaning products, as this is one of the group's specialties. The tone of these sessions is casual and friendly, and training for new members takes place while every-one else sits around gossiping about other matters and occasionally kibitzing about the training. All members are tested on the material (orally or in writing, depend-ing on whether they are literate) and they are retested on those questions they got wrong. The knowledge they are tested on is not extensive, but it is easy to see how not knowing some of these things could lead to disaster. What is most striking about the process are the contrasts: between the informality of the actual training sessions and the formality with which both staff and older members describe them; between the tremendous variation in what is actually involved for different people going through the process and the absolute insistence that everyone go through it. It is not as much how it is done as that it is done at all that appears to be significant for the group.

The group has established clear standards for employers as well as workers. On the phone, Lilian asks for specific information about what the employer wants done. If she feels that the amount of work is unreasonable given the time paid for, she suggests that the worker may need more time or may need to leave some of the work undone. She makes clear that workers will not work extra time for free. She communicates this to workers as well. For instance, after listening to members complaining about unreasonably demanding jobs, she comments, "Don't do them. If you do them, they'll think it's possible for the next one who goes. Tell them it's not possible. You need to learn those phrases in English, to defend yourself. And if they insist, let them go. There are other jobs." Margarita at the Amigos cooperative would never have made such a comment. From Margarita's perspective, the most fundamental purpose of her work was to provide as many members with work as possible. To Lilian, on the other hand, this comment goes to the heart of what makes this work worthwhile—the development of dignified work for cooperative members.

Choices meetings are social and members clearly enjoy them. There are even several women who no longer need new jobs who continue to attend. Both the twice-weekly meetings are preceded by an English class, and one is preceded by the cleaning training. During meetings, members sit in a circle, and they have a time set aside for reports on their work, as well as for general "commentaries." Jobs are allocated according to an elaborate point system with which they are constantly tin-kering. About a quarter of the group gets a job each week, generally for four hours every week or two. Members who speak little English are encouraged by the group to be brave and take jobs, using the bilingual task sheet to communicate. Respon-sibility for running the meetings is supposed to be rotated. Although this goal is never completely realized, about half of the group participates by taking or reading minutes or by recording dues payments. In introducing the co-op to new members, the group's collective self-sufficiency is always emphasized. Victoria comments, "We maintain the group ourselves—no one else, not the mayor, not anyone, us."

There are constant complaints that some women come "*just* to get work." This is seen as a serious accusation, despite the fact that distributing work is the organi-zation's reason for existence. Since they charge dues for the right to take jobs, there is no mechanism through which they can exclude those who don't behave like "real" members. As a result, there are repeated debates over what to do about this problem. One woman expressed a sort of tacit consensus when she called out during one of these discussions: "It's a community. It shouldn't be just an agency!"

In fact, the group does operate far more like an occupational community than it does like an agency. Members trade tips constantly, developing and sharing strategies to deal with dirty houses and impossible employers in the same breath. During the English classes they ask the teacher to write out specific dialogues for them to memorize: "The house is big; I need more time." "I can't give you more time." "OK, I'll clean as far as I can get in the time I have." Someone comments that she got to a new house and found a filthy oven but no Ajax. What should she have done? Use baking soda, of course. She'd never heard that before. "It's amazing how you just keep on learning." "Yes, there's always more to learn." One member announces that she's giving up a job: "My boss keeps calling Lilian to complain. I told her that I do the work, not Lilian. If she has any problems she should talk to me. But she keeps calling Lilian. I'm not anyone's ward." Her decision to leave an otherwise unobjectionable job because she is being treated in a demeaning manner is supported without question by the group. Meetings serve as a context within which workers collectively set standards for themselves and for employers and in so doing redefine their work as dependent on training and deserving of respect.

This collective image of skilled work is carried onto the job and communicated to employers as part of an ongoing struggle for autonomy. A member comments: "It's good to have training. Sometimes an employer says, 'Don't do it that way, that way won't work,' and then I can say, 'Yes it will. I know because I have training.' 'Oh,' they say. . . . Once I worked for this very rich woman and I told her I had had training, and so she started asking me all these questions and I answered them all, and then she was very impressed and left me alone." Another member goes to the front of the room to tell this story:

> I went to clean a house, but the lady wasn't there. And the man didn't have any of the right products. He gave me Clorox to wash the floor—*hardwood* floors. I told him I couldn't, because it would go against my responsibility and my knowledge of cleaning. ["That's good," someone else responds, "That's why we have training. If you'd done it you'd have ruined the floor and they'd have put you in jail." She nods and continues.] Maybe he didn't like the way I talked to him, because when I was leaving he said, "Next time I'll have a list for you of what you should do," and I said to him, "OK, that's good. Next time I come I'll bring a list of the supplies I need to do the work." So he said "Oh" and then he drove me home.

Given our earlier discussion of why these women do domestic work, the stark contrast between Choices and Amigos is puzzling. After all, despite their varied life histories, women in both groups have ended up doing this work for essentially the same reason: because it is the best of a limited set of options. Moreover, the literature on immigrants' rising expectations suggests that those who have been here longer would be least satisfied with domestic work. Yet the women in Choices are far more positive about their work than are the women in Amigos. Clearly, the founders of the two groups began with somewhat divergent focuses, but these seem minor in comparison to their shared goals of creating domestic-worker cooperatives for Latina immigrants. How could initial differences in founders' emphases within an otherwise similar set of goals produce such sharp and enduring discrepancies in members' perceptions of their work? The answer lies in the structure of the labor market within which the co-ops are embedded and in the way in which the two sets of organizational priorities position their members in this structure.

A Bifurcated Market

Sassen-Koob points to the contemporary emergence of a two-tiered service economy composed of professionals and those who serve them, both at work and at home. What this analysis overlooks is the two-tiered nature of the domestic services market itself. For not only is there an increasing demand for domestic services from single, elite professionals (the "yuppie" phenomenon), but there is also an increasing demand for such services from the rising number of elderly people living alone on fixed incomes, from two-earner working-class families, and from single mothers who need cheap child care in order to work at all. These groups can afford very different pay scales and thus have different requirements and standards for their employees. Together they constitute a dual labor market within the bottom tier of the larger service economy.

In the Bay Area today, Latin American domestic workers are routinely paid anywhere from $5 to $10 hourly. Live-in salaries range between $300 and $1,000 monthly. In her study of Japanese-American domestic workers, Evelyn Nakano Glenn notes similarly broad discrepancies in pay among her respondents.[9] She attributes this to personalistic aspects of the negotiating process between domestic workers and their employers. However, such an explanation begs the question of how this tremendous range for negotiation came to exist in the first place. The variation is made possible in part by the social isolation of the work and by the lack of organization among both workers and employers. This atomization is compounded by ineffective state regulation; domestic work was not covered by the Fair Labor Standards Act until 1974, and even today it is often done under the table. However, hourly wages that vary routinely by factors of two or three must be produced as well as tolerated. What is the structure of demand for domestic work that has kept some wages so low, while allowing enterprising businesses to consistently raise the ceiling on prices at the other end of the spectrum?

Over the past thirty years, women have entered the paid labor force in ever-increasing numbes. This movement is a response both to the economic shifts mentioned by Sassen-Koob—the decline of (primarily men's) manufacturing jobs paying a "family wage" and the increasing availability of "feminized" service jobs—and to cultural shifts that have made paid work an acceptable choice for women even in the absence of financial need. This has led to the increasing commodification of what was once unpaid household labor, visible in the boom in restaurants and cleaning agencies and in the increasing demand for child care during the last two decades.

Like all large-scale shifts in a stratified society, these developments have had a differential impact on the lives and options of people located at different levels within it. Working-class and lower-middle-class women, having entered low-paid service occupations themselves, generally can afford to pay very little to replace their household labor if they are to gain anything at all from their own salaries. Professional women raising children alone often find themselves in a similar quandary. Women in such situations show up regularly at Amigos. A single mother who works part-time at the post office comes in to interview live-in help. She wants to pay only $400 a month. "I can't afford any more," she says, looking desperate. "All I need is someone strong and trustworthy who can look after the kids while I'm gone." Elderly people living alone on fixed incomes, another growing sector of the population, also need domestic help and have little leeway in what they can pay for it. A manager for a seniors' apartment building calls. "My boss gave me your flyer," he says. "I'm always on the lookout to find cheap cleaning help for them. The most important thing is that people be honest." For these groups, the search for domestic help is less a negotiation process with a single worker than it is a desperate search for anyone willing to accept the inevitably exploitative salary they have to offer.

At the other end of this spectrum are single professionals of both genders, an increasingly significant segment of urban consumers in an era of delayed marriage and childbearing. This group faces very different constraints in their relationships with domestic workers. Regardless of the hourly cost, a weekly housecleaning will absorb only a minuscule portion of any middle-class budget. And even middle-class couples seeking full-time child care can afford to negotiate for particular skills and services. There is considerable plasticity in the amount these employers can pay for domestic work.

Not surprisingly, recent years have seen an explosion of entrepreneurs focused on convincing such people that there is something worth paying more for. Young white middle-class women hang advertising posters in trendy restaurants implying that they are just like employers and so can "make your home feel like a home." Professional advertisements for personalized cleaning agencies abound. "Maid-to-Order" promises an ad in the local *Yellow Pages*: "Your chores are our business. Bonded and Insured." "You've Got It Maid," asserts another: "We'll do the cleaning, run your errands, wash the laundry, drop off and pick up the cleaning." In a community accustomed to professionalized personal services of all sorts—therapy, home decorating, personal shoppers—this rhetoric finds fertile ground.

Beneath the seemingly random pattern of wage variations among Bay Area domestic workers there lies a dual labor market constituted by two distinct sets of potential employers: the elderly, working-class parents and single mothers with the little money to spare; and professionals already accustomed to paying relatively high wages for work packaged as a personalized and professional service. What is remarkable is that the work done in these homes—vacuuming, dusting, scrubbing—remains similar. Insofar as there is any difference, it lies in the addition of child care to other duties in the *bottom* sector of the market.[10] It is the nature of the employer, rather than of the work, that is most significant in determining wages.

Creating Meaning

The founders of Choices and Amigos had different goals in creating the two cooperatives. Whereas Choices' founders focused on creating a collective context where women could support each other in the search for decent, long-term work, Amigos' founders focused on the creation of a clearinghouse where women with no other options could find enough work to survive. Thus, Choices emphasized job quality, whereas Amigos emphasized quantity. Ironically, due to the bifurcated market for domestic services, the strategies that emerged to accomplish these divergent priorities did not attract markedly different numbers of jobs, just different types of jobs. Whereas Amigos' marketing strategy ultimately located its workers in the bottom sector of the labor market, Choices' strategy located its members in the top. Members' differing attitudes toward their work took shape in this context. Within both groups, members' attitudes are revealed as strategies to create viable work-lives within differing structures of opportunity—as struggles at the boundaries of the possible.

The competitive atmosphere and low expectations of Amigos members can best be understood as a set of individual responses to the organization's marketing strategy and workers' consequent location in the bottom tier of the domestic services market. Members have little to gain from sharing work tips in a market in which their skill makes virtually no difference in their ability to get jobs. And in an organization in which resistance to employer exploitation is regarded by leaders as undermining the interests of the collective, mutual support is difficult if not impossible. Co-op members' perception that only individual strategies are worth focusing on, and that they share little but need and competition with other members of the group, is an accurate one within this limited framework.

In a similar vein, Amigos members' vision of domestic work as essentially unimportant, as a means rather than as an end in itself, reflects the constraints within which they are hired. There is no reason to struggle over the social construction of work when employers couldn't pay more for it even if they agreed it was worth more. In such an environment, Ana's comment that after ten years of domestic work she is still hoping to get training for other work, rather than attempting to improve the work she is doing, makes sense. In an organization in which collective action is precluded, individualized occupational strategies remain the only option. And located among employers who define workers as cheap labor, the obvious occupational strategy is one that leads out of the occupation entirely.

Choices' market strategy, on the other hand, locates its members in the top tier of the domestic services market. Choices members have taken advantage of the opportunities implicit in this situation by working for individual mobility through upgrading the occupation as a whole. They are collectively redefining domestic work as skilled labor, and on that basis struggling for increased pay and security and for autonomy and control over their work. They are in fact engaged in what in other contexts has been called a "professionalization project."[11]

This struggle takes place simultaneously in interactions with employers and within the group itself. Choices' advertising and intake process uses a white middle-class rhetoric that allows members to enter the top tier of the market. These first contacts introduce employers to a group of skilled workers.[12] Once on the job, workers emphasize their expertise. Comments about their training and their insistence that they be treated as experts who know and are accountable for what they are doing emerge as part of this project. However, it is not only employers who need to be convinced that these women are skilled workers; co-op members also need to be convinced of this. Group meetings become the arena in which members construct and reinforce their professionalized identity; thus the strikingly supportive atmosphere, the constant, repetitive discussions of cleaning techniques, the emphasis on the ritual of training and testing are all revealed as elements in the creation of a collective professional identity. Even the ongoing presence of women who no longer need new jobs makes sense. Members of the group have everything to offer each other, for they affirm their tenuous, shared status as skilled workers.

Understanding Choices as a professionalization project makes problematic my earlier portrayal of skilled workers entering the top tier of a preexisting "bifurcated market," however. It pushes us to reconceptualize the relationship between supply and demand in a more dynamic framework.[13] If the market for skilled workers already existed, a collective effort of this sort would not be necessary; workers could simply get training on an individual basis. Clearly, Choices is not creating this demand on its own. But just as clearly, the market for skilled domestic workers is not an outgrowth of unmediated demographic shifts. Rather, the co-op has joined a host of contemporary entrepreneurs already attempting to create a demand for professionalized personal services among the new middle class. Cooperative members are responding to the market and to the structure of constraints and opportunities they encounter within it; but as a collectivity, they are also part of redefining the market and thus expanding the range of possibilities they face. They are not only individuals lucky enough to have entered a context within which professionalization is possible; they are also members of a group that is part of the collective construction of that new structure of opportunity.

At bottom, the professionalization project is an emergent property of the interactive structure of the group itself—of the existence of an infrastructure that makes the development of a collective occupational strategy possible.[14] This process is made somewhat easier by the life histories of the women in the group. Choices members have generally been in this country longer than their counterparts in Amigos and tend to come from somewhat more middle-class backgrounds. Since they no longer expect to leave domestic work, they have an incentive to improve it. Similarly, their time in this country has given them some security, providing them with more latitude in picking and choosing jobs and consequently encouraging the development of domestic work as a career. In addition, their more middle-class backgrounds may have made them more likely to conceptualize their work—even work for which they initially had little respect—in professional terms. Thus, although neither class nor tenure in this country is completely correlated with membership in the two cooperatives, it is likely that the preponderance of long-term residents with middle-class backgrounds in Choices has been conducive to the development of a professionalization project. However, it is the structure of

Choices that has provided a context within which these characteristics could make a difference. Amigos does not provide a space within which workers can develop a collective strategy; as a result, each worker faces the market as an individual. Since domestic work is only partially professionalized, this means that Amigos members enter the market as unskilled, immigrant labor, with all the handicaps that such a label implies. Choices members, on the other hand, participate collectively in the redefinition of this work as skilled, and so realize the potential benefits of their class background and tenure in this country within the context of a more powerful occupational identity.

The Social Organization of Domestic Work

This analysis raises a final set of questions, for while it explains the differential ability of the women in these two cooperatives to professionalize their work, it does not explain why domestic workers have so rarely attempted—and even more rarely sustained—such projects in the past.[15] To understand this shift, we need to look more closely at the evolving social organization of domestic work itself, at the constellation of social relations within which the work is performed.

Until recently, domestic workers in this country were seen by employers, and at times saw themselves, as bound by the web of affective and paternalistic connections that constitute relations in the family. This patriarchal relationship reflected the fact that domestic workers shared both home and workplace with their employers. Not only did the domestic worker live in her employer's home, but her workplace was generally the mistress's workplace as well. These overlapping arenas lodged the worker securely within the family, leaving little room for the development of an independent occupational identity.

The overlap between worker and employer living spaces was the first of these linkages to erode. Live-in work began to decrease in frequency during the 1920s,[16] when the young white women, native and foreignborn, who had previously dominated the occupation began leaving to enter factories. They were replaced by Japanese and Mexican immigrants and by Black women migrating from the South. Unlike their white predecessors, their mobility into other jobs was barred by racism. Many did domestic work all their lives, instead of as a prelude to other work. As a result, they were generally unwilling to sleep in their employers' homes, and the occupation began to reshape itself to the fact that domestic workers had their own families. This shift to "day-work" was the first significant break in the mistress-servant relationship.[17]

The overlap between worker and mistress workplaces did not begin to erode until much later. Until quite recently, most women who could afford domestic help did not work outside the home. As a result, servants joined the mistress of the house in a realm in which emotions were defined as central and contractual relationships as irrelevant.[18] However, as middle-class women moved out of the home, they blurred the boundaries of this realm and changed the relationship of domestic workers to the household in the process. It is easier to construct a house as a workplace when it contains only workers (or more likely a single worker) than it is when it is shared with those for whom it is "home." Similarly, employers who do paid work are less committed to seeing housework as a "labor of love" than they were when they did it full-time themselves. Thus, the increase in the labor market participation of "mistresses" has meant that paid domestic work is increasingly done in a capitalist wage-labor context, rather than in a feudal master-servant context.

In 1974 domestic work was brought under the aegis of minimum wage laws for the first time. Although wages continued to be paid primarily under the table, many employers responded to this new expectation by paying for fewer hours of cleaning per month (frequently for the same amount of cleaning as before[19]). This speed-up further weakened the personal ties between worker and employer. Seeing workers' time as costly, employers who previously used domestic workers as company and confidantes[20] were less likely to stop their work to socialize. Like other shifts in the social organization of domestic work, the imposition of minimum wage laws made the occupation less personal and affective and more contractually defined.

In recent years, agencies have entered the field in growing numbers. They hire people and send them out to private homes in which they may never see the employer whose home they are cleaning.[21] Although many employers continue to find workers through informal routes, this absolute separation of worker and employer spheres is important both because it is expanding so rapidly and because it embodies a transformation of domestic work from servant to wage labor.

Domestic workers' evolution from the servants of one employer to wage laborers for many has opened up new possibilities both for exploitation and for resistance. Unlike their predecessors, domestic workers today can separate their work from their relationships with particular employers; thus, they can forge a collective identity based on the work itself. And in the current capitalist context, such an ability carries new payoffs. The struggle over domestic work is no longer primarily a struggle to delineate the limits of the employer-employee relationship; instead, it is a struggle over whether the work is to be defined as skilled or unskilled labor. Within the context of a feudal relationship, the redefinition of the servant's work as skilled would not necessarily have resulted in a materially different status. Today, it can make the difference between security and insecurity. Thus, the emergence of grass-roots efforts at professionalization today, rather than in earlier periods, can be understood within the context of the changing social organization of domestic work. The shift from servant to wage laborer provided both the opportunity and the incentive for this new form of struggle.

A New Sort of Agency?

Although the social organization of domestic work has shifted over time, the migrant origins of the work force have shown remarkable stability. This should come as no surprise. In both academic and more popular contexts, there is a pervasive sense that immigrant labor is a distinct component of the labor force, filling specific low-level functions in developed capitalist economies.[22] Several authors provide analyses that point at immigrants' structured inability to organize as the key both to the ongoing function of immigrant labor within capitalist economies and to the consignment of immigrants to menial, dead-end, low-paid jobs.[23] Domestic work is certainly a paradigmatic example of such a job, as well as of an occupation that has proved resistant to organizing for most of its history.

However, such analyses preclude the possibility of change because they ignore agency. Immigrants cannot organize by definition, thus there is no reason to examine the features of immigrants' daily life that foster or impede the development of collective identity and strategies. However, among human beings, nothing is precluded by definition. The existence of a group like Choices pushes us to reexamine such assumptions and to focus on changes in the social organization of the work immigrants do, as well as on specific collective projects that are initiated within this new work context.

Domestic work has evolved over the last two decades in directions that have weakened the connection between worker and employer and consequently increased the possibility of connection among workers. The creation of an organization such as Choices—one that provides an infrastructure of space, time, and predictability within which the emergence of collective identity is supported—becomes particularly important in this context. It is important because it provides a space within which immigrant workers can begin to organize and so to resist their consignment to "dirty work" within the capitalist economy.

In any particular context, organizing can shift some constraints and not others. Thus, in today's economy, there is no way for a new group to evade the credentialing requirements struggled for by others, and as individuals Choices members still have no access to those credentials. However, they do have access to domestic work, and collectively, they are able to effect change there. Thus we do not see these women moving into more prestigious and powerful occupations. What we see instead is the beginning of a transformation of domestic work itself from unskilled to skilled, from humiliating to respectable, from minimum wage to its double, from employer-controlled to worker-controlled, from "dirty" work to "clean."

Afterword: Ethnography for What?

Immersed in another world, watching, analyzing, gossiping, matching hypothesis to reality—moment by moment, participant observation is deeply engaging. But the analysis is another story. In the privacy of head and home I can only sustain research as part of a larger project to understand the world in order to change it. This made choosing a site particularly unnerving. I wanted a guarantee that whatever I chose would illuminate something meaningful.

During those first hectic weeks I scoured the area looking for a site. Inspired by the political success of the Rainbow Coalition, I was eager to explore the creation of inclusive identities at the grass-roots level. To my frustration and surprise, no one in the area was organizing with this as an explicit focus. This situation in itself was food for analysis, but it certainly didn't qualify as participant observation. Eventually, I settled on two Central American domestic-worker cooperatives in the hope that a cross-national "Latino" identity would emerge in such a setting even if it was not an organizational goal.

Then followed weeks of frustration. I went to meeting after meeting. Whenever the problem was an exploitative white employer, the discussion centered around

"Latinos." "At last," I thought, "now *this* is oppositional identity." But then a co-op member would complain that someone else had gotten a job unfairly, and national identities would surface once again. As I chatted with people I sometimes tried to slip my questions into conversation: "By the way, do you identify more as a 'Latino' or as a Salvadoran?" It never worked. It sounded absurd, and they looked at me with amused tolerance: "She's a nice girl, if a bit slow." It soon became evident that their identities were—like my own multiple allegiances—flexible, dependent on context. Regardless of how important identity formation might be in the broader political context, my focus on it obscured rather than revealed the particularities of what was going on.

So I kept attending meetings, enjoying the people more and more, but increasingly unsure that anything of importance was taking place. All they talked about in Amigos was unemployment and poverty and each other, and in Choices they talked constantly about cleaning: week in and week out they discussed how to polish silver and clean windows and . . . Some days I went stir-crazy, coming home and typing out pages and pages of field notes about individual traumas I couldn't fix and heroic feats of cleaning that seemed to celebrate exploitation. A typical excerpt from my field notes in this period reads: "There's no real 'political' work going on here—no discussion of members' social location in terms of race or gender or any power issue at all—so I'm continually thrown back on looking at the organizational dynamics. Everything seems very straightforward—'let's make money'—and I don't know how to get at how people see themselves in this process."

Then somewhere in the second month I began to worry less about where I thought their interests belonged and to listen more to what they were saying. In Amigos they were talking about precarious survival at the edges of an exploitative market, but in Choices something else was happening: they were talking about cleaning as skilled work. I brought my field notes into class, and people kept asking how the women in Choices could possibly speak positively about such dirty work. This was the same question I had struggled with, but hearing it from others it felt wrong. The constant discussions at Choices had changed my vision of housework as necessarily demeaning. I began to question my underlying assumptions about cleaning as work, and about the "legitimate" political bases of identity. Was cleaning more demeaning than plumbing? Why did I assume that identity organizing would necessarily build on race or gender? As I examined my own perspective, I began to take in their world more fully. I realized that whereas Amigos' members were not constructing a collective identity, Choices' members were. It was not the identity I had expected, but nonetheless they were forming a self-respecting vision of themselves as a collectivity, a vision based on their experience of their work.

I began the project determined that my work be useful not only to other researchers, but to activists working within a particular political framework. For a long time, I was so focused on that framework that I was capable of seeing little else. It was only once my expectations had been repeatedly frustrated that I was able to see the autonomous (and political) identities that were actually emerging before me. However, with the analysis behind me, a new set of issues arises. Now that I have come to understand processes that do not fit neatly into a preexisting political agenda, there are no longer obvious groups or institutions who could use the information I have gathered. Thus, finding those who might want this piece of the puzzle becomes a new and ongoing task. As much as it required energy to cull these images, it will take energy to incorporate their analysis into a broader political context of knowledge and action.

I thank the members of Choices and Amigos for the warmth, tolerance, and good humor with which they welcomed me into their midst. I also thank John Lie for supporting me in pushing the limits of my analysis, and Mary Romero for insightful comments on the manuscript.

Notes

1. The names of the cooperatives and people discussed here are fictional. All conversations quoted in this chapter—except for those with the staff at Choices and the classroom exercises—were conducted in Spanish.

2. Michael Piore, *Birds of Passage*; Judith Rollins, *Between Women*.

3. One of the foremost proponents of this position is Thomas Sowell. For instance, in *Ethnic America*, he attributes the fact that Irish immigrants often worked as domestic servants, whereas Italian immigrants generally did not, to a divergence in cultural attitudes toward gender and family. See Stephen Steinberg, *The Ethnic Myth*, for an alternate explanation of this history based on dramatic differences in the gender composition of the two immigrant flows.

4. Saskia Sassen, *The Mobility of Labor and Capital*; Saskia Sassen-Koob, "New York City: Economic Restructuring and Immigration," "Changing Composition and Labor Market Location of Hispanic Immigrants in New York City, 1960–1980," "Labor Migrations and the New International Division of Labor," and "Immigrant and Minority Workers in the Organization of the Labor Process."

5. In *The Mobility of Labor and Capital* Sassen points out that the distribution of immigrants' occupations in their countries of origin is significantly more "bimodal" than is the distribution of their occupations in the United States. Once here, there is a convergence between those of distinct occupational statuses upon a limited set of jobs. She comments: "The basic factor at work is not so much immigrants' failure or success to carry out their intended occupations, but the characteristics of the occupational structure in the U. S. and the kinds of labor needs it generates" (p. 76).

6. Steven Wallace, "Central American and Mexican Immigrant Characteristics and Economic Incorporation in California."

7. The group officially accepts both men and women. However, it is so difficult to find jobs for men that they are generally put on a waiting list and very few are in the group at any given time. Given the difference in the structure of the labor market for men and women, I only discuss the women in this paper.

8. The difference in number of years in this country and the class background of members of the two groups is striking. The difference in tenure in this country is primarily a reflection of the fact that Central Americans tend to immigrate during their late twenties. Thus, in selecting for older women, Choices also effectively selects for those who have been here longer. Similarly, earlier immigrants from Central America tended to come from a somewhat higher class background than the compatriots they left behind. (On these demographic issues see Wallace, "Central American and Mexican Immigrant Characteristics.") In recent years, according to groups working

with refugees in the Bay Area, these disparities have evaporated. Thus, the difference in class background of the two cooperatives' members reflects shifts in the demographic composition of immigrant flows from Central America over time and is also an artifact of Choices' over-forty membership criterion.

9. Evelyn Nakano Glenn, *Issei, Nissei, War Bride*.

10. Others have noted that an important strategy in transforming domestic work is the elimination of certain tasks. In "Sisterhood and Domestic Service" Mary Romero comments: "Chicana domestics use several methods to define themselves as professional housecleaners. One method involves eliminating personal services, such as babysitting, laundry and ironing" (p. 339).

11. See Magali Sarfatti Larson, *The Rise of Professionalism*, p. 50. I use the term *professionalization projects* in Larson's sense to refer to an occupation's ongoing effort to increase its status, rather than to refer to an occupation's already-achieved status. My usage departs from Larson's in that he generally uses the concept to discuss occupations that involve higher education and external credentialing. In this sense, my use of the term in the context of a low-status occupation is unusual. Nonetheless, since the goal of professionalization is to raise the status of an occupation by redefining the work as skilled and getting external support for this definition, to refuse to apply the term to any occupation that has not already gained this external support is to conflate success with "truth." Any sense we have that this strategy cannot be used in currently low-status occupations is a better indication of the overwhelming success of those who have pursued this strategy in the past than it is of the futility of such efforts among those beginning the attempt today.

12. Even the group's relatively high wage scale (for Latina workers) communicates members' professionalism to prospective employers. It not only weeds out those with less money to spare but serves as a marker for those with more discretionary income that there is something worth paying for. In commenting on the impact of raising prices at Choices, the group's first staff person observed: "The lower our prices, the more calls I got saying 'Why should they [co-op members] get $5 when I can get an English-speaking girl who will do it for $4?' It seems to me that if people pay more, they think they're getting something better."

13. For a more general discussion of this relationship see John Lie, "Visualizing the Invisible Hand."

14. In her work on Chicana domestic workers in the Southwest, Mary Romero also found them "modernizing" and "professionalizing" the occupation; see her "Chicanas Modernize Domestic Service" and "Sisterhood and Domestic Service." What is particularly interesting about Romero's work is that although the women she interviewed were not members of a formal collective, she saw their membership in an "informal network" as a central element in this process. "The controlled environment created by the use of the informal network provides the avenue for Chicanas to establish their self-definition as experts" ("Chicanas Modernize Domestic Service," p. 332).

15. Phyllis Palmer, "Housework and Domestic Labor," p. 87. She notes that eight projects were set up by the National Council of Household Employment in 1964 to create a pool of "certified" domestic workers. Their goal was to simultaneously improve the status of Black domestic workers and increase the amount of help available to (white) working wives and mothers. The projects were never able to break even and eventually folded. In light of the discussion that follows concerning the changing character of domestic work over the last three decades, both the timing and the failure of these projects take on a new significance.

16. Rollins, *Between Women*.

17. Glenn, *Issei, Nissei, War Bride*; Rollins, *Between Women*.

18. Bonnie Thorton Dill, "'Making Your Job Good Yourself.'"

19. Rollins, *Between Women*, p. 69.

20. Ibid.

21. Palmer, "Housework and Domestic Labor."

22. Mary Jo McConahay, "The Intimate Experiment"; James Fallow, "The New Immigrants"; Manuel Castells, "Immigrant Workers and Class Struggles in Advanced Capitalism"; Sassen, *The Mobility of Labor and Capital*; Piore, *Birds of Passage*.

23. Castells, "Immigrant Workers and Class Struggles"; Sassen, *The Mobility of Labor and Capital*; Piore, *Birds of Passage*.

Works Cited

Castells, Manuel. "Immigrant Workers and Class Struggles in Advanced Capitalism: The Western European Experience." *Politics and Society* 5 (1975): 33–66.

Dill, Bonnie Thornton. "'Making Your Job Good Yourself': Domestic Service and the Construction of Personal Dignity." In *Women and the Politics of Empowerment*, edited by A. Bookman and S. Morgan, pp. 33–52. Philadelphia: Temple University Press, 1988.

Fallow, James. "The New Immigrants: How They're Affecting Us." *The Atlantic*, November 1983.

Glenn, Evelyn Nakano. *Issei, Nissei, War Bride: Three Generations of Japanese American Women in Domestic Service*. Philadelphia: Temple University Press, 1986.

Larson, Magali Sarfatti. *The Rise of Professionalism: A Sociological Analysis*. Berkeley: University of California Press, 1977.

Lie, John. "Visualizing the Invisible Hand: From Market to Mode of Exchange." Harvard University, Ph. D. dissertation, 1988.

McConahay, Mary Jo. "The Intimate Experiment." *Los Angeles Times Magazine*, February 19, 1989.

Palmer, Phyllis. "Housework and Domestic Labor: Racial and Technological Change." In *My Troubles Are Going to Have Trouble with Me: Everyday Trials and Triumphs of Women Workers*, edited by Karen B. Sacks and D. Remy, pp. 80–91. New Brunswick, N. J.: Rutgers University Press, 1984.

Piore, Michael. *Birds of Passage: Migrant Labor and Industrial Societies*. Cambridge: Cambridge University Press, 1980.

Rollins, Judith. *Between Women: Domestics and Their Employers*. Philadelphia: Temple University Press, 1985.

Romero, Mary. "Chicanas Modernize Domestic Service." *Qualitative Sociology* 11 (1988): 319–34.

———. "Sisterhood and Domestic Service: Race, Class and Gender in the Mistress-Maid Relationship." *Humanity and Society* 12 (1988): 318–46.

Sassen, Saskia. *The Mobility of Labor and Capital*. Cambridge: Cambridge University Press, 1988.

Sassen-Koob, Saskia. "Immigrant and Minority Workers in the Organization of the Labor Process." *Journal of Ethnic Studies* 8 (1983): 1–34.

———. "Labor Migrations and the New International Division of Labor." In *Women, Men and the International Division of Labor*, edited by J. Nash and M. P. Fernandez-Kelly, pp. 175–204. Albany: State University of New York Press, 1983.

————. "New York City: Economic Restructuring and Immigration." *Development and Change* 17 (1986): 85–119.

Sowell, Thomas. *Ethnic America: A History*. New York: Basic Books, 1981.

Steinberg, Stephen. *The Ethnic Myth: Race, Ethnicity and Class in America*. Boston: Beacon Press, 1981.

Wallace, Steven. "Central American and Mexican Immigrant Characteristics and Economic Incorporation in California." *International Migration Review* 20 (1986): 657–71.

17 Chicanas in White-Collar Jobs

"You Have to Prove Yourself More"

DENISE A. SEGURA

> I think you have to prove yourself more just because you are—number one—a woman, and then [because] you are Latino. So, it's like you have two forces that I think people subconsciously or consciously judge.
>
> [Chicana professional worker #5a]

Increasing numbers of Chicanas (women of Mexican descent)[1] are striving to get and keep white-collar jobs. Their efforts are constrained by a complex interplay of institutional and individual factors: the historical subordination of Mexicans in the United States (Barrera 1979); sex and race-ethnic discrimination embedded in large organizations (Baron and Newman 1990; Nelson and Tienda 1985); negative stereotypes held by employers and coworkers (Ybarra 1988); and family work over-load (Segura 1989a). When Chicanas secure white-collar jobs, they tend to find work in female-dominated clerical occupations. These jobs, often dismissed by labor-market researchers as a low-wage ghetto, nevertheless represent a consider-able step upward for Chicana workers, particularly when they are in large, stable organizations (Pesquera 1985; Segura 1986, 1989b).

Approximately half of all Chicana labor-force participants work in female-dominated white-collar jobs, mostly clerical (Malveaux and Wallace 1987; Dill, Cannon, and Vanneman 1987). While this is an impressive growth from 1980 lev-els, substantially lower proportions of Chicanas than non-Hispanic women work in professional/managerial white-collar occupations (14.1 percent and 28 percent, respectively) (U. S. Bureau of the Census 1991b).

Chicanas' movement into white-collar jobs contributes to growing heterogene-ity in the work force, although it has eroded neither occupational segregation nor inequality at work and in the family. This paper explores how 152 Chicana white-collar workers in a major public university view their employment experiences and family responsibilities in ways that contribute to the production of gender and gender/race-ethnicity in the labor market and in the larger ethnic community. I explore how job satisfaction among these women reflects one aspect of their repro-duction of traditional gender and race-ethnic relations. Specifically, I suggest that work activities can affirm one's gendered relation to the world and reinforce one's gender/race-ethnic sense of self, particularly when the clients are racial-ethnic minorities. I also examine the workplace barriers Chicanas encounter, such as sexual harassment and racial-ethnic discrimination, and how their effects can strengthen a gender/race-ethnic sense of self. Finally, I argue that Chicanas' activities at home and their seemingly irrational satisfaction with the unequal division of household labor actually represent rational ways of accommodating themselves to the relatively rigid constraints imposed by gender and race-ethnicity. These actions and their interpretations offer another lens to view mechanisms critical to the maintenance of the ethnic community, and of gender and labor-market inequality.

Reproducing Gender and Chicano Ethnicity

The theoretical reference point for this paper is the perspective originally developed by West and Zimmerman (1987), and usefully applied to other empirical data on women's work (Berk 1985).[2] This framework views gender and race-ethnicity not just as categorical statuses, but as dynamic, interactional accomplishments. It presumes that in the course of daily affairs—work, for example—we present, reaffirm, and reproduce ourselves as belonging to, and competently representative of, gender and racial-ethnic categories. Thus, the worker not only *is* Chicana, she also "does" Chicana. And work activities provide ample opportunities for the reaffirmation of membership in good standing of that group.

Female-dominated jobs offer unique occasions for women to "do gender," or enact and thus reaffirm what we take to be the "essential nature" of women (West and Zimmerman 1987; West and Fenstermaker n.d.). When an occupation involves "helping others," or "serving men," etc., women can simultaneously affirm themselves as competent workers, and also reinforce social conceptualization of their "essential" femininity within the organization, for the clientele, and among themselves.

Fenstermaker, West, and Zimmerman observe: "the demands of gender do not *compete* for attention on the job; together they form *one of the dimensions of the job* that is daily enacted by participants" (1991:301, emphasis added). Hochschild's (1983) study of what she terms "emotional labor" in two occupations—flight attendants and bill collectors—details the different expectations for male and female workers required by the employer, clients, and among the workers themselves. Unlike female flight attendants, males were not sought by customers (or trained by the organization) for nurturance or gentleness, nor were they expected to display constant cheerfulness. Male flight attendants also tended to be promoted more quickly than women. Hochschild's study offers one instance of how both institutions and workers are held accountable for the "doing of gender" and affirms Fenstermaker et al.'s contention that, "regardless of position, the *practice* of gender and its complex relation to the practice of work will support inequality on the job" (1991:299).

The notion of gender as an accomplishment acquires other nuances when women have children and families to care for. In the United States, women continue to do the vast majority of household labor even when they are employed full-time (Berk 1985; Hochschild 1989). Moreover, most household members view the typical asymmetric division of household labor as "fair" (Berk 1985). One explanation for the tenacity of this attitude among men and women is that such judgments concerning equity involve many more considerations than efficiency or effort. Berk

(1985:204) argues that, when women engage in housework and child care, one social product is "a reaffirmation of one's *gendered* relation to the work and to the world. In short, the 'shoulds' of gender ideals are fused with the 'musts' of efficient household production." The result is what we have in the past thought of as "irrational" and "unfair" household arrangements.

The notion of gender as a situated accomplishment allows for real interaction between gender and variations in women's material conditions or circumstances, including race-ethnicity. Zinn defines "racial ethnic" groups as referring to

> groups labeled as races in the context of certain historical, social, and material conditions. Blacks, Latinos, and Asian Americans are racial groups that are formed, defined, and given meaning by a variety of social forces in the wider society, most notably distinctive forms of labor exploitation. Each group is also bound together by ethnicity, that is, common ancestry and emergent cultural characteristics that are often used for coping with racial oppression. The concept racial ethnic underscores the social construction of race and ethnicity for people of color in the United States. [1990:80, note 1]

Ethnicity is marked by a set of norms, customs, and behaviors different from the dominant or majority ethnic group as well as "a shared feeling of peoplehood" (Gordon 1964; Keefe and Padilla 1987). Chicano race-ethnicity encompasses both psychological processes of group attachment (identity, attitudinal orientation, and preferences) and behavioral manifestations (cultural knowledge, language use, and traditions) (Garcia 1982:296). While no single reason can account for the persistence of Chicano culture and the racial-ethnic community, causal factors stem from treatment by the majority group and the racial-ethnic minority group and from the interaction between them that occurs within social institutions (e.g., the labor market and the family) (Keefe and Padilla 1987; Zinn 1980). This suggests that, like gender, Chicano race-ethnicity is socially constructed through interaction and dynamically maintained by both institutions and individuals. Thus, with this framework, we can pose not just the "intersection" of race-ethnic and gender categories, but an *interaction* in the true sense of the term. Chicanas become not just female *Chicanos*, nor just women workers. And their experiences at work—as they simultaneously produce both worker *and* Chicana—are unique (Fenstermaker, personal communication).

Zinn observes that, in general, "it has been assumed that one's ethnic identity is more important than one's gender identity" (1980:23). Moreover, she notes that discussions of gender and race-ethnicity have been limited in scope and typically situated within the context of the family. Within the racial-ethnic community, Chicano race-ethnicity is affirmed in the family when Spanish is taught, cultural values instilled, racial-ethnic pride emphasized, and interaction with other Chicanos esteemed.

Within the labor market, Chicano race-ethnicity is reinforced by discrimination (both objective and perceived) and social exclusion from the dominant group (Barrera 1979; Nelson and Tienda 1985). In addition, there are other, less obvious ways that Chicano race-ethnicity may be affirmed. Even as occupations contain a dimension for "doing gender," there may be a dimension for "doing Chicano race-ethnicity" as well. That is, organizations may structure jobs in ways that reaffirm Chicanos' sense of themselves as members of a unique racial-ethnic group (e.g., using bilingual workers as interpreters without additional pay). Or, Chicanos may themselves act in ways that either consciously or unconsciously serve the Chicano community. As one example of the first possibility, Chicanos who work in jobs structured to "serve" a racial-ethnic clientele (e.g., minority students) may encounter a reward system that affirms their racial-ethnic identification while doing their job. In the second case, Chicanos who work in jobs that are not overtly structured to accomplish race-ethnicity may nonetheless reaffirm their racial-ethnic identity. They often remain in white-collar jobs despite experiencing social isolation or discomfort because they feel that such "success" indirectly enlarges the options for others in the racial-ethnic community.

For Chicanas, accomplishing race-ethnicity is even more complex since their social identity involves gender and embraces the family and the labor market in ways that may have profound implications for Chicano culture. That is, insofar as women's employment is typically viewed as "for the family," such employment may not offer a dynamic avenue for challenging gender inequality or male privilege at home (Zavella 1987; Segura 1989a). This possibility is strengthened when Chicanas work in jobs that affirm both their traditional gender and/or gender/race-ethnic sense of themselves. Also militating against a forceful challenge to gender inequality is women's household work, often eulogized as part of a distinct cultural heritage under assault by outside social pressures (Mirandé and Enriquez 1979; Zinn 1982, 1979, 1975; Segura 1989a). For Chicanas to challenge traditional patterns involves integrating personal empowerment with the politically charged issue of culture-ethnic maintenance. Thus, the need or motivation to continue "traditional" patterns may be more complex for Mexican women inasmuch as doing housework or child care is the site of accomplishing not only gender, but culture/race-ethnicity as well. This dilemma adds another dimension to our understanding of the tenacity of Chicana inequality. The following section explores the ways gender and gender/race-ethnicity are affirmed in the lives of Chicana white-collar workers.

Method and Sample

In Fall 1989/Winter 1990, in collaboration with Beatriz Pesquera of the University of California, Davis, I administered a 20-page questionnaire on "women and work issues" to all Hispanic-identified women employed at a large public university in California.[3] The questionnaire included a battery of closed-ended questions concerning work, the intersection of family and work, gender ideology, feminism, ethnicity, and political ideology. One hundred and fifty-two women completed the questionnaire, representing a response rate of 47.5 percent. In addition, we conducted follow-up interviews with 35 randomly selected informants.[4] The purpose of the interviews was to explore in greater depth the meanings of work, gender, and ethnicity for this group of women. This paper is an exploratory analysis of these survey and interview data for their implications for the reproduction of gender, race-ethnicity, and labor-market stratification.

Background Characteristics

Most of the survey respondents are of Mexican (Chicano) descent (85 percent) with the rest either Latin American or Spanish (Hispanic) origin. All but fifteen women were born in the United States. All of the women express a great deal of pride in their ethnicity and a majority also feel that maintaining Chicano culture is important. Sixty percent of the respondents are bilingual in Spanish and English.

All but three women received high school diplomas; 118 have educations beyond high school; 43 have a B. A. degree or above. Their educational levels are much higher than the California norm for Chicanas (11th grade). Ninety-four women (61.8 percent) are presently married or partnered, 45.8 percent (n = 43) are married to Chicano men, 10.6 percent (n = 10) are married to "other Hispanic" and 40.4 percent (n = 38) have non-Hispanic husbands. Three women declined to state their husbands' ethnicity. The respondents' ages range from 20 to 60 years old, with an average age of 36.5 years. One hundred and eleven women have children. The mean number of children is 2.1.

Occupations

Chicanas' employment profiles and my textual analysis of their interviews reveals that their experiences at work—their social experiences, discrimination, harassment, or acceptance—all took on gendered and/or racial-ethnic features. By and large, the women work in environments that are homogeneous in terms both of gender (59.2 percent report all-female coworkers)[5] and race-ethnicity (80 percent report all-Anglo coworkers) and reproduce gender/race-ethnic hierarchies (only 29 women have minority women supervisors).

Of the 152 respondents, 41.4 percent (n = 63) work in jobs we classified as "lower-level clerical"; 28.9 percent (n = 44) are "upper-level clerical workers"; 5.9 percent are "technical aides and service workers" (n = 9); while 19.7 percent are "professional/managerial workers" (n = 30).[6] Six women declined to provide information about their occupations. The mean income of the respondents is $23,288 annually.[7]

The informants' average incomes are above those of many women workers.[8] This income profile allows me to explore the intersection of gender and race-ethnicity among Chicanas in the more privileged tiers of the working class. It is important to note, however, that the form and contours the intersection of gender and race-ethnicity take among this group of women probably differ from that of Chicanas in different jobs with lower incomes. The benefit of the present analysis is that it attests the pervasive significance of gender and race-ethnicity to Chicanas' lives.

Findings

Job Satisfaction

Exploring what Chicanas like and dislike about their jobs offers one way to gain insight into how labor-market mechanisms maintain occupational segregation. When jobs with limited opportunities offer certain subjective rewards (e.g., quality personal interaction, "helping others") or help meet instrumental needs (e.g., economic subsistence), they provide important reasons for women to stay in them, thereby reinforcing existing labor-market boundaries (Segura 1989b; Zavella 1987; Pesquera 1985). The job characteristics valued by Chicanas may also provide insight into ways in which they accomplish gender and/or race-ethnicity. That is, when a Chicana indicates pleasure or displeasure with a specific job characteristic, she engages in self-reflection—a process that involves interaction with herself and the larger group to which she holds herself accountable. Insofar as a Chicana connects her job to a larger group, she may be affirming her gendered relation to the world and reinforcing her racial-ethnic sense of self.

Contradictory accounts exist regarding the role gender plays in workers' evaluations of their jobs (see England and Browne 1992 for a review of this topic). Some argue that women value social aspects of their jobs more than men and also place less emphasis on pay and career-related values (Crewley, Levitan, and Quinn 1973). Other research finds no significant gender difference in what workers value about their jobs when occupation and organizational level are taken into account (Brief and Aldag 1975). Using similar control variables, still other investigators find that women are more likely than men to emphasize competence to do the job and good personal relations on the job (Neil and Snizek 1987; Agassi 1979). Whether women and men like or dislike different aspects of their jobs overlooks one critical possibility: what workers do at work may reaffirm their gender and/or their race-ethnicity. It is equally possible that the intrinsic reward of ably "doing gender and/or race-ethnicity" may provide them with an additional incentive to stay on the job.

In the present study, 70.4 percent of the Chicana workers (n = 107) report being satisfied with their current jobs; only 21.7 percent (n = 33) indicate dissatisfaction. When asked to select three features of their jobs they liked most (out of a list of 10 items), 60.3 percent of the women replied "having control of my own work"; 56.3 percent chose "the pay"; 39.7 percent replied, "it makes me feel good"; 38.4 percent selected "doing different things at work"; 30.5 percent listed "my coworkers"; and 25.8 percent indicated "ability for me to make meaningful changes." I should note that about one-sixth of the women reported that they enjoyed more than three work features while seven replied that they liked nothing about their jobs.

There were a few interesting variations by occupational groups. A much higher proportion of lower-level clerical workers and technical aides/service workers listed "coworkers" as important to their job satisfaction (42.9 percent and 44.4 percent, respectively) than did either upper clerical (18.2 percent) or professional workers (17.2 percent). On the other hand, professional and upper clerical workers were much more likely to indicate their job "makes me feel good" (55.2 percent and 43.2 percent, respectively). Few women indicated they valued their jobs because of the "prestige" or "chances for promotions." Professional workers were the least likely to mention promotion as a valued feature of their jobs. Insofar as they esteem the social aspects of the job and place less emphasis on occupational prestige or promotion, survey respondents appear to confirm previous research on women's job satisfaction.

The in-depth interviews provide insight into the meanings women attach to social aspects of work as well as job features that make them "feel good." Women's accounts of their jobs reveal two major patterns. First, women discuss job features and job satisfaction in terms that affirm social conceptualizations of femininity. Second, their accounts reveal a sense of affinity or connection with Chicano ethnicity. For example, when I asked an upper clerical worker what she valued about her job, she replied:

> I need to do that because for your self-esteem to feel that you're doing something and you're helping other people accomplish themselves [is important]. In that sense it's good for my health and also for my kids. I think if they see that you're involved with something, it helps them reach beyond their own world to see that there is an outside world there. And that there's things that they can pursue that they enjoy.
>
> [upper clerical worker #64a]

This informant values her job for allowing her to "help others," a trait socially ascribed to the "feminine nature." Her commitment to affirm the feminine is captured by her insistence that helping others is "good" for her health and is maternally nurturant. Her subsequent opinion that her job enables her children to "reach beyond their own world" demonstrates solidarity with her racial-ethnic group's politicized view that Chicano youth have limited options (Ogbu 1978; Garcia 1981; Keefe and Padilla 1987). Moreover, gainfully employed in an upper clerical job, she sees herself as a role model for the larger Chicano community. Finally, her words underscore the centrality of "family" among the respondents—a dynamic consistent with the politics of Chicano cultural maintenance (Williams 1990; Keefe and Padilla 1987).

Other respondents worked in jobs structured to do "gender and race-ethnicity," or "help" racial-ethnic minority students or staff. One Chicana professional worker employed in this type of job stated:

> It is very satisfying when you're working with a Chicano student or with a black student who really wants to become a veterinarian. To see them being admitted to a vet school is really very satisfying and to see them graduate is just incredible. I just graduated my second class, and every year they'll say, 'Thanks!' And, God—the parents will say, 'We never thought we'd have a doctor in the family!' So, that's really neat to feel that way, but I'm still limited in that I'm not doing enough.
>
> [professional worker #10]

This informant, like others employed in jobs structured to "help" racial-ethnic minority students or staff, is satisfied when she is able to do the job competently. Critical here is that the gendered act associated with women—that of "helping others" intersects with bettering the racial-ethnic community, thereby allowing the respondent to simultaneously accomplish gender and race-ethnicity.

Many of the respondents (60.3 percent) reported they liked feeling "in control" of their job. When I explored what this meant, I found that Chicanas filtered their evaluation of their jobs through a gender and/or race-ethnic lens. That is, they valued job control as a means to better help others (a value associated with women) and also expand the job range of Mexican American women (a value associated with the ethnic community and women). As one lower clerical worker (#4) succinctly stated: "You're helping in some ways helping people in helping make a difference." In this way, the preference for on-the-job "control" implies a politicized sense of themselves as racial-ethnic women striving for social change.

About one-fifth of the respondents are dissatisfied with their jobs. Women with children tended to dislike their jobs if their supervisors were inflexible about taking time off and making up work. Since women bore the major responsibility for taking children to doctor appointments or caring for them when they were sick or on vacation, women valued jobs that offered them a degree of flextime. Women employed in lower-level clerical jobs tended to be unhappy with their pay. In general, women disliked their jobs when they felt they were not doing anything they perceived as "helpful" or "useful." As one woman, working in a laboratory setting, said:

> I need something that's useful and related to something that is happening in the world now. And what we're doing is really closely related to basic science and, for me, has no practical purpose. So, I don't feel—I was going to study plant sciences to save the world and I'm not doing anything now. I find that my research is not useful at all for people, so I really want to move out.
>
> [professional worker #212a]

This informant's words imply that not only was doing "useful" work critical to job satisfaction, it also enabled her to affirm her femininity and accomplish gender.

In general, the job characteristics Chicanas enjoy (e.g., "control," and "helping others") are not necessarily engaged in voluntarily, but rather form integral parts of the jobs as structured by this particular organization. Thus, Chicanas who "feel good" about helping minority students obtain information about financial aid or other resources are actually performing tasks essential to their jobs. In helping others, Chicanas affirm their gender and their race-ethnicity. The organization structures this enactment (e.g., specifications of the job description) and they are held accountable for it by their coworkers and clients (e.g., through performance evaluations). Chicanas' impetus to continue this process is intertwined with the process of identity as well as the larger politics of accessing jobs outside the purview of most Chicana workers in the state.

Sexual Harassment and Race-Ethnic Discrimination
Women's gendered and race-ethnic sense of themselves is reinforced by other, unrewarding features of the job. In this study, about one-third of the respondents reported experiencing sexual harassment (n = 50), while nearly 44 percent (n = 67) said they had encountered discrimination based on gender and/or race-ethnicity. Sexual harassment and discrimination reinforce Chicanas' sense of on-the-job vulnerability and their social inequality. In addition, the way in which women describe sexual harassment and employment discrimination reveals how gender and gender/race-ethnic boundaries are maintained in the organizational setting. While main-

taining these boundaries is not the same as the accomplishment of gender on the job, it provides a context in which it occurs.

Women interviewed in this study believe that sexual harassment is one of the most underreported problems of the organization. They aver that women often do not know the definition of sexual harassment and are reluctant to pursue a complaint out of fear of recrimination. Or, as one informant (#155a) put it: "You have to pick your battles."

Sixty percent of the women who indicated having experienced sexual harassment reported "doing something about it." Usually this meant "telling the person to stop," "talking with friends and family," or "complaining to the appropriate person-nel officer." Eleven women did "nothing" and another nine women acted as though nothing had happened.

Chicanas voice outrage when women (especially themselves) were cast in the role of instigators rather than victims by coworkers and/or supervisors:

> Everyone likes to pretend it [sexual harassment] doesn't happen. When you go from one position to the next in this university it's so small that bosses know each other and say, 'Hey, this woman—watch out for her.' So, you get blackmailed that way. And so you sort of have to be careful in how you handle it—you don't want to give that person a chance to get out of it. So, if you really want to nail him, you'd better go through the proper channels and make sure that when you do it you do it well.
>
> [professional worker #102a]

Implicit in this informant's words is the sense that women who assert themselves in ways that directly confront men risk retaliation by those participating in the inter-personal networks of supervisors and other workers. Bosses warn each other. In her assertiveness, the Chicana worker violates *all* relevant expectations of the group: as a worker, as a woman, and as a Chicana; she becomes a threat to the organization, and especially vulnerable to informal workplace sanctions.

Sexual harassment reinforces Chicanas' sense of vulnerability and subordination to men within the organization. Women express anger when sexual harassment occurs, but view it as a job hazard that needs to be handled with care. Within this constrained setting, women are expected to meet debilitating gender expectations in a way that denigrates their sense of self even as it reconfirms their secondary standing in the institution.

A problem of equal or greater magnitude is discrimination based on Chicanas' combined gender/race-ethnicity. It is noteworthy that with few exceptions (n = 9), survey respondents did not privilege one form of discrimination over the other. Rather, they felt their experiences reflected *both* gender and race-ethnicity.

During their interviews, Chicanas spoke passionately of their first hand experi-ences with on-the-job discrimination. Almost to a woman, they argued that employers, coworkers, the organization, and society itself maintain pejorative, stereotyped images of Chicana and Hispanic women:

> When people look at us they don't *see us* [her emphasis]. They just see the stereotypes that they have gotten from the movies or somewhere . . . they think we are all unedu-

cated. They have this 'indito' under the cactus plant idea. I've had people say, 'I didn't know that there were any educated people in Mexico that have a graduate degree.' I think we stumble against the wall because they're looking at us across a barrier that is their imagination.

[professional worker #212a]

One lower clerical worker described negative stereotypes more succinctly:

That we like to be pregnant. We don't like to take birth control. We're 'mañana' [tomorrow] oriented. We're easy. We're all overweight and I guess we're hot [laughs]— and submissive.

[lower clerical worker #153a]

Chicanas feel they are held accountable or judged in terms of their deviance from or conformity to these one-dimensional stereotypes. Chicanas claim that supervisors, coworkers, and the institution draw on these negative images when they evaluate their credentials or previous work experience:

I think that society as a whole sees Mexican women as the good family role models, but they don't see them as also being just as good in the workplace. Just as capable. So, I think that they have a view that's limiting their role—what they [Chicanas] can do.

[professional worker #176a]

Another Chicana declared:

I think you have to demonstrate that you can do a job—I mean I've seen it! In interviews with a white candidate, they see it written on the paper and they say, 'Isn't this great!' But, when you bring a Latina woman in, it's almost like they're drilled: 'Tell us'; 'Give us examples'; 'How long did you do it?' Some say to prove yourself and that's what I feel. You always have to prove yourself that you are just as good even when it's all there. It's all written. You almost have to fight harder to demonstrate that you can do a job just as well!

[upper clerical worker #64a]

This particular informant told me that she had resisted interpreting her experience as evidence of gender/racial-ethnic discrimination. In this regard, she is very similar to the majority of the women interviewed. Survey respondents typically tried to downplay the salience of gender/racial-ethnic discrimination in their personal lives although most (70 percent) considered it a feature of the organization and society at large. All the women interviewed believe that women of Mexican descent have a "harder time" getting good jobs than either Anglo men, Anglo women, or Latino men.

Women who believed they had experienced discrimination condemned it and described its nuances at length. Several told of "subtle discrimination," i.e., comments that devalue their culture and/or features of their combined gender/race-ethnicity:

. . . it's subtle discrimination. I haven't gotten a job because of, or I don't know if I have gotten a job because of my color. You know, subtle stuff—that subtle baloney that people pass you over because they think that women of color aren't as brilliant as they [Anglos] are. That sort of thing. Actually, they can be condescending to me.

[upper clerical worker #155a]

Another said:

I'm usually asked because of my accent—they say, 'You have a funny accent.' And I always say, 'I'm Mexican.' And people are really surprised. They say, 'You don't look Mexican.' And so I ask, 'How many Mexican people do you know?' And they say, 'Oh, just you.'

[professional worker #212a]

The Chicana respondents argued that differences in skin color, accents, language skills, and cultural mannerisms shaped their occupational chances. One respondent said: "They want someone to fit the mold, and if you don't fit the mold . . ." (#102a). Interestingly, many of the women reporting that they had not personally experienced job discrimination (although they were careful to note their belief in its importance) attributed it to their fair or light complexions:

Maybe I haven't felt as much discrimination because I'm not—I'm kind of fair complected. So, a lot of people don't know, or don't even assume that I'm Mexican. They're real surprised when I say, 'Yeah, I'm Mexican.'

[professional worker #5]

Many women also offered analyses of the consequences of gender/race-ethnicity for Chicana employment inequality. Some women argue that discrimination is the primary reason Chicanas are overrepresented in lower-level positions in the organization. Other women assert that the organization often "punishes" Chicanas who try to "push" their way into a promotion either by denying them the job or actually downgrading it. For example:

This position that I have now, before me was a Word Processing Supervisor.[9] None of them [previous job incumbents] had the work load that I have now. In fact, they just surveyed my job, and it's increased 130 percent. Yet, I'm a Senior Word Processor. I've had to fight tooth and nail to be classified back. Even then, it's been procrastinated. They know it has to be done, but why is it taking so long? It's just obvious. It just makes you think—those were all white women prior to me. What's the difference?

[upper clerical worker #64a]

This informant's case was being investigated. Few women, however, felt able to officially challenge job discrimination within the organization. Integral to their reluctance is their sense that they lack credibility in the institution due, in part, to pejorative stereotypes that symbolize essential parts of the gendered and raced expectations that are constantly being played out in social interaction and, ultimately, situate Chicanas in a socially subordinate position.[10] As one upper clerical worker said:

> . . . one time I wanted a job at [unit x] and a white woman got it because she'd already been in the position. I should have gotten the job. But they didn't even interview me because they knew I was completely qualified for the position. And so I thought; well, I could take it further, but if you take it further that means [unit x] would never hire me because I was a troublemaker.
>
> [upper clerical worker #155a]

This respondent's words point to the power of real or imagined social control mechanisms to cap instances of discrimination as well as maintain inequality at work. In every instance, the burden of proof is on the woman. Further, whether or not she succeeds in proving discrimination at work, she will be stigmatized as a "troublemaker." As a troublemaker, she risks incurring the wrath of coworkers, supervisors, and the organization itself. This reaction may be even stronger in the case of Chicanas, given their social image as "passive" and "nurturing good mothers" that is reinforced, moreover, by their responsibilities at work.

Discrimination at work plays an important role in reinforcing gender and/or race-ethnic boundaries in the organization. Research on ethnicity indicates that individual and institution-level discrimination help maintain a "sense of peoplehood" among the group. Chicanas interpret their personal experiences of discrimination as part of the shared experiences of the larger racial-ethnic community. While most of the Chicanas in this study assert that maintaining their culture is important to them, discrimination within an institution serves to hold them accountable to this resolution. In this way, the organization reinforces Chicanas' gender/race-ethnic sense of themselves.

Chicanas' racial-ethnic identity is not only maintained by negative events such as discrimination or by intrinsic rewards on the job. Women in the present study also affirm their race-ethnicity by organizing and/or participating in a variety of cultural activities in the community. In addition, one-third of the survey respondents belonged to a Hispanic Workers Advocacy group at their worksite. Women feel this group promotes a positive image of Chicanos/Latinos and will help erode the power wielded by negative cultural stereotypes currently embedded in the institution.

The Intersection of Family and Work
An analysis of social dynamics that contextualize Chicanas' options and maintain their social inequality would be incomplete without considering the family (Smith 1987; Zavella 1987). Motherhood is simultaneously a source of joy and a powerful constraint on employment and occupational mobility. Coltrane argues that "the routine care of home and children . . . provide opportunities for women to express and reaffirm their gendered relation to men and to the world" (1989:473). Among the 111 Chicana respondents with children, family caretaking constrains their

chances for mobility in the world of work. It also forms one way they accomplish gender and culture.

One way Chicanas strive to manage the contradictions of overwork is to try carving out two separate worlds where, in reality, there is but one world and one woman trying to meet the expectations of children, coworkers, supervisors, and her own ambitions. As one woman said:

> For the most part, my job doesn't interfere too much with home. When I leave work, I leave my work. I switch stations to do whatever I need to do for the family. But, there are times when, yes, work does tend to tire you out and you do carry it home with you in terms of less energy and not having the energy to deal with the family. That's really hard, especially when both of you come in very tired and you sort of want the other one to do something because you're too tired to deal with it. Then it's hard. The poor kids, they don't understand. They just know that they're hungry and 'how come you guys won't feed us?'
>
> [professional worker #102a]

This woman speaks to the dilemma of reconciling what Hochschild refers to as the "competing urgencies" of family and work.[11] Interestingly, women in this study downplayed the spillover between work and family. In the surveys and in their interviews, women consistently reported that their jobs "almost never" (27 percent) or only "occasionally" (47.7 percent) interfered with their abilities to manage their family responsibilities. Yet, their discussions of the intersection of family and work reveal they are experiencing considerable tension and stress in this relationship.

Ironically, ideological changes that have expanded the domain of women's competencies may impede women's articulation of their stress meeting family and work responsibilities. As one woman argues:

> I think as women, maybe the progress has been kind of negative in some aspects. You know, we go out and say that we can do this—we can work, we can raise a family, and all that. And yet at the same time, I feel like maybe we've hurt ourselves because we can't do it all. I don't believe there is superwoman.
>
> [professional/managerial worker #5a]

An additional constraint felt by many of the Chicana workers is their responsibility to maintain Chicano cultural traditions and forms. One woman said:

> In order to be valued we have to be wives and mothers first. That cultural pressure is the most difficult to overcome.
>
> [professional worker #10]

This informant struck a chord that resonated throughout the study: Mexican/Latina women take on much of the caretaking work in the household as an expression of Mexican culture.[12] Charged with cultural socialization of offspring, Chicanas often avoid debating their partners about the household division of labor. An overwhelming majority of our survey respondents reported "little" (39.4 percent) or "no" (40.4 percent) difference of opinion on the household division of labor between married women and their spouses. Yet, when asked about the actual division of labor, women reported doing most of the housework and wished their husbands/partners would do more.

Traditional gender roles and gender ideologies are particularly resistant to change when they are framed within what Caufield (1974) terms a "culture of resistance." Consistently, Chicanas refuse to engage in sustained struggle with husbands/partners over the division of household labor even though they admit they are, as one Chicana professional worker (#6) said, "too stressed and torn between career and family responsibilities to feel good about the accomplishments!" Rather, Chicanas conform to their community's gendered expectations, reaffirming both their womanhood and their culture:

> I'm just happy [about] who I am and where I come from. Our women, Latino women, do things just a little bit differently because of who we are and where we came from. There are certain things that we do . . . for our husbands that I know that other women, white women, have problems doing . . . for instance—and I've seen it because my brother-in-law was married to a white woman. You're eating and you go to the stove to maybe serve yourself a little more. It's just normal, I think. You're brought up with that real nurturing with, 'Honey, do you want some more?' . . . And her comment was, 'Well, he can get up by himself.' Just the real independence on their side, and I think we're brought up a little more nurturing to our male counterparts. Maybe there's more machismo there too—whatever. It's the way you're brought up.
>
> [upper clerical worker #64a]

The desire to affirm their gender and their race-ethnic culture is strengthened in those cases where women work in jobs that value services to other women and/or Chicanos on the campus. As one Chicana professional worker (#6) said:

> Chicanas feel that working—we see ourselves as social change agents. We see it as being done in a partnership basis with our families. We get hurt by things that people in our culture do, but we don't turn against them. Maybe that hurts in the end, but I think we want to keep a forged relationship and a partnership. As painful as it may be. And that's where I want to be. Yes.

Summary and Conclusion

This study has demonstrated ways in which gender and race-ethnicity are affirmed in the labor market among selected Chicana white-collar workers. By considering both the features of jobs that Chicanas value and dislike and the perceived barriers to success at work that they encounter in the organization, I have identified mechanisms that reinforce occupational segregation by gender and gender/race-ethnicity.

There is, however, another outcome of Chicana employment. Chicanas' job performances and their concurrent fulfillment of family responsibilities mutually reinforce the accomplishment of culture and ethnicity. Whereas traditional Marxist and feminist analyses view market labor as potentially "liberatory" by increasing women's economic clout (e.g., Engels [1884] 1968; Smith 1987; Moore and Sawhill 1978; Hartmann 1981; Ferree 1987), this study finds the opposite. That is, while women usually enjoy their jobs, work is not so much "liberatory" as intensifying their accomplishment of gender both in the tasks they do at work as well as the sex-typed tasks they continue to do at home. Moreover, their attachment to family is linked ideologically to the survival of the culture, rendering their accomplishment of gender an overt act of racial-ethnic and cultural politics. This particular finding may well be a neglected truth in many women's lives.

The Chicanas of this study also tend to work with Chicano students or assist male faculty under the supervision of white women or males (in academic departments)—a dynamic that reinforces gender and gender/race-ethnic hierarchies at work. This scenario does not provide a strong point of departure to engage in gender critiques either at home or in the workplace.

Chicana workers in this study have a clear sense of their socially imposed limits, but struggle to survive and wrest meaning from worlds where their multidimensional experiences and constraints defy easy solutions and answers. The complexity of their struggle is captured by an informant's observation that became the subtitle of this paper: "you have to prove yourself more." But, while Chicanas prove their competence at work and in the family, they not only reproduce gendered social relations but simultaneously affirm their culture and racial-ethnic identity as well.

Acknowledgments

I gratefully acknowledge the constructive criticism and support offered by Sarah Fenstermaker, Karen Miller-Loessi, and Beatriz M. Pesquera on earlier drafts of this paper and the research assistance provided by Marisela Marquez. I alone am responsible for whatever shortcomings remain. This research was supported in part by funding grants from the Academic Senates of the University of California, Davis, and the University of California, Santa Barbara, as well as the University of California Consortium on Mexico and the United States (University of California, Mexus). A Ford Foundation Postdoctoral Fellowship is currently supporting the final phases of the project.

Notes

1. The terms "Chicana" and "Chicano" refer respectively to a woman and to a man of Mexican descent residing in the United States without distinguishing immigrant status. "Chicano" also refers generically to the category of persons (male and female) who claim Mexican heritage (e.g., the "Chicano" community). These labels offer an alternative to the more common ethnic identifiers, "Mexican" and "Mexican American" (Garcia 1981). Other terms associated with people of Mexican descent include "Hispanic" and "Latino." Both of these terms typically include Spaniards and a variety of ethnic groups who were colonized at one time by Spain. Readers interested in the history and significance of different labels used by the Mexican-origin population are referred to Tienda (1981), Garcia (1981), and Penalosa (1970).

2. I gratefully acknowledge Sarah Fenstermaker's help in clarifying the theoretical underpinnings of gender as dynamic, interactional accomplishments. I also add that any remaining ellipses are my responsibility.

3. One shortcoming of this study is that I do not distinguish native-born Chicanas from foreign-born Mexican women. There is little published work on women of Mexican descent that makes this distinction. Also, relatively few of the informants in both studies indicated they were foreign-born Mexicans or Latinas. Readers interested in the differences between native-born and foreign-born Mexican women are referred to Tienda and Guhleman (1985) and Ortiz and Cooney (1984).

4. At present, Beatriz Pesquera and I are planning to interview an additional 15 women. We do not expect to find meaningful departures from the interview data reported here. Our intention is to expand and enrich our existing qualitative database for future work on gender ideology and ethnic identity among Chicana workers.

5. It is important to note that we believe that many of the women had a rather broad interpretation of "coworkers" that embraced academic personnel. Strictly speaking, faculty are not coworkers of the white-collar workers of this study. Our knowledge of the research site indicates that the gender of administrative support staff (which includes our categories of upper clerical and lower clerical) is overwhelmingly female. Professional and service/technician occupations are more heterogeneous by gender.

6. Our occupational categories were derived in consultation with the personnel manual of the research site and two personnel analysts. In general, lower clerical occupations (levels 1–3 in this organization) are nonsupervisory. Upper clerical occupations (levels 4–6) are often supervisory. Professional occupations include managers of academic and staff units as well as a variety of specialized jobs that are mainly administrative (e.g., counselor, personnel analyst) or scientific (staff research associate). Service workers and technicians tended to be lower-paid workers in laboratories (laboratory helper) or custodians. One important limitation of this case study is that relatively few women in the latter category answered the questionnaire (n = 9) or answered our call for an oral interview.

7. These figures obscure the income range of the respondents. Fourteen women earned less than $15,000; 33 earned between $15,000–$19,999; 57 earned between $20,000–$24,999; 21 earned between $25,000–$29,999; 13 earned between $30,000–$34,999; 11 earned more than $35,000.

8. National median incomes in 1989 for white female full-time workers were $19,873 and $16,006 for Hispanic females (U. S. Bureau of the Census 1991a).

9. The specific occupations and units mentioned by this informant have been changed to protect her anonymity.

10. One example of how gendered and raced expectations are played out in interaction is a Chicana being called to account for why her skin is so light. This "accounting" is one way in which, through interaction, stereotypes or the static part of master statuses are actually created, re-created, and reproduced.

11. This phrase was coined by Hochschild and quoted in Rubin (1983).

12. It is important to note that the literature that focuses largely on samples of white women reports similar findings. Gender, culture, race, and ethnicity are readily and easily invocable to justify an asymmetrical division of household labor. Nevertheless, the Chicanas in this study are unique insofar as they invoke their gendered responsibilities to Chicano culture.

Works Cited

Agassi, Judith B. 1979. *Women on the Job: The Attitudes of Women to Their Work*. Lexington, MA: Lexington Books.

Baron, James N., and Andrew E. Newman. 1990. "For What It's Worth: Organizations, Occupations, and the Value of Work." *American Sociological Review* 55:155–175.

Barrera, Mario. 1979. *Race and Class in the Southwest: A Theory of Racial Inequality*. Notre Dame, IN: University of Notre Dame Press.

Berk, Sarah Fenstermaker. 1985. *The Gender Factory: The Apportionment of Work in American Households*. New York: Plenum.

Brief, A. P., and R. J. Aldag. 1975. "Male-Female Differences in Occupational Attitudes within Minority Groups." *Journal of Vocational Behavior* 6:305–314.

Caufield, Mina Davis. 1974. "Imperialism, the Family, and Cultures of Resistance." *Socialist Revolution* 2:67–85.

Coltrane, Scott. 1989. "Household Labor and the Routine Production of Gender." *Social Problems* 36:473–491.

Crewley, Joan F., Teresa E. Levitan, and Robert Quinn. 1973. "Facts and Fiction about the American Working Woman." Ann Arbor: Survey Research Center, University of Michigan.

Dill, Bonnie Thornton, Lynn Weber Cannon, and Reeve Vanneman. 1987. "Pay Equity: An Issue of Race, Ethnicity and Sex." Washington, DC: National Commission on Pay Equity.

Engels, Frederick. [1884] 1968. *Origin of the Family, Private Property, and the State*. Moscow: International Publishing.

England, Paula, and Irene Browne. 1992. "Trends in Women's Economic Status," *Sociological Perspectives* 35:17–51.

Fenstermaker, Sarah, Candace West, and Don H. Zimmerman. 1991. "Gender Inequality: New Conceptual Terrain." Pp. 289–305 in *Gender, Family, and Economy: The Triple Overlap*, edited by R. Lesser-Blumberg. Newbury Park, CA: Sage.

Ferree, Myra Marx. 1987. "The Struggles of Superwoman." Pp. 161–180 in *Hidden Aspects of Women's Work*, edited by Christine Bose, Roslyn Feldberg, and Natalie Sokoloff. New York: Praeger.

Garcia, John A. 1981. "Yo Soy Mexicano. . . . : Self-Identity among the Mexican Origin Population." *Social Science Quarterly* 62:88–98.

———. 1982. "Ethnicity and Chicanos: Measurement of Ethnic Identification, Identity, and Consciousness." *Hispanic Journal of Behavioral Sciences* 4:295–314.

Gordon, Milton M. 1964. *Assimilation in American Life: The Role of Race, Religion, and National Origin*. New York: Oxford University Press.

Griswold del Castillo, Richard. 1984. *La Familia: Chicano Families in the Urban Southwest, 1848 to the Present*. Notre Dame, IN: University of Notre Dame Press.

Hartmann, Heidi. 1981. "The Family as the Locus of Gender, Class, and Political Struggle: The Example of Housework." *Signs: Journal of Women in Culture and Society* 6:366–394.

Hochschild, Arlie R. 1983. *The Managed Heart: Commercialization of Human Feeling*. Berkeley: University of California Press.

Hochschild, Arlie R. [with Anne Machung]. 1989. *The Second Shift, Working Parents and the Revolution at Home*. New York: Viking.

Keefe, Susan E., and Amado M. Padilla. 1987. *Chicano Ethnicity*. Albuquerque: University of New Mexico Press.

Malveaux, Julianne, and Phyllis Wallace. 1987. "Minority Women in the Workplace." Pp. 265–298 in *Women and Work: Industrial Relations Research Association Research Volume*, edited by K. S. Koziara, M. Moskow, and L. Dewey Tanner. Washington, DC: Bureau of National Affairs.

Mirandé, Alfredo, and Evangelina Enriquez. 1979. *La Chicana*. Chicago: University of Chicago Press.

Moore, Kristin A., and Isabel U. Sawhill. 1978. "Implications of Women's Employment for Home and Family Life." Pp. 201–205 in *Working Women: Theories and Facts in Perspective*, edited by Ann H. Stromberg and Shirley Harkess. Palo Alto: Mayfield.

Neil, Cecily C., and William E. Snizek. 1987. "Work Values, Job Characteristics, and Gender." *Sociological Perspectives* 30:245–265.

Nelson, Candace, and Marta Tienda. 1985. "The Structuring of Hispanic Ethnicity: Historical and Contemporary Perspectives." *Ethnic and Racial Studies* 8:49–74.

Ogbu, John U. 1978. *Minority Education and Caste: The American System in Cross-Cultural Perspective*. New York: Academic.

Ortiz, Vilma, and Rosemary Santana Cooney. 1984. "Sex-Role Attitudes and Labor Force Participation among Young Hispanic Females and Non-Hispanic White Females." *Social Science Quarterly* 65:392–400.

Penalosa, Fernando. 1970. "Toward an Operational Definition of the Mexican American." *Aztlan: Chicano Journal of the Social Sciences and the Arts* 1:1–12.

Pesquera, Beatriz M. 1985. "Work and Family: A Comparative Analysis of Professional, Clerical and Blue-Collar Chicana Workers." Ph. D. diss., University of California, Berkeley.

Rubin, Lillian B. 1983. *Intimate Strangers: Men and Women Together*. New York: Harper and Row.

Segura, Denise A. 1986. "Chicana and Mexican Immigrant Women in the Labor Market: A Study of Occupational Mobility and Stratification." Ph. D. diss., University of California, Berkeley.

———. 1989a. "The Interplay of Familism and Patriarchy on the Employment of Chicana and Mexican Immigrant Women." Pp. 35–53 in *Renato Rosaldo Lecture Series Monography*, vol. 5. Tucson: Mexican American Studies and Research Center, University of Arizona.

———. 1989b. "Chicana and Mexican Immigrant Women at Work: The Impact of Class, Race, and Gender on Occupational Mobility." *Gender and Society* 3:37–52.

Smith, Dorothy E. 1987. "Women's Inequality and the Family." Pp. 23–54 in *Families and Work*, edited by N. Gerstel and H. E. Gross. Philadelphia: Temple University Press.

Tienda, Marta, 1981. "The Mexican American Population." Pp. 502–548 in *Non-Metropolitan America in Transition*, edited by A. H. Hawley and S. M. Mazie. Chapel Hill: University of North Carolina Press.

Tienda, Marta, and P. Guhleman. 1985. "The Occupational Position of Employed Hispanic Women." Pp. 243–273 in *Hispanics in the U. S. Economy*, edited by G. J. Borjas and M. Tienda. New York: Academic.

U. S. Bureau of the Census. 1991a. "Money Income of Households, Families, and Persons in the United States: 1988 and 1989." *Current Population Reports*, Series P-60, No. 172. Washington, DC: U. S. Government Printing Office.

———. 1991b. "The Hispanic Population in the United States: March 1990." *Current Population Report*, Series P-20, No. 449. Washington, DC: U. S. Government Printing Office.

West, Candace, and Sarah Fenstermaker. n.d. "Power, Inequality and the Accomplishment of Gender: An Ethnomethodological View." In *Theory on Gender/Feminism on Theory*, edited by Paula England. New York: Aldine. Forthcoming.

West, Candace, and Don H. Zimmerman. 1987. "Doing Gender." *Gender and Society* 1:125–151.

Williams, Norma. 1990. *The Mexican American Family, Tradition and Change*. New York: General Hall.

Ybarra, Lea. 1988. "Separating Myth from Reality: Socio-economic and Cultural Influences on Chicanas and the World of Work." Pp. 12–23 in *Mexicans at Work in the United States*, edited by M. B. Melville. Houston: Mexican American Studies Program, University of Houston.

Zavella, Patricia. 1987. *Women's Work and Chicano Families*: *Cannery Workers of the Santa Clara Valley*. Ithaca, NY: Cornell University Press.

Zinn, Maxine Baca. 1975. "Chicanas: Power and Control in the Domestic Sphere." *De Colores, Journal of Emerging Raza Philosophies* 2:19–31.

———. 1979. "Chicano Family Research: Conceptual Distortions and Alternative Directions." *Journal of Ethnic Studies* 7:59–71.

———. 1980. "Gender and Ethnic Identity among Chicanos." *Frontiers* 5:18–23.

———. 1982. "Mexican-American Women in the Social Sciences." *Signs: Journal of Women in Culture and Society* 8:259–272.

———. 1990. "Family, Feminism and Race." *Gender and Society* 4:68–82.

Knock 'Em Dead

18

Work on the Killfloor
of a Modern Beefpacking Plant

DONALD D. STULL

Entering one of the Durham buildings, they found a number of other visitors waiting; and before long there came a guide to escort them through the place. They make a great feature of showing strangers through the packing plants, for it is a good advertisement. But Ponas Jokubas whispered maliciously that the visitors did not see any more than the packers wanted them to.

—Upton Sinclair, *The Jungle*

The Tour

The doors to the guard station were marked in Spanish and Vietnamese—but not in English. The uniformed guard behind the glass window said to sign in, mentioning who we represented and the time. After we all finished, he let us inside the high chain-link fence, where we were met by someone who led us down a long walkway and into the plant. From there we were ushered through the cafeteria and into a training room, given brand new white hardhats and smocks along with yellow foam-rubber earplugs. As we clumsily adjusted the plastic headbands inside the hardhats, buttoned up our smocks, and removed the earplugs from their plastic envelopes, a middle-aged Anglo man dressed in a golf shirt, polyester western dress jeans held up by a trophy buckle, and snakeskin boots began to speak.

"Welcome to IBP. IBP is the largest beefpacking company, and this is the largest and most sophisticated plant in the world. Please do not talk to the employees, for their safety and yours, since they are operating machinery and using knives. And please stay together for your safety. Because of the high noise level, and since you'll be wearing earplugs, we won't be able to answer your questions in the plant, but we will return here after the tour and you can ask questions then."

Our guide was a Vietnamese man in his early thirties. We followed him through two heavy swinging metal doors and out onto the "killfloor," where we were met by a moving row of dead cows, suspended upside down on meathooks, their tongues hanging out, their limbs jerking. As they passed by, like monstrous red and black quivering shirts being called up at the dry cleaners, an Anglo man clipped off their hooves with a tool resembling large pruning shears, while above us, on a catwalk, a Latina slapped plastic sheets onto their skinned rumps.

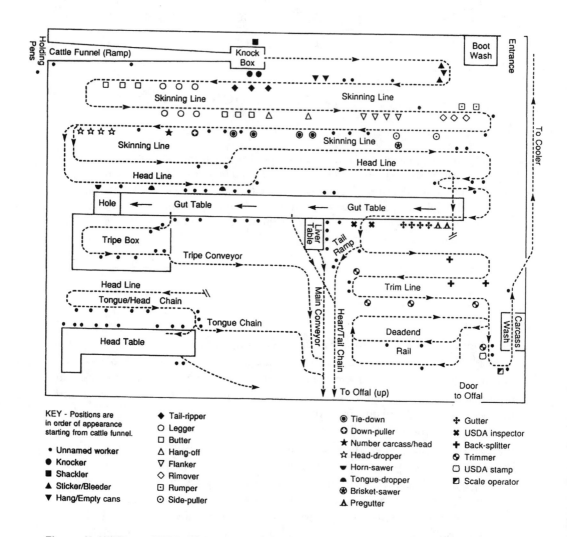

KEY - Positions are
in order of appearance
starting from cattle funnel.

• Unnamed worker	◆ Tail-ripper	◉ Tie-down	✠ Gutter
● Knocker	○ Legger	⊘ Down-puller	✖ USDA inspector
■ Shackler	□ Butter	★ Number carcass/head	✚ Back-splitter
▲ Sticker/Bleeder	△ Hang-off	☆ Head-dropper	◎ Trimmer
▼ Hang/Empty cans	▽ Flanker	▼ Horn-sawer	⬡ USDA stamp
	◇ Rimover	▲ Tongue-dropper	▨ Scale operator
	▣ Rumper	⊛ Brisket-sawer	
	☉ Side-puller	▲ Pregutter	

**Figure 1. Killfloor of IBP's Finney County plant, Summer 1989. Stations on the lines
and locations on the floor are keyed to the text. Not all jobs and operations are
depicted.** *Drawing by* Laura Kriegstrom Poracsky.

Forty-five minutes later, back in the training room, we removed our earplugs and took off our smocks and hardhats, still dazed by what we had experienced. The man in the snakeskin boots (who turned out to be the personnel manager) asked if we had any questions. For almost an hour, he cheerfully answered our questions, taking great pleasure in his statistics and in our wonder at "the Cadillac of all packing plants."

"Here at the Finney County plant, we kill between 30,000 and 32,000 head of cattle a week. Since many feedyards in this area have a capacity of about 40,000 head, we empty the equivalent of about one feedyard per week. Every day we receive 101 trucks of live cattle and load out one truck of boxed beef every twenty-two minutes of every day, seven days a week. From hoof to box, the longest a cow will stay in this plant is six days; the prime time is two to three days.

"There is little demand for hanging beef anymore. About 95 percent of what we send out is boxed beef—the only carcasses we sell are those that do not grade out to our specifications. IBP boxes only the best—quality grades Prime, Choice, and Select, and yield grades 1, 2, and 3.[1] Those that don't meet our specifications are sold as hanging beef to other packers in the area.

"This plant can slaughter about 350 head of cattle an hour. The number of head we can process depends on whether we're doing 'bone-in' or 'bone-out.' Bone-out is largely for institutional buyers, such as hospitals and restaurants, and requires more cuts, since most of the bones are removed. It's heavy work—and hard—we can do about 350 head an hour on bone-out. Bone-in is mainly what the housewife will buy at the local grocery store, and it moves a lot faster—400 head an hour or more. They do 240 cuts of meat here; 9 of ground beef alone!

"Right now, this plant has 2,650 employees and an annual payroll of $42 million. Each job is ranked, and paid, according to importance and difficulty. There are seven levels. Starting pay for someone just off the street with no experience on a level-1 job is $6.40 an hour in Processing, $6.70 in Slaughter. The base for level-7 employees is $9.40 in Processing, $9.58 in Slaughter. After six months you get an automatic 50-cent raise and another 72 cents at the end of one year. We have profit sharing and yearly bonuses. IBP is self-insured. We offer an excellent insurance package—health, dental, vision, retirement, disability, alcohol and drug abuse coverage. Line workers are eligible for coverage after six months.

"Absenteeism normally averages 1.7 percent. We compensate for absenteeism by having more workers on a shift than we absolutely need. If too many show up, we assign the extra workers to different tasks, which helps them qualify for more than one job, or we experiment with new techniques."

In spite of the ease with which he threw out statistics in response to our questions, the man in the snakeskin boots neatly side-stepped a query about the rate of worker turnover. Instead, he informed us that "more than a thousand of our workers have been in this plant for two or more years. As plants get older, their workforce becomes more stable. Most workers stay on the same job for about a year. By then they are getting bored and usually bid to another job.

"We have an internal job posting system here at IBP. Current employees are given the opportunity to apply for and fill jobs before we hire from outside. New hires are placed wherever the need is greatest. After the initial ninety-day probationary period, you can bid on other jobs and move around the floor. The more jobs you are qualified for, the more competitive you are for supervisory jobs. Each supervisor oversees forty-five employees and has a trainer working under him. Although it helps, supervisors don't have to be qualified on the jobs they oversee. We look around the plant for workers who show real promise—leadership, potential, interpersonal communications skills. The supervisor runs his own business out there; he is responsible for his crew's production and is given daily reports on its output.

"We stress safety here. We spend $1 million a year on training and employ twenty-eight hourly trainers. Each new hire receives three days of orientation, then comes back each day for thirty minutes of stretching exercises until he gets into shape to do his job. Depending on their job, each worker may wear as much as $600 worth of safety equipment—hardhat, earplugs, cloth and steelmesh gloves, mail aprons and leggings, weight-lifting belts, or shin guards. They don't have to buy any of this equipment. Knife users normally carry three knives. Each one is owned by IBP and has its own identification number. The workers use the same knives as long as they work here. They grow very attached to their knives, they know their feel, and this helps them do a better job. Knives are turned in at the end of the day for sharpening and are picked up at the beginning of the next shift. They also carry sharpening steels with them and sharpen their knives while they work."

"With all those knives, they must cut themselves a lot?" one of us asked. "The most common injuries are punctures, not lacerations," he replied. "These wounds usually occur when a knife slips and pokes the other hand. Such injuries are usually caused by workers not wearing their safety equipment. But we've had very few such injuries so far this year. In fact, we won the President's Award for the best safety record of any IBP plant."

As I listened to him speak, I recalled the signs admonishing safety scattered along the corridors, interspersed with printouts of crew performance records highlighted in yellow. In their margins were handwritten calls for the team to pull together. On the stark walls of the training room three charts showed stretching and flexibility exercises for wrists and fingers. Next to the door was a large poster entitled "5 Reasons to Stay Non-Union." Underneath was a picture of cops in riot gear and newspaper headlines about the lengthy plant closure and the number of people injured at a strike at the Dakota City plant.

"The list of products we produce at this plant is almost never-ending. We separate the white and red blood cells right here in the plant and each is used for different things. Blood is used to make perfume. Bone meal is used as a feed additive. Kodak is the biggest buyer of our bone gelatin, which is used in making film paper. Intestines are used to string tennis rackets. The hairs from inside the cow's ears are used for paintbrushes. Spleens are used in pharmaceuticals.

"Processing begins at 6:05 A.M. Slaughter starts an hour later. Workers get a fifteen-minute break after about two and a half hours and a thirty-minute lunch break after about five-and-a-half hours. The day shift, we call it 'A' shift, ends at 2:35. 'B' shift begins at 3:05. In between shifts we do a quick, dry cleanup. From midnight to 6:00 A.M. we contract out for a wet cleanup, which holds down bacteria."

Our heads were swimming. There was so much more we wanted to know, but we were exhausted from trying to absorb it all and remember even a fraction of the facts and figures he glibly tossed back in response to our questions. The man in the snake-skin boots made no attempt to hurry us, and he seemed a little disappointed when we could no longer think of anything more to ask. As we uneasily shuffled in tacit recognition that this adventure was about to end, someone asked, "Do you get any flak from the animal rights people?" "Not really," he quipped; "most people enjoy a good steak."[2]

So began my research on beefpacking and beefpacking workers. Even as I write this, three years later, my fieldnotes still evoke the awe and excitement I felt that day as I followed our guide through a confusing maze of men, machines, and meat. Only now am I beginning to comprehend the place and the process. Try as I might, I can never convey the sights, sounds, smells of this massive factory where almost three thousand men and women toil on "disassembly" lines killing, bleeding, skinning, gutting, sawing, boning, cutting, trimming, shrink-wrapping, boxing, and loading hundreds of cattle an hour, sixteen hours a day, six days a week. I can only try to give a sense of what the killfloor of one modern plant is like, what the workers do, how they feel about their work, and the strategies adopted by their supervisors to maximize their productivity, often at the cost of their safety.

Methodology

> There are learned people who can tell you out of the statistics that beef-boners make forty cents an hour, but, perhaps, these people have never looked into a beef-boner's hands.
>
> —Sinclair, *The Jungle*

While finagling a tour of a beef plant is not so hard, doing ethnographic research on beefpacking and beefpacking workers certainly is. Politely but firmly, IBP and Monfort declined my request to participate directly in a study of ethnic relations in Garden City that I was directing, forcing me to rely primarily on indirect methods of data collection concerning work and worker relations on the plant floor.

I conducted formal, audiotaped interviews with packinghouse line workers and supervisors, with feedyard managers, and with others familiar with cattle feeding and beefpacking. And I was able to draw on interview materials collected by other team members. I subscribed to *Beef Today* and went on every plant tour I could. I attended monthly workers' compensation hearings, which offered detailed job descriptions and graphically demonstrated why meat-packing is America's most dangerous industry. I enrolled in Meat and Carcass Evaluation at Garden City Community College to learn more about the industry, make contacts, and gain regular entry into "the cooler," where carcasses are graded for quality and cutability. Perhaps the only person ever to pursue postdoctoral training at a community college, I received an "A" in the course and am learning to speak, though haltingly, an arcane jargon of "cutters" and "canners"; of "bloom" and "KPH"; of "bullers," "black baldies," and "heiferettes." I helped tag carcasses for Beef Empire Days as they snaked along the chain at IBP, being skinned and gutted before entering the cooler. One afternoon, I helped my instructor tag the carcasses of one hundred cattle for the Certified Angus Board (CAB). A couple of times I rode on the work train out to IBP to pick up tallow and hides, taking pictures and even managing to get onto the Hides floor.

But it was in Tom's Tavern that I did much of my research on work in the packing plants. There I could meet a cross-section of Garden City—beefpacking line workers and supervisors, farmers and feedyard cowboys, dentists and accountants—the well-to-do and the unemployed; Anglo Americans, African Americans, and Mexican Americans; Latino immigrants up from Mexico or perhaps Central America, even an occasional Vietnamese; old-timers and newcomers alike. Without ready access to the packinghouse floors, Tom's offered the best opportunity to talk candidly with workers. In its relaxed atmosphere, people spoke often and openly about their work. I soon became a "regular," playing Trivial Pursuit or hearts with a circle of devotees, shuffleboard and pool with friends and acquaintances. On Thursdays—payday at the packinghouses—I helped tend bar from midnight till closing at 2:00 A. M., waiting on, listening to, and talking with thirsty line workers coming off "B" shift. On "zoo day"—Sunday—the only day off for packers and many others, I worked from 10:00 P. M. till 2:00 A. M.

Tending bar allowed me to meet and sound out potential interviewees, and productive interviews came from these contacts. I could listen to and participate in conversations with a wide range of people, many of whom I would never have talked with otherwise. My research was well known, if somewhat mysterious, and a cause for suspicion among some. Bartending gave me "real" work in the eyes of those who found it odd that a college professor spent most of his time sitting around talking to people.

The description of jobs and plant layout that follows is based on five formal interviews and several informal conversations with a long-time Slaughter worker with extensive experience in several jobs. The information "Enrique" provided has been supplemented by my own observations, as well as formal interviews and informal conversations with other current and former workers. This description is based on research during 1988 and 1989, although the job descriptions and plant layout refer to the summer of 1989—changes in personnel and specific jobs have taken place since then. The lack of cooperation from plant management and my inability to spend more than short, sporadic periods in the plant may at times lead to gaps in my knowledge.

Background

> The *Appeal* was a "propaganda" paper. It had a manner all its own—it was full of ginger and spice, of Western slang and hustle. . . . The people of Packingtown had lost their strike, if ever a people had, and so they read these papers gladly, and twenty thousand were hardly enough to go round.
>
> —Sinclair, *The Jungle*

The literature on today's meatpacking industry presents an interesting paradox. Talk of consumer trends, and of new developments in procurement, processing, and marketing, fill the trade journals. Newspapers carry articles on meat safety, cattle ranching's environmental impact, the dangers of red meat for health-conscious consumers; stories on the changing workforce and hazardous working conditions even appear from time to time. But scholarly treatises are spotty at best, and more often than not are found in obscure reports. Skaggs (1986) presents the most comprehensive history of meatpacking in America, but he stops in 1983 and pays scant attention to the nature of work in the plants. Wood's (1980) history of the Kansas beef industry focuses on beef production and devotes only eighteen pages to the period after 1940. Economists look at the impact of restructuring on productivity (Carnes 1984) and occupational hazards (Personick and Taylor-Shirley 1989); geographers describe the industry's recent restructuring (Broadway 1990) and its impact on local communities (Broadway 1994).

As policy analysts and cattle producers debate the consequences of packer concentration and vertical integration (Center for Rural Affairs 1990; National Cattlemen's Association 1989), activists decry the suffering of animals during slaughter (Birchall 1990) and even suggest "ecotage" (Mooney 1989). Reporters from the *Kansas City Star* win a Pulitzer Prize with their exposé of the U.S. Department of Agriculture (USDA), which includes revelations of tainted meat, inadequate inspection procedures, and serious conflicts of interest (McGraw 1991; McGraw and Taylor 1991). Hidden cameras reveal the contamination that can result from high-speed, streamlined inspection procedures in beef plants on ABC's "Prime Time Live." k. d. lang tells her fans that "meat stinks," and Linda McCartney says she couldn't kiss a man who was a meat eater. Jeremy Rifkin launches "Beyond Beef," an eight-year campaign intended to cut American beef consumption in half.

Amid all this hullabaloo, surprisingly little is said about meatpacking workers and the nature of their work. Slayton (1986) and Barrett (1990) tell of life in Back of the Yards and work on the floors of Chicago's packinghouses at the turn of the century. Hardy Green (1990) gives an insider's view of the protracted strike against the Hormel plant in Austin, Minnesota, in 1985–1986. But descriptions of work on the chains and lines of modern meatpacking plants are few and far between. Remy and Sawers (1984) offer a glimpse of the floor at the "Square Deal Packing Company" in their analysis of the consequences of retrenchment for women and Blacks. Until recently, only Thompson (1983) has described in detail what it is like to work in a modern packing plant.

This chapter seeks to turn attention to meatpacking workers, to their work and how it influences their lives and the communities in which they make their homes. While the story that follows is set in Garden City, Kansas, it could just as easily have been told about beef and pork workers in any number of towns in Kansas, Nebraska, or Iowa. (For complementary descriptions of work in modern beef plants and the consequences for local communities, see Broadway and Stull 1991; Stull and Broadway 1990; Stull, Broadway, and Erickson 1992.)

Power and Authority on the Floor

> Jurgis was like a boy, a boy from the country. He was the sort of man the
> bosses like to get hold of, the sort they make a grievance they cannot get
> hold of. When he was told to go to a certain place, he would go there on
> the run. . . . If he were working in a line of men, the line always moved
> too slowly for him, and you could pick him out by his impatience and rest-
> lessness. That was why he had been picked.
>
> —Sinclair, *The Jungle*

On the packinghouse floor authority is circumscribed, the hierarchy rigid. Job
type—and status—are marked by the color of the hardhat everyone must wear. The
floor supervisor is a greenhat; the general foreman a yellowhat, as are the three line
supervisors or foremen. Each is assisted by a leadman, or bluehat. Below them are
the whitehats—the hourly line workers.

Bluehats are "utility people" or "leadmen." They should know how to perform
most, if not all, of the jobs on their line; to fill in as needed and assist the yellowhat
in other ways. Whitehats jokingly call them "back scratchers" and "peter shakers,"
and they often say the way to become a bluehat is to "suck up" to your supervisor—
take him hunting, buy him beer. The bluehat's job includes keeping tabs on whitehats and "writing them up" for infractions.

"Jim" says supervisors should practice the "Three Fs": "Be firm, be fair, and be
friendly." Beginning supervisors may be told to practice the Three Fs in training
sessions, but on the line it's a different matter.

> "Dave" has worked at the plant for three years. They made him a bluehat, but there
> was "too much bullshit" and he asked to go back to being a whitehat. He found keep-
> ing tabs on those workers who were on the yellowhat's "shitlist" especially distasteful.
> There are plenty of ways a supervisor can find to fire you if he gets it in for you. Dave
> knows them all because when he first came to work his yellowhat took a liking to him
> and taught him the ropes. For example, you are allowed 6 minutes for a "piss break."
> But there is no way you can get to the bathroom, take off all your gear, take care of
> business, wash up, put your gear back on, and get back on the line in 6 minutes—espe-
> cially for women who are having their period. But the supervisor can enforce that (as
> well as deny or simply ignore the worker's request altogether) by having his bluehat
> keep time on the person and hound that person out or easily build a case for firing
> him. (Stull fieldnotes 1/27–2/20/89:5)

Write-ups may be issued for many reasons—failure to show up for work or call
in sick, safety infractions, horseplay, taunting or arguing with another worker, or
simply not being able to do the job. If you are written up, you have to sign the
form. If you refuse to sign, you are sent home.

> If you can't do your job the supervisors will tell you, "Either do your job or go home."
> Enrique has been used as a translator in several instances, and apparently language dif-
> ficulties contribute to some Hispanics being fired. He spoke of Hispanics who were

told by the supervisor to "go home." When they returned to work the next day, they were told they had abandoned their post and were terminated. However, Enrique says yellowhats are now being held more accountable, that you can appeal a write-up, and in some cases supervisors have been reprimanded for bad write-ups. (Stull fieldnotes 6/14–19/89:11–12)

The company does not control worker behavior with the threat of write-ups alone. When the plant found punitive measures were not significantly reducing accidents, it adopted incentives. If a line goes fifteen days without an accident, its members get a free lunch; thirty days gets five pounds of hamburger; sixty days a cap; still longer brings a jacket. This system has proved successful, although yellowhats still carry green cards to write workers up for infractions (Stull fieldnotes 7/12–16/89:12).

Supervisors and bluehats are not the only ones who exert power on the floor. Whitehats may contest for power among themselves, crossing over and back across the thin line between horseplay and open conflict.

A couple of times that same week I got hit by the heads. See, I was working on my head, I grabbed it like this, and with my steel, like that, pulling on the meat, and the other guy, when the other head came, instead of throwing it in the front of me so after I finish with mine I can grab it myself, he threw it straight and hit me with the head. . . . And he hit me a couple of times and they just laughed. The second time I got mad and I threw him a head. He, of course, got mad, but he stopped it, too. . . . The person that is going to do something like that, he won't do it when the foreman is there, he will wait until he's not in sight. . . .

I was threatened a couple of times with knives . . . on the floor. You know, there is somebody joking, throwing you pieces of fat or something. . . . So one time I was washing my boots, I wash them with a pressure hose, and he threatened me with a knife. And I just told him . . . "Just drop it." . . . I talk to a lot of people, and sometimes joke, not heavy, though. I know when to stop. And I tell them, too, when they are getting out of hand. I never had any trouble in the floor. . . . The only problem that I had that got threatened that time was with a Vietnamese guy. . . .

Q: With the knife?

A: [Yes.] It was an air knife, those round ones. [We were in the boot wash] washing up. That time I got smart, so I wash him off with a pressure hose when he turn around. I said, "If you can't take any jokes then don't joke." He said, "Forget about it." And he did. So that's how far it got. (Stull interview 8/13/89:35, 37–38)

From the Knocker to the Cooler: Work on the Killfloor

Then the party went across the street to where they did the killing of beef—where every hour they turned four or five hundred cattle into meat. . . . [T]here were fifteen or twenty lines, and the men moved from one to another of these. . . . [I]t was only a couple of minutes to knock fifteen or twenty cattle and roll them out. . . . The manner in which they did this was something to be seen and never forgotten. They worked with furious intensity, literally upon the run. . . . It was all highly specialized labor, each man having his task to do; generally this would consist of only two or three specific cuts, and he would pass down the line of fifteen or twenty carcasses, making these cuts upon each. . . . There were men to cut it, and men to split it, and men to gut it and scrape it clean inside. There were some with hoses which threw jets of boiling water upon it, and others who removed the feet and added the final touches. In the end . . . the finished beef was run into the chilling room, to hang its appointed time.

—Sinclair, *The Jungle*

The Skinning Line

Cattle arrive in trucks a few hours before slaughter. They are unloaded into holding pens, weighed, given a lot number, and when their time comes, driven onto a ramp, or *funnel*. The funnel gradually narrows as it winds upward to the *knock box* high above the killfloor. There each animal is immobilized, as two *knockers* take turns applying cylindrical stun guns to each animal's forehead. On impact, the gun discharges a .25-caliber cap that propels a short steel piston into the skull, causing a displaced skull fracture and unconsciousness. Underneath the knockers stands the *shackler*, who wraps a hook and chain around the animal's left hind hoof—easier said than done, since its legs may be jerking from the stun. As each animal (referred to in both the singular and plural as "cattle") is knocked and shackled, it falls forward and down onto a mechanized overhead trolley and swings out onto the floor, hanging upside down from its left hind hoof.

After traveling the full width of the floor, the suspended animal makes a 90-degree turn to meet the *sticker*. Holding a knife with a four-inch blade, he deftly makes an incision in the hide at the base of the throat, careful not to pierce the throat itself. The *can-hanger*[3] then hooks a stainless-steel cylinder under the animal's open throat. The *bleeder* quickly severs an artery and blood gushes into the cans, spilling over to drench the workers and run through the grated floor beneath their feet. The three stand shoulder to shoulder like gladiators, wearing hockey helmets and face masks for protection from flailing hoofs and their own knives, which are sometimes knocked into their faces. The bleeder deals the fatal blow, but dying is a process. Signs of life such as muscle twitches and jerking limbs may continue well down the line.

After the bleeder, the chain makes another 90-degree turn. Ten feet or so down the chain, the cans, now full of blood, are emptied into a vat and placed on a hook, for their ride on the chain back to the can-hanger by way of a "box," where they are washed with high-pressure water spray. Farther down the line, severed heads and carcasses are washed in similar "boxes."[4]

Because the hide is hard to cut, the sticker exerts more effort than the bleeder, who reaches up inside the cattle's throat to slice an artery. The can-emptiers do not face the same risk of being kicked by the cattle as the can-hangers, but they must lift and empty the heavy cans. So at break, stickers and bleeders, can-hangers and can-emptiers, switch positions. They switch again after lunch. Since there is no break after lunch, they switch again the following morning to maintain equity.

The skinning line is the hardest of all the lines on the killfloor because

> the hide is the hardest part, the toughest thing to cut. Those knives have to be pretty
> sharp in order to do a good job. . . . So if you're working with the butt knife, man,
> your hands swell, get blisters and everything, and finally [workers] have to either move
> out or they have to tell the foreman they want to move out, [take] some other job that
> you don't need to use a knife. It's up to them. A lot of people quit. (Stull interview
> 6/19/89:6)

As the cattle pass by the can-emptier on the second leg of the snaking journey
through the killfloor, most of the work stations are on raised grated platforms. The
knockers stand high above the floor; the sticker and the bleeder, the can-hanger
and can-emptier, stand on the floor. Most of the rest of the workers stand on
grated steel platforms at varying heights off the floor, depending on what part of
the carcass they work on.

The skinning begins with the *tail rippers*, who "cut out the ass" (rectum), slice
the hide all the way to the cod, and remove the pizzle (penis) if it is a bull—a dangerous job because the cattle are often still kicking. The *first legger* removes the
hoof from the loose hind leg and slits the hide down the full length of the rear
flank. Then three *first butters* skin down the loose leg, "peeling" the whole round
(hindquarter). At this point, the carcass is still on the chain. The *first hang-off*
inserts a hook attached to a roller (the "trolley") in a tendon between two bones in
the gam (in the hock of the loose leg) and places it on the "rail" above the workers.

The carcass was initially suspended from its left hind leg. Now it hangs on the
trolley from its right hind leg. Three *second leggers* take the chain off the left hind
leg, then cut the hoof off and slice the hide the length of the leg up to the first
joint. The *second butters* peel the round on the loose leg, and the *second hang-off* puts
a trolley in the loose leg and places it on the rail. The carcass now travels down the
rail suspended by both hind legs; both rounds are now peeled.

The cattle are now traversing the floor for the third time, while *flankers*,
rimovers, and *rumpers* skin more and more of the carcass. Interspersed among them,
others remove ears, horns, and hooves. Doing a good job, and doing it right, is
vital—if you don't, it will soon take a toll on your body.

> Those guys know what they're doing, because if they don't do it right, boy, that gets
> hard. Any job that you do, if you don't do it right, you get tired in a flash, because that
> chain is going too fast to keep up with it if you're not doing it right. (Stull interview
> 6/19/89:5)

If something goes wrong, *redhats*—maintenance workers—weighed down by
sagging implement belts are summoned by prearranged blasts on sirens. Maintenance crews are on duty around the clock in rotating shifts—six weeks on grave-
yard, six weeks on swings, six weeks on days.

> There's a lot of breakdown. . . . You replace what you can, but you're just barely keep-
> ing ahead of the game, keeping things running. . . . At this point they're more inter-
> ested in keeping it running than they are in maintenance. They're more interested in

keeping it running as a basis of putting the product out than, you know, the fights with equipment. I foresee that is going to be the downfall here sooner or later. (Maintenance worker 5/9/89:4–5)

When the flank and the rump have been peeled, the *side-puller* attaches a machine by the same name to the hide on both sides of the carcass, which hangs limply upside down. The push of a button sends an electrical shock coursing through the carcass—it contracts, arches its back, and the hide is stripped cleanly away from the ribs. (Carcasses are shocked at several stages in the slaughter process: initially to stimulate blood loss before the cans are emptied, later to hasten rigor mortis and to keep them from being torn apart by the massive skinning machines.)

The scissor-like *tie-down* machine grasps the head as the *banana bar* skins the loin and hindquarters; the *down-puller* then strips the hide from the back and shoulders down over the foreshanks and the head. Another electrical charge is needed at this point, otherwise the head and forequarters would be pulled off by the massive down-puller. Even so, carcasses with backs broke in skinning are a common sight. Hides travel beneath the floor on a conveyor belt out of Slaughter and over to the Hides building, where they are first bathed in a brine solution, then bailed and shipped out to tanneries by rail.

After the hide is removed, the carcass and the head are numbered; the head is then "dropped" (severed) and placed on a hook.

Figure 2: Here a worker is "hanging" a tongue on a hook. With the head beside it, the tongue will travel "down the line" for inspection and further processing. (Courtesy of *MEAT&POULTRY* Magazine.)

The Head Line

Skinned heads, resting on hooks inserted at the base of the skull, proceed down the "head line," then make a turn at a right angle onto the "head table"—a grisly sight as they round the U at one end of the building, naked with eyes and tongues still intact.

Workers with air-powered saws cut the horns flush with the skull, then wash the head by inserting a long metal tube into the back of the skull, which shoots water out the nose and mouth to clean the inside of the skull. Tongues are "dropped," then "hung" on a hook. Heads and tongues travel, side by side, down the line on hooks into a "box," where they are sprayed with a fine mist of water.

USDA inspectors check the glands of the tongue for disease by making incisions both inside and outside the head. On down the line, workers take the tongue apart, trim fat from its side, remove the windpipe, and put it on the conveyor headed to Rendering. Tongues go on the chain to Offal, there to be packed for shipping.

Meanwhile, whitehats on the head table use straight knives, hydraulic machines with tigerlike claws, and Whizard knives—circular blades, operated by a lever, with teeth like a hacksaw—to remove the lower jaw, then loosen, separate, and save meat from the jaw, cheek, and head. Once every bit of flesh has been removed, skulls are split open with a hydraulic machine, then pushed into a hole, later to be ground up for bone meal or gelatin. Brains are saved, washed, and bagged. "And that's the end of the line for the heads," says Enrique.

The Gut Table

While heads make their way down their own line, carcasses move toward the gut table. The *brisket-sawer* splits the sternum. Two *pregutters* then slice the length of the belly, remove the bladder, and open the skin from the cod to where the brisket saw stopped. The stomach sags. Five *gutters*, sometimes six, pull the paunch and viscera out and "drop" them on a conveyor belt. This is very hard because the steam rising from the still-warm insides and chest cavity makes it difficult to see. If the viscera do not come loose from their own weight, they are cut loose and proceed in a pile down the gut table.

> You watch these guys who gut cattle, the gutters themselves, they're removing the viscera with as much skill as a surgeon. They're standing there, they're soaking wet a lot of time from the heat, you know the moisture coming up off the table, and they're working inside this hot carcass all day, and their skill level is a helluva lot more than just a common laborer. (Respondent with wide industry experience 3/30/89:22)

The guts come down the conveyor belt in two lines as five USDA inspectors stand on both sides of the table, looking them over. One inspector checks carcasses as they move on down the line, another the livers, the other three stomachs and hearts. Any diseased or contaminated organs are condemned with blue dye and discarded down "the hole." Once the viscera pass USDA, they are sorted and processed. Hearts are separated from lungs, then hung on hooks headed for Offal; livers are stamped with "USDA" and then boxed, sealed, and placed on a conveyor

Figure 3: Processing, or Fabrication, floor of modern beef plant. Here carcasses are broken down, fat and bone removed, then boxed for shipment to customers. (Courtesy of *MEAT&POULTRY* Magazine.)

belt; lungs and windpipes are separated; "rounds" (intestines) are saved. A worker hangs tripe on a chain that carries it into the "tripe box," there to be washed and bleached, then weighed, boxed, and placed on a conveyor belt that moves past the head table, rising steadily till it exits the killfloor on the second floor.

The Trim Line
After the gut table, carcasses move onto the "trim line," where tails are removed, washed, then hung, interspersed between hearts on a chain, which travels to Offal where they are sealed in plastic, boxed, labeled, and frozen.

Next come the *back-splitters*, arguably the most important job in Slaughter. Using a Jarvis Buster IV saw—a large band saw suspended from the rail above—the back-splitter cuts the carcass in half from bottom to top, since the carcass hangs upside down. He must do his job with great precision, splitting the backbone exactly in half. A bad cut costs the company money.

The carcass, now split in two, passes by a series of *trimmers* who remove pieces of hide, dirt, internal organs—anything missed earlier. USDA inspectors watch for pieces of liver, pus, bad kidneys—anything that should not be there. Carcasses failing inspection are railed off to the "deadrail" or "deadend rail," where a yellowhat from the trim line, and maybe one or two whitehats, fixes the problem.

The USDA inspector then rechecks these carcasses, and they are pushed back onto the main rail.

The carcass is given a USDA stamp, weighed, and labeled, after which it exits the killfloor behind a plastic "wall" or "fence." It cools in the hotbox for twenty-two to twenty-four hours, then enters the cooler, where it is given a yield and quality grade. From the cooler the carcass goes to Processing, where it is broken down into subprimal cuts, shrink-wrapped, then boxed for shipment to wholesale and retail outlets (see Erickson 1994 for a discussion of work on the Processing floor). In all, the trip from knock box to cooler takes a mere forty-two minutes, in which time a steer or a heifer is transformed from an animal to a carcass (Stull fieldnotes 2/21/89:6). In two or three days, it will be shipped out in boxes as meat.

Discussion

> Jurgis would find out these things for himself if he stayed there long enough; it was the men who had to do all the dirty jobs, and so there was no deceiving them; and they caught the spirit of the place, and did like all the rest.

> —Sinclair, *The Jungle*

In spite of a "century of progress" since Upton Sinclair wrote *The Jungle*, I am struck by how little the industry—its work or its workers—has really changed. Knockers still start the killing, but now they use a stun gun instead of a sledgehammer. Splitters are still the most expert and highly paid workers on the killfloor, deftly cutting carcasses in half with Jarvis Buster IV band saws on moving platforms, where once they used massive cleavers. Today's luggers carry 200-pound beef quarters into refrigerated semis, rather than boxcars. Still, stickers and gutters, trimmers and droppers wield razor-sharp knives as they turn 400 cattle an hour into meat.

Beefpacking plants remain massive factories, in so many ways reminiscent of the turn of the century. They continue employing hundreds or even thousands of workers to toil on their disassembly lines. And immigrants are still attracted to packinghouse jobs because command of English is not required, and wages are relatively high. But instead of the German, Irish, Lithuanian, and Polish workers of Sinclair's day, today's packinghouses are crowded with Southeast Asian refugees, Mexican migrants, African Americans, Latinos, and Anglos from our farms and cities.

Yes, the "chain" connecting meatpacking's past and present runs strong. Companies still "make a great feature of showing strangers through the packing plants, for it is a good advertisement" (Sinclair 1985:43). And somewhere in between pointing out the "wonderful efficiency" of the plant, the unbelievable speed with which they kill and disassemble cattle, and the "many strange and unlikely products (that come from) such things as feet, knuckles, hide clippings, and sinews" (Sinclair 1985:50), the guide will chuckle and say: "They don't waste anything here. IBP markets every part of the cow but the moo. My father used to work at IBP before me, and he used to tell me that the little toy boxes that moo were made by IBP"

(Stull fieldnotes 7/22/88:1). The group laughs, and he is pleased that we should take this ancient witticism as his own.

Training

As in Jurgis's time, new hires are placed in jobs according to vacancies and prior experience.

> When they start . . . they have to be in the job the foreman assigns them, or in other words where they need them, and if that person doesn't make it there, he can ask to be changed or has the choice to quit. And it's easier to make a person quit when they start because they are hurting all over and they want a change, and they won't change them because they need them there. And they are all with bandages. (Slaughter worker 7/16/89:10)

Training new employees should be vitally important in an industry where workers with no previous experience, often with limited English skills, are expected to perform precise tasks rapidly. The company claims to provide each worker with extensive orientation and training. Workers say training consists of little more than watching and imitating the person you are to replace for a day or two—then you are on your own. The company, after all, does not want to pay two people to do the job of one.

> Q: What did [your] training consist of?
> A: I just started that job. They should have trained me for two weeks, and they only trained me for four days, and they wanted to leave me after two days. . . . Initially they had me just watching and doing one or two [pieces] while the other ones were working the place. Nobody told me how to grab the steel to do the job or how to handle it—just by look. I had to stay there and look and try to just imitate what the other ones were doing. (Enrique 6/4/89)

Such training practices at first seem counterproductive to the packers' avowed goal of high productivity, but Enrique goes on to explain.

> Q: Doesn't that mess up the line speed and stuff?
> A: No, because what it does is it puts a burden a little more to somebody else down the line, that other person that has already been there for quite a while and they are used to it. . . . It's a little bit more to the one next in the line, coming down in the line, because the person they put there is not going to do it right, so it just puts a little bit more work to the next one. But when they see it's a new [worker], they take it. They try kind of helping out. There are some people, they don't, but they complain, but they still do it. (6/4/89:2–3)

In part, new workers receive inadequate training because the leadmen, who serve as trainers, spend much of their time filling in for absentees on the line. The man in the snakeskin boots says they compensate for absenteeism by having more workers on a shift than are absolutely needed. But workers complain of "short crews," which they attribute to attempts to cut costs. A former supervisor put it this way:

> We're shorthanded out there, just continuously. Seems like we never have enough people, and when we do get crewed somebody quits or gets fired or bids off. And normally the bluehat is just like anybody else, just out there filling a position, a position that needs filling. He doesn't get a chance to train very often, which isn't right. And that's not how it's designed to work, but that's how it works most generally. (Stull interview 5/29/89:18)

Probation

Hourly workers are assigned to their initial job and are on probation ninety days. After successfully completing the probationary period, the worker is given seniority and may "bid" on any "posted" job within the same department (Slaughter, Processing, Hides, Offal, etc.). Workers may not bid out of their own department. The qualified bidder with the highest seniority "wins" a job. A worker who wins a new job and "can't stay with it" is "frozen" in his prior job for six months before again becoming a "qualified bidder."

Whether a worker is on probation or has won seniority, he is subject to strict rules and rigid sanctions. Probationary employees may be discharged without notice or recourse. All employees are "written up" for being late or absent without an excuse, excessive excused absences, failure to report on-the-job injuries, overstaying lunch or relief breaks, deliberate discourtesy, horseplay, substandard job performance. Workers with four such infractions within a calendar year are discharged. More serious offenses bring even quicker termination—malicious mischief that results in property damage or injury, gambling, alcohol or drug use, theft, abusive or threatening language. Fighting, even in the parking lot, results in immediate discharge—with so many knives so close at hand, it cannot be otherwise (National Beef Packing Company n.d.: 19).

For whitehats, and their supervisors, the work is hard. One Mexican immigrant called it *esclavitud*—slavery. "They make you hump for your seven or eight dollars. The first ninety days it's tough till you get in shape. I'm a supervisor, and I'm not supposed to work hard, but I bet I run ten miles a day in my job. It's not a place to be if you don't like to work" (Stull fieldnotes 8/7/88:7).

Communication and Interaction

Communications must be quick and to the point; workers have little time for idle conversation, or even work-related discussion, as carcasses whiz by at 400 or more an hour. When communication does take place, it is restricted to workers at the same or nearby stations, or with yellowhats or their bluehats.

Interaction with co-workers is a function of proximity. It is also a function of the job itself—how demanding it is and how many people do it. Once a job is mastered, especially if several workers share the same task, there may be time for a bit of conversation and rest. Still, interaction is largely confined to those at the same or nearby work station. Workers are allowed two scheduled breaks a day—fifteen minutes approximately two and a half hours into their shift and thirty minutes for lunch after about five and a half hours. Breaks, as well as starting and quitting times, are staggered down the line.

To the outsider, IBP's Slaughter lunchroom appears segregated by ethnicity and gender. Mexican immigrants occupy the northeast and southwest corners; Southeast Asians sit at a couple of tables in the middle of the room; an Anglo couple sits across from one another near the south wall. There are exceptions—an Anglo sitting with Hispanics here and there, an Asian and a Hispanic woman sitting at a center table. When only a few workers are on break, they quietly watch the color television that runs continuously from atop its perch at the southeast corner. When the lunchroom is crowded, most pay little attention to it. Instead, they visit among themselves, often sharpening their knives or rubbing down their steels.

This clustering is only partly explained by workers' preferences to socialize with others of the same sex or ethnic group. Those from the same station also congregate together. For example, workers from the cooler always sit at a table in the northeast corner—the part of the lunchroom closest to their station. In Slaughter, fifteen or twenty workers at a time go on break. Who one sits by is thus a *combination* of ethnic, gender, and personal bonds *and* work station proximity. While those of the same ethnic group will sit with one another if they have the opportunity, ties developed on the line may take precedence.

In spite of tension between supervisors and line workers, between members of different ethnic groups, common workplace experiences help build shared concerns and identity that transcend ethnic boundaries. The community's general antipathy toward packinghouse workers serves to reinforce their common identity. All are subjected to the power and authority of large and indifferent corporations, who appear to value machinery and daily quotas over the welfare of their workers.

The Price of Work: Tales from Workers' Compensation Hearings

> There is another interesting set of statistics that a person might have gathered in Packingtown—those of the various afflictions of the workers.
>
> —Sinclair, *The Jungle*

On the killfloor—indeed throughout the plant—production quotas, driven by daily fluctuations in the fat-cattle and boxed-beef markets, take precedence over other considerations, including safety and equipment maintenance. And chain speed takes a heavy toll on the workers, not only in the high job turnover that plagues the industry, but on the very bodies and lives of line workers. Investigations by the Occupational Safety and Health Administration (OSHA) reveal that the packers go to great lengths to camouflage the incidence and prevalence of injuries. They say they are trying to reduce risk by ergonomics and better training, not to mention extensive safety equipment, but they are quick to point out that by its very nature meatpacking has always been—and always will be—dangerous. This may be, and it certainly will be as long as chains run fast, as long as cheap meat is prized above human welfare. But let us hear from the workers themselves. What follows are a few cases from monthly workers' compensation hearings I attended in Garden City in 1988 and 1989. They tell not only of the work and the risks that attend it but of the true price of our meat—the price in human suffering, in broken bodies and lives.

His wife drove him over from Dodge. He was in his mid-30s, did not finish high school in Vietnam, could not speak English, and had worked only in meatpacking since coming to the U. S. He wore sandals in spite of the morning chill, but kept on his heavy coat throughout his testimony.

His attorney and the company both brought their own interpreter: his was a young man, the company's was a woman in her mid-30s who someone said was a restaurateur. The lawyers argued over whose interpreter should be used during the hearing—the judge decided in Solomonic fashion that the claimant's interpreter be used in examination and the company's in cross-examination. When it came time to cross-examine, the company attorney chose to stick with the young man.

"Huong" was fired for allegedly failing to call in sick, though he says he did. He was a cow-sticker, and he got down off the stand to graphically demonstrate his job. He earned $256 a week. On November 18, 1987—some 26 months ago—he was knocked unconscious when a carcass fell on him. He was carried to the plant office by co-workers, then taken to Dr. X by his Hispanic supervisor—no interpreter accompanied them.

After examining him, the doctor—the one the company always uses—signed a card giving him two days off. When Huong asked for a week off (how I'm not sure), Dr. X got mad, tore up the slip, and sent him back to work immediately, prescribing "light duty" and one hour of physical therapy a day for five or six days. When he got back to work his light duty turned out to require lifting 60-pound meat trays. The next day he called in sick and was then "terminated" (fired). He has not worked since and still has problems with his ears, head, and chest.

Since the accident, Huong has seen several doctors, including a Vietnamese physician in town, all of whom have told him he cannot work. He has borrowed $5,000–6,000 from friends, but he still owes on doctor bills and has been refused treatment for failure to pay. He moves back and forth between Wichita and Dodge City, living with friends and borrowing money from them.

The judge concluded from testimony that Dr. X could not understand Huong, didn't want to be bothered, failed to note the extent and severity of his injuries, and just sent him back to work. He ordered 70 days of vocational rehabilitation. (Stull fieldnotes 1/16–1/20/89:6–8)

What was left unsaid, but understood by all, was that Dr. X is the "company doctor" for both the packing plants—his diagnoses have more to do with the company's welfare than those of the workers he sees.

John was 32 years old, an Anglo from the next county to the north. He graduated from high school in 1974 and received an associate of arts degree in auto mechanics in 1986. He had been a manual laborer before he began working for IBP in September 1987. He started as a knocker on "B" shift. His first injury came in January 1988.

"I was knocking—killing—cows. They run cattle through like a revolving chute, a restrainer, and the animals weren't being cleaned and the (stun) gun kept misfiring, so it bounced off most of the time. Instead of knocking them once, you had to knock them two or three times. It kicked my right arm back into the cow's head. (As that occurred, did you have physical problems?) My back hurt real bad, on my shoulder blade, the top part of my back."

Attorney: Did you report that to anyone?

John: Yes, the foreman and then the nurse.

Attorney: As a result of notifying the foreman and the nurse was your job changed in any way?

John: Yes, ma'am. I went home the night my back was hurting and I saw the nurse, and then I came (in the next night) and then I had to cut ears and tails.

Attorney: What happened on January 12, 1988?

John: The trolley that lowered the cows, that the cows were hanging from, came loose at the back. It's like a roller, it's got a hook in it. The hook goes through the cow's leg. It weighs about 5 or 6 pounds, and it came down and hit me in the shoulder blades.

Attorney: Did you report the incident to anyone?

John: There was a foreman standing right beside me when it happened.

Attorney: Did you receive medical treatment as a result of that injury?

John: No.

Attorney: Did you request medical treatment?

John: No.

Attorney: Why didn't you request treatment?

John: I was scared.

Attorney: What do you mean you were scared?

John: When I went in the first time, and they sent me into the nurse, they just kept telling me that if I couldn't tell them what it was that happened to hurt my back I couldn't see the doctor. And I kept saying, "The guns aren't going off right." And they said that I had to be more specific, and I didn't know how to be more specific.

On February 2, John slipped and fell in a pool of frozen blood, landing on his buttocks and then his back. The next day he could not get out of bed. IBP did not at first provide medical treatment, so John went on his own. His doctor prescribed painkillers and nothing more. IBP subsequently sent him to the company doctor. He referred him to another physician for examination, who diagnosed a soft tissue problem and told John to go back to work. John did not feel able to go back to work and when he asked to see another doctor he was terminated. The date was February 15.

Attorney: Currently do you feel capable of employment?

John: No.

Attorney: Why not?

John: I can't do anything. My back hurts, right above the belt line. I have to change positions, lay down for a while, sit for a while. Sitting, laying, I change positions about 20–30 times per night, walking. I don't pick up anything, and just sometimes, heck, one time that I wanted to get up and I just, everything didn't work, and I just fell flat on my face. (Stull fieldnotes and audiotape transcriptions 8/14/88)

"Rock 'n' Roll Ron" is Anglo, in his mid-20s, an on-again, off-again regular at Tom's. He has worked at Monfort for five months; before that he worked at National Beef in Liberal for two years. He was hitchhiking from Florida to California and stopped off in Liberal because he heard there were jobs. He applied at National and was hired the next day. He told them he would only work in Loadout, "I've never used a knife and don't know how." He's worked in Loadout ever since. He figured he'd work a couple of months, earn some money, then continue on to California—he hasn't made it yet.

Loadout works three eight-hour shifts, seven days a week—other crews work two shifts, five days a week. He likes Loadout, in part because it is safe, but he says that many guys bid out of Loadout to get "knife jobs" because the pay is better. It's the most dangerous and dirty jobs that pay the best; he says that people aren't that concerned about injuries, they want the money. He makes $6.75 an hour. When the Teamster's contract goes into effect in September, his pay will go to $7, but it really won't make any difference to him since it'll be eaten up in union dues.

The last time I'd seen him he was on crutches with a full leg brace. I asked him about it, and he said that in early June he was picking up a 100-pound box of chuck and the handles on the box gave way and fell on his knee, tearing ligaments and cartilage. It's his first injury in two and a half years in meatpacking. He expected to be put on workers' comp, but that's not what happened. "The company doctor wanted no part of it" and sent him instead to a bone specialist here in town, who recommended light duty. He said his light duty consisted mainly of sitting around drinking coffee from 8 to 4 every day. Lately, he's been nailing cardboard onto wooden slats that the boxes sit on in the trucks.

He goes off light duty on Monday and is anxious to get back to his old job, even though his leg is still not completely healed. But he is afraid of being fired. One reason he thinks he didn't get workers' comp and may get fired is because after his accident he "failed the piss test." The accident took place on a Friday on the "B" shift. Normally drug testing is done immediately after accidents, but because it happened on a weekend he was not tested till Monday—he tested positive for alcohol and drugs. The implication was that he would have tested clean had he been tested immediately, but I have my doubts.

He said there is a lot of drug use at the plant, much of it sold by supervisors: "If you want some coke, go to a supervisor." Many workers also use speed, in part to keep up with the line. Boxes weighing from 40 to 120 pounds come down the line every 10 seconds or so, sometimes even faster. You can't stop just because they are heavy and you're tired. "It gets you in great shape and makes an old man of ya real quick—both at the same time." (Stull fieldnotes 8/5/88:17–21)

Case 5 was a 40-year-old Anglo with severe pains from her shoulders to her fingertips.

She must cross her arms and clench her fists to fight the pain. She found it hard, if not impossible, to work, to do housework, even to turn pages while reading. ["Do you read?" "Sometimes." "Do you turn pages?" "It hurts, that's why I said sometimes."]

She'd been a housewife till 1986 when she went to work at the packinghouse. She worked there till September 1987. At the time she was terminated she was making $359 a week. This was the first paying job she ever held. She was forced to go to work when a divorce left her with two boys, now 19 and 17, to support.

She started out in Slaughter on the "head table" cutting sinew off skulls. The heads go around the chain at about 6 per minute and she had to make 5–7 cuts per head. After she cut the sinew off, she put it in a bucket.

She began developing problems in her fingers and shoulders and as a result she was moved to "brains," where she took brains out of skulls, put them in a bucket, and when the bucket weighed about 30 pounds, she carried it to a different station and emptied it. Much of her job was to wash, weigh, and put the brains in a box. She also massaged the membrane that covers the brain, removing it—this involved the constant motion of her fingers.

The sinew cutting and the brain cleaning were part of the same process. There were two cutters—one Black, one Vietnamese. Also working with her were several women and a supervisor named "Rudolfo." At times she was the only person doing the brains, other times not.

The new job did little to alleviate the pain in her arms and shoulders, and she was often helped to lift her load by one of the men on the line. She calculated that when working on the brains, she lifted a 30-pound bucket every 5 minutes and performed approximately 1,800 squishing movements per hour with her hands in removing the membrane.

She complained of her pain to her supervisor. First she was sent to the company doctor, then to a local specialist, then back to the company doctor, then to a specialist in Wichita. This specialist had her taken off work, but the company then canceled her subsequent appointments with him, which meant she had to go back to work. They later sent her to a specialist in Denver. Ultimately she was terminated.

She still has the pain; she can't use her fingers at all now and keeps her hands clenched because it hurts to open them. She stays at home, where she does only minimal housework. Her new husband, whom she met at work, still works for the company. He and her boys do most of the cooking and cleaning.

The company position is that her pain is not related to work but is caused by an underlying emotional problem. Their attorney questioned her emotional state, attacked her personality, and tried to suggest that divorce was the cause of her problem. The judge intervened and stopped this line of questioning. (Stull fieldnotes 8/14/88:13–15)

The pathos in this case and many others like it shows in the testimony of a Hispanic man against another employer later the same day: "Only thing I know is labor. I can't go back to being a lugger. I lugged beef for 9 years. That's the only thing I really know" (Stull fieldnotes 8/14/88:19).

Conclusion

> Upton Sinclair provided a voice to the great masses of immigrants who
> had come to America yearning to be free and comfortable and who had
> found instead the wage slavery and misery of mill, factory, sweat-shop,
> and slum. Jacob Riis had shown *How the Other Half Lives* in 1890; Sinclair
> showed how more than the other half worked in 1905—in conditions of
> physical danger, insecurity, fear, exploitation, corruption, and filth.
>
> —Ronald Gottesman, Introduction to *The Jungle*

Sadly, Gottesman's words ring no less true for meatpacking workers of his own day
than for those of Sinclair's—the killfloor is still a jungle. After all, the Beef Trust
has merely been replaced by the "Big Three." Concentration and vertical integration are worse now than in 1890, when the packers' excesses contributed to the passage of the Sherman Antitrust Act.

The public has not changed all that much either. It is still much easier to hit
them in the stomach than in the heart. Thanks in large measure to *The Jungle*, the
Pure Food and Drug Act and the Meat Inspection Act, both passed in 1906, soon
after the book's publication, have (until the recent revelations on "Prime Time
Live") dispelled serious doubts about what might be lurking in our burgers. Today
we are more likely to worry about global emissions of methane, animal rights, and
cholesterol, while the packers and producers keep an uneasy eye on the steady
decline in Americans' consumption of red meat as they try to come up with ever
leaner cuts of meat "to fit into today's balanced diet."

We wince and, perhaps for a moment or two, our hearts go out to packing-plant
line workers and their families when we read of the deaths of three maintenance
workers overcome by toxic fumes in a blood-collection tank at the National Beef
Packing plant in Liberal, Kansas (*Garden City Telegram* 1991), or the twenty-five
who died in the fire at the Imperial Food Products chicken plant in Hamlet, North
Carolina, later the same year (Tabor 1991). But all too soon, our hearts once again
give way to our stomachs, and if we think of meat processing at all, it is to worry
about hormone-laced steaks or salmonella-infected chicken.

But meat-processing workers are the miner's canary for us all. Their unions have
been busted, their wages slashed. And their work is the most dangerous—in 1988
the probability of injury was .39 in meatpacking, compared to .13 in manufacturing overall (U. S. Department of Labor 1989). We now know "butcher's wrist" as
carpal tunnel syndrome, one of the more common and debilitating forms of cumulative trauma disorder (CTD). CTDs make up a quarter of the injuries in meatpacking (Austin 1988). In 1988, they accounted for 48 percent of *all* occupational
illness—up 30 percent since 1981—with an estimated cost of $27 billion a year in
medical bills and lost time on the job. But record OSHA fines have not slowed the
chains in packing plants (*U.S. News & World Report* 1990): the price of cattle has
been up, the demand for beef down. So are the profit margins. Workers are still
cheap—and expendable. Despite health and environmental concerns, price remains
the major reason consumers buy less beef. Until we are willing to pay more for our

meat—and until we demand fair wages and decent working conditions for meat-packing workers—the jungle will remain in our midst.

> The peculiar bitterness of all this was that Jurgis saw so plainly the meaning of it. In the beginning he had been fresh and strong . . . but now he was second-hand, a damaged article, so to speak, and they did not want him. They had got the best out of him—they had worn him out, with their speeding-up and their carelessness, and now they had thrown him away! And Jurgis would make the acquaintance of others of these unemployed men and find that they had all had the same experience. (Sinclair 1985:149)

Acknowledgments

What I have learned about beefpacking—its work and its workers—is conditioned by how I learned it, by who has collaborated with me, and who has not. In this description of work and its consequences, the voices are at times mine, at others those of my native teachers and collaborators. I am indebted to Gale Seibert, my instructor in Meat and Carcass Evaluation at Garden City Community College, my classmates, and the many beefpacking workers who patiently tried to instruct me in the ways of cattle, meat, and men. I have tried to render faithfully what I saw, heard, and was told, but these many teachers bear no responsibility for my errors or interpretations. I also wish to acknowledge the Ford Foundation's Changing Relations Project, the General Research Fund of the University of Kansas, and a sabbatical leave in providing the necessary funding and time to conduct my fieldwork. Michael Broadway, Janet Benson, and Carol Warren read drafts of this chapter and provided me with helpful comments. Finally, I am grateful to MEAT&POULTRY Magazine for kindly providing pictures of Slaughter workers and to Laura Kriegstrom Poracsky for transforming my arcane sketching into a real map.

Notes

1. Beef carcass quality grade (QG) is determined by degree of marbling (intramuscular fat) and maturity. Color, texture, and firmness of lean meat in the ribeye at the twelfth rib are considered in assigning one of eight USDA quality grades. Yield grade (YG) measures cutability—the percentage of boneless, closely trimmed retail cuts from the round, rib, loin, and chuck. Yield grades range from 1.0 (54.6 percent) to 5.9 (43.3 percent) (Boggs and Merkel 1984). USDA graders assign both quality and yield grades to each carcass by sight. Quality grade determines the value of the carcass—a Choice carcass brings about $8 more per hundredweight than one graded Select. Graders have about seven seconds to assign both a QG and YG to each carcass (Seibert 1989).

2. The information presented in the question-and-answer period after the tour is from several sessions over more than a year (Stull fieldnotes 6/17/88, 7/10/88, 7/22/88, 5/6/89). Although it did not come in a single session, or in such a flowing narrative, most is from the man in the snakeskin boots. Supervisors, line workers, and industry observers at times dispute some of these facts, and the conclusions drawn from them.

3. The job titles used in this description combine IBP line worker terminology and my own. Whenever I know the proper IBP term, I use it; when I don't, I make one up, using various sources as guides. The general rule of thumb appears to be to name the job after the activity (e.g., dropping heads). Terminology varies somewhat from plant to plant. In the journey from knocket to cooler, not all jobs are presented—space and reader interest prohibit a complete description. Photographs of work on

the killfloor presented in this chapter were *not* taken at an IBP plant. The photos are, in fact, several years old and do not necessarily represent the present state of technology in modern beefpacking plants. But given the general ban on photographs of their installations imposed by IBP and other major packers, these prints do convey a good sense of what the work looks like.

4. I was never able to get officials to say how much water is actually used at the Finney County plant, but Fund and Clement (1982:53) claim IBP uses 400 gallons of rinse water per animal per day. If this figure is correct it means that with a daily slaughter capacity of 6,000 head, IBP uses as much as 2.4 million gallons of water a day, six days a week! This estimate is probably conservative, since company officials say they use 600–650 gallons per head at their Lexington, Nebraska, plant, which opened in November 1990.

Works Cited

Austin, Lisa. 1988. "Riskiest Job in Kansas Escapes Close Scrutiny." *Wichita Eagle-Beacon*, December 4.

Barrett, James R. 1990. *Work and Community in the Jungle: Chicago's Packinghouse Workers, 1894–1922.* Urbana: University of Illinois Press.

Birchall, Annabelle. 1990. "Kinder Ways to Kill." *New Scientist*, May 19, pp. 44–49.

Boggs, Donald L., and Robert A. Merkel. 1984. *Live Animal Carcass Evaluation and Selection Manual.* 2nd ed. Dubuque, Iowa: Kendall/Hunt.

Broadway, Michael J. 1990. "Recent Changes in the Structure and Location of the U. S. Meatpacking Industry." *Geography* 75(1):76–79.

———. 1994. "Beef Stew: Cattle, Immigrants and Established Residents in a Kansas Beefpacking Town." In *Newcomers in the Workplace: Immigrants and the Restructuring of the U.S. Economy*, edited by Louise Lamphere, pp. 25–43. Philadelphia: Temple University Press.

Broadway, Michael J., and Donald D. Stull. 1991. "Rural Industrialization: The Example of Garden City, Kansas." *Kansas Business Review* 14(4):1–9.

Carnes, Richard B. 1984. "Meatpacking and Prepared Meats Industry: Above-Average Productivity Gains." *Monthly Labor Review*, April, pp. 37–42.

Center for Rural Affairs. 1990. *Competition in the Livestock Market, Report of a Task Force.* Walthill, Neb.: Center for Rural Affairs.

Erickson, Ken C. 1994. "Guys in White Hats: Short Term Participant Observation among Beef-Processing Workers and Managers." In *Newcomers in the Workplace: Immigrants and the Restructuring of the U.S. Economy*, edited by Louise Lamphere, pp. 78–98. Philadelphia: Temple University Press.

Fund, Mary, and Elise W. Clement. 1982. *Distribution of Land and Water Ownership in Southwest Kansas.* Whiting: Kansas Rural Center.

Garden City Telegram. 1991. "Three Workers Found Dead at Liberal's National Beef Packing." *Garden City Telegram*, June 10.

Gottesman, Ronald. 1985. "Introduction." In Upton Sinclair, *The Jungle*, pp. vii–xxxii. New York: Penguin.

Green, Hardy. 1990. *On Strike at Hormel: The Struggle for a Democratic Labor Movement.* Philadelphia: Temple University Press.

McGraw, Mike. 1991. "A Case of Very Vested Interest." *Kansas City Star*, December 10.

McGraw, Mike, and Jeff Taylor. 1991. "Deadly Meat: Poor Inspection Exposes Public to Health Risks." *Kansas City Star*, December 10.

Mooney, Rick. 1989. "The Strong Arm of Earth First." *Beef Today* 5(7):12–13.

National Beef Packing Company. n.d. Employee Policy and Procedure Manual. Twenty pp. author's files.

NCA Beef Industry Concentration/Integration Task Force. 1989. *Beef in a Competitive World*. Englewood, Colo.: National Cattlemen's Association.

Personick, Martin E., and Katherine Taylor-Shirley. 1989. "Profiles in Safety and Health: Occupational Hazards of Meatpacking." *Monthly Labor Review*, January, pp. 3–9.

Remy, Dorothy, and Larry Sawers. 1984. "Economic Stagnation and Discrimination." In *My Troubles Are Going to Have Trouble with Me: Everyday Trials and Triumphs of Women Workers*, edited by Karen B. Sacks and Dorothy Remy, pp. 95–112. New Brunswick, N. J.: Rutgers University Press.

Seibert, Gale. 1989. Class Lecture for Meat and Carcass Evaluation, Garden City Community College, January 31.

Sinclair, Upton (first published in 1906) 1985. *The Jungle*. New York: Penguin.

Skaggs, Jimmy M. 1986. *Prime Cut: Livestock Raising and Meatpacking in the United States, 1607–1983*. College Station: Texas A&M University Press.

Slayton, Robert A. 1986. *Back of the Yards: The Making of a Local Democracy*. Chicago: University of Chicago Press.

Stull, Donald D., and Michael J. Broadway. 1990. "The Effects of Restructuring on Beef-packing in Kansas." *Kansas Business Review* 14(1):10–16.

Stull, Donald D., Michael J. Broadway, and Ken C. Erickson. 1992. "The Price of a Good Steak: Beef Packing and Its Consequences for Garden City, Kansas." In *Structuring Diversity: Ethnographic Perspective on the New Immigration*, edited by Louise Lamphere, pp. 35–64. Chicago: University of Chicago Press.

Tabor, Mary B. W. 1991. "Poultry Plant Fire Churns Emotions over Job Both Hated and Appreciated." *New York Times*, September 6.

Thompson, William E. 1983. "Hanging Tongues: A Sociological Encounter with the Assembly Line." *Qualitative Sociology* 6:215–237.

U.S. News & World Report. 1990. "On-the-Job Straining: Repetitive Motion Is the Information Age's Hottest Hazard." *U.S. News & World Report*. May 21, pp. 51, 53.

U. S. Department of Labor, Bureau of Labor Statistics. 1989. *Occupational Injuries and Illnesses in the United States by Industry*. Washington, D. C.: Government Printing Office.

Wood, Charles L. 1980. *The Kansas Beef Industry*. Lawrence: Regents Press of Kansas.

19

Women's Resistance in the Sunbelt

Anglos and Hispanas Respond
to Managerial Control

LOUISE LAMPHERE AND PATRICIA ZAVELLA

Over the last twenty years, the composition of the industrial labor force in the United States has changed as more women have continued to work while having children, and semi-skilled and skilled jobs have been increasingly filled by people of color and immigrant workers, especially women. At the same time, U. S. manufacturing has experienced a radical restructuring, primarily characterized by the decline of heavy industry, the movement of light industry to the South and West as well as to the Third World, and the introduction of Japanese management techniques as a way of shoring up American productivity. In this climate, women were seen as more docile workers than men, and managers deliberately attempted to control women's labor through various strategies and practices. Understanding the conditions under which women consent to or resist managerial control means that we need a more complex analysis of women's position as industrial workers, one that takes account of restructured and relocated industries, the new array of management practices, and the diversity among women workers.

This essay focuses on women's resistance to management control and its relation to ethnic difference in apparel and electronics firms in Albuquerque, NM. These factories were part of "sunbelt industrialization," the building and expansion of manufacturing facilities in the West and South that began in the early 1980s. In Albuquerque, many of these new facilities were enthusiastic innovators in the growth of "participative policies" that were catching on in U. S. firms a decade ago. We examine women's resistance in three plants and illustrate the array of resistance strategies we found. These responses range from individual strategies of resistance at Leslie Pants, an apparel factory with hierarchical management, to collective resistance through a union drive at Health Tech, a plant that makes surgical sutures and has a participative structure, to minimal resistance and a climate of consent at Howard Electronics, a participative plant that manufactures electronic thermostats.

We look at the strategies and tactics for resisting management control that have been developed by both Anglo and Mexican American women.[1] The racial/ethnic composition of the workers is important in these workplaces, for the work force was predominantly Hispana. We argue that women of different racial/ethnic backgrounds had similar work experiences and resistance strategies in particular workplaces, and women's resistance was shaped by management policies, the labor process, and the wage structure rather than racial/ethnic differences per se. In this

period when ethnicity and race are seen as a source of major divisions among workers, it is important to understand when women have common reactions to their
work situations and to build models that illuminate the complexity and variability
in women's perceptions and behavior on the job.

Our project consisted of intensive interviews conducted in 1982 and 1983 with
working mothers and their husbands. In all, we interviewed 53 young mothers
employed in electronics and apparel plants, including 37 Hispanas and 16 Anglos;
of these, 38 were married and 15 were single mothers. We located our interviewees
through a variety of sources: sympathetic plant managers who referred us to the
personnel manager or plant nurse for names of potential interviewees, suggestions
through union officers, contacts through friends or colleagues, and names of other
working mothers through women we had already interviewed. Since we were
unable to get access to plant records and since union membership lists did not indicate if workers were mothers with small children, we relied on a "snowball sample"
based on contacts with both workers and managers. Interviews were conducted sep-
arately with women and their spouses in their homes and involved two long tape
recorded sessions for both the husband and the wife.[2] In writing this essay, we have
used the 31 interviews from three plants (Leslie Pants, Health Tech, and Howard
Electronics) since these represent the range of management systems and worker
strategies we found within the study.

All of the mothers we interviewed had young children under school age, and
most of them had entered the labor force during high school and had continued to
work after marriage. When their children were born, many returned to work after
their six-week maternity leaves expired. These sunbelt mothers were committed to
remaining in the labor force and juggled the demands of work and family lives.

In Albuquerque these industrial workers occupy a relatively privileged place in
the local economy. The electronics and apparel plants studied were built between
1972 and 1982, and they were branch plants of larger multi-national companies.
The work force was not an immigrant one, but consisted primarily of high-school
educated workers. A handful of the women had some vocational training at the
local community college or through the military. Our Hispana informants were
predominantly third-generation born in the United States, whose first language
was English. Within the larger Albuquerque economy, male jobs in construction
and service are much more vulnerable than female jobs. Most of the women were
earning between $5.00 and $6.50 an hour in 1982, but the importance of their paychecks varied depending on the husband's wages and job status. Of the 38 couples
interviewed, 30 (79 percent) were those in which the wives were coproviders or
mainstay providers; that is, they earned almost as much as their husbands or had a
more stable job—one with good benefits that was less likely to be lost during reces-
sionary layoffs.[3]

Building a Framework to Study Resistance
in the Context of Management Policies

Since 1975 the U. S. economy has undergone a structural transformation as many
industrial plants began to close or to move their operations abroad. Women in

these industries, such as apparel, textiles, electrical products, and shoes, have often been faced with layoffs and job loss (Rosen 1987). At the same time, working-class families have become more dependent on female wages, and wives have stayed in the labor force while their children are young, often going back to work after a six-week maternity leave.

Managers have begun to transform the work-place in response to foreign competition, attempting to make U. S. companies more productive. Borrowing management techniques developed in Japan after the U. S. occupation and building on the "Quality of Work Life" (QWL) movement of the 1970s, corporations have turned to various forms of "participative management," instituting quality circles, team structures, and various forms of open-door management.

Following Perkins, Nieva, and Lawler (1983:5–15), we define participative management in terms of the wide range of personnel and management policies that characterize "high-involvement plants." Such firms have a flat organizational structure with few levels between the plant manager and shop-floor workers, a mini-enterprise or teamwork structure, and a strong emphasis on egalitarianism in the way work and leisure areas are designed. There is usually a commitment to employee stability, heavy emphasis on training, pay based on the attainment of "skill levels," and job enrichment whereby workers have some control over the organization of work. Our interviewees came from seven different plants: three with traditional hierarchical management structures and four that were of the high-involvement type. These latter four firms did not have strict assembly lines, allowed workers to rotate jobs, and did not enforce quotas or use piece-rate systems. Often there were equal benefits for blue-collar and white-collar employees, no time clocks or special parking places for management, and a plant-wide work culture designed to build a loyal work force. Two of these plants organized production in teams with facilitators rather than supervisors.

Many, particularly management consultants and business school professors, have been enthusiastic about the potential of participatory management techniques to reform more hierarchical and traditional management structures and to revolutionize the U. S. workplace at all levels (see Peters 1987: 282–896; Ouchi 1981). Others have seen the darker side of the QWL movement, calling line speed up, just-in-time inventory control, and manipulative team meetings a system of "management by stress" (Parker and Slaughter 1988: 16–30).[4]

Robert Howard emphasizes the manipulative aspects of participative management where workers are led to "feel in control," but where power remains with management (Howard 1985: 127–29). Guillermo Grenier expands on this theme and considers the way in which teams are used to "debureaucratize control." While power differences are de-emphasized in company rhetoric, a manager's authority is in fact widened and peer pressure is used to create a compliant work force. "The trick is to make workers feel that their ideas count and their originality is valued while disguising the expansion of managerial prerogatives in the manipulative arena of pop psychology. By depending less on impersonal rules and more on personality characteristics, today's manager effectively de-bureaucratizes the control mechanism of the firm" (Grenier 1988: 131).

In our discussion of women's resistance at Health Tech we take a position similar to Grenier. However, we also want to examine one of several workplaces we studied where resistance did not erupt into a struggle over a union drive, where management participatory policies were less ambitious and global, and where women, on the surface at least, appreciated the positive aspects of nonhierarchical management. Our argument here is not that participatory management has lost its manipulative character, or that managers don't subtly pressure workers to become loyal, but that women pick and choose from among the panoply of management practices, voicing favorable responses especially to those that help mediate the contradictions they face as workers *and* mothers. Indeed, they still may engage in individual tactics and strategies of resistance when it comes to gaining some control over the labor process.

Our approach to resistance owes much to scholars who have analyzed the workplace and work culture. Susan Porter Benson and Barbara Melosh, for example, implicitly include the notion of resistance in their definition of work culture as "the ideology and practice with which workers stake out a relatively autonomous sphere of action on the job." They see work cultures as "a realm of informal, customary values and rules that mediate the formal authority structure of the workplace and distances workers from its impact." They argue that "work culture is created as workers confront the limitations or exploit the possibilities of their jobs. . . . Generated partly in response to specific working conditions, work culture includes both adaptation and resistance to these structural constraints" (Benson 1986).

Following Richard Edwards (1979), we see the labor process and management policies as systems of control. They involve the exercise of power and as such always promote resistance. As Foucault suggests, "There are no relations of power without resistances; the latter are all the more real and effective because they are formed right at the point where relations of power are exercised; resistance to power does not have to come from elsewhere to be real, nor is it inexorably frustrated through being the compatriot of power. It exists all the more by being in the same place as power" (1980, 142). The exercise of power at the point of production also brings about consent, accommodation, quiescence, and approval (see Burawoy 1979; Shapiro-Perl 1979). Resistance can include a number of individualistic tactics, the "everyday resistance" or "weapons of the weak" described by James Scott in his study of Malay Peasants (1985).

In examining resistance on the shop floor, we have used the language of "tactics and strategies" emphasizing the simultaneously positive and reactive nature of resistance. Workers are both attempting to carve out a space where they can control the labor process and resisting management's system of control. It is important to note, as Dorrine Kondo reminds us, that individual actions may simultaneously include resistance and consent. In other words, these strategies may invoke subversion and the attempt to control the production process but simultaneously bind workers more firmly to management's control mechanisms and to compliance with the firm's policies (Kondo 1990: 223–24).

For those researchers who focused on particular workplaces where both white women and women of color were employed, women's tactics and strategies on the job emerged as a central theme. Using individualized strategies, women have resisted the fragmentation of their labor processes (Lamphere 1979; Sacks and Remy 1984) and attempted to gain control and autonomy within particular worksites or in relation to individual employers (Glenn 1986; Rollins 1985; Romero 1992). Some women have struggled to "bring the family to work" so as to "humanize the workplace" (Lamphere 1985, 1987), while others have consented to exploitative conditions in part because of their economic vulnerability and family constraints (Shapiro-Perl 1984).

Other researchers have demonstrated how women of color and white women have engaged in collective resistance, including joining labor organizations in service and clerical settings (Costello 1991; Milkman 1985; Sacks 1984), striking for union recognition in canneries and the garment industry (Ruiz 1987; Coyle, Hershatter, and Honig 1980), or successfully pursuing race and sex discrimination suits in canneries (Zavella 1987, 1988). These collective actions ultimately created significant changes in particular worksites or in large sectors of some industries. Only a few researchers, however, have examined how women of different racial groups in the same worksite engaged in individual or collective resistance (Ruiz 1987; Sacks 1988).

In our study, we seek to situate resistance along a continuum and to recognize that resistance, consent, and unarticulated quiescence form a range of responses to new forms of management practice. Here the women themselves often made contradictory assessments of their work situations. On the one hand, they appreciated management policies that helped them mediate the tensions they experienced being mothers and workers (policies like flex-time) or that promised a more egalitarian workplace ("open door" management). On the other hand, women had a sharp sense of the importance of wresting control over their work from management. These seemingly contradictory responses took various forms depending on the firm's organization of work, its pay system, its management policies, and its work culture. For the women we studied, their positions in the labor process, struggles with their jobs, and particular relationships with supervisors and other management were important in the development of work strategies even more than either provider role or racial/ethnic status.

Individual Tactics in an Apparel Plant

At Leslie Pants, women confronted a system of hierarchical control. Like most apparel plants, Leslie was organized into several lines, where bundles of pants progressed from one sewer to the next. The small parts like pockets and belt loops were assembled first, then the side pockets, fly, belt, and side seams. Each section of the line was supervised by a floor lady and workers were paid on a piece rate. The essence of the piece-rate system is that a worker's wages depend on the level of efficiency she reaches. Efficiency is defined as the number of hip pockets or belt loops sewn in a day to reach a base rate or 100 percent efficiency, which in 1982 was $4.25 an hour. This takes a great deal of hand/eye coordination and an ability to pace oneself throughout the day; a worker must always keep an eye on how many bundles need to be done in order to maintain or increase her level of production.

Individuals developed a set of tactics and strategies for gaining a measure of control over their work.

While these tactics could be seen as a measure of resistance—an attempt to keep from capitulating entirely to management's methods of extracting production from workers—they also ensnare women in the system itself, keeping them working to improve their percentage. As they do so, women are encouraged by the system of rewards held out by management and by the lively work culture created by managers and aimed at building a loyal work force.

The cases of Dolores Baca, a Hispana, and Mary Pike, an Anglo, illustrate the ways that women can be more or less successful in developing tactics and strategies for dealing with the piece-rate system. For both, resistance never became a confrontation with management, but was part of a "mixed consciousness" illuminating the field of contradictory power relations where a sharp sense of how to wrest some control over one's work was placed alongside an appreciation for management incentives, health benefits, profit sharing, and company celebrations.

Dolores Baca, a coprovider, had worked in the plant for eight years. Her husband, Albert, was a grocery-store stocker. Dolores's job at Leslie Pants helped stabilize their marriage. Both she and Albert would have preferred that he provide economic support while she remain at home to care for their infant daughter: "I wish I could stay home and take care of the baby. But we can't afford it, you know. So I got to work and my mother takes care of my baby." Albert agreed: "I really wish that she could stay home, you know, instead of [the baby] having to stay with her grandma." In 1982, Dolores was working on "belt loops," but had been trained to hem pants as well. She was making $5.37 an hour, had recently reached 110 percent, and was trying to maintain a new level of 120 percent so her wages would increase.

Similarly, Mary Pike, an Anglo coprovider, struggled to keep her piece-rate average up to 78 percent on the new job (elastic waistbands) she was assigned after returning from her pregnancy leave. Mary had only been employed for a year and returned six weeks after her baby was born because "I had to go back and start getting the paychecks." Her husband, Don, had lost his high-paying job in the New Mexico oil fields and had been fortunate to find a job at Leslie Pants in another city. But the factory closed and they both transferred to Albuquerque: "When they announced they were closing the plant, I was in tears. Here I was about three months pregnant, losing all the insurance, and both my husband and I were losing jobs. I was really scared. It was a hard blow just to go to Leslie Pants after he'd been working on the oil rig, making $11 an hour, and we had bought this trailer." Mary made $5.11 an hour, and her job at Leslie Pants was crucial for their family survival.

During training or retraining, both women developed tactics to deal with the piece-rate system that pushes workers to produce as quickly as possible while maintaining accuracy; mistakes will be returned for repairs, resulting in lost time and wages. This begins first when a woman is introduced to "the method" or routine for doing a job that is written up in a manual called a "blue book." Dolores had worked out a way to by-pass the method and developed her own "tricks of the trade":

They do expect for you to go by "the method," that's what the instructor is for. To show you the method and how to do it in order to be faster. Sometimes you're doing that, but sometimes you think, "I can do it this other way, and it'll be faster for me." But they do come around and check you to see if you're on your [prescribed] method. Once I see her coming I right away go back to my [prescribed] method, you know. But to me doing it the way where I feel more comfortable and faster at it, I do it that way.[5]

Mary, in contrast, had difficulty mastering her new job of sewing on elastic waistbands. One of her biggest problems was dealing with cutting-room mistakes, in this case "shaded parts." She absorbed the mistakes herself, doing repairs when garments were returned to her. "If they're shaded, the parts, like say the bands are dark brown and the pants are a little beige or something, if you sew it on, you get it back. You get pretty quick at ripping out too. But it does take a long time to make repairs on the operation." Dolores, facing a similar problem, used the strategy of going to her supervisor: "Like now we've been having problems with our loops. They've been like overlapped. And we've been having trouble with that because they're too fat on the bottom and we can't fold them and they don't look right like that, you know, [so we] throw them away. So we've been having problems with that, but we do go straight to our supervisor or line manager." Here the supervisor was crucial in getting new loops, so that Dolores and other workers on the same operation would not lose pay. Dolores's tactics, which included devising her own method and getting help from her supervisor, allowed her to successfully maintain her piece-rate average, while Mary, trying to cope with some of the same problems, used similar individual strategies but was struggling rather than succeeding.

Dolores was typical of several women we interviewed who were experienced workers, employed at Leslie Pants between three and nine years. They were in jobs they knew well and were not struggling with work difficulties. Mary was one of several workers who were having problems. These women tended to be relatively new workers being retrained on a new job while they were simultaneously experiencing machine difficulties or trouble with cutting-room mistakes. The piece-rate system could potentially produce competition among workers where it is difficult to even meet the piece rates (Lamphere 1987), yet that did not seem to happen here. Instead, many women expressed an individualized ideology that "how much you earn is really up to you." Mary, for example, did not emphasize competition among workers, but acknowledged that cutting-room mistakes or machine problems got in the way of producing more quickly.

The piece-rate system acts almost automatically to extract labor from workers as they push each day to increase their pay. At Leslie Pants, management buttressed the piece rate with a system of rewards and incentives, which included good benefits. Each trainee or retrainee graduated from the program when she reached 100 percent efficiency, but further recognition was given to those who reached 110 percent and 120 percent. Graduations were held on Thursdays, and those being recognized were presented with a diploma and were given a soft drink or coffee and brownies during the morning break. As Dolores Baca described the system,

"First they give you little flags, and then with 100 percent you get a pin that says Leslie Pants and then you get a flag that says 100 percent [which goes above the worker's machine]. And then your 110, you get another pin and your flag for 110." Dolores, who had just received her pin for reaching 100 percent on belt loops, said that the recognition made her feel "proud, happy, 'cause you're working so hard 'cause, you know, you want to make money see. And you feel happy that you have already made it, and you know you can make it every day, and you can make some money, you know."

When a worker maintained 130 percent for 7 weeks, she joined the President's Club. An 8 x 10 color photo of each member was posted on the wall in the front entryway to the shop floor. Members were taken out to lunch yearly by the plant manager and thanked for their effort on behalf of the plant. Dolores, as well as other interviewees, was positive about the President's Club: "I like it but you got to work, you got to work hard to get into it." Some women, like Tony Sena, emphasized how difficult it was to maintain high levels of production because of daily layoffs during the recession or disruptions in the production process. Tony was trying to achieve 110 percent on hang pockets but had difficulty accruing the 32 hours per week for 2 weeks necessary to get the award, since she had been sent home early several days a week due to a reduced number of orders. Nevertheless, reactions to the reward system were positive and some interviewees showed us their certificates and pins. Unlike the Rhode Island apparel plant studied by Lamphere (1987), at Leslie there was no sense that the system was an unnecessary embarrassment that merely showcased management's goals. Instead, workers felt that the plant really depended on the 130 percent workers to keep production up.

In some apparel plants the piece-rate system combined with strong supervisory control can create worker competition or disgruntlement with supervisors (Lamphere 1987). At Leslie Pants preventing this divisiveness was crucial to management, which sought to "keep up the morale" through the creation of a strong plant-wide work culture. This included sponsorship of nonwork activities that ranged from picnics to raffles, and included contests at Halloween and Christmas. By co-opting workers' organizational skills and cultivating worker participation in plant activities, the firm prevented the possibility of a strong women's work culture of resistance. The plant manager was quite clear about this when he noted, "If a manager takes care of his people, then there are no problems." Otherwise one might "tap out" the available labor pool or encourage unionization.

Management was very successful in creating a labor force that contained a number of high producers (members of the President's Club). On the whole, tactics or strategies to control their own labor remained at an individual level, between a woman, her work, her machine, and her supervisor. The lack of a strong set of resistance strategies at a collective level was due to management's ability to make the piece-rate system more palatable through nonmonetary rewards like membership in the President's Club and monetary incentives like good benefits and a profit-sharing plan. Morale and loyalty were further encouraged through a wide range of company-sponsored picnics, raffles, and other forms of entertainment. Resistance did not go very far and co-optation was more characteristic as women came to see their goals as consonant with those of the company.

Participatory Management, Teams, and a Union Drive

Our second example is Health Tech, the firm that in 1982 represented the most participatory of the plants we studied and, at the same time, the plant that generated the most conflict over the nature of participative management. Health Tech produced surgical sutures, and most workers were engaged in swaging (pronounced "swedging"), attaching surgical thread to curved needles and winding the thread to ready it for packaging. During the course of our interviews, the company was the site of a union drive. The drive met with a great deal of company resistance, and in May 1983, the union was defeated in an election by a two-to-one margin.

We focus on the experiences of three women: Lucille Sanchez, an anti-union activist and Hispana mother of three; Bonnie Anderson, an Anglo mother of three who was a union supporter; and Annette Griego, a Hispana single parent and strong union supporter. We use these three cases to show how a woman's place in the production process, her relationship with "facilitators," and her family situation influenced her participation in the union drive as a form of resistance. In addition, we draw attention to the process of the drive itself and the dialectical relationship that evolved as workers responded to management tactics and vice versa.[6]

Coprovider Lucille Sanchez's husband was a truck driver for a local beverage company who earned slightly more than her hourly wage. She believed that her job paid well and had good security, which was very important to her. She first stated, "I like everything about that job." Then she recalled that she did not like the rotating shifts. "[My husband] doesn't like me to work, but he knows that I have to. If it was up to him, he'd rather have me home, especially since we had the last baby." She agreed with her husband that it would be better if she remained at home, taking care of their three children, but she continued working mainly for economic reasons.

Unlike Lucille, Bonnie Anderson was a mainstay provider. Her husband had been laid off for eight months in 1982 as a cement truck driver because of the recession in the construction industry. Bonnie's wages and benefits were the main source of support for her spouse and three sons. She worked at Health Tech as a swager, using a machine to attach surgical thread to curved needles. She enjoyed her job because of good coworkers and the challenge of beating the clock, but did not like that when her machine broke down it was counted against her. She characterized her job as having relatively good job security, but it did not have good pay, and the possibilities for promotion were difficult since whether "they liked me" would play a big role in getting a better job. She was strongly committed to working, "It was hard for me to give it up," but also believed that "if [a woman] has got kids, I think it's important for her to stay home, if she enjoys it. [But] sometimes you can stay home with your kids and not be a good mother. But I think your kids are important." Her husband "always backed me, whatever I wanted to do, he would back me. If I wanted to work, fine, if I didn't that was okay too." Once he got laid off, however, her job became crucial for family support.

Annette Griego, a young widow was a sole provider for herself and her son, although she shared household expenses with her sister and sister's boyfriend. She had became pregnant at 16, married her son's father, and then began living with her divorced mother after her own marital separation and then her husband's suicide. Annette began living with her sister soon after the birth of her son in 1978 and started working at Health Tech in 1981.

At the time of our interview, Annette was part of a committee that had just passed out a union leaflet and come "above ground," which caused a lot of tension at work. Her facilitator quit holding team meetings because they were talking about pro-union issues. Annette was strongly committed to her job. She liked her coworkers and the fact that "management isn't always on your back . . . 'cause we don't let them get on our back," indicating a strong sense of collective resistance. She did not like the fact that workers were pressured to work fast (in order to attain 110 percent efficiency), yet if they made their quota or even went over, there was no reward. "I don't like that about the job—you can work your hardest and do twice as much as the person next to you and you can be getting the same pay." She appreciated the good benefits, that the plant was in a convenient location for her commute to work, and that the company allowed workers to make up missed work. The disadvantages of the job were the low pay, the pressure to work faster, and the management's attempts to get workers to produce more than at their other plants, which were unionized: "As it is, our [production] numbers are too high. They're comparing us to the other plant. But you backtrack and say if we compare them to the other plant, they are making 40–50 percent more. They only have to make 67 percent and then after that it's all bonus and incentive. Not only that, they have down time—anytime you're not swaging, you get down time. We don't get that."

Annette also had a difficult time coping with Health Tech's policy of rotating shifts—alternating between working first and second shifts every two weeks. Annette's sister also alternated three shifts as manager of a fast-food place. Annette divided child care with her live-in sister and her mother (who lived 20 miles from Albuquerque) and had a complicated system that sometimes meant that her son spent the night at his grandmother's home. Characterizing this arrangement, she said, "Sometimes things get kind of hectic."

The "team concept" at Health Tech entailed a massive restructuring of management/worker relations. Each team had a "facilitator"—not a supervisor or "boss"—who meted out rewards and punishments, but rather someone who focused on the interpersonal relationships within a team. In addition, the hiring prerogatives of management were shared with the team. Two team members interviewed prospective employees and if the evaluation was negative, the person usually was not hired. Teams were also involved in evaluation for raises and even firing. Team meetings were supposed to be occasions when team members could discuss ways to help each other meet the production targets of reaching 100 percent efficiency at the end of a 12- or 18-month period.

There was, however, a contradiction between management's participative ideology and its practice. It was this contradiction that brought about the union drive. Workers in Channel and Drill Swaging (who were attaching surgical needles to thread) had difficulty meeting the weekly efficiency levels as they were being trained. They were working on machines that had come from another plant and often broke down. They were penalized for "down time" and couldn't "keep their numbers up." Team meetings for those under several of the facilitators became "just one big tattletale session." As Bonnie, one of the first workers hired in the new plant and assigned to Channel Swaging (Team A), explained, the facilitator "was always on us about numbers. It was always his job if our numbers didn't come up. And why did we do so poorly that week. We'd have to go around the table [to explain why their numbers reached only 67 percent rather than 80 percent efficiency, for example]. I hated that. It was so embarrassing. It really was." Bonnie also found it difficult to participate in the firing of a teammate, for example, someone who was "a good worker and a good person" but whose numbers "weren't there" because he had some trouble with his machine.

The problem for Annette was that she was having machine difficulties and her numbers were low: "When they first started using gut in channel swaging, I was the first one to work with it. I had to learn. The facilitator had me trying different dyes to find out which dyes the needles worked best with and stuff like that. So my numbers dropped then too." These difficulties were probably related to Annette's view that as long as they were working under a learning curve, with higher rates expected as their training progressed, they should have been paid on a piece rate or bonus system. She also felt the numbers were too high: "They are always comparing us to the other plant. But their swagers have been there an average of 15–20 years, and we've only been swaging a year or a year and a half."

Lucille's difficulties didn't occur in the beginning, but only when she needed to maintain 100 percent efficiency during her "demonstration period" of 13 weeks. She learned both the drill swaging technique and how to wind the sutures quickly; she was asked to train new employees in the drill department in March. She continued training until December 1981 and then began a period of 13 weeks of "demonstration" in winding. "Well, in the winding department it took several weeks and I was performing like at 97 or 98 percent. I couldn't get over that 98 or 99 hump. My last week in demonstration is when I went on a daily basis to 117, 124 and that averaged out to make up for the other weeks when I hadn't made the 100 percent. So, I took a big step without realizing what position I was putting myself into, and then not only that, I was the first person to demonstrate. That made the pressure more severe. You know, there was lots of people behind you and lots of people against you. It was really hard." Lucille felt that other team members were not supportive and that she was not given credit and praise for finishing her demonstration (and getting a raise). However, this did not dampen her overall enthusiasm for her job; she gave her work top ratings on all aspects from pay to supervisor and job security.

Women responded to the labor process and pay system in Channel and Drill differently. Many, especially in the more demanding Channel Department, developed tactics to deal with the pressures of producing, but also came to feel that the numbers were too high, that it would be difficult to go through demonstration, and even that a piece-rate system that would reward faster production would be more fair. Women in Drill, like Lucille, had less difficulty learning the drill-swaging technique, but most felt pressure to work harder to attain 100 percent efficiency, working quickly, while avoiding defects.

Within a year of when the plant opened, workers like Bonnie and Annette in the Channel and Drill swaging teams had come to feel that workers were unfairly treated and that the team concept was not really "participation." They had begun to see through company ideology and feel that their participation was really only on the surface and under the control of management. They formed an organizing committee and contacted Amalgamated Clothing and Textile Workers Union with the goal of forming a union.

Management's response was twofold. At the level of tactics, they imposed sanctions on union activists, divided them from other workers, and prevented new workers from voting for the union. In terms of ideology, management used notions of participation and democracy to discredit unionism. They argued that a union would interfere with the effort to get everyone to participate and the company would "lose flexibility" in implementing the high-involvement design. One company document stated, "We give everyone a chance to represent themselves without a 'third party' such as a union."

Management responded swiftly to the campaign. Team meetings became the arena in which the facilitator could mold anti-union opinions, often calling on those who had already taken an anti-union stance to pressure their peers. For example, one facilitator at a team meeting provoked an anti-union discussion of the Coors strike in Colorado, using comments from a female personnel administrator whom he had invited to a meeting to voice pro-company sentiments. Lucille, a member of his team, became a vocal supporter of the company and helped organize an anti-union committee. At team meetings she was always available to chime in with her anti-union opinions. In another team, this same facilitator effectively isolated one of the pro-union women and turned others against her. He allowed and even encouraged her best friend to demand this woman's resignation from the newly formed Compensation Committee since she was "untrustworthy" and unable to represent her coworkers' opinions because she was a union activist. At a larger meeting later that week, he asked her to stand up and be identified, further embarrassing her and separating her out as a "trouble-maker." She felt she was "being harassed for her political opinion" and eventually resigned.

About four months after the campaign started, the management planned two firings and then later fired two other women—all members of the union organizing committee. The firings created a climate of fear that the union was never really able to overcome, even though activists filed unfair labor practice grievances for these firings and for another firing that took place at a later date. Facilitators carefully screened new employees and hired only anti-union recruits. They continued to isolate union supporters, breaking up conversations between activists and other workers and branding union supporters as "losers" and pro-company workers as "winners."

During the last two months of the campaign, management stepped up its efforts, sending anti-union memos home in paychecks, showing anti-union films, initiating a Union Strike Contest, asking employees to guess how many strikes the union had engaged in between 1975 and 1983, and pushing their campaign motto, "Be a Winner! Vote No." In such a climate, it is not surprising that the union lost, getting only 71 votes, while 141 employees voted against the union.

While men in the plant were evenly divided on the union issue (22 for and 23 against), women voted against the union 72 percent to 29 percent. Furthermore, only 24 percent of the Hispanas voted for the union while 40 percent of the non–Mexican American women (Anglos, Blacks, and Asian Americans, about 10 altogether) did so. Many Hispanas and several Anglos and Black women who had earlier been supportive of the union backed away during the last few months of the campaign. For example, 37 Hispanas and 7 Anglo and Black women had signed a petition sponsored by the union asking the company to investigate a bad smell that was pervading the plant; later they did not vote for the union. Had they continued to support the union, the union would have won.

While the gap between a participative philosophy and company practice along with difficulties at the point of production fostered the union drive, company tactics created a climate of fear, making the company rhetoric about the team concept and not needing a "third party" seem a safer avenue. For many women, this was the best job they had ever had, and it was too important to risk.

Participative Management and Making Thermostats

At other plants in Albuquerque, managers have been able to implement participative management in ways that pushed the contradictions between management ideology and shop floor practice in a different direction. Women in these plants did not break open the contradiction revealing the gaps between "participation" and the power exercised by management. Instead women held in tension their critique of the demands placed on them and their sense of management's willingness to incorporate worker views on the production process and thus downplay the hierarchy of decision making. Interviewees appreciated the open-door policy, job rotation, and a chance to talk with the plant manager over coffee and vote on plant-wide holiday schedules. Howard Electronics, which produced electronic thermostats, is an example of this kind of plant. By 1991, the plant had developed a team structure that went even further than the one at Health Tech. Rather than having two assembly lines, the plant now has a number of teams, one for each part of the assembly process. The teams have a facilitator and meet weekly as they do at Health Tech; however, in addition, members of each team are "crosstrained" on all the jobs for which the team is responsible. Most importantly, the teams manage their own budgets, keep track of production, and conduct their own quality control. Teams have replaced supervisors and indeed many of the middle-level management positions at the plant.

Anita Alvarez was an electronics assembler at Howard in 1982. She had had electronics training and had previously worked at two other electronics factories. When her husband became unemployed, she applied at Howard and for a while was a mainstay provider. At the time of our interview, her husband worked as a custodian and she was a coprovider. She characterized her job as having good pay and job security, but found opportunities for promotions "pretty hard [to get]."

In 1982, women reported on the ways in which management incorporated their views and flexibly enforced quotas or absence regulations. Anita, who had faced an unrealistic quota of testing 200 Liquid Crystal Displays an hour, talked to her supervisor, who told her, "That's all right, you just do the work, and if you can't put it out, you can't. " It was not surprising that she felt, "The advantage is probably that I can say whatever I feel like, and they'll listen to me. If I have changes I want to make, I'll go up there and I'll say it and they'll listen. . . . [The firm is] like one big family."

Linda Henry, an Anglo single parent and sole provider, worked at Howard Electronics as an assembly operator, inserting electronic components on the printed circuit board on the thermostat. She had worked previously for 14 years as a dental assistant, but left because the benefits were much better at Howard Electronics. To Linda, the most important aspects of a job were good pay, job security, and opportunities for promotion. She was satisfied with her pay and job security, but worried that she would not be able to advance because "it's hard without the basic training." She was committed to her job because "for the position I'm in [as a single parent] with my two little children, I need the job security and I need the good pay. And I mainly need the free benefits which we have."

Linda delivered a cogent critique of the way in which management had raised the rates on stuffing boards four times over the previous year, thus making it impossible to earn any incentive pay. Instead of being resentful, she emphasized the plant's participative policies. "They made it a point to come out and talk to you every day, and they made it a point to see how you like it and if you were happy. . . . They didn't segregate you like say, they were the office and you were the factory."

Both women emphasized their supervisors' efforts to create a friendly and egalitarian atmosphere. As Anita said, "You don't find very many supervisors that come and sit down and eat lunch with you and act like [they're] not even a supervisor, you know." Even those we interviewed who were more critical of the plant emphasized the job security, and the good pay and benefits the plant offered.

For English-speaking Hispanas and Anglos who are products of the U. S. public school system, participative management draws upon a series of notions inherent in U. S. cultural descriptions of the self in a democratic society. Pamphlets written by each Howard team for visitors who tour the plant stress self-sufficiency, responsibility, "team spirit," competition (for awards like "Team of the Week" and "Team of the Month") as well as quality. The ideology of participation and management's "listening to what I have to say" both evoke a sense of democracy and egalitarianism.[7]

In work places like Howard, women come to see themselves as "individuals," "team members," and employees who have "ownership of quality," not as women who are being pushed to higher and higher levels of production. In a political economy like Albuquerque's where there are few good jobs for women, this is a powerful and highly seductive system. Some of these jobs may disappear due to plant buyouts, a decline in military spending, and future recessions in the electronics industry, but the few women who hold remaining jobs will continue to appreciate the advantages of working in "new participatory plants."

Conclusion

Mexican American and Anglo women had similar reasons for entering the labor force, and they worked in comparable positions regardless of their ethnicity. All of these women were in the lowest but most numerous positions in each plant, working as sewing operators and electronics assemblers. While the majority of the labor force was Hispana, they were raised and educated in the United States, much like their Anglo counterparts, they had similar job training, and they worked in departments that were not segregated by ethnicity or race. Thus all the women experienced the features of their jobs—whether the wages and benefits were good, whether there was job security or possibilities for promotions—in similar terms.

Moreover, there was no neat relationship between a woman's provider role and her resistance to managerial control. One might expect that those women in the most dire economic circumstances, the sole and mainstay providers, would be the most conservative and would avoid "rocking the boat" while at work. Instead we found that some of the most vulnerable of our interviewees, like single parent Annette Griego at Health Tech and mainstay provider Bonnie Anderson, were the most militant. In contrast to other single parents in their firm and to most of the Hispana married women—who could rely on their spouses' wages—Annette and Bonnie withstood management's harassment and actively supported the union. Anglo and Hispana women alike (including coprovider Lucille Sanchez) voted against the union. Both of the married interviewees at Leslie Pants, one a Hispana coprovider and one an Anglo mainstay provider, felt ambivalent about their work, but both worked hard to try to increase their wages through partially accepting the company's piece rate and reward culture. And at Howard Electronics, where participative management had been successfully introduced, where management allowed employees some say over the speed of their work, and where the workers were treated with respect, both Hispana coprovider Anita and Anglo single parent Linda were relatively satisfied with their jobs, although they realized there were few opportunities for advancement.

Resistance developed very differently in each of these three settings. At Leslie Pants, the hierarchical apparel plant, tactics and strategies to control one's work remained at the individual level, as women carved out their own approach to the piece-rate system while accepting and becoming part of management's overall reward structure and plant-wide work culture. In contrast, at Health Tech, which operated through a similar set of learning curves but without piece-rates, workers forged similar individual tactics but also came to resist at a group level the firm's new participative structure and ideology. And finally, at Howard, a more flexible production process with participative management features again kept tactics to an individual level while pulling women into a system that drew successfully on U. S. cultural notions of participation, self-sufficiency, and egalitarianism.

We have shown that women's work in each of these factories posed different constraints, depending on a woman's place in the production process, management's attempts to create a firm work culture, and management's degrees of success in creating conditions in which women could gain some control over their labor. While all of these women were confined to "women's jobs," each originally sought work in the factories because they were regarded as having good jobs, and each strategized in her everyday work to make the most of the opportunities provided. In this sense, Hispanas and Anglos had more similar experiences of work in sunbelt factories than they had differences on the job.

Acknowledgments

Pat Zavella would like to thank Barbara Laurence and especially Melissa Hemler for their technical assistance above and beyond.

Notes

1. We use Mexican American and Hispana interchangeably. For a discussion of ethnic identity among our sample see Lamphere et al. 1993; Zavella 1993.

2. Lamphere interviewed Anglo women, while Patricia Zavella and Jennifer Martinez interviewed Hispanas. Anglo husbands were interviewed by Felipe Gonzáles and Victor Mancha, while Gary Lemons talked with Anglo husbands.

3. In our sample, 11 Hispano and 8 Anglo couples were coproviders, 7 Hispano and 4 couples were mainstay providers, and 15 women were sole providers. Eight couples (7 Hispano and 1 Anglo) were secondary providers, but none of them are discussed here. The term "secondary provider" is derived from Hood (1983) to indicate that women's contribution to family income is significantly less (usually at least 30 percent) than their spouses' income. We do not wish to imply that the women's wages were "pin money" or not important.

4. Others, particularly Rehder and Smith (1986) and Brown and Reich (1989), have been much more positive about the New United Motor Manufacturing Co, Inc. (NUMMI) plant, playing down issues of line speed and stress, and emphasizing increased worker involvement (including the active presence of the union) and productivity.

5. As Jennie Garcia, an interviewee who had been an instructor for four years, noted, not all instructors insist that their trainees follow the "blue book." "But if you see that somebody's making their goal and is producing more . . . why do anything?"

6. See Lamphere and Grenier (1988) for a more detailed explanation of why the union drive failed.

7. In 1992, Leslie Pants broke with tradition in the apparel industry and converted its assembly line organization to a team structure. Each team of 36 operators is organized into mini-teams of four to eight workers who each learn two or three operations and help one another maintain quality control. Management pays a flat hourly rate of $7.30 an hour, plus a bonus of 30 cents an hour if the team produces fewer than 2.9 flaws in every 100 pairs of pants. The company instituted the new system to improve quality and boost worker morale. Perhaps Leslie Pants will be able to follow Howard Electronics in the successful implementation of a participative management style.

Works Cited

Benson, Susan Porter. 1986. *Counter Cultures: Saleswomen, Managers, and Customers in American Department Stores, 1890–1940.* Urbana: University of Illinois Press.

Brown, Clair, and Michael Reich. 1989. When Does Union-Management Cooperation Work? A look at NUMMI and GM–Van Nuys. *California Management Review.* 31(4): 26–44 (Summer 1989).

Burawoy, Michael. 1979. *Manufacturing Consent: Changes in the Labor Process under Monopoly Capitalism*. Chicago: University of Chicago Press.

Costello, Cynthia B. 1991. *We're Worth It!: Women and Collective Action in the Insurance Work Place*. Urbana: University of Illinois Press.

Coyle, Laurie, Gail Hershatter, and Emily Honig. 1980. Women at Farah: An Unfinished Story. In *Mexican Women in the United States: Struggles Past and Present*. Ed. M. Mora and A. del Castillo. Los Angeles: University of California, Chicano Studies Research Center, 117–144.

Edwards, Richard. 1979. *Contested Terrain: The Transformation of the Workplace in the Twentieth Century*. New York: Basic Books.

Foucault, Michel. 1980. *Power/Knowledge: Selected Interviews and Other Writings*. New York: Pantheon Books.

Glenn, Evelyn Nakano. 1986. *Issei, Nissei, War Bride: Three Generations of Japanese American Women in Domestic Service*. Philadelphia: Temple University Press.

Grenier, Guillermo J. 1988. *Inhuman Relations: Quality Circles and Anti-Unionism in American Industry*. Philadelphia: Temple University Press.

Hood, Jane. 1983. *Becoming a Two-Job Family: Role Bargaining in Dual Worker Households*. New York: Praeger.

Howard, Robert. 1985. *Brave New Workplace*. New York: Penguin Books

Kondo, Dorinne K. 1990. *Crafting Selves: Power, Gender, and Discourses of Identity in a Japanese Workplace*. Chicago: University of Chicago Press.

Lamphere, Louise. 1979. Fighting the Piece Rate System: New Dimensions of an Old Struggle in the Apparel Industry. In *Case Studies in the Labor Process*. Ed. A. Zimbalist. New York: Monthly Review Press, 257–276; 8.

———. 1985. Bringing the Family to Work: Women's Culture on the Shop Floor. *Feminist Studies* 11(3):519–40.

———. 1987. *From Working Daughters to Working Mothers: Immigrant Women in a New England Industrial Community*. Ithaca: Cornell University Press.

Lamphere, Louise, and Guillermo Greiner. 1988. Women, Unions, and "Participative Management": Organizing in the Sunbelt. In *Women and the Politics of Empowerment*. Ed. Ann Bookman and Sandra Morgan, 227–56. Philadelphia: Temple University Press.

Lamphere, Louise, Patricia Zavella, Felipe Gonzáles, and Peter B. Evans. 1993. *Sunbelt Working Mothers: Reconciling Family and Factory*. Ithaca: Cornell University Press.

Milkman, Ruth, ed. 1985. *Women, Work, and Protest: A Century of U. S. Women's Labor History*. Boston: Routledge and Kegan Paul.

Ouchi, William G. 1981. *Theory Z: How American Business Can Meet the Japanese Challenge*. Boston: Addison-Wesley.

Parker, Mike, and Jane Slaughter. 1988. *Choosing Sides: Unions and the Team Concept*. Boston: South End Press.

Perkins, Dennis N. T., Veronica Nieva, and Edward Lawler. 1983. *Managing Creation: The Challenge of Building a New Organization*. New York: Wiley.

Peters, Tom. 1987. *Thriving on Chaos: Handbook for a Management Revolution*. New York: Alfred A. Knopf.

Rehder, Robert R., and Marta Medaris Smith. 1986. Kaizen and the Art of Labor Relations. *New Management* (October).

Rollins, Judith. 1985. *Between Women: Domestics and Their Employers*. Philadelphia: Temple University Press.

Romero, Mary. 1992. *Maid in the U.S.A.* New York: Routledge.

Rosen, Ellen Israel. 1987. *Bitter Choices: Blue-Collar Women in and out of Work*. Chicago: University of Chicago Press.

Ruiz, Vicki L. 1987. *Cannery Women, Cannery Lives: Mexican Women, Unionization and the California Food Processing Industry, 1930–1950*. Albuquerque: University of New Mexico Press.

Sacks, Karen Brodkin. 1984. Computers, Ward Secretaries, and a Walkout in a Southern Hospital. In *My Troubles Are Going to Have Trouble with Me: Everyday Trials and Triumphs of Women Workers*. Ed. K. Sacks and D. Remy. New Brunswick: Rutgers University Press, 173–192.

———. 1988. *Caring by the Hour: Women, Work, and Organizing at Duke Medical Center*. Urbana: University of Illinois Press.

Sacks, Karen Brodkin, and Dorothy Remy, eds. 1984. *My Troubles Are Going to Have Trouble with Me: Everyday Trials and Triumphs of Women Workers*. New Brunswick: Rutgers University Press.

Scott, James C. 1985. *Weapons of the Weak: The Everyday Forms of Peasant Resistance*. New Haven: Yale University Press.

Shapiro-Perl, Nina. 1979. Labor Process and Class Relations in the Costume Jewelry Industry: A Study in Women's Work. Ph. D. diss., Department of Anthropology, University of Connecticut, Storrs.

———. 1984. Resistance Strategies: The Routine Struggle for Bread and Roses. In *My Troubles Are Going to Have Trouble with Me: Everyday Trials and Triumphs of Women Workers*. Ed. K. Sacks and D. Remy. New Brunswick: Rutgers University Press, 193–208.

Zavella, Patricia. 1987. *Women's Work and Chicano Families: Cannery Workers of the Santa Clara Valley*. Ithaca: Cornell University Press.

———. 1988. The Politics of Race and Gender: Organizing Chicana Cannery Workers in Northern California. In *Women and the Politics of Empowerment*. Ed. A. Bookman and S. Morgen. Philadelphia: Temple University Press, 202–224.

———. 1993. Feminist Insider Dilemmas: Constructing Identity with Chicana Informants. *Frontiers, a Journal of Women's Studies* 13(3):53–76.

Spirits of Resistance

20

AIHWA ONG

This article focuses on the off-stage voices of factory women, the self-perceptions which have emerged, partly in reaction to the external caricatures of their status, but mainly out of their own felt experiences as wage workers in changing Malay society. I have argued elsewhere that in a society undergoing capitalist transformation, it is necessary not only to decipher the dominant gender motifs which have become the symbols of relations of domination and subordination, but also to discover, in everyday choices and practices, how ordinary women and men live and refashion their own images and culture. Disparate statements, new gestures, and untypical episodes will be used to demonstrate how concepts of gender and sexuality became transmuted through the new experiences of the emergent Malay working class.

The contradictory experiences of Malay factory women indicate that we need to reformulate the relationships among class, resistance, and consciousness. Frederick Engels rather hastily asserted that the first condition for the liberation of women from their oppressed status was to bring the whole female sex into public industry (1972: 137–38).

The first condition of women's induction into industry was subjection to increased external control. This is not to deny that wage employment has also had gradual, corrosive effects on the extraeconomic relationships which continued to bind workers to their families and community. In Telok, it was the particular insertion of Japanese industrial organization into the *kampung* milieu which has preserved female compliance with male authority and slowed individuation from the fabric of rural society. Ronald Dore has remarked elsewhere that the Japanese factory system "enhances enterprise consciousness; it also . . . does less to develop individualism" (1973: 215). Of course, extrafactory influences can undo corporate restraints of self-expression.

For the village adolescent girl working in a Japanese factory, her meager earnings became a means to venture further afield, to explore and acquire a shifting, partial view of the widening social universe. New relationships, ideas, and images imparted a fresh self-consciousness and promptings to greater individual determination in thought and behavior. Assertion of individual versus family interests has its source in a new subjectivity constituted as much by educational practice, state agencies, and the media as by the labor process. In the factories, consciousness of mistreatment *as human beings (manusia)* by particular foremen or the management *(majikan)* was partial and discontinuous; there was no coherent articulation of exploitation in class or even feminist terms. At the most, one may say that the following instances of individualistic conduct, acts of defiance, and violent incidents were scattered tactics to define and protect one's moral status; as such they confronted the dehumanizing aspects embedded within capitalist relations of production. At issue is not a conscious attack on commodity relations but rather the self-constitution of a new identity rooted in human dignity.

A New Subjectivity

In Sungai Jawa, the most acceptable form of self-assertion among factory women was their control of savings, i.e., after family contributions had been deducted from their wages. Out of the 35 workers I interviewed at length, two-thirds came from families with five to nine siblings still at home. By routinely contributing half or more of their monthly wage packet, these working daughters gained a measure of self-esteem which made the low wages somewhat more tolerable. One young woman gave a practical assessment of her economic situation.

> Factory workers regard the work they hold not to be of high rank. But although factory work is low status, they help their families if they can. So they feel a little satisfaction—but not much.

Another woman worked out the family budget in which she and her brother paid for vegetables and other foodstuffs while their father bought the rice. She said that such an arrangement could be "considered fair" *(jadi kira adillah juga)*.

Yet another operator chafed at her low wages and complained that her co-workers did not have the proper perspective with which to compare their earnings or situation with conditions in urban-based factories. She commented:

> (T)he workers, they cannot differentiate between the section in which they work and other divisions. Thus, the party above [i.e., the management] likes their ignorance and they work as if they are imprisoned *(kena kongkong)*. As we Malays say, "like a frog beneath the coconut shell," they don't know about other things.

A few factory women were concerned not with looking for better conditions in factory work but viewed their wages as a means to improve their technical qualifications in order to compete for better jobs. Seventy percent of the interviewed workers had Form Three to Form Six certificates; one-third were using a portion of their factory earnings to pay for typing or academic classes which they attended after the factory shift. These classes were based in urban institutions, usually in Klang, and the commuting involved additional expenses. Most of the operators aspired to permanent careers in government service, stating that they would not stop work even if they got married and had children, because civil employment was well-paid and secure. Some factory workers had voiced interest in becoming policewomen, and one, in becoming a nightclub singer or firefighter.

For most adolescent girls in the *kampung*, looking for a steady job has become the rule once they left or dropped out of school. Earlier generations of young women had fewer years of schooling, married in their teens, and only worked intermittently for wages in village smallholdings or estates. With the introduction of mass education, better communications, and establishment of the factories, village girls wanted to seek their own employment and earn their own income of their own accord and not just under family pressure. For instance, an 18-year-old woman from the rice district of Sabak Bernam had left a large family of girls to stay with her married sister in Sungai Jawa in order to work in the FTZ. When asked why the public looked askance at outstation factory women, she answered:

> Maybe village people regard female workers as less than sweet *(kurang manis)* because a nice woman in their view stays in the house. But because in this era women and men are of the same status *(sama taraf)* then we also want to seek experiences like men, in earning a living, looking for a job. . . .

Seeking work for their own economic interest also meant facing the uncertainty of their market situation, compared to the relative security of peasant families who could make a living off their own land. When asked whether her economic situation could be considered better than her parents', a factory woman replied:

> I feel that [comparing] myself with my parents, their work situation is better. Since I work in the private sector, the management at whatever time . . . . can throw me out *(bolih membuangkan saya)* . . . but in their work, my parents are self-employed and there is no one who can prevent them [from working].

Another woman noted, however, that it was nevertheless preferable that there was factory employment for women, since it was increasingly difficult for men to find work in the *kampung*. Although rural women sought in factory employment a source of independent wealth, in practice, their low wages, the unavoidable claims of their families, and insecurity of employment did not provide a sufficient basis for economic independence.

For the majority of factory women then, their modest savings were employed as a means of compensation for hard work, low wages, and family support. Shopping expeditions after payday, when *kampung* women go into town, were consumption activities to make up for long hours lost to the factory. "Leisure" became detached from "work" as the rhythm of their lives changed. A village woman described her joyful splurge in town.

> After getting my wage I straight away go to Klang to *jolli jolli*. I go to the movies and walk around. I buy knickknacks for the house, and sometimes I buy clothes.

"Making jolly with money" *(jolli duit)* was also part of the overall attempt by some rural women to change their status from ascribed *(kampung)* to attributional. In their excursions into towns and farther places, young village women were exposed to an alternative status system based on the attributes of an urban-based, Westernized culture. Some working women demonstrated this alternative status largely defined by consumption and "presentation of self" (Goffman 1959). They went into town in their Malay *baju kurong* and returned in mini-skirts or tight T-shirts and jeans. Whereas in the recent past the painted face was a mark of prostitution, regular visits by "Avon ladies" to even remote villages have increased *kampung* cosmetic sales fourfold in two years.[1] Village women were said to be willing to spend a great deal to achieve the "Electric Look." Such a code of dressing may be construed as simply consumerism, an attempt to ape urban "youth culture." However, it was also a deliberate mechanism to distance themselves from the *kampung* community and seek acceptance in the urban milieu. For some women, such inventive presentation of self also challenged *kampung* definition of male and female sexuality. A village woman observed with some hostility:

> (I)t is not nice the way [some factory women] attempt to imitate male *style*. Like, they want to be *rugged*. For instance, men wear *"Wrangler,"* they want to follow suit . . . some of them straight away take on the attributes of men in their clothing, they forget their sex. If they are already very *bebas* they forget that they themselves are women.

Indeed, *kampung* women increasingly sought rights previously limited to men. Almost all factory women chose their potential spouses either directly, through correspondence, or by accepting a suitor's overtures. This autonomy was directly based on their earning power, since increasingly, village women were expected to save and contribute towards their own wedding expenses and bridal furnishings. Most village parents have given up arranging marital unions for their children, although "go-betweens" were still hired to formalize matches privately initiated by the couple itself. In a few cases, especially when the family had no male head, the young women simply announced to their mothers that they were getting engaged. Some mothers were even unaware of their daughters' courtship and simply went along with their personal arrangements for marriage. A village mother told me that young women could meet potential husbands all over the place—in the factories, in towns, on their way to work—and there was no possible way, nor inclination, on the part of the parents to monitor their daughters' social contacts with men. Most young women I interviewed would not let their parents pick their future spouses, the usual retort being "What if I don't like him?"

Such self-determination and ability to resist parental authority increased young women's awareness of control over a personal life separate from that of the family. One heard numerous cases of young working women running away from home to escape intolerable domestic situations. For instance, a 21-year-old operator from Banting was ordered by her mother to marry a well-off man in his forties. She told me that she rejected the match and planned to resign from ENI and go stay with her married sister in Kuala Lumpur. A 19-year-old woman confided to the factory nurse that she had been involved in an incestuous relationship with her widowed father for three years. The negative result of her pregnancy test was a source of relief to the factory medical staff since they were uncertain about what to do with the case. Subsequently, the woman took her own decision and sought refuge with her maternal grandmother in town. Even with limited economic independence, village women demonstrated an emerging sense of personal responsibility in dealing with the consequences of their action, thereby challenging *kampung* notions about the helplessness of *budak budak*.

Individuation in economic matters, attitudes, and conduct has led a small but growing number of rural women to bypass *kampung* conventions and cross different social boundaries on their own. While "illicit" love between single people or persons not married to each other has always been part of village society, we may say with some confidence that "dating" practices have become more common with the large-scale participation of young women and men in wage employment. What has changed is that affairs between single persons, which in former times usually culminated in marriage, now have less certain outcomes as village elders lose their ability to enforce social norms over an increasingly mobile and dispersed population. Since the opening of the FTZ, four cases of abortions have been reported among unmarried factory women in the area. A woman from Sungai Jawa had her illegitimate child in the home of a married sister and then gave the infant up for adoption in another village. Other unwed factory women who became pregnant had abortions outside the *mukim*, and thereafter sought employment in other villages and towns. Female relatives provided sympathy and material support to help these women begin life anew.[2]

In venturing beyond the socially confined circumstances of *kampung* life, factory women also came into increasing daily contact with other Malaysians. Talking about her workplace, an operator disclosed her widening social horizon:

> (T)here I have friends from Pahang, Trengganu all from far away. . . . For instance, if they come from Negri Sembilan, I come to know their customs and traditions . . . the way of life in their state.

Other young women began to associate, for the first time in their lives, with non-Malays as co-workers and friends.

> (W)e get to mix widely with peoples other than Malays—Indians, Chinese and others who are not Malaysians. My thinking has already changed little by little as I get to know their mannerisms, their ways. Previously, before we had experience, when we were not yet *bebas*, we did not get to know their ways, but now little by little we are learning about other races.

The proletarianization of rural Malays and increasing daily association with workers of other ethnic identities do not inevitably lead to a political movement which would replace ethnic hostility with class consciousness, as some scholars have claimed (Zawawi and Shahril 1983). The structuring of social relations and class interests along ethnic lines by industry, state agencies, and groups founded on communal interests would continue to constitute the "reality" whereby ordinary people conducted their lives and achieved practical consciousness. In the Telok industrial system, which by economic calculation and political expediency was a miniature replica of the wider ethnic and gender divided society, conflicts produced by unequal relations of production often took on ethnic tones.

Unleashed Spirits: The World Decentered

> The basis [of capitalist society] is that a relation between people takes on the character of a thing and thus acquires a "phantom objectivity," an autonomy so strictly rational and all-embracing as to conceal every trace of its fundamental nature: the relation between people.
>
> Lukács (1982: 83)

As capitalist development reworks the basis of social relations, the changing sense of personhood and of things is most intensively experienced in the realm of production. However, consciousness of injustice and being treated "like things" among neophyte factory women was partial, discontinuous, and seldom articulated. Sporadic forms of protest, both overt and covert, were not so much informed by a specific class consciousness as by the felt violation of one's fundamental humanity.

As elsewhere in the Peninsula, the self-definition of Malay peasants in Telok was still overlaid with noncapitalist native status categories, primarily extraeconomic, which still prevailed in contexts increasingly defined by capitalist relations.[3] Self-definition among rural Malays was at once localized and universal: *orang kampung* versus *orang asing* (villagefolk versus outsiders); *orang Islam* and the legal term *bumiputra* vis-à-vis *orang asing* (in the sense of persons outside the Islamic-Malay community). This social consciousness, as Hobsbawm has commented about non-capitalist cultures, was simultaneously lilliputian and global; it often went beyond any consciousness of "classness" among agrarian peoples (1971:10). As I have argued elsewhere, peasant adherence to noncapitalist worldview has been used to advantage by capitalist enterprises both to enhance control and to disguise commodity relations. However, the noncapitalist universe can also furnish rural people with a moral critique of the dehumanizing aspects of market relations.[4] In Telok, culturally-specific forms of protest and retaliation in the corporate arena were directed ultimately not at "capital" but at the transgression of local boundaries governing proper human relations and moral justice. A young woman from Sungai Jawa disclosed her sense of having been tricked into working under unjust conditions by the management:

> For instance, . . . sometimes . . . they want us to raise *production*. This is what we sometimes contest *(bantahlah)*. The workers want just treatment *(keadilan)*, as for instance, in relation to wages and other matters. We feel that in this situation there are many [issues] to dispute *(bertengkar)* over with the management—because we have to work three shifts and when the *midnight shift* arrives we feel sort of drowsy and yet have to

use the *microscope*, and with our wages so low we feel as though we have been tricked or forced *(seolah macam dipaksa)*.

This is why we ask for justice because we have to use the *microscope*. . . . Justice because sometimes they exhaust us very much as if they do not think that we too are human beings *(manusia)* . . . so that from time to time we must protest, that they should not rap *(menutuk)* us too much.

Most factory operators, less outspoken, nevertheless felt the same sense of having been taken. They resorted to indirect resistance which was culturally consistent with their subordinate female status. Capitalizing on beliefs in their emotional instability and susceptibility to male power, factory women reacted in expected ways to intolerable demands. Crying was a common response to verbal abuse which could deflect disciplinary action. Some operators who could not keep up with repeated orders to attain high production targets deliberately slowed down their normal pace of work, became careless in the assembly of components, or simply lost their temper. In their resistance to being treated like things, mounting work pressures *(tekanan)*, and harsh *(keras)* foremen, workers often cultivated an unconcerned, uncomprehending *(tidak apa)* attitude towards orders and the technical details of production. A common tactic was to make excuses to leave the shopfloor by citing "female problems" which had to be attended to in the locker room. Alternately, they sought release to adjourn to the prayer room, confronting foremen who tried to limit prayer time. Thus, cultural conformity and covert resistance fed on each other as factory women in daily life fought for and held on to a residual space for the preservation of human dignity. However, the locker room and prayer room, as refuge from work discipline and surveillance, were also the places in which operators were seized upon by vengeful spirits.

The rural Malay universe is still inhabited by spirits which move easily between human and nonhuman domains. Thus, familiar spirits such as *toyol* help their masters reap wealth out of thin air, while the *pontianak* birth demon threatens the life of newly born infants. Another group consists of possessing spirits which are associated with special places marking the boundary between human and natural worlds. These include (1) aboriginal (Negrito) and animal spirits inhabiting old burial grounds, strangely shaped rocks, hills, or trees; (2) holy men or well-known ancestors *(datuk)* dwelling in sacred abodes *(kramat)*, such as grave sites and natural objects; and (3) *syaitan* (evil spirits) of Islamic origin. Malays believe that women lacking in spiritual vigilance become possessed by angry spirits *(kena hantu)* when the victims wander unsuspectingly onto the sacred dwelling places of spirits. In his study of spirit seances in Kelantan villages, Clive Kessler observes that middle-aged women were particularly susceptible to spirit affliction, possibly because of their vulnerable social status at this phase of their life cycle (1977). Susan Ackerman maintains that in rural Malacca threats of spirit possession operate as a sanction against self-assertion on the part of young Malay women engaged in industrial work (1979: 13). Over the past decade, spirit possession episodes have proliferated among the young Malay women who flock in the thousands to urban institutions. Newspaper reports of the sudden spate of "mass hysteria" among young Malay women in boarding schools and modern factories have interpreted their causes in terms of "examination tension," "the stresses of urban living," "superstituous beliefs," and, less frequently, "mounting pressures" which induced "worries" (*keciwa*) among female operators.[5]

The Management View of "Mass Hysteria"

The late 1970s produced a flurry of newspaper reports on "mass hysteria" in free trade zones.[6] In 1975, forty Malay operators were seized by spirits in a large American electronics plant based in Sungai Way. A second large-scale incident in 1978 involved some 120 operators in the microscope sections. The factory had to be shut down for three days and a spirit-healer (*bomoh*) was hired to slaughter a goat on the premises. The American director wondered how he was to explain to corporate headquarters that "8,000 hours of production were lost because someone saw a ghost."[7] In late 1978, a Penang-based American microelectronics factory was disrupted for three consecutive days when fifteen women became afflicted by spirit possession. A factory personnel officer told reporters:

> Some girls started sobbing and screaming hysterically and when it seemed like spreading, the other workers in the production line were immediately ushered out. . . . It is a common belief among workers that the factory is "dirty" and supposed to be haunted by a *datuk*.[8]

The victims were given injectable sedatives while hundreds of other female workers were sent home. A *bomoh* was called to ritually cleanse the factory premises, but workers' demands for a feast (*kenduri*) elicited no response. A few days after the incident, I interviewed some workers about "filth" (*kotor*) in the factory. They pointed out that the production floor and canteen areas were "very clean," but factory toilets were "filthy" in two senses: pollution by soiled sanitary napkins and by evil spirits. In recounting the incident, a worker remembered that a piercing scream from one corner of the shopfloor was quickly followed by cries from other benches as women struggled against spirits trying to possess them. They would struggle so hard that sometimes ten supervisors could not control one afflicted worker who would shout "Go away!" Most spirit incidents were also linked to the appearance of *datuk* apparitions, sometimes headless, gesticulating angrily at the operators. A third example occurred in 1980 when spirits afflicted 21 women workers in a Japanese factory based in Pontian, Kelantan. As they were being taken to ambulances, some victims screamed, "I will kill you, let me go!"[9]

In Kuala Langat, spirit possession incidents among Malay factory women reiterated themes of filth, angry spirits, fierce struggles, and rites of exorcism. Interviews with factory managers and workers reveal contrasting interpretations of the episodes: biomedical causes versus pollution-violation imagery. At ENI, the personnel manager said that the first spirit affliction occurred five months after the factory began operation in 1976. Thereafter, we had our counter-measure. I think this is a method of how you give initial education to the workers, how you take care of the medical welfare of the workers. The worker who is weak, comes in without breakfast, lacking sleep, then she will see ghosts!

Those who had had two previous experiences of affliction were dismissed for "security reasons." Village elders protested, claiming that ghosts in the factory were responsible for the women's condition. The manager agreed but pointed out that these "hysterical, mental types" might hurt themselves when they flailed against the machines, risking electrocution. In his view, "hysteria" is a symptom of the women's rural-urban transition. "They move from home idleness to factory discipline. The ghosts disturb only the new girls." In contrast to managers in other firms who operated on the "basis of feelings," he used a "psychological approach" to deal with recurrent spirit visitations:

> You cannot dispel *kampung* beliefs. Now and then we call the *bomoh* to come, every six months or so, to [waving his hand vaguely] pray, walk around. Then we take pictures of the *bomoh* in the factory and hang up the pictures. Somehow, the workers seeing these pictures feel safe, [seeing] that the place has been exorcised.

Similarly, whenever a new section of the factory had been constructed, the *bomoh* was sent for to sprinkle holy water, thereby assuring workers that the place is rid of ghosts. Furthermore, the factory nurse periodically toured the shopfloor to encourage female workers to talk over their problems with the "industrial relations assistant." Complaints of "pain in the chest" (*sakit dada*) meant that the workers were emotionally upset and should be allowed to go to the clinic. The nurse also recommended that spirit possession victims be sent home for a day or two on medical leave. However, neither she nor the industrial relations assistant was consulted about the policy to sack workers after their third affliction. She noted:

> It is an experience working with a Japanese company; they do not consult women. To tell you the truth, they don't care about the problem except that it should go away.

EJI also commenced operations in a spate of spirit possession incidents. The production supervisor told me that in the following year, a well-known *bomoh* and his retinue were invited to the factory *surau* where they read the *yasin* prayer over a basin of "pure water." Those who had been visited by the devil drank from it and washed their faces, a healing ritual which made them immune to future spirit attacks. A *kenduri* of saffron rice and curry chicken was served to managers and officers, but not a single operator (or victim) was invited. A month after the ritual, spirit attacks resumed, but involving smaller numbers (one or two) of women in each incident. The *bomoh* claimed that the *hantu* controlling the factory site was "very kind"; he merely showed himself but did not disturb people. Now spirit attacks occurred only once a month. Last year, the supervisor sent home a possessed woman who was all rigid, with eyes turned inwards. She had put up a terrific struggle. Since the nurse could not do anything to help, the victim was given special leave of up to a week, to be healed by the *bomoh* in her home village. The supervisor admitted, "I think that hysteria is related to the job in some cases." He explained that workers in the microscope sections were usually the ones to *kena hantu*, and maybe they should not begin work doing those tasks. However, he quickly offered other possible interpretations. There was one victim whose broken engagement had incurred her mother's wrath; at work she cried and talked to herself, saying, "I am not to be blamed, not me!" Another worker, seized by possession, screamed, "Send me home, send me home!" Apparently, her mother had taken all her earnings. What do the spirit attacks really mean to factory workers themselves?

In Their Own Voices

I wish to discover, in the vocabulary of spirit possession, the unconscious beginnings of an idiom of protest against labor discipline and male control in the modern industrial situation. Spirit visitations to both foreign and local factories with sizeable numbers of young Malay female workers engender devil images which dramatically reveal the contradictions beteen Malay and capitalist ways of apprehending the human condition. Joan M. Lewis has suggested that women's spirit possession episodes are "thinly disguised protest . . . against the dominant sex." By "capitalizing on their distress," the victims of spirit possession called public attention to their subordinate position and sought to alleviate it (1971: 31, 85). In the following cases, spirit imageries reveal not only a mode of unconscious retaliation

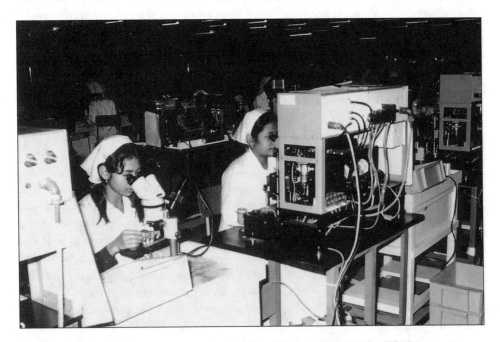

Figure 1: "Through a Glass Darkly": Malaysian Women Electronics Workers.
(Courtesy of International Development Research Center, Social Science Division, Ottawa. Reprinted by permission of Aihwa Ong and State University of New York Press.)

against male authority but fundamentally a sense of dislocation in human relations and a need for greater spiritual vigilance in domains reconstituted by capitalist relations of production.

An ENI operator described one incident which occurred in May 1979:

> It was the afternoon shift, at about nine o'clock. All was quiet. Suddenly, [the victim] started sobbing, laughed and then shrieked. She flailed at the machine . . . she was violent, she fought as the foreman and technician pulled her away. Altogether, three operators were afflicted. . . . The supervisor and foremen took them to the clinic and told the driver to send them home. . . .

> She did not know what happened . . . she saw a *hantu*, a were-tiger. Only she saw it, and she started screaming. . . . The foremen would not let us talk with her for fear of recurrence. She was possessed, maybe because she was spiritually weak. She was not spiritually vigilant so that when she saw the *hantu* she was instantly afraid and screamed. Usually, the *hantu* likes people who are spiritually weak, yes. People say that the workplace is haunted by the *hantu* who dwells below . . . well, this used to be all jungle, it was a burial ground before the factory was built. The devil disturbs those who have weak constitutions . . . [therefore] one should guard against being easily startled, or afraid.

In a separate interview, another female worker told me what happened after the "*penyakit histeria*" (hysteria affliction) broke out:

> The work section was not shut down, we had to continue working. Whenever it happened, the other workers felt frightened. They were not allowed to look because [the management] feared contagion. They would not permit us to leave. When an incident breaks out, we have to move away. . . . At ten o'clock they called the *bomoh* to come . . . because he knew that the *hantu* had already entered the woman's body. He came in and scattered flour all over the area where the incident broke out. He recited prayers over [holy] water. He sprinkled water on places touched by the *hantu*. . . . The *bomoh* chanted incantations (*jampi jampi*) chasing the *hantu* away. He then gave some medicine to the afflicted. . . . He also entered the clinic, *jampi jampi*.

> [After their recovery, the victims] never talk about [their affliction] because they don't remember . . . like insane people, they don't remember their experiences. Maybe the *hantu* is still working on their madness, maybe because their experiences have not been stilled, or maybe yet their souls are now disturbed (*jiwa terganggu*).

Other interviews elicited the same images: the erection of the FTZ on the burial grounds of aboriginal groups; disturbed earth and grave spirits swarming through the factory premises; weretigers roaming the shopfloor. Women not spiritually vigilant were possesed by the *hantu*. The *bomoh* was hastily summoned to perform exorcist rites. Recovering victims suffered from amnesia, their souls not properly healed. A woman told me about her aunt's fright in the EJI prayer room.

She was in the middle of praying when she fainted because she said . . . her head suddenly spun and something pounced on her from behind.

Furthermore:

Workers saw "things" appear when they went to the toilet. Once, when a woman entered the toilet she saw a tall figure in the midst of licking sanitary towels ["*Modess*" supplied in the cabinet]. It had a long tongue, and those sanitary towels . . . cannot be used anymore.

These vivid images of harassment by spirits on the factory floor and places of "refuge" like the prayer room and toilets are symbolic configurations of the violation, chaos, and draining of one's essence. Pervasive threats of possession induced the need for vigilance, looking behind one's back and over the shoulder to guard one's body and soul against violation. The *bomoh* has become a fixture of transnational production operations in Malaysia; however, his slaughter of chickens or goats on factory premises has been insufficient to placate the unleashed, avenging spirits of a world torn asunder.

A medical model is increasingly replacing native interpretations of spirit attacks. Using terms like *penyakit histeria*, some operators have come to accept scientific explanations of these events, as offered by the management. Thus, one operator mused:

They say they saw *hantu*, but I don't know. . . . I believe that maybe they . . . when they come to work, they did not fill their stomachs, they were not full so that they felt hungry. But they were not brave enough to say so.

The male technician gave an even more alien reading of the women's afflictions, as much to convince the anthropologist as himself.

I think that this [is caused by] a feeling of *complex*, that maybe *inferiority complex* is pressing them down, their spirit, so that this can be called an illness of the spirit (*penyakit jiwa*), *conflict jiwa*, *emotional conflict*. Sometimes, they see an old man, in black shrouds, they say, in their microscopes, they say. . . . I myself don't know how. They see *hantu* in different places. . . . Some time ago an *emergency* incident like this occurred in a boarding school. The victim fainted. Then she became very *strong* like *a strongman or a strong girl*. It required ten or twenty persons to handle her. . . .

If indeed spirit possession episodes provided female workers the guise to launch attacks on male staff members, they certainly never came close to challenging male authority on the factory floor or elsewhere. In effect, the enactment of "ritualised rebellion" (Gluckman 1958) by Malay women in modern factories did not directly confront the real cause of their distress, and instead, by operating as a safety valve, tended to reinforce existing unequal relations which are further legitimized by scientific notions of female maladjustment. A woman in ENI talked sadly about her friend, dual victim of spirits and industrial discrimination:

At the time the management wanted to throw her out, to end her work, she cried. She did ask to be reinstated, but she has had three [episodes] already.... I think that whether it was right or not [to expel her] depends [on the circumstances], because she has already worked here for a long time; now that she has been thrown out she does not know what she can do, you know.

In circumstances calling for the denial of oppressive conditions, some operators slipped into the vacuous state induced by popular music. Malay, Hindustani, and Chinese tunes, adjusted to a soothing level, alternating by the hour, were piped into the shopfloor. It helped them forget their bodily aches or the work they were doing because they were borne along in daydreams. Others cultivated a spiritual vigilance through performing more prayers, to shield themselves against attacks by malevolent spirits.

More direct tactics have emerged for silent renegotiations of rules on the shopfloor. Some operators, without the guise of spirit possession, have undertaken deliberate but surreptitious attacks on factory equipment. Such machine wrecking is to be differentiated from the preunion tradition of early English labor movements which, by publicly attacking factory property, engaged in "collective bargaining by riot" (Hobsbawm 1964: 6–7).[10] In the Telok FTZ, the subversive acts were spontaneous, carried out by individual workers independently of each other. When production targets seemed unbearable, or a foreman had been especially harsh, operators registered their private vengeance by damaging the very components that they had painstakingly assembled. Others stalled the machines and thus interrupted production. The cumulative effect of countless subversive acts, as evidenced in thousands of defective components at the end of the month, constituted an anonymous protest against mounting work pressures rather than a collective action with specific demands on the management. The Malay technician quoted above explained this subterranean resistance.

There is certainly a lot of *discipline* ... *but when there is too much discipline*, ... it is not good. Because of this the operators, with their small wages, will always contest. They often break the *machines* in ways that are not apparent.... Sometimes they damage the *products*.... This is something entirely up to the *individual operator*, [an action taken] on their own. I feel that it is indeed proper that they do this because their wages are small and we cannot *blame* them. *Blaming operator is nothing* [sic] because ... if they have problems they are not about to tell anyone. Because others will not listen to their complaints ... Because they do not have a union. I cannot [propose wage increases on their behalf] because if you value yourself you want to get *promotion* if you can, and so we can't talk about this [to the management]. Thus, all that I do is behind the scenes. Because if one cares about one's future, one's *career*, then one is forced to keep quiet. Thus, even if one sympathizes with the operator (*simpati dengan operator*), one is not brave enough to speak up.

In the absence of a union, covert revolts sometimes developed into acts of retaliation against factory men, the intimate supervisors as well as tormentors of operators in daily life. Factory women on occasion manipulated their kinsmen's sense of honor by gossiping and crying about mistreatment in the FTZ. In 1976, an Indian foreman was set upon, "beaten and badly hurt on the face and stomach by an unknown gang," according to EJI records. A Malay assistant foreman coming to his aid was also beaten up. According to an informal questioning of workers, the fore-man deserved punishment because he refused workers their 15-minute breaks, insulted them about personal matters, followed women into the locker room, and threatened to terminate their employment whenever he felt necessary. He became blacklisted among village youths. In spite of the incident, the foreman was retained and told to modify his conduct. Of the operators he had terrorized, only one resigned in protest. One Chinese foreman was beaten up for dating an operator. Another Chinese foreman said that this was only part of the story. All male super-visors in the factory, he claimed, had been privately warned by Malay youths that reports of their mistreatment of women workers would invite physical retaliation. Operators pointed fingers at foremen who were said to restrict their rights to pray, to move about on the shopfloor, or who pressed them too hard to attain high pro-duction targets. *Kampung* youths, in the tradition of enforcing rough justice and set-tling scores, were ready to make covert attacks on the blacklisted factory men. Possibly, in the case of the Chinese foreman, his romance with a Malay worker marked him out as a scapegoat to be used as a warning to all male factory staff. There had been at least two other incidents of nocturnal attacks on male workers—none of local origin—outside the FTZ gates. Rural youths not only empathized with the women's harassment in the workplace, they were also resentful of these outsiders, both non-Malays and Malays, placed in daily contact with nubile Malay women.

The policing of rural society by young men focused on deviant social behavior, particularly when "outsiders" were involved. *Kampung* elders gave tacit approval to such activities, including attacks on outside men who were perceived to be infring-ing on local territory and young women. Any untoward behavior, such as frequent visits to the home of an unmarried woman, could be considered as "dishonoring" her reputation. Such an intrusion was to be redressed by youths waving staves to warn off the culprit, ripping up his bicycle/motorcycle tires, or giving him a thrash-ing. This *kampung* mode of enforcing social norms has come to constitute the shad-owy side of rural relations with "strangers" at the FTZ. The two *mukim* policemen usually feigned ignorance of such violent incidents since they were regarded as within the province of *kampung* leaders. Factory managers too avoided direct con-frontation over the incidents, preferring to negotiate privately with local headmen and policemen over possible measures to reduce attacks against factory men. For their part, the "protection" village youths extended to working women compen-sated for their reduced sense of "honor," intangible values in effect purchased by female earnings which helped sustain rural livelihood.

The lamentations of possession victims decry the dislocations experienced by peasants in an industrializing world. The issue is not one of "false consciousness" or everyday forms of resistance which may culminate in large-scale rebellion. In the factories set up by transnational corporations, the constitution of new subjec-tivities unavoidably calls forth countertactics which proceed against neither capitalism nor the state. The spirit imageries of filth and violation speak out against male oppression as well as a deep sense of moral decentering, insisting on an ancient equality rooted in common (ungendered) humanity. Where self-regulation failed, the inscription of microprotests on damaged microchips constituted an anonymous resistance against the relentless demands of the industrial system. These nomadic tactics, operating in diverse fields of power, speak not of class revolt but only of the local situation.

The *syaitan* hovers over the passage of Malay peasants from a moral economy to an economy of commodities. Inducted into production systems where principles of assembly, disassembly, and reassembly are the cybernetics of control, Malay women have emigrated to the state of twentieth century homelessness. In constructing substitute homes and new identities, Malay working classes may recreate a collective consciousness which will transcend particularistic, *kampung* bonds.

Glossary of Malay Words Used in Text

baju kurong   loose tunic and sarong worn by Malay girls and women
bebas   at liberty; not restrained in speech and behavior
bomoh   Malay spirit-healer
budak budak   children; also maidens
datuk   grandfather; honorary title for a man of high status
EJI   Electronics Japan Incorporated—one of the plants studies by author
ENI   Electronics Nippon Incorporated
FTZ   Free Trade Zone
hantu   spirits, often harmful to human beings, associated with a place, animal, or deceased person
kampung   village
kenduri   feast, usually marking rite-of-passage ceremony or religious occasion
mukim   subdistrict; smallest administrative unit, headed by a **penghulu**
surau   islamic prayer room or house
Sungai Jawa   village in which auhtor conducted field research
Telok   sub district in which author conducted field research

Notes

1. *Sunday Mail,* Jan. 27, 1980.
2. Jamilah Ariffin notes that newspaper reports of abandoned infants outside urban FTZs indicated the inability of unwed factory women to cope with critical life situations (1980:56). These factory women in cities probably did not have easy access to female kin, the basic source of emotional and social support in rural society.
3. For a description of the indigenous status classificatory system in the Malay states, see Gullick (1958) and Milner (1982). Social rank and prestige were derived from the political system based on the sultanate. In Telok, the traditional strata of *raja, orang besar*, and *rakyat* were still regarded as culturally salient even though the traditional prestige system has been restructured and emasculated under British colonial rule and modern state formation. For instance, the term *orang besar* applied to surviving members of aristocratic families has been bestowed on contemporary power holders of "common origins": civil servants and elected representatives who constitute the upper stratum of rural society (A. Kahar Bador 1973).
4. See, for example, Wolf (1969); Scott (1976); Nash (1979); Taussig (1980).
5. For a report on "hysteria-exam blues link," see *New Straits Times*, Oct. 23, 1981.

6. For media interpretations of "mass hysteria" among factory women, see *Asiaweek*, Aug. 4, 1978; *Sunday Echo*, Nov. 27, 1978; *Mimbar Sosialis*, June/July 1978.

7. See Linda Lim (1978) for one view of this incident.

8. *Sunday Echo*, November 27, 1978.

9. *New Straits Times*, Sept. 26, 1980.

10. However, in their motivations the Malay workers were comparable to the Luddites in that it was not the machines per se to which they objected, but the new relations of production of which the machines were part (see Hobsbawm 1964: 11).

Works Cited

Ackerman, Susan E. 1979. "Industrial Conflict in Malaysia: A Case Study of Rural Malay Female Workers." Unpublished manuscript.

Bador, A. Kahar. 1973. "Social Rank, Status-Honour and Social Class Consciousness among the Malays." In *Modernization in Southeast Asia*, edited by Hans-Dieter Evers. Singapore: Oxford University Press.

Dore, Ronald. 1973. *British Factory—Japanese Factory: The Origins of National Diversity in Industrial Relations*. Berkeley: University of California Press.

Engels, Frederick. 1972. *The Origins of the Family, Private Property and the State*. New York: International Publishers [orig. pub. 1884].

Gluckman, Max. 1958. *Analysis of a Social Situation in Modern Zululand*. Manchester: Manchester University Press [The Rhodes-Livingstone Papers, no. 28].

Goffman, Erving. 1959. *The Presentation of Self in Everyday Life*. New York: Anchor Books.

Gullick, J. M. 1958. *Indigenous Political Systems of Western Malays*. London: Athlone Press.

Hobsbawm, Eric. 1964. *Labouring Men: Studies in the History of Labour*. London: Routledge & Kegan Paul.

———. 1971. "Class Consciousness in History." In *Aspects of History and Class Consciousness*, edited by I. Meszaros. London.

Jamilah Ariffin. 1980. "Industrial Development in Peninsular Malaysia and Rural-Urban Migration of Women Workers: Impact and Implications." *Jurnal Ekonomi Malaysia*, 1: 41–59.

Kesser, Clive S. 1977. "Conflict and Sovereignty in Kelantan Malay Spirit Seances." In *Case Studies in Spirit Possession*, edited by Vincent Crapanzano and V. Garrison. New York: J. Wiley and Sons.

Lewis, Joan M. 1971. *Ecstatic Religion: An Anthropological Study of Spirit Possession and Shamanism*. Harmondsworth: Penguin Books.

Lim, Linda. 1978. *Women Workers in Multinational Corporations: The Case of the Electronics Industry in Malaysia and Singapore*. University of Michigan, Occasional Paper no. 9.

Lukács, Georg. 1982. *History and Class Consciousness: Studies in Marxist Dialectics*. Translated by Rodney Livingstone. Cambridge, Mass: MIT Press [orig. pub. Berlin, 1968].

Milner, Anthony C. 1982. *Kerajaan: Malay Political Culture on the Eve of Colonial Rule*. Tucson: University of Arizona Press.

Nash, June. 1979. *We Eat the Mines and the Mines Eat Us: Dependency and Exploitation in Bolivian Tin Mines*. New York: Columbia University Press.

Scott, James C. 1976. *The Moral Economy of the Peasant: Subsistence and Rebellion in Southeast Asia*. New Haven: Yale University Press.

Taussig, Michael. 1980. *The Devil and Commodity Fetishism in South America*. Chapel Hill: The University of North Carolina Press.

Wolf, Eric. 1969. *Peasant Wars of the Twentieth Century*. New York: Harper and Row.

Zawawi Ibrahim and Shahril Talib. 1983. "Neither Rebellions nor Revolutions: Everyday Resistance of the Malay Peasantry Under Capitalist Domination." *Ilmu Masyarakat*, 2 (Apr.–June): 25–41.

Part Five

Colonizing Gender and Sexuality

Representation and Practice

The Politics of Race and Sexual Morality

in Twentieth-Century Colonial Cultures

ANN L. STOLER

The shift away from viewing colonial elites as homogeneous communities of common interest marks an important trajectory in the anthropology of empire, signaling a major rethinking of gender relations within it. More recent attention to the internal tensions of colonial enterprises has placed new emphasis on the quotidian assertion of European dominance in the colonies, on imperial interventions in domestic life, and thus on the cultural prescriptions by which European women and men lived (Callan and Ardener 1984; Knibiehler and Goutalier 1985; Reijs et al. 1986; Callaway 1987; Strobel 1987). Having focused on how colonizers have viewed the indigenous Other, we are beginning to sort out how Europeans in the colonies imagined themselves and constructed communities built on asymmetries of race, class and gender—entities significantly at odds with the European models on which they were drawn.

These feminist attempts to engage the gender politics of Dutch, French and British imperial cultures converge on some strikingly similar observations; namely that European women in these colonies experienced the cleavages of racial dominance and internal social distinctions very differently than men precisely because of their ambiguous positions, as both subordinates in colonial hierarchies and as active agents of imperial culture in their own right. Concomitantly, the majority of European women who left for the colonies in the late 19th and early 20th centuries confronted profoundly rigid restrictions on their domestic, economic and political options, more limiting than those of metropolitan Europe at the time and sharply contrasting with the opportunities open to colonial men.

In one form or another these studies raise a basic question: in what ways were gender inequalities essential to the structure of colonial racism and imperial authority? Was the strident misogyny of imperial thinkers and colonial agents a byproduct of received metropolitan values ("they just brought it with them"), a reaction to contemporary feminist demands in Europe ("women need to be put back in their breeding place") or a novel and pragmatic response to the conditions of conquest? Was the assertion of European supremacy in terms of patriotic manhood and racial virility an expression of imperial domination or a defining feature of it?

In this paper I examine some of the ways in which colonial authority and racial distinctions were fundamentally structured in gendered terms. I look specifically at the administrative and medical discourse and management of European sexual activity, reproduction and marriage as it articulated with the racial politics of colonial rule. Focusing on French Indochina and the Dutch East Indies in the early 20th century, but drawing on other contexts, I suggest that the very categories of "colonizer" and "colonized" were secured through forms of sexual control which defined the domestic arrangements of Europeans and the cultural investments by which they identified themselves.[1] Gender-specific sexual sanctions demarcated positions of power by refashioning middle-class conventions of respectability, which, in turn, prescribed the personal and public boundaries of race.

Colonial authority was constructed on two powerful, but false, premises. The first was the notion that Europeans in the colonies made up an easily identifiable and discrete biological and social entity; a "natural" community of common class interest, racial attributes, political affinities and superior culture. The second was the related notion that the boundaries separating colonizer from colonized were thus self-evident and easily drawn (Stoler 1989). Neither premise reflected colonial realities (see for example, Cooper 1980; Drooglever 1980; Ridley 1983; Prochaska 1989; Comaroff (this volume)). Internal divisions developed out of conflicting economic and political agendas, frictions over appropriate methods for safeguarding European privilege and power, competing criteria for reproducing a colonial elite and for restricting its membership.

This latter, the colonial politics of exclusion, was contingent on constructing categories, legal and social classifications designating who was "white," who was "native," who could become a citizen rather than a subject, which children were legitimate progeny and which were not. What mattered were not only one's physical properties but who counted as "European" and by what measure.[2] Skin shade was too ambiguous; bank accounts were mercurial; religious belief and education were crucial but never enough. Social and legal standing derived not only from color, but from the silences, acknowledgments, and denials of the social circumstances in which one's parents had sex (Martinez-Alier 1974; Ming 1983; Taylor 1983). Sexual unions in the context of concubinage, domestic service, prostitution or church marriage derived from the hierarchies of rule; but these were negotiated and contested arrangements, bearing on individual fates and the very structure of colonial society. Ultimately inclusion or exclusion required regulating the sexual, conjugal and domestic life of *both* Europeans in the colonies and their colonized subjects.

Colonial observers and participants in the imperial enterprise appear to have had unlimited interest in the sexual interface of the colonial encounter (Malleret 1934:216; Pujarniscle 1931:106; Loutfi 1971:36). Probably no subject is discussed more than sex in colonial literature and no subject more frequently invoked to foster the racist stereotypes of European society. The tropics provided a site of European pornographic fantasies long before conquest was underway, but with a sustained European presence in colonized territories, sexual prescriptions by class, race and gender became increasingly central to the politics of rule and subject to new forms of scrutiny by colonial states (Loutfi 1971; Gilman 1985:79).[3]

While anthropologists have attended to how European, and particularly Victorian, sexual mores affected *indigenous* gendered patterns of economic activity, political participation and social knowledge, less attention has been paid to the ways in which sexual control affected the very nature of colonial relations themselves (Tiffany and Adams 1985). In colonial scholarship more generally, sexual domination has figured as a social metaphor of European supremacy. Thus, in Edward Said's treatment of orientalist discourse, the sexual submission and possession of Oriental women by European men "*stands for* the pattern of relative strength between East and West" (1978:6). In this "male power-fantasy," the Orient is penetrated, silenced and possessed (1978:207). Sexuality illustrates the iconography of rule, not its pragmatics; sexual assymetries are tropes to depict other centers of power.

Such a treatment begs some basic questions. Was sexuality merely a graphic substantiation of who was, so to speak, on the top? Was the medium the message, or did sexual relations always "mean" something else, stand in for other relations, evoke the sense of *other* (pecuniary, political, or some possibly more subliminal) desires? This analytic slippage between the sexual symbols of power and the politics of sex runs throughout the colonial record and contemporary commentaries upon it. Certainly some of this is due to the polyvalent quality of sexuality; symbolically rich and socially salient at the same time. But sexual control was more than a "social enactment"—much less a convenient metaphor—for colonial domination (Jordan 1968:141); it was, as I argue here, a fundamental class and racial marker implicated in a wider set of relations of power (Ballhatchet 1980).

The relationship between gender prescriptions and racial boundaries still remains unevenly unexplored. While we know that European women of different classes experienced the colonial venture very differently from one another and from men, we still know relatively little about the distinct investments they had in a racism they shared (Van Helten and Williams 1983; Knibiehler and Goutalier 1985; Callaway 1987). New feminist scholarship has begun to sort out the unique colonial experience of European women as they were incorporated into, resisted and affected the politics of their men. But the emphasis has tended to be on the broader issue of gender subordination and colonial authority, not more specifically on how sexual control figured in the construction of racial boundaries per se.[4]

The linkage between sexual control and racial tensions is both obvious and elusive at the same time. While sexual fear may at base be a racial anxiety, we are still left to understand why it is through sexuality that such anxieties are expressed (Takaki 1977). If, as Sander Gilman (1985) claims, sexuality is the most salient marker of Otherness, organically representing racial difference, then we should not be surprised that colonial agents and colonized subjects expressed their contests— and vulnerabilities—in these terms (see Chatterjee 1989).

An overlapping set of discourses has provided the psychological and economic underpinnings for colonial distinctions of difference, linking fears of sexual contamination, physical danger, climatic incompatability, and moral breakdown to a European colonial identity with a racist and class-specific core. Colonial scientific reports and the popular press are laced with statements and queries varying on a common theme: "native women bear contagions"; "white women become sterile in the tropics"; "colonial men are susceptible to physical, mental and moral degeneration when they remain in their colonial posts too long." To what degree are these statements medically or politically grounded? We need to unpack what is metaphor, what is perceived as dangerous (is it disease, culture, climate or sex?) and what is not.

In the sections that follow I look at the relationship between the domestic arrangements of colonial communities and their wider political structures. Part I examines the colonial debates over European family formation, over the relationship between subversion and sex in an effort to trace how evaluations of concubinage, morality and white prestige more generally were altered by new tensions within colonial cultures and by new challenges to imperial rule.

Part II examines what I call the "cultural hygiene" of colonialism. Focusing on the early 20th century as a break point, I take up the convergent metropolitan and colonial discourses on health hazards in the tropics, race-thinking and social reform as they related to shifts in the rationalization of colonial management. In tracing how fears of "racial degeneracy" were grounded in class-specific sexual norms, I return to how and why biological and cultural distinctions were defined in gender terms.

The Domestic Politics of Colonialism: Concubinage and the Restricted Entry of European Women

The regulation of sexual relations was central to the development of particular kinds of colonial settlements and to the allocation of economic activity within them. Who bedded and wedded with whom in the colonies of France, England, Holland and Iberia was never left to chance. Unions between Annamite women and French men, between Javanese women and Dutch men, between Spanish men and Inca women produced offspring with claims to privilege, whose rights and status had to be determined and prescribed. From the early 1600s through the 20th century the sexual sanctions and conjugal prohibitions of colonial agents were rigorously debated and carefully codified. In these debates over matrimony and morality, trading and plantation company officials, missionaries, investment bankers, military high commands and agents of the colonial state confronted one another's visions of empire, and the settlement patterns on which it would rest.

In 1622 the Dutch East Indies Company (VOC) arranged for the transport of six poor but marriageable young Dutch women to Java, providing them with clothing, a dowry upon marriage and a contract binding them to five years in the Indies (Taylor 1983:12). Aside from this and one other short-lived experiment, immigration of European women to the East Indies was consciously restricted for the next 200 years. Enforcing the restriction by selecting bachelors as their European recruits, the VOC legally and financially made concubinage the most attractive domestic option for its employees (Blussé 1986:173; Ming 1983:69; Taylor 1983:16).

It was not only the VOC which profited from such arrangements. In the 19th and early 20th centuries, salaries of European recruits to the colonial armies, bureaucracies, plantation companies and trading enterprises were kept artificially low because local women provided domestic services for which new European recruits would otherwise have had to pay. In the mid-1800s, such arrangements were *de rigueur* for young civil servants intent on setting up households on their own (Ritter 1856:21). Despite some clerical opposition, at the end of the century concubinage was the most prevalent living arrangement for European colonials in the Indies (Ming 1983:70; Taylor 1983:16; van Marle 1952:486).

Referred to as *nyai* in Java and Sumatra, *congai* in Indochina and *petite épouse* throughout the French empire, the colonized woman living as a concubine to a European man formed the dominant domestic arrangement in colonial cultures through the early 20th century. Unlike prostitution, which could and often did result in a population of syphilitic and therefore non-productive European men, concubinage was considered to have a stabilizing effect on political order and colonial health—a relationship that kept men in their barracks and bungalows, out of brothels and less inclined to perverse liaisons with one another.

Concubinage was a contemporary term which referred to the cohabitation outside of marriage between European men and Asian women; in fact, it glossed a wide range of arrangements which included sexual access to a non-European woman as well as demands on her labor and legal rights to the children she bore (Pollman 1986:100; Lucas 1986:86).[5] Native women (like European women in a later period) were to keep men physically and psychologically fit for work, marginally content, not distracting or urging them out of line, imposing neither the time-consuming nor financial responsibilities that European family life was thought to demand (Chivas-Baron 1929:103).[6]

To say that concubinage reinforced the hierarchies on which colonial societies were based is not to say that it did not make those distinctions more problematic at the same time. Grossly uneven sex ratios on North Sumatran estates made for intense competition among male workers and their European supervisors, with *vrouwen perkara* (disputes over women) resulting in assaults on whites, new labor tensions and dangerous incursions into the standards deemed essential for white prestige (Stoler 1985a:33; Lucas 1986:90–91). In the Netherlands Indies more generally an unaccounted number of impoverished Indo-European women moving between prostitution and concubinage further disturbed the racial sensibilities of the Dutch-born elite (Hesselink 1987:216). Metropolitan critics were particularly disdainful of such domestic arrangements on moral grounds—all the more so when these unions *were* sustained and personally significant relationships, thereby contradicting the racial premise of concubinage as an emotionally unfettered convenience.[7] But perhaps most important, the tension between concubinage as a confirmation and compromise of racial hierarchy was realized in the progeny that it produced, "mixed-bloods," poor "indos," and abandoned "*métis*" children who straddled the divisions of ruler and ruled and threatened to blur the colonial divide.

Nevertheless, colonial governments and private business tolerated concubinage and actively encouraged it—principally by restricting the emigration of European women to the colonies and by refusing employment to married male European recruits. Although many accounts suggest that European women chose to avoid early pioneering ventures, and this must have been true in some cases, the choice was more often not their own (cf. Fredrickson 1981:109). Nor were the restrictions on marriage and women's emigration lifted as each colony became politically stable, medically upgraded and economically secure, as it is often claimed. Conjugal constraints lasted well into the 20th century, long after rough living and a scarcity of amenities had become conditions of the past. In the Indies army, marriage was a privilege of the officer corps while barrack concubinage was instituted and regulated for the rank and file. In the 20th century, formal and informal prohibitions set by banks, estates and government services operating in Africa, India and Southeast Asia restricted marriage during the first three to five years of service, while some prohibited it altogether (Moore-Gilbert 1986:48; Woodcock 1969:164; Tirefort 1979:134; Gann and Duignan 1978:240).

The marriage prohibition was both a political and an economic issue, defining the social contours of colonial communities and the standards of living within them. But, as significantly, it revealed how deeply the conduct of private life and the sexual proclivities which individuals expressed were tied to corporate profits and to the security of the colonial state. Nowhere were the incursions on domestic life more openly contested than in North Sumatra in the early 1900s. Unseemly domestic arrangements were thought to encourage subversion as strongly as acceptable unions could avert it. Family stability and sexual "normalcy" were thus linked to political agitation or quiescence in very concrete ways.

Since the late 19th century, the major North Sumatran tobacco and rubber companies neither accepted married applicants nor allowed them to take wives while in service (Schoevers 1913:38; Clerkx 1961:31–34). Company authorities argued that new employees with families in tow would be a financial burden, risking the emergence of a "European proletariat" and thus a major threat to white prestige (Kroniek 1917:50; *Sumatra Post* 1913). Low-ranking plantation employees protested against these company marriage restrictions, an issue which mobilized their ranks behind a broad set of demands (Stoler 1989:144). Under employee pressure, the prohibition was relaxed to a marriage ban for the first five years of service. This restriction, however, was never placed on everyone; it was pegged to salaries and dependent on the services of local women which kept the living costs and wages of subordinate and incoming staff artifically low.

Domestic arrangements thus varied as government officials and private businesses weighed the economic versus political costs of one arrangement over another, but such calculations were invariably meshed. Europeans in high office saw white prestige and profits as inextricably linked and attitudes toward concubinage reflected that concern (Brownfoot 1984:191). Thus in Malaya through the 1920s, concubinage was tolerated precisely because "poor whites" were not. Government and estate administrators argued that white prestige would be imperiled if European men became impoverished in attempting to maintain middle-class lifestyles and European wives (Butcher 1979:26). In late 19th-century Java, in contrast, concubinage itself was considered to be a major source of white pauperism; in the early 1900s it was vigorously condemned at precisely the same time that a new colonial morality passively condoned illegal brothels (Het Pauperisme Commissie 1901; Nieuwenhuys 1959:20–23; Hesselink 1987:208).

What explains such a difference? At least part of the answer must be sought in the effects concubinage was seen to have on European cultural identity and on the concerns for the community consensus on which it rests. Concubinage "worked" as long as the supremacy of *Homo Europeanus* was clear. When it was thought to be in jeopardy, vulnerable or less than convincing, as in the 1920s in Sumatra, colonial elites responded by clarifying the cultural criteria of privilege and the moral premises of their unity. Concubinage was replaced by more restricted sexual access in the politically safe (but medically unsatisfactory) context of prostitution, and, where possible, in the more desirable setting of marriage between "full-blooded" Europeans (Taylor 1977:29). As we shall see in other colonial contexts, such shifts in policy and practice often coincided with an affirmation of social hierarchies and racial divisions in less ambiguous terms. Thus, it was not only morality which vacillated but the very definition of white prestige—and what its defense should entail. What upheld that prestige was not a constant; concubinage was socially lauded at one time and seen as a political menace at another. Appeals to white prestige were a gloss for different intensities of racist practice, gender-specific and culturally coded.

Thus far I have treated colonial communities as a generic category despite the sharp demographic, social and political distinctions among them. North Sumatra's European-oriented, overwhelmingly male colonial population, for example, contrasted sharply with the more sexually balanced mestizo culture which emerged in 17th- and 18th-century colonial Java.[8] Such demographic variation, however, was not the "bedrock" of social relations (Jordan 1968:141); sex ratios derived from specific strategies of social engineering, and were thus political responses in themselves. While recognizing that these demographic differences and the social configurations to which they gave rise still need to be explained, I have chosen here to trace some of the common politically gendered issues which a range of colonial societies shared; that is, some of the similar—and counter-intuitive—ways in which the positioning of European women facilitated racial distinctions and new efforts to modernize colonial control.[9]

Racist But Moral Women: Innocent But Immoral Men

Perhaps nothing is as striking in the sociological accounts of colonial communities as the extraordinary changes which are said to accompany the entry of European-born women. These adjustments shifted in one direction; toward European lifestyles accentuating the refinements of privilege and the etiquettes of racial difference. Most accounts agree that the presence of these women put new demands on the white communities to tighten their ranks, clarify their boundaries and mark out their social space. The material culture of French settlements in Saigon, outposts in New Guinea, and estate complexes in Sumatra were retailored to accommodate the physical and moral requirements of a middle-class and respectable feminine contingent (Malleret 1934; Gordon and Meggitt 1985; Stoler 1989). Housing structures in Indochina were partitioned, residential compounds in the Solomon Islands enclosed, servant relations in Hawaii formalized, dress codes in Java altered, and food and social taboos in Rhodesia and the Ivory Coast became more strict. Taken together, the changes encouraged new kinds of consumption and new social services catering to these new demands (Boutilier 1984; Spear 1963; Woodcock 1969; Cohen 1971).

The arrival of large numbers of European women thus coincided with an embourgeoisement of colonial communities and with a significant sharpening of racial lines. European women supposedly required more metropolitan amenities than men and more spacious surroundings to allow it; their more delicate sensibilities required more servants and thus suitable quarters—discrete and enclosed. In short, white women needed to be maintained at elevated standards of living, in insulated social spaces cushioned with the cultural artifacts of "being European." Whether women or men set these new standards is left unclear. Who exhibited "overconcern" and a "need for" segregation (Beidelman 1982:13)? Male doctors advised French women in Indochina to have their homes built with separate domestic and kitchen quarters (Grall 1908:74). Segregationist standards were what women "deserved," and more importantly what white male prestige required that they maintain.

Colonial rhetoric on white women was riddled with contradictions. At the same time that new female immigrants were chided for not respecting the racial distance of local convention, an equal number of colonial observers accused these women of being more avid racists in their own right (Spear 1963; Nora 1961). Allegedly insecure and jealous of the sexual liaisons of European men with native women, bound to their provincial visions and cultural norms, European women in Algeria, the Indies, Madagascar, India and West Africa were uniformly charged with constructing the major cleavages on which colonial stratification rested (Spear 1963:140; Nora 1961:174; Mannoni 1964 [1950]:115; Gann and Duignan 1978:242; Kennedy 1947:164; Nandy 1983:9).

What is most startling here is that women, otherwise marginal actors on the colonial stage, are charged with dramatically reshaping the face of colonial society, imposing their racial will on African and Asian colonies where "an iron curtain of ignorance" replaced "relatively unrestrained social intermingling" in earlier years (Vere Allen 1970:169; Cohen 1971:122). European women were not only the bearers of racist beliefs, but hardline operatives who put them into practice, encouraging class distinctions among whites while fostering new racial antagonisms, no longer muted by sexual access (Vere Allen 1970:168). Are we to believe that sexual intimacy with European men yielded social mobility and political rights for colonized women? Or, even less likely, that because British civil servants bedded with Indian women, somehow Indian men had more "in common" with British men and enjoyed more parity? Colonized women could sometimes parlay their positions into personal profit and small rewards, but these were *individual* negotiations with no social, legal or cumulative claims.

Male colonizers positioned European women as the bearers of a redefined colonial morality. But to suggest that women fashioned this racism out of whole cloth is to miss the political chronology in which new intensities of racist practice arose. In the African and Asian contexts already mentioned, the arrival of large numbers of European wives, and particularly the fear for their protection, followed from new terms and tensions in the colonial encounter. The presence and protection of European women was repeatedly invoked to clarify racial lines. It coincided with perceived threats to European prestige (Brownfoot 1984:191), increased racial conflict (Strobel 1987:378), covert challenges to the colonial order, outright expressions of nationalist resistance and internal dissension among whites themselves (Stoler 1989:147).

If white women were the primary force behind the decline of concubinage as is often claimed, they did so as participants in a broader racial realignment and political plan (Knibiehler and Goutalier 1985:76). This is not to suggest that European women were passive in this process, as the dominant themes in their novels attest (Taylor 1977:27). Many European women did oppose concubinage not because of their inherent jealousy of native women, but, as they argued, because of the double standard it condoned for European men (Clerkx 1961; Lucas 1986:94–95).[10] The voices of European women, however, had little resonance until their objections coincided with a realignment in racial and class politics.

Dealing with Transgressions: Policing the Peril

The gender-specific requirements for colonial living, referred to above, were constructed on heavily racist evaluations which pivoted on the heightened sexuality of colonized men (Tiffany and Adams 1985). Although European women were absent from men's sexual reveries in colonial literature, men of color were considered to see them as desired and seductive figures. European women needed protection because men of color had "primitive" sexual urges and uncontrollable lust, aroused by the sight of white women (Strobel 1987:379; Schmidt 1987:411). In some colonies, that sexual threat was latent; in others it was given a specific name.

In southern Rhodesia and Kenya in the 1920s and 1930s, preoccupations with the "Black Peril" (referring to the professed dangers of sexual assault on white women by black men) gave rise to the creation of citizens' militias, ladies' riflery clubs and investigations as to whether African female domestic servants would not be safer to employ than men (Kirkwood 1984:158; Schmidt 1987:412; Kennedy 1987:128–147). In New Guinea the White Women's Proctection Ordinance of 1926 provided "the death penalty for any person convicted for the crime of rape or attempted rape upon a European woman or girl" (Inglis 1975:vi). And as late as 1934, Solomon Islands authorities introduced public flogging as punishment for "criminal assaults on [white] females" (Boutilier 1984:197).

What do these cases have in common? The rhetoric of sexual assault and the measures used to prevent it had virtually no correlation with the incidence of rape of European women by men of color. Just the contrary: there was often no evidence, *ex post facto* or at the time, that rapes were committed or that rape attempts were made (Schmidt 1987; Inglis 1975; Kirkwood 1984; Kennedy 1987; Boutilier 1984). This is not to suggest that sexual assaults never occurred, but that their incidence had little to do with the fluctuations in anxiety about them. Secondly, the rape laws were race-specific; sexual abuse of black women was not classified as rape and therefore was not legally actionable, nor did rapes committed by white men lead to prosecution (Mason 1958:246–247). If these accusations of sexual threat were not prompted by the fact of rape, what did they signal and to what were they tied?

Allusions to political and sexual subversion of the colonial system went hand in hand. Concern over protection of white women intensified during real and perceived crises of control—provoked by threats to the internal cohesion of the European communities or by infringements on their borders. While the chronologies differ, we can identify a patterned *sequence* of events in which Papuan, Algerian, and South African men heightened their demands for civil rights and refused the constraints imposed upon their education, movements or dress (Inglis 1975:8, 11; Sivan 1983:178). Rape charges were thus based on perceived transgressions of political and social space. "Attempted rapes" turned out to be "incidents" of a Papuan man "discovered" in the vicinity of a white residence, a Fijian man who entered a European patient's room, a male servant poised at the bedroom door of a European woman asleep or in half-dress (Boutilier 1984:197; Inglis 1975:11; Schmidt 1987:413). With such a broad definition of danger, all colonized men of color were potential aggressors.

Accusations of sexual assault frequently followed upon heightened tensions within European communities—and renewed efforts to find consensus within them. In South Africa and Rhodesia, the relationship between reports of sexual assault and strikes among white miners and railway workers is well documented (van Onselen 1982:51; Kennedy 1987:138). Similarly, in the late 1920s when labor protests by Indonesian workers and European employees were most intense, Sumatra's corporate elite expanded their vigilante organizations, intelligence networks and demands for police protection to ensure their women were safe and their workers "in hand" (Stoler 1985b). In this particular context where the European community had been blatantly divided between low-ranking estate employees and the company elite, common interests were emphasized and domestic situations were rearranged.

The remedies intended to alleviate sexual danger embraced a common set of prescriptions for securing white control: increased surveillance of native men, new laws stipulating severe corporal punishment for the transgression of sexual and social boundaries, and the creation of areas made racially off limits. This moral rearmament of the European community and reassertion of its cultural identity charged European women with guarding new norms. While instrumental in promoting white solidarity, it was partly at their own expense. As we shall see, they were nearly as closely surveilled as colonized men (Strobel 1987).

While native men were legally punished for alleged sexual assaults, European women were frequently blamed for provoking those desires. New arrivals from Europe were accused of being too familiar with their servants, lax in their commands, indecorous in speech and dress (Vellut 1982:100; Kennedy 1987:141; Schmidt 1987:413). The Rhodesian immorality act of 1916 "made it an offence for a white woman to make an indecent suggestion to a male native" (Mason 1958:247). In Papua New Guinea "everyone" in the Australian community agreed that rape assaults were caused by a "younger generation of white women" who simply did not know how to treat servants (Inglis 1975:80). In Rhodesia as in Uganda, women were restricted to activities within the European enclaves and dissuaded from taking up farming on their own (Gartrell 1984:169; Kennedy 1987:141). As in the American South, "etiquettes of chivalry controlled white women's behavior even as [it] guarded caste lines" (Dowd Hall 1984:64). A defense of community, morality and white male power affirmed the vulnerability of white women and the sexual threat posed by native men, and created new sanctions to limit the liberties of both.

Although European colonial communities in the early 20th century assiduously monitored the movements of European women, some European women did work. French women in the settler communities of Algeria and Senegal ran farms, rooming houses and shops along with their men (Baroli 1967:159; O'Brien 1972). Elsewhere, married European women "supplemented" their husbands' incomes, helping to maintain the "white standard" (Tirefort 1979; Mercier 1965:292). Women were posted throughout the colonial empires as missionaries, nurses and teachers; while some women openly questioned the sexist policies of their male superiors, by and large their tasks buttressed rather than contested the established cultural order (Knibiehler and Goutalier 1985; Callaway 1987:111).

French feminists urged women with skills (and a desire for marriage) to settle in Indochina at the turn of the century, but colonial administrators were adamantly against their immigration. Not only was there a surfeit of widows without resources, but European seamstresses, florists and children's outfitters could not compete with the cheap and skilled labor provided by well-established Chinese firms (Corneau 1900:10, 12). In Tonkin in the 1930s there was still "little room for single women, be they unmarried, widowed or divorced"; most were shipped out of the colony at the government's charge (Gantes 1981:45). Firmly rejecting expansion based on "poor white" (*petit blanc*) settlement as in Algeria, French officials in Indochina dissuaded *colonies* with insufficient capital from entry and promptly repatriated those who tried to remain.[11] Single women were seen as the quintessential *petit blanc*, with limited resources and shopkeeper aspirations. Moreover, they presented the dangerous possibility that straitened circumstances would lead them to prostitution, thereby degrading European prestige at large.

In the Dutch East Indies, state officials identified European widows as one of the most economically vulnerable and impoverished segments of the European community (Het Pauperisme Commissie 1901:28). Professional competence did not leave European women immune from marginalization. Single professional women were held in contempt as were European prostitutes, with surprisingly similar objections.[12] The important point is that numerous categories of women fell outside the social space to which European colonial women were assigned; namely, as custodians of family welfare and respectability, and as dedicated and willing subordinates to, and supporters of, colonial men. The rigor with which these norms were applied becomes more comprehensible when we see how a European family life and bourgeois respectability became increasingly tied to notions of racial survival, imperial patriotism and the political strategies of the colonial state.

White Degeneracy, Motherhood and the Eugenics of Empire

de-gen-er-ate (adj.) [L. *degeneratus*, pp. of *degenerare*, to become unlike one's race, degenerate < *degener*, not genuine, base < *de-*, from + *genus*, race, kind: see genus]. 1. having sunk below a former or normal condition, character, etc.; deteriorated. 2. morally corrupt; depraved-n. a degenerate person, esp. one who is morally depraved or sexually perverted-vi-at'ed, at'ing 1. to decline or become debased morally, culturally, etc. 3. Biol, to undergo degeneration; deteriorate. [*Webster's New World Dictionary* 1972:371]

European women were essential to the colonial enterprise and the solidification of racial boundaries in ways that repeatedly tied their supportive and subordinate posture to community cohesion and colonial peace. These features of their positioning within imperial politics were powerfully reinforced at the turn of the century by a metropolitan bourgeois discourse (and an eminently anthropological one) intensely concerned with notions of "degeneracy" (Le Bras 1981:77). Middle-class morality, manliness and motherhood were seen as endangered by the intimately linked fears of "degeneration" and miscegenation in scientifically construed racist beliefs (Mosse 1978:82).[13] Due to environmental and/or inherited factors, degeneracy could be averted positively by eugenic selection, or negatively by eliminating the "unfit" (Mosse 1985:87; Kevles 1985:70–84). Eugenic arguments used to explain the social malaise of industrialization, immigration and urbanization in the early 20th century derived from the notion that acquired characteristics were inheritable and thus that poverty, vagrancy and promiscuity were class-linked biological traits, tied to genetic material as directly as nightblindness and blonde hair.

As part of metropolitan class politics, eugenics reverberated in the colonies in predictable as well as unexpected forms. The moral, biological and sexual referents of the notion of degeneracy (distinct in the dictionary citation above) came together in how the concept was actually deployed. The "colonial branch" of eugenics embraced a theory and practice concerned with the vulnerabilities of white rule and new measures to safeguard European superiority. Designed to control the procreation of the "unfit" lower orders, eugenics targeted "the poor, the colonized, or unpopular strangers" (Hobsbawn 1987:253). It was, however, also used by metropolitan observers against colonials, and by colonial elites against "degenerate" members among themselves (Koks 1931: 179–189). While studies in Europe and the U. S. focused on the inherent propensity of the poor for criminality, in the Indies delinquency among "European" children was biologically linked to the amount of *"native blood"* among children of poor Indo-Europeans (Braconier 1918:11). Eugenics provided not so much a new vocabulary as it did a medical and moral basis for anxiety over white prestige which reopened debates over segregated residence and education, new standards of morality, sexual vigilance and the rights of certain Europeans to rule.

Eugenic influence manifested itself, not in the direct importation of metropolitan practices such as sterilization, but in a translation of the political *principles* and the social values which eugenics implied. In defining what was unacceptable, eugenics also identified what constituted a "valuable life": "a gender-specific work and productivity, described in social, medical and psychiatric terms" (Bock 1984: 274). Applied to European colonials, eugenic statements pronounced what kind of people should represent Dutch or French rule, how they should bring up their children and with whom they should socialize. Those concerned with issues of racial survival and racial purity invoked moral arguments about the national duty of French, Dutch, British and Belgian colonial women to stay at home.

If in Britain racial deterioration was conceived to be a result of the moral turpitude and the ignorance of working-class mothers, in the colonies, the dangers were more pervasive, the posibilities of contamination worse. Formulations to secure European rule pushed in two directions: on the one hand, away from ambiguous racial genres and open domestic arrangements, and on the other hand, toward an upgrading, homogenization and a clearer delineation of European standards; away from miscegenation toward white endogamy; away from concubinage toward family formation and legal marriage; away from, as in the case of the Indies, mestizo customs and toward metropolitan norms (Taylor 1983; van Doorn 1985). As stated in the bulletin of the Netherlands Indies' Eugenic Society, "eugenics is nothing other than belief in the possibility of preventing degenerative symptoms in the body of our beloved *moedervolken*, or in cases where they may already be present, of counteracting them" (Rodenwaldt 1928:1).

Thus, whites in the colonies adhered to a politics of exclusion that policed their members as well as the colonized. Such concerns were not new to the 1920s (Taylor 1983; Sutherland 1982). As early as the mid-18th century, the Dutch East Indies Company had already taken "draconian measures" to control pauperism among "Dutchmen of mixed blood" (*Encyclopedie van Nederland-Indie* 1919:367). In the same period, the British East Indies Company legally and administratively dissuaded lower-class European migration and settlement, with the argument that it might destroy Indian respect for "the superiority of the European character" (quoted in Arnold 1983: 139). Patriotic calls to populate Java in the mid-1800s with poor Dutch farmers were also condemned, but it was with new urgency that these possibilities were rejected in the following century as challenges to European rule were more profoundly felt.

Measures were taken both to avoid poor white migration and to produce a colonial profile that highlighted the vitality, colonial patriotism and racial superiority of European men (Loutfi 1971:112–113; Ridley 1983:104). Thus, British colonial administrators were retired by the age of 55, ensuring that "no Oriental was ever allowed to see a Westerner as he aged and degenerated, just as no Westener needed ever to see himself . . . as anything but a vigorous, rational, ever-alert young Raj" (Said 1978:42). In the 20th century, these "men of class" and "men of character" embodied a modernized and renovated colonial rule; they were to safeguard the colonies against physical weakness, moral decay and the inevitable degeneration that long residence in the colonies encouraged and the temptations that interracial domestic situations had allowed.

Given this ideal, it is not surprising that colonial communities strongly discouraged the presence of nonproductive men. Dutch and French colonial administrators expressed a constant concern with the dangers of unemployed or impoverished Europeans. During the succession of economic crises in the early 20th century, relief agencies in Sumatra, for example, organized fund raisers, hill station retreats and small-scale agricultural schemes to keep "unfit" Europeans "from roaming around" (Kroniek 1917:49). The colonies were neither open for retirement nor tolerant of the public presence of poor whites. During the 1930s depression when tens of thousands of Europeans in the Indies found themselves without jobs, government and private resources were quickly mobilized to ensure that they were not "reduced" to native living standards (Veerde 1931; Kantoor van Arbeid 1935). Subsidized health care, housing and education complemented a rigorous affirmation of European cultural standards in which European womanhood played a central role in keeping men *civilisé*.

Colonial medicine reflected and affirmed the slippage between physical, moral and cultural degeneracy in numerous ways. The climatic, social and work conditions of colonial life gave rise to a specific set of psychotic disorders affecting *l'equilibre cerebral*, predisposing Europeans in the tropics to mental breakdown (Hartenberg 1910; Abatucci 1910). Neurasthenia was a major problem in the French empire and supposedly accounted for more than half the Dutch repatriations from the Indies to Holland (Winckel 1938:352). In Europe and America, it was "the phantom disease . . . the classic illness of the late 19th century," intimately linked to sexual deviation and to the destruction of the social order itself (Gilman 1985:199, 202).

While in Europe neurasthenia was considered to signal a decadent overload of "modern civilization" and its high-pitched pace, in the colonies its etiology took the *reverse* form. Colonial neurasthenia was allegedly caused by a *distance* from civilization and European community, and by proximity to the colonized. The susceptibility of a colonial male was increased by an existence "outside of the social framework to which he was adapted in France, isolation in outposts, physical and moral fatigue, and modified food regimes" (Joyeux and Sice 1937:335).[14]

The proliferation of hill stations in the 20th century reflected these political and physical concerns. Invented in the early 19th century as sites for military and sanatoria, hill stations provided "European-like environments" in which colonials could recoup their physical and mental well-being by simulating the conditions "at home" (King 1976:165). Isolated at relatively high altitudes, they took on new importance with increasing numbers of European women and children, considered particularly susceptible to anemia, depression and ill health.[15] Vacation bungalows and schools built in these "naturally" segregated surroundings provided cultural refuge and regeneration (Price 1939).

> [Young colonial men] are often driven to seek a temporary companion among women of color; this is the path by which, as I shall presently show, contagion travels back and forth, contagion in all senses of the word. [Maunier 1932:171]

Racial degeneracy was thought to have social causes and political consequences, both tied to the domestic arrangements of colonialism in specific ways. *Metissage* (interracial unions) generally, and concubinage in particular, represented the paramount danger to racial purity and cultural identity in all its forms. It was through sexual contact with women of color that French men "contracted" not only disease but debased sentiments, immoral proclivities and extreme susceptibility to decivilized states (Dupuy 1955:198).

By the early 20th century, concubinage was denounced for undermining precisely those things that it was charged with fortifying decades earlier. Local women who had been considered protectors of men's well-being were now seen as the bearers of ill health and sinister influences; adaptation to local food, language and dress, once prescribed as healthy signs of acclimatization, were now sources of contagion and loss of (white) self. The benefits of local knowledge and sexual release gave way to the more pressing demands of respectability, the community's solidarity and its mental health. Increasingly French men in Indochina who kept native women were viewed as passing into "the enemy camp" (Pujarniscle 1931:107). Concubinage became the source not only of individual breakdown and ill health, but the biological and social root of racial degeneration and political unrest. Children born of these unions were "the fruits of a regrettable weakness" (Mazet 1932:8), physically marked and morally marred with "the defaults and mediocre qualities of their [native] mothers" (Douchet 1928:10).

Concubinage was not as economically tidy and politically neat as colonial policy makers had hoped. It concerned more than sexual exploitation and unpaid domestic work; it was about children—many more than official statistics often revealed— and who was to be acknowledged as a European and who was not. Concubine children posed a classificatory problem, impinging on political security and white prestige. The majority of such children were not recognized by their fathers, nor were they reabsorbed into local communities as authorities often claimed. Although some European men legally acknowledged their progeny, many repatriated to Holland, Britain or France and cut off ties and support to mother and children (Brou 1907; Ming 1983:75). Native women had responsibility for, but attenuated rights over, their own offspring. They could neither prevent their children from being taken from them nor contest paternal suitability for custody. While the legal system favored a European upbringing, it made no demands on European men to provide it; many children became wards of the state, subject to the scrutiny and imposed charity of the European-born community at large.

European pauperism in the Indies reflected broad inequalities in colonial society, underscoring the social heterogeneity of the category "European" itself. Nonetheless, as late as 1917, concubinage was still seen by some as its major cause and as the principal source of *"blanken-haters"* (white-haters) (Braconier 1917:298). Concubinage became equated with a progeny of "malcontents," of "parasitic" whites, idle and therefore dangerous. The fear of concubinage was carried yet a step further and tied to the political fear that such Eurasians would demand economic access and political rights and express their own interests through alliance with (and leadership of) organized opposition to Dutch rule (Mansvelt 1932; Blumberger 1939).[16]

Racial prejudice against *métis* was often, as in the Belgian Congo, "camouflaged under protestations of 'pity' for their fate, as if they were *'malheureux'* [unhappy] beings by definition" (Vellut 1982:103). As objects of charity, their protection in Indochina was a cause célèbre of European women—feminists and staunch colonial supporters—at home and abroad (Knibiehler and Goutalier 1985:37). European colonial women were urged to oversee their "moral protection," to develop their "natural" inclination toward French society, to turn them into "partisans of French ideas and influence" instead of revolutionaries (Chenet 1936:8; Sambuc 1931:261). The gender breakdown is clear: moral instruction reflected fears of sexual promiscuity in *métisse* girls and the political threat of *métis* boys turned militant men.

European Motherhood and Middle-Class Morality

> "A man remains a man as long as he is under the watch of a woman of his race." [George Hardy quoted in Chivas-Baron 1929:103]

Rationalization of imperial rule and safeguards against racial degeneracy in European colonies merged in the emphasis on particular moral themes. Both entailed a reassertion of European conventions, middle-class respectability, more frequent ties with the metropole and a restatement of what was culturally distinct and superior about how colonials ruled and lived. For those women who came to join their spouses or to find husbands, the prescriptions were clear. Just as new plantation employees were taught to manage the natives, women were schooled in colonial propriety and domestic management. French manuals, such as those on colonial hygiene in Indochina, outlined the duties of colonial wives in no uncertain terms. As "auxiliary forces" in the imperial effort they were to "conserve the fitness and sometimes the life of all around them" by ensuring that "the home be happy and gay and that all take pleasure in clustering there" (Grall 1908:66; Chailley-Bert 1897). Practical guides to life in the Belgian Congo instructed (and indeed warned) *la femme blanche* that she was to keep "order, peace, hygiene and economy" (Favre 1938:217), "perpetuate a vigorous race," while preventing any "laxity in our administrative mores" (Favre 1938:256; Travaux du Groupe d'Etudes Coloniales 1910:10).

This "division of labor" contained obvious asymmetries. Men were considered more susceptible to moral turpitude than women, who were thus held responsible for the immoral states of men. European women were to create and protect colonial prestige, insulating their men from cultural and sexual contact with the colonized (Travaux . . . Coloniales 1910:7). Racial degeneracy would be curtailed by European women charged with regenerating the physical health, the metropolitan affinities and the imperial purpose of their men (Hardy 1929:78).

At its heart was a reassertion of racial difference which harnessed nationalistic rhetoric and markers of middle-class morality to its cause (Delavignette 1946:47, Loutfi 1971:112; Mosse 1978:86). George Mosse describes European racism in the early 20th century as a "scavenger ideology," annexing nationalism and bourgeois respectability such that control over sexuality was central to all three (1985:10,

133–152). If the European middle class sought respectability "to maintain their status and self-respect against the lower-classes, and the aristocracy," in the colonies respectability was a defense against the colonized, and a way of more clearly defining themselves (Mosse 1985:5). Good colonial living now meant hard work, no sloth, and physical exercise rather than sexual release, which had been one rationale for condoning concubinage and prostitution in an earlier period. The debilitating influences of climate could be surmounted by regular diet and meticulous personal hygiene over which European women were to take full charge. Manuals on how to run a European household in the tropics provided detailed instructions in domestic science, moral upbringing and employer-servant relations. Adherence to strict conventions of cleanliness and cooking occupied an inordinate amount of women's time (Hermans 1925; Ridley 1983:77). Both activities entailed a constant surveillance of native nursemaids, laundrymen and live-in servants, while reinforcing the domestication of European women themselves (Brink 1920:43).

Leisure, good spirits, and creature comforts became the obligation of women to provide, the racial duty of women to maintain. Sexual temptations with women of color would be curtailed by a happy family life, much as "extremist agitation" on Sumatra's estates was to be averted by selecting married recruits and by providing family housing to permanent workers (Stoler 1985a). Moral laxity would be eliminated through the example and vigilance of women whose status was defined by their sexual restraint, and dedication to their homes and to their men.

The perceptions and practice that bound women's domesticity to national welfare and racial purity were not applied to colonial women alone. Childrearing in late 19th-century Britain was hailed as a national, imperial, and racial duty, as it was in Holland, the U. S. and Germany at the same time (Davin 1978:13; Smith-Rosenberg and Rosenberg 1973:35), Bock 1984:274; Stuurman 1985). In France, where declining birth rates were of grave concern, popular colonial authors such as Pierre Mille pushed mothering as women's "essential contribution to the imperial mission of France" (Ridley 1983:90). With motherhood at the center of empire building, pronatalist policies in Europe forced some improvement in colonial medical facilities, the addition of maternity wards, increased information and control over the reproductive conditions of European and colonized women alike. Maternal and infant health programs instructed European women in the use of milk substitutes, wet nurses and breastfeeding practices in an effort to encourage more women to stay in the colonies and in response to the many more that came (Hunt 1988). But the belief that the colonies were medically hazardous for white women meant that motherhood in the tropics was not only a precarious but a conflicted endeavor. French women bound for Indochina were warned that they would only be able to fulfill their maternal duty "with great hardship and damage to [their] health" (Grall 1908:65).

Real and imagined concern over individual reproduction and racial survival contained and compromised white colonial women in a number of ways. Tropical climates were said to cause low fertility, prolonged amenorrhea and permanent sterility (Rodenwalt 1928:3; Hermans 1925:123). Belgian doctors confirmed that "the woman who goes to live in a tropical climate is often lost for the reproduction of the race" (Knibiehler and Goutalier 1985:92; Vellut 1982:100). The climatic and medical conditions of colonial life were associated with high infant mortality, such that "the life of a European child was nearly condemned in advance" (Grall 1908:65; Price 1939:204).

Imperial perceptions and policies fixed European women in the colonies as "instruments of race-culture" in what proved to be personally difficult and contradictory ways (Hammerton 1979). Childrearing manuals faithfully followed the sorts of racist principles that constrained the activities of women charged with childcare (Grimshaw 1983:507). Medical experts and women's organizations recommended strict surveillance of children's activities (Mackinnon 1920:944) and careful attention to those with whom they played. Virtually every medical and household handbook in the Dutch, French and British colonies in the early 20th century warned against leaving small children in the unsupervised care of local servants. In the Netherlands Indies, it was the "duty" of the *hedendaagsche blanke moeder* (modern white mother) to take the physical and spiritual upbringing of her offspring away from the *babu* (native nursemaid) and into her own hands (Wanderken 1943:173). Precautions had to be taken against "sexual danger," uncleanly habits of domestics, against a "stupid negress" who might leave a child exposed to the sun (Bauduin 1941; Bérenger-Féraud 1875:491). Even in colonies where the climate was not considered unhealthy, European children supposedly thrived well "only up to the age of six" when native cultural influences came into stronger play (Price 1939:204; Grimshaw 1983:507). In the Dutch East Indies, where educational facilities for European children were considered excellent, some still deemed it imperative to send them back to Holland to avoid the "precocity" associated with the tropics and the "danger" of contact with *Indische* youths not from "full-blooded European elements" (Bauduin 1941:63).

> We Dutch in the Indies live in a country which is not our own . . . we feel instinctively that our blonde, white children belong to the blonde, white dunes, the forests, the moors, the lakes, the snow. . . . A Dutch child should grow up in Holland. There they will acquire the characteristics of their race, not only from mother's milk but also from the influence of the light, sun and water, of playmates, of life, in a word, in the sphere of the fatherland. This is not racism. . . . [Bauduin 1941:63–4]

But even in the absence of such firm convictions, how to assure the "moral upbringing" of European children in the colonies remained a primary focus of women's organizations in the Indies and elsewhere right through decolonization.[17] In many colonial communities, school age children were packed off to Europe for education and socialization. In those cases European women were confronted with a difficult set of choices which entailed separation either from their children or husbands. Frequent trips between colony and metropole not only separated families, but also broke up marriages and homes (Malleret 1934:164; Grimshaw 1983:507; Callaway 1987:183–184). The important point is that the imperial duty of women to closely surveil husbands, servants and children profoundly affected the social space they occupied and the economic activities in which they could feasibly engage.

Shifting Strategies of Rule and Sexual Morality

> Though sex cannot of itself enable men to transcend racial barriers, it generates some admiration and affection across them, which is healthy, and which cannot always be dismissed as merely self-interested and prudential. On the whole, sexual interaction between Europeans and non-Europeans probably did more good than harm to race relations; at any rate, I cannot accept the feminist contention that it was fundamentally undesirable. [Hyam 1986a:75]

The political etymology of colonizer and colonized was gender and class specific. The exclusionary politics of colonialism demarcated not just external boundaries but interior frontiers, specifying internal conformity and order among Europeans themselves. I have tried to show that the categories of colonizer and colonized were secured through notions of racial difference constructed in gender terms. Redefinitions of sexual protocol and morality emerged during crises of colonial control precisely because they called into question the tenuous artifices of rule *within* European communities and what marked their borders. Even from the limited cases we have reviewed, several patterns emerge. First and most obviously, colonial sexual prohibitions were racially assymetric and gender specific. Thus racial attributes were rarely discussed in nongendered terms; one was always a black *man*, an Asian *woman*. Secondly, interdictions against interracial unions were rarely a primary impulse in the strategies of rule. Interracial unions (as opposed to marriage) between European men and colonized women aided the long-term settlement of European men in the colonies while ensuring that colonial patrimony stayed in limited and selective hands. In India, Indochina and South Africa in the early centuries—colonial contexts usually associated with sharp social sanctions against interracial unions—"mixing" was systematically tolerated and even condoned.[18]

Changes in sexual access and domestic arrangements have invariably accompanied major efforts to reassert the internal coherence of European communities and to redefine the boundaries of privilege between the colonizer and the colonized. Sexual union in itself, however, did not automatically produce a larger population legally classified as "European." On the contrary, miscegenation signaled neither the absence nor presence of racial prejudice in itself; hierarchies of privilege and power were written into the *condoning* of interracial unions, as well as into their condemnation.

While the chronologies vary from one colonial context to another, we can identify some parallel shifts in the strategies of rule and in sexual morality. Concubinage fell into moral disfavor at the same time that new emphasis was placed on the standardization of European administration. While this occurred in some colonies by the early 20th century and in others later on, the correspondence between rationalized rule, bourgeois respectability and the custodial power of European women to protect their men seems strongest during the interwar years when Western scientific and technological achievements were in question, and native nationalist and labor movements were hard pressing their demands.[19] Debates concerning the need to systematize colonial management and dissolve the provincial and personalized satraps of "the old-time *colon*" in the French empire invariably targeted and condemned the unseemly domestic arrangements in which they lived. British high colonial officials in Africa imposed new "character" requirements on their subordinates, designating specific class attributes and conjugal ties that such a selection implied (Kuklick 1979). Critical to this restructuring was a new disdain for colonials too adapted to local custom, too removed from the local European community, and too encumbered with intimate native ties. As in Sumatra, this hands-off policy distanced Europeans in more than one sense: it forbade European staff both from personal confrontations with their Asian fieldhands and from the limited local knowledge they gained through sexual ties.

I have focused here on the multiple levels at which sexual control figured in the substance, as well as the iconography, of racial policy and imperial rule. But colonial politics was obviously not just about sex; nor did sexual relations reduce to colonial politics. On the contrary, sex in the colonies was about sexual access and reproduction, class distinctions and racial privileges, nationalism and European identity in different measure and not all at the same time. These major shifts in the positioning of women were not signaled by the penetration of capitalism per se but by more subtle changes in class politics, imperial morality and as responses to the vulnerabilities of colonial control. As we attempt broader ethnographies of empire, we may begin to capture how European culture and class politics resonated in colonial settings, how class and gender discriminations not only were translated into racial attitudes, but themselves reverberated in the metropole as they were fortified on colonial ground. Such investigations should help show that sexual control was both an instrumental image for the body politic, a salient part standing for the whole, and itself fundamental to how racial policies were secured and how colonial projects were carried out.

Notes

1. Here I focus primarily on the dominant male discourse (and less on women's perceptions of social and legal constraints) since it was the structural positioning of European women in colonial society and how their needs were defined *for*, not *by*, them which most directly accounted for specific policies.

2. See Verena Martinez-Alier (1974) on the subtle and changing criteria by which color was assigned in 19th-century Cuba. Also see A. van Marle (1952) on shifting cultural markers of European membership in the 19th- and early 20th-century Netherlands Indies.

3. See Malleret (1934:216–241). See also Tiffany and Adams, who argue that "the Romance of the Wild Woman" expressed critical distinctions between civilization and the primitive, culture and nature, and the class differences between repressed middle-class women and "her regressively primitive antithesis, the working-class girl" (Tiffany and Adams 1985:13).

4. Many of these studies focus on South Africa and tend to provide more insight into the composition of the black labor force than into the restrictions on European women themselves (Cock 1980; Gaitskell 1983; Hansen 1986). Important exceptions are those which have traced historical changes in colonial prostitution and domestic service where restrictions were explicitly class specific and directly tied racial policy to sexual control (Ming 1983; Van Heyningen 1984; Hesselink 1987; Schmidt 1987).

5. As Tessel Pollmann suggests, the term *nyai* glossed several functions: household

manager, servant, housewife, wife and prostitute. Which of these was most prominent depended on the character of both partners and on the prosperity of the European man (1986:100). Most colonized women, however, combining sexual and
domestic service within the abjectly subordinate contexts of slave or "coolie," lived
in separate quarters, and exercised very few legal rights; they could be dismissed
without reason or notice, were exchanged among European employers and most significantly, as stipulated in the Indies Civil Code of 1848, "had no rights over children recognized by a white man" (Taylor 1977:30). On Java, however, some *nyai*
achieved some degree of limited authority, managing the businesses as well as the
servants and household affairs of better-off European men (Nieuwenhuys 1959:17;
Lucas 1986:86; Taylor 1983).

6. While prostitution served some of the colonies for some of the time, it was economically costly, medically unwieldy and socially problematic. Venereal disease was difficult to check even with the elaborate system of lock hospitals and contagious disease
acts of the British empire and was of little interest to those administrations bent on
promoting permanent settlement (Ballhatchet 1980; Ming 1983). When concubinage was condemned in the 1920s in India, Malaya and Indonesia, venereal disease
spread rapidly, giving rise to new efforts to reorder the domestic arrangements of
European men (Butcher 1979:217; Ming 1983; Braconier 1933; Ballhatchet 1980).

7. See Ritter, who describes these arrangements in the mid-19th century as a "necessary evil" with no emotional attachments, because for the native woman, "the meaning of our word 'love' is entirely unknown" (1856:21).

8. On the differences between Java's European community which was sharply divided
between the *totoks* (full-blooded Dutch born in Holland) and the *Indisch* majority
(Europeans of mixed parentage and/or those Dutch born in the Indies), and Sumatra's European-oriented and non-*Indisch* colonial community, see Muller (1912),
Wertheim (1959), van Doorn (1985), Stoler (1985b).

9. Similarly, one might draw the conventional contrast between the different racial
policies in French, British and Dutch colonies. However, despite French assimila-
tionist rhetoric, Dutch tolerance of intermarriage, and Britain's overtly segregationist stance, the similarities in the actual maintenance of racial distinctions through
sexual control in these varied contexts is perhaps more striking than the differences.
For the moment, it is these similarities with which I am concerned. See, for example,
Simon (1981:46–48), who argues that although French colonial rule was generally
thought to be more racially tolerant than that of Britain, racial distinctions in
French Indochina were *in practice* vigorously maintained.

10. Although some Dutch women in fact championed the cause of the wronged *nyai*,
urging improved protection for nonprovisioned women and children, they rarely
went so far as to advocate for the legitimation of these unions in legal marriage
(Taylor 1977:31–32; Lucas 1986:95).

11. See the French Archive d'Outre Mer, Series S.65, "Free Passage Accorded to Europeans," including dossiers on "free passage for impoverished Europeans," for example GG 9925, 1897; GG 2269, 1899–1903.

12. Cf. van Onselen (1982:103–162), who argues that the presence of European prostitutes and domestics-turned-prostitutes in South Africa was secured by a large, white
working-class population, and a highly unstable labor market for white working-
class women. Also see van Heyningen, who ties changes in the history of prostitution among continental women in the Cape Colony to new notions of racial purity
and the large-scale urbanization of blacks after the turn of the century
(1984:192–195).

13. As George Mosse notes, the concept of racial degeneration had been tied to miscegenation by Gobineau and others in the early 1800s but gained common currency in

the decades that followed, entering European medical and popular vocabulary at the turn of the century (1978:82–88).

14. Adherence to the idea that "tropical neurasthenia" was a specific malady was not shared by all medical practitioners. Those who suggested that the use of the term be discontinued did so on the belief that neurasthenia in the tropics was a pyschopathology caused by social, not physiological, maladjustment (Culpin [1926] cited in Price 1939:211).

15. On the social geography of hill stations in British India and on the predominance of women and children in them, see King 1976:156–179.

16. French government investigations, accordingly, exhibited a concern for "the *métis* problem" which was out of proportion with the numbers of those who fell in that category. While the number of "Indos" in the Indies was far greater, there was never any indication that this social group would constitute the vanguard of an anticolonial movement.

17. See, for example, the contents of women's magazines such as the *Huisvrouw in Deli* for which the question of education in Holland or the Indies was a central issue. The rise of specific programs (such as the *Clerkx-methode voor Huisonderwijs*) designed to guide European mothers in the home instruction of their children may have been a response to this new push for women to oversee directly the moral upbringing of their children.

18. I have focused on late colonialism in Asia, but colonial elite intervention in the sexual life of their agents and subjects was by no means confined to this place or period. See Nash (1980:141) on changes in mixed marriage restrictions in 16th-century Mexico and Martinez-Alier on interracial marriage prohibitions in relationship to slave labor supplies in 18th- and early 19th-century Cuba (1974:39).

19. See Adas (1989) for a discussion of major shifts in colonial thinking during this period.

Works Cited

Abatucci. 1910. Le milieu africain considéré au point de vue de ses effets sur le système nerveux de l'européen. Annales d'Hygiène et de Médecine Coloniale 13, 328–335.

Adas, Michael. 1989. Machines as the Measure of Men: Scientific and Technological Superiority and Ideologies of Western Dominance. Ithaca: Cornell University Press.

Arnold, David. 1979. European Orphans and Vagrants in India in the Nineteenth Century. The Journal of Imperial and Commonwealth History 7:2, 104–27.

———. 1983. White Colonization and Labour in Nineteenth-Century India. The Journal of Imperial and Commonwealth History 11:2, 133–158.

Ballhatchet, Kenneth. 1980. Race, Sex and Class under the Raj: Imperial Attitudes and Policies and Their Critics, 1793–1905. New York: St. Martin's Press.

Baroli, Marc. 1967. La vie quotidienne des Français en Algérie. Paris: Hachette.

Bauduin, D. C. M. 1941 (1927). Het Indische Leven. 'S. Gravenhage: H. P. Leopolds.

Beidelman, Thomas. 1982. Colonial Evangelism. Bloomington: Indiana University Press.

Bérenger-Féraud, L. 1875. Traité Clinique des Maladies des Européens au Sénégal. Paris: Adrien Delahaye.

Blumberger, J. Th. Petrus. 1939. De Indo-Europeesche Beweging in Nederlandsch-Indie. Haarlem: Tjeenk Willink.

Blussé, Leonard. 1986. Strange Company: Chinese Settlers, Mestizo Women and the Dutch in VOC Batavia. Dordrecht: Foris.

Bock, Gisela. 1984. Racism and Sexism in Nazi Germany: Motherhood, Compulsory Sterilization, and the State. In When Biology Became Destiny: Women in Weimar and Nazi Germany. New York: Monthly Review Press, 271–296.

Boutilier, James. 1984. European Women in the Solomon Islands, 1900–1942. *In* Rethinking Women's Roles: Perspectives from the Pacific. Denise O'Brien and Sharon Tiffany, eds. Berkeley: University of California Press, 173–199.

Braconier, A. de. 1913. Het Kazerne-Concubinaat in Ned-Indie. Vragen van den Dag 28, 974–95.

———. 1917. Het Pauperisme onder de in Ned. Oost-Indie levende Europeanen. *In* Nederlandsch-Indie (1st yr.), 291–300.

———. 1918. Kindercriminaliteit en de verzorging van misdadiq aangelegde en verwaarloosde minderjarigen in Nederlandsch Indie. Baarn: Hollandia-Drukkerij.

———. 1933. Het Prostitutie-vraagstuk in Nederlandsch-Indie Indisch Gids 55:2, 906–928.

Brink, K. B. M. Ten. 1920. Indische Gezondheid. Batavia: Nilmij.

Brou, A. M. N. 1907. Le Métis Franco-Annamite. Revue Indochinois (July 1907):897–908.

Brownfoot, Janice N. 1984. Memsahibs in Colonial Malaya: A Study of European Wives in a British Colony and Protectorate 1900–1940. *In* The Incorporated Wife. Hilary Callan and Shirley Ardener, eds. London: Croom Helm.

Butcher, John. 1979. The British in Malaya, 1880–1941: The Social History of a European Community in Colonial Southeast Asia. Kuala Lumpur: Oxford UP.

Callan, Hilary, and Shirley Ardener, eds. 1984. The Incorporated Wife. London: Croom Helm.

Callaway, Helen. 1987. Gender, Culture and Empire: European Women in Colonial Nigeria, London: Macmillan Press.

Chailley-Bert, M. J. 1897. L'Emigration des femmes aux colonies. Union Coloniale Francaise-conférence, 12 January 1897. Paris: Armand Colin.

Chenet, Ch. 1936. Le role de la femme française aux Colonies: Protection des enfants métis abandonnés. Le Devoir des Femmes, 15 February 1936, p. 8.

Chivas-Baron, Clotide. 1929. La femme française aux colonies, Paris: Larose.

Clerkx, Lily. 1961. Mensen in Deli. Amsterdam: Sociologisch-Historisch Seminarium voor Zuidoost-Azie. Publication no. 2.

Cock, J. 1980. Maids and Madams. Johannesburg: Ravan Press.

Cohen, William. 1971. Rulers of Empire: The French Colonial Service in Africa. Stanford: Hoover Institution Press.

———. 1980. The French Encounter with Africans. White Response to Blacks, 1530–1880. Bloomington: Indiana University Press.

Comaroff, John. 1989. Images of Empire Contests of Conscience: Models of Domination in South Africa. American Entomologist 16:4, 661–685.

Cool, F. 1938. De Bestrijding der Werkloosheidsgevolgen in Nederlandsch-Indie gedurende 1930–1936. De Economist, 135–47; 217–243.

Cooper, Frederick. 1980. From Slaves to Squatters. New Haven: Yale University Press.

Corneau, Grace. 1900. La femme aux colonies. Paris: Librairie Nilsson.

Courtois, E. 1900. Des Règles Hygiéniques que doit suivre l'Européen au Tonkin. Revue Indo-chinoise 83, 539–541; 564–566; 598–601.

Davin, Anna. 1978. Imperialism and Motherhood. History Workshop 5, 9–57.

Delavignette, Robert. 1946. Service Africain. Paris: Gallimard.

Douchet. 1928. Métis et congaies d'Indochine. Hanoi.

Dowd Hall, Jacquelyn. 1984. "The Mind That Burns in Each Body": Women, Rape, and Racial Violence. Southern Exposure 12:6, 61–71.

Drooglever, P. 1980. De Vaderlandse Club, 1929–42. Franeker: T. Wever.

Dupuy, Aimé. 1955. La personnalité du colon. Revue d'Histoire Economique et Sociale 33:1, 77–103.

Encylopedie van Nederland-Indie. 1919. S'Gravenhage: Nijhoff and Brill.

Etienne, Mona, and Eleanor Leacock. 1980. Women and Colonization. New York: Praeger.

Fanon, Frantz. 1967[1952]. Black Skin, White Masks, New York: Grove Press.

Favre, J. L. 1938. La Vie aux Colonies. Paris: Larose.

Fredrickson, George. 1981. White Supremacy. New York: Oxford University Press.

Gaitskell, Deborah. 1983. Housewives, Maids or Mothers: Some Contradictions of Domesticity for Christian Women in Johannesburg, 1903–39. Journal of African History 24, 241–256.

Gann, L. H., and Peter Duignan. 1978. The Rulers of British Africa, 1870–1914. Stanford: Stanford University Press.

Gantes, Gilles de. 1981. La population française au Tonkin entre 1931 et 1938. Memoire. Aix-en-Provence: Institut d'Histoire des Pays d'Outre Mer.

Gartrell, Beverley. 1984. Colonial Wives: Villains or Victims? In The Incorporated Wife. Hilary Callan and Shirley Ardener, eds. London: Croom Helm, 165–185.

Gilman, Sander L. 1985. Difference and Pathology. Ithaca: Cornell University Press.

Gordon, R., and M. Meggitt. 1985. Law and Order in the New Guinea Highlands. Hanover: University Press of New England.

Grall, Ch. 1908. Hygiène Coloniale appliquée. Paris: Baillière.

Grimshaw, Patricia. 1983. Christian Woman, Pious Wife, Faithful Mother, Devoted Missionary: Conflicts in Roles of American Missionary Women in Nineteenth-Century Hawaii. Feminist Studies 9:3, 489–521.

Hammerton, James. 1979. Emigrant Gentlewomen. London: Croom Helm.

Hansen, Karen Tranberg. 1986. Household Work as a Man's Job: Sex and Gender in Domestic Service in Zambia. Anthropology Today 2:3, 18–23.

Hardy, George. 1929. Ergaste ou la Vocation Coloniale. Paris: Armand Colin.

Hartenberg. 1910. Les Troubles Nerveux et Mentaux chez les coloniaux. Paris.

Hermans, E. H. 1925. Gezondscheidsleer voor Nederlandsch-Indie. Amsterdam: Meulenhoff.

Hesselink, Liesbeth. 1987. Prostitution: A Necessary Evil, Particularly in the Colonies: Views on Prostitution in the Netherlands Indies. In Indonesian Women in Focus. E. Locher-Scholten and A. Niehof, eds. Dordrecht: Foris, 205–224.

Het Pauperisme Commissie. 1901. Het Pauperisme onder de Europeanen, Batavia: Landsdrukkerij.

———. 1903 Rapport der Pauperisme-Commissie. Batavia: Landsdrukkerij.

Hobsbawm, Eric. 1987. The Age of Empire, 1875–1914, London: Weidenfeld and Nicholson.

Hunt, Nancy. 1988. Le bébé en brousse: European Women, African Birth Spacing and Colonial Intervention in Breast Feeding in the Belgian Congo. International Journal of African Historical Studies 21:3.

Hyam, Ronald. 1986a. Empire and Sexual Opportunity. The Journal of Imperial and Commonwealth History 14:2, 34–90.

———. 1986b Concubinage and the Colonial Service: The Crewe Circular (1909). The Journal of Imperial and Commonwealth History 14:3, 170–86.

Inglis, Amirah. 1975. The White Women's Protection Ordinance: Sexual Anxiety and Politics in Papua. London: Sussex University Press.

Jordan, Winthrop. 1968. White over Black: American Attitudes Toward the Negro, 1550–1812. Chapel Hill: University of North Carolina Press.

Joyeux, Ch. and A. Sice. 1937. Affections exotiques du système nerveux. Précis de Médecine Coloniale. Paris: Masson.

Kantoor van Arbeid. 1935. Werkloosheid in Nederlandsch-Indie. Batavia: Landsdrukkerij.

Kennedy, Dane. 1987. Islands of White. Durham: Duke University Press.

Kennedy, Raymond. 1947. The Ageless Indies. New York: John Day.

Kevles, Daniel. 1985. In the Name of Eugenics. Berkeley: University of California Press.

King, Anthony. 1976. Colonial Urban Development. London: Routledge & Kegan Paul.

Kirkwood, Deborah. 1984. Settler Wives in Southern Rhodesia: A Case Study. *In* The Incorporated Wife. Hillary Callan and Shirley Ardener, eds. London: Croom Helm.

Knibiehler, Y. and R. Goutalier. 1985. La femme au temps des colonies. Paris: Stock.

———. 1987 Femmes et Colonisation: Rapport Terminal au Ministère des Relations Extérieures et de la Cooperération. Aix en-Provence: Institut d'Histoire des Pays d'Outre-Mer.

Koks, Dr. J. Th. 1931. De Indo. Amsterdam: H. J. Paris.

Kroniek. 1917. Oostkust van Sumatra-Instituut. Amsterdam: J. H. de Bussy.

Kuklick, Henrika. 1979. The Imperial Bureaucrat: The Colonial Administrative Service in the Gold Coast, 1920–1939. Stanford: Hoover Institution Press.

Le Bras, Hervé. 1981. Histoire secrète de la fécondité. Le Débat 8:76–100.

Loutfi, Martine Astier. 1971. Littérature et Colonialisme. Paris: Mouton.

Lucas, Nicole. 1986. Trouwverbod, inlandse huishousdsters en Europese vrouwen. In Vrouwen in de Nederlandse Kolonien. J. Reijs, et al., eds. Nijmegen: SUN, 78–97.

Mackinnon, Murdoch. 1920. European Children in the Tropical Highlands. Lancet 199:944–945.

Malleret, Louis. 1934. L'Exotisme Indochinois dans la Littérature Française depuis 1860. Paris: Larose.

Mannoni, Octavio. [1950] 1964. Prospero and Caliban. New York: Praeger.

Mansvelt, W. 1932. De Positie der Indo-Europeanen. Kolonial Studien, 290–311.

Martinez-Alier, Verena. 1974. Marriage, Class and Colour in Nineteenth Century Cuba. Cambridge: Cambridge University Press.

Mason, Philip. 1958. The Birth of a Dilemma: The Conquest and Settlement of Rhodesia. New York: Oxford University Press.

Maunier, M. René. 1932. Sociologic Coloniale, Paris: Domat-Montchrestien.

Mazet, Jacques. 1932. La Condition Juridique des Métis. Paris: Domat Montchrestien.

Mercier, Paul. 1965. The European Community of Dakar. In Africa: Social Problems of Change and Conflict. Pierre van den Berghe, ed. San Francisco: Chandler, 284–304.

Ming, Hanneke. 1983. Barracks-Concubinage in the Indies, 1887–1920. Indonesia 35 (April):65–93.

Moore-Gilbert, B. J. 1986. Kipling and "Orientalism." New York: St. Martin's.

Mosse, George. 1978. Toward the Final Solution. New York: Fertig.

———. 1985 Nationalism and Sexuality. Madison: University of Wisconsin Press.

Muller, Hendrik. 1912. De Europeesche Samenleving. Neerlands Indie. Amsterdam: Elsevier: 371–384.

Nandy, Ashis. 1983. The Intimate Enemy: Loss and Recovery of Self under Colonialism. Delhi: Oxford University Press.

Nash, June. 1980. Aztec Women: The Transition from Status to Class in Empire and

Colony. *In* Women and Colonization: Anthropological Perspectives. Mona Etienne and Eleanor Leacock, eds. New York: Praeger, 134–148.

Nieuwenhuys, Roger. 1959. Tussen Twee Vaderlanden. Amsterdam: Van Oorschot.

Nora, Pierre. 1961. Les Francais d'Algerie. Paris: Julliard.

O'Brien, Rita Cruise. 1972. White Society in Black Africa: The French in Senegal. London: Faber & Faber.

Pollmann, Tessel. 1986. Bruidstraantjes: De Koloniale roman, de njai en de apartheid. *In* Vrouwen in de Nederlandse Kolonien. J. Reijs, et al., eds. Nijmegen: SUN, 98–125.

Price, Grenfell A. 1939. White Settlers in the Tropics. New York: American Geographical Society.

Prochaska, David. 1989. Making Algeria French: Colonialism in Bone, 1870–1920. Cambridge: Cambridge University Press.

Pujarniscle, E. 1931. Philoxène ou de la literature coloniale. Paris.

Reijs, J., E. Klock, U. Jansz, A. de Wildt, S. van Norden, M. de Baar. 1986. Vrouwen in de Nederlandse Kolonien. Nijmegen: SUN.

Ridley, Hugh. 1983. Images of Imperial Rule. New York: Croom Helm.

Ritter, W. L. 1856. De European in Nederlandsch Indie. Leyden: Sythoff.

Rodenwalt, Ernest. 1928. Eugentische Problemen in Nederlandsch-Indie. Ons Nageslacht, 1–8.

Said, Edward W. 1978. Orientalism. New York: Vintage.

Sambuc. 1931. Les Métis Franco-Annamites en Indochine. Revue du Pacifique, 256–272.

Schmidt, Elizabeth. 1987. Ideology, Economics and the Role of Shona Women in Southern Rhodesia, 1850–1939. Ph. D. dissertation, University of Wisconsin.

Schoevers, T. 1913. Het leven en werken van den assistent bij de Tabakscultuur in Deli, Jaarbock der Vereeniging "Studiebelangen." Wageningen: Zomer, 3–43.

Simon, Jean-Pierre. 1981. Rapatriés d'Indochine. Paris: Harmattan.

Sivan, Emmanuel. 1983. Interpretations of Islam. Princeton: Darwin Press.

Smith-Rosenberg, Carroll, and Charles Rosenberg. 1973. The Female Animal: Medical and Biological Views of Woman and Her Role in Nineteenth-Century America. Journal of American History 60:2, 332–356.

Spear, Percival. 1963. The Nabobs. London: Oxford University Press.

Stoler, Ann. 1985a. Capitalism and Confrontation in Sumatra's Plantation Belt, 1870–1979. New Haven: Yale University Press.

———. 1985b. Perceptions of Protest. American Ethnologist 12:4, 642–658.

———. 1989. Rethinking Colonial Categories: European Communities and the Boundaries of Rule. Comp. Studies in Society and History 13:1, 134–161.

Strobel, Margaret. 1987. Gender and Race in the 19th and 20th Century British Empire. *In* Becoming Visible: Women in European History. R. Bridenthal et al., eds. Boston: Houghton Mifflin, 375–396.

Stuurman, Siep. 1985. Verzuiling, Kapitalisme en Patriarchaat. Nijmegen: SUN.

Sutherland, Heather. 1982. Ethnicity and Access in Colonial Macassar. *In* Papers of the Dutch-Indonesian Historical Conference. Leiden: Bureau of Indonesian Studies, 250–277.

Takaki, Ronald. 1977. Iron Cages. Berkeley: University of California Press.

Taylor, Jean. 1977. The World of Women in the Colonial Dutch Novel. Kabar Seberang 2, 26–41.

———. 1983 The Social World of Batavia. Madison: University of Wisconsin Press.

Tiffany, Sharon, and Kathleen Adams. 1985. The Wild Woman: An Inquiry into the Anthropology of an Idea. Cambridge, MA: Schenkman Publishing Co.

Tirefort, A. 1979. 'Le Bon Temps': La Communauté Francaise en Basse Cote d'Ivoire pendant l'Entre-Deux Guerres, 1920–1940. Troisème Cycle, Centre d'Etudes Africaines, Paris.

Travaux du Groupe d'Etudes Coloniales. 1910. La Femme Blanche au Congo. Brussels: Misch & Thron.

Van Dorin, Jacques. 1983. A Divided Society: Segmentation and Mediation in Late-Colonial Indonesia. Rotterdam: CASPA. 1985 Indie als Koloniale Maatschappy. *In* De Nederlandse samenleving sinds 1815. F. L. van Holthoon, ed. Assen: Maastricht.

Van Helten, J., and K. Williams. 1983. 'The Crying Need of South Africa': The Emigration of Single British Women in the Transvaal, 1901–1910. Journal of South African Studies 10:1, 11–38.

Van Heyningen, Elizabeth B. 1984. The Social Evil in the Cape Colony 1868–1902: Prostitution and the Contagious Disease Acts. Journal of Southern African Studies 10:2, 170–197.

Van Marle, A. 1952. De group der Europeanen in Nederlands-Indie. Indonesie. 5:2, 77–121; 5:3, 314–341; 5:5, 481–507.

Van Onselen, Charles. 1982. Studies in the Social and Economic History of the Witwatersrand 1886–1914. Vol. 1. New York: Longman.

Veerde, A. G. 1931. Onderzock naar den omvang der werkloosheid op java, November 1930–Juni 1931). Koloniale Studien, 242–273; 503–533.

Vellut, Jean-Luc. 1982. Materiaux pour une image du Blanc dans la société coloniale du Congo Belge. *In* Stréréotypes Nationaux et Préjuqés Raciaux aux XIXe et XXe Siècles. Jean Pirotte ed. Leuven: Editions Nauwelaerts.

Vere Allen, J. de. 1970. Malayan Civil Service, 1874–1941: Colonial Bureaucracy Malayan Elite. Comparative Studies in Society and History 12, 149–178.

Wanderken, P. 1943. Zoo leven onze kinderen. *In* Zoo Leven Wij in Indonesia. Deventer: Van Hoever, 172–187.

Wertheim, Willem. 1959. Indonesian Society in Transition. The Hague: Van Hoeve.

Winckel, Ch. W. F. 1938. The Feasibility of White Settlements in the Tropics: A Medical Point of View. Comptes Rendus du Congrès International de Géographie Amsterdam. Leiden: Brill, 345–56.

Woodcock, George. 1969. The British in the Far East. New York: Atheneum.

22 The Empire's Old Clothes[1]

Fashioning the Colonial Subject

JEAN COMAROFF

It might be argued that modern European empires were as much fashioned as forged—that as social fields, they arose as much from the circulation of stylized objects as from brute force or bureaucratic fiat. The banality of imperialism—of the mundanities that made it ineffably real—has seldom been given its due by colonial historians, although most would probably agree that cultural revolutions must root themselves in rather humble ground. Even the most formal of economic structures may be shown to arise from ordinary transactions. Marx understood this well; after all, he vested his mature account of capitalism in the unobtrusive career of the commodity, that "very queer thing" (Marx 1967,1:71) whose seemingly trivial production, exchange, and consumption built the contours of a whole social world.

This insight turns out to be highly relevant to an understanding of European colonization in nineteenth-century South Africa, especially the project of those "humane imperialists" who hoped to found God's Kingdom in the savage wilderness. The civilizing mission merged bourgeois Protestantism with imperialism; both were fueled by expanding industrial capital. But the record of such evangelism speaks less of a theological crusade than of an effort to reform the ordinary, a pursuit in which common objects were as central as the Holy Book. Particularly striking was the place of dress in this enterprise: clothes were at once commodities and accoutrements of a civilized self. They were to prove a privileged means for constructing new forms of value, personhood, and history on the colonial frontier.

In what follows, I relate these sartorial adventures to the more general British effort to incorporate African communities into a global economy of goods and signs. These stylized transactions were not mere representations of some "real" history being made on the ground; they themselves began to generate a new cultural economy. Both parties to the colonial encounter invested a great deal in the objects that passed between them; for these goods were "social hieroglyphics" (Marx 1967,1:74), encoding in compact form the structure of a world in the making.

My immediate case is that of the Nonconformist mission to the Tswana peoples of Southern Africa, a project that relied heavily on recasting local modes of consumption. Consumption, here, must be understood in its nineteenth-century European context, one that idealized the market and its integrative powers—its ability to convert primitive difference into a unified system of value (a "commonwealth"). Along with its Protestant ardor, the civilizing mission professed the faith that commodities could conjure new desires, bodily disciplines, and exertions; indeed, new forms of society *tout court*. And nowhere was this faith more visible than in the realm of self-presentation, especially in modes of dress.

My argument will trace one strand of a more encompassing colonial encounter.[2] I explore the Nonconformist campaign to cover African "nakedness"; in particular, to make the southern Tswana susceptible to the aesthetics of European fashion. This project was driven by a clear sense that civilization was promoted by encouraging discerning consumption. The aim was to draw would-be converts into the system of surplus production by evoking a competitive urge to produce new identities with coded things. The case centers on a feature quite common in European colonialism: its early moments frequently focused not only on making non-Western peoples want Western goods, but on teaching them to use them in particular sorts of ways (cf. Sahlins 1989). Indeed, imperialists and their merchant associates often sought to prevail by transplanting highly specific regimes of consumption; their conscious concerns at this stage dwelled less on brute extraction or productive reform than on trade that seemed capable of forging new self-sustaining orders of desire, transaction, and wealth. The sense that culture is constructed through consumption, then, is clearly no mere figment of the "post-modern" or "post-industrial" imagination, as some have assumed (Baudrillard 1973; cf. Appadurai 1993). It is as old as capitalism itself.

Attempts to explain the rise of colonialism—and the rest of modern industrial society—in terms of the logic of expanding European *production* alone tend to miss this point. Yet we have long realized that imperialism was a more complex cultural process, both in motivation and in outcome. The effort to clothe Africa, for instance, was driven as much by the urge to civilize as to garner profits, at least in crude material terms. Already by the early nineteenth century, commodity consumption was indissolubly linked to the production of civilization. Thus, when British mission propagandists advertised the commercial opportunities available in Africa, they did so to glean support for what they saw as a more profound moral enterprise. But while they drew alike from the gospels of Jesus and Adam Smith, the evangelists would learn that commerce and civility were not always hand in glove. Though the churchmen shared a faith in commodities characteristic of their culture, they were also aware of the contradictions of competitive consumption, especially in light of their Puritan heritage. In time, they would try vainly to stem the materialism they had set in motion, especially as it engaged with the more cynical designs of colonial capital.

In outline, I argue that attempts to reform Tswana consumption had unintended outcomes—that they played powerfully into the making and marking of new social classes, rupturing existing communities of signs (Volosinov 1973) and hastening the conversion of local systems of value to global currencies. But these efforts also set off playful processes of experimentation and synthesis. For novel goods spurred the African imagination, and in the early years, many refused to "buy in" to European cultural dictates, epitomized by the mission's strict codes of dress. Old elites were especially resistant to such sartorial discipline, seeing it as a foreign assault on their subjects. But, as the century wore on, few Tswana would escape the constraints of the colonial economy, and their room for creative manoeuvre was severely reduced. Forced to be more dependant on the market, the majority would adopt a dress that—more than any other medium—made visible their marginal place in the new imperium. Experimental syntheses were replaced by a more enduring style; its female form (a "folk" costume to the European eye) contrasting with the work garb that became the uniform of male migrants here and elsewhere in South Africa. Women's dress seemed to "ethnicize" what had become a peasantariat, a unit in the national reserve army of "tribal" labor. Their dress would be made almost entirely from store-bought materials. Yet these commodities would be used to craft a novel conservatism, an existence beyond the exigencies of innovation and endless metropolitan mimicry that defined black petite bourgeois culture.

"Ethnic" dress, in fact, seemed part of an effort to stabilize a radically compromised identity. It was also a mark of displacement from the centers of social and cultural production. Fashion seems especially appropriate for this task in the modern world, for it epitomizes the power of the commodity to encompass the self: not only does fashion's insistence on "pure contemporaneity" render those who do not wear it "out of date" and parochial (Faurschou 1990, 235); it also confirms the fact that, in a commodity culture, identity is something owned *apart* from one's self, something that must continuously be "put on" and displayed (Bowlby 1985, 27–8; see Williamson 1992, 106). This turns out to be a crucial aspect of the remaking of African space and time, African selves and societies under colonialism.

The Heathen Body

From the start, in Southern Tswana communities, the most tangible signs of the European presence were worn on the backs of the people themselves. Clothing is a "social skin" (Turner n.d.) that makes and marks social beings everywhere. But the early evangelists came from a world in which distinctions of dress were crucially implicated in the work of "self-fashioning" (Greenblatt 1980; Veblen 1934). Their activities suggest that, at least in this Christian culture,[2] clothedness was next to godliness: it was easier for a camel to pass through the eye of a needle than for the ill-clad to enter the Kingdom of Heaven.

At the core of the Protestant mission lay a tension between inner and outer verities, the life of the spirit and of the sensuous world. Dress epitomized this conflict. It was a fitting means for showing self-improvement, but it was also the stuff of the flesh. Unless it could effect moral reform that was more than skin deep, it remained an exterior overlay or vain deception. The concern with dress revealed what was often a vain effort to fuse the cultivation of the body with the conversion of the spirit. At the same time, the evidence suggests that many Southern Tswana acknowledged the ritual resonance of dress—albeit from their own perspective, one that gave voice to a distinct understanding of the colonial encounter. As they read them, European gestures with clothes were unambiguously embodied and pragmatic.

These gestures began with, and were at first frankly preoccupied by, the covering of African "nakedness." A complex trope here, "nakedness" in mission prose implied more than mere savage degeneracy. It spoke also of darkness, disorder, and pollution. Pioneer evangelist Robert Moffat (1842, 287) expresses a widely shared sense of the rampant heathen body threatening the fragile cultural order built on the frontier:

> As many men and women as pleased might come into our hut, leaving us not room even to turn ourselves, and making every thing they touched the color of their greasy red attire. . . . They would keep the housewife a perfect prisoner in a suffocating atmosphere, almost intolerable; and when they departed, they left ten times more than their number behind [i.e., lice]—company still more offensive.

There is no effort to disguise the distaste for African intruders who breach the bounds of domestic propriety. Moffat's prose is not without precedent. The notion of the "greasy native" had gained currency in the texts of late eighteenth-century travelers and anatomists (Comaroff and Comaroff 1991:104), probably reflecting the use of animal fat and butter as cosmetics in much of South and East Africa, where a gleaming skin radiated beauty and projected status (Comaroff 1985, 110).[3] But for the Europeans, the epithet carried more prurient associations. It suggested a lascivious stickiness, a body that refused to separate itself from the world, leaving (as an unnamed writer put it) red, "greasy marks upon everything" (Read n.d.). Nothing could have been further from the cool, contained, inward-turning person of the mission ideal; a self both "discreet" and "discrete."

The bogey of bestial bodies was well rooted in the English imperial imagination. First the Irish, then Native Americans had been seen as dirty primitives in animal hides (Muldoon 1975). In each case, the trope was tuned to the tenor of its times. Hence, in early nineteenth-century Africa, the "lubricated wild man of the desert" contrasted with the "clean, comfortable and well-dressed believer" as did "filthy" animal fat and skin with the "cotton and woollen manufactures of Manchester and Leeds" (Hughes 1841, 523). The early evangelists assumed that the benefits of "decent dress" would be self-evident to the Africans: while Moffat (1842, 348) found it understandable that Tswana might at first oppose Christian doctrine, he thought it "natural" that they would adopt Western attire "for their own comfort and convenience." But appeals to practical reason are always also moral injunctions: Rybczynski (1986) has shown that the concept of "comfort," seemingly so transparently physical, is itself an historical construct denoting a set of material and moral assumptions born of bourgeois domestic order.

Of course, the Nonconformists were heirs to a moralistic language that had long waxed eloquent on the issue of shame and modesty. The frequent eruption of corporeal images in staid mission prose confirms their preoccupation with the erotic. It also lends credence to the claim that, in order to extract power from the repressed body, modern Protestantism had constantly to evoke it (Foucault 1978, 115f). One early churchman told the Tlhaping that the Word would melt their flinty savage hearts, bringing forth penitent tears and "wash[ing] away all the red paint from their bodies" (Comaroff and Comaroff 1991, 214). Redness and rudeness were made one, for the daubed body invoked a brace of nineteenth-century associations, from the "rouge" of female depravity to "Red" Indian warpaint. The

Tswana had to be made aware of their brazen nakedness, their sinful passion. If they were to become vessels of the Spirit, their corporeality had to be reconstructed: confined, turned inward, and invested with self-consciousness and shame.

Western dress was both a sign and an instrument of this transformation. To the European and African alike, it would become the most distinctive mark of association with the mission (Etherington 1978, 116), a fact graphically conveyed to the British public in pictures sent from the field. In the oft-illustrated incident of Moffat ministering to an "abandoned mother" (Comaroff and Comaroff 1991, 110–11), for example, the evangelist's black assistant, a male convert, stands attentively behind his mentor, faithfully replicating his dress (Figure 1). By contrast, the heathen lies in tatters in the bush, her breasts flagrantly bare. Absent altogether from the heroic scene is the mission wife, primary agent of the early campaign to clothe Africa.

African Adornment

The Western trope of "nakedness"—which implies a particular conception of bodily being, nature, and culture—would have made little sense to Tswana prior to the arrival of the missions. In South Africa, what the nineteenth-century missionaries took to be indecent exposure was clearly neither a state of undress nor impropriety in indigenous eyes (although other aspects of body presentation, including uncovered genitals and undressed hair were considered uncouth in Tswana adults). African dress and grooming were scanty by European standards, but they conveyed—

Figure 1: "The Abandoned Mother: A Scene in the Life of Robert Moffat."
Source: Reproduced from Adam & Company, *The Life and Explorations of Dr. Livingstone* (1874).

as such things do everywhere—complex distinctions of gender, age, and social identity. In their seeming nakedness, the Africans were fully clothed.

What was most unsettling to the evangelists was the place of apparel in the whole Tswana social order. As I have said, in the European world, discerning consumption was the major index of social worth. In fact, consumption was increasingly set off from production as a gendered and markedly female sphere of practice. Women's domestic demesne centered on the display of adornments that would signal the status of their male providers, men whose own attire, as befitted their endeavors, was relatively sober and unelaborated (Turner n.d.). Moreover, while men of the bourgeoisie controlled the manufacture and marketing of clothes, the labor which produced textiles and garments was largely that of poor women and (in the early years) children, members of the lower orders who were conspicuously excluded from the stylish self-production that engrossed their more privileged sisters.

Other Kinds of Clothes

Above all else, it struck the evangelists as unnatural that, while Tswana women built houses, sowed, and reaped, "men ma[d]e the dresses for themselves and the females" (London Missionary Society [LMS] 1824). Refashioning this division of labor was integral to reforming "primitive" production in all its dimensions; and this, in turn, required the creation of a distinct (feminine) domestic world centered on reproduction and consumption. In this regard, the churchmen were disturbed by the fact that, although it was marginally distinguished by rank, female attire was largely uniform. In direct contrast to bourgeois fashion, it was mainly men's clothes that signaled social standing here (cf. Kay 1834,1:201). European observers pronounced male dress to be quite varied, even dandyish (LMS 1824, 1828).

Such distinctions apart, however, Tswana costume seemed to be unremittingly rude and rudimentary. For the most part, those of the same sex and age dressed alike (Schapera 1953, 25). Nonetheless, it soon struck the Europeans that indigenous clothes also spoke of status. In contrast to infants who wore nothing but medicated ornaments, adults of both sexes wore long skin cloaks (*dikobò*; sing. *kobò*) that were significant "sign[s] of wealth" (LMS 1824, see also Willoughby n.d., unfiled notes, 14).[4] Cloaks were first donned at the conclusion of male and female initiation, denoting the onset of sexual and jural maturity (Comaroff 1985, 105f); interestingly, during lapses from full participation in social life—such as after bereavement—people put on their *dikobò* inside out. Royal males wore especially fine karosses, often incorporating the pelts of wild beasts, although that of the leopard was reserved for reigning chiefs (Philip 1828,2:126). The skin cape was to prove extremely durable in this economy of signs, surviving amidst a riot of market innovations to give a distinctive stamp to Tswana "folk" style, where it lived on, in the form of the store-bought blanket, as a crucial element of "tribal" costume.

Early accounts suggest that Tswana were especially creative in fashioning new ornaments that seemed to radiate personal identity. They favored shining surfaces (recall the glossy cosmetics) and a gleaming visibility that contrasted markedly with the dullness of mission modes, which countered "flashiness" with a stress on personal restraint and inward reflection. Plenty of evidence shows that novel adornments made with sparkling buttons and glass beads found their way into the interior, for by the early nineteenth century, the latter had become a widespread currency linking local and monetized economies. But bright beads were not all equally desirable; Campbell (in LMS 1824) notes that Tswana "greatly prefer[red] the dark blue color." This is intriguing for, as we shall see, dark blue was to be the shade favored for the dress of converts by the mission. If Campbell was correct, the Europeans' chosen hue had a fortuitous precedent, having been associated with prestige of foreign origin. Blue beads were globules of exchange value, imaginatively congealed into local designs. Clear blue appears to have had no other place in indigenous artistic schemes: patterns on housefronts, pottery, and ritual artifacts tended to play on the three-way contrast of black, red, and white (Comaroff 1985, 114). It is tempting to suggest that blue—so clearly the color of the mission and its materials (as well, in Tswana poetics, as the pale, piercing eyes of whites)—was the pigment of exogenous powers and substances. The Christians would certainly wield the blues in their effort to counter "heathenism," for when it came to heathens, they saw red.

Civility, Cloth, and Consumption

The evangelists would try to force Tswana bodies into the straightjacket of Protestant personhood. The Nonconformists acted on the implicit assumption that, in order to reform the heathens, it was necessary to scramble their entire code of body management; thus "decent" Western dress was demanded from all who would associate with the church. Tswana soon appreciated the role of clothes in this campaign. When Chief Montshiwa of the Tshidi Rolong perceived that the Christian influence in his realm had begun to extend even to his own kin, he ordered his daughter publically "to doff her European clothing, . . . to return to heathen attire" (Mackenzie 1871, 231). His royal counterparts elsewhere also fastened on to such discernable signs of allegiance, and many struggles ensued over the right to determine individual dress. From the first, Southern Tswana treated objects of Western adornment as signs of exotic force; those introduced by the mission were soon identified as *sekgoa*, white things (Burchell 1824,2:559). But some items of European clothing had preceded the mission into the interior,[5] where people often seem to have treated them as bearers of alien power (Burchell 1824,2:432). An early report from Kuruman tells how the Tlhaping chief addressed his warriors prior to battle in a "white linen garment," his heir wearing an "officer's coat" (Moffat 1825, 29). In a published account of this incident, Moffat (1842, 348) revealed that the garment was actually a chemise of unknown origin. Such attire seemed to lend potency to indigenous enterprise, in part because its qualities resonated with local signs and symbols. White, the usual color of the baptismal gown (itself, to the untrained eye, much like a chemise) was also the color of the transformative substances placed on the human body during rites of passage (Comaroff 1985, 98). Similarly, the military uniforms carried inland from the colony by Khoi soldiers might have had cogent connotations associated with this mediating population. But the interest they evoked seems also to have been fed by what appears to have been a long-standing Tswana concern with the dress of combat (Comaroff 1985, 112; Comaroff and Comaroff 1991, 164).

European costume, in short, opened up a host of imaginative possibilities for Southern Tswana. It offered an enhanced language in which to play with new social identities, a language in which the mission itself would become a pole of reference. In the early days, before the Christians presented a palpable threat to chiefly authority, royals monopolized the Western garments that traveled into the interior. These were worn in experimental fashion, often in ceremonial audiences with visiting whites (Philip 1828,2:126–27). Already at this point, several aspects of the synthetic style that would be much in evidence later on in the century seem to have taken shape—among them, the combination of European garments with skin cloaks. This was a form of mixing that the evangelists abhorred, yet would never manage to eradicate.

But the missions would expend great effort and cost to ensure that, in Moffat's (1842, 505) telling words, the Africans would "be[come] clothed and in their right mind." As Western dress became more closely associated with expanding evangelical control, the early phase of playful experimentation came to an end. By the 1830s, once a regular mission presence had been established, most senior royals turned their backs on the dress of *sekgoa*, identifying with an ever more assertively marked *setswana* (Tswana ways). Some were said to "ridicule . . . and even abuse . . ." those kin who "laid aside" the dress of their "forbears" (Smith 1939,1:3 37).

I have noted that the campaign to clothe black South Africa was inseparable from other axes of the civilizing mission, especially the effort to reform agricultural production. Thus in order to dress Tswana—or rather, to teach them to dress themselves—women had to be persuaded to trade the hoe for the needle, the outdoor for the indoor life (Gaitskell 1988). In this endeavor, the Nonconformists largely relied on the "domesticating" genius of the "gentler sex": on their own wives and daughters (cf. Hunt 1990), most of whom started sewing schools almost at once (Moffat 1842, 505); these also served as a focus for the exertions of female philanthropists in Britain, who sent pincushions and needles with which to stitch the seams of an expanding imperial fabric. Recall that, in precolonial times, clothing was made of leather; an extension of animal husbandry, it was produced by men. It is not surprising, then, that sewing schools had limited appeal at first. In the early years, moreover, there was no regular supply of materials. But by the late 1830s, once merchants had been attracted to the stations, those Tswana women most closely identified with the mission had begun to take in sewing for payment (Moffat 1842, 17). This was one of several areas in which the evangelists encouraged commercial relations well ahead of a formal colonial labor market.

Even if the missionaries had succeeded immediately in persuading Tswana to clothe themselves, local manufacture would have fallen short of the task. Thus the Christians appealed to the generosity of the Great British public. The growth of the fashion industry encouraged obsolescence and by this time had already provided a steady supply of used garments (or recycled commodities) for the poor and unclad at home and abroad. When, in 1843, the Moffats returned to Cape Town from a visit to the United Kingdom, they sailed with 50 tons of "old clothes" for

the Kuruman station (Northcott 1961, 172). The famous David Livingstone, some-
time missionary among the Tswana, was scathing about the "good people" of England who had given their cast-off ballgowns and starched collars to those "who had
no shirts" (Northcott 1961, 173). But a letter from Mrs. Moffat ([1841] 1967,
17–18) to a woman well wisher in London shows that she had thought carefully
about the adaptation of Western dress to African conditions:

> The materials may be coarse, and strong, the stronger the better. Dark blue Prints, or
> Ginghams . . . or in fact, any kind of dark Cottons, which will wash well—Nothing
> light-colored should be worn outside. . . . All the heathen population besmear them-
> selves with red ochre and grease, and as the Christians must necessarily come in con-
> tact, with their friends among the heathen, they soon look miserable enough, if
> clothed in light-colored things. . . . *I* like them best as Gowns were made 20 or 30 years
> ago. . . . For little Girls, Frocks made exactly as you would for the Children of the poor
> of this country, will be the best.

The priority was clearly the proper clothing of women and children. And while any
European clothes, even diaphanous ballgowns, were better than none, more
somber, serviceable garb was ideal. Dark blue garments, especially, resisted the
stains of a red-handed heathenism that threatened to "rub off" on the convert.
Indigo-dyed prints, now being mass-produced with raw materials drawn from other
imperial outposts, conformed well to the long-standing European association of
dark hues with humility, piety, and virtue. Their ochre and grease aside, Mrs. Moffat suggested, African converts were like the virtuous British poor, whose inability
to produce their own wealth was marked by their exclusion from the fashion system
and by the dismal durability of their dress. Great efforts would also be made to stir
a desire for self-improvement in these neophyte Christians.

The fact that Mary Moffat wrote about such matters to a woman was itself predictable. Not only the acquisition and maintenance but also the despatch of clothing in the form of charity had become a key element of a feminized domestic
economy (Davidoff and Hall 1987). But such recycling carried its own dangers: it
could inhibit ambition in the poor. Care had to be taken not to evoke indigence.
Here the churchpeople put their faith in the sheer charm of commodities. Comfortable and attractive garments, they hoped, would awaken the desire for property
and self-enhancement, for a life of righteous getting and spending.

And so, through the effort of mission wives and their European sisters, the germ
of the fashion system arrived on the African veld. It bore with it the particular features of the culture of industrial capitalism: an enduring impetus toward competitive accumulation, symbolic innovation, and social distinction (Bell 1949). But its
export to this frontier also underscored the deep-seated contradictions in the material expression of the Protestant ethic. Ascetic angst focused most acutely on female
frailty. For, in as much as the fashion system made women its primary vehicles, it
strengthened the association of femininity with things of the flesh. Willoughby
(n.d., unfiled notes, 14) was far from alone in grumbling that many Tswana women
were soon enthralled with ridiculous hats and expensive garments. Also, while the

Nonconformists might have striven to produce an elite driven by virtuous desires, they had also to justify the lot of the less fortunate majority. They had, in other words, to sanctify poverty and the postponement of physical pleasure in the interests of eternal grace. Their most humble adherents remained the deserving recipients of charity, dressed in strong dark blue cottons whose color and texture were to become synonymous with the mission rank-and-file. This would be the nucleus of rural "folk," whose style and predicament would come to typify Tswana peasant-proletarians in modern South Africa.

As the century wore on, the evangelists would devote their energies increasingly to the creation of a black petite bourgeoisie. But in the early years, they encouraged "improvement and self-reliance" as an ideal for all; hence their attempts to bring traders and, with them, the goods needed to make Christians. In 1833, Rev. Archbell began to pursue merchants for his Wesleyan station among the Seleka Rolong; and by 1835, Moffat had persuaded one "Mr. Hume," a long-term factor catering to the "demand for British commodities," to base himself at Kuruman. The mission played a large role in stimulating demand, not just for ready-made garments, cotton prints, and sewing goods, but for all the elements of the European sartorial economy. The Nonconformists, for instance, stressed the fact that, unlike "filthy skins," clothes had to be washed and repaired, binding wives and daughters to an unrelenting regime of "cleanliness"—epitomized, to this day, by the starched and laundered uniforms of the black women's Prayer Unions. It was a form of discipline that the mission monitored closely, ensuring brisk sales of soap and other cleansing agents (cf. Burke 1990).

From 1830 on, mission reports speak with pleasure of "decent raiments" worn by their loyal members. They also note that trade was healthy and that there was a growing desire among Southern Tswana to purchase European apparel (Moffat 1842, 219; Read 1850, 446). Not only was the clothing of the heathen masses under way but a distinct and sedately styled Anglophile elite was increasingly visible (Read 1850, 446).

Self-Fashioning on the Frontier: The Man in the Tiger Suit

The growing supply of Western apparel in the interior toward mid-century also had another effect on the Tswana, one less palatable to the mission. It incited what the Christians saw as an absurd, even promiscuous syncretism (Moffat 1842, 506):

> A man might be seen in a jacket with but one sleeve, because the other was not finished, or he lacked material to complete it. Another in a leathern or duffel jacket, with the sleeves of different colours, or of fine printed cotton. Gowns were seen like Joseph's coat of many colours, and dresses of such fantastic shapes, as were calculated to excite a smile in the gravest of us.

Such descriptions give a glimpse of the Tswana bricoleur tailoring a brilliant patchwork on the cultural frontier. To the evangelist, they offered a disconcerting distortion of the worthy self-fashionings he had tried to set in motion. Such "eccentric" garb caused the Christians much anxiety. As Douglas (1966) might have predicted, it came to be associated with dirt and contagion. By the turn of the century, state health authorities were asserting that "natives who partially adopted our style of dress" were most susceptible to serious disease (Packard 1989, 690).

If the selective appropriation of Western attire flouted British codes of costume and decency, it also called into question the authoritative norms of Nonconformism. This was particularly evident in the counterpoint between the colorful, homemade creations of most people and the "uniforms" introduced by the mission to mark the compliance of those in its schools and associations. (The latter attire, being both novel, yet closed to stylish innovation, anticipated subsequent "folk" dress.) But the creative *couture* contrived by so many Southern Tswana suggests a riposte to the symbolic imperialism of the mission at large. It speaks of a desire to harness the power of *sekgoa*, yet evade white authority and discipline. The bricoleur contrasted, on one hand, with those who ostensibly rejected everything European, and, on the other, with those who identified faithfully with church aesthetics and values. Style, here, was clearly implicated in the making of radically new distinctions. And as the colonial economy expanded into the interior, the means for such fashioning was increasingly available through channels beyond the control of the mission.

Indeed, as the century progressed, the growing articulation of the Southern Tswana with the regional political economy was tangible in their everyday material culture. For a start, the volume of goods pumped into rural communities rose markedly. A visitor to Mafikeng in 1875 (Holub 1881,2:14) reported that, apart from a small elite, the population persisted in its patchwork of indigenous and European styles. But the makeup of the mixture had subtly altered. Mafikeng was then a Christian Tshidi-Rolong village that had no mission presence. Still, store-bought commodities amounted to a growing proportion of its cultural melange. British aesthetics were being used in ever more complex ways; both in the honor and in the breach they marked widening social and economic differences.

The deployment of Western style was particularly evident in the changing garb of "traditional" rulers and royals. As noted above, they had responded to the earlier missionary challenge by assertively reverting to *setswana* costume—and by insisting that their Christian subjects do likewise. By the late nineteenth century, however, with the colonial state ever more palpably upon them, few but the most far-flung of Tswana sovereigns harbored illusions about the habits of power. Some, in fact, sought to outsmart the evangelists at their own game; Mackenzie (1883, 35) records the fascinating case of Chief Sechele, who, in 1860, had a singular suit tailored from "tiger" (i.e., leopard) skin "in European fashion." According to the missionary, the Kwena ruler wished "to make himself a white man." But the matter was surely more complex. In crafting the skin, itself a symbol of his office, the chief seems to have been making yet another effort to mediate the two exclusive systems of authority at war in his world, striving, perhaps, to fashion a power greater than the sum of its parts. Other rulers, most notably the Tshidi and Ngwaketse chiefs (Holub 1881,1:291), chose to dress themselves in highly fashionable garb, clothes whose opulence set them off from their more humble Christian subjects—missionaries included. These early examples of royal dandyism involved only male dress; but the nascent local bourgeoisie had already begun, like its European counterpart, to signal status on the bodies of its women, whose clothing became ever more nuanced and elaborate (see Willoughby c.1899, 25, 48).

Migrants, Merchants, and the Costume of the Countryside

In the closing decades of the century, labor migration had the greatest impact on Southern Tswana dress. Whites in the interior had insisted, from the beginning, that "natives" with whom they sustained contact should adopt minimal standards of "decency"—covering at least their "private" parts. Men who interacted regularly with whites soon took to wearing trousers, and those who, in later years, journeyed to the new industrial centers had little option but to conform to the basic rules of respectability pertaining to public places. By then, however, the Christians had already established a widespread "need" for European garments, if not necessarily for European styles. Schapera (1947, 122) is not alone in claiming that the desire for such commodities as clothes drove migrants to urban areas in the first place.

Perhaps, perhaps not. Desire is rarely a motivation that can be recuperated with certainty. In any case, it is never a sufficient explanation for large-scale social processes. The migration of Southern Tswana to the cities occurred in the wake of regional political and ecological forces that impoverished local populations. Nor was the consumption of European fashions a specifically urban affair. Willoughby (n.d., unfiled notes, 14) indicates that, by the late nineteenth century, Tswana living near rural mission stations had learnt well how to craft themselves with commodities; some spent "as much on clothes in a year as would keep my wife well-clad for Ten Years." Nonetheless, it is clear that those who did migrate to the industrial centers were immediately confronted by an array of "Kaffir Stores" that pressed upon them a range of "native goods" designed for the neophyte black proletarian.[6]

Advertisements attest that clothes were by far the most significant commodities sold by urban "Kaffir storekeepers."[7] Their sheer volume at the time suggests that migrants were devoting a high proportion of their earnings to self-fashioning. And the standardization and range of goods indicates that some customers, at least, were putting on the dress of industrial capitalism, with its distinctions between labor and leisure, and manual and non-manual toil. Contemporary advertisements also invoked class distinctions: texts aimed at literate Africans, for instance, suggested that discerning taste coffered distinction. The moral economy of mission and marketplace overlapped ever more neatly.

Rural Transformations

In rural areas, too, important transformations were unfolding. The closing decades of the century were marked by the proliferation of a striking array of local fashions. Style had become integral to the internal stratification of local Tswana communities as they were drawn more tightly into the regional political economy. Among the evidence, a published collection of photographs, *Native Life on the Transvaal Border*, produced circa 1899 by the Rev. Willoughby of the London Missionary Society, gives intriguing insight into the development of local material culture, especially with respect to dress and domestic design.

The pictures suggest that the contrasts discernible a couple of decades before had undergone transformation. Wealthy royals remained the most expensively and stylishly clad (Figure 2), but they were now less distinguishable from the Christian elite, which also dressed itself in elaborate (if sober) versions of current English fashion. This convergence stemmed, in part, from the fact that overrule had established new Eurocentric hegemonies; the expansion of the bureaucratic state had continued to erode the bases of chiefly power and had enhanced the status of those schooled by the mission. Moreover, nominal membership in the church now extended to most Tswana, including senior royals. Here, as elsewhere, class distinctions were literally tailor-made. Style did not just reflect new Southern Tswana alliances; it was part of their fabrication.

The crowd scenes in the pictorial archive offer little evidence of "heathen dress" among adults, although it clearly remained common among youths and unmarried girls (Figure 3). Having acquired the status of the primitive and childlike, such clothing might still have been worn by adults in areas not yet penetrated by the white gaze. But most Tswana chiefs had become aware of the stigmatizing implications of "backwardness," and were themselves urging their subjects to dress in European style. In such a climate, the evangelists testified proudly that "traditional costume" was all but extinct (Willoughby c. 1899, 84).[8]

Feminizing the "Folk" on the Ethnic Periphery

But history has a habit of leaping across such rigid breaks. In this respect, perhaps the most telling feature of Willoughby's pictures is found on the middle ground

Figure 2: "A Native Bride" and "Sekgome, The Only Son of Chief Khama."
Source: Illustration no. 26, page 25 and illustration no. 14, page 15, reproduced from Willoughby, *Native Life on the Transvaal Border.* London: Simpkin, Marshall, Hamilton, Kent & Co., Ltd, (1899).

Figure 3: "Rising Generation."
Source: Illustration no. 53, page 49, from Willoughby, *Native Life on the Transvaal Border.*

between the elite and those in childish "heathen" attire: the appearance of ordinary people, especially women. By now, almost all Southern Tswana had been drawn into a world dominated by commodity manufacture. Yet unlike their elites, who strove to effect Eurocentric models, the rank-and-file developed a distinctive style, one that shaped industrial materials to a heightened sense of *setswana*. Neither straightforwardly Western nor "authentically" indigenous, this style combined elements of both to signify a novel sense of anachronism: that of membership in a marginalized, "ethnic" culture. Like the dress of other peripheral peoples in South Africa (cf. Mayer 1961, 25–26) and Europe, it drew on global commodities to mark the fact that its wearers were being refigured as quaint premoderns, existing at the exploitable edge of an empire. But the costume was not conjured up *ex nihilo*. Its elements were drawn from the different cultural schemes articulated along the new frontiers. In short, these Tswana women and men did not simply don imperial designs. They opted, in the main, for a dress that defied fashion in important respects, one that configured an enduring identity at a distance from white markets and morals.

Notwithstanding local variation, this kind of clothing takes on a recognizable identity in a Eurocentric world. It is the "folk costume" of rural peoples, of those marginalized by "modernity," whose greatest elaboration is often expressed in the garb of women (cf. Nag 1991; Hendrickson 1986). Of course, this is not invariably the case. In much of West Africa, where elites gestured not only to Christian Europe but to the Muslim world, male dress became the more elaborate bearer of refashioned ethnic identities in colonial and postcolonial contexts. How do we account for such differences? The answer seems to lie in the manner in which local communities are caught up in encompassing empires, a process that draws them into world economies even while they remain rooted, in important respects, in their own regimes of production and exchange. It has become commonplace to observe that, while they change existing arrangements, such processes also reinforce certain indigenous practices, recreating them as "traditions" used to bound local identities in a world of exploding horizons.

And here is the point. In the first instance, Western colonizers often set out to extract labor from men. Where this involved the commoditization of local agriculture or the establishment of plantations, both sexes were usually pressed into service. But the rise of industrial capitalism in the colonies initially tended to favor male migration to new centers. This, it is true, did not always preclude the movement of women (White 1988); but low male wages were frequently subsidized by females farming in the countryside. In South Africa, this process was so marked that the rural areas became, in many respects, female domains. Indeed, women became icons of a "tribal" home centered beyond the reaches of modern economy, society, and history.

Is it any wonder then that in the signifying economy of such "modernizing" processes, "native" women often come to embody "tradition," the latter often rooted in a newly nuanced sense of the rural? Made by colonizing forces into premodern counterparts of European females, they were set apart from modern centers of production in devalued "domestic" enclaves. (Later, in South Africa, these would be termed, quite literally, "*home*lands.") Here they reproduced and represented the "tribal" essence—the cheap labor—that fueled the economy of empire.

To underscore the point, our photographic evidence from the turn of the century shows that the clothing of the migrant male rank-and-file was largely limited to khaki jackets, shirts, and trousers. This standard proletarian uniform for black males made little ethnic distinction. By contrast, the visual archive confirms that non-elite Tswana women became the prime bearers of emergent "tribal" markings of a particularly modern sort. Attesting to a generic "ethnicity," their costume secured the rural pole of the hyphenated condition of the "peasant-proletarian" (Figure 4): the tight-bodiced dresses of indigo cotton print, their full skirts worn over several petticoats; the appliquéd patterns of darker-blue fabric around the hem; the blankets or shawls, wrapped about the upper body at all times, except during strenuous labor; and the dark twill headscarves. Some elements of this costume were transformations of precolonial dress: blankets were worn like precolonial cloaks and were referred to by the same term, *dikobò*. In contrast, the "hampering long dresses and innumerable petticoats" (Mears 1934, 94) and the modest headscarves clearly expressed the moral imperatives of Victorian mission garb and the somber regularity of its rank-and-file.

This composite costume was the product of a specific conjuncture, a particular pastiche of African and European elements that captured precisely the paradoxical relation of difference and sameness remaking colonized peoples into serialized "ethnic" populations. Characteristic of such styles—indeed, crucial to their historical meaning—is a "conservatism," which might (as the Southern Tswana case attests) be a relatively recent feature. This is more than the marked anachronism typical of "invented traditions"; it is a repeated invocation of the very moment of articulation that radically redefined "local" identities in Eurocentric terms. Herein lies the essence of so-called "folk costume" in southern Africa and elsewhere.

Figure 4: "Cottar's Saturday Night—Secwana [Tswana] Version."
Source: Illustration no. 52, page 48, from Willoughby, *Native Life on the Transvaal Border.*

Conclusion

What this history seems to reveal, then, is the complex dynamics at play in the incorporation of African communities into the European colonial world; how such communities became engaged with forces capable of re-creating them as both "local" and primordially parochial. I have suggested that we gain purchase on such global processes by pursuing their roots in the small-scale transactions that generate them. But these were no ordinary transactions, for this is a history centered on the worldwide extension not only of European Christian culture, but of industrial capitalism. Whatever mechanisms it might have utilized, colonization here relied heavily on the magic of commodities to build new consuming subjects and new relations of difference.

We have seen that the early exposure to British commodities and consumption encouraged Tswana to deploy alien objects in diverse and creative ways. But these objects were themselves embedded in forms of relations destined to transform African societies. Clothes bore with them the threads of a macroeconomy; they were a ready-made means of engaging indigenous peoples in the colonial market in goods and labor. And such processes reveal how the mantle of wider politico-economic forces came to rest on individual persons, redefining them as bearers of a ready-made identity.

But such processes were neither all-or-none, nor mechanical in their effects. Changing modes of dress show that commodity culture played into existing African societies in complex ways. As the century wore on, all Tswana were confined by the rising colonial state, most being tied to its cultural imperatives and its market in goods and labor. European norms of dress and comportment came increasingly to define public space in terms of an aesthetics of civility, one that positioned whole populations within a hierarchical scheme. Indeed, the restriction of black "ethnic" identities to a diminished sphere of self-expression was central to the founding of the colonial state, which strove to monopolize the production of value. As this account has shown, these were profoundly gendered and class-ridden processes, resting on novel forms of selfhood, production, beauty, and status; in recounting such histories, class is not separable from race, or race from gender.

It is within this context that we must view the paradoxical emergence of rural "folk dress," which speaks at once of structural regulation, of selective self-expression, and of the unevenness of commoditization—even within well-colonized social fields. For, while such dress evoked the moral economy of the mission, it also defied the other half of the Protestant message—the injunction to fashion new identities through ever increasing consumption. Significant features of this style would endure for decades—or rather, be actively reproduced as "tradition." And although it bore the imprint of Christian discipline, this costume also marked itself as anachronistic, its blanketed elegance conveying—to the metropolitan eye—an unmistakable aura of independence and reserve. The dress was iconic of the predicament of its wearers: it was made increasingly from foreign materials, yet it marked a locally tooled identity, elaborating in unforeseen ways on the possibilities presented by a commodity culture. The conservatism of their attire might have made rural Tswana women hostage to a discriminatory "tradition," but it also entailed an effort to limit dependency on the market and the fashion system, on the restless urge for advancement through endless consumption. In its more assertive forms, then, ethnic dress has acted like other enclaved commodities on the margins of the modern melting-pot (cf. Comaroff and Comaroff 1992:127f). It serves to stem the force of mainstream economies and cultures as they take control of local worlds.

Notes

1. Here I invoke the title—if not the content—of Dorfman's (1983) well-known book. Many people have responded to this material in one or another form; John Comaroff and Brad Weiss provided particularly rich insights, many of which are reflected in the text.

2. For an extended discussion of the Nonconformist (Wesleyan and London Missionary Society) engagement with the Southern Tswana peoples, see Comaroff and Comaroff (1991); for a detailed account of the role of dress in this history, see Comaroff and Comaroff (n.d., chap.5).

3. This is not to imply that Christian evangelists—even Protestants—were all alike in this respect. The link between dress, self-construction, and self-improvement seems to have been especially strong among Nonconformists, who stressed the methodical reform of personal habit.

4. Brad Weiss sharpened my sense of the importance of this issue.

5. Some linen goods seem to have found their way to northern Tswana from the east coast in the early nineteenth century, probably via Arab traders (Moffat 1825, 64).

6. For a more detailed account of the African clothing market in Kimberley at the time, see Comaroff and Comaroff (n.d., chap.5).

7. Such advertisements were common in papers like *The Diamond Fields Advertiser* in the late 1860s (see Comaroff and Comaroff n.d., chap.5).

8. This contrasts with the situation among many Nguni peoples where, for structural reasons (Comaroff 1985, 30), the impact of Christianity created more clearly distinct populations, such as the "Red" (that color again!) and "School" communities of the Xhosa, described by Mayer in the mid-twentieth century (Mayer 1961, 24f).

Works Cited

Appadurai, Arjun.
   1993. Consumption, Duration, and History. *Stanford Literary Review*, 10(1–2):11–33.
Baudrillard, Jean.
   1973. *The Mirror of Production*. St. Louis: Telos Press
Bell, Quentin.
   1949. *On Human Finery*. New York: A. A. Wyn.
Bowlby, Rachel.
   1985. Modes of Shopping: Mallarmé at the Bon Marché. In *The Ideology of Conduct: Essays in Literature and the History of Sexuality*. Ed. Nancy Armstrong and Leonard Tennenhouse. New York: Methuen.
Burchell, William J.
   1822–4. *Travels in the Interior of Southern Africa*. 2 vols. London: Longman, Hurst, Rees, Orme, Brown & Green.
Burke, Timothy.
   1990. "Nyamarira That I Love": Commoditization, Consumption, and the Social History of Soap in Zimbabwe. Paper read at the Africa Studies Seminar, May, at Northwestern University, Evanston, IL.
Comaroff, Jean.
   1985. *Body of Power, Spirit of Resistance: The Culture and History of a South African People*. Chicago: University of Chicago Press.
Comaroff, Jean, and John L Comaroff.
   1991. *Of Revelation and Revolution: Christianity, Colonialism, and Consciousness in South Africa*. Vol.1. Chicago: University of Chicago Press.
Comaroff, John L., and Jean Comaroff.
   1992. *Ethnography and the Historical Imagination*. Boulder: Westview Press.
   ———. n.d. *Of Revelation and Revolution*. Vol.2. Forthcoming.
Davidoff, Leonore and Catherine Hall.
   1987. *Family Fortunes: Men and Women of the English Middle Class, 1780–1850*. Chicago: University of Chicago Press.
Dorfman, Ariel.
   1983. *The Empire's Old Clothes: What the Lone Ranger, Babar, and Other Innocent Heroes Do to Our Minds*. New York: Pantheon Books.
Douglas, Mary.
   1966. *Purity and Danger: An Analysis of Concepts of Pollution and Taboo*. London: Routledge & Kegan Paul.
Etherington, Norman.
   1978. *Preachers, Peasants, and Politics in Southeast Africa, 1835–1880: African Christian Communities in Natal, Pondoland, and Zululand*. London: Royal Historical Society.
Faurschou, Gail.
   1990. Obsolescence and Desire: Fashion and the Commodity. In *Postmodernism in Philosophy and Art*. Ed. Hugh Silverman. London: Routledge.

Foucault, Michel.
   1978. *The History of Sexuality*. Trans. R. Hurley. New York: Pantheon Books.
Gaitskell, Deborah.
   1988. Devout Domesticity? Continuity and Change in a Century of African Women's
      Christianity in South Africa. Paper read at the Meeting of the African Studies Asso-
      ciation, Chicago, IL.
Greenblatt, Stephen Jay.
   1980. *Renaissance Self-Fashioning: From More to Shakespeare*. Chicago: Chicago Univer-
      sity Press.
Hendrickson, Carol E.
   1986. *Handmade and Thought-woven: The Construction of Dress and Social Identity in
      Tecpán, Guatemala*. Ph. D. diss., University of Chicago.
Holub, Emil.
   1881. *Seven Years in South Africa: Travels, Researches, and Hunting Adventures, between the
      Diamond-Fields and the Zambesi, 1872–79*. 2 vols. Trans. E. E. Frewer. Boston:
      Houghton Mifflin.
Hughes, Isaac.
   1841. Missionary Labours among the Batlapi. *Evangelical Magazine and Missionary
      Chronicle*, 19:522–23.
Hunt, Nancy Rose.
   1990. "Single Ladies on the Congo": Protestant Missionary Tensions and Voices.
      Women's Studies International Forum, 13:395–403.
Kay, Stephen.
   1834. *Travels and Researches in Caffraria*. 2 vols. New York: Harper & Brothers.
London Missionary Society.
   1824. Kurreechane. *Missionary Sketches*, no. 25, (April). London: London Missionary
      Society.
   ———. 1828. Sketch of the Bechuana Mission. *Missionary Sketches*, no. 43 (October).
      London: London Missionary Society.
Mackenzie, John.
   1871. *Ten Years North of the Orange River: A Story of Everyday Life and Work among the
      South African Tribes*. Edinburgh: Edmonston & Douglas.
   ———. 1883. *Day Dawn in Dark Places: A Story of Wanderings and Work in Bechwanaland*.
      London: Cassell. Reprint, 1969. New York: Negro Universities Press.
Marx, Karl.
   1967. *Capital: A Critique of Political Economy*. 3 vols. Ed. F. Engels. New York: Interna-
      tional Publishers.
Mayer, Philip.
   1961. *Townsmen or Tribesmen: Conservatism and the Process of Urbanization in a South
      African City*. Cape Town: Oxford University Press.
Mears, W. Gordon A.
   1934. The Educated Native in Bantu Communal Life. In *Western Civilization and the
      Natives of South Africa*. Ed. I. Schapera. London: George Routledge & Sons.
Moffat, Mary.
   [1841] 1967. Letter to a Well-Wisher. *Quarterly Bulletin of the South African Library*
      22:16–19.
Moffat, Robert.
   1825. Extracts from the Journal of Mr. Robert Moffat. *Transactions of the Missionary
      Society*, 33:27–29.
   ———. 1842. *Missionary Labours and Scenes in Southern Africa*. London: Snow.
Muldoon, James.
   1975. The Indian as Irishman. *Essex Institute Historical Collections*, 3:267–89.
Nag, Dulali.
   1991. Fashion, Gender, and the Bengali Middle Class. *Public Culture*, 3:93–112.

Northcott, William C.
  1961. *Robert Moffat: Pioneer in Africa, 1817–1870*. London: Lutterworth Press.
Packard, Randall M.
  1989. The "Healthy Reserve" and the "Dressed Native": Discourses on Black Health
      and the Language of Legitimation in South Africa. *American Ethnologist*, 16:686–703.
Philip, John.
  1828. *Researches in South Africa; Illustrating the Civil, Moral, and Religious Condition of the
      Native Tribes*. 2 vols. London: James Duncan.
Read, James.
  1850. Report on the Bechuana Mission. *Evangelical Magazine and Missionary Chronicle*,
      28: 445–47.
  ———. n.d. *Rivers of Water in a Dry Place: An Account of the Introduction of Christianity
      into South Africa, and of Mr. Moffat's Missionary Labours, Designed for the Young*. Lon-
      don: Religious Tract Society.
Rybczynski, Witold.
  1986. *Home: A Short History of an Idea*. New York: Viking Penguin.
Sahlins, Marshall D.
  1989. Cosmologies of Capitalism: The Trans-Pacific Sector of the World System. *Pro-
      ceeedings of the British Academy for 1988*, 1–51.
Schapera, Isaac.
  1947. *Migrant Labour and Tribal Life: A Study of Conditions in the Bechuanaland Protec-
      torate*. London and New York: Oxford University Press.
  ———. 1953. *The Tswana*. London: International African Institute, 1991. Revised ed., I.
      Schapera and J. L. Comaroff. London: Kegan Paul International.
Smith, Andrew
  1939. *The Diary of Dr. Andrew Smith, 1834–1836*. 2 vols. Ed. P. R. Kirby. Cape Town:
      Van Riebeeck Society.
Turner, Terence S.
  n.d. *The Social Skin*. Unpublished manuscript. Published in abridged form in *Not Work
      Alone*. Ed. J. Cherfas and R. Lewin. London: Temple Smith.
Veblen, Thorstein
  1934. *The Theory of the Leisure Class: An Economic Study of Institutions*. New York: Mod-
      ern Library.
Volosinov, V. N.
  1973. *Marxism and the Philosophy of Language*. Trans. L. Matejka and I. R. Titunik. New
      York: Seminar Press.
White, Luise.
  1988. Domestic Labour in a Colonial City: Prostitution in Nairobi, 1900–1952. In
      Patriarchy and Class: African Women in the Home and the Workforce. Ed. Sharon
      Stichter and Jean Parpart. Boulder: Westview Press.
Williamson, Janice.
  1992. I-less and Gaga in the West Edmonton Mall: Towards a Pedestrian Feminist
      Reading. In *The Anatomy of Gender: Women's Struggle for the Body*. Ed. Dawn H. Cur-
      rie and Valerie Raoul. Ottawa: Carleton University Press.
Willoughby, William C.
  c.1899. *Native Life on the Transvaal Border*. London: Simpkin, Marshall, Hamilton,
      Kent.
  ———. n.d. Clothes. Willoughby Papers. Selly Oak Colleges, Birmingham, U. K.

23   Mudwomen and Whitemen

A Meditation on Pueblo Potteries

and the Politics of Representation[1]

BARBARA A. BABCOCK

Out in this desert we are testing bombs.

—Adrienne Rich[2]

The petit-bourgeois is a man unable to imagine the other.... But there is a figure for emergencies—Exoticism.

—Roland Barthes[3]

As my title implies, I am concerned with the objects of others and the constitution of the colonial Other, the constructions of gender and ethnicity, and the problematics of alterity and interpretation. This meditation on the representation of the Pueblo subject within Anglo-American discourse is both a re-visionary and experimental text—a rereading through juxtapositions. "Re-vision," in Adrienne Rich's now classic definition, entails "the act of looking back, of seeing with fresh eyes, of entering and old text from a new critical direction." This particular re-vision was occasioned by my leaving the Southwest and my work with Pueblo women and their potteries in 1987 and returning to it after a year in the Ivy League. My essay is experimental in being a pastiche of images, quotations, and reflections—the sherds of over a decade of studying ceramics and culture.[4]

I owe the first part of my title, "mudwomen and whitemen," to Nora Naranjo-Morse, a Pueblo potter and poet. In 1989 we participated in a symposium on figurative ceramics at the Heard Museum, and Nora read a poem she had written about the difficulty she had selling her first pieces because they were strange, not identifiable, not "traditional" Santa Clara black pottery; about how devastating it is to put your heart into a piece and then have it judged and dismissed. It was titled "Mudwoman's First Encounter with the World of Money and Business." Her laughter, her parody of self and other seems like the right place to situate this review of over a century of oppression, appropriation, and commodification. Better her poem than the scholar's statement that, "grasping for cultural legitimacy and survival in the industralized West in the past century, native peoples have accepted the economic option of coverting culture into commodity."[5]

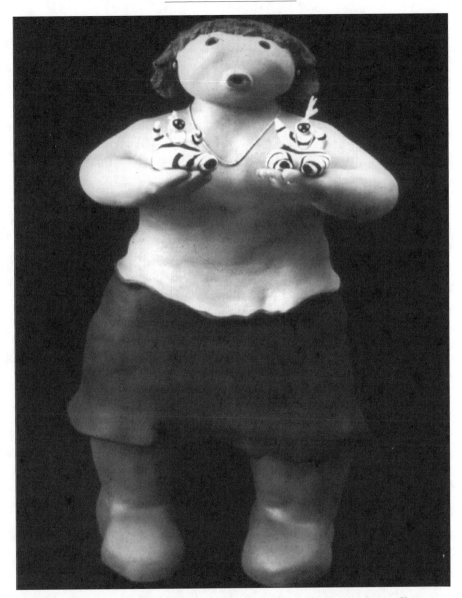

Figure 1: Pearlene, ceramic self-portrait by Nora Naranjo-Morse, Santa Clara Pueblo, 1987. Courtesy of Nora Naranjo-Morse and the Heard Museum, Phoenix, Arizona.

As I struggle to put this critique together, I envy Nora her poetry, her pottery, and especially Pearlene, her ceramic self-portrait and alter ego who "can say or do anything she wants" (Figure 1). "Pearlene," Nora says, "is a woman who doesn't know where she is, and it doesn't matter. She is the antithesis of the characteristics of Pueblo women that anthropologists love to point out." There is no question that Pearlene destabilizes the authorized narrative of traditional Pueblo pottery—the

Figure 2: Olla Maiden: Thomas Moran talking to an Acoma Woman. Original caption, "On the Line of the Santa Fe Railroad, Acoma Pueblo, Arizona [sic]."
Courtesy of Special Collections, The University of Arizona Library.

story of use and beauty told again and again by photographers, painters, collectors, and scholars (Figure 2).[6]

The "potteries" of my title is Pueblo English. Cultural critique in one word. The idea of a proper collective "pottery" is inconceivable from the Pueblo point of view. Every piece of pottery is a made being with a unique voice and spirit. But "politics"? Or "conflict *and* clay," as I once suggested in a lecture on Cochiti potteries? In response to presentations and proposals I have made in the last decade

Figure 3: Helen Cordero in her Cochiti Pueblo home, 1979, shaping a Storyteller with twenty-five children for an exhibit at the Denver Museum of Natural History. Photography by Dudley Smith. Courtesy of the Denver Museum of Natural History; Denver, CO, negative no. 4–79082–9A.

concerning the work of Cochiti potter Helen Cordero (Figure 3), I've been told by Pueblo ceramic scholars and feminists alike that a little old Pueblo lady shaping dolls of mud is charming but trivial and unproblematic—affirming yet again that even, perhaps especially, among scholars, "the non-Western woman is the vehicle for misplaced Western nostalgia." I suppose we have progressed, for a century ago they said "eccentric" or "grotesque," and they called such figures *monos* (monkey, mimic, fool, or mere doll) and dismissed them as "tourist trash."[7]

And so I ask, what about these very "relations of power whereby one portion of humanity can select, value, and collect the pure products of others"? What about the way that Anglo America has been imagining, describing, and fetishizing the Pueblo Southwest for over a century? And why, indeed, has the study of pottery "generated more literature than any other aspect of Southwest culture"? Why was Nampeyo the symbol of Hopi culture in the minds of white Americans, and why did Maria Martinez become *the* single most famous Native American artist? What about "the pervasive metaphorical elision of colonized, non-European, and female" and the fact that woman is the "main *vehicle*" for "the representation of difference and otherness within mass culture"? And that raises the issue of the inverse relation "between relative empowerment and objectified portrayal in popular culture"—the fact that "the Indian appears everywhere . . . as a mystified ideal, yet nowhere in dominant discourse do Indians speak with their own unmediated voices."[8]

It is late July, 1988. Kit Hinsley and I are driving from Alamogordo to Las Cruces through White Sands Missile Range. It is shimmering hot. I have been away from the desert long enough to forget how you can see as well as feel the heat. I have missed the dryness, the emptiness, and the clarity of this landscape. I look at the map to see how many miles to Tucson. Along the road we're on I read, "U. S. 70 closed during short periods of firing." That prompts discussion of Trinity, Titan missiles, and the military omnipresence in the Southwest. No sooner said than we are halted by a military policewoman, who tells us that testing is about to begin and that we will have to wait at least an hour. She points us in the direction of the visitor center.

Inside it is cool and dark and soft as only fifty-year-old adobes are. The contents, however, are not so comforting. In the main hall are books for sale about desert flora and fauna, about southwestern Native Americans, and about the day the sun disappeared. An adjoining exhibit hall contains similar definitions, representations, and textualizations of natural, cultural, and technological objects and events. Displays juxtapose Mimbres pottery and other prehistoric Pueblo artifacts with the natural history of White Sands against a photographic background of missiles and mushroom clouds. This is a shrine naturalizing, domesticating, and celebrating nuclear power and militarism.

In the tourist shop, the same three classes of objects and images are for sale—vials of white sand and plastic missiles along with Indian souvenirs made in Taiwan. "Authentic" Indian-made pottery, jewelry, weaving, and painting are in a side room, dominated by a huge buckskin on which is painted a "traditional" Pueblo woman. Kit urges me to take a picture. I don't have to. It is, as the cover of the 1987 *Insight Guide—American Southwest* (Figure 4) confirms, ubiquitous—a Pueblo woman with a pot on her head, encircled and frozen in time.

What preoccupies me and keeps returning to haunt our conversations for hours and weeks and months to come is the juxtaposition of Pueblo pottery, women, and nuclear power. They pasted a picture of Rita Hayworth on the bomb. They made it in Maria Martinez's backyard. Pueblo women cleaned Los Alamos labs and

Figure 4: Olla maiden cover illustration, *Insight Guide—American Southwest*. (Hong Kong: APA Publications, 1987.) Courtesy of APA publications.

houses, and these "maids," Charlie Masters recalls, gave the Anglo lab workers "splendid pieces" of Indian pottery. A number of scientists and their wives "went native," for San Ildefonso Pueblo was one of the few places off the hill they were permitted to escape to. "It was this group," Masters tells us, "who changed, temporarily, the entire economy of northern New Mexico with their free-handed spending and their sudden demand of a handicraft people for something like mass production." They decorated their drab quarters with "strange and beautiful" Pueblo pots and carried these "pieces of New Mexico earth" back to Berkeley, Chicago, and Princeton as mementos of their wartime experience. Not surprisingly, in the recent opera *Los Alamos*, the voice and symbol of Mother Earth is Morning Star, ancient Indian maiden and contemporary waitress. Apart from the literal Los Alamos connection, the dialectic of nuclear destruction and Pueblo pottery is perhaps inevitable, overdetermined in a postmodern culture that "continually constitutes itself through its ideological constructs of the exotic," escaping from the power relations of modern society into, in this case, "the artistic otherworldliness" of the Pueblo.[9]

For this very reason, the *Insight Guide* olla maiden, posed to sell the Southwest, raises "ambiguous and disturbing questions about the aesthetic appropriation of non-Western others—issues of race, gender, and power." What does it mean not only that the Other is frequently presented as female—the feminization that Said discusses in *Orientalism*—but that women and the things they make are both symbols and sources of cultural identity, survival, and social continuity, and also are mediators between cultures, vehicles of exchange and change? "It is," Gayatri Spivak has observed, "women's work that has continuously survived within not only the varieties of capitalism but other historical and geographical modes of production." For centuries pottery has been *the* primary Pueblo trade item, and pottery is women's work.[10]

In the past century pottery making has played a key role in the Pueblos' transition from an agrarian to a cash economy—a process that began with the Smithsonian Institution's first collecting expedition to the southwestern pueblos in 1879 and was accelerated by the coming of the railroads to New Mexico in the 1880s and Fred Harvey's marketing campaigns in the early decades of this century. Women sold potteries and demonstrated pottery making to railroad passengers, and images of women with pots were sold on Harvey/Santa Fe Railway postcards and playing cards as well as booklets and brochures and calendars (Figure 5). As Marta Weigle has suggested, both the collecting of Pueblo potteries and the imaging of Pueblo women as "civilized" artisans using or selling their wares to tourists signify the transformation and domestication of the "savage," nearly naked, male warrior of the first Santa Fe Railway publications.[11]

This raises what I see as a key question and a paradoxical problematic, and politically charged situation: What happens when indigenous Pueblo "signifiers of stability"—women and potteries—become valued items of exchange, cultural brokers, and agents of change precisely because they embody a "synchronic essentialism" for postindustrial Anglo consumers? Why has a traditionally dressed woman shaping or carrying an olla (a water jar) become *the* metonymic misrepresentation of the

Figure 5: Comely Indian maidens and aged squaws meet the train and sell their wares. This image of Pueblo Indians selling pottery at Laguna, NM, was reproduced both as a "phostint" postcard, with the preceding caption, and as the five of clubs in "The Great Southwest Souvenir Playing Card, made and published exclusively for Fred Harvey" in 1911. Courtesy of Marta Weigle.

Pueblo, and why has Anglo America invested so much in this image for well over a century? In *The Conquest of America* Todorov suggests part of the answer. If, he argues,

> instead of regarding the other simply as an object, he [*sic*] were considered as a sub-ject capable of producing objects which one might then possess, the chain would be extended by a link—the intermediary subject—and thereby multiply to infinity the number of objects ultimately possessed. This transformation, however, necessitates that the intermediary subject be maintained in precisely this role of subject-producer-of-objects and kept from becoming like ourselves.[12]

Examples of such image maintenance abound. As early as 1540 Castaneda, the chronicler of the Coronado expedition, reported that Pueblo women made "jars of extraordinary labor and workmanship, which were worth seeing." Under American occupation three centuries later, Lieutenant James W. Albert, with the advanced guard of the "Army of the West," made an "Examination of New Mexico" in 1846 and 1847 (with illustrations by C. R. Graham). Olla maidens are prominently featured in the foreground of the etchings of the Rio Grande pueblos of San Felipe, Santa Ana, and Santo Domingo. In his ethnographic reconnaissance for the Smithsonian Institution in 1879, Frank Hamilton Cushing painted similar images in words. He recalled his first evening at Zuni as follows:

> As I sat watching the women coming and going to and from the well, "How strangely parallel," I thought, "have been the lines of development in this curious civilization of an American desert with those Eastern nations and deserts." Clad in blanket dresses, mantles thrown gracefully over their heads, each with a curiously decorated jar in her hand, they came one after another down the crooked path. A little passageway through the gardens between two adobe walls to our right led down rude steps into the well which, dug deeply in the sands, had been walled up with rocks, like the Pools of Palestine, and roofed over with reeds and dirt. Into this passageway and down to the dark, covered spring they turned, or lingered outside to gossip with newcomers while awaiting their chances, meanwhile slyly watching, from under their black hair, the strange visitors from "Wa-sin-to-na." These water-carriers were a picturesque sight as with stately step and fine carriage they followed one another up into the evening light, balancing their great shining water-jars on their heads.[13]

Within the same decade, in essays also written for popular periodicals and later collected in *The Land of the Pueblos*, Susan Wallace described Pueblo men as ploughing with a crooked stick, "the [O]riental implement in the days of Moses" and found much "to remind [her] of Bible pictures" in Hispanic villages along the Rio Grande:

> [T]he Mexican women, straight as a rule, carrying water-jars on head or shoulder, like maidens of Palestine. Now and then an old black shawl, melancholy remnant of the gay rebosa [sic], shrouding an olive forehead, suggested the veiled face of the gentle Rebecca.

And, in the summer of 1890, anthropologist John G. Owens described an evening at Zuni remarkably like the one Cushing had witnessed:

> Just before dark, the squaws all go to the spring to get an olla of water. I went over this evening to see them. It reminded me of the pictures of Palestine. . . . It certainly is a classic sight.

Again and again, this picturesque sight is figured in classical and biblical terms.[14]

It is probably neither insignificant nor coincidental that, at the same time that such inscriptions of Pueblo women and their potteries were proliferating, an anonymous article appeared in an 1880 *Harper's Weekly* on the revitalization of pottery among the women of Cincinnati, Ohio: "Handling dear old mother earth . . . does not leave much time for hysteria." The implied and valued proper role of woman—as well as relations between culture and nature, and production and reproduction—in this statement are made explicit almost a century later. In 1972

Marxist anthropologist Claude Meillassoux theorized "pre-capitalist formations" such as turn-of-the-century Zuni as follows:

> [A]gricultural self-sustaining formations . . . rely less on the control of the means of material production than on the means of human reproduction: subsistence and women. Their end is reproduction of life as a precondition to production. Their primary concern is to "grow and multiply" in the biblical sense. They represent comprehensive integrated, economic, social and demographic systems ensuring the vital needs of all the members . . . of the community. A change towards a material productive end, the shift from production for self-sustenance and self-perpetuation to production for an external market, must necessarily bring a radical transformation, if not the social destruction of the communities, as indeed we witness the process nowadays.

Even more recently the following imagined conversation took place in the midst of an unstable African political situation between a CIA operative and a KGB agent in the best-selling spy thriller *Tass Is Authorized to Announce* . . . :

> [The Russian:]   "In this age of the rat race, only woman remains a symbol of stability, that is, beauty."
> [The CIA agent:]   "That's not bad. . . . Sell it to me, Ivan. *Beauty as a symbol of stability*. Ten dollars? Fifteen then. Imagine the report I could write for the swine back home."[15]

What these "classic" statements and images share is that he is speaking for and representing her and that she is valued because she is, if only in his imaginary projections, outside history, outside industrial capitalism. For many decades now Pueblo women have rarely worn *mantas* on an everyday basis or walked around with pots on their heads unless they were paid to do so. Such "picturesque" scenes exemplify "aesthetic primitivism," which is a form of colonial domination. Both Bhaba and Ong have pointed out that "colonial discourse produces the colonized as a fixed reality which is at once an 'other' and yet entirely knowable and visible"; that "by and large, non-Western women are taken as an unproblematic universal category." "The language of occupation" posits women as "receptacles and products of desire," for repeatedly "a female colored body serves as a site of attraction and symbolic appropriation."[16]

I have already implicated Edward Said's *Orientalism* in my argument, because I think that the Southwest *is* America's Orient. Like the Orient, the Southwest is an idea that has "a history and a tradition of thought, imagery, and vocabulary that have given it reality and presence in and for" the rest of America. And, as the preceding verbal and visual images amply attest, this Anglo-American tradition is explicitly figured in the trope of Orientalism. Repeatedly, "travellers passing Pueblo villages of the Southwest in the [eighteen] eighties were invited to recall the villages of ancient Egypt and Nubia, Ninevah and Babylon, rather than to aboriginal study the remains of American life; the people were 'like the descendants of

Rebecca of Bible fame.'" Contrary to what Pomeroy implies, however, such Orientalizing was not simply an 1880s phenomenon. In 1896 Philip Embury Harroun won a ten-dollar prize from Eastman Kodak for a photo of a San Juan Pueblo woman titled *A New Mexican Rebecca*. In 1920 Harriet Monroe compared Pueblo dances to Homeric rites and Egyptian ceremonies. A few years later, in introducing the Santa Fe Railway's "Indian Detours," Erna Fergusson lured the traveller as follows: "Motorists crossing the southwestern states are nearer to the primitive than anywhere else on the continent. They are crossing a land in which a foreign people, with foreign speech and foreign ways, offer them spectacles which can be equaled in few Oriental lands."[17]

In this romantic dichotomizing and essentializing discourse that modern industrial America began producing about the Southwest in the late nineteenth century, the image of an olla maiden is a primary and privileged signifier and one in which considerable material investment has been and continues to be made. The 1987 *Insight Guide* cover and countless other recent olla maiden images by contemporary artists and photographers attest that the nostalgic aestheticism of the 1800s has persisted at great profit for well over a century. Unsettled Indians were unsettling, and this authorized image of the "civilized," domestic, and feminized Pueblo was popularized at the very moment when "wild" nomadic Apaches were still killing whitemen and eluding General Crook in these same southwestern spaces. Late nineteenth-century authors such as Susan Wallace repeatedly juxtapose the "peace-loving," "pastoral" "maidens of Palestine" with the savage, bloodthirsty "Bedouins" of the desert. The Indian wars ended, but the Oriental tropology persisted, especially in the lyrical and escapist vision of Fred Harvey and Santa Fe Railway advertising. Advertising that was intent on selling the Southwest as "a last refuge of magic, mountains, and quaint ancestors"—"a gentle, peaceful, and picturesque people."[18]

Calendars, playing cards, postcards. It was a sell whose time had come. Between the Civil War and World War II, America had become, in Warren Sussman's words, "a hieroglyphic civilization"—a culture that understands itself and others chiefly in terms of visual symbols. At the same time, the arts and crafts movement had produced countless statements such as the preceding about Cincinnati pottery making. For an America which saw premodern craftsmanship as an antidote for modern ills, a technological America desirous of elegant articles of common use with, in Charles Eliot Norton's words, "something of human life in them," what could be better than the "timeless, authentic beauty" of a Pueblo pot? And who could better serve as an idealized alternative to modernity than a primitive "mudwoman" who, as Evans-Pritchard has assured us, "does not desire things to be other than they are"? An Indian mother shaping Mother Earth and gracefully carrying her burdens was/is indeed something of a bourgeois dream of an alternative redemptive life as well as an imagistic transformation of an unmanageable native into a manageable one. Modern power, Foucault argues, replaces violence and force with the "gentler" constraint of uninterrupted visibility. The camera replaces the cannon, and "the gaze" becomes a technique of power/knowledge, as the unruly other is managed through the creation and exploitation of a new kind of visibility.[19]

"The relegation of the tribal or primitive to either a vanishing past or an ahistorical, conceptual present" influences not only the Western valuation but the production and consumption of ethnic art, and that in turn profoundly affects gender relations within tribal communities with regard to the reproduction of culture for sale. Scholars and popularizers have been consistent in their refusal to see Pueblo women in their "psychological, social, and colonial complexity." Natives, especially female artisan natives, were co-opted into

> scripted ethnic stereotypes, not merely as part of the inevitable choreography of denial that characterized face-to-face interracial relations in contemporary America, but with increasing psychosocial investment in the fiction it perpetuated. . . . [T]hey learned to market, as well as elaborate, their own ethnicity,

and in the process they assumed powers and prerogatives that had once belonged to their husbands. Similarly, the repeated imaging of Pueblo pottery as useful beauty denies its complex embodiment of spiritual, commercial, and political, as well as aesthetic, factors. For both pots and potters, the olla maiden stereotype has not only influenced aesthetics—it has had profound economic and political consequences.[20]

Shortly after the turn of the century George Pepper went to New Mexico to collect for the American Museum of Natural History. A photo taken at Cochiti Pueblo in 1904 shows Mrs. Pepper and an Indian man packing potteries to be shipped to New York, and as the figures in the foreground attest, these barrels contained something more than utilitarian bowls and jars. Between 1875 and 1905, Cochiti and Tesuque potters produced an astonishing array of human and animal figures in addition to bowls and jars decorated with figurative designs. Many were satiric potraits of the whitemen, for one response of tribal peoples everywhere to Western invasion and domination has been to mock and caricature the light-skinned alien. Then and now, Pueblo men mimed the whiteman in clown performances on dusty plazas, and Pueblo women shaped his image in clay. Few whitemen who bought these figures, which were described as "eccentric" or "grotesque," realized that they were in fact portraits of themselves. These *monos* were not regarded highly, and because traders such as Jake Gold of Santa Fe encouraged the manufacture of these "primitive idols," they were (and still are) frequently dismissed as "tourist junk" and as wholly "commercial" in origin.[21]

In an 1889 note titled "The Debasement of Pueblo Art," William Holmes urged that the manufacture of such forms be discouraged and that museums not deign to collect or accept them. Collector and dealer Thomas Dozier was similarly disparaging. In his "Statement to the Trade for 1907," he attributed the manufacture of such "odd and attractive pieces" to "idle dallying in lazy moments" and predicted that, "in this utilitarian age, *she* cannot always go on making toys." From the perspective of these and countless other anthropologists and collectors, Pueblo potters playing and playing with the outsider's games did not make for a vision of authenticity, of timeless, useful, and subjugated beauty. The scholars were even more successful than the Spanish clergy in suppressing idolatry. As a consequence of this attitude, historic figurative ceramics have been more or less invisible, gathering dust in museum basements and attics for over a century. One can still view many exhibits and read countless books, catalogues, and essays on Pueblo pottery and not encounter a single figurative form. The pervasiveness of this use-and-beauty bias is also evident in souvenir postcards, photo albums, books, slides, and now even videotapes. Bowls and jars are featured as "authentic" items of everyday use. Figurines are basely commercial. To give but one example, an image of a Tesuque potter making "raingods," published in a 1930s souvenir folder of American Indian life, is captioned "Indian girl moulding lucky bucks."[22]

In contrast to these "tourist atrocities," the shapes that scholars call "utility ware" are, in fact, "receptacles of desire," for repeatedly authenticity is produced by removing such objects from their current historical situation or, even if photographed in the pueblo, by re-dressing the present in the past. In the established tradition of Charles Lummis and Edward Curtis, history is airbrushed out. Clearly, Ruth Benedict did not invent the stereotype of the peaceful, poetic, feminine Pueblo. She simply called it "Apollonian." To the extent that potteries are seen at all as containers of cultural value, as well as art objects to decorate Anglo lives, they are described as reiterating, affirming this world view. Nor is this view specific to the Pueblo, for it is widely assumed that primitive and folk art is tradition bound and conflict free. The idea that conflict, as well as clay, may be shaped in Pueblo ceramics is simply absent from the literature.[23]

When Helen Cordero shaped the first Storyteller doll in 1964, she engendered a revolution in Pueblo ceramics, caused a dislocation in the economy of cultural representations, and forced a taxonomic shift in Anglo classifications and valuations of Pueblo ceramics. When I first encountered a Storyteller figure (see Figure 3), I read it as female and as a powerful image of generativity, of reproductive power. I soon learned that this was not simply another image of a Pueblo mother, of which Helen herself has made several, but a male figure: "It's my grandfather. He's giving me these. He had lots of stories and lots of grandchildrens, and we're all in there, in the clay." In studying these grandfather Storytellers, which are also images of cultural reproduction, I have discovered that synchronic essentialism and significations of stability in Pueblo art and culture are not entirely a matter of Anglo projection. Without pottery to store water and grain, settled Pueblo existence as it developed and was lived for centuries in the southwest deserts was literally inconceivable. Not surprisingly, therefore, the existence and well-being of the people was connected to the creation and maintenance of clay figures. Pueblo religion centers on reproduction or, in Haeberlin's terms, "the idea of fertilization." Connections between human fertility and agricultural subsistence were frequently made and have been the subject of both ritual and iconography, and a consistent theme in ceramic self-representation, for almost two thousand years.[24]

In the first half of this century, pottery production at Cochiti declined, as it did in many other pueblos. While scholars, collectors, traders, and writers were soon encouraging pottery revivals, they discouraged figurine manufacture and the production of "tourist atrocities." Santa Fe organizations such as the Indian Arts Fund and the Southwest Association for Indian Affairs combined aestheticism and activism, and in the 1920s supporters such as Mary Austin, Mabel Dodge Luhan, and Natalie Curtis promoted Indian art as a way to build popular sympathy for Indian political and religious freedoms and the preservation of Indian culture. The problem then and now was that they decided what counted as Indian art. Clearly, figurines did not.

Remembering her childhood, Helen Cordero has said, "For a long time pottery was silent in the pueblo." Among the few figurative forms that continued to be made at Cochiti, the figure of a woman holding a child, a water jar, or a bowl of bread was the most popular and was called "a singing mother," "a madonna," or "a singing lady." When Helen shaped the first Storyteller in response to Alexander Girard's request for a larger figure with more children, she revised the singing mother tradition in two significant respects: she made the primary figure male, rather than female; and she placed more than a realistic number of children on him. Helen's reinvention of this important mode of cultural production and tradition of representation controlled by women (pottery) transformed an image of natural reproduction into a figure of an important mode of cultural reproduction (storytelling) that is controlled by men and that both embodies and expresses generativity, the root metaphor of Pueblo culture.

By 1973 when the Museum of International Folk Art mounted its "What Is Folk Art?" exhibit, the success and popularity of Helen's Storyteller was such that at least six other potters had imitated her figure. A decade later over fifty other Cochiti potters and no fewer than 150 potters throughout the New Mexico pueblos were shaping Storytellers and related figurines. Many of these imitations are female figures, and as far as Helen is concerned, they are not "really" Storytellers: "They call them 'Storytellers,' but they don't know what it means. They don't know it's after my grandfather. At home, no womens are storytellers." When Helen Cordero insists upon the ancestral and masculine attributes of her Storyteller, she is both explicitly and implicitly "authorizing" her creation: explicitly, by invoking her biological connection to ancestral authority and power; implicitly, by identifying her pottery with a sacred masculine activity, a tradition that is both patriarchal and genealogical.

Women do tell stories at Cochiti, but they do not tell *the* stories—the sacred origin myths and legends. As Helen's uncle Joe Trujillo once remarked, "Our kivas are like men's clubs. Religion is a man's business with Indians." If women are practically peripheral, they are symbolically central to this "man's business," which involves a transcendental appropriation of the female principle. Moreover, in this world in which discourse is controlled by men, women's ideas or models of the world about them find expression in forms other than direct expository speech, and for generation upon generation of Pueblo women, pottery making has been a primary and privileged mode of expression. If Pueblo potteries were once a primary mode of production, a necessity of life, they were also and still are symbolic forms, containers of cultural values, models *of* and *for* reproduction and regeneration. But even here, men have traditionally controlled the marketing and distribution of pottery and other forms of communication with the outside world. Acculturation, automobiles, and an Anglo art market that names and wants to know its Indian artists have changed all that. Women have assumed control of activities and monies that were once their husbands' prerogatives.[25]

In the summer of 1982, when a Cochiti tribal officer tried to persuade the council to prohibit the women from having shows and demonstrating pottery making despite the obvious economic benefit to the pueblo, he was reasserting the traditional male role of mediating with the outside world and protecting what "he" deemed sacred discourse. He was also attempting to reinvoke his right to appropriate, control, and re-present female generativity and creativity. Perhaps he realized that in the remarkable revival of figurative pottery that Storytellers have engendered, women potters have done much more than reshape traditional roles in terms of economics, mobility, and communication. By creating Storytellers and other mythic and ceremonial figures, such as Turtles and Drummers, rather than bowls and jars, and in exhibiting and demonstrating their art, they are telling stories about storytelling and have assumed the right to re-present and interpret to the outside world at least some of the aspects of the very discourse in which they are displaced. Helen Cordero and her sisters are manipulating considerably more than clay. They are reproducing culture "with a difference."

As a consequence of Helen Cordero's creativity, Pueblo figurative pottery has also been rediscovered and redefined by Anglo consumers. There are now several categories for figurative pottery—other than "Pottery, Miscellaneous"—at Santa Fe's Indian Market, figurines win major prizes, and shapes once dismissed as "tourist junk" and relegated to museum attics and basements are now on display and commanding high prices. Nonetheless, it is doubtful if, from the white man's point of view, the shape of Pueblo pottery has *really* changed. In 1987 *American Indian Art* published a special issue on pottery that included two essays on historic and contemporary figurative ceramics—the latter shaped by Nora Naranjo-Morse. The cover, however, featured a very traditional, early nineteenth-century Acoma olla.

I don't think there's any question that Nora's Pearlene goes beyond such nostalgic Anglo categories of Pueblo women and Pueblo potteries. She got written about but did not appear on the cover of that glossy Indian art magazine, and I can guarantee that this Pueblo woman's representation of herself as postcolonial Pearlene will not be featured on any guidebooks to the Southwest. Nor is she likely to be the subject of Native American artists such as R. C. Gorman, Amado Peña, or Robert Redbird. Or Anglo Southwest artists such as Ross Stefan, Jacqueline Rochester, or Bill Schenck. They have very different ideas about these "mudwomen" than Nora Naranjo-Morse does. Fictions that sell. They don't want Pearlene, with all her ambiguity of dependency and rupture, for "man dreams of an Other not only to possess her but also to be ratified by her." They want those shiny polychrome acoma ollas (see Figure 2) that look like "ancient" potteries are supposed to.[26]

To conclude this meditation on aesthetic appropriation and mystification: On October 15, 1989, *Money* magazine ran an ad in the *New York Times Magazine* titled "Adobe Sonata." Imaged as "the rewards of Money" was a casually elegant couple embracing at a grand piano in a Santa Fe adobe living room decorated with traditional ollas. The caption reiterated that "to live in Santa Fe is to live amid the

grandeur of nature and the beauty of the inspired artist's creation. The readers of
MONEY magazine can easily afford to reflect this harmony in the paintings and
crafts that illuminate their homes." In the late twentieth as in the late nineteenth
century, such images not only are "invested with indescribable romance" but have
become commonplace significations of incredible investment. Nine years ago
Helen Cordero's potteries were photographed against a pastoral, Edenic background to advertise the 1980–81 Colorado Springs Symphony season and its sponsor, Otero Savings. The poster tells us that the art objects are from the Otero
Savings Collections and that "the Otero Savings Blue Ribbon Collection reflects a
corporate promise to offer excellence to all. The Indian art mirrors the Otero
image of quality and lasting value."

In fin de siècle remarks that an "immense amount of romance is wasted on the
old mud houses" and "tiresome pottery fragments," Susan Wallace might well be
describing present-day Santa Fe. Adobes and ollas and olla maidens (see Figure 2)
and countless advertisements such as the preceding confirm that

> the need of our society both to engulf Others and to exploit "otherness" is not only a
> structural and ideological phenomenon; it has been at the root of the very develop-
> ment of capitalism, founded as it is on imperialist relations. . . . Economically, we need
> the Other, even as politically we seek to eliminate it. . . . Capitalism feeds on different
> value systems and takes control of them, while nourishing their symbolic difference
> from itself. . . . [D]ifferent systems of production . . . which are suppressed by capital-
> ism are then incorporated into its imagery and ideological values: as "otherness," old-
> fashioned, charming, exotic, natural, primitive, universal—

the timeless beauty of a Santa Clara Pueblo pot shaped by, yet another ad tells us,
"the warm hands of man." Confirmation yet again, as Luce Irigaray has pointed
out, that "commodities, women, are a mirror of value of and for men." When
"mudwoman encounters the world of money and business," she cannot but confront the nostalgic aestheticism, synchronic essentialism, feminization, and utilitarian biases that have shaped the Anglo valuation and imaging of Pueblo potteries.
Among other things, Pearlene discovers that "tradition remains the sacred weapon
oppressors repeatedly hold up whenever the need to maintain their privileges,
hence to impose the form of the old on the content of the new, arises."[27]

Notes

1. This essay is dedicated to Helen Cordero, who has shared her life and work with me
   and by so doing has revised my own; to Marsie Cate, who has given me a home in
   New Mexico and never not challenged my own romantic vision of Pueblo life; to
   Marta Weigle, friend and fellow interpreter of the regional web of commodification
   in which our lives and work are entangled; and to Kit Hinsley, who has inspired, sustained, and contributed to this re-visioning. I would also like to thank Jay Cox for
   research and computer assistance; Linda Degh and Richard Bauman for inviting me
   to an Indiana University conference, "Folklore and Social Transformation" (Bloomington, November 1988); the editors of the *Arizona Quarterly* for inviting me to
   their first conference on American Literatures and Cultures (Tucson, March 1989);

and John MacAloon for asking me to be Ford Foundation Lecturer in the social sciences at the University of Chicago (May 1989). These three presentations occasioned the rereading and rethinking that resulted in this essay, first presented at a Winterthur Conference in 1989—"The Material Culture of Gender/ The Gender of Material Culture"—and forthcoming in a book of the same title.

2. Adrienne Rich, "Trying to Talk with a Man," in *Poems Selected and New, 1950–1974* (New York: W. W. Norton & Co., 1975), 185.

3. Roland Barthes, *Mythologies* (New York: Hill & Wang, 1986), 151–52.

4. Adrienne Rich, "When We Dead Awaken: Writing as Re-Vision," in *On Lies, Secrets and Silence: Selected Prose, 1966–1978* (New York: W. W. Norton & Co., 1979), 35. For further discussion of the "question of how the third-world subject is represented within Western discourse," of "the mechanics of the constitution of the Other," see Gayatri Spivak, "Can the Subaltern Speak?" in *Marxism and the Interpretation of Culture*, ed. by Cary Nelson and Lawrence Grossberg (Urbana: University of Illinois Press, 1988), 271–313.

5. The Heard Museum, *Earth, Hands, Life: A Ceramics Figures Symposium* (January 21–22, 1989); Edwin Wade, "The Ethnic Art Market in the Southwest, 1880–1980," in *Objects and Others: Essays on Museums and Material Culture*, ed. by George W. Stocking, Jr. (Madison: University of Wisconsin Press, 1985), 167; for more on the commodification of ethnicity in New Mexico, the cooptation of the Pueblo and their marketing, and elaborating their own ethnicity, see Sylvia Rodriguez, "Art, Tourism, and Race Relations in Taos: Toward a Sociology of the Art Colony," *Journal of Anthropological Research* 45 (1989): 77–99. Nora Naranjo-Morse's poems have now been published in *Mud Woman: Poems from the Clay* (Tucson: University of Arizona Press, 1992).

6. The Heard Museum, *Earth, Hands, Life* (January 22, 1989). For examples of the official and predominantly utilitarian narrative of Pueblo ceramics, see especially Alfred E. Dittert, Jr., and Fred Plog, *Generations in Clay: Pueblo Pottery of the American Southwest* (Flagstaff: Northland Press, 1980); David L. Arnold, "Pueblo Artistry in Clay," *National Geographic* 162, no. 5 (November 1982): 593–605; Jonathan Batkin, "Pottery: The Ceramic Tradition," in *Harmony by Hand: Art of the Southwest Indians*, ed. by Patrick Houlihan (San Francisco: Chronicle Books, 1987), 74–106; and Jonathan Batkin, *Pottery of the Pueblos of New Mexico, 1700–1940* (Colorado Springs: Taylor Museum, 1987).

7. Aihwa Ong, "Colonialism and Modernity: Feminist Re-Presentations of Women in Non-Western Societies," in *Feminism and the Critique of Colonial Discourse*, ed. by Deborah Gordon, *Inscriptions* 3/4 (1988): 85; for discussion of nineteenth-century Cochiti ceramic "grotesques," which were in fact portraits of the whiteman, see Barbara A. Babcock, "Pueblo Clowning and Pueblo Clay: From Icon to Caricature in Cochiti Figurative Ceramics," *Visible Religion* 4/5 (1986): 280–300; and "'Those, They Called Them Monos'": Cochiti Figurative Ceramics, 1875–1905," *American Indian Art* 12, no. 4 (Autumn 1987): 50–57, 67. Only two essays have dealt at all with the relationship between politics and potteries, with the shaping of conflict as well as clay in Pueblo ceramics, and those quite recently: Edwin L. Wade, "Straddling the Cultural Fence: The Conflict of Ethnic Artists within Pueblo Societies," in *The Arts of the North American Indian: Native Traditions in Evolution*, ed. by Edwin L. Wade (New York: Hudson Hills Press, 1986), 243–54; and Barbara A. Babcock, "'At Home No Womens Are Storytellers': Potteries, Stories, and Politics in Cochiti Pueblo," *Journal of the Southwest* 30, no. 3 (Autumn 1988): 356–89.

8. James Clifford, "Histories of the Tribal and the Modern," in *The Predicament of Culture: Twentieth-Century Ethnography, Literature, and Art* (Cambridge: Harvard University Press, 1988), 213; Batkin, "Pottery: The Ceramic Tradition," 77; Helen Carr,

"Woman/Indian: 'The American' and His Others," in *Europe and Its Others; Proceedings of the Essex Conference on the Sociology of Literature*, Vol. 2, ed. by Francis Barker et al. (Colchester: University of Essex, 1985), 46; Judith Williamson, "Woman Is an Island: Femininity and Colonization," in *Studies in Entertainment: Critical Approaches to Mass Culture*, ed. by Tania Modleski (Bloomington: Indiana University Press, 1986), 101; Rodriguez, "Art, Tourism, and Race Relations in Taos," 87.

9. Charlie Masters, "Going Native," in *Standing By and Making Do: Women of Wartime Los Alamos*, ed. by Jane S. Wilson and Charlotte Serber (Los Alamos: The Los Alamos Historical Society, 1988), 117–30; Marc Neikrug, "Los Alamos" (unpublished manuscript, 1988); Clifford, *Predicament*, 272; Helen Carr, "In Other Words: Native American Women's Autobiography," ed. by Bella Brodzki and Celeste Schenck (Ithaca: Cornell University Press, 1988), 151.

10. Clifford, *Predicament*, 197; Edward W. Said, *Orientalism* (New York: Vintage Books, 1979); Gayatri Spivak, *In Other Worlds: Essays in Cultural Politics* (New York: Methuen, 1987), 83–84.

11. Frank Hamilton Cushing, "My Adventures in Zuni," *The Century Magazine* 25, no. 1 (November 1882): 191–207; 25, no. 4 (February 1883): 500–11; 26, no. 1 (May 1883): 28–47; David Snow, "Some Economic Considerations of Historic Rio Grande Pueblo Pottery," in *The Changing Ways of Southwestern Indians: A Historic Perspective*, ed. by A. Schroeder (Glorieta: Rio Grande Press, 1973), 55–72; Terry Reynolds, "Women, Pottery, and Economics at Acoma Peublo," in *New Mexico Women: Intercultural Perspectives*, ed. by Joan M. Jensen and Darlis A. Miller (Albuquerque: University of New Mexico Press, 1986), 279–300; Wade, "Straddling the Cultural Fence," 243–54; Marta Weigle, "From Desert to Disney World: The Santa Fe Railway and the Fred Harvey Company Display the Indian Southwest," *Journal of Anthropological Research* 45 (1989): 115–137; T. G. McLuhan, *Dream Trucks: The Railroad and the American Indian, 1890–1930* (New York: Harry N. Abrams, Inc., Publishers), 34.

12. Homi K. Bhabha, "The Other Question," *Screen* 24, no. 6 (November–December 1983): 24; Tzvetan Todorov, *The Conquest of America: The Question of the Other* (New York: Harper & Row), 175–76.

13. Cheryl J. Foote and Sandra K. Schackel, "Indian Women of New Mexico, 1535–1680," in Jensen and Miller, *New Mexico Women*, 21; James W. Albert, "Report of Lieutenant J. W. Abert, of His Examination of New Mexico, in the Years 1846–47," in *Notes of a Military Reconnaissance, From Ft. Leavenworth, in Missouri, to San Diego in California, Including part of the Arkansas, Del Norte, and Gila Rivers* by Lt. Col. W. H. Emory (Washington: Wendell and Ven Bethuysen, Printers, 1848), 417–548; Cushing, "Adventures in Zuni," 197.

14. Susan Wallace, *The Land of the Pueblos* (New York: Columbian Publishing Co., 1891), 43, 51, 52; John G. Owens to Deborah Stratton, July 20, 1890, John G. Owens Papers, Peabody Museum Archives, Harvard University.

15. "Cincinnati Art Pottery," *Harper's Weekly*, no. 1202 (January 10, 1880): 342; Claude Meillassoux, "From reproduction to production: A Marxist approach to economic anthropology," *Economy and Society* 1, no. 1 (February 1972): 101–2; Julian Smyonov, *Tass Is Authorized to Announce . . .* (New York: Riverrun Press, 1987), 73.

16. For discussion of "aesthetic primitivism" in the representation of Native American women, see Carr, "In Other Words," 146; Bhabha, "The Other Question," 23; Ong, "Colonialism and Modernity," 82; Trinh T. Minh-ha, "Introduction," in *She, The Inappropriate/d Other*, ed. by Trinh T. Minh-ha, *Discourse* 8 (Fall–Winter 1986–87): 8; Clifford, *Predicament*, 5.

17. Said, *Orientalism*, 5; E. Pomeroy, *In Search of the Golden West: The Tourist in Western*

America (New York: Alfred A. Knopf, 1957), 39; quoted in Marta Weigle and Kyle Fiore, *Santa Fe and Taos: The Writer's Em, 1916–1941* (Santa Fe: Ancient City Press, 1982), 17; quoted in D. H. Thomas, *The Southwestern Indian Detours: The Story of the Fred Harry/Santa Fe Railway Experiment in "Detourism"* (Phoenix: Hunter Publishing, 1978), 196. For more on Orientalizing in the imaging of Pueblo women, see Babcock, "'A New Mexican Rebecca': Imaging Pueblo Women," *Journal of the Southwest* 32:4 (1990): 400–37.

18. Clifford, *Predicament*, 268, points out that while Said is right to identify an essentializing and dichotomizing discourse as an element of colonial domination, such discourse is not specific only to the tradition of Orientalism; Santa Fe Railway ads, quoted in McLuhan, *Dream Trucks*, 19, 45.

19. Warren I. Sussman, *Culture as History: The Transformation of the United States in the Twentieth Century* (New York: Pantheon Books, 1984); T. J. Jackson Lears, *No Place of Grace: Antimodernism and the Transformation of American Culture, 1880–1920* (New York: Pantheon Books, 1981). See especially Chapter 2: "The Figure of the Artisan: Arts and Crafts Ideology," Charles Eliot Norton quoted, 66; E. E. Evans-Pritchard, *The Position of Women in Primitive Societies and Other Essays in Social Anthropology* (New York: The Free Press, 1965), 45; Michel Foucault, "The Eye of Power," in *Power/Knowledge: Selected Interviews and Other Writings, 1972–1977*, ed. by Colin Gordon (New York: Pantheon Books, 1980), 146–65, and *Discipline and Punish: The Birth of the Prison* (New York: Pantheon Books, 1977). See also Nancy Fraser's discussion of "Foucault on Power," in *Unruly Practices: Power, Discourse, and Gender in Contemporary Social Theory* (Minneapolis: University of Minnesota Press, 1989), 17–34.

20. Clifford, *Predicament*, 201; Carr, "In Other Words," 150; Rodriguez, "Art, Tourism, and Race Relations in Taos," 93; for further discussion of the effects of pottery revivals on Pueblo gender arrangements, see Wade, "Straddling the Cultural Fence," and Babcock, "'At Home No Womens Are Storytellers.'"

21. For further discussion of Pueblo portraits of the whiteman in both ceramic caricature and Pueblo ritual clowning, see Jill Sweet, "Burlesquing 'The Other' in Pueblo Performance," *Annals of Tourism Research* 16 (1989): 62–75, and Barbara A. Babcock, "Ritual Undress and the Comedy of Self and Other: Bandelier's *The Delight Makers*," in *A Crack in the Mirror*, ed. by Jay Ruby (Philadelphia: University of Pennsylvania Press, 1982), 187–203; "'Arrange Me into Disorder': Fragments and Reflections on Ritual Clowning," in *Rite, Drama, Festival, Spectacle*, ed. by John J. MacAloon (Philadelphia: ISHI Press), 102–28; "Pueblo Clowning and Pueblo Clay"; and "'Those, They Called Them Monos.'"

22. William H. Holmes, "The Debasement of Pueblo Art," *American Anthropologist* 2 (1899): 320; Thomas S. Dozier, "About Indian Pottery," *Statement to the Trade for 1907* (Santa Fe, 1907); in "On Collecting Art and Culture," *Predicament*, 232, Clifford remarks that playing and playing with the outsiders' games "does not seem worth salvaging"; for representative texts on Pueblo pottery, see note 6.

23. Trinh T. Minh-ha, "Introduction," 8; for discussion of the production of authenticity by removing objects from their current historical situation, see Clifford, *Predicament*, 228; Trinh T. Minh-ha, *Woman, Native, Other: Writing Postcoloniality and Feminism* (Bloomington: Indiana University Press, 1989), 89 ff., similarly discusses "planned authenticity" as a "product of hegemony" which "constitutes an efficacious means of silencing the cry of racial oppression"; Sylvia Rodriguez, "Art, Tourism, and Race Relations in Taos," 83, makes this same point regarding the Indian paintings of the Taos painters; Ruth Benedict, *Patterns of Culture* (Boston: Houghton Mifflin, 1934); Babcock, "'At Home No Womens Are Storytellers.'"

24. For discussion and documentation of the revolution in Pueblo figurative ceramics engendered by the Storyteller, see Barbara A. Babcock and Guy and Doris Monthan, *The Pueblo Storyteller: Development of a figurative Ceramic Tradition* (Tucson: University of Arizona Press, 1986); statements by Helen Cordero were made in conversations with me between 1988 and 1986; H. K. Haeberlin, "The Idea of Fertilization in the Culture of Pueblo Indians," *Memoirs of the American Anthropological Association* 3 (1916).

25. Quoted in Edith Hart Mason, "Enemy Bear," *The Masterkey* 22 (1948): 85. For further discussion of traditional gender roles and the disturbance thereof as a consequence of the manufacture of pottery for sale, and of the Storyteller revolution in particular, see Babcock, "'At Home No Womens Are Storytellers.'"

26. *American Indian Art Magazine* 12, no. 4 (Autumn 1987): "Pottery Issue"; in her "Introduction," p. 4, Trinh T. Minh-ha discusses "the ambiguous relation of dependency and rupture that the female writing/speaking/looking subject maintains towards both the West and men"; Simone de Beauvoir, *The Second Sex* (New York: Vintage Books, 1974), 170.

27. Susan Wallace, *The Land of the Pueblos*, 13; Judith Williamson, "Woman Is an Island," 112; Luce Irigaray, "Women on the Market," in *This Sex Which Is Not One* (Ithaca: Cornell University Press, 1985), 177; Trinh T. Minh-ha, *Woman, Native, Other*, 106.

24 Warriors or Soldiers?

Masculinity and Ritual Transvestism

in the Liberian Civil War

MARY H. MORAN

Cynthia Enloe urges us to look closely at the process by which nationalist and ethnic movements are militarized and the relationship between this process and changes in gender ideology. "Put simply, no person, no community, no national movement can be militarized without changing the ways in which femininity and masculinity are brought to bear on daily life" (1993:20). Enloe reminds us that militarization is neither an inevitable nor a "natural" step for nationalist movements; that it involves, more than anything else, a *mental* transformation in the way people think about men, women, and their respective duties as citizens. By defining militarism as a set of *beliefs*, Enloe opens the way for a truly anthropological analysis of the "uses of masculinity in the mobilization of national consciousness" (1993:11). Her feminist analysis cautions us to see that the deployment of new masculinities are not without consequences for corresponding changes in what it means to be a woman. She makes clear that lack of attention to women's experience in nationalizing and militarizing movements leaves maleness itself unproblematized. In her 1991 paper at the American Anthropological Association meetings, Enloe stated simply: "It takes a lot of power to turn a man into a soldier and a woman into the wife or mother of a martyr."

Militarization in the nationalist context, therefore, is a contested process with gender used as an instrument by all sides. Some struggles may take place between women and men, as when women, in their identity as mothers, begin to challenge, resist, or protest such processes as conscription or violence against civilians. But the struggle may just as likely take place *among* men (or women) over competing, often ethnically linked, notions of maleness or femaleness. Violent state-making, therefore, always includes a struggle over the meaning of masculinity and femininity and in this contest commodified markers of gender identity are frequently called into play. Recent events in the West African country of Liberia provide a graphic illustration of these processes, as well as of the West's consumption of a bizarre and horrifying representation of Africa.[1]

Since early 1990, Liberia has been gripped by civil war, chaos, and genocide on an appalling scale. With half the population of two and a half million displaced, approximately 20,000, dead, and an international West African military force occupying the capital of Monrovia, armed bands loyal only to their own commanders roam the countryside (U. S. Committee for Refugees 1992). Coinciding with the

Iraqi invasion of Kuwait and ensuing U. S. involvement in the Gulf War, the Liberian tragedy was all but ignored by the international press. More recently, as the stalemate has dragged on, Liberia has been eclipsed by Somalia as the new source of press images and reports on political and economic chaos in Africa. Few remember that, only two years ago, experts on the Horn were warning that, without intervention, Mogadishu could become "another Monrovia."

At the height of the crisis, what reporting there was seemed designed for Western consumption within a discourse of savage "tribal" warfare. References to Conrad's *Heart of Darkness* were ubiquitous and seemingly obligatory in publications ranging from *Esquire* and *Soldier of Fortune* magazines on one extreme to *The New York Times* and the *National Review* on the other. The "tribal" nature of the violence and sensational accounts of torture, witchcraft, cannibalism, and the macabre seem to have been deliberately emphasized in implicit contrast with the "clean" and honorable war waged by the Western powers during the same period.

Of all the unfathomable aspects of the Liberian war, however, what seems to have most intrigued Western journalists was the widespread use by rebel soldiers of looted women's clothing, bras, and wigs. Labeled "inexplicable" (Jameson 1991: 36), "without explanation" (Johnson 1990: 46), and simply "bizarre" (Daniels 1991:18), this wartime transvestism seemed to contradict every taken for granted notion of the unambiguous masculinity of war; a soldier wearing a wedding dress or negligee and a blond wig is hardly a soldier in the Western sense of the term. Although fascinated with these transvestite soldiers, foreign journalists abandoned explanation or understanding in favor of simple voyeurism. Against the backdrop of indigenous Liberian gender constructions and the recent history of military rule, this paper seeks to explain the transvestite soldier not as soldier but as warrior, an altogether more complex and multi-layered identity. At the same time, I will argue that, while at the beginning of the conflict the indigenously defined warrior represented an explicit critique and rejection of the state-identified soldier, the warrior's ludic attributes have been recuperated and perverted in the attempted state-making of competing military leaders. Following many others, this may be only the latest betrayal of the Liberian people.

The Conflict

Liberia's history as a nineteenth century benevolent project to repatriate "Free People of Color" from the United States "back" to Africa is generally well known (for an extended discussion, see Boley 1983; Liebenow 1987; Sawyer 1992). From independence in 1847 until the military coup of 1980, the state apparatus was controlled by a small elite defined in both class and ethnic terms. Recent scholarship, much of it by Liberians, is beginning to challenge the standard "morality play" version of Liberian history (see especially Burrowes 1989). This account featured arrogant, culturally alienated Americo-Liberians who reproduced the slave society they had known in the antebellum south by oppressing and victimizing the nobly savage natives. It is now clear that the national elite, despite obsessive concern with endogamy and genealogy, was closely allied both biologically and politically with their counterparts among the indigenous people (Burrowes 1989; Dunn and Tarr

1988). During the 133 years of the First Republic, the repatriate state slowly expanded from a few settler enclaves along the coast to exert at least nominal control over the peoples of the interior. As was the case elsewhere in Africa, these peoples were not organized into neatly circumscribed "tribes" but held overlapping and sometimes competing identities and loyalties to a range of named units, including towns, town clusters and their temporary confederacies, and cross-cutting clans and lineages (see d'Azevedo 1969–70; McEvoy 1977). Although there were attempts to set up administrative divisions along language and "tribal" lines, there was little interest on the part of the state in codifying ethnic units. Indigenous people stood in relation to those tracing descent from the American settlers as a relatively undifferentiated (and, until the 1960s, unenfranchised) whole. While groups like the Vai and Mandingo were recognized as distinctive and somewhat superior due to their literacy and practice of Islam, no rigid hierarchy of indigenous ethnic groups was produced during this period. Assimilation to the repatriate lifestyle and upward mobility within the national bureaucracy were achieved on an individual rather than group basis, and indigenous warfare through the mid-twentieth century was characterized by conflict *within* so-called "tribal" units rather than between them.

In 1980, a small group of non-commissioned soldiers successfully challenged the long tenure of the repatriate state. Initially viewed in class terms as the triumph of the poor and oppressed over the rich and corrupt, the military regime and subsequent Second Republic soon began to take on a decidedly ethnic caste. Samuel K. Doe, who emerged from the group of coup plotters first as a spokesman and only later as the "chairman," belonged to the Krahn linguistic group, one of the smallest, most geographically isolated and least nationally assimilated units in Liberia. Doe, who weathered several attempted counter-coups in the early days, swiftly moved to surround himself with friends and relatives from his home area. Identification with the new power-brokers was quickly extended to anyone speaking one of the many dialects of the Krahn language. As early as 1983, Liberians were saying with a mixture of resignation and impatience, "First Congo[2] man's turn to eat, now Krahn man's turn to eat. When my own turn to eat?"

Through the mid-1980s, a period of rigged elections and more attempted coups, Doe, with the help of U. S. and Israeli funding and "advisors," transformed the elite military corps into a solidly Krahn division. Furthermore, he began retaliating not only against his enemies and competitors as individuals, but against their home regions as well. In 1985–86, following a nearly successful coup attempt by a former comrade, Doe ordered bloody attacks on the Gio and Mano peoples of the north, resulting in an estimated 4,000 civilian deaths (U. S. Committee for Refugees 1992:5). In late 1989, rebel leader Charles Taylor brought about 200 Libyan trained mercenaries through this region, triggering another assault on the Gio and Mano by Doe's army. This time, the people had had enough; new recruits swelled Taylor's little band to over 10,000 in a few months and full-scale ethnic massacres, perpetrated by both sides, were underway. The Western press, when they have reported on the situation at all, have presented an almost perversely decontextualized account of "ancient tribal hatreds," simmering for generations, suddenly unleashed.

Taylor's National Patriotic Front of Liberia (NPFL) never achieved the complete military victory he craved, due to both breakaway factions from his own forces and the intervention of a peace keeping force from the Economic Community of West African States (ECOWAS). The stalemate dragged on even after Doe's death at the hands of the breakaway Independent National Patriotic Front (INPFL), and continues with a new rebel group formed from the remnants of Doe's army now challenging Taylor for control of the hinterland. Out of the chaos, a distinct enactment of indigenous concepts of gender and violence seemed to briefly emerge, then was quickly subsumed into a new discourse of militarization. Three possible masculine identities: the soldier, the warrior, and the commando, briefly competed for dominance. From what I can deduce, the commando appears to have triumphed.

The Soldier

Liberia's national military originated with a nineteenth century Frontier Force dependent upon conscripts from the indigenous population. The twentieth century Armed Forces of Liberia (AFL) was stratified to reflect the society at large, with the officer corps made up of repatriates and the bulk of the troops drawn from young, minimally educated rural men and the urban unemployed. Rank and file soldiers were frequently abused, underpaid, and forced to perform unremunerated labor for officers and government officials. In the rice riots of 1979, the troops demonstrated their solidarity with urban protesters by refusing orders to fire on the crowds, assisting in looting, and defending protestors from the Monrovia police. Soldiers were celebrated as heroes and saviors following the 1980 coup. A praise song of the time mocked the former elites; "Congo woman born rogue, Market woman born soldier," explicitly contrasting the powerful effectiveness of the new heroes with the corruption of the old guard. Doe and his military government were the self-styled People's Redemption Council and a stature of a simple, rank and file soldier clutching an M-16 rifle[3] was erected in the center of Monrovia, an image that was also stamped on newly minted coins. Even when harassing civilians or setting up petty extortion schemes with expatriate merchants, soldiers clung to the belief that they had "saved" the country; that the people owed them a debt of gratitude and it was indeed their "turn to eat."

As an image of ideal masculinity, the soldier was presented as disciplined, progressive, and committed to the betterment of the nation and the protection of its people. This imagery was part of an ongoing reconstruction of Liberian nationalism which sought to distance itself from the Congo-dominated past, emphasizing the liberation and "redemption" of the indigenous people by their own young men. The soldier was, at the same time, a generic category, not recognizably Liberian or even African, but part of a universal, world-wide militarized masculinity. This identity was paradoxically located both in the ideal of self-sacrifice to protect home and family and in commitment to values beyond the local and particularistic. All enlisted men (and women) were comrades in arms; distinctions of language and ethnicity were to be subsumed and covered over by the same camouflage uniform.

It did not take long for this ideal masculine type to become eroded by the increasing ethnic tension within the military and the resentment of the civilian population. By the election of 1985, it was clear that only soldiers were keeping an increasingly unpopular administration in power. The soldier was now synonymous with Doe himself and "soldier time," as this historical period became known, was a time of fear and economic hardship. By the summer of 1990, as rebel groups closed in on Monrovia, AFL soldiers were throwing away their uniforms, deserting in droves, hoping to blend in with the civilian population. The soldier had become completely discredited, a figure of derision, corrupt, cowardly, and ineffectual in the face of a real adversary. That adversary, in casting itself in opposition, required some other model of militarized masculinity, one that evoked a power greater than the M-16. The rebels, drawn from the rural population and staging their attacks from the forest, turned to an older and more potent, although less clearly Western, masculine ideal, that of the indigenous warrior.

The Warrior

The warrior as a construction of ideal masculinity takes a diversity of forms among indigenous Liberian cultures. In this section, I draw on my 1982–83 fieldwork with one of these groups, the Glebo of Cape Palmas, in the southeastern part of the country. There is clear evidence, however, of regional commonalties in the ritualization of warfare and of the association of warrior status with the elemental forces of nature, in particular, with the forest. Among the Glebo, the adult men's age group, the *sidibo*, or warriors, were formerly responsible for the defense of each town. Led by their officers or "war priests," the *sidibo* danced before going into battle to "bury themselves" in case they were killed in action. Since the last intergroup wars among southeastern peoples ended in the 1930s, such dances occur as part of the funeral ceremonies for elder men. They provide a visual enactment of the warrior ethic in Glebo society.

Significantly, women also perform "war dances" in honor of the death of an elder woman. This is consistent with a cultural construction of gender as enacted rather than essentialist (see Moran 1990). Women are frequently said to be "warriors" in contexts where they must face pain and even death with courage, such as childbirth. Their war dances, however, display little that is warlike, with an emphasis on the performance of intricate steps and the waving of white handkerchiefs.[4] Men's war dances, on the other hand, clearly demonstrate the techniques of traditional warfare, including ambush and sneak attacks, and incorporate the brandishing of cutlasses and firing of ancient rifles and shotguns. Yet, what appears as aggressive masculinity is subtlety undermined by elements of the warriors' costume. In every one of the twenty or more war dance performances I observed in the field, at least one or two men added bras or negligees to the standard warrior dress of raffia skirt and shredded wild animal skins. The juxtaposition of these feminine articles with other warrior elements was striking, unmistakable, and consistent from one performance to the next. When asked to explain their inclusion, informants replied simply "for play."

If we take "play" as indicating an ability to recombine elements at will, a creative freedom, then the informant statement may be taken as signifying the power of playing with cultural symbols. Only the strong, the brave, the hard of heart can claim to be a warrior, a neither masculine nor feminine status. Warriors are free to play with gender identity, to draw power from the deliberate conflation of categories, to demonstrate that qualities of courage, strength, and supernatural prowess are not limited by biological endowment. This is why the women's dance, while overtly containing none of the violent imagery, is also a war dance. In enacting their status as warriors, men incorporate items of feminine clothing to signify their transcendence of gender as an arbitrary and culturally located identity; power is inherent in combination, not separation, in mixing rather than purifying an essential maleness.

Interestingly, it is items of western manufacture, wigs, bras, and so on, that represent the mixing of gender elements in these performances. This contrasts with another indigenous form of transvestism, in which men dress as and impersonate the women of their own communities. Among the Glebo, this takes place in the context of a dance performed for a woman who has died young, still in her childbearing years (the women's war dance, like that of the men, is performed for an elder). Young men dress as women in long-sleeved shirts, cloth wrappers, and head-ties in order to participate in a dance honoring one of their age mates. Robert Leopold, working among the Loma to the north and west, has analyzed similar cases of ritual transvestism, also associated with funerals, as enacting the relationship between lineages as wife-givers and wife-receivers. In this case, men impersonate women by wearing head-ties and carrying items associated with women's economic roles, such as fishing baskets and cooking sticks (Leopold 1991:212–215). In the Glebo men's war dance, female associated items are not the only Western products appropriated by the dancers. Commodities from Halloween masks to inflatable beach balls are incorporated, again signalling the warriors' transcendence of the West's control over these products. Exotic Western items are bent to serve other purposes than those for which they were created. The power of the warrior is manifest in the ability to meld Western and indigenous, masculine and feminine, constructing the authentic not in opposition to the imported, but as an intrinsic part of it.

The appropriation of women's wigs and dresses by rebel troops in the first two years of the civil war, I would argue, can be read as an attempt to retrieve the power of the indigenous warrior as well as an implicit protest against the soldier as the agent of an oppressive state. It also represents the rejection of a static, externally defined masculinity stripped of its local referents. Responding to the brutal, mechanized violence of the AFL, NPFL and INPFL fighters turned to a no less bloody but different tradition of ritualized violence, one which was not intelligible to Western observers with their single standard of militarized masculinity. After an initial attempt to explain transvestite elements as disguise, reporters simply wrote off what they were seeing as bizarre and unfathomable, further evidence of the ultimate "darkness" and unknowability of Africa.

The Commando

There is some evidence that rebel leaders have attempted to manipulate the warrior imagery for their own purposes, although the amount of control exercised by commanders over troops in the field has been questionable from the start. An April 1992 article in *The New York Times* reports on the numerous posters and paintings of Charles Taylor decorating his interior "capital" of Gbarnga. "Recently, Mr. Taylor's face has begun to appear with the world 'ghankay' written in bold letters underneath. Ghankay means warrior in Gola, one of Liberia's main languages" (Noble 1992:A3).[5] Rather than nationalist leaders creating new versions of masculinity for consumption by their followers, this seems to be a case of the leader attempting to clothe his personal ambitions with the legitimacy of "tradition." But it may already be too late.

The transformation of soldiers into warriors is no simple reinterpretation of imported or imposed gender constructions into a more "authentic" idiom. As quickly as the warrior emerged in the context of orchestrated ethnic antagonism, it was just as quickly transmuted into something else. There is evidence that the "fashion" among young rebels has already shifted. "In 1990, reporters watched a bizarre crew of rebels take over the [Firestone Rubber] plantation. These fighters dressed in drag and women's wigs, careening around in looted vehicles in search of people from rival tribes to slaughter. Two years later, the commandos are wearing jeans and t-shirts" (Associated Press 1992).

Cynthia Enloe urges us to be sensitive to the uses of Western popular culture in the construction of militarized masculinities worldwide: "Today there is anecdotal evidence, for instance, that the American film 'Rambo' has been used to build morale by insurgent men in the Philippines and Chile, but we know little about how the masculinist meanings insurgents derived from their clandestine video viewings have shaped their relationships with women inside and outside of the national communities" (1993:18). In Liberia, the "commando," clearly based on American film imagery, appears to provide the newest model of militarized masculinity. One reporter has commented that the camp of Prince Johnson, leader of the breakaway INPFL, "resembled a Hollywood B-type horror film written by a scriptwriter on acid" (Jameson 1991:33). Taylor's bodyguard, made up of non-Liberian mercenaries trained in Libya, have the title or rank of "Special Commando" (Jameson 1991:37) and interviews with both leaders indicate that they are consciously trying to live up to a hyper-masculine adventure film ideal. The password for getting past checkpoints at one rebel camp was: "Commando!" "Brave, Strong, Intelligent!" (Jameson 1991:33).

Unlike the warrior, the commando fights not in the service of the local community but for competing leaders with national aspirations. The young men do not necessarily share these goals, and appear to join the cause either for revenge, the hope of immediate personal gain, or only fleeting loyalty to the "field marshall" of the moment (Tokpa 1992:10–12). All the dangerous elemental force of the warrior has been unleashed without the social context and ritual hierarchy that once controlled and directed it. The result is true chaos, not the playful, inventive visual chaos of the indigenous warriors' costume, but Schwarzenegger and Stallone in wigs and wedding dresses, a disrupted gender discourse that serves no purpose but destruction and death. Like the soldier, the warrior in the service of violently ethnicized state making is a warrior no longer, but a commando who bears only the trace of an emergent, alternative masculinity, a possibility lost.

The Reconstruction of Femininity

It is difficult to tell, at a distance and through the selective reports of male journalists, how Liberian women have reacted to this shift in masculine identities. Have they resisted or supported the transformation, and how have their own understandings of manhood, womanhood, and nationality been altered? Militarization as a process privileges masculinity, but at the same time reconstructs the feminine as its complementary opposite (Enloe 1993:22). Several sources report the presence of armed women among the rebels, particularly in the entourages of leaders and commanding officers. Prince Johnson apparently refers to his group of over two hundred female bodyguards as his "wives" (Jameson 1991:37), a usage which clearly implies that their services are sexual as well as protective. Henrique F. Tokpa, who interviewed a number of young rebels at a training camp on the campus of Cuttington University College, reports that about four and a half percent (or 250 out of 6,000) of the trainees were female (1992:14–15). The women made what seem to be subtle complaints about sexual exploitation but gave few other clues as to their feelings about militarization (1992:15). Other reports indicate that not all female recruits were willing volunteers; some appear to have been commandeered sexually and then "joined" for their own protection (Jameson 1991:35).

Published photographs of female rebels depict them wearing military uniforms and clutching weapons that appear too large for them. The figures are difficult to identify as women, especially given the knowledge that both Taylor and Johnson have been known to arm boys as young as nine. As Western observers, we take it for granted that women will take on the clothing and accoutrements of men in times of war. This form of transvestism, deemed acceptable and unremarkable in the West, is rarely commented upon. We assume that women entering formerly all-male domains like the military, police, or even the upper echelons of capitalist business will dress "like men" in order to both disguise their sexuality and to try and capture some semblance of men's authority (Young 1992:273). Recall, however, that Glebo women performing their war dance do *not* dress as male warriors; they are able to take on the authoritative, highly valued status of warriors without also taking on men's regalia.

While some female rebels are depicted as indistinguishable from men, however, something quite different seems to be happening with those most associated with the male leadership. Jameson writes:

> Like his mentor, Khadaffi, Taylor has also established an Amazonian personal bodyguard. His wife and sister dress in tight-fitting cammies [camouflage uniforms] with matching handbags, high heels, and pistol holsters. Reeking of perfume and bristling with sidearms and assault rifles, they hover around Taylor in a comic parody of the "commando" bodyguard (1991:37).

What is the meaning of this feminization of military dress? To Western observers, transvestism practiced by men with their wigs and negligees is intriguing; bizarre, yes, but worthy of repeated comment. When practiced by women, it is only a "comic parody." To the participants, however, it may be the women's transvestism that is the most disruptive of expected gender norms. As we have seen, there are models in several indigenous Liberian cultures for men to wear clothing clearly belonging to women. On the contrary, although commonplace in Monrovia, women in trousers were quite rare and somewhat shocking in rural Liberia well into the early 1980s. What is incongruous about Taylor's bodyguard, to Liberian eyes, may be the camouflage and the guns, not the handbags and perfume.

The more important question, following Enloe's analysis, is how might participation in armed struggle alter the status of women within the fractured nation state? Is it the sexual role of those women closely associated with the leaders which is manifest in the adding of feminine accessories to the standard uniform, or is this a new kind of transvestite "play"? Does this mark a difference between the privileges of the women who surround Taylor and Johnson and those on the front line of battle? It is clear that the vast majority of Liberian women have experienced the war as victims and refugees, rather than as direct participants. What place in the nation will they claim for themselves, when and if peace comes? Will they attempt to construct a new kind of nationalism, in opposition to the militarism that has brought so much suffering and destruction?

Again, the evidence is sketchy and any analysis would be somewhat premature, since a new reunited Liberia has yet to be achieved. We can only ask, at this point, whether the experience of civil war has allowed some women to break the "confines of domesticity and carve[d] out a space in the public arena through nationalist activism" (Enloe 1993:3). Given that "domesticity" and "the public arena" are constructed quite differently in Africa than in the West (Hansen 1992; Sudarkasa 1986), perhaps the question should be, how much or how little have a few women been incorporated into the "commando" ethic and what are the implications of this for future Liberian nationalisms? In Enloe's words, how can we understand "those pushes and pulls employing gender to fashion a national community in somebody's, but not everybody's image" (Enloe 1993:26)?

Conclusion

Enloe notes that militarization is a process "riddled with gendered contradictions" (1993:23). Sometimes these contradictions may be made visually manifest, as in the striking case of Liberia's transvestite warriors, both male and female. But visually enacting these contradictions provides no guarantee that they will be easily or nonviolently resolved, as Liberia's long national nightmare sadly shows. In the indigenous military tradition, the status of warrior was tied neither to gender nor nation; it was a state of being to which individuals, situated by kinship and other highly localized identities, might gain access by transcending their social selves. The colonial and postcolonial periods saw the professionalization of organized violence and its integration into the state apparatus. The soldier which emerged from this process was constructed not only in national but in class terms; thus the military coup of 1980 could be presented as a revolutionary uprising of the oppressed, led by an unusually disciplined, nationalist yet ethnically authentic proletariat. The fragility of this construction was evident in the contradiction between the soldier as modern, progressive patriot *and* as representative of those autochthonous people who predated the modern state. It was this unstable image which dissolved into ethnic hostility as Doe abandoned nationalism for simple self-preservation.

The most recent model of militarism, based on exported Western images, is the most lethal and terrifying. Unlike the incorporation of Western objects as a demonstration of power, as in the indigenous warrior's costume, the leaders of Liberia's warring factions seem to be desperately trying to achieve power by emulating and reproducing Western images. Rebel women are drawn into this mode of representation in a process that may "liberate" them from feminine convention yet ironically emphasizes and commandeers their sexuality. The relationship of this contested reinterpretation of gender to the nationalism which will define post-war Liberia is still unknown.

Notes

1. This paper was originally written for and presented at the 1991 Annual Meeting of the American Anthropological Association in Chicago. At those same meetings, I heard the original version of Enloe's paper and recognized its significance for the Liberian material. A revised version was presented in 1992 at the Annual Meeting of the American Ethnological Society in Memphis; I would like to thank the organizer of that session, Colleen Ballerino Cohen, and the discussant, Linda Layne, for their insightful comments (not all of which, unfortunately, can be dealt with here).
2. "Congo" in Liberian English is an often derogatory term for a person of settler or "Americo-Liberian" descent. "Eating" is a widely used metaphor for any pleasurable activity, including sex.
3. The M-16 rifle is the basic American-made, Vietnam-era weapon marketed to U. S. client states.
4. In former times, Glebo women, through their parallel political institutions and tradition of collection action, could choose either to support or veto men's decisions to go to war with neighboring towns (see Moran 1989, 1990).
5. Gola is not a "main language" in Liberia, as it is spoken by less than 5 percent of the population (Liebenow 1987:35). The Gola are, however, the indigenous group from which Charles Taylor, usually considered a Congo, claims maternal descent and they have, as a group, the reputation of fierce warriors.

Works Cited

Asociated Press.
1992. Army of Children Terrorizes Liberia. *Springfield* (Massachusetts) *Union.* July.

Boley, G. E. Saigbe.
1983. *Liberia: The Rise and Fall of the First Republic.* New York: St. Martin's Press.

Burrowes, Carl Patrick.
1989. *The Americo-Liberian Ruling Class and Other Myths: A Critique of Political Science in the Liberian Context.* Philadelphia: Temple University Institute of African and African-American Affairs, Occasional Paper No. 3.

Daniels, Anthony.
1991. Heart of Darkness. *National Review.* June 10, pp. 17–18.

d'Azevedo, Warren L.
  1969–70. A Tribal Reaction to Nationalism, Parts I-IV. *Liberian Studies Journal* 1:1–21; 2:43–64; 3:99–116.
Dunn, D. Elwood, and S. Byron Tarr.
  1988. *Liberia: A National Polity in Transition*. Metuchen, N.J.: The Scarecrow Press.
Enloe, Cynthia.
  1993. Feminism, Nationalism and Militarism: Wariness Without Paralysis? In *Feminism, Nationalism and Militarism*. C. Sutton, ed. Washington D.C.: Association for Feminist Anthropology and International Women's Anthropology Conference.
Hansen, Karen Tranberg, ed.
  1992. *African Encounters with Domesticity*. New Brunswick: Rutgers University Press.
Jameson, John.
  1991. Rap Revolution and the Prince of Darkness. *Soldier of Fortune*. March, pp. 32–39.
Johnson, Denis.
  1990. The Civil War in Hell. *Esquire*. December, pp. 43–46, 219–221.
Leopold, Robert Selig.
  1991. *Prescriptive Alliance and Ritual Collaboration in Loma Society*. Ph.D. dissertation, Department of Anthropology, Indiana University.
Liebenow, J. Gus.
  1987. *Liberia: The Quest for Democracy*. Bloomington: Indiana University Press.
McEvoy, Frederick D.
  1977. Understanding Ethnic Realities Among the Grebo and Kru Peoples of West Africa. *Africa* 47:62–79.
Moran, Mary H.
  1989. Collective Action and the "Representation" of African Women: A Liberian Case Study. *Feminist Studies* 15:443–460.
  1990. *Civilized Women: Gender and Prestige in Southeastern Liberia*. Ithaca: Cornell University Press.
Noble, Kenneth B.
  1992. In Liberia's Illusory Peace, Rebel Leader Rules Empire of His Own Design. *The New York Times*. April 14, p. A3.
Sawyer, Amos.
  1992. *The Emergence of Autocracy in Liberia*. San Francisco: Institute for Contemporary Studies Press.
Sudarkasa, Niara.
  1986. The "Status of Women" in Indigenous African Societies. *Feminist Studies* 12:91–103.
Tokpa, Henrique F.
  1992. Why They Joined the Rebel Movement: Views from "Small Soldiers" and Its Implications for Liberia's Future. Paper presented at the Liberian Studies Association Meetings.
U.S. Committee for Refugees.
  1992. *Uprooted Liberians: Casualties of a Brutal War*. Washington, D.C.: American Council of Nationalities Service.
Young, Malcolm.
  1992. Dress and Modes of Address: Structural Forms for Policewomen. In *Dress and Gender: Making and Meaning*. R. Barnes and J.B. Eicher, eds. Pp. 266–285. Oxford: Berg Publishers.

The Gendered Politics and Violence 25
of Structural Adjustment

A View from Jamaica

FAYE V. HARRISON

An Ethnographic Window on a Crisis

"The ghetto not'ing but a sad shanty town now." This is what one of my friends and informants sadly remarked to me upon my 1992 visit to "Oceanview," a pseudonym for an impoverished slum neighborhood with a roughly 74 percent formal unemployment rate in the downtown district of the Kingston Metropolitan Area. Times were so hard that the tenements had deteriorated beyond repair. The conspicuous physical decline was a marker of the deepened socioeconomic austerity accompanying what some critics (e.g., *Race & Class* 1992) now consider to be the "recolonization" of Jamaica by "the new conquistadors"—the policies and programs that the International Monetary Fund (IMF), the World Bank, and the Reagan and Bush administrations of the United States government designed to "adjust" and "stabilize" the country's revived export-oriented economy. These strategies for delivering third world societies from collapsing economies are informed by a development ideology that euphemizes the widening social disparities that have been the outcome of policies imposing an unbearable degree of austerity on living conditions. Hence, these policies have sacrificed ordinary people's—especially the poor's—basic needs in health care, housing, education, social services, and employment for those of free enterprise and free trade.

Since 1978, I have observed and conversed with Oceanview residents about the social, economic, and political conditions shaping their lived experiences and struggles for survival in this neighborhood (e.g., Harrison 1987a,b; 1988; 1991a,b). The late 1970s was a time of economic hardship and political turbulence, a time when the People's National Party's (PNP) democratic socialist path to economic development and social transformation was vehemently contested, blocked, and destabilized by political opponents both within and without the country and by the concerted economic force of an international recession, quadrupled oil prices, and a massive flight of both domestic and foreign capital. Life was certainly hard then, but, as one resident commented, "Cho, mahn [sic]; tings worse now." Despite the bright promises of political and economic "deliverance" made by the Jamaica Labour Party (JLP) and its major backer, the Reagan and later Bush administrations of the U. S. government, the 1980s and early 1990s—under the leadership of a much more conservative PNP—brought only a deepened poverty to the folk who people the streets and alleys of slum and shantytown neighborhoods like Ocean-view. This deepening poverty is reflected, for example, in a serious decline in the conditions of public health. The implementation of structural adjustment policies has brought about alarming reductions in government health-care expenditures and promoted the privatization of more costly and less accessible medical care (Phillips 1994, 137). Those most heavily burdened by the impact of these deteriorating social conditions and capital-centered policies are women (Antrobus 1989) who serve as the major "social shock absorbers" (Sparr 1992, 31; 1994) mediating the crisis at the local level of households and neighborhoods. Nearly 50 percent of all Kingston's households are female-headed, giving women the major responsibilities for making ends meet out of virtually nothing (Deere et al. 1990, 52–53). Concentrated in the informal sector of the economy, these women along with their children are most vulnerable to the consequences of malnutrition, hunger, and poor health: rising levels of morbidity and mortality (Phillips 1994, 142; Pan American Health Organization/World Health Organization 1992).

To appreciate and understand the effects, contradictions, and meanings that constitute the reality of a structurally adjusted pattern of production and trade, we must examine the everyday experiences, practices, discourses, and common sense of real people, particularly those encouraged to wait—and wait—for social and economic benefits to trickle down. In the interest of an ethnographically grounded view of Jamaica's current economic predicament, I present the case of Mrs. Beulah Brown, an admirable woman whose life story I collected over several years, to help elucidate the impact the ongoing crisis has on the everyday lives of ordinary Jamaicans, particularly poor urban women and those who depend most on them. A longtime household head and informal-sector worker like so many other Jamaican women, Mrs. Brown was once a community health aide with a government program that provided much needed health services to a population to which such care would not have been available otherwise. Mrs. Brown would not have gotten or held that job for the years that she did without "the right political connections," something, unfortunately, that too few poor people ever obtain. Although visible benefits from membership in the local PNP group may have set her apart from most of her neighbors, the centrality of patronage-clientelism in local and national politics makes a former political client's experience an insightful window on the constraints and vulnerabilities built into Jamaica's political and economic policies.

Highlights from Mrs. Brown's life story lead us to the more encompassing story of postcolonial Jamaica's experience with debt, export-led development, and structural adjustment, and their combined impact on women workers as well as on neighborhood-level negotiations of crisis.

A Hard-Working Woman's Story within a Story

In the 1970s Beulah Brown, then a middle-aged woman responsible for a two-generation household and extended family, worked as a community health aide under the combined aegis of a government public health program and a local urban redevelopment agency, two projects that owed their existence to the social-policy orientation of the reformist PNP administration. Mrs. Brown had begun her employment history as a worker in a factory manufacturing undergarments. However, she preferred household-based self-employment over the stringent regimentation of factory work. A woman with strong civic consciousness and organizing skills, she had worked her way into the leadership of the PNP group within the neighborhood and wider political division. By the late 1970s, she was no longer an officer; however, her membership in the party was still active.

Mrs. Brown was so effective at working with patients and exhibiting good citizenship that she was widely recognized and addressed as "Nurse Brown," the term "nurse" being a title of utmost respect. When Mrs. Brown made her daily rounds, she did more than expected of a health aide. She treated her patients as whole persons with a range of basic needs she felt obligated to help meet. To this end, she saw to it that they had nutritional food to eat, clean clothes to wear, and neat and orderly rooms in which to live. She was especially devoted to the elderly, but she also invested considerable energy in young mothers who were often merely children themselves. She shared her experiences and wisdom with them, admonishing them to eat healthy foods, read good books, and, given her religious worldview, "pray to the Lord Jesus Christ" so that their babies' characters and personalities would be positively influenced while still in the womb.

When I initially met her, Mrs. Brown was responsible for caring for her elderly father, her handicapped sister, her sister's three daughters, and her own two daughters. At earlier times she had even minded a young niece who eventually joined her other siblings and mother, another of Mrs. Brown's sisters, in Canada. Despite many hardships, Beulah managed her household well enough to see to it that the children were fed, clothed, and schooled. Indeed, one of her nieces, Claudia, is now a nurse in New York City, and—"by the grace of God"—her eldest daughter, Cherry, is a graduate of the University of the West Indies. Unfortunately, Marie, the daughter who still remains at home, had difficulty getting and keeping wage work, whether in an office or factory, so she decided to make and sell children's clothes so she could work at home while minding her children. Despite the economic uncertainty of informal sector work, Marie appreciates its flexibility and the freedom from the "downpressive" (oppressive) industrial surveillance about which a number of former factory workers in Oceanview complain.

Because the community health aide job did not bring in enough income to support the household, Mrs. Brown found ways to augment her income. Mainly she made dresses, a skill and talent she had cultivated over most of her life. Years ago she had even had a small shop in Port Antonio that catered to locals as well as foreign tourists. That was before she gave up everything—her shop and her husband—to return home to Kingston to care for relatives who were going through some hard times. Besides her dressmaking enterprise, Mrs. Brown also baked and sold meat patties, bought and sold cheese, and sold ice from the deep freezer she had purchased with remittances from her twin sister in England and help from her church. Through political party connections gained through her earlier activism in the local PNP group, she also saw to it that her sister got a job cleaning streets in the government Crash Programme. Although her family managed better than most of their neighbors, survival was still an everyday struggle.

In the mid-1980s, Mrs. Brown lost her health aide job. The Community Health Aide Program suffered massive losses due to the retrenchment in public-sector employment stipulated by the structural-adjustment and stabilization measures imposed by the IMF and World Bank. Luckily, the layoff came around the time when the girls she had raised were coming of age and could work to support themselves and their families. By 1988, the household was made up of only Beulah, her second daughter, Marie, and Marie's three small children. Everyone else had moved on to independent residences in Kingston or emigrated to the U. S. and Canada to live with relatives, "a foreign," overseas. This dispersal relieved the household of considerable financial pressure, but to make ends meet Beulah still had to intensify her informal means of generating income. She did more dressmaking and added baking wedding and birthday cakes to her list of money-making activities.

No matter how much work she did, she never seemed to be able to do more than barely make ends meet. With the devaluation of the Jamaican dollar and the removal of subsidies on basic consumer items like food, the costs of living had increased dramatically. What more could she do to keep pace with the inflationary trend designed to make Jamaican exports more competitive on the international market? She knew that she would never resort to the desperate illicit measures some of her neighbors had taken by "tiefing" ("thiefing") or dealing drugs. She simply refused to sell her soul to the devil for some of the "blood money" obtainable from the activities of local gangs—now called posses—that move from Kingston to the U. S. and back trafficking in substances like crack cocaine. Increasingly, especially with political patronage becoming more scarce, drug trafficking has become an important source of local subsistence and small-scale investment. However, the price paid for a life of crime is too high. She lamented that too many "youts" (youths) involved in the drug economy make the return trip home to Jamaica enclosed in deathly wooden crates.

Like most Caribbean people, Mrs. Brown has long belonged to and actively participated in an international family network extending from Jamaica to Great Britain, Canada, and the U. S. (Basch et al. 1994). Her sisters abroad had often invited her to visit them, and they had also encouraged her to migrate so that she, too, could benefit from better opportunities. Before the mid-1980s, Mrs. Brown had been determined to remain at home caring for her family. Moreover, she loved her country, her church, and her party, and she wanted to help shape the direction of Jamaica's future. She strongly felt that someone had to remain in Jamaica to keep it going on the right course. Everyone couldn't migrate. "My home is here in Jamaica," she insisted adamantly.

These were her strong feelings *before* structural adjustment hit the heart of her home: her refrigerator, deep freezer, and kitchen table. In 1990 alone, the cost of chicken—a desirable entree to accompany rice and peas on Sunday—went up three times. The cost of even more basic staples also rose, making items such as fresh milk, cornmeal, and tomatoes (whose price increased 140 percent) more and more unaffordable for many people (Statistical Institute of Jamaica 1991).

Between 1987–92, Mrs. Brown travelled abroad twice for extended visits with relatives in England, Canada, and the U. S. While away for nearly a year at a time, she "did a likkle babysitting and ting" to earn money that she was able to save for her own purposes. Her family treated her "like a queen," buying her gifts ("good camera, TV, radio, and ting"), not letting her spend her own money for living expenses, and paying for her air transportation from point to point along her international itinerary. The savings she managed to send and bring back home were key to her Oceanview household's survival. Her transnational family network, and the geographical mobility it offered, allowed her to increase her earnings by taking advantage of the marked wage differential between Jamaica and the countries where her relatives live (Ho 1993, 33). This particular financial advantage has led even middle-class Jamaican women to tolerate an otherwise embarrassing and humiliating decline in social status to work as nannies and domestic helpers in North American homes. International migration within the Caribbean region as well as between it and major metropoles has been a traditional survival strategy among Jamaicans since nineteenth century post-emancipation society.

Harsh circumstances forced Mrs. Brown to join the larger wave of female emigrants from the Caribbean who, since the late 1960s, have outnumbered their male counterparts (Deere 1990, 76; Ho 1993, 33). Thus far, Mrs. Brown has remained a "visitor," but she acknowledges the possibility and perhaps even the probability that some day soon she will join her sisters as a permanent resident abroad. Meanwhile, she continues to take care of business at home by informally generating and allocating resources within the kinship-mediated transnational social field within which her local life is embedded.

Mrs. Brown's story and many others similar to it are symptomatic of the current age of globalization, marked by a deepening crisis that policies such as structural adjustment and its complementary export-led development strategy attempt to manage in favor of the mobility and accumulation of transnational capital. Mrs. Brown's story, however, is only a story within a story about the dramatic plot-thickening details of Jamaica's nonlinear struggle for development and decolonization. Let us now place Beulah Brown's lived experience in a broader context, and, in so doing, illuminate the forces and conditions that differentially affect Jamaica's hardworking women, particularly those who work in the informal sector and free trade zone. As we shall see, their dilemmas and struggles are closely interrelated.

Once upon a Time: Dilemmas of Development

Deep into Debt

Postcolonial Jamaica, like many other third world and southern hemisphere countries, is beset by a serious case of debt bondage. Jamaica is embroiled in a crisis that can be traced back to the economic turmoil of the mid-1970s. By 1980, when the conservative JLP ousted the democratic socialist PNP from power, Jamaica's debt had doubled due to the extensive borrowing undertaken to absorb the impact the receding international economy was having on the country, to offset massive capital flight (a domestic and international panic response to the PNP's move to the left), and to underwrite state-initiated development projects. To stabilize and reinvigorate the collapsed economy, the JLP administration, with the support and guidance of the Reagan administration, relied on the IMF and the World Bank for massive loans to redress its critical balance of payments and fiscal deficits. Consequently, the country's indebtedness grew by leaps and bounds. As a result, Jamaica now owes more than U. S. $4 billion. Its debt servicing exceeds what it receives in loans and grants (Ferguson 1992, 62), and it devours 40 percent of the foreign exchange it earns from its exports, which are supposed to jump start the economy into a pattern of sustained development. The development strategy pursued since 1980—one that privileges private-sector export production—has been underwritten by these relations of indebtedness. The IMF, World Bank, and the U. S. government's Caribbean Basin Initiative (CBI) and USAID have delimited terms for Jamaica's economic restructuring that further integrate the island into a global hierarchy of free-trade relations. This global hierarchy is not only class- and racially-biased (Köhler 1978); it is also fundamentally gendered (Antrobus 1989; Enloe 1989; Sparr 1994).

The Path to Economic Growth and Social Crisis

The debt-constrained, export-led, and free trade–based development path that the Jamaican economy is following has failed to deliver the masses of Jamaican people from the dilemmas of persistent poverty and underdevelopment. Benefits from this development strategy have not trickled down the socioeconomic ladder. However, what have trickled down are the adverse effects of drastic austerity measures, which are the strings attached to aid from the IMF and World Bank. These strings stipulate that the government de-nationalize or privatize public sectors of the economy, cut back social services and public employment, devalue the Jamaican dollar, impose restraints on wages, liberalize imports, and remove subsidies and price controls on food and other consumer goods (Antrobus 1989, 20). These measures along with the stipulated focus on export production have resulted in increased unemployment, a decline in real wages for those fortunate enough to have regular incomes, a dramatic rise in the costs of living, and, with these, an increase in malnutrition and hunger, a general deterioration in public health, and an escalating incidence of drug abuse and violence—including violence against women (Antrobus 1989, 23). Conditions are so severe that economist Clive Thomas (1988, 369) poignantly argues that poor people cannot afford to live as well as nineteenth century slaves whose access to protein, carbohydrates, fuel, and work tools was more adequate. Those bearing the heaviest burden in coping with today's social and economic austerity are women, a large proportion of whom have the responsibility—whether they are formally employed or not—to support households and family networks (Bolles 1991).

Although it has sacrificed ordinary people's basic needs, the debt bondage and free trade strategy has successfully restored "the military and economic foundations of U. S. superiority . . . incorporating the Caribbean Basin countries into the U. S. military-industrial complex" (Deere et al. 1990, 157). A central aspect of the CBI has been the increased sale of U. S. exports to the Caribbean (McAfee 1991, 43). Exports from the Caribbean that receive duty-free entry into the U. S. market are produced in foreign, and to a considerable extent, U. S. controlled free-trade zones where items (usually those of apparel and electronics) are assembled from raw materials and capital goods imported from the U. S. In other words, the Caribbean has become an offshore site for branch plants that are not generating the backward linkages and horizontal integration necessary for stimulating the domestic sectors of Jamaica's economy.

Gender Inequality in Globalization

Transnational capital has appropriated the enterprising freedom to repatriate profits without any enforced obligations to invest in the host country's future; it has enjoyed the freedom to employ workers, to a great extent female, whose labor has been politically, legally, and culturally constructed to be cheap and expendable. As Enloe (1989, 160–163) argues, economic globalization depends upon laws and cultural presumptions about femininity, sexuality, and marriage that help to lower women's wages and benefits. For instance, transnational garment production has taken advantage of and reinforced the patriarchal assumptions that activities such as sewing are "natural" women's tasks requiring no special skill, training, or compensation; that jobs defined as skilled belong to men, who deserve to be remunerated for their special physical strength and training; that women are not the major breadwinners in their households and families and are really supported by their fathers or husbands (Safa 1994); and finally that women's needs should not direct the policies and practices of business management and development specialists.

The profitability, capital mobility, and structural power (Wolf 1990) constitutive of globalization are fundamentally gendered phenomena marked by a masculinist logic. Present-day strategies to adjust, stabilize, and facilitate capital accumulation implicate constructions of femininity and masculinity that, in effect, legitimate the superexploitation of the productive and reproductive labor of women, with women of color bearing the heaviest burdens (see Enloe 1989; Deere et al. 1990; Antrobus 1989) and being the most vulnerable targets of structural violence—the symbolic, psychological, and physical assaults against human subjectivities, physical bodies, and sociocultural integrity that emanate from situations and institutions structured in social, political, and economic dominance (Köhler 1978).

The misogynous symbolic assault against women is reflected in the language and images of promotional materials addressed to prospective investors in trade journals and industrial magazines as well as in fliers and posters at trade shows. For instance, a Jamaica Promotions Corporation (JAMPRO) advertisement highlighting investment opportunities on the island, features an image of a black woman's shapely lower back, protruding buttocks (in Jockey briefs), and upper thighs (National Labor Committee 1992, 44). Inscribed across the underpants in large white print is the phrase: "A brief example of our work." Below this, under a sentence attesting to the high quality and productivity of Jamaican factories, is found in smaller print the statement: "From jeans to jackets—from suits to shorts—smart apparel manufacturers are *making it* in Jamaica" (emphasis added). "Making it" can be construed as a double or triple entendre evoking manufacture and profitmaking as well as the more risqué connotations associated with female anatomy. The implicit set of meanings being manipulated relates to the hypersexuality that historically racist/sexist ideology has attributed to women of African descent. Jamaican female labor is *cheap* in the dual sense of low labor costs and the myth of unrestrained sexual availability. Drawing on stereotypic notions of African-Caribbean "promiscuity," the advertisement informs prospective manufacturers that they can "make it" with Jamaican female workers without any legal strings attached or longterm commitment. The foreign manufacturer can take advantage of this lucrative situation for at most—and often less than—75 cents an hour or anywhere from 13 percent to 24 percent of what is paid to American apparel workers (McAfee 1991, 83). According to a 1988 survery, 80 percent of Kingston's free-trade zone workers earn less than U. S. $15 a week (McAfee 1991, 86). Although wonderful incentive for the investor, from the vantage point of the worker, this wage purchases less than 40 percent of a family's food needs (McAfee 1991, 24).

Beyond its decided class bias, Jamaica's current approach to development has a definite gender bias in that women's productive and reproductive roles are expected to bear the brunt and absorb the highest risks of both the export-growth and austerity facets of present-day policies. Caribbean feminist Peggy Antrobus (1989, 19) argues that structural adjustment policies in particular presuppose "a gender ideology [that is] fundamentally exploitative of women's time, labor, and sexuality." Poor women, whether employed in free-trade-zone factories or whether informally eking out a meagre livelihood in their ghetto households and neighborhoods, bear the burden of policies and programs that, in effect even if not in design, contribute to what George Beckford (1972) called the "persistent poverty" characteristic of plantation and post-plantation societies in the throes of recolonization (*Race & Class* 1992) in late twentieth-century capitalism.

The Trickle-Down Effects of Free Trade Zones

The free-trade or export-processing zones established under JAMPRO and the program organized under section 807 of the U. S. Special Tariff Provisions represent a "type of unregulated trade, investment and employment . . . that the [World] Bank believes ought to be in effect worldwide." The recipients of generous incentives, free trade zones do not pay "import duties and taxes on stock dividends," and they are free to transfer their profits from host countries. A state within a state, the free trade zone is unfriendly to unions (McAfee 1991, 84–85), and it has been given the license to exploit its host country's laborers, who are often forced to work overtime without any notice and denied sufficient time and facilities for rest and lunch breaks. In some cases, workers are frisked before they are allowed to use the restroom and, in the worst situations, are only permitted access to the restroom once a day (Ferguson 1992, 68–69; McAfee 1991, 85).

When export-processing-zone workers contest the free trade zone's cheap labor policy and, consequently, organize for better wages and work conditions, they risk being fired and blacklisted, which precludes their finding work in any other free-trade-zone factory. Despite the severe risks, Jamaican women have not accepted dehumanizing conditions without responding organizationally. For instance, in March 1988 2,000 women from Kingston's free trade zone went on a three-day strike (*Jamaican Weekly Gleaner* 1988a–d). The women complained of verbal and physical abuse, unreasonably low pay, and the lack of union representation. Initially, then Prime Minister Edward Seaga appointed a joint union-management council to investigate the workers' complaints; however, he eventually gave in to pressure from factory owners, who threatened that they would close down their plants if the government failed to live up to promises it made and if workers continued to exhibit "poor work attitudes."

Economic Desperation in the Informal Sector

Seaga's attitude that, no matter how bad the situation, free-trade-zone jobs are better than no free-trade-zone jobs is shared by many workers, who prefer these jobs over the insecure, unstable, and aggressively competitive work found in the informal economic sector (Deere 1990). Free-trade-zone workers, nonetheless, are extremely vulnerable to losing their jobs. If they exhibit behavior that management construes as nonproductive and reflective of poor work attitudes, they face abuse or summary termination. Moreover, they are apt to be made expendable if factory owners decide to move on to more lucrative grounds in a country better able to enforce a cheaper wage labor force.

While wage workers frequently augment their income with informal means of generating additional income, close to 40 percent of Jamaican women—as compared with 12 percent of the male labor force—work primarily in the informal economy, where they predominate in household service and petty commerce (Deere 1990, 67; Bolles 1991; Harrison 1991b). To maximize survival, informal-sector workers have to balance the competitive spirit of "aggressive hustling" with the cooperative spirit sustaining the extended kin and friendship networks through which goods, services, and cash are circulated for the sake of basic survival. In light of the increasing scarcity of cash, these extended exchange networks allow their impoverished participants to meet basic needs outside of formal market transactions.

While many women prefer factory jobs over informal means of subsistence, the reality is that there are few such job opportunities available. Moreover, the built-in expendability of free-trade-zone labor means that the export-processing proletariat cannot enjoy any real distance from the day-to-day reality of the informal sector and the people—like Beulah and Marie Brown—who operate within its sphere. While the full-time informal work force includes those with no recourse but the "underground" economy, there are, nonetheless, petty entrepreneurs for whom small-scale self-employment represents a meaningful source of livelihood preferable to work conditions in the free trade zone. Local residents' social criticism of the factory regime may amount to unemployed workers rationalizing the resentment they feel for being excluded from a wage-work opportunity. On the other hand, their criticism may also be an expression of a local knowledge cognizant of the contradictions and iniquities of the prevailing model of development, and its structure of employment/unemployment.

Many analysts claim that the individuated and present-day-oriented "aggressive hustling" characteristic of informal-sector activities "hinders the development of a sense of collective struggle" and contributes to "the fragmentation of the working class and a deterioration of its institutions" (Deere 1990, 11–12). This predicament, they argue, "further deepens the social crisis." Under what circumstances can a sense of collective struggle emerge among those without any recourse but "hustling" to survive? What role does gender politics play in the development of collective consciousness-of-kind in the sociopolitical space of structural unemployment and informal-sector work? These are questions that inform the following analysis of the structural violence of poverty in the slum where Beulah Brown's story began.

Negotiating Crisis in a Downtown Constituency

Everyday life is literally a struggle against "sufferation" in a place like Oceanview where unemployment is extremely high; the violent rivalry between gang-organized clients of the country's two major political parties, the PNP and JLP, runs rampant; "Babylon," or what the Rastafari call the oppressive society and its repressive state apparatus, reveals the fullness of its terror-provoking face; and (paraphrasing Roger Abraham's [1983] book title) men-and-*women*-of-words engage in verbal performances punctuated by questions concerning the meaning of freedom and sovereignty for "sufferers" and "likkle people" who struggle to survive in a national context in which independence has represented a redefined legal status unaccompanied by a fundamental social and economic metamorphosis (Lewis 1968). The rising expectations and unfulfilled promises of independence and decolonization have wrought in the folk experience and sociopsychology a deep sense of disappointment, alienation, and anger, which informs agency among Oceanview's sufferers.

No-Man's-Land and Centerwomen's Space

According to most Kingstonians' cognitive maps, the uptown-downtown division is a central dimension in local social class and political geography. Also, within the space of the expansive downtown ghetto zone, partisan boundaries demarcate loci of safety, danger, and neutrality, all of which are contingent and subject to recodification. The neighborhoods that are viewed as "no-man's-lands" to most middle-class people, who are afraid to be "caught dead" most places downtown, are highly contested sites that are often reduced to virtual war zones, especially during election campaigns.

These ghetto zones or "no-man's-lands" are also gendered, as suggested by this figure of speech. Territories within and between neighborhoods have been masculinized and paramilitarized according to a cluster of sociocultural criteria grounded in a popular imagination shaped and promoted by the violence-glorifying, B-rated movies imported from the U. S. during the 1960s and early 1970s. More importantly, local constructions of masculinity are grounded in what Lacey (1977, 159) calls the guns/ganja/organized crime nexus that has internationalized Jamaican marijuana production and distribution since the late 1960s (Harrison 1990). Aided and abetted by the routinized gang-centered political violence through which many politicians expropriate power, the gunman syndrome that has swept across Jamaica's urban ghettoes draws upon and reconfigures traditional notions of lower-class African-Jamaican masculinity that privileges such "reputational" attributes as virility, physical prowess, toughness, and defiance of authority (Wilson [1973] 1995; Whitehead 1986). Accordingly, masculinity is constructed in terms of the ability to be tough and defiant enough to use violence to conquer and control women and weaker men. In light of the salience of achieving a sense of social balance, this militarized manhood is most valued when it is balanced out by the "respectability" of being able to satisfy at least some of the material needs of one's offspring and "babymother" by "living by the gun." If a relative balance between reputation and respectability is not achieved, the gunman is judged to be "wicked"—a form of moral weakness.

Gunman values do not, however, stand uncontested. The paramilitarized masculinity of political gangs, drug posses, and their turfs and war zones is challenged both by peaceful men of street-corner networks, who manage to negotiate political neutrality, and by those women who claim local spaces and convert them into the sanctuaries, safety zones, and neutral interfaces (cf. Feldman 1991) of such nonpartisan fields of power as open markets, schools, churches, mutual-aid associations, and some "yards" or coresidential compounds. Peace-making women, similar in many respects to the "centerwomen" that Sacks (1984) analyzes in the context of workplace struggles in North Carolina, mobilize social power rooted in the familistic values and skills that enable and empower them to engage in effective communication, goal and priority setting, decision making, and conflict mediation and resolution.

In Oceanview, government- and political party-based domains are typically the primary and most visible loci of power, but at certain junctures partisanship and its attendant conflicts have been contained by truces negotiated and sustained for varying (but usually limited) periods of time. During peaceful phases, women-centered networks and associations (particularly the nonpartisan and multipurpose Blessed Sacrament School PTA, to which Beulah Brown belonged) have been visible agents of the microcultural change that has heightened social solidarity and consciousness-of-kind (cf. Vélez-Ibañez 1983). However, these periods of calm and collective identity are vulnerable to being subverted by the victimization and violence that accompany electoral campaigns.

The Structure and Meanings of Violence

The worst case of political violence was in 1980 when the heated rivalry between the PNP's democratic socialism and the JLP's free-market strategy set the stage for an unprecedented level of violence. Kingston came to be described as the "Beirut of the Caribbean" and life in Oceanview was "the worst nightmare," as one local resident described to me. More recently, in early 1993, the *Jamaican Weekly Gleaner* (1993a–c) published numerous articles, some with front-page headlines, on violence and the general election that took place in March of that year. Whether the expected level of violence could be contained was a major concern expressed by journalists, politicians, the police commisioner, and a respected priest who runs a mission in a downtown ghetto.

Violence—whether perpetrated by politicized gangs, criminals, the police, or men against women—is an integral feature of life in Oceanview. It is a phenomenon that conditions the climate affecting not only local and national politics but also economic activities and patterns of association and social interaction. Oceanview residents are forced to live with and against violence that provides a basis, though not the sole one, for the meanings invested in local evaluations of the legitimacy of government and its policies of development and political participation. As an instrument and process in power contests, violence is constitutive of the sociocultural forms and meanings that inform and negotiate the terms of interaction, conflict, and political culture. Throughout Jamaica's history, violence has generated politically and culturally salient meanings since the initial colonization of the island and the subsequent formation of an exploitative plantation slavery society. Violence has not only served as an instrument of domination, it has also been deployed in protest and resistance, as exemplified in the case of slave rebellions and *marronage* in which the moral economy and cultural politics of slavery were forcefully contested (Campbell 1977).

In its duality, violence is salient in Jamaicans' historical memory and present-day experience, and in places like Oceanview its salience is reproduced in a local *realpolitik* that has been buttressed by the growing pattern of militarization affecting the state as well as criminal forces like drug posses. State militarization has been underwritten by CBI aid from the U. S., which has determined that regional security and U. S. dominance be achieved in the Caribbean Basin by any means necessary (see Harrison 1987a, 32; Barry et al. 1984). The broader context within which physical violence in its various forms can be situated is that of structural violence. According to Köhler's (1978) and other peace researchers' conceptualization, structural violence encompasses such assaults and violations against human rights and dignity as food shortages and hunger, pollution and environmental degradation, and police brutality—conditions engendered by the "situations, institutions, and social, political, and economic structures" (Haviland 1990, 458) that characterize the polarized economic growth associated with the concerted IMF/World Bank/CBI strategy for development.

As suggested above, the structural violence of development relies upon constructions of masculinity and femininity that help produce and reproduce the mobility and accumulation of transnational capital. Violence-legitimating constructions of masculinity are implicit in U. S.-supported, military-industrial policies implemented in Jamaica. In either direct or indirect ways, the managers and protectors of the postcolonial—or *neo*colonial—social order (namely, politicians, policemen, and army officers) are expected to take high, "manly" risks and negotiate danger to ensure such desired outcomes as profitability, law and order, and counter-insurrection. Even tourism advertisements appropriate images of legitimately militarized males in police or army uniforms (and welcoming, available, and compliant females in colorful peasant attire) in order to sell the comfort and safety of Jamaica's beach resorts to prospective foreign tourists (Enloe 1989, 32).

In Jamaica's clientelist political system, a form of "democracy by default" (Edie 1990), the managers of the postcolonial social order commonly expropriate and enforce their power through paramilitary means: deploying ghetto "forces" or partisan street gangs. The success of this tactic depends, of course, on a social construction of ghetto masculinity that privileges the dauntless toughness of living by the gun. Such a value is rooted in the forms of complicity and cooptation embodied in the current hegemonic structure of masculinized power.

Gendered Fields of Regenerative Power

Oceanview's struggle over war and peace, over repressive militarism and people-centered democracy is also a struggle over the reconstruction of both gender and development. On the sociopolitical terrain of peace mobilization, local agents contest and renegotiate the terms and meanings of gender identity, power, work, and development, especially as they apply to local community life.

Sociopolitical agency is constituted in gendered fields of power. Gendered politics, through which dominant gender ideologies are sometimes challenged and refashioned, plays an integral part in the microcultural processes that periodically give rise to emergent forms of class-cognizant solidarity. Such episodes enable wider networks of men and women to coalesce and defy the legitimacy of the state, whose seductively divisive rituals of marginality (Vélez-Ibañez 1983) trap clients into vicious cycles of disenfranchisement.

During the 1970s and 1980s, Oceanview's political trajectory encompassed three phases (circa 1975, 1978–79, 1984–85) in which local social relations were marked by peaceful, bilateral, nonsectarian alliances, extra-local cohort formation, and increased inter-local consciousness-of-kind (Harrison 1987b). At these junctures there was a heightened recognition of the local consequences of underdevelopment and polarized economic growth, and a more explicitly articulated awareness of a connection between, on one hand, local poverty and political victimization and, on the other, national (and international) development strategies. At these moments of truce and reconciliation, the values and social power characteristic of women-centered sanctuaries and safety zones became more widespread.

Through the micro-transformative practices of these phases of reconciliation and solidarity, networks of local women in conjunction with peace-seeking men expressed their opposition to political violence, the politicization of scarce wage-work opportunities (generally public sector controlled), and the cultural construction of violence-glorifying definitions of ghetto manhood. In the process of contesting the paramilitarization of local masculinity as well as the masculinization of power in clientelist and partisan political spheres, these women redefined the meaning and purview of their womanhood. They reinterpreted and extended the meanings of the cultural principles of regeneration and reproduction invested in many African Caribbean notions of womanhood and mothering. According to folk sensibilities, mothering is a shared, cooperative-kin-network-based configuration and set of practices that involves nurturing, counseling, and healing dependents as well as fulfilling the obligations of meeting family needs through participation in the public arenas of work and sociopolitical engagement.

Oceanview's centerwomen applied these traditional principles to the extended, supra-kin public domain of neighborhood redevelopment—the term "redevelopment" signifying the renewal and reconstruction of the locality as a community and fictive kindred. Through their praxis in nonpartisan, multipurpose arenas like the Blessed Sacrament School PTA, these ghetto women asserted their collective familial responsibility and motherlike authority to challenge routinized political and criminal violence and to contest the hegemony of masculinist notions of power in the space of their everyday lives and lived experience. The polluted and violated space of the partisan political constituency was, hence, reclaimed and purified as an extended "yard." At once a space and a cluster of social relationships, a yard—especially as a metaphor for greater inclusiveness and cooperation—is reminiscent of the symbolically charged notion of "family land" that is believed to be the source of cosmopolitical and physical regeneration for both biological reproduction and folk-centered economic development (Carnegie 1987). Through truce-making efforts, centerwomen and their male allies reconstituted their base of survival by reclaiming the contested urban space of no-man's-land and converting it into a shared place of community.

Local articulations of social criticism and community solidarity confront nationwide forces that reduce ghetto sufferers to dispensable clients and pawns sacrificed to the secular deities of what Vélez-Ibañez (1983) calls "rituals of marginality." The challenge to the gender and class ideologies embedded in the syndrome of political violence and in current poverty-perpetuating policies is a key element in the grassroots politics of survival and rehumanization found in places like Oceanview. Underpinning this woman-centered praxis is a deep, potentially subversive knowledge of a longstanding tradition of resisting and contesting the status quo and of celebrating the power of the relatively powerless to imagine—and struggle for—a community that privileges freedom. The freedom imagined is not that of capital mobility and accumulation, but that which is wedded to social justice and equality. Oceanview's centerwomen, like their counterparts throughout Jamaica and the Caribbean, are catalysts in grassroots responses to a crisis that reverberates transnationally, affecting both southern and northern hemispheres. Grassroots mobilizations—in the form of action groups, cooperatives, nongovernment organizations, and social movements—are expressing the urgent concerns and grievances of households, communities, and the informal sector in ways that the established political parties and trade unions have not (Deere et al. 1990, 101, 106). It is not at all surprising that in light of "the specific ways in which the crisis impinges upon women" they "have been among the first to protest and organize in new ways."

End of Story within a Story—for Now

Tired from feeling the weight of her 63 years, especially the past 10 of them, Mrs. Brown complained to me about the prohibitive costs of living and the unjust formula being used to devalue the Jamaican dollar so as to make the economy more penetrable for foreign investment. "And all at the people's expense!" As we waited at the airport for my departure time, she remarked that she didn't know how she could have made it through all her trials and tribulations if it weren't for the grace of God who gave her industry, creativity, and a loving family as gifts; her church, upon which she had always been able to depend for both spiritual guidance and material aid; and Blessed Sacrament School, its PTA, and the various other activities and community services based on the grounds of that strategic local sanctuary from political warfare and economic desperation. When she was abroad she raised a respectable sum of money from her relatives and friends for the church and school that have helped sustain her family through plenty of hard times. She insisted that no amount of "gunshot or war" could ever dissuade her from giving back to and continuing to be a part of the vital organs of support and solidarity that have been integral to her sense of moral and sociopolitical agency. While committed to her Oceanview network of support and praxis, Mrs. Brown appreciated the freedom to go as she pleased or needed to and from the various sites of her international family.

It was time for me to go to my exit, so we kissed and hugged each other good-bye as we had done several times before. We promised to write and phone until we were able to meet again—whether in Jamaica or in the U. S. After all, she smiled, she had many other stories to tell me about her life as a hardworking Jamaican woman making her way in a difficult world.

I am back home now, but I can't help but think—and worry—about Beulah and Oceanview in light of the global restructuring that affects life in the Caribbean as well as in the U. S., where the implementation of first world versions of structural adjustment are being felt and confronted. The economic restructuring occurring in the U. S. is only a variation on a wider structural adjustment theme reverberating across the globe. Policies implemented in the U. S. resemble the austerity measures the IMF and World Bank are imposing on "developing" nations: cutbacks in social spending and public investments in housing, education, and health care; deregulation of airline, trucking, banking, finance, and broadcasting industries; corporate union-busting; currency devaluation; divestment of public enterprises; the increasing privatization of public services; and dramatic alterations of the tax system, shifting the tax burden away from wealthy individuals and large corporations (Sparr 1992, 30–31).

Probing the political and moral economy of poverty in "the field" (cf. D'Amico-Samuels 1991) has led me to reconceptualize analytical units and boundaries in ways that discern and utilize points of articulation and conjuncture between, for instance, Beulah Brown and myself, and Jamaica and the U. S., for a deeper, more broadly situated, and more personally grounded understanding of structural adjustment's gendered assaults—its invidious structural violence.

Works Cited

Abrahams, Roger D.
    1983. *The Man-of-Words in the West Indies: Performance and the Emergence of Creole Culture*. Baltimore: The Johns Hopkins University Press.
Antrobus, Peggy.
    1989. Crisis, Challenge and the Experiences of Caribbean Women. *Caribbean Quarterly* 35(1&2):17–28.

Barry, Tom, et al.
   1984. *The Other Side of Paradise: Foreign Control in the Caribbean*. New York: Grove Press.

Basch, Linda, Nina Glick Schiller, and Cristina Szanton Blanc.
   1994. *Nations Unbound: Transnational Projects, Postcolonial Predicaments, and Deterritorialized Nation-States*. Langhorne, PA: Gordon and Breach Science Publishers.

Beckford, George.
   1972. *Persistent Poverty: Underdevelopment in Plantation Economies of the Third World*. New York: Oxford University Press.

Bolles, A. Lynn.
   1991. Surviving Manley and Seaga: Case Studies of Women's Responses to Structural Adjustment Policies. *Review of Radical Political Economy* 23(3&4):20–36.
   1992. Common Ground of Creativity. *Cultural Survival Quarterly* (Winter):34–37.

Campbell, Mavis C.
   1977. Marronage in Jamaica: Its Origins in the Seventeenth Century. In *Comparative Perspectives on Slavery in New World Plantation Societies*. Ed. Vera Rubin and Arthur Tuden. *Annals of the New York Academy of Sciences* 292: 446–80.

Carnegie, Charles V.
   1987. Is Family Land an Institution? In *Afro-Caribbean Villages in Historical Perspective*. *ACIJ Research Review* no. 2. Kingston: African-Caribbean Institute of Jamaica: 83–99.

D'Amico-Samuels, Deborah.
   1991. Undoing Fieldwork: Personal, Political, Theoretical, and Methodological Implications. . In *Decolonizing Anthropology: Moving Further toward an Anthropology for Liberation*. Ed. Faye V. Harrison. Washington, D. C.: American Anthropological Association.

Deere, Carmen Diana, et al.
   1990. *In the Shadows of the Sun: Caribbean Development Alternatives and U. S. Policy*. Boulder: Westview Press.

Edie, Carlene.
   1990. *Democracy by Default: Dependency and Clientelism in Jamaica*. Boulder: Lynne Rienner Publishers.

Enloe, Cynthia.
   1989. *Bananas, Beaches, and Bases: Making Feminist Sense of International Politics*. Berkeley: University of California Press.

Feldman, Allen.
   1991. *Formations of Violence: The Narrative of the Body and Political Terror in Northern Ireland*. Chicago: University of Chicago Press.

Ferguson, James.
   1992. Jamaica: Stories of Poverty. *Race & Class* 34(1):61–72.

Harrison, Faye V.
   1987a. Crime, Class, and Politics in Jamaica. *TransAfrica Forum* 5(1):29–38.
   1987b. Gangs, Grassroots Politics, and the Crisis of Dependent Capitalism in Jamaica. In *Perspectives in U.S. Marxist Anthropology*. Ed. David Hakken and Hanna Lessinger. Boulder: Westview Press.
   1988. The Politics of Social Outlawry in Urban Jamaica. *Urban Anthropology and Studies in Cultural Systems and World Economic Development* 17(2&3):259–277.
   1990. Jamaica and the International Drug Economy. *TransAfrica Forum* 7(3):49–57.
   1991a. Ethnography as Politics. In *Decolonizing Anthropology: Moving Further toward an Anthropology for Liberation*. Ed. Faye V. Harrison. Washington, D. C.: American Anthropological Association.

1991b. Women in Jamaica's Urban Informal Economy: Insights from a Kingston Slum. In *Third World Women and the Politics of Feminism*. Ed. Chandra T. Mohanty et al. Bloomington: Indiana University Press.

Haviland, William.
1990. *Cultural Anthropology*. 6th ed. Fort Worth: Holt, Rinehart and Winston.

Ho, Christine G. T.
1993. The Internationalization of Kinship and the Feminization of Caribbean Migration: The Case of Afro-Trinidadian Immigrants in Los Angeles. *Human Organization* 52(1):32–40.

Jamaican Weekly Gleaner.
1988a. JIC [Joint Industrial Council] for Free Zone Workers. 14 March, 13.
1988b. Textile Workers Strike to Get "a Better Deal." 14 March, 28.
1988c. More Garment Workers Strike. 21 March, 24.
1988d. Free Zone Operators "Going Public" with Grouse. 28 March, 5.
1993a. Peace Treaty Signed. 26 February, 3.
1993b. Nomination Day Violence. 19 March, 2.
1993c. Landslide Election Marred by Bungling, Violence. April 2, 4.

Köhler, Gernot.
1978. Global Apartheid. *World Order Models Project*. Working Paper, No. 7. New York: Institute for World Order.

Lacey, Terry.
1977. *Violence and Politics in Jamaica, 1960–70: Internal Security in a Developing Country*. Manchester: Manchester University Press.

Lewis, Gordon K.
1968. *The Growth of the Modern West Indies*. New York: Monthly Review Press.

McAfee, Kathy.
1991. *Storm Signals: Structural Adjustment and Development Alternatives in the Caribbean*. Boston: South End Press.

National Labor Committee.
1992. *Preliminary Report: Paying to Lose Our Jobs*. New York: National Labor . Committee Education Fund in Support of Worker and Human Rights in Central America.

Pan American Health Organization/World Health Organization.
1992. *The Health of Women in the English Speaking Caribbean*.

Phillips, Daphene.
1994. The IMF, Structural Adjustment and Health in the Caribbean: Policy Change in Health Care in Trinidad and Tobago. *Twenty-first Century Policy Review* 2(1&2):129–149.

Race & Class.
1992. *The New Conquistadors*. 34(1) (July–Sept.):1–114.

Sacks, Karen Brodkin.
1984. Computers, Ward Secretaries, and a Walkout in a Southern Hospital. In *My Troubles Are Going to Have Trouble with Me: Everyday Trials and Triumphs of Women Workers*. Ed. Karen Brodkin Sacks and Dorothy Remy. New Brunswick: Rutgers University Press.

Safa, Helen.
1994. *The Myth of the Male Breadwinner: Women and Industrialization in the Caribbean*. Boulder: Westview Press.

Sparr, Pamela.
1992. How We Got into This Mess and Ways to Get Out. *Ms*. March/April,130.
1994, ed. *Mortgaging Women's Lives: Feminist Critiques of Structural Adjustment*. London: Zed Books.

Statistical Institute of Jamaica.
  1991. *Statistical Yearbook of Jamaica*. Kingston: Statistical Institute of Jamaica.

Thomas, Clive Y.
  1988. *The Poor and the Powerless: Economic Policy and Change in the Caribbean*. New York: Monthly Review Press.

Vélez-Ibañez, Carlos.
  1983. *Rituals of Marginality: Politics, Process, and Culture Change in Urban Central Mexico, 1969–74*. Berkeley: University of California Press.

Whitehead, Tony Larry.
  1986. Breakdown, Resolution, and Coherence: The Fieldwork Experiences of a Big, Brown, Pretty-Talking Man in a West Indian Community. In *Self, Sex, and Gender in Cross-Cultural Fieldwork*. Ed. Tony Larry Whitehead and Mary Ellen Conaway. Urbana: University of Illinois Press.

Wilson, Peter J.
  [1973] 1995. *Crab Antics: The Social Anthropology of English-Speaking Societies of the Caribbean*. Reprint, Prospect Heights, IL: Waveland Press.

Wolf, Eric.
  1990. Distinguished Lecture: Facing Power—Old Insights, New Questions. *American Anthropologist* 92(3):586–596.

The Mirror of Exploitation   26

DEVON G. PEÑA

In 1970, when Donald Baerresen published his plant location guide for investors curious about the Border Industry Program (BIP), it was widely presumed that Mexico's maquiladora workers would be a reliable source of cheap, quiescent, productive, and apolitical labor. Instead, over the years, tens of thousands of workers have participated in organized struggles. They have done so in a manner wholly antagonistic to and autonomous from the logic of the global assembly line and the systems of labor control that perpetuate the terror of the machine (Peña 1983; 1984; 1987).

In seeking alternatives to dominant institutions, maquila workers have invented new organizations and ideologies. In the process, they have discovered a new awareness of their own "agency," that is, of their ability to transform the world, however real or illusive that may turn out to be. The dynamic subjectivity of maquila workers, their conscious militancy, is nevertheless associated with myriad forms of subaltern struggle: go-slows, work stoppages, political protests, and autonomous organizing. In creating this subjectivity—a consciousness of themselves as agents of history if not as owners of their own destiny—Mexican working-class women are reappropriating the right to self-activity and developing a social-change orientation. In the process, Mexican women workers are also redefining the nature of development itself and their identities as members of a broader, historically located community (Staudt 1987; Young 1987).

These struggles and organizations are not new in the history of working-class insurgency internationally. Indeed, these women workers are perhaps just examples of what Marx called a "class-for-itself." However, in the context of the border region, these struggles and organizations are a quantum leap forward in the political life of Mexican women industrial workers. It is, as Chela Delgado once told me, quite a difference to go from being a household servant to being an industrial laborer and then an agitator for workers' rights. Restriction of output, sabotage, work stoppages, political protests, and the establishment of independent organizations are all indicative of an ongoing process of political recomposition among maquila workers. Drawing from their experiences in the industrial workplace, women workers are inventing new organizational forms by circulating their struggles beyond the confines of the shop floor back to their families and communities. Maquila women workers are challenging established ideologies, attitudes, relations of power, and orientations to family and community (Staudt 1987; Young 1987).

But these are more than just ideological challenges to dominant discourses and values. Maquila workers have established independent unions, student-worker-peasant coalitions, legal-aid centers, and other autonomous organizations intended to redirect the path of development in the border region. Experimenting with new forms of organization, including self-managed cooperatives, women workers are refusing development as defined by the imperatives of collective global capital. The subjectivity of maquila workers is increasingly antagonistic toward the terror of the machine. Capital's pretensions at possessing universal models of development are being challenged by the fierce refusal and unbounded creativity of third-world women.

Centro de Orientación de la Mujer Obrera (COMO) has consistently articulated a set of unique struggles and demands over a quarter century of social justice and labor activism. COMO gained prominence as a nodal point of struggle by committing itself to directly involving maquila workers in self-managed cooperatives, radical pedagogies and alternative educational programs, participatory democracy, and autonomous organizing efforts on the shop floor and in the working-class community of Ciudad Juárez. An important aspect of this struggle is the establishment of worker-owned, self-managed cooperatives. These cooperatives, many of which are still economically viable, are the prototypes of alternatives to global Fordism.

The Mirror of Double Exploitation: A History of COMO

The history of COMO spans more than two decades from its humble origins in 1968. The women's center has gone through six stages of development, each with different organizational forms, changing ideological outlooks, and expanding constituencies. The center's formative phase dates to the period between 1968 and 1974. The second, between 1975–77, involved the consolidation and formalization of the center. The third, from 1978 to 1983, witnessed the emergence of *autogestion* (self-management) as the basic organizational principle. This period also saw the growth of rank-and-file initiatives, as workers brought their own struggles to COMO. Between 1983–85, the organization experienced a period of retrenchment initiated after a series of internal and external evaluations. During this fourth period, a funding crisis occurred and the center briefly functioned as a volunteer organization with a more limited political agenda.

The fifth phase, 1985 to 1990, sustained the departure and disengagement of Guillermina Valdés from the directorship of COMO and saw new relationships with striking maquila workers (especially Texscan and RCA) develop. Since 1991 with the death of Guillermina Valdés, the center has reemerged under the leadership of her daughter, Luchi. COMO is once again supporting independent worker coalitions and offering alternative education programs.

Origins and Formation: 1968–74

In 1967, María Villegas was a nurse practitioner at the sprawling RCA factory complex in Bermúdez Industrial Park on the eastern edge of Ciudad Juárez. In 1967, Guillermina Valdés was a member of a philanthropic organization, Grupo Damas. The "Women's Group" was made up of middle-class professionals who were interested in solving the problems of working women in Juárez. María Villegas was struggling with RCA management over health issues affecting the workers. At the time, the RCA plant was among the largest in the border, with close to three thousand regular, full-time workers. In an interview I conducted with María in 1983, she recalls the events that led her to develop what she characterized as "working-class consciousness":

> I believed my work consisted solely in making sure the workers got sick less. Well, the indoctrination [*el coco-wash*] did not last for long. I began to realize workers often came to my nursing station only to relieve themselves from the tensions of the [assembly] line. After observing the production line it occurred to me that the working conditions and working materials . . . caused many of these problems. I began to ask management for things to protect the health of the workers. They told me I was being fussy [*necia*], and that the things I was asking for were not needed. It was over a period of one to three years my transition to . . . working-class consciousness (interview with María Villegas, January 1983).

María's efforts then turned to organizing RCA workers into self-help groups that held meetings inside the plant and after work. These groups informally discussed occupational health and safety, stress, and sexuality. About this time, María first met Guillermina Valdés. She recalled the circumstances surrounding their first meetings and her idea of what an organization like COMO might be like:

> I told her that I dreamed of a group that would orient women workers, not help them like the boss, but rather in their self-orientation. I mean an intrinsic or integral orientation. We had to recognize that workers carried strong values. . . . The workers only had their labor power, but that has a lot of value. Guillermina agreed. . . . [She] is very intuitive, she has a tremendous ability to synthesize and adapt (interview with María Villegas, January 1983).

During this formative period, COMO's ideological leanings tended toward a combination of *beneficiencia* or *assistencialismo*. Beneficiencia involves a philosophy of "interpersonal helping."

This dual aspect of the center's formative ideological outlook reflected Guillermina's affinity for the theoretical teachings of Eric Fromm and Paolo Freire as much as María's working-class perspective and experience at RCA, which emphasized an awareness of the systemic causes of problems faced by workers.

The formation of COMO was also strongly influenced by Guillermina's theoretical knowledge. Initially, while COMO attempted to gain a beachhead in the maquilas, Guillermina emphasized a philanthropic orientation and beneficiencia approach designed to improve human relations through personal change and development of self-esteem. Over time, she came to understand this in more profoundly ideological and political ways as well.

As a result of the Guillermina-Villegas partnership, COMO developed a collaborative relationship with management in order to carry out its mission of serving maquila workers. With the approval and consent of maquila management, the center briefly offered "promotional courses" inside the assembly plants. This work largely focused on presenting a more positive social image of the Mexican working-class woman, on understanding social problems like drug abuse, alcoholism, and marital conflict, and on facilitating discussion about physical and mental hygiene. Five factories contracted with COMO to teach these courses (Fernández-Kelly 1982, 21–22; Yudelman 1987, chap. 1; Kopinak 1989). But the basic organizational nucleus during this period was drawn from RCA and Grupo Damas. The latter published a magazine called *La Mujer*, which promoted a positive image of working-class women in the border region. Many of the articles focused on topics like assertiveness, consciousness raising, stereotypes, and social problems (drug and alcohol abuse, promiscuity). COMO also organized the Casa para Jóvenes, an educational youth hostel where classes and seminars were held for adolescents and young adults in Júarez.

In 1973, the women's center received a public building located in Colonia Exhípodromo, a lower- middle- and working-class neighborhood in south-central Ciudad Júarez. This building became COMO's permanent headquarters and greatly enhanced the organization's independence from the maquila industry and its proponents. It has a set of office suites, classrooms, a library and archive collection, a general assembly room, a kitchen area, and several conference rooms, some of which were eventually converted into child-care space and production areas for an apparel workers' cooperative, Guille. After COMO moved into the Exhípodromo building, Guillermina, Maria, and other organizers established their first contacts with the garbage dump workers *(pepenadores)*, who were among the first to participate in the establishment of the worker-owned, self-managed cooperatives that became the hallmark of COMO's accomplishments after the mid 1970s.

Towards the end of this formative period, COMO's relations with maquila management became strained. The organizers found themselves increasingly at odds with managers and open hostilities emerged. Guillermina and María became much more concerned with advising workers about health hazards in the workplace than with just improving their self-image. But COMO did more than just inform workers about workplace conditions. Instead, the organizers began pressuring management to improve working conditions, especially health hazards and medical services. This constituted a critical turning point in the relationship between the organization and maquila workers. Freed of managerial constraints and influence, the center became increasingly receptive to the rank-and-file initiatives of assembly plant workers. The maquila workers circulated struggle to COMO and in the process radicalized the organization even more (*El Fronterizo* 1979; *El Diario de Júarez* 1980; *El Correo* 1989; Simenthal 1981).

Consolidation and Formalization: 1975–77

During this period former maquila workers moved into direct administrative-, support-, and organizing-staff positions at COMO. Various international, national, and local events influenced the organization's increasing militancy: Mexico was in the grip of a deep recession dating back to 1973–74; the International Year of Women in 1975 culminated in a conference in Mexico City that COMO staff attended; 1976 brought a *peso* devaluation and an exodus of capital from Mexico partly fueled by Echeverria's lame-duck attempts at agrarian and political reforms. The economic and political climate during this period strengthened COMO's activist orientation. The number of maquila workers in Juárez increased from 3,800 in 1968 to more than 20,000 in 1976, in effect expanding the center's chosen constituency.

During this period, COMO established its first two worker-owned, self-managed cooperatives: Guille and SOCOSEMA. Guille is an apparel cooperative originally organized by COMO and seamstresses laid off from their jobs in the private maquila sector. Most of the original members of Guille were fired from their jobs due to "declining productivity." They were older than the average maquila worker and were more likely to have children. Early on, COMO established child-care for members of the cooperatives as well as the student-workers who were attending classes (SOCOSEMA 1975; *El Fronterizo* 1980; Fernández-Kelly 1982; 1983; and Peña 1983). SOCOSEMA is a garbage recycling and recovery operation collectively owned and managed by dump workers and their families.

> For the first time, COMO successfully transferred its learnings obtained by workers during their employment in the factories to the experience of cooperative formation. Mass production, fragmentation of labor processes, quality control, were all criteria implanted by [Guille] in the organization of its work (Fernández-Kelly 1982, 24–25).

Was COMO merely reproducing the terror of the machine in its cooperatives by adopting the principles of Fordist mass production? Hortencia, who worked at Guille for 13 years before retiring, had this to offer about her experience in the cooperative:

> Sure, we produced big quantities of the same product. . . . And we had a division of labor. But things were totally different compared to working in the private maquilas. . . . At Guille things were better organized. We were careful to spread our work out evenly over the year so that there was always plenty to do. . . . We also produced more than just one thing, and we changed the product lines from time to time. . . . We also decided things for ourselves. I mean the administration of the cooperative. Everything was in our hands. Who to sell the products to. Who to go to for supplies, work mate-rials. How to organize the work. Figuring out the members' shares in profit. How much to invest back into production. Defining our benefits and so on . . . You could switch jobs if you got bored or tired. And if you had trouble with your task there was no one around to scream at you or threaten you. Instead, someone would always be there to help you get the job done. This reduced our stress and made working at Guille a joy. A thing you looked forward to . . . It was just a much healthier environ-ment to work in (interview with Hortenia, January 1982).

Other members of Guille felt that a job in the cooperative was better than working in the maquilas because "you don't get sexually harassed and you have a large com-munity of women around you that makes you feel safer" (comment from Guille worker, 23 July 1989). My observations of labor process organization at Guille during 1981–83 led me to believe that the cooperative was adept at implementing a variety of job rotation schemes that lessened stress and boredom. The degree of democratic decision making also created a relaxed, almost jovial, atmosphere in the work areas. But could this be simply a case of self-management as self-exploitation? It is worth noting that the work week for members of the Guille cooperative averaged 38 hours, much lower than the average of 45–48 hours for maquila workers. I never witnessed speed-up or rate-busting at Guille. The absence of wage or supervisory hierarchies also clearly reduced work-related stress and conflict.

The establishment of the first two cooperatives was another important turning point in COMO's development. From 1975 forward, the center focused much of its efforts on linking factory struggles with community organizing, drawing largely from its experiences with Guille and SOCOSEMA. During this period, COMO not only promoted cooperatives, but itself took the first steps toward a self-managed organizational form. Maquila women workers began to develop their own initiatives and utilized the center as a place to strengthen their own networks or as a source of political and economic support.

Between 1975 and 1977, the educational program was reorganized and formalized. Prior to 1975, courses at COMO were, for the most part, informally organized, often spontaneous, and covered largely unrelated subjects ranging from consciousness-raising to weaving and other handicrafts. Curriculum development after 1975 incorporated areas of concern and interest expressed by maquila workers. Course offerings came to include English, psychology, library science, typing and other clerical skills, weaving, and even yoga. Additionally, a variety of experimental training programs in nursing, social work, public education, personnel management, and secretarial work were initiated.

Self-Management, Community, and Labor Activism: 1978–83

From 1978 through 1983, COMO underwent major changes in its scope of activities, political agendas, organizational structure, and funding base. Formal incorporation was completed in January 1978. The center was recognized by UCECA (Unidad Coordinadora para el Empleo, Capacitacion, y Adiestramiento or the Coordinating Unit for Employment, Capacity Building, and Training). UCECA is equivalent to the U. S. Manpower and Training Administration and is a federal agency promoting on-the-job training for industrial workers. Formal incorporation and recognition by UCECA legitimized COMO as a viable community-based organization. In addition, for the first time, the center received funding from the Inter-American Foundation (IAF) in 1978 (US$182,000) and in 1980 (US$160,500). A key development throughout 1980–83 involved the establishment of a program of *promotores externos*, student-workers acting as community organizers and labor activists. This program formalized the role of maquila women workers as agents of community organizing, self-management, and labor struggles and provided a stable vehicle for articulating links between factory and community struggles.

It was largely through the organizing activities of promotores that COMO asserted and maintained its presence in the working-class community. The promotores played a primary role in supporting the cooperative movement, circulating solidarity among different sectors of the Júarez working class, and developing outreach in the form of intensive basic education centers (CEBIS, Centros de Educación Basica Intensiva, Mexico's frontline to reduce illiteracy in "marginal areas"). Promotores provided ongoing advice, counseling, and logistical support to farmworkers and farmers (*ejidetarios*) in the Júarez Valley, worker cooperatives, and maquila workers' independent unions and coalitions. This organizing strategy provided maquila workers with an opportunity to begin redefining their social roles, attitudes, and the very nature of community development in Júarez. The desire to encourage "social promotion" required a more systematic educational program, and this led to the establishment of a critical, neo-Freirean curriculum. In 1979, COMO began developing and implementing a new educational program. The program offered *certificados de auxilio* (auxilary certificates endorsed by UCECA) in four main areas: public education (mainly the training of literacy instructors for the CEBIS), personnel management (discontinued in 1982), public sector nursing, and social work. Before pursuing specialized training in one of the four areas, all student-workers attended the *tronco común*, a six-month-long promotional course focusing on consciousness-raising, critical analysis of the maquiladoras, study of transnational capitalism, and workers' recognition of their history-making and social change capacities.

A related innovation during this period involved the *brigadas de investigación* (research brigades). The brigadas provided a vehicle for student research in their own communities and factories. Brigada research was linked to a variety of other activities and struggles. Research tied into the *autodidáctica* (self-teaching) activities of the student-workers. The entire learning process unfolded in dialectical fashion: concepts and problems were collectively identified in class; groups split up into collaborative teams that designed and conducted field research; the teams returned to class and assessed research findings in a collective discourse, criticizing earlier views and perspectives; then, the teams returned to their communities or factories to apply their research findings.

The praxeological unity between external promotion, the tronco común, and the brigadas represented an immense leap forward in COMO's organizational diversity, networking capacity, and ability to conduct field-based research. During this period, the center blended self-management, self-directed and social problem-solving education, and change-agent principles. Workers' autonomy and community self-organizing were increasingly important as guiding principles. The role of COMO in the CEBI educational outreach centers demonstrates the search for unity among external promotion, training, and research activities.

In the course of conducting research, external promoters use a tactic referred to as "socially relevant activity." whereby members of a particular targeted community participated in the research and planning process.

> Through us, people in the community can pool together knowledge of their own communities. . . . We serve like a local nucleus for meetings and discussions. . . . Even in Colonia Libertad CEBI, the children we teach get involved in researching the prob-

lems of the community. I remember one time we had asked the children to go out and learn about the housing in the area. These kids ... are eleven, twelve, sometimes younger or older. But they can do these things very well; they are very eager. A few of them came back and told us they had found some houses that looked like fire hazards. ... This led to agitation for building materials and better fire protection (interview with COMO promotora, February 1982).

By 1981, the majority of promotores and students associated with COMO were former maquila workers. Juárez assembly plants had over 40,000 employees, but there had been periods with serious layoffs, plant closings, relocations, violence against striking workers, and wage reductions (especially between 1974–75 and 1976–80). Of course, there was also the incessant speedup of the Fordist assembly lines. Many of the workers laid off by plant closings, those who left the plants exhausted by productivity pressures, and those who were terminated for their militancy, came to COMO as students, volunteer and paid staff members, or drifting activists.

Workers' lived experiences in the factories had a definite impact on their development as social promoters and labor activists. Many of the women maquila workers who joined COMO in 1980–81 had participated in output restriction networks or had been active in rank-and-file "grievance groups," independent unions, and informal worker coalitions. (Of the 60 student-workers at COMO who were part of my 1981–82 survey study, 80 percent had participated in slowdowns and more than 70 percent had participated in work stoppages, including full-blown wildcat strikes). One former maquila worker, who continued her involvement with farmer cooperatives in the Juárez Valley through the 1980s and early 1990s, noted the importance of her experiences on the assembly line: "As much as I hated my job in the factory, I have to admit that I learned a lot. ... I learned that workers can do a lot of self-organizing. Maybe it's the way the plant itself is organized. ... There was a lot of order, a lot of interdependency" (interview, February 1982). Juárez has a remarkably persistent history of confrontations between "popular sectors" and *charrista* unionists, military and police forces, and maquila management. It is also a history marked by manipulation or suppression of popular movements through graft, patronage, violence, and harassment. During the period that I was at COMO, from 1981 through 1984, there were repeated bridge and road blockades by cotton farmers, student occupations of buildings at the regional agricultural college, and protest marches by land squatters and maquila workers. Some of these protests triggered violent responses from the police and military forces (*El Fronterizo* 1981; Martinez 1978). Maquila workers were involved in many of these protests. Moreover, former maquila workers headed the establishment of labor law and occupational health and safety study groups both within COMO and in other organizational settings.

Between 1968 and 1981, all sectors of the Juárez working class experienced "generalized austerity and marginality" (COMO 1981). Maquila workers shared a similar set of experiences involving hardships with subsistence, housing, and health. They articulated these as a common set of demands and struggles in order to unite the various sectors into one mass movement. COMO's strength during this period resided in the resilience, autonomy, creativity, and linkaqe-building capacities of its external promoters, the former maquila workers. Maquila workers and other groups not formally affiliated with the center circulated the struggle *through* the organization. In other words, COMO, particularly between 1979–83, became a nerve center for the self-organizing activities of maquila workers, farmers and farmworkers, *colonos* and squatters, and progressive educators, researchers, and lawyers.

By 1981, activities focused on building links with other sectors of the working class. By then, an estimated 4,000 maquila workers had participated in educational, outreach, and external promotion programs, while another 2,000 had worked with the organization in establishing self-managed cooperatives. Hundreds of maquila workers had participated in brigada research projects and equal numbers were members of the informal self-help groups that gravitated to COMO. These rank-and-file initiatives had a profound impact on the organization's development. The activity of maquila workers at a number of Júarez assembly factories circulated struggles to the center, increasing the organization's involvement in industrial conflicts.

Throughout 1981–83, the tronco común shifted emphasis toward a range of shop floor-oriented problem-solving projects. During this same period, I was a guest researcher, lecturer, and technical consultant at COMO. Guillermina Valdés asked me to teach classes in the tronco común during the fall 1981 and 1982 semesters. My involvement as a lecturer led to my direct participation in the brigada research projects of the student-workers. The brigadas pursued some new concerns, including the political and wage effects of deskilling, defining strategies for industrial apprenticeship programs and self-managed, community-based cooperatives, and exploring the appropriateness of north-to-south technology transfers and recognition of deskilled labor's inventive force (COMO 1984; Peña 1984). Discussions in the tronco común also focused on the history and forms of capitalist labor process organization, labor struggles in Mexican history with an emphasis on the contributions of women, and new forms of working-class organization. The center provided the ideological and analytical resources for the development of these initiatives. As one former RCA worker observed:

> The struggles were germinating [*brotando*] because we were working in two spaces, the factory and COMO. It was like living a double life. But we had the benefit of a place where we could critically discuss and analyze the problems that we confronted in the factory. COMO was a mirror for us. *El espejo de la doble explotacion* (The mirror of double exploitation). It was at COMO that I came to understand my exploitation as a woman and as a worker. And if what you saw in the mirror was ugly, then you had to take the responsibility, and you had to improve your methods of resistance, in challenging the exploitation (interview, July 1984).

"Germinating" their militancy in individual, usually isolated acts of resistance and sabotage, and then moving to informal, shop floor group actions (work stoppages), maquila student-workers at COMO were gradually transformed into full-fledged organizers. Of the 60 student-workers I interviewed in 1981–82, over 30 percent were members of informal shop floor networks compared to only 15 percent of the total sample of 223 (Peña 1983, 455).

Crisis and Retrenchment: 1983–85

Since 1978, COMO has had close relations with scholars from the U. S., Mexico, Canada, and Western Europe. But in 1981–82, the center increased its capacity to undertake independent research projects with an aim toward social action. Important advances were made in terms of methodological rigor, funding, policy relevance, and linkage with other researchers (Fernández-Kelly 1982, 37–38). These advances were exemplified by COMO's first, and unfortunately last, major sponsored research project: its capstone study of industrial apprenticeship in the maquiladoras (COMO 1984; Peña 1984; Valdés de Villalva 1989). This research project was critical to the development of what Guillermina Valdés called a "transference methodology," a plan for transferring maquila workers' tacit skills and working knowledge to other branches of production and community organizing efforts. Research would contribute to the transference of skills through an "inductive apprenticeship" in industrial production. By revaluing the knowledge and skills of the industrial worker, the transference methodology challenged the conclusions of most researchers who depicted maquila workers as unskilled or deskilled. And it explicitly linked industrial apprenticeships with the formation of worker-owned, self-managed cooperatives:

> The systematization of this knowledge, linked to an adequate methodology that complements what the workers already know . . . would permit groups of women workers to establish their own companies, taking advantage of . . . the national conjuncture that has pushed cooperative societies as a form of creating employment (COMO 1982, 12).

This strategy for worker-directed development issued a serious challenge to transnational corporations operating maquilas in the border region. It empowered workers to confront major problems posed by the dominant model, namely: extremely dangerous productivity pressures and other hazards, high turnover rates, and a refusal by management to recognize skilled labor.

Throughout this period, COMO's strategy for autonomous development was based on the principles of workers' self-organization and community self-reliance, especially in order to counter policies seen as fetters to economic democracy and social justice:

> The woman worker will count with a tool, a weapon that will permit her to demand that the development policies of the border zone are not exclusively focused on promotion and attraction of transnational firms, or for exportation only, but rather [focused] on an authentic industrialization of the zone, coherently linked to the national economy (COMO 1982, 12).

The women's center envisioned a project that would eliminate dependence on transnationals for employment and on local intermediaries for basic goods. The key to self-reliance and economic democracy lay in developing worker- and community-owned cooperatives as centerpieces of a grand experiment in autogestión.

By 1983, COMO had arrived at a crossroads. In an internal evaluation prepared by COMO staff, members identified a number of central problems: rejection of the women's center by the maquiladoras; continuing limits on job opportunities for graduates; insufficient funding and overdependence on volunteers; a lack of administrative experience in organizing and maintaining the cooperatives; ineffective acceptance by UCECA; little development of the personnel management training program; and the decline of the workers' council (*conselo obrero*), which had been established in 1981 to formalize worker participation in the center's administration.

Moreover, an external evaluation proved cumbersome and somewhat damaging. Between 1982 and 1984, the IAF, as COMO's main source of funding, directed the external review, which concluded that the organizational structure, while "flat" and lacking hierarchy, was too dependent on its director (Guillermina Valdés), particularly in the areas of information and communication. This evaluation, however, mistakenly assumed that the core group of 22 paid staff members was in fact the center's organizing nucleus, while my research demonstrates the independence of maquila student-workers in relation to the staff and director.

To a fault, the IAF ignored the subaltern life of the organization, very likely because the evaluators did not spend enough time observing the dynamics of small groups and informal networks and instead focused on executing a formal evaluation design. Though student-workers from the maquilas and other groups from the working-class community used COMO as a liberated political space for self-organizing struggles, the evaluation team completely overlooked this activity. These subaltern and subrosa dynamics were by their nature not self-evident; they remained hidden as intimate whispers and off-the-record conversations workers shared between classes or on the way home or to work. These were personal narratives and could not have been detected through formal interviews or discussion sessions with the staff and director.

Unfortunately, the IAF evaluation produced serious political problems in Washington, D. C. Some COMO student-workers and staff interpreted the external review as a political effort by unknown opponents to undermine the organization's already fragile economic base (conversations with former student workers and COMO staff). In fact, after the election of Ronald Reagan in 1980, the IAF board of directors was reorganized to include a number of new political appointees, including Thomas Enders, a hawkish anti-communist from the State Department and a frequent, hostile opponent of funding for self-management and alternative development projects in Latin America. By the end of March 1984, the IAF had terminated funding for COMO. If I may indulge in some speculation, it may very well be that the "transference methodology" was the real reason that the IAF terminated funding. Indeed, the project was perhaps just too radical for the Reagan IAF to stomach.

Another aspect of organizational crisis during 1983–84 had to do with the declining and less direct role of the center's staff in industrial workers' struggles. For a time, the core staff became somewhat ambivalent and restrained about becoming directly involved in the struggles of industrial workers. This was not a consequence of co-optation or a less militant stance. There were historical reasons for this. After 1981, the core staff increasingly shifted focus from supporting labor struggles in the maquilas to promoting cooperative economic development. However, the defeat of the Acapulco Fashions independent union strike left many former student-workers who had been active in that struggle feeling frustrated. They may have misread the center's intentions and strategies. In any event, by the end of 1984 fewer rank-and-file activists were gravitating to COMO, and fewer informal groups and coalitions were meeting there to network.

Late in September 1984, COMO, having exhausted funding resources, was forced to operate with a significantly reduced, all volunteer staff. From this time until the spring of 1985, liaison with the co-ops had been all but eliminated. The organization was in a period of retrenchment. The cooperatives continued to function as economically viable and independent entities. SOCOSEMA survived a particularly difficult period of political attacks by corporate and governmental powers, including a threatened takeover of the municipal dump by a proposed consortium of Mexican and U. S. investors. The Guille also survived and to this day remains a profitable enterprise under complete worker ownership and self-management. The various farm co-ops also survive, despite continued problems with access to fertilizer and equipment credits and accounting battles with Rural Bank (*Banrural*) officials. The threat of NAFTA to the farm co-ops remains to be seen. And, despite the end of COMO's involvement with the CEBI training programs, a former promotora continues to direct nine projects in Ciudad Júarez.

Beyond the loss of paid staff and students, the main casualty of this crisis was the tronco común. Reduced in scope and then discontinued during the fall of 1984, the promotional course was an important source of rank-and-file activity between 1979–83. The tronco común, through the formation and activities of the research brigades, had undoubtedly increased the level of autonomous struggles circulated by the student-workers. Unfortunately, without funding and adequate staff, these struggles would no longer be mobilized by COMO. A wonderful liberated political space had been severely damaged.

Departures, New Links, Two COMOs? 1985–90

A former staff member of the IAF describes the situation after 1985 as involving the co-optation of COMO by the PRI (Partido Revolucionario Institucional) (Yudelman 1987, 28; Kopinak 1989). The PRI and the Education Ministry had approached the center earlier with promises of financial support, but the offers were always firmly rejected. In mid-1985, after Guillermina Valdés resigned from the COMO directorship and assumed a full-time position with CEFO (later El Colegio de la Frontera Norte), the Mexican government provided a six-month, $50,000 grant to fund a program for Júarez working-class men and women. By the summer of 1986, COMO was apparently back on track with a full-time, paid staff of eight and seven part-time teachers on contract (Yudelman 1987, 28).

In 1988, Kopinak interviewed Guillermina Valdés de Villalva and concluded that, after 1985, there were in reality "two COMOs." As Kopinak states:

Men are the visible leaders of the government funded COMO, and it serves young men who work in the informal sector as well as women and men maquiladora workers. . . . The second COMO is the St. John the Baptist Community. . . . Villalva says that it was the economic crisis and the political stress it has caused in Mexico since 1986 which has created the separation and distance between the two COMOs (Kopinak 1989, 233).

Kopinak argues that Guillermina Valdés used her contacts and experience in the religious community to organize the "new" COMO. Guillermina, in fact, had a longstanding relationship with the more progressive segments of the Charismatic Catholic movement in Júarez dating back to the early 1970s.

> Villalva was an intellectual who had a lifelong commitment to social justice; while she herself was an atheist, she had been intellectually interested in how U. S. Blacks and Chicanos had used religion in their respective civil rights movements. She was socially involved in her community giving lectures from a Marxist perspective in the technical schools and colleges on issues such as Mexican migrant laborers to the U. S., commuting workers, etc. Her work with priests who were also committed to reducing the sense of anomie in Júarez led to discussions about whether the holy spirit could be seen as the new person who needed to emerge in order to deal with societal changes (Kopinak 1989, 229).

In March 1984, after the IAF had terminated funding, Guillermina was stricken with a serious illness that required hospitalization in Houston, TX. During this illness, she experienced a second "religious conversion" that led to a more intimate relationship with the St. John the Baptist community. Many of Guillermina's closest professional colleagues were privately dismayed by this conversion. They viewed her renewed religiosity with skepticism. But as Kopinak argues:

> Since Villalva was already deeply involved in building COMO when she underwent her [first] conversion, she began to link the religious and the political in her work there, developing a systematic leadership training process which incorporated both. This was a female leadership because women were more likely to be maquiladora workers and to be religious. When I interviewed her in 1968, she said that she did not agree with Mother Teresa that one should follow people to the grave without political support and help. Villalva considered it naive to think that religious ideas do not have political ramifications (Kopinak 1989, 231).

I agree with Kopinak that, after 1985 and COMO's temporary retrenchment, Guillermina began to search more earnestly for alternative ways of organizing working women and marginalized communities. Many of SOCOSEMA's members were also involved in the St. John the Baptist community (a Charismatic Catholic organization). It is not surprising that Guillermina continued her activist work through the religious Left.

When I was at COMO during 1981–84, Guillermina and I had several lengthy discussions about religion and politics. We both shared an interest in liberation theology. I recall telling her that the Vírgen de Guadalupe had been an important symbol in the Chicano farmworkers' struggle during the 1960s and 1970s. She responded by stating that perhaps it was time to invent new symbols for the struggle.

An Untimely Death, New Political Agendas: 1991–92

In September 1991 a Continental commuter flight from Laredo to Houston crashed; all aboard died. Guillermina Valdés was among the ill-fated passengers. Her death is one of the most profound losses in recent memory for those of us committed to workplace democracy and environmental justice. Guillermina did not create the struggle, but she channeled and sustained it. She did not invent the pedagogy of the oppressed, but she made it relevant to the working women of Mexico's *frontera*. She did not create theories of workplace democracy and sustainable development, but in her practice she was the definitive champion of both. She did not invent liberation theology, but she blended religious conviction with political commitment in a manner few are capable of emulating.

There can be no worthy epitaph for Guillermina, for there is not a gravemarker large enough to support one that would do justice to her legacy. I can offer the last words she said to me during an interview in July 1989:

> The maquilas are constantly changing. They always have. And they have always had the necessity of changing. A necessity . . . that is born of the workers' resistance. This presents a special challenge for us. We too must change, adapting our struggles, our organizations and ideologies, to counteract the capitalist strategy. . . . I predict that by the year 2000, there will be thousands of maquilas with more than a million workers. What will our border be like then? It is already burdened with too many people, too much pollution, too many factories, too much of everything except hope. And, to answer your question about my future direction, . . . I see myself directing my work to creating hope. But not without action. Hope without action is, well, hopeless. But to resort to action without hope is to indulge the worst of human impulses: the idea that we can act in the world without values, orientation, or a view of what the good life should be; *must* be.

Since Guillermina's death, the two COMOs continue to be active, viable organizations. The St. John the Baptist "COMO" maintains its relationship with the worker cooperatives. This will remain the case as long as co-op members are committed to religious life and as long as these experiments in workplace democracy are economically stable. For a short time, the official COMO was directed by an *ex-obrera*. A group of workers and staff members asked Guillermina's daughter, Luchi, to assume the directorship, which she did late in 1991 (interview, February 1992). The tronco común has been reactivated with the familiar emphasis on the activities of the research brigades. This is not surprising given the historically salient role of the brigadas in COMO's research and organizing programs.

COMO has consistently survived crisis; in fact, it is hard to envision a developmental stage in the organization's history that was free of some type of crisis and change. As long as maquila and other workers experience conflict and exploitation in their workplaces there will be a need for an organization like COMO to step into the breach caused by the corruption of official unions and arbitration boards and the ineffectiveness of legal strikes. With the emergence of Luchi as director, workers will continue to circulate their struggles to the women's center out of necessity and because they recognize and value the legacy left by a spirited and imaginative organizer who spoke directly to their needs and strategies.

Como and Sustainable Development in the U.S.-Mexico Border

Many of the women workers in Juárez who became students at COMO during the late 1970s through early 1980s redefined their political identities by actively participating in the circulation of struggles from the factory to the community and by experimenting with alternatives in community development and self-organization. I want to suggest that the alternative forms of struggle and organization created by maquila workers constitute a refusal of capitalist *mal*development. The subjectivity of maquila workers, as members of a socially constituted and historically located community, was channeled through COMO in an increasingly antagonistic relation to the "objectivity" of transnational capitalist accumulation. Capital's pretensions at possessing universal models of development, especially in the organizational form of the maquiladoras, were challenged by the refusal of Mexican working-class women to acquiesce in the reduction of their lives to mere cogs in assembly lines.

A community of women workers, activists, and organizers *separated* from and opposed capital's twisted concept of development. This involved not just the establishment of autonomous organizations like COMO but the development of separatist identities. When workers in Ciudad Juárez sought to be something other than exploited labor in transnational factories, they crafted a separate, independent model of economic and cultural existence. The separatist identity politics of maquila workers refused maldevelopment, especially the reduction of their lived experiences to mere exploited labor power. Workers rejected the dehumanization that comes with the terror of the machine.

These struggles and forms of organization may seem reformist in their outlook. The refusal of maldevelopment and the emergence of separatist identities imply the existence of an organized radical opposition. It matters little that these activists and organizers were not a representative majority of maquila workers, as more strict empiricists might insist, but that these oppositional tendencies exist.

Because of the way COMO and the workers redefined development, their perceived social needs were bound to conflict with capital's reduction of the human being to mere labor power. Working for maquilas, assembling gadgets for the universal market, increasingly interfered with the ability of many of these workers to fulfill self-defined needs in the context of the living conditions in their communities. The primacy of fulfilling individual and community needs was therefore a counterpoint to the dictates of capitalist accumulation. This was the significance of COMO's transference methodology. Struggles that seek to meet these needs are revolutionary not because they are championed by "leftist vanguards" but because they are collectively articulated in the community as autonomous forms of self-development and self-valorization (Negri 1984). Maquila women are not just redefining needs, they are outlining the blueprints of alternative economic and political institutions to fulfill those needs. And perhaps most importantly, they are organizing in a space separate from the delusive universe of capitalist values.

The history of COMO suggests that there are alternatives in the border region to maquiladora industrialization. The establishment and lifespan of the worker-owned, self-managed cooperatives gives some indication of what these alternatives might look like. Despite the temporary fragmentation of COMO after 1985, the cooperatives continue as viable, creative examples of working-class autonomy. As alternatives to the maquilas, these cooperatives offer a model for future experiments in workplace democracy and sustainable development.

Works Cited

Centro de Orientación de la Mujer Obrera (COMO). 1981. Estudio económico y social de la industria maquiladora en Cd. Júarez. Unpublished research report. Cuidad Júarez, Mexico.

———. 1982. Propuesta para una investigación del aprendizaje industrial en las maquiladoras. Unpublished research proposal. Cuidad Júarez, Mexico.

———. 1984. Primer taller de aprendizaje en la producción y tranferencía de tecnologia en la industria de maquila de exportación. Cuidad Júarez, Mexico: COMO/Fundación Frederick Ebert (mimeographed).

El Correo. 1989. Las maquiladoras utilizan compuestos químicos daños. 19 June.

El Diario de Júarez. 1980. Tóxicos y ruidos en maquiladoras afectan el aparato reproductor humano: El COMO exije atención. 3 August.

El Fronterizo. 1979. Largo camino ha recorrido el COMO en sus 10 años de vida: Una mujer nueva para un mundo cambiante. 26 August.

———. 1980. Operan dos cooperativas en el Centro de la Mujer Obrera. 8 May.

———. 1981. Daño el bloqueo de campesinos. 27 October.

Fernández-Kelly, María Patricia. 1982. The Centro de Orientacion de la Mujer Obrera. Program evaluation report prepared for the Inter-American Foundation. Program in United States–Mexican Studies, University of California, San Diego, CA.

———. 1983. *For We Are Sold, I and My People: Women and Industry in Mexico's Frontier*. Albany, NY: State University of New York Press.

Kopinak, Kathryn. 1989. Living the Gospel Through Service to the Poor: The Convergence of Political and Religious Motivations in Organizing Maquiladora Workers in Júarez, Mexico. *Socialist Studies/Etudes Socialistes: A Canadian Annual* 5.

Martinez, Oscar. 1978. *Border Boom Town: Cúidad Júarez since 1948*. Austin: University of Texas Press.

Negri, Toni. 1984. *Marx beyond Marx: A Political Reading of the Grundrisse*. South Hadley, MA: Bergin and Garvey.

Peña, Devon G. 1983. The Class Politics of Abstract Labor: Organizational Forms and Industrial Relations in the Mexican Maquiladoras. Ph. D. diss., Department of Sociology, University of Texas, Austin.

———. 1984. Skilled Activities among Assembly Line Workers in Mexican-American Border Twin-Plants. *Campo Libre* 2: (Winter–Summer): 1–2.

———. 1987. Tourtousidad: Shop Floor Struggles of Female Maquiladora Workers. In

Women on the U.S.-Mexico Border: Responses to Change. Ed. Vicki Ruiz and Susan Tiano. London: Allen and Unwin.

Simenthal, Raul Flores. 1981. La industria maquiladora: Falsa alternative al desempleo y la marginacion del hombre. *Diario de Júarez*. 8 July.

Sociedad Cooperativa de Selecionadores de Materiales, S. A. (SOCOSEMA). 1975. *Desarrollo integral de una comunidad*. Cuidad Júarez, Chihuahua: SOCOSEMA.

Staudt, Kathy. 1987. Programming Women's Empowerment: A Case from Northern Mexico. In *Women on the U.S.-Mexico Border: Responses to Change*. Ed. Vicki Ruiz and Susan Tiano. London: Allen and Unwin.

Valdés de Villalva, Guillermina. 1989. Aprendizaje en la producción y tranferencía de tecnologia en la industria de maquila de exportación. In *Reestructuración industrial: maquiladoras en la frontera Mexico-Estados Unidos*. Ed. Jorge Carillo. Mexico City: Consejo Nacional para la Cultura y las Artes and Colegio de la prontera Norte de Mexico.

Young, Gay. 1987. Gender Identification and Working-Class Solidarity among Maquila Workers in Cuidad Júarez. In *Women On the U.S.-Mexico Border: Responses to Change*. Ed. Vicki Ruiz and Susan Tiano. London: Allen and Unwin.

Yudelman, Sally W. 1987. *Hopeful Openings: A Study of Five Women's Development Organizations in Latin America and the Caribbean*. West Hartford, CT: Kumarian Press.

Index